Eat Not This Flesh

Eat Not This Flesh

Food Avoidances from Prehistory to the Present

Second Edition
Revised and Enlarged

FREDERICK J. SIMOONS

THE UNIVERSITY OF WISCONSIN PRESS

The University of Wisconsin Press
114 North Murray Street
Madison, Wisconsin 53715

3 Henrietta Street
London WC2E 8LU, England

5   4   3   2   1

Printed in the United States of America

This is a revised and enlarged edition of *Eat Not This Flesh: Food Avoidances in the Old World*, published in 1961 by the University of Wisconsin Press.

Library of Congress Cataloging-in-Publication Data
Simoons, Frederick J.
Eat not this flesh: food avoidances from prehistory to the
present / Frederick J. Simoons. — 2nd ed., rev. and enl.
564 p.   cm.
Includes bibliographical references and index.
ISBN 0-299-14250-7   ISBN 0-299-14254-X (pbk.)
1. Food habits. 2. Meat. 3. Fish as food.   I. Title.
GT2865.S55   1994
394.1'6—dc20   94-5915

*For my brother Dan,
and our friends of youth:
Bernie Sobel, Russ Kendig,
and Pete and Rose Lewesky*

What's one man's poison, signor,
Is another's meat or drink.

—Beaumont and Fletcher, *Love's Cure*

CONTENTS

ILLUSTRATIONS

PREFACE

My interest in prejudices against flesh foods goes back forty years when, with my wife, I spent a year at doctoral field research in Ethiopia in 1952–53. Our field base was at Gondar, a city in the province of Begemder and Semyen located just north of Lake Tana, source of the Blue Nile. Gondar is on the Ethiopian Plateau in the *wayna dega,* "grape highland" (5,500–8,000 feet above sea level), a region of considerable ethnic diversity where most Ethiopians live. Most numerous of Begemder and Semyen ethnic groups are the Amhara (Christian Semites), but we also found good numbers of Moslems, Falasha (Jews), Christian and pagan Cushites, and, in the lowland along the Sudan border, pagan tribal people. Though my research focussed on agriculture and animal husbandry, I was especially struck by the curious attitudes the various ethnic groups express toward animal flesh of one sort or another. We never saw pigs in the province because all its peoples—Christians and pagans as well as Jews and Moslems—consider pigs unclean and refuse to keep them or to eat pork. Hippopotami were once plentiful in Lake Tana, but the only group to hunt them and eat their flesh, the Wayto, are looked down on for this. Moslems have no objections to eating camelflesh, but Christians refuse to do so because they consider this a Moslem custom. And, though dogs are eaten in much of sub-Saharan Africa, none of the Ethiopian groups we dealt with eat dogs, for dogflesh, too, is considered unclean. Leaving Ethiopia at the end of our stay, we travelled overland across Africa, enjoying the country but also asking questions about flesh foods that people ate.

Intending to write an article on the distribution of prejudices against pork, dogflesh, horsemeat, and camelflesh in Africa, I decided that I could not understand those prejudices unless I expanded my horizons to include Eurasia as well. The result was the first edition of this book, *Eat Not This Flesh,* which was published in 1961. In the three decades since that date, my research has taken me to Europe, India, Southeast Asia, and China, and to a broader interest in food and food habits in the Old World from a geographic and culture-historical perspective. When, three years ago, Amedeo Bertolo, editor with the Italian publisher Elèuthera, asked me to make minor changes in *Eat Not This Flesh* preparatory to their publishing the book in Italian, it was like meeting an old acquaintance again after many years. As I looked over the book, however, I quickly decided that it was quite out of date and that, instead of minor changes, major ones were called for. After all, three decades had passed since that book first appeared. Knowledge relevant to the subject had advanced considerably over that time, and I had boxes of notes accumulated over the years. When the Italian edition was finished, I decided that a revised English-language edition was needed, too, and that is what follows.

My thanks are extended to the many people in villages, towns, and cities, from Ethiopia to Nigeria, from Afghanistan to Thailand, and from Singapore to China, who have willingly given their time to explain to me, a strange foreigner, their views of food and food acceptability. I also thank the Department of Geography, Eastern Washington University, for making department facilities available to me, and the libraries at Eastern Washington University and Washington State University for similar assistance. Suggestions for improving the manuscript were made by Kenneth F. Kiple, Deryck O. Lodrick, Sidney W. Mintz, Calvin W. Schwabe, and my editor, Robin Whitaker.

Spokane, Washington   F. J. S.
June 1993

Eat Not This Flesh

1 INTRODUCTION

Behold the mighty Englishman
He rules the Indian small
Because being a meat-eater
He is full ten feet tall.

—Narmadashankar, nineteenth-century Gujarati poet

Nutritional Importance of Foods of Animal Origin

In the Western world, the dietary image of meat, milk, and eggs has suffered lately because of fears of heart disease. This has encouraged vegetarians to repeat an observation they have made for centuries. Meat and fish, and even eggs and milk, they insist, are not essential for adequate nutrition, which can be obtained on a purely vegetarian diet. Despite the validity of this observation, foods of plant origin are generally lower in protein than ones of animal origin. In addition, because vegetable protein has fewer essential amino acids than animal protein, it cannot be converted into body protein as readily. Thus, vegetarians may be at risk of protein deficiency, and those vegetarians who reject eggs and dairy products as well as flesh risk deficiencies of minerals (calcium, phosphorus, iron) and vitamins (B_{12}). They must, therefore, be constantly vigilant in following a purely vegetarian diet. The danger is that, through ignorance or poverty, they will not make a proper selection of foods. The nonvegetarian has an easier task, for animal foods are rich in various nutrients, and especially valuable as compact sources of easily digested protein.

Nutritionists have long been concerned with the widespread deficiency of protein found among the world's peoples, though their focus in recent decades has shifted from protein deficiency alone, to protein-calorie deficiency, a more widespread phenomenon around the world.

3

In both conditions, the protein component is a critical one, as demonstrated by the research of Robert McCarrison in India. McCarrison concluded that the general good health, vigor, size, and robustness of the Punjabis of the northwest derived from their much higher intake of protein, largely from milk and milk products. The poor health, lack of energy, small stature, and weakness of the Bengalis of eastern India, on the other hand, McCarrison attributed largely to their low protein intake. Studies by J. B. Orr and J. L. Gilks in East Africa found equally striking differences.[1] The pastoral Maasai (Masai) of Kenya, whose diet includes substantial amounts of milk, blood, and flesh, are tall, vigorous, and healthy. Their agricultural Kikuyu neighbors, who live almost exclusively on millet, maize, sweet potatoes, and yams, are smaller, weaker, and less resistant to certain tropical diseases, as well as to tuberculosis and pneumonia. Indeed, the contrast in nutritional state between the two peoples was so great that the average Maasai woman was as strong as the average Kikuyu man. Admittedly, the East African and Indian cases are extreme, but similar differences, though usually less striking, are common among the world's peoples.

General Shortage of Foods of Animal Origin through History, and the Craving for Flesh

Through history, most peoples have consumed only small quantities of meat and other foods of animal origin. In China, the world's most populous nation, traditional diet included little or no dairy products and very small amounts of meat and eggs. For 1931–37 it was estimated that per capita consumption of meat, poultry, and fish was about thirty-four pounds annually (in the United States, by contrast, such consumption was nearly five times as great). Eggs were much more expensive in traditional China than most foods of plant origin, and peasants, who accounted for the overwhelming share of China's people, saved for themselves only a small percentage of their eggs, to be consumed as a treat at important occasions. Indeed *annual* consumption of eggs in Chinese villages in 1929–33 was estimated to be only eight per adult-male unit, or forty-one per family.[2] In Peking (Beijing), a 1926–27 household budget survey found that only half of lower-income families used any eggs at all. It also found that consumption of one egg per capita per week was reached only among families with incomes of eighty dollars a month.[3] Similar patterns of low milk, egg, and meat consumption were found among most agricultural peoples of the non-Western world, with ordinary folk obtaining flesh on rare occasions, usually on holidays or at other festive times.

Among the Miskito Indians studied in Nicaragua by Nietschmann, meat is central to the thinking of people, and more critical than anything else in the food quest.[4] The Miskito characterize good times as ones having an abundance of meat, and bad times as ones when meat is lacking. Without meat, women may even refuse to prepare food, or they do so without enthusiasm. Hyndman reports that the Wopkaimin of New Guinea have similar strong concerns about meat, and prefer meat rather than plant foods.[5] They also distinguish between the "real meat" of animals such as swine and cassowaries and the "second-class meat" of animals such as lizards, snakes, frogs, and fish—a category that includes plant foods as well.

This calls to mind the "meat hunger" that is common among peoples of sub-Saharan Africa. Most of these peoples are agricultural, but some, such as the Hadza of Tanzania, are hunters and gatherers. Hadza diet consists mainly of plant foods, but, despite this, they consider such food as completely inadequate. For them, meat is the preferred food, and, when there is not enough of it to please them, they claim to be suffering from hunger even though, in fact, they may be well fed.[6] The Bemba of Zambia have a special word, "*ubukashya*," for their craving for meat. When meat is abundant, people dance through the night and work again the following day. They attribute this outburst of energy to the strength gained from eating meat, though anthropologist Audrey Richards insists that the Bemba reaction to the presence of meat goes far beyond its nutritional value.[7] Among the Lele of Zaire, people consider it an insult to offer a vegetable meal to a guest. Discussion of social occasions centers on the quantity and type of meat served, and if the Lele have no meat or fish to eat, they may choose to drink palm wine and go to sleep without eating.[8] Such meat hunger is also found elsewhere in Zaire, as well as in the Central African Republic and the Cameroons. Meat hunger in these three lands does not correlate with a general shortage of food, and peoples usually have words to differentiate between hunger in a general sense and lack of meat.[9] The phenomenon, moreover, is found mainly among forest dwellers, whose seasonal shortages of flesh are less severe than those of savanna dwellers. Despite this, forest dwellers consider those shortages as very serious, which has led de Garine and Pagezy to suggest that meat hunger is a form of psychological stress brought on by a decrease in availability of a highly prized food but with a quite minor decrease in intake of protein and calories.[10] The phenomenon of meat hunger needs further investigation, but it is clear that it is a widespread phenomenon among peoples living at a subsistence level.

Vegetarian Rejection of Flesh Foods

In sharp contrast with the peoples who crave flesh, are Old World vegetarians, a conspicuous element in the food scene since antiquity. The hearth of Old World vegetarianism is India, a land whose peoples, through history, have ranged from avid meat-eaters to strict vegetarians who reject meat, fish, and eggs, and sometimes other foods they view in a similar light.[11] Vegetarianism is an integral part of the teachings of Hinduism and Buddhism, the great religions of Indian origin, and is based on the concept of ahimsa, noninjury to all living creatures. Within India, however, one finds the strongest commitment to ahimsa and vegetarianism not in Hinduism or Buddhism, but in Jainism. Despite the small numbers of Jains in India today (1994 est.: 3.6 million, or about 0.4 percent of India's population), they are an influential pro-ahimsa force, setting an example that non-Jains often emulate.[12] Indeed, one of the best ways to appreciate vegetarian thinking in India is to read the religious tracts put out by Jains,[13] and to talk to them and consider their behavior relating to animal life. Because bees are often killed in collecting wild honey, Jains look on it as impure and will neither consume honey themselves nor give it to others.[14] To avoid accidentally killing insects and other tiny creatures, a Jain monk may wear a cloth mask to cover his nose and mouth.[15] Out of similar concerns, devout Jains have carried brushes to sweep the path as they walk. They have eaten only during daylight hours, and have avoided various fruits that commonly contain worms.[16] Such behavior, however different it may be from normal behavior in the West, derives from deeply felt religious views, and finds expression in ways that would warm the hearts of animal lovers everywhere. They build substantial brick towers in towns and cities where birds can feed and rest in safety (Figure 1). They have established and supported charitable institutions called *pinjrapoles,*

1. Birdhouse in a Gujarati town (photo by Deryck O. Lodrick).

which are committed to taking care of aged and infirm animals of various sorts.[17] A *pinjrapole* of special note is the Jain Charity Hospital for Birds in Old Delhi. It was set up solely to care for ill and injured birds that people bring from throughout the urban area.[18] The birds are fed and cared for, and if they recover sufficiently they are set free. When we visited the hospital, its top story was filled with thousands of lively, chirping birds that were nearly well and soon to be freed. A possible bad side of Jain ahimsa concerns is the story from one Indian city of Jain

dogs and cats becoming malnourished and requiring treatment because
meat is excluded from their diet. When the animals are brought to an
animal shelter for treatment and meat is included in their diet, they
recover and are returned to their owners.

If one were to seek a cartoon that best illustrates the way Indian
vegetarians rank other peoples in terms of their eating habits, few, if
any, would equal the one published by Godbole several decades ago.[19]
The cartoon is captioned "As they rise to the humanitarian ideal," and
it features a lighthouse with waves beating against its foundation. On
the outside of the lighthouse is a ramp winding around the structure
to its top. Making their way up the ramp are several human beings.
At the lowest level is a so-called barbarian, who is identified as eating
anything raw or cooked. Not much farther up the ramp is an individual
representing those Europeans, Americans, Chinese, and other peoples
who eat any animal except humans. Still higher up are other individuals—one who eats all kinds of meat except pork, another who eats all
meats except beef, and still another who consumes no meat but does eat
fish and eggs. One level higher is a European vegetarian who presumably consumes no meat or fish but does eat eggs. One is dealing with
a moral hierarchy based on the strictness with which vegetarianism is
observed. The goal, and highest moral state, involves the most complete commitment to ahimsa. Thus, at the top of the ramp are strict
vegetarians, identified as Jains and Hindus who eat no meat, fish, or
eggs, and humanitarians, for whom all life is sacred. Radiating from
the top of the lighthouse, moreover, are beacons of light labelled "LIVE
AND LET LIVE."

Some Indian vegetarians have even given up milk and milk products
on the grounds that their use amounts to nothing less than stealing
from a young animal the milk of its mother. Indeed, Devadatta (sixth
century B.C.), the Buddha's cousin and follower, urged that milk and
curd be banned for Buddhist monks. Though his request was denied,
when Devadatta left the Buddhist fold to set up a competing sect, dairy
products were presumably forbidden to monks in the new sect.[20] Devadatta's sect died out sometime after the fourth century A.D., but if it
had triumphed over Buddhism, one would expect that vegetarianism of
an even stricter sort would have been disseminated across Asia.

In Hinduism, vegetarian observance is important because meat and
blood, presumably obtained by killing, are, by their natures, impure.[21]

One would not, therefore, offer meat to respectable Hindu gods. In Mysore, for example, Harper has observed that supernatural beings are of three kinds—"all-good" (who cause good things to happen to people), "good-bad" (who may act for or against a person's well-being), or "all-bad" (who hurt people)—and that this is reflected in their diet.[22] All-good gods, who are Sanskritic and of highest ritual status, are vegetarian. Good-bad deities, local figures of second rank, will eat meat; and "all-bad" spirits, who are evil, irritable, destructive, and who demand blood, are lowest in ritual standing, and, indeed, if a human has contact with such a spirit, calamity will result.[23] Among humans, meat eating or avoidance is usually involved in caste ranking. Brahmins, as priests, are the most steadfast of vegetarians, though members of many other castes share their vegetarian commitment.[24] This is illustrated by the case of Gandhi, who was a member of the Bania caste (traders, moneylenders, and shopkeepers).[25] As a boy, Gandhi, like his vegetarian parents, rejected all flesh food. Once, presumably urged on by non-Hindu students, he tried to eat flesh in the hope of gaining physical strength of the sort the British rulers had.[26] As part of the experiment, the boys recited the words of the Gujarati poet Narmadashankar, quoted at the beginning of this chapter, but for young Gandhi the affair was a fiasco:

It began to grow on me that meat-eating was good, that it would make me strong and daring, and that, if the whole country took to meat-eating, the English could be overcome . . . It was not a question of pleasing the palate. I did not know that it had a particularly good relish . . . We went in search of a lonely spot by the river, and there I saw, for the first time in my life—meat. There was baker's bread also. I relished neither. The goat's meat was as tough as leather. I simply could not eat it. I was sick and had to leave off eating. I had a very bad night afterwards. A horrible nightmare haunted me. Every time I dropped off to sleep it would seem as though a live goat were bleating inside me, and I would jump up full of remorse . . . If my mother and father came to know of my having become a meat-eater, they would be deeply shocked. This knowledge was gnawing at my heart.[27]

Despite widespread commitment to vegetarianism, Hindus make an exception for members of the warrior *varṇa*, the Kṣatriyas, who consume meat without a loss in status. This is because they believe that meat is required for physical strength and military prowess.[28] The association is well-illustrated among the Tamils of South India, who call nonvegetarian restaurants by the Indian-English term "military hotels," because, even though they are open to all, they serve "warrior food." [29] Also of interest in South India, meat and alcoholic beverages (the latter are also impure) are considered the most suitable offerings to demons, who are noted for their turbulence and lack of moderation.[30] Among the Rājputs, that aristocratic caste of warriors and rulers of western, northern, and central India, wine drinking [31] as well as meat eating are considered necessary for full effectiveness. Meat and wine, it is said, stimulate the production of semen, which, in turn, contributes to bravery and strength and prepares Rājputs for battle. Meat and wine are also viewed as stimulating lust,[32] which, in turn, results in more children, more sons, and ultimately more warriors.[33] It is interesting that in the one section of a Lucknow-area Brahmin caste (*jati*) whose people are allowed to consume meat on certain occasions—a striking departure from Brahmin dietary behavior and that of most members of their caste—many persons explain their deviance in terms of warrior forefathers who, like Rājputs, ate meat to increase their strength.[34] On the other hand, Rājputs themselves are not oblivious to general Hindu thinking about meat eating. Some appear uneasy about their use of wine and meat, and a few who are seriously interested in religion have even given up the practices.

Buddhism has been far more effective than Hinduism and Jainism in diffusing ahimsa and vegetarianism to foreign lands, especially Southeast Asia, Tibet, Mongolia, China, Japan, and Korea. In China, where both Buddhist and Taoist influences have encouraged kindness to animals and vegetarianism, people believe that the gods do not like the killing of animals, that eating flesh is incompatible with the highest degree of purity, and that vegetarian practice will help one achieve a better afterlife. In spite of this, pure vegetarianism has generally been practiced in China only by clergy, devout laymen, and by widows, though others might eat vegetarian meals once or twice a month. An exceptional case is the island of Pootu (Puto Shan) off the coast of Chekiang, where in mid-1930s more than half the population consisted of Buddhist monks, who were strict vegetarians. There was a prohibition against importing meat products of any kind, and neither eggs nor meat could be bought on the island.[35]

In the Near East and the Mediterranean area, vegetarian practices have generally been observed scrupulously only by clergy and very devout laymen. Vegetarianism was common in ancient Persia among the priestly and learned class of the Magi.[36] Chaldean Christians of modern Turkey, Iraq, and Iran still require that a candidate for the patriarchate of their church shall never have eaten meat, and that his mother shall not have done so during her pregnancy and nursing.[37] An occasional religious group, such as the followers of Mani,[38] forbade flesh food to all believers, but this was exceptional. Even where vegetarianism was not widely followed, there sometimes occurred, as in ancient Greece,[39] the belief in a former golden age when people killed no animals and consumed no flesh; a related belief was that flesh food did not promote either individual temperance and frugality or piety and the contemplative life.

There have also been vegetarians in Western Europe, including religious-minded persons and others, though their numbers have been less impressive than their vociferousness. An extreme example is the English scholar Joseph Ritson (A.D. 1752–1803). Ritson contended that even the appearance of animal flesh is repugnant, that it reminds the thoughtful person of a dead body along the road being eaten by vultures or ravens, or perhaps even a cannibal feast. He argued that animal food is not necessary for attaining strength or size, and in fact injures health and mental well-being. He contended further that killing animals for food develops cruelty and ferocity, and leads to human sacrifice and cannibalism.[40] It is difficult to imagine a wider gulf than the one between such committed vegetarians and persons who sacrificed[41] an animal and ate its flesh, after offering it to a deity, as a moral act of self-denial and communion with the supernatural.[42]

Rejection of Specific Foods of Animal Origin

Among the most interesting avoidances of foods of animal origin are those involving milk and dairy products, an entire class of foods. This is a topic on which I have written elsewhere,[43] and in this book the focus is on one avoidance, of fish, which is general in the sense that it embraces a wide range of species, and on a half dozen more specific avoidances, of pork, beef, chicken and eggs, horsemeat, camelflesh, and dogflesh. All the avoidances we consider are widespread in the Old World, have persisted since antiquity, have interesting and sometimes unusual socio-religious associations, and often have led foreign observers to amusement and scorn. This was clearly shown by the classical

Greek poet Anaxandrides in addressing his Egyptian contemporaries: "I could not bring myself to be an ally of yours, for neither our manners nor our customs agree, but stand a long distance apart from each other. You worship the cow, but I sacrifice it to the gods. You hold the eel to be a mighty divinity, we hold it by far the mightiest of dainties. You eat no pork, but I like it very much." [44]

I had thought of including a chapter on the use and avoidance of eels, and another on cats (which were also sacred in ancient Egypt). Unfortunately, literary evidence proved to be scanty, and I leave those interesting topics to some subsequent scholar. I was, however, able to find a wealth of information on pork, to which we turn first.

2

And the swine, though he divide the hoof, and be clovenfooted, yet he
cheweth not the cud; he is unclean to you.
Of their flesh shall ye not eat, and their carcase shall ye not touch . . .
—Leviticus 11:7–8

Pork Avoidance in the Near East and the Mediterranean Area

As one might expect, the principal center of pork avoidance in the
Old World today is the Near East, where Moslems, who strongly reject
pork, account for a large part of the population. This center cannot,
however, be understood simply in terms of Islam, for anti-pork feeling was known there long before the rise of Islam and even in modern
times is found among certain non-Moslem groups. Where strong feeling against the use of pork occurs elsewhere in the Old World, it can
frequently be traced to Near Eastern influence, whether through diffusion of Near Eastern religions; through a return to ways of the old
religions, as among Seventh-day Adventists; or through the spread of
Near Eastern cultural attitudes unrelated to religion.

Early History

The widespread occurrence of pork rejection in the Near East today
and the strength of feeling about it contrast curiously with what appears
to have been the initial situation there. In late Paleolithic times, many
peoples of the region hunted wild swine and ate pork, the preferred
habitat of wild swine being moist, sheltered areas such as swamps;
reeds bordering rivers, lakes, other bodies of water; or thick forests.
Despite the fact that wild boars are among the most formidable and
dangerous of animals, such hunting continued in the area through Neolithic times into later periods. But already by about 7000–6000 B.C.

13

2. Seth (*left*) and Horus (*right*) at the coronation of Rameses II (from J. Gardner Wilkinson, 1878).

the domestic pig, apparently domesticated from wild *Sus scrofa* of the region, appeared in southeastern Europe and the Near East.[1] Its flesh supplemented or replaced that of its wild brethren, as shown by the occurrence of domesticated pig remains in an impressive number of prehistoric and early historic sites.[2]

In ancient Egypt, the domestic pig was either introduced from nearby Southwest Asia or domesticated locally, and its remains have been uncovered at various sites dating from Neolithic (c. 5000–4000 B.C.) and Predynastic (c. 4000–3100 B.C.) times.[3] For many years, various scholars held the view that in Predynastic times, though domestic pigs were common in Lower Egypt, the Nile Delta, they were rare or relatively rare in Upper Egypt.[4] Partly on those grounds, Kees and certain other scholars argued that Predynastic Upper Egyptians had negative views toward pigs and pork.[5] They suggested further that when Upper Egyptians conquered Lower Egypt to unify the land, they

3. Pigs in ancient Egypt: (a) sows with young; (b) young pigs; (c) boars (from J. Gardner Wilkinson, 1878).

prohibited the use of pigs for sacrifice and food, though the prohibition affected only upper levels of society, especially the ruler, royal officials, and priests. Kees also claimed that the pig had an association with the god Seth in Predynastic times, and that the prohibition of pork related to a myth about hostility between the gods Seth and Horus (Figure 2).[6]

Kee's hypothesis is in accord with certain evidence: that in ancient Egypt the pig is seldom represented (Figure 3) or mentioned in texts, and that pig bones are absent in tombs. Kees is also right that pigs were quite important in Lower Egypt. Recent archeological excavations have shown that this was so from Neolithic times onwards. Indeed, at two delta sites, perhaps because of unusually abundant food resources, the importance of pigs was extraordinary.[7] Contrary to Kees's hypothesis, however, is recent evidence of domestic pigs in Predynastic and later sites in Upper Egypt,[8] where they accounted for 7 percent of all animal bones, including wild animals, at Predynastic Hierakonpolis. In addition, the assemblage of herd animals, including the pig, at Neolithic

Merimde-Benisalame in Lower Egypt was quite similar to that at Predynastic Hierakonpolis and Naqada in Upper Egypt.[9] The percentage
of pigs in sites south of the delta, moreover, compares favorably with
those for many prehistoric sites in Southwest Asia.[10] The new evidence
for Neolithic and Predynastic sites in Egypt, as well as later ones, led
Hecker to conclude that the delta may not have been the sole area important in pig breeding in ancient Egypt, that in all likelihood pigs
were "fairly common throughout Egypt."[11] Richard W. Redding's recently published summary of the archeological data, including some
new since Hecker wrote, is in keeping with Hecker's conclusion.[12]

Another major element in Kees's hypothesis is that the antipathy of
Seth and Horus goes back to Predynastic times and that the pig, symbolizing Seth, was involved in the controversy. There is a convincing
myth of this sort, involving Horus, Seth, and the pig, in the Coffin
Texts, which date from c. 2150–1650 B.C.: "And Rē‹ [the sun-god]
said: 'Look again at yonder black pig.'[13] And Horus looked at this black
pig, and Horus cried out because of the condition of his injured Eye,
saying: 'Behold, my Eye is like that first wound which Seth inflicted
on my Eye,' and Horus became unconscious in his presence.[14] And Rē‹
said: 'Put him on his bed until he is well.' It so happened that Seth
had transformed himself into a pig and had projected a wound into his
[Horus's] Eye. And Rē‹ said, 'The pig is detestable to Horus.' 'Would
that he were well,' SAID THE GODS. THAT IS HOW THE DETESTATION OF
PIG CAME ABOUT FOR HORUS'S (SAKE) BY THE GODS WHO ARE IN THE
SUITE." The next spell, in which Horus is also involved, ends with the
words "NOT TO BE SAID WHEN EATING PIG."[15] What the above suggests
to me is that the pig, which was associated with Seth, came to be held
in contempt by Horus and certain other gods, and that, though Egyptians might continue eating pork, it was not proper to do so in rites
associated with Horus. Spell 157, first of the Coffin Texts quoted above,
also included the observation: "Now when he [Horus] was a child, his
sacrificial animal was a pig before his Eye had suffered." This suggests
that at one time, before Seth in the form of a pig had damaged Horus's
eye, pigs had been acceptable as sacrificial animals to Horus. Also found
in the Coffin Texts is the myth of Seth as the murderer of Osiris, Horus's
father,[16] who shared Horus's hostility to Seth.

If, however, one looks for evidence of a link between Seth and the pig
in times earlier than the Coffin Texts, matters become quite clouded.

4. The Seth animal (from J. Gardner Wilkinson, 1878).

The earliest-known Egyptian funerary literature is the Pyramid Texts,[17] taken from Old Kingdom pyramids of the late fifth and sixth dynasties (dating from about 2345–2181 B.C.). In the Pyramid Texts, one finds most elements, or hints of them, that occur in the Coffin Texts mentioned above. Among them are the conflict between the two deities, the gouging out of Horus's eye by Seth, and the killing of Osiris by Seth. The pig, however, is not identified with or associated with Seth that early unless one accepts questionable translations, or the proposition that the pig was "the Seth animal," a creature whose identity is a matter of controversy (Figure 4).[18] If one seeks to extend the matter still further back, into Predynastic times, one faces even greater uncertainty. As te Velde has observed, the origins of the Seth-Horus myth are "lost in the mists of the religious traditions of prehistory,"[19] and even the existence of Seth and the Seth animal in Predynastic times is a matter of controversy.[20] In view of the above, I consider it prudent to follow J. G. Griffiths, a leading authority on Seth, who has concluded that an early tie between Seth and the pig is doubtful, and that convincing evidence is lacking for such a tie in Old Kingdom times.[21]

In texts later than the Coffin Texts, on the other hand, the pig is a prominent element in the myth of Seth and Horus. One text is the Book of the Dead,[22] earliest copies of which are said to date from the mid-fifteenth century B.C. (New Kingdom times), but which drew on the Coffin Texts and Pyramid Texts of earlier times. Additional evidence of anti-pig sentiment in the New Kingdom is found in inscriptions and representations in burial places of pharaohs that relate to the gods Seth and Horus, in which Seth was belittled and the pig, which was associated with him, was disparaged, speared, or beaten.[23] Such evidence is found in the tomb of Horemheb (who ruled from 1348 to 1320 B.C.), the sarcophagus of Sethos I, and the tomb of Rameses VI (1156–1148 B.C.).[24]

It is unclear what the impact all the above may have had on the general status of pigs in Egypt and on the acceptability of pork as food. J. G. Griffiths has written me of his "a priori objection" to the view that the reviling of one animal, the pig, should be tied to the reviling of one deity, Seth, in a polytheistic system. The question is whether one can explain the origin of the lowly status of the pig in Egypt (Figure 5) in terms of its association with Seth, or whether it derives from other factors. In either case, the archeological evidence clearly shows that pigs continued to be kept.[25] Paton has observed that pigs were not considered impure in the third or fourth dynasties (c. 2686–2498 B.C.),[26] and Darby and associates, that tolerance of pigs seems to have typified the entire period of the Old Kingdom.[27] In a sixth-dynasty tomb dating to about 2340 B.C., moreover, there is a controversial "pig-kissing" scene in which a man is holding what may be a pig and has his mouth in contact with the animal's snout.[28] The man may be force-feeding the animal, but whatever he is doing, it is hard to imagine such intimacy with an impure animal. Though some say that the pig-kissing scene is more likely one of dog kissing, evidence from "the tale of the eloquent peasant"[29] is incontrovertible. That tale, which is set at the close of the First Intermediate period (c. 2181–2040 B.C.), depicts pigs as respectable animals owned by a minor official in Upper Egypt. In a weighing of the Middle Kingdom evidence (2133–1786 B.C.), furthermore, Darby and associates[30] found nothing to suggest a ban on pork, legal or implied. Equally significant is the fact that King Sesostris I (1971–1928 B.C.) appointed an official to care for the royal farms and named him overseer of swine,[31] that King Amenophis III (1417–1379 B.C.) pre-

5. Other images of the pig in ancient Egypt.

Top: Soul of a deceased man in the form of a pig after the deceased has been weighed and found wanting by Osiris, judge of the dead. The pig, an unclean animal, is transported in a boat guarded by two baboons, symbolic of Thoth, who recorded the deeds of dead persons. Standing at the right is Anubis, lord of the dead. Saite Dynasty, 664–525 B.C. (from J. Gardner Wilkinson, 1878).

Right: Horus spearing a wild boar. Ptolemaic-Roman period (from E. A. W. Budge, 1904, as redrawn by W. J. Darby et al., 1977).

sented a thousand pigs and a thousand piglets to the temple of Ptah at
Memphis, and that King Sethos I (1318–1304 B.C.) permitted pigs to
be kept at the temple of Osiris at Abydos.[32] The above strongly suggests
that the pig was a respectable animal during the Middle Kingdom and
into New Kingdom times (1570–1085 B.C.). Kings owned pigs. They
presented pigs to temples. And pigs were bred in the temple grounds
of Osiris at Abydos, most sacred place in all Egypt.[33]

Especially interesting in ancient Egypt are the ties certain rulers had
with Seth. This was true of two kings of the second dynasty (c. 2890–
2685 B.C.), one of whom identified himself with Seth, and a second,
with both Seth and Horus.[34] It was also true of kings of the fifteenth
and sixteenth dynasties (1674–1567 B.C.), which, however, are considered foreign (Hyksos) and Sethian.[35] During New Kingdom times after
the Hyksos dynasties, two kings took Sethos as a throne name.[36] Of
particular note is King Sethos I, whose name means "the Sethian" or
"one dedicated to Seth." During his reign, one of the four principal
divisions of the Egyptian army was named for the deity Seth. As we
have seen, Sethos also permitted pigs at the temple in Abydos. On the
other hand, Seth was not among the deities represented there, and on
Sethos's sarcophagus there is a pig-humbling scene.[37] The implication
is that the deity Seth was losing ground. This fits with the fact that
after the twentieth dynasty (1200–1085 B.C.), last dynasty of the New
Kingdom, no new temples seem to have been built for Seth. Nor is
there evidence that his existing temples were renovated after that date.[38]

The New Kingdom evidence clearly shows that the pig was involved
in religious controversy and belittled, yet one cannot be certain, for
that period, whether Egyptians in any significant numbers rejected the
flesh of pigs at all times. The matter is made clear only in writings
of the Greek historian Herodotus (c. 484–425 B.C.).[39] Herodotus observed that most Egyptians did not eat pork, except that once a year
they sacrificed pigs and ate pork at a celebration to the moon and to
Osiris (called Bacchus by Herodotus). Poor people who could not afford to buy pigs for this celebration made and baked pigs of dough
and sacrificed them. Pigs were also used in the Nile Delta for treading
in the seed after sowing. At the same time they were regarded as so
unclean that a respectable Egyptian who accidentally brushed against
a pig cleansed himself by rushing to the Nile and plunging in without
undressing. Contact with a swineherd was equally polluting, and swine-

herds constituted a separate class. Other Egyptians did not intermarry with them, and they were considered too defiled to enter the temples. Should they have entered a temple, swineherds would not only have fouled a ritually pure and sacred site, but also their uncleanness would have been transmitted to other worshippers.[40] The writings of Greeks and Romans following Herodotus do not always portray the pig in a consistent way.[41] They do, however, reveal an ambivalence about swine among Egyptians. They also indicate that pork rejection was present, especially among priests, but that, despite this, pigs continued to be kept and eaten.[42]

The ancient Hebrew attitude toward the pig is clearer and more consistent. As shown in the quotation at the start of our chapter, Leviticus pictures the pig as unclean and forbids its flesh.[43] Other biblical passages, such as the proverb likening an attractive woman who lacks good taste to "a golden ring in the snout of a sow,"[44] also indicate the lowly position of swine. In later times, there was an effort in the Talmud to refrain from even using the name for swine, referring to them instead as "another thing" (a thing not to be referred to by name).[45] In addition, swine breeding and keeping swine among flocks were banned.[46] There are, however, some statements in Isaiah, in sections probably added to the book from 400 to 200 B.C., which suggest that certain Hebrews had secret religious meetings at which they ate pork.[47] But it was the feeling that the pig is unclean that prevailed among the Hebrews, and that caused the avoidance of pork to become symbolic of their religion. During the reign (175–164 B.C.) of the Seleucid conqueror Antiochus Epiphanes, who put strong pressure on the Hebrews to abandon their religion in favor of the Greek gods, they were tested to determine their willingness to accept the new ways by being compelled to eat the flesh of a pig that Antiochus had sacrificed.[48] In one instance, the old scribe Eleazar was forced to put pork in his mouth. He then spat it out, choosing to die rather than break the law of his faith.[49] Some Hebrews evidently did acquiesce in pork eating, for a little later when John Hyrcanus I was high priest (c. 135–105 B.C.), he found it necessary to issue a decree prohibiting the practice.[50] There are various references to pigs and pig keeping in New Testament times. One is the story of how Christ cured the madman (or madmen) from across the Sea of Galilee by driving the demons who possessed him into a herd of swine.[51] These pigs, however, probably belonged to Gentiles, for Hebrews con-

tinued to regard pig keeping as the lowliest of occupations, debased and
dishonorable.

As for peoples who preceded the Hebrews in Palestine, we shall
see later that remains of domesticated pigs have been uncovered in
various Bronze Age sites. Evidence has also been presented that swine
played a role in ritual. In an underground "place of worship" (c. 1800–
1600 B.C.) uncovered at Tell el-Fârʿah (likely Tirzah,[52] a Canaanite city
mentioned in the Bible), for example, bones of a young domesticated
pig were found, along with a jar containing bones of a pig embryo.
De Vaux explains these as the remains of a ritual killing, perhaps in
connection with magic or spirits of the underworld.[53] Further suggestions of ritual use of pigs are found at Beth-shan, another Canaanite city
mentioned in the Bible. At Beth-shan a pottery cult object was found
with a top that resembled the head of a pig, and pieces of similar objects
were uncovered in a temple of the god Mekal (Mukol). Beth-shan had
been occupied by Egyptians from the fifteenth until the eleventh century B.C., and there is evidence that Mekal may have been a local form
of the Egyptian deity Seth.[54] Other evidence comes from Gezer, also
mentioned in the Bible, where very few pig bones were uncovered overall, but some were found at what the excavator believed to be a place
where sacrifices were carried out. If that description is accurate, this,
too, implies that pigs were ritually killed, perhaps in connection with
supernatural beings associated with agriculture or the underworld.[55] At
an Early Bronze Age shrine at Et-Tell, certain alabaster fragments, according to de Vaux, are those of the hindquarters of a pig which is tied,
"a victim dressed for sacrifice."[56] De Vaux also mentions a bronze figure,
possibly a wild boar, from Megiddo (sixteenth century B.C.) that had
some ritual purpose.[57] Some of this, along with other evidence suggesting that pigs had a ritual role in Bronze and Iron Age Palestine, has
been discussed by Hesse.[58] He finds some of it contradictory, and, in any
case, is unconvinced that pigs played a role in cult activities in Iron Age
Palestine, even among the Philistines. That this statement may apply to
Canaanites, as well, is suggested by the fact that pigs are not included
on the lists of animals offered to deities at the ancient Canaanite, or
Northwest Semitic,[59] city of Ugarit in Syria.[60] Despite the weakness for
the case that the pig was used for sacrifice in established cults, to me it
nevertheless seems likely that, as was true in neighboring lands, pigs
were sometimes ritually killed on an individual or family basis.[61]

Evidence is more abundant for the Hittites, those Indo-Europeans of Anatolia who were a major power in the Near East in the second millennium B.C. The Hittites kept pigs, a trait they may have acquired independently or from the non-Indo-European Hatti. The latter are believed by most scholars to have preceded the Hittites in Anatolia and to have been the majority population in the heart of Hittite country.[62] Most Hittite pigs seem to have been free-ranging scavengers which, unlike other livestock, normally survived entirely on garbage. The Hittites had laws that provided compensation for damage done by pigs and for losses through the theft of pigs and piglets. The size of payments for loss indicates that pigs were not valued as highly as other meat animals. Though pork seems to have been acceptable enough to have been consumed at a funeral feast, pigs, unlike common cattle, sheep, and goats, were not among the usual sacrificial animals of the Hittites. Instead, they were chthonic animals that served as scapegoats in rites of magic, purification, and the removal of evil,[63] as when a piglet, along with a man and other animals, was ritually killed by troops who had been defeated in battle. The carcasses of pigs used in such rituals seem to have been thrown away, burned, or buried afterwards. The Hittites also prepared likenesses of pigs in dough, perhaps for similar purposes. They used a clay representation of a pig, as well as sow's milk, in a ritual involving a ruined house. Some documents link pigs with dogs, which also ate garbage, as being among the most humble of animals, ones that were usually impure. Thus, on three occasions in a single text, the approach of pigs was said to be defiling. In keeping with the above, neither pigs nor dogs were permitted to enter a temple, and particularly not its kitchen. One text of instructions for temple officials says that, if a pig or dog comes near temple implements of wood or fired clay, and the kitchen official does not dispose of them but instead offers the god food from an impure implement, "then to him the gods will give excrement and urine to eat and drink."[64] Harry A. Hoffner, a leading authority on the Hittites, is also certain that pig keepers were held in low esteem, and that it was insulting to call people swineherds.[65]

In Mesopotamia, archeological discoveries, representations of wild boars and domestic pigs, and mention of swine in inscriptions[66] permit a reasonable understanding of the role of pigs. In Sumer (c. 3000–2000 B.C.), people hunted wild swine, which were common in swampy areas, and kept domestic pigs in herds that normally survived by scavenging, along with supplements of grain or its by-products.[67] In a collection of Sumerian proverbs translated by Samuel Noah Kramer, the pig was referred to more often than any other animal being killed for its flesh, and often with humor: (1) "The fatted pig is about to be slaughtered, and so he says: 'It was the food which I ate!'" (2) "The pork butcher slaughters the pig, saying: 'Must you squeal? This is the road which your sire and your grandsire travelled, and now you are going on it too! (And yet) you are squealing!'" (3) "He was at the end of his means, and so he slaughtered his pig!"[68]

The Sumerians had special swineherds as well as pig butchers who supervised the killing of pigs and preparation of their flesh.[69] In one Sumerian proverb there is an allusion to the pig as an unclean animal, but in others it is clear that there was no ban against eating pork and nothing strange about it. Pork, like fish, was among the foods frequently banned in connection with particular rites and at specified times.[70] One reads, for example, that swine were not slaughtered during the month Teshrītum, seventh month of the year,[71] and that pork, along with several other foods, was specifically banned on the second and fifth days of that month.[72] Normally, however, pork appears to have been consumed without risk, and one document mentions a suckling pig delivered to the royal palace at Ur for roasting purposes.[73] That pork, especially fat pork, was a prestigious Sumerian food is further indicated by a proverb saying that fat pork "was too good for slave girls," that they had to be satisfied with lean flesh.[74]

How important were pigs compared with other domestic animals? The sign for pig was found frequently on tablets uncovered at the Sumerian city of Uruk.[75] At Tell Asmar (ancient Eshnunna), the bones of domesticated pigs were so plentiful (27 percent of all animal bones) that Max Hilzheimer concluded that the pig was the most important domestic animal raised for food.[76] On the other hand, swine are virtually unknown on cylinder seals,[77] and are mentioned infrequently on the Drehem tablets (c. 2100–2000 B.C.),[78] records of a sizable government livestock operation that obtained animals as taxes, loot from conquered peoples, gifts to royalty, and offerings at temples.[79] One may conclude from this that, as contrasted with sheep, goats, and common cattle, pigs were of quite minor importance at Drehem and of little or no importance in temple sacrifices. On the other hand, they were probably more important in ritual than the Drehem tablets suggest. I say this because pigs were also killed on an individual or family basis in connection with spirits of the earth. In this regard, one reads of a Sumerian lord of underworld spirits who appeared as a swine, and was called lord of swine.[80]

At Matarrah in northern Mesopotamia the bones of pigs (both wild and domesticated) amounted to 25 percent of all animal bones.[81] The pig also played a significant economic role among the Semites of northern Mesopotamia early in the Agade period (following 2370 B.C.), judging from tablets, written in Old Akkadian, that dealt with everyday economic matters at the city of Gasur (later Nuzi). The tablets include information on an exchange of barley for a pig, on barley issued as feed for pigs, on fat pigs that seem to have been given to people, and on an inventory of pigs in various cities.[82] The pig seems to have been dealt with in a businesslike manner much like common cattle, sheep, grain, flour, and other economic products.

In Babylonia and Assyria, wild swine were eaten, though their flesh and that of domestic pigs was banned, as in Sumer, on certain days.[83] Domestic pigs were urban scavengers whose value among the Babylonians is shown by the code of laws of Hammurabi (1792–1750 B.C.), which set a high penalty for the theft of pigs belonging to temples or householders.[84] Pigs, especially young, undefiled animals, were also killed in rites of healing and exorcism,[85] commonly as a substitute for a person who was ill and possessed by evil spirits.[86] One such rite is described on a tablet from the royal library of the Assyrian king Ashurbanipal (reigned c. 668–627 B.C.) at Nineveh.[87] The rite involved removing the bristles of a slain suckling pig, and placing them, as symbolic of human hair, on the head of the sick man. The heart of the pig, which had also been removed, was placed over the man's heart. Pig blood was sprinkled along the sides of the man's bed, and the carcass was opened and spread out over the man's body. The man was then cleansed by washing him with pure water "from the deep." As the rite continued, an appeal was read: "Give the pig in his [the man's] stead, and give the flesh as his flesh, the blood as his blood, and let him [the evil spirit] take it; its heart (which thou hast set on his heart) give as his heart, and let him take it." The evil spirit possessing the sick man was urged to leave his body and enter that of the slain pig, and a kindly spirit was asked to take its place. In cases like the one just described, the pig's flesh possessed by the evil spirit was impure and was presumably cast away or destroyed. At the same time, even though Assyrians were Semites, no impurity seems to have been attached beforehand to the animal—admittedly a young one—for its bristles, heart, blood, and carcass were in direct contact with, or near, the sick man.

Of special note in rites requiring pig killing was Lamashtu (Sumerian: Lamar), the Assyrian demon of childbed fever, who was hostile to "pregnant women, young mothers, and their babies."[88] Lamashtu is often depicted in Mesopotamia as suckling a young pig and a puppy, or standing in a field with a pig nearby.[89] The nursing of young animals by women is widespread in the modern world,[90] and some believe it likely that women nursed pigs during the Paleolithic period,[91] when hunters, after killing a nursing sow or some other nursing animal, brought home infant animals to be reared as members of the human family. Such a practice would have facilitated the domestication of dogs and pigs, and may explain their widespread sacrificial and ritual role in planting cultures.[92] In light of the above, it has been suggested that Lamashtu may have been a demonized version of an ancient fertility goddess.[93]

There are also reports of taming and fattening wild boars in Mesopotamia,[94] and of swamp boars being offered in temple sacrifice,[95] but de Vaux insists that the pig's use in Mesopotamian cult activities was minor, that its major ritual role was of the sort described above, in exorcising evil spirits.[96] Whatever its uses, the pig continued to be kept in Mesopotamia. After the death of Persian pretender Cyrus in 401 B.C., the Greek mercenaries and their Persian allies pledged allegiance to each other by slaughtering a bull, a ram, and a boar, dipping their weapons in the blood, and swearing an oath.[97] On their march upcountry to safety, the Greeks obtained hogs' lard and pork in Armenia and encountered pigs among the Drilai in Pontus.[98] Thus, from the time of the Sumerians down to the March of the Ten Thousand, pigs were kept and their flesh was eaten by various peoples in Southwest Asia.

In spite of the above, in Southwest Asia there were ambiguous feelings toward pigs similar to those found in Egypt. Saggs has suggested that in Mesopotamia pigs were numerous in early times, and that their flesh and lard were acceptable foods. In later times, he writes, a ban on pork developed, and pigs became taboo to all deities.[99] The date Saggs gives for this is "after 1400" B.C.[100] Pork continued to be consumed in Mesopotamia, as shown by reports[101] that in Assyria pork was eaten but was a food of the lower classes, and that in Babylonia in the time

6. Shamash (*seated*) (from William Hayes Ward, 1910).

of Nebuchadrezzar II (605–562 B.C.), people, including the poor, ate
pork, but it was not acceptable to deities.[102] The latter is well illustrated
in a popular saying recorded on an eighth-century B.C. Assyrian tablet:
"The pig is unholy . . . bespattering his backside, making the streets
smell, polluting the houses. The pig is not fit for a temple, lacks sense,
is not allowed to tread on pavements, an abomination to all the gods, an
abhorrence [to the (personal) g]od, and accursed by Shamash." [103] I will
say more later about Shamash (the Sumerian Utu) (Figure 6),[104] Assyrian
sun-god and god of justice. Here, however, I would observe that such
a perception of the pig fits with an Assyrian dream-book which states

that if, in a dream, one eats pork, it is an unlucky omen foretelling the anger of the gods.[105]

In Hellenistic and Roman times, the ritual associations of swine in Phoenicia, Syria, and Anatolia were often noted.[106] In Haran, now in southernmost Turkey, city residents were forbidden to eat pigs, but on a certain day every year they sacrificed swine, offered them to their gods, and ate as much pork as they could lay their hands on.[107] The pig is said to have been sacred to Astarte at Byblos in southern Lebanon,[108] and Porphyry (c. A.D. 234–305) wrote that the Phoenicians did not sacrifice pigs to their deities or eat pork.[109] Lucian (c. A.D. 120–180) wrote that at Hierapolis, a city in northern Syria sacred to Atargatis, people neither sacrificed pigs nor ate pork, with some saying it was because pigs were abominable, others, because they were holy animals.[110] In either case, it is said, such a ban was not found in other parts of Syria.[111]

In Anatolia proper, several religious cults were foci of pork avoidance. At Comana in Pontus, a center of the worship of the ancient Anatolian goddess of fertility Ma, people, to maintain the purity of the temple, neither ate pork nor permitted it in the city.[112] Similarly, at Castabus in the Carian Chersonese in southwest Anatolia, people who had eaten pork or come into contact with pigs were forbidden entry to the sanctuary of Hemithea.[113] Contact with swine also constituted one of the first categories of impurity for the followers of Men Tyrannus, an Asiatic deity worshipped widely in Anatolia. Perhaps best known of such cults in Anatolia, however, is the Phrygian cult of Cybele, the mother goddess. Worship of Cybele originated in prehistoric times, and became important in Galatia, Lydia, and Phrygia early in historical times. Julian (A.D. 331–363) said that the followers of Cybele abstained from pork during their sacred rites because the pig was regarded as an animal belonging to the earth and because its flesh was impure and coarse.[114] Pausanias (second century A.D.) reported that the people of Pessinus in Galatia, most sacred city of the cult of Cybele, did not eat pork; and he recounted the explanation given him, which centers on one of the myths of Attis, Cybele's son and lover, who figured prominently in her worship.[115] This was the account of a poet of the fourth century B.C., Hermesianax, who said that Attis was a Phrygian who migrated to Lydia and was so honored by the Lydians that Zeus sent a boar to destroy their fields. The boar killed Attis and some of the Lydians; hence the Galatians of Pessinus abstain from swine.[116]

In the Aegean region people seem to have kept sizable numbers of pigs from Neolithic times onwards.[117] The works of both Greek and Roman writers indicate that pork was a favorite meat and was considered more nutritious than other foods. Hippocrates (c. 460–377 B.C.), for example, wrote that pork, when not overly fat or lean, was the best of all meats.[118] Artemidorus Daldianus (second century A.D.) wrote that to dream of eating pork is very auspicious because it is more appetizing than the flesh of other animals.[119] Galen stated that, if professional athletes went for one day without pork and were given instead an equal amount of any other food, they immediately became weaker, and that if this persisted for several days, they lost weight. Aëtius, Oribasius, and the authorities succeeding Galen agreed in his judgment.[120] Pliny commented that in Rome the flesh of both domestic pig and wild boar was much esteemed, and that hogs' fat was highly regarded for medicinal purposes.[121] Martial wrote of his fondness for young milk-fed pigs;[122] and Juvenal and other writers of the period mentioned wild boar as a favorite delicacy of Roman epicures.[123] The boar hunt was an exciting event, and at the time of the late republic, wild boars were sometimes confined by well-to-do Roman gentry in private parks (*vivaria*), in part for the pleasure it gave the owners to observe them, and in part to have them readily available for slaughter for guests at special dinners.[124] At a dinner held by Trimalchio in Nero's day, a huge wild pig was brought in on a dish. On its head was a cap, and suspended from its tusks were two small baskets containing dates. Around the swine were arranged small piglets made of dough as if they were nursing, to identify the larger animal as a sow. Live birds had been placed inside the pig, and when the server cut through the sow's side with a knife, the birds emerged and flew off.[125] The Romans and Greeks also provided pork as food for the dead, and it was said in Rome that places where bodies are being buried are not really graves "until the proper rites are performed and a pig is slain."[126]

Among the Greeks and Romans, pigs were also sacrificed to deities,[127] whether for public purposes[128] or private ones, as of an unofficial group, family, or individual.[129] In early Rome, pigs were third in the hierarchy of common sacrificial animals,[130] following common cattle and sheep, and, in some cases, males of all three species were offered at one sacrifice, made only to Mars, under the name *suovetaurilia* (a boar, ram, and bull).[131] The wild boar was viewed as a terrifying adversary, and both

Greek and Roman warriors sometimes had images of boars on their helmets and shields.[132] On the other hand, the pig also had a special association with agricultural fertility, perhaps because of its ability to reproduce and its habit of turning up the soil.[133] In Rome, sows or pregnant sows were favored by goddesses such as Ceres (goddess of plant growth and agriculture) and her close associate Tellus (who had similar concerns), and boars were favored by male gods such as Mars (in early times likely a god of fertility).[134]

Archeological remains in Greece and the Balkans indicate that the pig has been associated with agricultural rites in the region since Chalcolithic and Neolithic times, long before the great Indo-European migrations. Gimbutas, using early Greek myths as well as images from sites in prehistoric eastern and southeastern Europe, has presented clear evidence of a close association between the pig and fertility goddesses.[135] The most convincing images are of Chalcolithic age (c. 5500/5000– 3500 B.C.), one a clay figure of a pregnant vegetation goddess wearing a pig mask, and others, sculptured pigs impressed with grain in the same way that it was impressed on the vegetation goddess herself.

In classical Greece, the role of sacrifice was so great that butchers' methods of killing animals had to agree with those used in sacrifice. Animals not killed in that manner, and animals not acceptable for sacrifice (usually wild animals were not offered to deities), could not be sold in butcher shops. "In other words," writes Marcel Detienne, "all comestible meat must result from a sacrificial killing."[136] The pig was a common sacrificial animal, and the pig or piglet was also the least expensive of the early sacrificial animals,[137] the normal victim at rites of purification[138] and at sacrifices to Demeter (*de* = "earth" or "cereal"; *meter* = "mother"),[139] goddess of agriculture (Figure 7), whose cult came to overlie that of Ceres in Rome. Though the pig was also sacrificed to other deities,[140] it was sacred to Demeter, and archeologists have uncovered in her shrines pig bones and representations of pigs, whether alone or being carried by women; there are also reports of representations of Demeter herself carrying or walking with a pig.[141] A major Greek festival involving Demeter, as well as her daughter, Persephone/ Kore,[142] was the Thesmophoria, most noted of the secret cult rites of ancient Greece,[143] and, in the view of some scholars, a survival from the Neolithic.[144]

7. Pig for sacrifice to Demeter and Persephone (from Maxime Collignon, 1901).

The Thesmophoria was an autumn planting festival, a many-sided affair with fertility concerns,[145] which was observed at various places in Greece, including Athens and Eleusis, where it was known as the Greater of the Eleusinian Mysteries. Though the carrying out of blood sacrifice was normally the realm of men in Greece, the Thesmophoria was a notable exception,[146] where men were excluded from the proceedings, and where those who killed pigs were usually married women of good families.[147] Killing was carried out in two ways. One involved throwing live pigs into an opening in the earth's surface, a crevice where the animal was not eaten but left to decay. The second involved slaughtering pigs on an altar, and later cooking and eating their flesh.[148] Apparently the eating of pork at the Thesmophoria was a solemn sacrament, in which, according to Frazer, the worshippers symbolically ate the body of the deity.[149] Additional testimony to fertility concerns is the fact that decayed meat from the previous year's festival was collected by women, brought to the altar, and sown with seed to assure a good crop.[150] It was especially fitting, therefore, that when, in the fourth century B.C., the city of Eleusis was given the right to issue its own coins, the pig was selected to appear on them to symbolize its mysteries.[151]

In Crete, like mainland Greece a center of the worship of Demeter, the pig was considered sacred, and one report indicates that nothing could induce people to eat its flesh.[152] This suggests the possible intrusion into the Greek and Roman world of Asian influences, for Crete was one of the avenues by which Oriental elements entered the Mediterranean world.

If a specific rejection of pork was present in Greece and Rome, it may have been introduced along with Asian deities. One likely candidate is the Phrygian Cybele with her lover Attis. Cybele was present in ancient Greece.[153] In Rome, she was introduced in such a direct and auspicious way as to enhance the possibility that Asian elements would be accepted at the same time.[154] In addition, there are reports of restrictions on her Roman devotees' use of pork.[155] A second candidate is the Syrian Adonis, who resembled Attis in some ways; whose followers presumably did not, as a rule, sacrifice pigs or eat pork;[156] and who in Greece was associated with the goddess Aphrodite. Ordinarily in Greek communities pigs were not sacrificed to Aphrodite, goddess of love and fertility and lover of Adonis.[157] Though the Greeks did not know why this was so, in those places where the pig was sacrificed in the rites of Aphrodite,[158] it may have been at special rituals in which Adonis was implicated along with Asian influence.[159]

Since the Rise of Christianity

In early Christianity there was considerable controversy over the food bans in Leviticus.[160] The result was that Christianity, despite its roots in Judaism, did not adopt the Jewish view that the pig is an unclean animal whose flesh should not be eaten. On the contrary, Christians spread the use of pork, both through conversions from Judaism and through the gradual elimination in the Greek and Roman world of earlier cults associated with the rejection of pork. Even in Egypt, with its ancient and curious attitudes toward the pig, the animal apparently became acceptable again and pork eating became more general.

Yet old attitudes persisted in Judaism and perhaps, too, in some of the unchronicled cults that survived in the Near East and Mediterranean. With the establishment of Islam, moreover, there arose a new champion of the ancient negative attitudes toward the pig and pork. The Prophet Mohammed, who had been swayed by Jewish law and may, in a general sense, have sought to imitate Jewish food laws, banned the flesh of swine.[161] The pig was the only animal singled out in this way in the Koran, where the ban was repeated more than once.[162] There is a hypothesis, advanced in an article by Diener and Robkin, that the Islamic prohibition of pork was established by the emerging Islamic state in an effort to control the peasantry, and to obtain rural agricultural surpluses for urban centers.[163] This hypothesis, while considered interesting by those who commented on their article, was also judged by many to be unconvincing or contrary to historical evidence.[164] Whatever factors led to the ban's introduction, it served to distinguish Moslems from their Christian adversaries, and from the seventh century on it was rapidly diffused by the faithful from an essentially pigless Arabia into regions of pig keeping in Asia, Africa, and southern Europe. Islamic rejection of the pig and pork was commonly accompanied by strong feelings of revulsion and scrupulous avoidance of both pigs and their flesh.[165] Some Moslems, such as those of Egypt, so abhorred swine as to consider everything touched by them contaminated and worthless.[166] The writings of Western travellers contain abundant references to Moslems ridiculing Christian pork eating. At the close of the fifteenth century, moreover, Venetian merchants were required to pay a substantial sum for the right to keep a pig at their establishment in Alexandria.[167] Christian minorities living in Moslem lands were special targets, and some, as a result, gave up pig keeping and denied that they ate pork. The Armenians who lived in Turkey prior to the First World War adapted in an unusual way. Since they could not follow a normal form of pig keeping, many of them would capture young wild swine to raise for their flesh.[168]

The contrast between Moslem and Christian practices has made the present-day pattern of pig keeping in the Mediterranean and Near East fairly simple. Christians on the north shores of the Mediterranean generally keep pigs and eat pork, though Moslems of the Balkans do not.[169] In North Africa, pork has been eaten by European Christian settlers in various places and by at least some Coptic Christians of Egypt.[170] To the east of the Mediterranean, pork is rejected by Orthodox Jews and Moslems, including the Nuṣayrīs (Alawites) of northern Syria,[171] whose religion appears to be a syncretism of Islam and the ancient Haranian religion, as well as by such cults as the Yezidis of Kurdistan [172] and the Mandaeans of southern Iraq and Iran.[173] The Christians of Syria and Lebanon eat pork.[174] It has been substantiated, too, that the Druse do not hesitate to eat it, and that, if they seem to abstain, it is during their stay in the cities and by imitation or from fear of the Moslems.[175]

In Israel, both Arab and foreign Christians, as well as some non-observant Jews, eat pork, with pork working its way into Israeli menus because it is superior in taste to the low-quality beef available there.[176] The threat to pig keeping in Israel today comes from strict Jews who have pushed for legislation to restrict or eliminate pig keeping and the processing and sale of pork, though they have often been thwarted by secularists. As described by Zucker in 1972, there had been a supreme court ruling that blocked attempts at obtaining a complete ban on the keeping of pigs and marketing of pork in Israel, but the struggle continued on a local level, with traditional forces enjoying some success. There were laws intended to keep pigs out of sight, as behind tall hedges or walls, or under cover when moved by truck. The government also limited pig keeping to northern areas of Israel in the hope that the practice would be restricted mainly to Christians living there. Unfortunately, from the traditionalist perspective, a Marxist collective farm (kibbutz) in the Nazareth area of the north soon became the nation's leader in raising pigs and selling pork. Tel Aviv, in turn, had ordinances forbidding stores from exhibiting pork in their windows, and restaurants from listing the words for pork, ham, or bacon on their menus. The response to the latter ban was understandable: some restaurants began to call pork white steak or special steak, and one chain of sandwich shops designated it oink. Strict Jews were still able to deny kosher certification to restaurants that served pork, which meant that observant Jews could not eat in them. On the other hand, Jews who were strictly observant were estimated to constitute a mere 15 percent of Israel's population, too few to be essential to a restaurant's survival. It must have been a frustrating situation for all concerned. As a rabbi in Tel Aviv observed: "I am afraid not many people follow the Bible anymore. They want to eat pork and the government won't ban its sale."[177] Despite his frustration, parliamentary proposals of one sort or another continued to be made. In 1985, Prime Minister Shimon Peres supported one such proposal to ban the sale of pork.[178]

At the end of 1990, moreover, the government, now under new

leadership, proposed a ban on the marketing of pork by Jewish firms, in a concession to get a small ultraorthodox political party to join its coalition. In an initial response, several nonkosher butchers staged a protest in central Jerusalem by distributing free ham sandwiches to the public. In early 1993, the processing and selling of pork by Jews still continued in Israel, and, because of demand from Russian Jewish immigrants, Jewish pork sellers are now found in communities where they had not been present previously. This has been greeted with considerable hostility and harassment by earlier residents, who also blame the newly arrived Russians for other social problems. In the town of Kiryat Shmonah, occupied mainly by Sephardic Jews from the Near East, one earlier resident was quoted as saying, "What have the Russians brought to this town? . . . Pork and prostitution. That's it, pork and prostitution." A rabbi, in turn, observed that the Russians introduced an alien culture to the town, that townfolk were faced with Jews "selling pork and putting up Christmas trees. We didn't expect them to be Zionists," he said, "but we thought that at least they would come as Jews. But to many people here, the immigrants seem like strangers, rather than part of the Jewish nation." [179]

Returning to the Islamic world, one notes that though almost all Moslems have condemned pork as unacceptable food, two tenth-century Persian doctors apparently upheld its use. One is Avicenna, who, in his classification of foodstuffs, included pork among foods that strengthen the blood.[180] A second is Haly Abbas, who spoke favorably of it as a food.[181] The eating of wild[182] and domestic pigs as food has also survived here and there.[183] One reads of certain Islamic sects in Kurdistan (the Ahle Hagg, for example) permitting pork as food.[184] Among the Indonesians and certain Berbers of North Africa, moreover, people persisted in pig keeping and pork eating long after becoming Moslems. Xavier de Planhol says that, in the Middle Ages, Ghomara nonconformists of the Rif permitted the consumption of pork.[185] He also says that formerly people raised swine in most of the mountain core of the Rif, a wooded environment eminently suited since antiquity to the practice.[186] It was only a few generations ago, in fact, that the Berbers of Iherrushen and Ikhuanen in northern Gzennaya, Morocco, stopped raising pigs after one of their leading men returned from a pilgrimage to Mecca. Elsewhere among the Berbers of Morocco, pig keeping apparently persisted even later, although people were very secretive about it. Carleton Coon could not say with certainty whether people kept swine in the Rif or Senhaja when he was there in the late 1920s, but he suspected that they did. The pigs were bred from animals trapped in the mountains and brought home. They fed on acorns and roots on the mountainside during the daytime, and at night were kept in houses. People were careful to remove them before guests arrived, and never took them to market or admitted keeping them.[187] In Coon's time, pork, apparently from wild boars, was also made into sausages or dried in the sun to form kadids. Because some people ridiculed the eating of pork kadids, connoisseurs in some places ate them secretly and in others called them by different names when strangers were present.[188]

Under Western influence the prejudice against pork seemed to have declined somewhat among Moslems in the Near East. With the end of European colonialism following the Second World War and the subsequent rise of Islamic fundamentalism, however, the direction of the struggle has again been reversed.

Europe beyond Greece and Rome

In preagricultural Europe, the wild pig, along with deer, aurochs, and wild equines, was among the animals most sought by hunters. With the coming of the Neolithic, these and other wild animals continued to be hunted, but domestic common cattle, sheep and goats, and pigs became much more important as providers of flesh.[189] As agriculture spread from the far southeast of Europe, where conditions favored sheep and goats, into better-wooded lands to the north and west, pigs initially gained in relative importance because they are well suited to wooded habitats.[190] As agricultural expansion and forest clearing continued, however, the relative importance of sheep increased, though pigs have continued to play a major economic role up to the present.

For various northern Europeans, boars or hogs were often associated with war or combat.[191] Swine were also believed to associate with evil forces, and were thus considered sinister and able to predict the weather.[192] Like the ancient Greeks and Romans, Slavic, Baltic, Germanic, and Celtic peoples also associated swine with crop fertility. This is well illustrated in the account by Tacitus (c. A.D. 56–120) of a Germanic (or Estonian) tribe along the Baltic that had a cult of the mother goddess symbolized by boar's masks worn to protect against danger of all sorts.[193] The association is also revealed in the sanctity of the

8. Modern drawing of Freyr riding a boar (from Thomas Bulfinch, 1898).

boar to Freyr, principal Scandinavian god of fertility, and to various other deities who dealt with fertility. Boars were sacrificed to Freyr. The god is depicted in a mythical scene as riding his "golden-bristled boar" (Figure 8). He is described in a chariot pulled by that boar. He himself may have appeared as a boar. His sister, the goddess Freyja, is called sow and is associated with swine, and with love, sensuality, birth, death, and war.[194] The figure of a boar is found on the lid of an early cremation urn uncovered in Germany, and "boar-crested helmets" (Figure 9) were among the most highly valued possessions of early kings in Sweden, who claimed descent from Freyr. Boar-crested helmets are mentioned several times in *Beowulf*, that Old English epic believed to have been composed in the eighth century. An Anglo-Saxon helmet of that sort has been uncovered in a grave in England, presumably placing its wearer under the protection of Frey (= Freyr) or Freya (= Freyja).[195]

Associations between swine and fertility persist in local traditions

9. Early Swedish warriors wearing boar-crested helmets (from O. Montelius, 1888).

and practices in northern Europe even today. In parts of Kurland in
Latvia, for example, the pig is regarded as the grain spirit, whose fertil-
izing power is concentrated in its tail. When the first barley is planted,
a pig tail is stuck in the soil in the hope that the barley will reach a
similar height. In certain places in White Russia, pig bones are believed
to keep the cereal crop safe from damage by hail, and elsewhere pig
ribs are added to a flax seedbag in the hope that plants will mature
well and be of good size. In Scandinavia, one finds the tradition of the
"Yule boar," involving use of the final stalks of harvest cereal to prepare,
ordinarily at Christmastime, a cake in the image of a pig. This cake is
kept and fed to plow horses at the time of spring sowing with wishes
for an abundant harvest.[196] In a similar vein, people of the Scania area
in Sweden set the salted head of a pig, along with its feet and tail, on
the table at Christmastime.[197] These were not eaten, however, until the
initial plowing in springtime, when some was consumed by men and
some was given to the plow horses.[198]

The ancient Celts also had swine gods or goddesses, as well as divine
swineherds, magic swine, boar-crested helmets, coins on which swine
were depicted, models and other representations of swine (Figure 10),

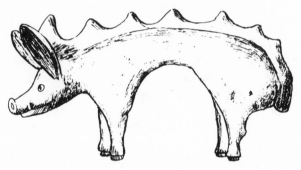

10. Early bronze figures of boars found in Middlesex, England (from John Arnott MacCulloch, 1918; see MacCulloch 1916–32).

and burials that contained pig bones and even entire joints of pork as food for the afterlife. In Irish myths, pork was so typical at feasts provided to dead warriors in the afterworld that, on occasion, the lord of the feast was pictured as a man with a pig in his arms. Swine are also common in Celto-Roman sculpture in mainland Europe, including, as in Ireland, a boar carried by a deity. Celtic tales from the British Isles contain numerous references to the hunting of swine, to mighty supernatural swine, and to powerful swineherds. Certain Celts, in an effort to assure good crops, would bury pork in their fields or mix it with seed before sowing their cereal. In addition, they sacrificed swine, regarded pork as the best of all flesh foods, and ate it with enthusiasm, as indicated in Irish folktales of great feasts at which huge swine were consumed. In Christian times, several Irish saints were swineherds before joining the clergy, and monasteries in Ireland kept swine and also obtained pork from wild boars that were hunted.[199] Próinséas Ní Cha-tháin has suggested that the visionary and magical powers of pig herders may have stemmed from the acorns consumed by their pigs or by the herders themselves, or from oak leaves they chewed. He bases this on the fact that, as among other Indo-Europeans, oaks had special sanctity for the Celts. In Ireland sacred oaks served in inauguration ceremonies. In addition, certain major Irish saints, such as Columba and Brigid, were associated with an oak.[200]

Against the above background, it is somewhat surprising to find an account referring to a prejudice against pork in the highlands of Scot-land.[201] This, however, has been explained in terms of the sanctity of pigs.[202] On the other hand, it is said that in northeast Scotland the pig was regarded as unclean, and its bite was believed to cause cancer.[203] At sea, the men of several villages would not pronounce the word "swine," which was a word of ill omen. Yet, despite this, the people ate pork, and soup made of fresh pork was considered a remedy for many dis-eases. Apart from this and other local bans that may have occurred, from temporary penetrations of Islam and from the settlement of non-pork-eating Jewish migrants there, Europeans beyond Moorish Spain and the Balkans remained relatively isolated from the great struggle between those who used pork as food and those who rejected it.[204] I say "relatively" because the conflict did appear even in northern Europe. In-deed, some say that the triumph of Christianity over Islam and Judaism in Russia came about partly because Vladimir (d. A.D. 1015), earliest Christian ruler in that land, decided that the continued use of pork (and strong liquor) was essential for survival in a land with a rigorous climate like his.[205] In any case, when Europeans began their colonial ex-pansion following the explorations of Christopher Columbus and Vasco da Gama, they took a more active part in favor of pig keeping and pork eating in far-flung parts of the world. Today, Europe as a whole has more pigs (185.6 million in 1989) than any region of the Old World except China.

Africa South of the Sahara

Africa south of the Sahara has long been deeply embroiled in the controversy over the status of the pig and the acceptability of its flesh as human food. In early times, that controversy involved only limited parts of sub-Saharan Africa, where wild forms of *Sus* seem to have occurred only in the Sudan and Ethiopia, and domestic pigs appear to be newcomers except in the same two countries.[206] It seems most likely that domestic pigs were introduced at some unknown, but pre-Islamic, date to the Sudan from Egypt by way of the string of Nubian agricultural villages that cling to the banks of the Nile.[207]

Once the domestic pig reached the more humid country south of Khartoum, it spread into areas away from the river in the Sudan, and probably then found its way into Ethiopia.[208] It does not seem, however, that in pre-European times the domestic pig was diffused farther into mainland Africa than this. Why it should have failed to spread farther cannot be determined precisely. The tropical forests of Africa at first glance appear to be as well suited to pig keeping as the forests of tropical Asia. However, one should not overlook the fact that tropical Africa is affected by tsetse-borne sleeping sickness, and that the pig, along with other domesticated animals, is susceptible to the disease. In early times, this may have been a deterrent to the spread of pig keeping in the same way that in modern times it has limited pig keeping in forested areas. Another deterrent to the early spread of pigs southward was anti-pig sentiment. That sentiment is reported in modern times for certain cattle peoples of eastern and southern Africa, and, if it was present in early times, these peoples may have hindered the southward spread of domestic pigs. More clearly involved were Ethiopian groups who, since antiquity, have looked on pigs as unclean and refused to keep them or eat pork. The antipathy today occurs not only among Moslems and Jews (Falasha) but also among Christians and unassimilated pagan Cushites such as the Qemant,[209] who also reject the flesh of its distant relative, the hippopotamus.[210] There are reports of pig keeping among various tribal groups in the Sudan borderlands of Ethiopia, and even among certain Galla of southern highland Ethiopia.[211] Such pig keeping has long been under pressure, however, and likely this represents the last stand of the domestic pig among highland peoples. It is no surprise to read that in 1989 Ethiopia as a whole had an estimated total of only twenty thousand pigs.

Pig keeping in the Sudan area was clearly under pressure from the north starting in the seventh century, when Moslems overran Egypt. Although the Nubian Christian kingdoms along the Nile held out for several centuries, they were overthrown one by one as Islam gradually spread southward, and pig keeping was abandoned. After the capitulation of the Nubian Christians at Ibrīm in 1173, the Moslem conquerors performed acts symbolic of their victory over Christianity. They burned the cross taken from the church. They jailed and tortured the bishop. In addition, they killed all seven hundred pigs found in the community.[212] Nevertheless, pig keeping probably persisted farther south in Nubia until the fall of Dongola in the fourteenth century and of Alwa in the early sixteenth century. The further expansion of Islam has brought about a continuing recession of pig keeping in the Sudan belt. The practice has survived mainly among groups that have remained pagan,[213] as among certain peoples of the Nuba Mountains and the Sudan-Ethiopian borderlands, though a few Moslem groups, such as the southern Fung, are said to keep pigs.[214] Even these are now coming under increasing pressure from Islam. Many Nuba already have abandoned pig keeping and speak with contempt of their unconverted brethren who continue to eat pork.[215] A similar abandonment of pig keeping has occurred along the border between the Sudan and Ethiopia, where tribal people have been under pressure not only from Islam in the Sudan but also from Christianity in Ethiopia.[216]

At the same time that Islam was bringing about the decline of pig keeping in the Sudan, Europeans were introducing domestic pigs to Africa, following the Portuguese voyages of exploration in the fifteenth century.[217] From the west coast, pigs spread into the interior, except where sleeping sickness or Islamic or other prejudice blocked their way.[218] In East Africa the introduction of pig keeping had been hindered by the presence of the Arab coastal settlements, and, there and in southern Africa (used throughout to refer to the region south of the middle course of the Zambesi River), by the reluctance of various non-Arab peoples to accept them. Though in some cases this may have resulted from Islamic influence, in others it may simply have been due to the strangeness of the animal or a contempt developed by cattle people for a beast unsuited to their way of life. As in the Near East, some sub-Saharan groups who rejected the flesh of domestic pigs nevertheless ate the flesh of wild pigs, whether bush pigs (*Potamochoerus*), wart hogs (*Phaecochoerus*), or, where they were found, common pigs (*Sus*).[219]

Whatever their initial objection, many non-Moslem groups of Africa have since given way to European example and influence.[220] Pig keeping and pork eating have been adopted by many native groups, especially along the Guinea coast, in the Congo area, and in Angola. Among certain groups pigs occupy an important place in animal husbandry, but most keep only small numbers. Thus in 1989 sub-Saharan Africa as a whole had only about thirteen million domestic pigs, little more than Vietnam, a single, small country in Southeast Asia.

Not only is the keeping of domestic pigs found in sub-Saharan Africa, but also a few peoples of West and Central Africa have tamed and kept its relative, the bush pig or red river hog, for eating.[221] This may be an interesting step toward the domestication of an animal that would fit into the same ecological niche in African life as the domestic pig.

Iran and Inner Asia

Iran and Inner Asia (Central Asia) represent another major arena of struggle between pro- and anti-pig views. This is partly because the region contains many pastoral groups, who traditionally have been major actors in the struggle. It is also related to the region's geographic position between and ties with the European and Chinese centers of pig keeping on one hand and the Near Eastern center of pig and pork rejection on the other.

In Iran, archeological evidence indicates that in certain places pigs have been kept and eaten since Neolithic times. At the site of Hajji Firuz in northwestern Iran (which dates from 5500 to 5100 B.C.), pigs, most of them apparently domesticated, accounted for about a third of all animals used for food, exceeded only by caprines.[222] This, however, was not the general Neolithic pattern, judging from sites in western Iran,[223] where pigs, whether wild or domesticated, were of quite minor importance. Their importance seems to have increased in that region in Chalcolithic times, but it remained far less than that of sheep and goats, and less even than common cattle. Moreover, at Tal-e Malyan, site of the ancient highland Elamite city of Anshan (not far from the later Persian capital of Persepolis), only a handful of pig bones, most likely from wild swine, were found at levels dating from 3400 to 2800 B.C. and 2100 to 1800 B.C., and none from Middle Elamite levels (1600–1000 B.C.).[224] In a careful review of recently uncovered evidence of early animal use in eastern Iran and Baluchistan, Meadow mentions the wild boar for a few sites.[225] He also writes of a common cattle-sheep-goat complex during Neolithic times, and of early domesticated dogs. These domesticates were joined at some sites in the late third or early second millennium B.C. by camels, horses, and donkeys. Meadow does mention a few pig remains, along with those of domesticated water buffalo, for Balakot, at the far southeastern borders of Baluchistan, but he does not say whether the pigs were domesticated.

In the Avesta, holy book of the Zoroastrians, parts of which may date from the seventh century B.C., the wild boar is mentioned as strong, sharp-toothed, wrathful, swift, and pursuing,[226] but I have found nothing in that work to indicate that its flesh was consumed, or that domestic pigs were kept or eaten. This, as we shall see, parallels the situation of the pig in the *Rig-veda,* which resembles the Avesta in many ways. The failure of the Avesta to include domestic pigs is nevertheless surprising because bones of pigs (presumably domesticated) have been uncovered in Iron Age (c. 1200–550 B.C.), Achaemenid (c. 550–250 B.C.), and Early Parthian (c. 250–100 B.C.) levels at Jammeh Shuran in western Iran.[227] In the last two periods, moreover, they seem to have been far more important than they had been earlier. There is also documentary evidence from Achaemenid times that wild boars were hunted and their flesh eaten.[228] Such hunting of wild boars (Figure 11) continued into Sassanian times (A.D. 224–651),[229] and apparently their flesh was eaten.[230] In addition, the Pahlavi texts of the Zoroastrians, which date roughly to the ninth century A.D. (a time when most Iranians had already converted to Islam), contain references to domestic pigs. I have found no indication in those texts that they were impure. On the contrary, such pigs were killed for a sacred feast.[231] After that time, Islamic influence brought on a decline in the status of the pig among Zoroastrians. Today in Iran, neither the surviving Zoroastrians[232] nor Moslems eat pork, and in 1989 no pigs were reported in livestock statistics of the FAO (Food and Agriculture Organization of the United Nations) for that country. When a European in Iran ate ham or bacon, the Iranians called it nightingale's flesh to save face for the cook who prepared it.[233] Iranians also now regard the wild boar as unclean. A pious Moslem killed by a wild boar, it is said, has to remain in the fires of hell for five hundred years to become purified.[234] In view of their antipathy toward pigs, it is odd to read that Iranian grooms whenever possible keep a wild pig in the stable. They do this in the

11. Ancient Persian (?) hunter spearing a wild boar (from William Hayes Ward, 1910).

belief that pigs protect horses from the evil eye and that pig's breath is good for horses.[235]

The Scythians, horse people originally from Inner Asia, used no pigs for sacrifice according to Herodotus, and were not inclined toward pig keeping;[236] and for the early Turks, swine were taboo.[237] In Inner Asia today, pork is rejected by Moslem groups. It has also been rejected by certain non-Moslem peoples both there and in neighboring areas: Christian Cheremis who lived along the Volga River in European Russia in the last century,[238] Votyak (a Christian Finnic group of the Vologda region of European Russia), Lapps, and Yakut of Siberia.[239] With the Cheremis and the Votyak, the rejection of pork was apparently in imitation of Moslem groups, but the diffusion of Moslem ideas seems less certain for the Lapps and the Yakut.

Inner Asia nevertheless is transitional in its attitudes toward pigs and pork. Although the Selkup Samoyed apparently keep no pigs themselves, wealthier families eat pickled pork during wedding celebrations.[240] The Kara-Kirghiz (Burut) farmers, who live northeast of Afghanistan from the Pamir region into Chinese Turkestan, keep pigs.[241] Mongols have a strong bias against pigs, but have no prejudice against pork and usually will eat it whenever they visit a city like Peking. When they do settle down to farming, moreover, they may start at once to keep pigs, which can become their sole source of meat.[242]

Tibet presents an even more confusing picture of transition. Tibetan Buddhists believe that pigs must have been guilty of great evil in their previous lives to have been reborn in their present form. Because of their prior evil, the flesh of pigs, more than that of any other animal, is believed to contain "small black pills" which have magical powers and can send one to hell. Because of concern with spiritual injury, Tibetans avoid eating such flesh and even attempt to keep their dogs from consuming it. They also believe that pigs are unclean in their present state because, in feeding, they destroy other forms of life. High lamas avoid pork even if it is free of black pills because it is impure and Buddhist law bans it. Other lamas may occasionally eat it, and there is even one report of pork being served in monasteries. Certain Tibetan nomadic tribes also reject pork, though settled folk eat it to some extent, especially in places like Lhasa and Dartsendo (Kangting), where foreign habits are imitated.

Often in the past the peoples of Inner Asia who kept pigs were under strong pressure to abandon the practice. Until recently in this century, however, the struggle has gone in favor of the pig, for China and Russia were dominant in the area. Where pigs are found in the region, they have often been introduced: to western Turkestan by the Slavs, and to eastern Turkestan, or Sinkiang, from China.[243] Now, with the rise of vigorous Islamic fundamentalism, the situation is being reversed again.

East Asian Center of Pig Keeping

China has been a major center of pig keeping since antiquity. According to the traditional view, the domestic pig spread from the Near East, breeding with wild boars along the way, to reach China some millennia after its initial domestication. Some scholars, however, favor an independent domestication of pigs in Southeast or East Asia in antiquity, perhaps even before pigs were domesticated in the Near East.[244] This view seems to be supported by studies of pig cranial capacity[245] and pig taxonomy[246] that suggest that domestic pigs in Southeast Asia and China are descended largely from local wild swine. It is also supported by the occurrence of bones of domestic pigs in caves near Kweilin in South China, the bones dating to about 9300–7000 B.C.[247] There are serious questions about these dates. If, however, they prove to be valid, these may be the earliest domestic pigs known in the entire Old World. Bones of domestic pigs are also found in early Neolithic sites in North

China (c. 6500–5000 B.C.),[248] as well as in other early sites in North and Central China.

Swine were an important feature of every early northeast Chinese culture from the Neolithic down to and including Shang times (eighteenth to twelfth century B.C.). Indeed, pig bones are found in such enormous numbers as to suggest that pork was a dietary staple for Neolithic groups. The Shang Chinese, who kept both domestic pigs and an occasional wild boar in sties, also ate them in large numbers.[249] Perhaps the best illustration of the importance of the pig is the fact that the Chinese ideograph meaning "home" consists of the signs for roof and for pig.

In later times, the number of pigs has varied according to group and period. Whatever the variation, the pig has remained one of the most common domestic animals in China, and pork, a prized food. In traditional China, most people consumed very little meat, but the New Year's Day pig was cherished in the same way as the Thanksgiving turkey in the United States. According to a village survey conducted throughout China from 1929 to 1933, pork and lard supplied more than 70 percent of all animal calories consumed.[250] In more recent times (1989), China had 41 percent of all the pigs in the world, and its pig population was by far larger than that of any other country (349 million, compared with 55 million for the United States), and nearly twice that of the entire continent of Europe (185.6 million).

The pig in the traditional Chinese economy was a household scavenger that ate table scraps and other items that people could not eat. Sometimes pigs were even quartered so as to provide direct access to human excreta and garbage. The result was that they converted into flesh the nutrients that people were unable to digest. In addition, they may have performed a significant role in interfering with the life cycles or in killing human parasites that passed through their intestines.[251]

Pressure in China against keeping and eating pigs (as contrasted with vegetarian pressures against eating animals of any sort) has come principally from the sizable Moslem minority, who number at least seventeen million to twenty-five million, and may number as many as forty million to fifty million. Most are of Turkic, Mongol, or Arab extraction, and they are especially numerous in northwestern China. For pious Moslems, the very presence of a pig is an irritant, for it defiles the ground and pollutes the air.[252] The strictest Mongol Moslems refuse even to enter an ordinary Chinese house.[253] Some Moslems avoid the very word "pig," and refer to the animal as the black one. Chinese Moslems also use the oath "pig-defiled," which seems to puzzle non-Moslem Chinese, who do not regard the pig as an abominable animal.[254] In some regions, Chinese Moslems drink river water to avoid using the same well as their pig-keeping Chinese neighbors. When, during the Cultural Revolution, the insensitive demand was made in certain places that Moslems raise pigs, this, along with other violations of their traditional ways, understandably led to a furious reaction.[255]

Though they publicly avoid pork, in private Chinese Moslems may be quite lax. Some will eat pork if it is called mutton or some other name. Others, if on a trip alone without other Moslems to observe their behavior, may eat pork even without such evasions. This has led to the popular Chinese jibe "One Moslem travelling will grow fat, whereas two on a journey will grow thin."[256] Although the outcome is far from certain, one wonders whether the Chinese may have weakened Moslem rejection of pork, in this sense acculturating the Moslems in the same way they have done with other alien groups through history. Not only have the Chinese blunted Moslem pressure in China Proper, but they have also carried pigs wherever they have migrated and have encouraged other people to raise them. In Tibet, pigs are kept mainly by the Chinese.[257] In Inner Mongolia, most Chinese families have a pig or two, and pork is their most common meat.[258] On Taiwan, both Chinese settlers and some aboriginal groups keep pigs, and pork is the most important source of animal protein.[259]

Elsewhere in East Asia, pig keeping is important in many areas. Among the Manchu, as among the Chinese, pigs are valuable, prestigious animals. Not only are they used to pay the bride price and for ransom, but also pork is the principal flesh food and is offered to the spirits on ceremonial occasions.[260] The Koreans keep pigs in much the same way as the Chinese, though pork is too expensive for most people except on important occasions.[261]

In Japan proper, the situation is different. Bones of domesticated swine have not been found in Neolithic sites of the Jomon culture (fifth or fourth millennium to c. 250 B.C.).[262] Thus pigs may have been introduced rather late; and even then vegetarian feeling, encouraged by Buddhism, apparently kept consumption of pork low. Today, though traditional attitudes have broken down, relatively small numbers of Japanese have come to like pork because it is fatty and out of keeping with the greaseless cooking typical of the country.[263] It is true that many farmers in Japan now raise pigs, feeding them largely on waste and garbage, but for the most part they sell them for consumption by town and city people. In the Ryukyus, pig keeping is of greater importance than in Japan: not only is the pig the most important sacrificial animal, but also the remnant of an ancient cult survives in which pig skulls are associated with ancestor worship.[264]

The Indian Subcontinent

The Indian subcontinent stands in sharp contrast to China in its small pig population: about ten million in 1989 (no pigs were reported for the predominantly Islamic countries of Pakistan and Bangladesh, even though pigs are present in those countries). This number is so small primarily because of cultural attitudes, for in some parts of the subcontinent the pig could play just as important a dietary role as it does in Vietnam and China.

Wild boars (*Sus cristatus*) were among the fauna of early India, and even today they continue to survive in most parts of the country.[265] As for domestic pigs, they seem to have been known in the subcontinent since antiquity (fourth millennium B.C. or before). Indeed, at some early sites bones of young pigs are so numerous as to lead to the conclusion that pork was a dietary staple.[266] Remains of Indian pigs, whether from domesticated or wild animals, are also found in more than one site of the Indus Valley civilization (c. 2500–1700 B.C.), and there are indications that they were eaten.[267]

The earliest suggestions of feeling against the pig and pork in India come in the Vedic records. The Aryans apparently knew the wild boar in their homeland, and the first part of "*sū-kara,*" one of their names for the boar, is similar to the Latin root "*sus,*" from which the genus name *Sus* derives. The *Rig-veda* (1500–900 B.C.?) includes various references to the boar or wild boar. It is described as iron-tusked, destructive, and fierce. Certain demons and deities who have such qualities (such as weather gods) are called boars or are accompanied by wild boars. Other deities, in turn, hunted and killed them.[268] The Vedic records also reveal an association of the boar with various deities, and include boars and domestic pigs among the animals and things closely linked with fertility, water, and moisture, or that foretold rain.[269]

There is nothing in the *Rig-veda,* however, to suggest that wild boars were eaten. Nor is there a single reference to the flesh of domestic pigs being eaten in the *Rig-veda,* despite such statements about horses, rams, barren cows, bulls, oxen, and water buffaloes. Furthermore, neither Macdonell and Keith, in their summary of flesh food in the Vedic literature,[270] nor Om Prakash, in his book on food and drink in ancient India,[271] mentions pork as food in the Vedic period. On the other hand, the Aryans are believed to have used the word *"kola"* (boar or hog) in a derogatory way to refer to aborigines.[272] There are also specific early references to boars or village pigs as unclean animals and their flesh as forbidden food. Pigs were not among the normal sacrificial animals.[273] In the *Śatapatha Brāhmaṇa* (800–600 B.C.?), a vicious boar, a vicious ram, and a dog are mentioned as unclean animals.[274] In the *Vaikhānasa Gṛihya-sūtra* (500–100 B.C.?), a place of sacrifice walked on by a boar is depicted as unclean.[275] In the *Mānava Dharma-śāstra* (c. A.D. 100–300), one reads that a village pig, along with other unclean beings (among them, a dog and a menstruating woman), should not observe Brahmins eating.[276] In the *Vishnu Smṛti* (c. 100 B.C.—A.D. 400), a ceremony is said to be inauspicious if carried out in sight of a tame pig.[277] The grunt of a hog was also considered inauspicious in the Sanskrit literature.[278] In the *Mānava Gṛihya-sūtra,* one finds a statement that a dream in which a person observes pigs is unclean.[279] In the *Āpastamba Dharma-sūtra* (?500 B.C.—A.D. 200), a ban on the flesh of village pigs is mentioned along with bans on other unclean foods.[280] Other early documents on Hindu law[281] simply say that pigs or village pigs should not be eaten, but the *Mānava Dharma-śāstra*[282] not only lists village pigs as banned food, but also indicates that a "twice-born man [initiated member of one of the three highest classes] who knowingly eats . . . a village-pig [or certain other unclean foods, such as garlic and onions][283] will become an outcaste," and that if he eats such flesh unwittingly, he must perform penances. The *Chhāndogya Upanishad,* in turn, says that an evil person will be reborn as a pig or some other evil creature.[284] The strong suggestion is that the Aryans had no pigs when they entered India. They may have harbored anti-pig feelings before they arrived or developed them not long afterwards, perhaps in reaction to the ways of the pig-keeping peoples they conquered.

Pig keeping and pork eating seem to have been under pressure from the Aryans, but those practices nevertheless continued. There is a tradition that the Buddha himself died after eating pork, and, though this is based on a controversial translation,[285] one gathers from the Buddhist *Jātakas* (c. 450 B.C.) that pork, whether from wild, tame, or domestic pigs, was well liked.[286] There is also evidence (i.e., cut marks and charring of pig bones) uncovered at ancient Bhogavardhana (second century B.C. to third century A.D.) in Maharashtra which indicates that pork was eaten and suggests that bone marrow of young pigs was a delicacy.[287] It is true that Aelian (c. A.D. 170–235), basing his statement on reports of Ctesias (400 B.C.) and other Greeks, wrote that there were neither wild nor domesticated pigs in India, and that people there had strong feelings against pork, which they never consumed.[288] This may have been true of some people and places, but as a generalization it is incorrect. The situation described by Prakash for the Gupta period (early fourth to late fifth century A.D.) indicates that by then most Indians avoided pork and that those who did consume it were scorned by others.[289] Nevertheless, pigs continued to be killed for food even in the post-Gupta period, and one twelfth-century Hindu work even includes information on the best cuts of pork and on how to prepare and eat them.[290]

In modern India, the hunting and eating of wild boar has been reported among various groups, including certain Rājputs, members of that aristocratic warrior caste.[291] Tod, writing early in the nineteenth century, described a royal boar hunt conducted each spring by the Rājputs of Mewar in Rajasthan, at which boars were killed to honor the goddess Gaurī, to whom the pig is sacred. A royal kitchen was set up in the field, and a feast prepared with the flesh of the slain boars.[292] In a similar vein, members of one Bombay sect or caste, the Prabhus, consume a wild pig on one occasion each year as a religious obligation.[293] The boar was one of the reincarnations of the deity Vishnu, who sometimes came to the earth in that form.[294] Though sacrifice of pigs, like all animal sacrifice, is not permitted in the worship of Vishnu,[295] I have found nothing to suggest that the role of the boar as an incarnation of the deity has affected the status of pigs among his followers.

As for pig keeping and pork eating among present-day Hindus, it is a general rule that members of upper castes, and many lower castes as well, object to pig keeping and pork eating. It is true that members of some low castes do keep pigs and eat pork,[296] but other Hindus regard such groups as unclean in consequence. In the village of Rampura,

Mysore District, members of the pig-keepers' caste (*jati*) live on the outskirts of the settlement. Other people refuse to eat food prepared by these swineherds, to drink water from a vessel they have touched, or even to come into contact with them.[297] A number of low castes have understandably given up pigs and pork. The Balahi Hindu caste of untouchables in the Nimar District, Central Provinces, for example, banned pork because it was rejected by higher castes.[298] In Kerakat Subdistrict, Uttar Pradesh, another Hindu caste of untouchables, the Bhars, renounced pig keeping in an effort to raise their status. They remained untouchable, but are regarded more highly than other local Chamars who still keep pigs.[299] In the former Kotah State, two subcastes within the Chamar caste have rejected pork as food, though one inferior subcaste, which apparently derives its name from the word "pig," still eats pork.[300]

In light of its lowly position in general, it is surprising to find among Hindu Dravidians of South India that the domestic pig is among the traditional sacrificial animals (along with the chicken, water buffalo, sheep, and goat). In former times, pigs were unhesitatingly offered in blood sacrifices[301] to village goddesses whose concerns were with local matters, fertility, health, agriculture, and village well-being.[302] Pig killing, which may be a family or communal affair, was common at times of marriage, death, epidemic, and crop failure.[303] Sacrifices of pigs in South India were not made to the popular gods of Hinduism, Shiva and Vishnu, male Aryan gods worshipped in large Hindu temples. Nor did Brahmins ordinarily officiate at the sacrifices. Instead, those who directed the ceremonies were drawn from other castes.[304] That animal sacrifice in South India included animals such as the pig and water buffalo, which occupy lowly positions in general Hindu religious thinking today, suggests that they enjoyed a higher status among Dravidian peoples in antiquity.

The practice of making blood sacrifices of animals, including pigs, to village goddesses, is believed to be an ancient and essential element in the worship of village goddesses in South India.[305] It found its way into popular Hinduism by means of Śākta cults,[306] which focus not on male gods but on their wives, especially those of Shiva, who are worshipped as fertility goddesses, lovers, loyal spouses, or in terms of other female characteristics.[307] One such deity mentioned above is Gaurī, whose name means "yellow" or "light," and is also linked to the yellow-colored Gaura water buffalo and the yellow harvest. Another such deity is Satī ("virtuous"). At Satī's temple in Devīpātan, pilgrims sacrificed piglets by beating out their brains on stones and permitting the blood to run over the altar of the goddess. At the close of the last century, more than twenty thousand pigs were sacrificed in this way at one annual celebration at the temple. There is a tradition that the Devīpātan temple had been looted by an officer of the Moghul emperor Aurangzeb (who ruled from A.D. 1658 to 1707). In retribution, the officer was covertly captured, killed, and buried not far from the altar, and pilgrims would let the blood of sacrificial pigs drip on his grave.[308]

There are also reports of pigs being sacrificed by Hindus to certain male deities or demons for similar reasons.[309] As described in the Central Provinces of India early in this century, sacrificial pigs were supplied by certain members of the Kumhar caste (potters) who made their living by raising pigs.[310] The pigs were purchased by low-caste Hindus for sacrifice to, and propitiation of, Bhainsāsur, the buffalo demon. The purchasers could not touch the pigs, which were unclean to them. This is in keeping with the observation for South India that "food offered when exorcising demons or performing black magic never becomes *prasāda*" (consecrated),[311] but is cast out, burned, or "left at a burning ground."[312] In the sacrifice to Bhainsāsur, however, the Kumhars who carried out the sacrifice were permitted to take the dead pig home to eat. The Kumhars thus enjoyed a double benefit, the proceeds from selling the pig as well as its flesh to eat, whereas the sponsors of the sacrifice gained assurance that the buffalo demon would not trample their crops.

Of special note among Hindu pig-killing practices is the trampling and killing of pigs by common cattle at a festival in north-central India, after which people eat the flesh of the pigs. Lodrick has described this interesting practice in detail,[313] and here I would mention only a few of his observations. First, he notes that the practice of ritually killing a pig for the well-being of cattle seems to be an ancient one found widely in the Old World. In north-central India the pig-trampling ritual is associated with the Govardhan festival (in honor of cows) and is thus indirectly tied to the Purāṇas. This, he suggests, may give such killing a certain legitimacy among Hindus today, even though it is a clear violation of the ahimsa precept. Finally, Lodrick speculates, the practice in India may represent "a symbolic confrontation between opposing cultural traditions"—one pastoral and Indian, the other (agricultural and) Southeast Asian. In agreement with this are the practices, commonly associated with pig killing, of also killing chickens and feeding rice to the pig victim (chicken and rice are both Southeast Asian domesticates). Were it not for the fact that water buffaloes, also Southeast Asian domesticates, may also be used in the trampling, and that trampling of pigs with water buffaloes is also reported in South India,[314] Lodrick's hypothesis of symbolic confrontation would be quite convincing. It could be, of course, that water buffaloes are later additions to such ceremonies. If this were so, one could equally well conceive of the confrontation as between Aryan and pre-Aryan Indians, with the pig humbled in the same way that it was humbled by followers of Horus in ancient Egypt. Even without such symbolic meaning, the affair involves the killing of pigs in the interests of cattle.

Among Indian Moslems, anti-pig sentiments are as strong as those of Moslems in the Near East. One illustration of this, reported in the popular press in 1980, is an incident that occurred in Moradabad, southeast of New Delhi, when a pig entered a prayer ground where Moslems were celebrating the Id al-Fitr, an important festival marking the end of Ramadan. Suspecting that Hindus had intentionally driven the pig onto the prayer ground in order to defile the latter, infuriated Moslem worshippers attacked Hindus nearby. The episode ended after a fire fight with police, who had intervened, which left three policemen and twenty-four other persons dead and hundreds wounded by gunfire, stones, or other weapons. The curious aspect of the unfortunate Moradabad incident is that most Hindus also consider pigs to be unclean animals.[315]

As for other minority religions of India, pig keeping and pork eating are absent among Sikhs and Jains, though they do occur among Syrian Christians ("St. Thomas Christians") of South India,[316] an Indian community that claims to date back to the first century A.D.

Many tribal people of the subcontinent also keep pigs and ritually kill them and eat their flesh. They also commonly regard pork as a delicacy, and may make efforts, such as confining pigs or castrating males, to assure that the flesh is tender. Though tribal people may kill pigs at occasions of various sorts, commonly the affairs relate to wishes for fertility and well-being of people and their domestic plants and animals. The Adi of Arunachal Pradesh (formerly India's North-East Frontier

Agency), for example, kill pigs at a fertility rite at the start of the harvest season, as well as at times of pregnancy, marriage, and death. In the marriage sacrifice, the new wife cannot go to her husband's house until he has carried out the pig killing, for half of the pork goes to the father of the bride.[317] Individual families among the Raj Gonds of Adilabad buy and sacrifice a pig in their cultivated fields, usually when a crop is half-grown, in the hopes that the earth goddess will provide a good harvest.[318] The Reddi of Hyderabad, in turn, breed pigs for sacrifice to the earth goddess at the first sowing of the crops. They believe that the blood fertilizes the seed, an interesting parallel of the practice of the devotees of Demeter who stored the flesh of the sacrificed pig and sowed it with the seed to assure a good crop. The Reddi also killed pigs on other ceremonial occasions, and used them for paying fines.[319] In Orissa, the Saora kill pigs on a wide range of occasions. Among them are ones for assuring success in agriculture and childbirth, and honoring their supreme sun-god.[320] In Madhya Pradesh, the Laru Kaj, most important sacrifice of the Gonds, Baigas, and Pardhans (made also by lower Hindu castes), is intended to cure a sick person whose illness was brought on by the deity Narayan Deo, who is identified with the sun by local Hindus.[321] Pigs are also ritually killed on other occasions by tribal groups in Madhya Pradesh, with household killings apparently older and more important than communal ones.[322]

In view of their ritual importance, it is understandable that among tribal people owning and killing pigs may bestow high social standing. This contrasts with the situation among Hindus, where the very possession of pigs is a sign of low status. This is shown among various tribal groups in the displays which enhance a pig killer's social status. Among the Adi, for example, the man who ritually kills a pig displays the lower jaw and teeth outside his house, and, when he dies, half of all the jaws he has accumulated over the years are hung in front of his grave.[323]

Despite widespread pig keeping and pork eating by Indian tribal peoples, certain of them have restrictions on these practices. Some restrictions are probably associated with ancient beliefs and practices, such as the Saora ban on women eating pork.[324] Other restrictions, however, are related to Hindu influence. Thus, while pigs and pork are important in Reddi culture generally, one entire group of Reddi neither keeps pigs nor eats pork. This is believed to reflect the influence of Hindu religious teachers who have convinced these people that the pig is unclean.[325] Similar agitation by Hindu reformers is reported among the Bhumia and Gond of eastern Mandla, Madhya Pradesh. Though at one point the Bhumia made the decision that they would no longer eat pork, they soon found this too difficult and returned to pig keeping and pork eating. Among the Gond, some would not eat pork, and others, though they returned to pork eating, were reluctant to raise pigs. Instead, when they wanted pork, they would purchase a pig from their neighbors, the Bhumia.[326] Among the Ho, when social reformers loudly denounced pork they succeeded in getting upper classes to abstain from it.[327]

It is clear that anti-pig attitudes, fostered by Moslems and Hindus alike, are continuing to make progress in the Indian subcontinent. One small reversal of the trend has developed in former Portuguese Goa, where pigs are numerous in Christian villages and pork is a favorite Christian food and major source of animal protein.[328] Pigs are also kept and pork eaten by Christians along the west coast of Sri Lanka,[329] and in India, too, Christians, who number about twenty-four million today (1994 est.), must be reckoned with as a pro-pig force.

Southeast Asia

Despite the antiquity of the domesticated pig in Southeast Asia and the widespread occurrence of pig keeping and pork eating there, most parts of the region lack populations of pigs as dense, or systems of pig care as well developed, as those of China. The main exception is Vietnam, which has more pigs by far (11.6 million in 1989) than any other country in Southeast Asia, and probably more than all the rest of mainland Southeast Asia combined.[330] In the Tonkin Delta, almost every house has its square piggery enclosed by a crude railing and covered with a thatched roof. Pork and pork fat are so important in the delta that a woman does not return from market without pork, and the whole pig is consumed, skin and all.[331] The early people of this part of Vietnam, called Nan-Yüeh by the Chinese, were under Chinese rule for a millennium, and Chinese influence entered all aspects of their life. This may account for the importance of pigs and pork among the Vietnamese. At the same time, one should not overlook the fact that the early Nan-Yüeh had impressive credentials of their own. They developed a sophisticated system of aquatic agriculture that may have been the model for aquatic agriculture in South and Central China. In addition, they were an enterprising seafaring people responsible for introducing food plants and spices from Southeast Asia to China.[332] Thus it may be that the development of intensive pig keeping among the Chinese derived from Nan-Yüeh example, rather than the other way around. In any case, Vietnam in traditional times contrasted notably with its neighbor Cambodia, where Indian influence was stronger, where virtually all Khmer, the majority people, were Buddhists, and where Buddhism permeated the life of the people and was the official state religion. Buddhists, because of commitment to the concept of nonviolence, had strong objections not only to killing but also to rearing animals with the intention of killing them, and this was the principal reason why pig raising was so little developed. In most parts of Cambodia, pigs were raised only by the poorest Khmer peasants. Ordinarily a peasant would raise only one pig from time to time, and would sell it to a Chinese butcher for slaughter. Then, as he needed it, he would buy pork from the butcher, especially for festive occasions. Pig keeping was better developed among the Khmer in some places. This was especially true near larger settlements and rubber plantations where there was a large demand from Chinese and Vietnamese residents, or near an export market serving Vietnam.[333]

Among other groups of Southeast Asia, particularly tribal ones, the pig is often a free-ranging household animal and village scavenger. In many places the housewives own the pigs and develop strong ties to them.[334] A Thai household has no pigs if it does not have a woman capable of caring for them.[335] Among the Karen of Burma, in turn, a woman's pigs are killed when she dies so that their spirits may accompany her's into the next world.[336]

Some peoples of Southeast Asia seem to raise pigs as much for purposes of divination and offering to supernatural beings as for food. The Karen, for example, keep pigs chiefly to propitiate evil spirits,[337] and a Karen guilty of adultery or fornication must atone for his trespasses by sacrificing a hog to make the land fertile again.[338] Divination may involve using the pig's liver or gall bladder, or it may simply require drinking the animal's blood. The Karen use the gall bladder: a full and round bladder is a sign that the spirits are pleased and that good fortune, health, and abundance will follow.[339] The Sea Dyak of Borneo ask the pig an important question to be relayed to the supreme being. The deity inscribes his answer on the pig's liver, and, after slaughtering the pig, old men examine its liver, as well as its gall bladder, fat, and tendons, to obtain his response.[340] The Minahasa of Celebes follow a somewhat different procedure: the priest thrusts his head into the dead animal, drinks the blood, and begins to prophesy.[341] It is not known what role, if any, the need for animals in sacrifice and divination may have played in pig domestication in Southeast Asia. It is clear, however, that sacrifice and divination are prominent features of animal keeping among the tribal peoples of Southeast Asia and South China. It is also clear that those practices involve not just the pig but also a variety of domesticated animals, perhaps most notably bovines (water buffalo, common cattle, mithan) and chickens.

Whatever pressure Buddhism and Hinduism have exerted for the abandonment of pig keeping and pork eating in Southeast Asia, it has not been effective everywhere. On Bali, a surviving outlier of Hindu culture, pigs are still raised and pork relished by the general populace, though some Brahmins avoid pork along with beef and other flesh foods.[342] In Burma and Thailand, pork is eaten by Buddhists.[343] The main change many Thai have made to conform with their Buddhist beliefs is to avoid killing pigs themselves and to sell the pigs they raise at home to others for slaughter.[344] Then they may buy pork from others to meet their needs. Some accounts indicate that certain Thai obtain young pigs from local Chinese, fatten them, and then sell them back to the Chinese, but, whatever procedure they follow, the Thai do not regard pork as any less of a delicacy.

In contrast with Hinduism and Buddhism, the intrusion of Islam into Southeast Asia, especially in the Malay world, has brought about a considerable reduction in pig keeping and pork eating. The Malay Peninsula, according to Burkill, became a land without domestic pigs before the Chinese arrived, and pigs are still not found and pork is not eaten in Malay villages.[345] A similar situation prevails among the Moslem populations of Java, Sumatra, and other Indonesian islands. Anti-pig attitudes were carried by Moslems from Indonesia into the southern Philippines, where, for example, the Moro of Mindanao have given up pork. Among the Tawsug, one group included under the generic term "Moro," a pork eater is designated *kapil* (Christianized) and, if convicted by law, he is given a ritual whipping.[346] One even reads that certain Tuaran Dusuns of Borneo who, though they are animists, apparently reject pork so as not to be reviled by their Moslem neighbors.[347] The avoidance of pork, however, seems not to be observed by all Moslem Chams in Indochina. The Chams are a Malayo-Polynesian people who had been influenced by Hinduism and Buddhism, and, since about A.D. 1000, by Islam, with many of them being Moslem today. The Moslem Cham of Cambodia are said to be stricter than those of Vietnam. The latter, according to some early investigators, observed the Islamic ban on pork, but in the 1940s another investigator reported that they did not observe that ban.[348] There are also reports of pork eating or suspicions of pork eating by lax Moslems elsewhere in Southeast Asia.

This, together with the continuation of pig keeping and pork eating among various native groups who still follow traditional systems of belief or have become Christians,[349] as well as among Chinese and Western residents, makes it clear that the abandonment of pig keeping and pork eating in the region is far from complete. Indeed, there are significant pig populations in such largely Moslem lands as Malaysia (FAO estimate: 2.3 million in 1989) and Indonesia (6.5 million).

In the survival of pig keeping in the region, Christians deserve special credit, and so do Chinese settlers. In Malaya, not only do Chinese raise pigs, but in the past they also imported swine from abroad. Pig keeping also occurs among Chinese in Indonesia, as on Java, where many Chinese own pigs and maintain them on the outskirts of settlements with the help of Javanese herdsmen.[350] The Chinese on Sumatra keep pigs, too;[351] and on Indonesian Timor the Chinese, through bartering with natives of the interior since early in the last century, are credited with encouraging the latter to carry out a simple form of pig fattening.[352] Chinese restaurants, in turn, are the readiest source of the forbidden flesh for lax Moslems.

The Pacific Area

Domestic pigs were not introduced to Australia and Tasmania until European settlers arrived in the eighteenth and nineteenth centuries, for the Aborigines lived entirely by hunting, gathering, and fishing. Long before, however, pigs had spread from Southeast Asia to the east, along a southern route through Melanesia to the Fiji Islands, and along a northern route at least into the western end of the Micronesian chain of islands. Credit for introducing them into the eastern Pacific belongs to the Polynesians, who pushed eastward, either from Melanesia or Micronesia, at a date presumed by some to have been about the fourth or fifth century A.D. It is not certain whether they carried pigs with them in their initial movement into western Polynesia or obtained them later, perhaps from the Fijians. Eventually, however, they carried them across Polynesia as far as Samoa in the southwest, the Marquesas, Society, and Austral islands in the southeast, and Hawaii in the north. It is understandable that the pig is the most celebrated animal in Polynesian fable, as in the tale of giants who sailed from Tahiti to fight a man-eating pig, and of Hiro, born of the sun, who killed this pig.[353]

There were, however, certain places in Polynesia where pigs were not present in pre-European times. Some, New Zealand and Easter Island, are on the fringes of settlement. Others are coral atolls (including, among others, Pukapuka, Manihiki, and Rakahanga north of the Cook Islands), where, some claim, there was too little food to maintain pigs. Still others are high islands such as Aitutaki and Mangaia in the Cook Islands, and Mangareva in the Tuamotu Archipelago.[354] Traditional accounts on Mangareva suggest that pigs were present earlier but had become extinct,[355] which may have happened on other high islands, too.

In any case the absence of the domestic pig in certain Pacific islands had nothing to do with Islam, which had a limited and late presence in the area (e.g., the Moslem Indian minority in Fiji; Indonesians in West Irian). People were free to develop their own patterns of pig keeping. Moreover, when the Europeans arrived, pig keeping was stimulated by increased demand for pork in places where they settled, as well as by the introduction of pigs to most Polynesian groups who had lacked them. The Maori of New Zealand, for example, began to rear pigs extensively for food and for market, and were delighted with their acquisition.[356]

Despite European encouragement, a few peoples, such as those of Tikopia in Melanesia,[357] failed to take over domestic pigs, whether from indifference or other reasons. In some places in the New Hebrides, wild pigs are abundant in the countryside,[358] and this may reduce the need for people to keep domestic pigs. There are also scattered reports of group rejection of pork. In Australia, where European settlers introduced pigs, certain Aborigines, such as those of Victoria and Queensland, developed a repugnance for pork and pork fat, and, at least initially, refused to eat it.[359] The people of Tamara, an island off New Guinea, refuse pork because they believe that souls of the dead sometimes pass into the bodies of pigs.[360] Other cases of pork rejection apply only to particular types of animals or to particular members of society and are based on magical, religious, or totemic beliefs. Among the Kai of New Guinea, for example, agricultural laborers refuse pork for fear the flesh of the dead pig in the laborer's stomach will attract live pigs, whether wild or domesticated, to destroy crops in his field.[361] No inhabitant of the village of Osiwasiu, a settlement of the northern Massim in New Guinea, will eat wild pigs. Though people eat domestic pigs without hesitation, the flesh of wild pigs, they believe, makes one's stomach swell.[362] At the village of Boitaru, one Massim clan, the Malasi, whose totemic animal is the pig, avoids the flesh both of the wild pig and of domestic pigs that are yellowish-brown in color. They sell or exchange their brown pigs with men of other clans.[363] Most of the avoidances mentioned above do not represent a rejection of pork by an entire people, and are therefore not at all similar to the pork avoidance of the Moslems. They are little different from similar observances of non-Moslem aboriginal groups in Southeast Asia.

Methods of pig care in Melanesia, Micronesia, and Polynesia also resemble those found in Southeast Asia. The pig is a household animal that in some places is permitted to run loose and to scavenge for its food, and in other places is restricted in its movements. Some Melanesians permit their boars to run wild but blind their sows to keep them from wandering too far.[364] On Ifalik in Micronesia and in the Society Islands in Polynesia, on the other hand, hogs are commonly tethered to trees and fed.[365] In Manua, Samoa, people apparently permit pigs to run loose in the plantations but construct low stone walls to keep them from entering the village.[366] Elsewhere in Samoa large, stone-walled community pig enclosures are used ordinarily; to fatten their pigs, however, some people confine them in small stalls near their dwellings and feed them leftovers.[367]

Another similarity of the Pacific area with Southeast Asia is the importance of pigs for sacrifice to the gods and for slaughter on ceremonial occasions such as wedding and funeral feasts. The pig is also involved in the prestige structure of society. Certain prestigious persons commonly enjoy preferential rights in keeping pigs, in slaughtering them, and in eating their flesh. On Kiriwina in the Trobriand Islands, for example, the paramount chief is the only one permitted to own pigs, though lesser chiefs and important headmen sometimes enjoy similar privileges

within the areas of their control.[368] On Tonga, large pigs are reserved for
people of high rank,[369] and the flesh of pigs sacrificed to the gods was
formerly eaten by the priests.[370] On Pukapuka the chief obtains a special
portion of the slaughtered pig, though otherwise the pork is distributed
without reference to rank or status.[371] At a feast in the Cook Islands, the
head of the slaughtered pig is set before the high chief as the proper
share for a person of his status.[372]

Reports of restrictions on women eating pork further confirm the
association of pork eating with a position of prestige in society. The
Biara of New Britain did not permit women to eat pork,[373] nor did
the Society Islanders.[374] In the Marquesas Islands, pork was forbidden
to women at certain times,[375] whereas in Hawaii it was forbidden except
in special cases.[376]

In the Pacific area, New Guinea and certain adjacent islands of Melanesia have been singled out for their unusual focus on the pig, a "Melanesian pig complex" involving the raising of pigs and sponsoring of pig
feasts. Lowland New Guinea pig kills are rather small-scale affairs, but
in the highlands it is not unusual for dozens or even hundreds of pigs to
be butchered at a single pig feast.[377] Among pig-complex groups, pigs
are among a man's most valued possessions. They bestow prestige on
him. Among the South Kewa of New Guinea, for example, a person
wealthy in shells and pigs enjoys the right to wear a special hat and plays
a special role in the pig kill.[378] Pigs may so frequently serve in paying for
valuable objects that they can almost be regarded as currency. They may
be major factors in causing disputes among people,[379] and exchanges at
a pig kill may serve to suppress disputes that occur.[380] Pigs may also be
loaned to other people to incur complicated patterns of indebtedness. In
Malo, one of the New Hebrides, when a man has sacrificed a thousand
small pigs to the souls of his ancestors, he attains the highest nobility.[381]
In Malekula, another of the New Hebrides, people use pigs to exchange
for wives and for goods of various sorts. A man's status also depends on
the number and value of his pigs, which he tries to increase by careful
lending and borrowing.

Melanesian practices provide interesting parallels with those of
cattle-complex peoples in eastern and southern Africa,[382] where cattle
occupy a similar position in the prestige structure. New Hebrideans'
concern with the size and shape of their boars' tusks, for example, recalls the interest some cattle-complex peoples take in the size and shape

of cattle horns. It is not so much the size of the animal as the size and curvature of its tusks that determine a boar's value. Preferred tusks curl around to make two or three complete circles.[383] To encourage growth of tusk teeth, Malekulans take out the top canine teeth of their best male piglets when they are almost a year old. Should the pig reach the three-circle tusk stage, it is said to be "surcharged with power" with its tusk "the coiling snake and the spirit of earth."[384]

Another parallel between Melanesia and the African cattle complex is the attachment that develops between people and their animals. Malekulans, for example, say that pigs are life, progress, and power, and that without them life would be mere existence.[385] The Papuans of the Trans-Fly region in New Guinea not only take genuine pride in their mature pigs but also show strong affection for them. The woman who feeds a pig fondles and pets it, and when finally it is killed, she cries freely. The owner does not kill the pig, for as Papuans say, sorrow would make his arm too weak to use the bow.[386] Similarly, a man of the northern Massim sometimes has a remarkable fellowship with his pig. In this regard, there is a delightful record of a pig's doglike attachment to its master which led it to persist in following him on a trip despite all his efforts to send it home.[387]

The ultimate in affection is displayed by women who suckle their piglets. The practice of breast-feeding piglets, puppies, or both is a nearly universal custom among island peoples of the Pacific who had such animals. Among groups who did not possess pigs in pre-European times, moreover, women commonly took up the practice once they obtained pigs. On New Guinea, reports of the nursing of piglets are far more abundant than reports of nursing puppies. It is true that the ultimate fate of every village pig on New Guinea is to be killed and consumed at some ceremonial or ritual occasion, but this is usually to the accompaniment of the wails of the woman who raised it. Throughout New Guinea, moreover, a family that raises a pig is normally prohibited from eating its flesh after it has been killed. Among the Agarabi, for instance, people believe that for a woman to eat a piglet she has suckled would be no different from eating her own child.[388] This practice of not eating pigs you have raised is so widespread that one study of traditional exchange in New Guinea was even entitled *Your Own Pigs You May Not Eat*.[389]

Certain anthropologists from the 1930s through the 1950s focussed

on the wasteful aspects of the Melanesian pig complex, and Ralph
Linton went so far as to describe pig raising there as a type of pretentious
waste.[390] More recently, however, ecologically oriented anthropologists
have argued, on the contrary, that the system is effective in managing
pigs. Pigs eat feces and garbage, thereby helping keep villages clean.
Pig dung may serve to fertilize the soil. Grubbing by pigs breaks the soil
of exhausted gardens and makes it easier for them to be replanted. Pigs
convert mainly carbohydrate products, which are generally in abundant
supply, into high-quality protein and fat, of which, in most cases, there
is an overall shortage. Indeed, the pig can be looked on as a repository
of foodstuffs that are surplus at one time of the year and that otherwise
might be wasted. Pork, unlike many other foodstuffs, is available at
all times, and may provide an important protein supplement at times
of stress, such as sickness or the start of warfare. Ecologically oriented
anthropologists even consider the slaughter of large numbers of pigs
on festive occasions as reasonable, as eliminating excess animals that
threaten agriculture, and as assisting in the maintenance of ecological
balance.[391]

Origin and Spread of Pork Avoidance

Because in Western thinking the ancient Hebrews are so closely associated with the ban on pork, many Westerners have assumed that it
originated with them. Yet, despite the fact that the Hebrew pork ban
has been a matter of speculation for the past two thousand years, no
scholarly consensus has been reached as to its origin.

Hypotheses Advanced to Explain the Origin of the Ban on
Pork in the Near East

Four main explanations have been advanced for Hebrew food laws,
including the ban on pork. One is that they are arbitrary, make no
sense to humans, or can be understood only by Jehovah. The second is
that they came about because of hygienic concerns, because of danger
of illness or disease. The third is that, for the Hebrews, their food laws
served a symbolic purpose, with acceptable animals representing proper
human behavior, and banned ones, sinful behavior. The fourth is that
Hebrew food laws originated in their rejections of cultic practices of
alien peoples and of the worship of deities other than Jehovah.[392] In-

volved in both the third and fourth hypotheses is the notion that the Hebrews wanted to set themselves apart from other peoples. In recent decades, a fifth explanation—economic, environmental, and/or eco-logical—has been reintroduced by certain anthropologists to explain the ban on pork among Hebrews and other Near Eastern peoples. If one accepts the view that the Hebrew ban on pork, like the other food bans, was arbitrary, there is little incentive to seek its historical origins. If, on the other hand, one inclines toward the hygienic, symbolic, cultic, or economic-environmental-ecological hypotheses, a careful weighing of the historical record is necessary if one is to reach an acceptable answer.

Other hypotheses, not falling into the five categories identified above, have also been advanced to explain the Hebrew ban on pork, but, for one reason or another, are not taken seriously today. One is Porphyry's suggestion that pork was rejected by the Jews, as well as Phoenicians and Cypriots, because swine were not native to their lands.[393] Thus, in his view, the Hebrew rejection of pork is little dif-ferent from Greeks not eating camelflesh. We have seen, however, that wild swine were native to early Palestine,[394] and that, from early times onward, one people or another kept domestic pigs there.

The Hygienic Hypothesis

Deserving more serious attention is the hypothesis—or hypothe-ses—that the ancient Hebrews rejected pork on hygienic grounds. One such hypothesis is that pork decays rapidly in the high temperatures that characterize much of the Near East. Another is that a scavenging pig, which eats all kinds of filth and is itself physically dirty, may be dangerous to eat. A third is that the consumption of pork can lead to trichinosis.[395]

The hypothesis of pork decay is completely without support in the Bible. Nor, it should be emphasized, are temperatures in Palestine higher than in many other areas where pork is commonly eaten and where rapid decay presents no insurmountable health problem. If it were a major problem, the Hebrews, like other peoples of the Old World, could have banned pork in the hot season when the decay dan-ger was greatest,[396] or they could have consumed the flesh quickly, as in a great feast, or they could have preserved it.

The view that pork rejection springs from the eating habits or physi-cal dirtiness of the pig is one that has persisted since antiquity as an explanation for the Hebrew ban and those of other Near Eastern peoples.[397] Moses Maimonides (A.D. 1135–1204), a medieval rabbi, philosopher, and physician, is viewed as having been among the most influential early proponents of a hygienic explanation for the Hebrew ban. In his *Guide for the Perplexed,* Maimonides wrote that the principal reason the pig was abhorred in Hebrew law is that its habits and its food are quite dirty and disgusting.[398] If Hebrew law had permitted the eating of pork, he argued, markets and even homes would have been dirtier than any latrine, as is true among European Christians. Maimonides then cites, in an approving manner, a seer who wrote in the Babylonian Talmud, "The mouth of a swine is as dirty as dung itself." Maimonides also contends that, like other banned flesh, pork is unwholesome. Objections to Maimonides's explanation of Jewish food laws in terms of "rational restraint" have been raised by various Jewish religious scholars.[399] One objection sometimes made is that the Levitican code does not mention the eating habits of the pig as responsible for the ban on pork. Nor does it refer to the eating habits of other animals whose flesh was banned. Some argue further that if, nevertheless, banned animals had been singled out for their indiscriminate eating habits, why would the Hebrews have banned the flesh of some animals that are quite clean in that way, for example the hare, which eats mainly grass and other plant food?[400] Despite these objections, I am not ready to dismiss this hypothesis completely, and will return to it later.

The Trichinosis Hypothesis

It is so widely believed that fear of contracting trichinosis led the Hebrews to ban pork, that a detailed weighing of the hypothesis seems necessary. As background, several things must be borne in mind. First, virtually nothing is known about the place of origin of the parasite *Trichinella spiralis* or the time of its spread to Europe or the Near East. Thus, it is not certain that *T. spiralis* was even found in Palestinian domestic pigs at the time the Hebrew ban on pork was established. According to one early hypothesis, *Trichinella spiralis* came to Europe only in the eighteenth century because of a mass migration of rats from Southeast Asia. According to another early hypothesis, it came to England and Germany along with Chinese and Indochinese pigs introduced early in the nineteenth century. A more recent hypothesis, based on what is claimed to be the earliest historical record of trichinosis in

Krakow, Poland, is that *T. spiralis* reached Europe from Asia in the thirteenth century with the Mongol invasions.[401] At present, few trichinosis specialists give credence to the above hypotheses, in large part because the parasite is now known not to be host specific, but to occur widely around the world in many species of mammals, with transmission not only in a domestic cycle involving the pig, pork scraps, and, according to some observers, the rat,[402] but also in a sylvatic cycle involving wild animals.[403] As a result, a recent spread involving a single host has become increasingly unlikely. In addition, it is now known that one is not dealing, as was once believed, with a single form of the parasite *Trichinella spiralis,* but with multiple forms that differ in geographic occurrence, climatic needs, infectivity for pigs, humans, and other animal species, and in other ways.[404] It has become clear, according to W. C. Campbell, that an understanding of the epidemiology of trichinosis cannot be gained by concentrating on the pig and rat as "hosts par excellence of *T. spiralis*" or on conditions in better-developed areas of the world.[405] Thus, even though it seems likely that the parasite was found in humans in ancient Palestine, this cannot be taken as an absolute certainty, nor is it safe to cast the domestic pig as the sole culprit in transmission of the disease.[406]

A second point is that, though information on trichinosis in the modern Near East is quite scanty, it suggests that the disease is less serious as a public health problem than it has been in many other places. It is true that *Trichinella* are found today in various Near Eastern animal species, wild and domestic—including the wild boar and domestic pig—and there is a real possibility of humans contracting the disease from them. I have found no information on infection rates in wild and domestic swine in Israel, but in other Near Eastern lands these rates vary from very low to very high.[407]

As for human trichinosis, our main concern, the overwhelming number of Near Eastern people today are Moslems or Jews who do not eat pork, and who would be less likely to contract the disease. For Iran, apparently the only record of human trichinosis, a questionable case involving consumption of undercooked flesh of a wild boar, dates from 1966, and for Turkey it was only in 1977 that the first cases, also involving a wild pig, were reported.[408] There have been trichinosis epidemics among pork-eating groups in modern Lebanon, but, if present conditions prevailed in antiquity, they were quite uncommon. I say this because, although Christians account for roughly a third of Lebanon's population, no case of trichinosis in humans was reported from 1894 until 1939 (though several outbreaks have occurred since).[409] Israel, on its part, has a very small Christian population today (roughly 2 percent of the total), as well as some nonobservant Jews who eat pork. In addition, there are reports of wild swine being eaten by Moslems and Jews. An epidemic of trichinosis, for example, occurred late in the last century in the Lake Huleh area among Bedouins who ate the flesh of wild boar in a raw or partially cooked state.[410] Eating of undercooked pork must have been very rare, however, for in 1970 Yamashita was able to say that not a single case of human trichinosis had been recorded in Israel in more than eighty years.[411] Cases of trichinosis have been reported in Israel since, but until recently all infected persons requiring hospitalization had contracted the disease abroad. It was only in 1992 that one finds what is thought to be the first case of trichinosis acquired in modern Israel.[412] This involved members of an Israeli family who ate the flesh of a wild boar killed in hunting. As for Egypt, a lack of clinical reports of human trichinosis was one factor leading authorities there to conclude that trichinosis was absent in their country. Indeed, it was not until the 1970s that the first cases of human trichinosis were confirmed, though more have been reported since.[413] However one interprets these fragmentary data on human trichinosis in the Near East, they lend no support to the view that the disease was a major public-health problem in antiquity.

Another significant point is that neither the Hebrews nor any other people of the Near East knew of *Trichinella spiralis* or of the relationship of the parasite, the pig, and human disease. An awareness of that relationship came about only as a result of medical discoveries in Europe extending over a quarter of a century after Paget first discovered encysted *Trichinella* in a human cadaver in 1835. After this discovery, it took an additional twenty-five years before it was determined that it was pathogenic, after which the perception of *Trichinella* changed from that of "zoological curiosity to lethal pathogen."[414] Yet, with surprising modesty, some scientists quickly jumped to the conclusion that the Hebrews, by commonsense observation, had learned of that relationship thousands of years before. This conclusion, which was quickly accepted by many nonscientists, was reached without any supporting documentary evidence: there is nothing in the early historical record, whether the Bible or other sources, to indicate that the Hebrews or any other early Near Eastern people associated pork eating with the symptoms that may develop in trichinosis.

That such a conclusion should be reached so uncritically is surprising in view of the fact that no such commonsense association had been made in those parts of northern Europe where trichinosis was a much more serious problem. Why was it not discovered in Byelorussia (White Russia), where an 82.9 percent human trichinosis rate was once reported, the highest known anywhere in the world?[415] Why was the discovery not made in Germany, which, late in the last century, experienced regular outbreaks of human trichinosis? Even in the United States, which at one time was estimated to have three-fourths of all trichinosis-infected people in the world, that relationship had not been discovered by commonsense methods.[416] One reason is that, though there are severe outbreaks,[417] in most cases of trichinosis, symptoms are mild or absent. It was estimated some decades ago that in the United States there were 350,000 new infections each year, that only 4.5 percent may have shown symptoms, and that but a few hundred were reported.[418] The symptoms, moreover, are remarkable in their variety, and they mimic other conditions.[419] Even physicians, with the benefit of their medical training and equipment, have found trichinosis difficult to diagnose, and correct initial diagnosis is the exception rather than the rule. In fact, researchers have listed fifty diseases that have been mistakenly diagnosed in individuals suffering from trichinosis, and the list ranges alphabetically from acute alcoholism to undulant fever.[420]

It nevertheless remains a possibility that in cases of acute trichinosis the Hebrews or some other group by commonsense methods associated the first-stage symptoms (vomiting, diarrhea, fever, and general malaise) with eating pork. Such associations have been made in the modern world, as in cases in which ham was suspected of bringing on such symptoms, and in which the illness was actually called ham poisoning.[421] On the other hand, the association is not easy to make. The average incubation period in most individuals with trichinosis is ten days; people may develop symptoms a few hours after consuming infected meat, but it may be as long as fifty-one days before they appear.[422] During the period between exposure and the first appearance of symptoms, moreover, suspicion can easily fall on other causes. This is illustrated by the members of the German school inspection commission who ate together at an inn in 1845. One of the members had only a glass of red wine. The other seven drank white wine and ate a meal, which included ham, sausage, and cheese. The first member was unaffected, but the seven became ill, and four of them died. A judicial investigation was then made in which both the innkeeper and the meal were suspected, and in which the white wine was tested. The inquiry led to no conclusion, but the innkeeper could not dispel public suspicion and eventually was obliged to emigrate.[423]

Even if the Hebrews or some other ancient Near Eastern people had made the association, pork eating would not necessarily have been banned. In modern times, despite knowledge of the relationship between the disease and pork eating, there have been few serious suggestions that pork be banned. In the United States,[424] pork is not even routinely examined microscopically for trichinae, though Prussia (1877) then Germany (1900) have required such inspection for nine decades or more. American inaction derives largely from opposition of meat-packers who are concerned that such inspections would be too costly. Another objection is that inspection could not determine absolutely whether pork is free of trichinae, and would serve only to lull the public into a false sense of security.[425] Even the German inspection system has not altogether eliminated epidemics of trichinosis.[426] It is also interesting that, since discovery of the relationship between pork and trichinosis, not only has there been no general decline in pork eating but also even Jews are increasingly accepting pork as food.

The history of our knowledge of the disease casts further doubt on the trichinosis hypothesis. Before the discovery of *Trichinella spiralis,* it was common in Europe to attribute the Jewish ban on pork to fear of tapeworms,[427] which demonstrates the modern Western tendency to seek explanations in terms of disease. With the discovery of the pathogenicity of *T. spiralis* and the role of pork in bringing on trichinosis, certain writers added it to the tapeworm hypothesis, sometimes with a finality that increased over time. Asa Crawford Chandler, for example, in earlier editions of his *Introduction to Parasitology* wrote that there is little doubt that fear of *T. spiralis,* along with the pork tapeworm, led the early Hebrews to ban pork. By the 1955 edition, the statement had been strengthened, with "little doubt" becoming "without a doubt."[428] In the mind of Chandler and many members of the public as well, an assumption that fit with Western preconceptions had gradually evolved into accepted fact. Though some well-qualified scientists and scholars have persisted in their commitment to the trichinosis hypothesis,[429] subsequent research has failed to uncover any documentary evidence to support it. In full awareness of all the factors involved, Calvin W. Schwabe, a noted parasitologist, epidemiologist, and student of Near Eastern life and history, has concluded that it is impossible that the ancient bans on pork derived from fear of trichinosis.[430]

Some Jewish observers have objected to hygienic theories as presenting a false perspective on the reasons for banning the flesh of pigs and certain other animals. In the words of Isaac Abrabanel (A.D. 1437–1508),

God forbid that I should believe that the reasons for forbidden foods are medicinal! For were it so, the Book of God's Law would be in the same class as any of the minor brief medical books . . . Furthermore, our own eyes see that people who eat pork and insects and such . . . are well and alive and healthy at this very day . . . Moreover, there are more dangerous animals . . . which are not mentioned at all in the list of prohibited ones. And there are many poisonous herbs known to physicians which the Torah does not mention at all. All of which points to the conclusion that the Law of God did not come to heal bodies and seek their material welfare. . .[431]

Also casting doubt on the hygienic hypotheses is Harmer's observation that they disregard the fact that the core concept of the Hebrew ban is that the pig itself has a defiling nature, of which the refusal to eat pork is only one manifestation.[432] The pig, moreover, is merely one of many unclean animals. Implied here is the need, if one is to reach a satisfactory solution to the problem, to explain the basis on which animals as different as the camel, ostrich, hare, and pig came to be regarded as impure.

Economic, Environmental, and Ecological Hypotheses

Harmer's objection applies, as well, to the economic, environmental, and ecological hypotheses to which we now turn. In recent times, one of the best examples of such a hypothesis is that of anthropologist Carleton Coon. Coon, after rejecting hygienic explanations of the Hebrew dietary law against eating pork, suggested instead that it derives from population increase and environmental deterioration. According to his view, the pig was a splendid animal in the regional economy of the south and east Mediterranean lands at an early period when the environment was unexploited and animals could feed in the oak and beech woods on acorns, beechnuts, and truffles. With the increase of human population and the stripping of the oaks from the landscape to make room for olive trees, he contends, the ecological niche of the pig was destroyed. He goes further in claiming that the pig could survive in the new situation only by consuming foodstuffs that could better be used in feeding people directly. Under the changed conditions, says Coon, any man who kept pigs would be displaying his wealth and disturbing the ecological balance of the group in which he lived. In this way, he says, the pig was displaced.[433]

Marvin Harris has followed Coon in saying that, under conditions of environmental deterioration in the Near East, the keeping of pigs in any numbers was "ecologically maladaptive" and pork was banned "to remove temptation."[434] Harris, in an effort to demonstrate that the pig was unsuited to Near Eastern conditions, writes of it as "a creature that ate the same food as man . . . had to be provided with shade and mud-holes . . . from the beginning an economical and ecological luxury . . . [that] ate you out of home and, if you gave [the pig] a chance, used up your water as well." Its flesh, he admits, is tasty, but a "delectable temptation—the kind, like incest and adultery, that mankind finds difficult to resist."[435]

Diener and Robkin have effectively demonstrated that the pig can adapt to Near Eastern temperatures, climates, landscapes, and water resources, and has done so since antiquity.[436] For this reason, we will concentrate here on weighing the hypothesis of environmental deterioration against evidence from the Bible, other historical sources, and archeology.

Many present-day scholars have serious doubts about the biblical account of Moses, its date, accuracy, and usefulness as a historical document. Whatever position one takes in the matter, if environmental deterioration had been a factor in the Hebrew ban on pork, one might expect to find some hint of it in the books of Moses, who is credited by tradition with instituting the Hebrew ban on pork. One convincing piece of evidence would be a simple statement that Moses (thirteenth century B.C.?) banned pork because of concern with environmental deterioration and the ecological maladaptiveness of the pig. There is no such statement. Even without a statement linking the ban on pigs and pork to environmental deterioration and ecological maladaptiveness, one might hope to find some indication in the story of Moses (materials in the books of Moses may date from the time of Moses until roughly 400 B.C.)[437] that marked environmental deterioration had in fact taken place in Palestine in Moses's day. In the biblical account, Moses himself was not permitted by God to enter the Promised Land, so his information came primarily from two sources: from God and from Hebrew spies sent to scout and report on conditions. The spies brought back pomegranates, figs, and grapes from the Promised Land, which, they said, "floweth with milk and honey."[438] Later, Moses, in turn, is quoted as saying: ". . . the Lord thy God bringeth thee into a good land, a land of brooks of water, of fountains and depths that spring out of valleys and hills; a land of wheat, and barley, and vines, and fig trees, and pomegranates; a land of oil olive, and honey; a land wherein thou shalt eat bread without scarceness, thou shalt not lack any thing in it . . ."[439] He describes it further as a well-watered land "which the Lord thy God careth for: the eyes of the Lord thy God are always upon it, from the beginning of the year even unto the end of the year."[440]

One must recognize that many biblical scholars consider the biblical account of the exodus and the forty years in the desert not as a historical document but as "legendary and epic."[441] The biblical description of the land of Canaan is, from this perspective, not to be taken at face value, but to be viewed in the light of a poetic account of the Promised Land viewed against the background of Egypt and the Sinai Desert.[442] One must also recognize that the account may have been written several centuries after Moses. Despite this, the picture of the Promised Land contains not even a suggestion that serious environmental deterioration disturbed Moses or his followers.

Turning to the firmer ground of archeology, however limited that evidence may be, it is clear that, before the time of Moses, conditions in Palestine were arid or semiarid in many places, and that sheep and goats, not common cattle or pigs, were the most numerous domestic food animals.[443] Sheep and goats were the mainstay of the animal economy of Chalcolithic times (c. 4500–3500 B.C.), when there were groups ranging from pastoral nomads to seminomadic farmers who also practiced animal husbandry.[444] The Early Bronze Age (c. 3500–2000 B.C.) saw a movement toward greater sedentarization. Despite this, judging from Horwitz and Tchernov's survey of bones uncovered in Early Bronze Age levels in eight sites from different parts of Palestine (most from areas of Mediterranean vegetation), sheep and goats continued dominant.[445] On average, they were more than twice as numerous as common cattle, the next most common domestic animal. Pigs, on their part, were still fewer, altogether amounting to less than 10 percent of all animals.[446] In nine Middle and Late Bronze Age levels at sites in Palestine for which Hesse provides data that can be compared, sheep and goats were more numerous at seven, common cattle at two, and pigs at none.[447] In all sites but one where sheep and goats were dominant, they were from two to ten times more numerous than pigs—or even more.[448]

The numbers and geographic range of the domestic pig in Palestine did fluctuate in prehistoric times for various reasons, environmental and others.[449] One significant factor was increase or decrease in long-term precipitation and resulting changes in natural vegetation. In the Chalcolithic period, apparently a time of somewhat higher precipitation, pigs seem to have been more abundant in nondesert sites,[450] and some were even kept in a few villages in better-watered areas of the Negev Desert.[451] As for periods closer to the time of Moses, swine were found in all ten Middle and Late Bronze Age sites on which Hesse provides clear evidence.[452] In at least five of those sites, moreover, pigs amounted to more than 10 percent of all animals, and in one, a third.[453] This suggests that in places where conditions were at all suitable in Palestine, people kept pigs, and that in unusually favored places they could be of considerable importance.

Before looking further at archeological evidence, I would note that in the last several decades there has been a spirited debate about the Hebrews in Iron Age Palestine: who they were, where they came from, how they came into possession of that land, how their religion evolved, and what factors—socio-cultural, economic, and environmental—may have been involved.[454] Whatever the persuasion of the scholarly disputants, they are in agreement that the earliest Hebrews lived in thinly settled hill country whose population increased rapidly after roughly 1200 B.C.[455] Reconstructing the vegetation of the hill country at the time of earliest Hebrew settlement, however, is difficult because, as Stager has noted, few archeologists provide data useful for such reconstruction.[456] The climax vegetation of most of the hill country of Palestine, however, is described as forest and maquis.[457] A pollen diagram taken in a crater lake on the Golan Heights suggests that around 2000 B.C. "forest," with oaks usually dominant, was found there and in the west of northern Palestine.[458] In the Middle and Late Bronze ages (c. 2000–1200 B.C.), according to biblical historian and archeologist William F. Albright, the hills of Palestine were thinly settled and heavily forested along their western slopes and crests.[459] Joseph Weitz writes that in the uplands of Canaan the Hebrews found many forests containing oaks and dozens of other species of trees and shrubs.[460] Yohanan Aharoni writes that when the Hebrews arrived, settlement was thin in most hill regions of Palestine, much of which was forested with thick scrub.[461] Liphschitz and Waisel write of olive, oak, and other woody plants uncovered in the village of ʿIzbet Ṣarṭah in the low foothills of Ephraim in levels dating from the twelfth and eleventh centuries B.C.[462] The trees identified in the site still grow in the area today, and two woody species are identified as major elements in the Mediterranean maquis. Adam Zerfal writes of early Manasseh, an area rich in Hebrew archeology, as having hills covered primarily with maquis, and valleys, apparently occupied mainly by Canaanites, with widely spaced oaks and a parklike appearance.[463] One judges from the above and other such accounts that in Canaan there were woodlands as well as maquis, and that they contained tree species used for timber and capable of providing edible seed or fruit for pigs, among them evergreen oak, pine, olive, sycamore fig, and carob.[464]

I qualified "forest" with quotes above because, though forests are frequently mentioned in biblical accounts,[465] one cannot be certain what sort of vegetation was actually involved. As Martin Noth has observed, though the mountains of Palestine were originally forested, "one cannot assume a heavy forestation . . . [or] high trees [for] even in Old Testament times there were only greater or smaller remnants of primeval forests left."[466] One must be especially wary about biblical accounts of forests, because the usual Hebrew word for forest (yaʿar) seems to have been used in different senses. Today "yaʿar" is usually defined as "rough" (following the Arabic waʿar), as with rough country or a rough road.[467] The original meaning, however, seems to have been "richness," with a forest being a place with the richest vegetation. When used in the latter sense, however, one cannot be certain whether the word refers to a thicket, wood, or true forest.[468]

At the same time, significant forest areas remained in western Asia at the end of the Bronze Age and in succeeding centuries, though most was in shrubs or open woodlands rather than dense forests like those of northern Europe.[469] Oaks (especially the common oak, *Quercus callipri-*

nos; the Tabor oak, *Q. ithaburensis;* and the gall oak, *Q. infectoria*) were
the principal species in the woodlands of ancient Palestine. Regular
felling and browsing by goats and sheep have left most trees of *Q. cal-
liprinos,* an evergreen and the main species in the Judean and Galilean
hills, little more than shrubs today. At the same time, some very large
trees are found in modern Palestine, among them the well-known "oak
of Abraham," a sacred tree growing in Hebron.[470] *Q. ithaburensis* is a
deciduous species found in groves in the hills of Lower Galilee and at
one place in the Huleh Valley, "where there are about 200 giant trees
(50 feet high with trunks of 16 ft. or more in circumference)."[471]

This provides an idea of the size it was possible for oaks to reach in
the wooded areas of ancient Israel. In addition, oaks have long lives
and, when a tree is old or is chopped down, it can put out new shoots
from its "stump or roots that in time develop into a strong tree."[472] The
prophet Isaiah referred to such an ancient oak in Jerusalem which had
its branches removed and its trunk cut down regularly. Only a stump
might be left, "yet no sooner was [the tree] felled, than the stump
put forth 'holy seed,' sprouting new shoots."[473] One may conclude that,
since the uplands were thinly settled when the Hebrews first appeared
in Palestine, Palestine's oaks, with their considerable ability at regen-
eration, would have had an opportunity to survive and provide acorns
for pigs.[474]

Equally important in Palestine, wooded areas, which also contained
other plant and animal species that provided feed, seem to have been of
reasonable extent in antiquity, creating favorable conditions for modest
numbers of pigs. The "forest of Carmel," for example, was estimated to
have covered over 375,000 acres, and the "forest of Ephraim," roughly
250,000 acres.[475] Hyvernat and Hirsch, writing in the first decade of
this century, observed that in Galilee, where more than 13 percent
of the land was wooded, nearly half of the wooded area was dense
forest with roughly one-fourth "high wood" and three-fourths "low
wood."[476] It seems likely that at the time of Moses, when there were
far fewer human inhabitants, significantly larger areas of Palestine's
woods consisted of high wood. Even with oaks of only modest size,
apparently such wooded areas were suitable for acorn feeding. Though
deforestation has been widespread in the Mediterranean region and in
the Balkans, woodland-foraging by swine has continued right up to the
present day.[477] In former Yugoslavia, for example, domestic pigs have

been permitted to forage in nearby forests because, even though such forests are mere remnants of what they once were, they can still provide excellent pannage.[478]

Some writers have argued that, in the centuries immediately after Hebrew settlement, the upland areas of Palestine presented a problem, and that a substantial effort may have been required to clear land for adequate production of food crops.[479] This fits with the biblical account of the people of Ephraim and Manasseh, who complained about their lack of cultivable land. Whereupon Joshua, the Hebrew leader who, by biblical tradition, led the entry into the Promised Land, said: "Thou art a great people, and hast great power . . . the mountain shall be thine; for it is a wood, and thou shalt cut it down: and the outgoings of it shall be thine . . ."[480] Clearing of shrubs and trees is especially difficult in the mountains of Palestine because rock underlies the soil, and such plants are deep-rooted and most of them can regrow from underground stems and suckers. This created serious problems for cultivators with simple tools and methods of clearing; it required that "man . . . [fight] . . . bitterly to eradicate deep-rooting trees and shrubs," and perhaps not with quick and complete success.[481]

Over time, the situation continued to worsen as most woody vegetation was cut down to make way for cultivation; for building materials, fencing, implements, and fuel;[482] to deny an enemy cover during times of war; or for other reasons.[483] Accidental and deliberately set fires must have taken a toll, and the grazing of sheep and goats was a major destructive factor as well.[484] At the time of Moses, however, Palestine's wooded areas seem to have been adequate for pig herding on a modest scale.

Destruction of wooded areas had occurred in Palestine intermittently over a long historical period since the establishment of agriculture several thousand years before the beginning of the Christian Era.[485] Judging from the pig's effect on species of woodland plants elsewhere,[486] it is likely that it did its share of damage in Palestine. Nor can the Hebrews, as we have seen, be absolved of responsibility.[487] Far more serious destruction and environmental deterioration, however, seems to have come with the Arab conquest and a notable increase in the population of voracious sheep and goats.[488] Indeed, Taylor called Palestine's goats "Public Enemy No. 1" in the destruction of vegetation,[489] and many other scholars regard the goat, not the pig, as the villain in deforestation of the Mediterranean area.[490] This fits with the conclusion of geographer Xavier de Planhol that the banning of pork had a role in opening Mediterranean wooded country to sheep and goats, which led to significant deforestation. De Planhol calls attention to the fact that deforestation is particularly noticeable in the Islamic sections of the Mediterranean. He also notes that in Albania, in passing from Moslem to Christian sections, where pigs are kept, the amount of woodland immediately becomes much greater.[491] A strong case, therefore, could be made that, if indeed the early Hebrews, in the centuries following 1200 B.C., had sought to retard destruction of wooded areas by banning the keeping and eating of destructive animals, they would have focussed on goats and sheep.[492]

Such laws against raising sheep and goats were actually established in Palestine among Jews in the initial centuries of the Christian Era, and the rabbi Akiba is quoted as saying, "Those who rear [sheep and goats] and cut down good trees . . . will see no sign of blessing."[493] This reveals an awareness of the dangers of destroying trees, it is true, but this was more than a millennium after the time of Moses, and even then, it was sheep and goats that were singled out as destructive animals, not pigs.

The above review fails to find convincing evidence to support the hypothesis that environmental deterioration brought on the Hebrew ban on pigs and pork. On the contrary, conditions that existed in the uplands of Palestine at the time of Moses and in the next few centuries, while not ideal for pigs, seem to have been adequate for the Hebrews to have kept pigs in limited numbers—if they had a mind to do so. Yet, as Hesse has observed, archeological excavations of "Iron-Age sites in Palestine present a picture of mostly pigless deposits."[494] In addition, he points out that several locales, where in earlier times there had been considerable pig keeping, had virtually no pigs in the Iron Age. All three sites on the coastal plain where pig keeping was significant, moreover, were Philistine rather than Hebrew settlements.[495] The data presented by Hesse are consistent with the views that there were ethnic differences in attitude toward pigs in ancient Palestine, and that the Hebrew ban goes back to the beginning of the Iron Age.

Turning from Palestine to the Near East in general, the pig had, during periods of greater and lesser precipitation, fitted into village ecology for several thousand years before the Hebrew ban on pork is first recorded.[496] Moreover, it is by no means certain that the ban originated among peoples living in wooded areas. On the contrary, some of the earliest certain evidence of anti-pig feeling in the Near East (c. 1400 B.C. or before) is for Egypt and Mesopotamia, arid lands in great river valleys which, from the times of earliest agriculture, possessed no woods or forests in which pigs could feed. In those valleys, swine, wild and domesticated, were dependent for their food, not on acorns and other woodland products, but from scavenging in marshes, along river banks, and in fields. Much of their food, however, seems to have derived from human refuse thrown onto the streets.[497] As a result, pigs, wild and domesticated, did not lose their niches altogether because of further deforestation. Their basic environmental needs of shelter, plentiful water, soft ground for rooting, and mud for wallowing could be met in other places as well.[498] That such habitats exist even in modern times is clearly indicated by the fact that wild boars are quite numerous in the Huleh region and in the brushy banks of the Jordan River in Palestine.[499] They are also common in riverine thickets and other places with adequate food and moisture in Iran.[500] Pigs are still found in the marshes of southern Iraq, where there is a report of forty or more being killed in one day's hunt.[501] Pigs were also found in the marshy delta of Egypt until the end of the nineteenth century. Previous to that time, wild boars had been abundant and destructive of crops in the Nile Delta. In 1846 this led the government to order the elimination of the boars, and a large body of soldiers, led by nineteen officers, undertook the task. The result was that over eight hundred wild boars were shot.[502]

Nor should one overlook the versatility of pigs in their eating habits, which, as Grigson has noted, may include favorite foods, such as acorns, beechnuts, ferns, grasses, and broad-leafed herbs, as well as "insects, earthworms, corms, bulbs, roots and rhizomes, . . . ground-nesting birds, rodents, and carrion."[503] They will also consume spoiled fruit and vegetables and even human excrement, fully deserving the term "diversivores" used by Grigson.[504] Even in places lacking natural habitats with adequate food, pigs could have continued living as scavengers that consumed human refuse. This is what wild pigs do in India around Bikaner in arid Rajasthan. Large numbers of them enter the city at night to consume waste and other items thrown out by the residents, and indeed they flourish on such fare.[505] The Chinese have demonstrated the efficiency of garbage- and waste-feeding of pigs by developing what may be the most ecologically sophisticated system of pig keeping in the world. It is one that, as we have seen, not only enables China to support a pig population far larger than that of any other country, but also provides humans with over 70 percent of all dietary calories that come from animal sources. It is true that pigs are more numerous in the well-watered Rice Region of Central and South China (1.37 per farm in a 1929–33 survey), but they are also found in reasonable numbers in the semiarid Wheat Region of North China (0.52 per farm).[506] North China, I would emphasize, has amounts of annual precipitation comparable to those found in Palestine, Lebanon, and Anatolia, though it has far more severe winters to present an additional problem for pig keepers.

The conclusion I reach from the above is that, just as enterprising Chinese have been successful in keeping pigs in North China, Near Eastern peoples are capable of doing the same, and did, if their culture and religion permitted. As Brian Hesse has noted for Tel Miqne (Ekron) on the coastal plain of Palestine, the number of pigs jumped strikingly when the Philistines arrived in Early Iron Age I—the very time their numbers were being drastically reduced among Hebrews. This was because, unlike Hebrews, Philistines, or at least some of them, did not scorn pig keeping, and because pigs fitted well into the Philistine economy, for they "act as scavengers within a community, transforming the most diverse array of garbage into food for human consumption."[507] Pigs competed with humans for food in the Near East only to the degree that they were fed or stole foodstuffs that otherwise would have been eaten by humans. It is difficult to imagine that farmers there would not, like their counterparts elsewhere, be able to control or eliminate crop robbing by domestic pigs.[508] Among the Hittites, according to Hoffner, domestic pigs, unlike other livestock, survived on garbage alone, and records of fattening pigs on grain are rare.[509] Though this was not true everywhere in the ancient Near East,[510] it is hard to imagine early pig keepers indiscriminately providing pigs with food suited for direct consumption by humans. As Lord Ernle observed about medieval farmers in England, our present-day practice of buying grain for fattening pigs, "or of converting into pork or bacon farm-produce for which no ready market was available, scarcely entered into the heads of . . . farmers." On the contrary, pigs were expected "to be able to dig," that is, to support themselves. Feed was provided only to a sow that was farrowing or to pigs being fattened for consumption by wealthy families. Even then, cheap foods were used. These were items that were readily available and of poor quality, such as coarse barley, peas, beans, skimmed milk, buttermilk, and brewer's grains, which almost every family had at hand because beer making was a household affair.[511] This recalls the inscription on a Sumerian clay tablet, uncovered at Umma, dating from shortly before 2000 B.C. The inscription mentions a "reed-fed pig," which presumably fed itself in swampy areas or, though this seems less likely, was fed reeds that had been cut for it. The tablet goes on to say that the pig was also given fodder of fine bran.[512] The result at Umma was not to deprive humans of badly needed food, but to produce nutritious pork from reeds, which are unsuited for consumption by humans, and bran, a by-product of flour milling which even today is used mainly for animal feed.

I am convinced that any food provided to pigs in the ancient Near East was largely of this sort, and that any grain fed to pigs represented a small price to pay for their delicious flesh and services in removing household waste. In a study of Hierakonpolis in Early Dynastic times, Michael Hoffman concluded that living and/or ceremonial areas of elite structures that continued in use were relatively clean because of a conscious effort to remove all trash.[513] This, however, was not the case with homes of ordinary folk, whose organic trash was dumped near the home or even on the floors of houses. Robert Miller carried this matter further in a fascinating and well-documented article on pigs and their role in the subsistence economy of two workers' villages in ancient Egypt.[514] As background, Miller observes, like Harris, that pigs, along with dogs and chickens, do indeed need a range of nutrients similar to that required by humans. Whereas Harris sees this as leading to the pig taking food from the mouths of humans, Miller, like Diener and Robkin a decade before,[515] views it in quite a different light, in terms of mutual benefits accruing to both species. He observes that pigs, though they were not necessarily permitted to do so, are capable of surviving by scavenging alone. Because they can eat the entire range of human foods, moreover, pigs are ideally suited for consuming human waste.[516] They add to the ecosystem's productivity by speeding nutrient flow to smaller organisms and enhancing the value of manure available for use in gardens and fields. In balance, they also play a positive public-health function by consuming garbage and human feces and reducing health risks posed by fecally transmitted diseases and parasites, whether eliminating them altogether or interrupting their cycles of transmission. In addition, Miller observes, pigs represent valuable stores of food and energy available for human consumption whenever needed. He notes further that, not only were pigs useful in ancient Egypt, but that their usefulness has not ceased in Egypt even today. Of special interest in this regard are the *zabbālīn* of Cairo, refuse collectors who live in shantytowns near dumps outside the city and engage in garbage feeding and breeding of pigs. In the late 1970s, they were said to compose forty thousand families and to be mainly Coptic Christians originally from the Asyût (Assiout) area.[517] Miller describes *zabbālīn* pigs as "walking waste disposal units," and part of a "unique network of entrepreneurial technology."[518] The system makes excellent sense in both economic and ecological terms.

Returning to Palestine after the time of Moses, one sees that numerous remains of domesticated pigs, along with bones of humans and other animals, were found in one tomb at biblical Lachish (Tell ed-Duweir) dating from the eighth or early seventh century B.C., not long before destruction of the kingdom of Judah in 587 B.C.[519] Moreover, in Iron Age sites listed by Hellwing and Adjeman[520] and by Hesse,[521] though overall pig remains were rare (0.0–1.5 percent of all animal bones in sites other than those known to be Philistine), they were completely absent in only one or two. Individuals who kept pigs in the communities may have been non-Hebrews. Whoever they were, it is clear that a niche for the pig still existed and that, despite religious pressures, the niche was exploited on a small scale by enterprising individuals. Also of relevance are certain rabbinical writings, set down from roughly 100 B.C. to A.D. 200, that describe the pig as "the richest of all animals because it can find food everywhere." Swine breeders, in turn, are likened "to usurers because both grow rich easily and rapidly,"[522] indicating that pig rearing was quite profitable and implying that swine fitted well into certain ecological niches at that time. This is supported by Hesse's observation that in non-Hebrew Ashkelon in coastal Palestine in the Classical, Byzantine, and Islamic periods "pork was a mainstay of the diet."[523] Of special interest in this regard was the discovery of bones of domesticated pigs in the excavation of a synagogue and its environs at Khirbet Shemaᶜ in Upper Galilee, at medieval levels dating from the twelfth and thirteenth centuries A.D. The ethnic and religious composition of the population of Khirbet Shemaᶜ at that time is not known. It remains possible that its people were Christians, but it is believed to be much more likely that they were either Moslem Arabs or Eastern Jews.[524] Whoever the pig keepers of Khirbet Shemaᶜ may have been, their practice demonstrates once again that the pig continued to find suitable niches in the Holy Land.

Nor can one dismiss the fact that, despite strong anti-pig feeling among many of its people, Israel had a pig population estimated at 130,000 in 1989. Pigs have been kept in modern Israel not only by Christians but also by certain Jews, including Jewish communal settlements whose members have discovered that pigs fit well into the local agricultural system, converting into flesh waste products that otherwise would be discarded.

On the basis of the evidence reviewed above, it seems that the Harris hypothesis is simply off the mark. The principal problem of the pig keeper in Israel today is not the lack of such things as shade and mudholes, but the confusing web of legislation erected by anti-pig traditionalists.[525] As one observant reporter wrote, "It is not easy to raise pork in Israel, but it is profitable."[526] In other words, pig keeping is not an extravagance, as Harris suggests, but an activity that brings a good financial return.

The second part of the Coon hypothesis, that the abandonment of pig keeping occurred because people did not wish to display their wealth, is equally questionable. The historical record from the Near East shows that pig keeping and pig ownership were not restricted to the wealthy classes, nor was pork an expensive delicacy priced like Kobe beef today. Instead, pork was a reasonably priced food eaten by the lower classes among others. One judges, from records of the necropolis workmen's village at Thebes in Ramessid times, that pigs were of reasonable price. They were somewhat more expensive than fowl, sheep, or goats, but only a fifth the price of the usual garment (a skirt or loincloth) worn by the workmen.[527] Evidence such as this led Hecker to the tentative view that the "pig was more commonly eaten by the poorer classes."[528] In Middle Bronze Age Tell Jemmeh in Palestine, moreover, significant numbers of pig remains were uncovered in modest residences.[529] The same pattern seems to have prevailed in Babylonia and Assyria as well. Indeed, we have found no evidence that anywhere in the Near East the pig was an expensive creature kept exclusively by monied individuals.

Even if it had been, the historical record is full of accounts, from all parts of the world, of domestic animals, especially highly desired ones, being kept at great cost in habitats not well suited to them. Consider the horse in Arabia, where desert conditions are poorly suited to horses, but where Arabs have not only managed to keep them, but have also developed one of the most sought-after breeds in the world. Or consider common cattle in East Africa, where herding groups have such large populations of cattle as to bring on serious environmental deterioration. Yet men continue to increase the size of their herds, and government efforts to get them to reduce their cattle numbers have not met with notable success.

Nor does it follow that the early Hebrews would have given up eating pork, a tasty delicacy, even if much of the environment of Israel had become unsuited to pig keeping. It would have been quite reasonable for them to import pigs for slaughter and consumption, and even, because they were expensive, to consume them in a conspicuous manner. Such culinary display—conspicuous consumption—occurs among peoples everywhere,[330] and the more rare and costly a food item, the greater the status gained by the sponsor of the feast and the individuals consuming the food. In the case of bear's paw, a great delicacy among the Chinese, demand has been so persistent over millennia as to reduce the number of bears and even threaten their survival in many parts of the country. This has not led people to give up bear's paw, though it is so rare today that substitutions are commonly made (buffalo's foot and beef tongue are generally used instead of bear's paw in China today). In the cases of bird's nest and shark's fin, two other costly Chinese delicacies (bird's nests of the best quality in the early 1980s cost nearly three hundred dollars an ounce in Hong Kong, compared with about four hundred dollars for an ounce of gold), great efforts have been made to seek foreign sources of supply. Chinese entrepreneurs have developed trade networks to obtain nests from Southeast Asia to India in one direction, to Fiji in the other. The trade network for obtaining shark's fin is even broader, and at present extends to lands as distant as Mexico, Venezuela, and Norway. All the above leads me to conclude that the ecological hypothesis is as questionable as the hygienic hypothesis rejected by Coon. In this, I reach a conclusion similar to that of Diener and Robkin, who, after a careful weighing of the evidence on pork avoidance in the Near East, found the arguments advanced by Harris untenable.[531]

Symbolic and Cultic Hypotheses

Turning to symbolic and cultic hypotheses of the Hebrew flesh bans in Leviticus, one notes that only one reason is given for them, the need for "holiness," a word having the meaning of both " 'sanctification' (by emulating God's nature . . .) and 'separation' (from the impurities of pagans)."[532] One notes, for example, that immediately following the discussion of the flesh bans in Leviticus, Jehovah states: "For I am the Lord your God: ye shall therefore sanctify yourselves, and ye shall be holy, for I am holy."[533] One may properly ask why this explanation in terms of holiness, given in the Bible, should not be accepted at face value, why so many present-day secular observers insist that the actions of ancient Hebrews can have been based only on motives in conformity with a contemporary secular perspective. It appears that such observers are predisposed, by their limited perspective of the world, to reject a clear, reasonable, biblical explanation in favor of dubious explanations that are couched in terms of the present-day fashions of disease or ecology. Many early Jewish writers, as well as more recent ones,[534] have accepted the biblical explanation that the dietary laws were motivated by hopes of attaining a state of purity and holiness.[535] Isaac Klein writes of this position as follows: "The Torah regards the dietary laws as a discipline in holiness, a spiritual discipline imposed on a biological activity. The tension between wanton physical appetites and the endeavors of the spirit was traditionally explained as the struggle between . . . the good inclination, and . . . the evil inclination—the two forces that contend with each other for the mastery of the soul."[536] Another perspective on this position occurs in the *Siphrei*, a rabbinical exposition or commentary. "Let not a man say 'I do not like the flesh of swine'; on the contrary, he should say, 'I like it, but what can I do, seeing that the *Torah* has forbidden it to me?' "[537] Related to this is the view, found in certain rabbinical writings, that the Jewish dietary laws are a measure of a person's willingness to accept fully the laws of God. The holiness gained by Jews who adhere to those laws elevates them above other peoples.[538]

In keeping with the above are the views of Mary Douglas, set forth in her book *Purity and Danger*, published in 1966.[539] Douglas emphasizes holiness as an essential goal of the ancient Hebrews. In a state of holiness, they could approach God and receive his blessing, from which everything good derived. God's blessing produced order, which was essential to the well-being of the individual and the family as well as crops and domestic animals. If, on the other hand, God's blessing was denied, a person was at risk of all sorts of dangers, such as infertility and disease. The quest for holiness involved the notion that things should be complete, without imperfection. Thus sacrificial animals could have no blemishes, and ritual cleansing was required of persons who had become polluted, such as women in giving birth. Holiness also demanded that individuals fit into distinct categories that were to be kept apart. Sexual morality is thus holy, and incest and adultery are not, because the last two do not conform to the proper order of things. Turning to animals mentioned in the Levitican code, Douglas observed first that the ancient Hebrews were a herding people who kept sheep, goats, and cattle. These animals, she notes, had been blessed by God. They were, as a result, clean, and a person could enter the temple without purification after touching one of them. Their herd animals, moreover, served as models as to what other kinds of land animals were acceptable for eating: ungulates that chew the cud and have cloven hoofs. Land animals that failed to meet the criteria were unclean and unacceptable. The hare, for example, seems as if it were chewing the cud by its regular grinding of teeth, but is banned in the Levitican code because it does not have cloven hoofs. The pig was banned, Douglas argues, not because of its dirty eating habits, which were not mentioned in Leviticus, but because, though it has cloven hoofs, it does not chew the cud. The camel, in turn, was banned because, though it does chew the cud, it lacks cloven hoofs. As for other of the bans, fish are expected to have scales and fins, and water creatures that do not meet those criteria are unclean. Though the basis for classifying birds as unclean is not given in Leviticus, Douglas suggests that some of them (e.g., the cormorant) were unclean because, in addition to flying, they swim and dive. Had the penguin been known to the ancient Hebrews, she expects, it would have been unclean because it is wingless. Douglas's ingenious hypothesis provides a simple, reasonable answer to a question that has troubled observers for thousands of years: what basis could the Hebrews have had for banning as unclean the flesh of the unusually varied group of animals listed in Leviticus?

In subsequent publications,[540] written after criticisms of her hypothesis by other scholars, Douglas's views changed somewhat. She agreed with the criticism that, to explain those laws as they relate to animals, one must go beyond animal taxonomy and consider the broader social thinking and activities of the Hebrews. Her weighing of that evidence led her to conclude that an important wish of the Hebrews was to remain apart from other ethnic groups. As she observed, for the Hebrews "being holy means being set apart. The Israelites cherish their boundaries and want nothing better than to keep them strong and high."[541] As for the impurity of the pig, she agreed that her explanation in *Purity and Danger* was too simple, that it failed to answer the question of why the pig should be singled out for special abhorrence. She answers this by saying that the pig bore a burden of "multiple pollution" for the Hebrews. Not only was it a taxonomic anomaly, but it was also raised by non-Hebrews and ate carrion.[542] Also important, in her view, the conqueror Antiochus made the pig central in his campaign at forcing the Jews to abandon their faith. He sacrificed pigs on their altars and interpreted their willingness to eat pork as a sign of submission. For the Hebrews, in turn, the eating of pork became not merely abhorrent, but also "an act of betrayal" of their faith.[543]

Jean Soler, in a study first published in 1973, reaches somewhat similar conclusions by carefully weighing the Hebrew dietary laws found in the first five books of the Bible.[544] Like Douglas, he regards hygienic explanations to be "false leads." He argues further against seeking answers in terms of individual food items, and for the need to seek an overall explanation in the system of beliefs of the ancient Hebrews. One of the earliest beliefs, expressed in Genesis, is that God and humans are different, that for humans to be clean in the eyes of God, they must maintain that separateness from him, including dietary separateness. Human foods, Soler observes, initially came from the plants God created to assure the survival of mankind, whereas God's foods were the living creatures offered in sacrifice. For humans to kill freely for their own needs is wrong, for such killing by humans would be an improper intrusion into the domain of God, who alone has the right to take life away. This placed the eating of animals in a bad light, though the possibility of eating flesh arose in the distinction God made between flesh and blood. Blood, the "vital principle" of living creatures, belonged to God, but once an animal's blood was set aside, its flesh was desanctified and acceptable as human food. In Soler's view, the distinction between blood and flesh left the food structure of the Hebrews intact, since it merely involved elements that defined the permissible, that separated the clean from the unclean.

Implied in the above was a right enjoyed by the Hebrews at the time of Genesis to eat land animals of all sorts as long as their blood was separated and their flesh desanctified. Soler notes further that bans on eating specific animals are not present in Genesis, but first occur in Leviticus and Deuteronomy and date from the time of the covenant between Moses and God. That covenant, Soler emphasizes, focussed on the need for separating the Hebrews from other people. "I am the Lord your God, which have separated you from other people. Ye shall therefore put difference between clean beasts and unclean, and between unclean fowls and clean: and ye shall not make your souls abominable by beast, or by fowl, or by any manner of living thing that creepeth on the ground, which I have separated from you as unclean."[545] For Soler, the basic reason for the bans instituted by Moses was to separate the Hebrews from other peoples. The matter of why specific land animals were banned, while interesting and important, is a secondary matter relating to Hebrew views of killing and of what, from their experience, is normal for such animals. The first requirement, that land animals have a "hoofed foot," was intended to eliminate carnivores, who departed from God's original intent of vegetarianism, which involved animals as well as humans. The second requirement, that acceptable animals chew the cud, is seen by Soler as a further effort to include only true herbivores. Thus swine, which are omnivores, are eliminated by the second requirement, even though they have hoofed feet. Even land animals that meet the two tests for herbivores were not necessarily clean. They still had to conform to what the Hebrews viewed as the normal condition for land animals, to have cloven hoofs like their sheep, goats, and common cattle. Animals lacking cloven hoofs, like the horse and camel, may be true herbivores, but, because they depart from the norm, were considered to be blemished and unclean. Overall, in Soler's words, "the Mosaic logic is remarkable for its rigor, indeed its rigidity. It is a 'stiff-necked' logic. . . . It is self-evident that the very inflexibility of this order was a powerful factor for unification and conservation in a people that wanted to 'dwell alone.'"[546] In many ways, Soler's explanation of the animal bans of the ancient Hebrews resembles that of Douglas as set down in 1966. He differs with Douglas's views, however, in giving clear primacy to the Hebrew desire to maintain their ethnic separateness and a secondary position to taxonomy, to the criteria that were actually used to distinguish clean from unclean animals.

The works of Douglas, Soler, and biblical scholars of their persuasion[547] demonstrate the importance of viewing flesh bans in the context of the system of belief and behavior of the ancient Hebrews. Problems remain, however, even if one accepts the primacy of such beliefs in establishing the Hebrew ban on pigs and pork, for, as Jacob Milgrom has observed, "the food bans are certainly older than the rationale given them."[548] This fits with Roland de Vaux's conclusion that the prohibitions of animals in Leviticus, Chapter 11, "are certainly inherited from a primitive age."[549] It also agrees with Jacob Neusner's observation about Hebrew views of purity and impurity in general, that priests in biblical times "took over into their system [of belief] widespread attitudes" of their time.[550] In other words, the explanation of the feelings of Moses and the ancient Hebrews about pigs and pork lies beyond that given in the Bible.

This brings us again to the cultic hypothesis. One question is whether Moses and his followers, who had lived in Egypt, may have taken over anti-pig attitudes from Egyptian priests, who harbored such feelings in his day and long before. May those attitudes, on the other hand, have been in reaction to the pig honoring of Egyptian devotees of Seth in Canaan, where Egypt had a presence?[551] Another possibility is whether the ritual associations of the pig with "certain Canaanite-Syrian cults may have made the pig particularly reprehensible to the Hebrews. . .".[552] As we have seen, however, there is no archeological or literary evidence that the pig had a ritual role in established cults in Palestine. Nevertheless, one cannot dismiss the possibility that ritual killing of pigs by Canaanites or other non-Hebrews on an individual or family basis may have been sufficient to bring on a negative Hebrew reaction. Indeed, even their keeping and eating of pigs could have sufficed.

It is my view that development of anti-pig attitudes in antiquity did not follow a single path, that such attitudes were influenced by factors, or combinations of them, that differed from place to place. Some factors were unique to a particular people and time, as to the Hebrews. Other factors had an impact across vast regions through long historical periods. In my opinion, we, as Westerners, have focussed excessively on the

Hebrews and the Near East, and on hypotheses that fit with contemporary perspectives of hygiene, disease, and ecology. It is now time, I would argue, to cast the problem of the pig and pork in a broader geographic, historical, socio-economic, and religious perspective. I would also argue that the pig's eating habits are basic to an understanding of human antipathy to the pig and pork, and that these may go back to the earliest days of pig domestication. Where domestic pigs fed in woodlands or away from human settlements much of the time, as was common in early Western Europe, their eating habits may have received little negative notice. In a free-ranging situation near human settlements, on the other hand, people would have observed pigs eating all sorts of things repulsive to humans, including excrement and the bodies of dead animals, perhaps even humans. Sty pigs would also have been observed consuming dead creatures, whether their companions or others. In my opinion, such awareness of the dirty eating habits of domestic pigs may have led certain individuals or social classes to avoid pork from earliest times of domestication. On the other hand, because of reduced visibility and awareness, the avoidance was less stringently applied to wild swine, which is likely why many present-day peoples who abhor the flesh of domestic pigs nevertheless consume that of wild boars.[553]

Despite the dirty eating habits of domestic pigs, many people in the earliest days of pig keeping continued to eat pork. The matter, however, was one about which there was sensitivity and concern, presenting an invitation for activists of one sort or another to press for a broader ban, whether for members of their own occupation, social class, or whatever. The persons most likely to seize that invitation were priests and other persons especially concerned with maintaining their ritual purity, and, as a result, the rejection of pork in earliest times tended to be selective. Some persons of high ritual status and some classes or castes rejected pork, whereas others continued to eat it. In Egypt, Southwest Asia, and India such selective use and avoidance of pork persisted over several millennia—despite awareness of the dirty eating habits of swine.

This pattern is clear in the early literary accounts from Egypt to India. It is also clear that there were efforts to extend the ban on pork to all members of an ethnic or religious group—for example, all Jews or all Hindus. Bans on pork were also more likely to develop and persist among peoples who enjoyed a way of life that provided abundant animal protein of other sorts, which permitted them to survive quite well without pigs and pork. This would have been especially true of pastoral peoples living in steppes and deserts. They had numerous herd animals, whether sheep, goats, common cattle, or horses, and their habitats and ways of life were not suited to the keeping of swine. The ancient Near East and Inner Asia did contain a broad range of habitats, some suitable to pigs and others not. This is likely why some ancient archeological sites there contain an abundance of pig bones while others contain few, if any. Also of relevance are the facts that anti-pig feelings have been common among pastoral peoples in the arid and semiarid sections of Eurasia, and that in some cases these feelings may have spread from them to settled peoples. It may be that the widespread transition of the pig from acceptable to unacceptable food among Old World settled peoples was initiated largely by pastoral influence. The pig was kept widely among agricultural peoples in Europe, Asia, and North Africa in ancient times. There is also a long history of conflict between pastoralists and settled people, the former holding the latter in contempt for their manual labor, their carefully regulated lives, and their lack of spirit and individual courage in battle.

Kaj Århem has presented an interesting example of food symbolism among the pastoral Maasai of East Africa, and how it relates to their perception of neighboring agricultural and hunting groups.[554] Among the Maasai, Århem notes, people and their cattle share a symbolic identity. Cow's milk is the staple food of everyone, although, when it is in short supply, women and children may consume the milk of smaller animals. Meat is normally consumed on ritual occasions, which are frequent enough to make it an important dietary element. Plant foods are consumed by women and children, but they are not part of the ideal pastoral diet of adult men, which is observed with special strictness by warriors. The Maasai food system also serves to distinguish them from neighboring hunting or farming groups, whom they regard not as merely different in the ways that all ethnic groups differ from one another, but as basically different and inferior types of people. The Maasai have a high regard for grass, which represents cattle, fertility, and finally life itself. Cultivators have no respect for grass and, on the contrary, are destructive of pasture. Cultivators eat domesticated food plants, which the Maasai regard as tainted and unclean. Cultivators are also viewed as having ties with the earth, with nature, and the wild, and "*ilmeek*," the Maasai word for cultivators, contains elements of contempt. Though Århem does not mention pigs, it is not difficult to imagine the Maasai and other pastoral peoples regarding the pig and pork as alien to their way of life, part of the food systems of farmers, whom they hold in low regard.

Indeed, the widespread association of the pig with settled people in the Old World, sometimes a sacred animal in the worship of agricultural deities such as Demeter, makes it an ideal symbol for pastoralists to use for their settled rivals. I suspect that this association was made repeatedly by pastoralists, and it is clearly illustrated among the Mongols. Though Mongols do not reject pork, they have a prejudice against the pig that Owen Lattimore contends may be an instinctive response by pastoralists to the fact that they cannot successfully herd pigs, as farmers can.[555] They also seem to regard the pig as symbolic of the Chinese, for they call pigs black cattle and the Chinese, herders of black cattle,[556] just as in the fifteenth century the followers of Tamerlane called the emperor of Cathay the pig emperor.[557]

Other Possibilities

Pastoralists and Their Role.—In some cases, broad bans against pig keeping and pork eating may have been introduced to settled groups by pastoralists. The early Hebrews are an excellent possibility in this regard. We have noted the controversy about the early Hebrews: who they were, where they came from, and what factors led them to settle in the hills of Palestine. The traditional view, based on certain biblical accounts, is that the Hebrews were seminomads who emerged from the desert to invade and conquer the Promised Land. Among the prominent advocates of this conquest hypothesis is archeologist William F. Albright.[558] A second hypothesis, associated with Albrecht Alt, Martin Noth, and others, is based in part on early Egyptian records.[559] By this hypothesis, the Hebrews were seminomads who slowly infiltrated the Promised Land in a peaceful manner, and later came to fight and triumph over the Canaanites. A third hypothesis, drawing on sociological and anthropological thinking and associated particularly with George Mendenhall and Norman Gottwald,[560] is that of peasant rebellion, in which the Hebrews are seen not as outsiders but as lowland Canaanites, refugees ('Apiru, from which the term "Hebrew"?)[561] who, perhaps urged on by disgruntled mercenaries and pastoralists, withdrew into the hill country to escape oppression. A fourth hypothesis, advanced by Israel Finkelstein, is based on the lack of evidence that the Hebrews came from Canaanite urban centers to the west.[562] Like those who support the peasant rebellion hypothesis, however, Finkelstein sees the Hebrews as people whose origin is related to environmental, economic, demographic, and social change within the hills and steppe regions of Canaan. Also at odds with the peasant rebellion hypothesis are the findings of archeologist Adam Zerfal, that in Manasseh the Hebrews had migrated from arid lands to the east, beyond Canaan or at least beyond Manasseh, and had gradually changed from a herding economy to agriculture.[563] However the above differences are ultimately resolved— there are also variations and combinations of the hypotheses above— from my perspective it is significant that in most of them pastoralists of one sort or another are seen as playing a significant role in the evolution of early Hebrew life. This is true even of hypotheses that view the Hebrews as basically Canaanite, which may include pastoralist 'Apiru stirring up the peasantry; a small but influential pastoral minority coming from outside Palestine, as from the Sinai Desert with Moses to introduce the worship of Yahweh; or people who, as conditions changed, moved from a settled to a pastoral nomadic way of life and back again.[564] If this is true, it markedly increases the likelihood that pastoral influence may have contributed to the negative Hebrew opinion of the pig and pork. Also significant, the total number of "Israelites" was small initially, with one estimate of only about twenty thousand sedentary folk in early Iron Age I sites (following c. 1200 B.C.) west of the Jordan River.[565] This would have greatly enhanced the possibility of small numbers of pastoralists having a major influence on the entire population. Mendenhall has argued that the emergence of the Hebrew monotheism of Yahweh created an identity beyond the tribal level, and was consistently used to contrast Hebrew culture with that of the Canaanites.[566] The ban on pork, as argued by Douglas and Soler, would have provided the Hebrews still another means for distinguishing themselves from the Canaanites. Similar processes likely occurred in other places in the Old World as well, with anti-pig sentiments of pastoralists becoming entrenched by example, and sometimes through incorporation into the religions of the settled people. Commonly there was a long period of transition as the practices associated with the ancient agricultural gods were broken down and gradually gave way. During this time, survivals of ancient attitudes and practices respecting the pig created a situation that was both ambiguous and confusing, but with pork usually a food of ethnic minorities and lower castes or classes.

An Indo-European Contribution?—Such information as is available suggests that a great impetus to the spread of anti-pig feeling came during the second millennium B.C. This was a time associated with a notable rise in strength of Indo-European groups living north of the great civilizations of Asia. In India, the earliest evidence of anti-pig attitudes is for the Aryans, who seem to have come from the north-west sometime in the second millennium B.C. The earliest such evidence I have uncovered for Anatolia (c. 1650–1200 B.C.) is for the Indo-European Hittites, who seem to have come from the north at the beginning of the second millennium B.C. That the Hittites may have had a regional impact in attitudes toward the pig is suggested by W. M. Ramsay's observation about post-Hittite times. Ramsay identified striking differences in views of the pig existing between eastern Anatolia, on one hand, and western Anatolia and Greece, on the other.[567] The Halys River, according to Ramsay, was roughly the boundary between the two regions. To the east were pig haters, to whom the idea of having pigs in a sacred city was indecent and polluting. To the west were pig eaters, who used swine in their holiest ceremonies and who made images of the pig to bury with their dead. Though Ramsay did not mention the Hittites in explaining this phenomenon,[568] the Halys River marked the western boundary of the Hittite realms in Old Kingdom times (1700–1500 B.C.), and, even in the mid-fourteenth century B.C., Hittite settlement in the far northwest did not extend much beyond the Halys. There is also the interesting question, raised by James C. Moyer, whether the Hebrews, by direct contact or through intermediaries, came to regard the pig (and dog) in a negative manner because of their importance in Hittite ritual.[569] Moyer cites Hittite and biblical verses as providing striking support for this hypothesis. He also observes, "There is at least a strong likelihood that Israel considered the pig and dog unclean because of negative rituals associated with the Hittites or others."

Two other groups of Indo-Europeans also had a major role in Southwest Asia: the Indo-Aryan Kassites and Mitanni. These groups established themselves in Mesopotamia in the second millennium B.C., apparently as military elites with chariots and an unusual focus on the horse.[570] The Kassites established the second dynasty of Babylonia, which lasted from about 1600 to 1157 B.C. The kingdom of Mitanni flourished in northern Mesopotamia from about 1500–1360 B.C., and contended with the Egyptians and Hittites for control of Syria.[571] The Mitanni capital, Wassukkani, has still not been discovered. Knowledge of the Mitanni, therefore, derives largely from records found elsewhere, as on the tablets of Tell el-Amarna in Egypt; at Hattusas, the Hittite capital; and at cities subject to Mitanni rule. As a result, we have uncovered nothing to indicate what their attitudes toward pigs and pork may have been. According to Ghirshman, however, their early migrations took them by way of the same areas of Turkestan through which the Aryans of India also passed.[572] Whether or not the Indo-Aryan Kassites or Mitanni contributed to them, anti-pig attitudes in Mesopotamia are said to date from 1400 B.C., which coincides with their periods of dominance. One possible interpretation of the quotation about the Assyrian deity Shamash, given in my discussion of pigs in Mesopotamia, is that, though pigs were an abomination to all Assyrian deities, they were especially distasteful to Shamash, who abhorred and cursed them.[573] If this was the meaning intended, one wonders whether the cult of Shamash may have been one vehicle by which anti-pig sentiments, perhaps derived from Indo-Europeans, spread. I base this on the fact that Assyria was a northern frontier against Indo-Aryan incursions into Mesopotamia,[574] and on the likelihood that early syncretization took place among Aryan, Hittite, and Mesopotamian deities, including Shamash.[575]

Prior to the possession of Palestine by the Hebrews, Shamash (or Shemesh) was worshipped by the Canaanites. Several places bearing the god's name are mentioned in the Old Testament (ʿIr-Shemesh, "city of the sun"; Beth-Shemesh, "house of the sun"; and ʿEn-Shemesh, "spring of the sun").[576] It is possible that, as may have been the case in Assyria, the cult was strongly anti-pig, and that the Hebrews took over such views from this Canaanite cult, if not directly from Assyrians. Palestine, like Egypt, was also influenced by Indo-Europeans through trade, diplomacy, and war.[577] In this regard, Albright cites documentary evidence, dating from 1500 to 1300 B.C., which shows that there were many personal names in Syria and Palestine that were not Semitic, but Indo-Aryan or Hurrian.[578] He notes further that in Palestine a large number of the chiefs had Indo-Aryan names, and that such names apparently were more common in the upper classes. He believes it likely that we are dealing with a movement into the Fertile Crescent during the eighteenth century B.C. that was part of the same one that brought Indo-Iranians into Iran and India, and that, in Albright's view, "must have been unusually terrifying, since swift horse-drawn chariots were used by the invaders in battle." [579]

The matter of Proto-Indo-Europeans and the pig has long been a subject of controversy. There was a Proto-Indo-European word for pig, reconstructed as "*su-," which occurs among widely scattered later Indo-European peoples (Latin: "sus," Indic: "su-," English: "swine"). It may have applied to pigs in general (though the Indo-Iranian form was limited to wild pigs). In addition, "porko-," another word found in European languages, referred specifically to domestic pigs. Some linguists have argued that the first of the above terms applied to wild pigs among the Proto-Indo-Europeans, and the second, after Indo-European migration and contact with earlier agricultural peoples in Europe, came to refer to domesticated ones. This led to further speculation that the Proto-Indo-Europeans, who may have lived in the Pontic-Caspian region,[580] did not keep domesticated pigs, and that they came to know pigs only when they migrated westward across Europe.[581] At present, on both linguistic and osteo-archeological grounds, it is generally believed that the wild pig was hunted by Proto-Indo-Europeans and that the domestic pig also played a role, albeit a minor one, in their economy.[582] How, then, is it possible that certain Indo-Europeans, such as the Aryans, could have introduced anti-pig sentiments into lands where they migrated? My belief is that, even though domesticated pigs were kept in the Proto-Indo-European homeland, they were ill-suited to the pastoral or semipastoral way of life that developed among groups in more arid country to the east. Thus, the latter groups did not keep pigs and came to scorn both the pig and pig keeping. In accord with my view are observations by Matyushin [583] about archeological finds in the southern Urals and Inner Asia. In the southern Urals and nearby areas, he notes, bones of domesticated horses, sheep, and common cattle are found in nearly all early Neolithic sites. Pig bones, on the other hand, are absent in those sites, and, even though pigs were domesticated in the Near East by 7000 B.C. or so, they first appear in the southern Urals only in Late Bronze Age levels, following about 2000 B.C. In a recent review of archeological evidence, Shnirelman notes that, though stock breeding was found across the entire steppe belt from the Dnieper to the Volga in the Late Neolithic (c. 5800–4000 B.C.), pigs, which in general were far fewer than common cattle and sheep, were much less numerous in the eastern part of that belt.[584] Indeed, he points out that pigs were rare or absent altogether in more arid parts of that belt; that in the Volga-Ural steppe, virtually no bones of wild boars or domesticated pigs have been uncovered in Neolithic sites; and that, because pigs were unsuited to steppe conditions in that area, the people who migrated eastward along that southern route may not have had pigs, but sheep and common cattle. Shnirelman suggests further that these herding peoples may have developed a negative view of pork while migrating into the region which later developed into a pork taboo.[585] This he sees as the only plausible explanation for the migrants' failure to hunt wild boars. Such boars were common in river valleys in the steppe and in the forest steppe to the north, and were widely hunted by earlier and later peoples in Mesolithic and Bronze Age times. J. P. Mallory has made similar observations.[586] One is that, in the Pontic-Caspian area, pigs apparently were not kept in the east before the second millennium B.C., when pig bones are found in Bronze Age sites.[587] Another is that in the arid lands in Inner Asia, people of the Bronze Age Andronovo culture (1700–1200 B.C.), which many scholars accept as Indo-Iranian, were cultivators who kept common cattle, sheep, goats, and horses, but seem to have had "little or no place for the domestic pig."[588] One notes, in this regard, that at what is believed to be an Indo-Iranian kurgan burial site at Sintashta (c. 1500 B.C.) in the southern trans-Ural steppe, bones of sacrificial horses, common cattle, sheep, and dogs were found, whereas wild boars were rare and domestic pigs were not mentioned.[589] Mallory suspects that the unsuitability of Inner Asia to pig keeping may account for the poor preservation of the ancient Indo-European name for pig among Indo-Iranians east of the Ural Mountains.[590] I would add the observation by Epstein and Bichard that there are no domesticated pig remains in sites of the Afanasievo culture (c. 3000–1700 B.C.) of the Minusinsk Basin and Altai region, which preceded Andronovo, or in ones of the Late Bronze Age Karasuk culture (1200–700 B.C.), which succeeded it.[591] The Afanasievo people had copper implements. They are said to have been the earliest pastoralists in northern Asia, with horses, common cattle, and sheep. They were also hunters and fishers, who tended to live in small settlements, judged by some archeologists to have been seasonally used herders' camps. Physical anthropologists consider them

Europoid, most closely resembling groups living in the Pontic-Caspian area. Archeologists, in turn, have noted many similarities with cultures of the Pontic-Caspian.[592] The Karasuk people, by contrast, seem to have been Mongoloid and to have had close cultural ties with China. They appear to have been cultivators, but they had a strong pastoral element in their economy and may have been seminomads, with horses, camels, sheep, and common cattle.[593] The information above suggests that more than one ethnic group in prehistoric Inner Asia did not keep pigs. It also suggests that, like pastoral peoples of the region today, such groups may have been indifferent or hostile to pig keeping, that they passed those attitudes on to succeeding generations, and that when they migrated into neighboring areas they carried such views with them. This seems to have been the case with the Scythians, Iranian-speaking horse nomads who moved into the Pontic-Caspian steppe from Inner Asia in the first millennium B.C. Judging from Herodotus's observations, the Scythians had an indifference to pig keeping and did not use pigs in sacrifice. I am suggesting that other Indo-Iranian peoples, such as the Aryans, likely also carried such attitudes with them in their migrations. If I am correct, it is no accident that pigs were an acceptable sacrifice and even served in the "triple sacrifices" of Greeks (*trittua*) and Romans (*suovetaurilia*), but were not among the canonical lists of sacrificial animals of Indo-Iranian Avestans or the Vedic Indians.[594] Indeed, the pig's place in the hierarchy of sacrificial animals among Vedic Indians has been described as "beyond the pale."[595]

The resolution of the problem of anti-pig attitudes among early Indo-Europeans, especially pastoralists in Inner Asia, is best left to linguists, archeologists, and historians. Here I would observe only that certain of these peoples likely deserve far more credit than they have received for disseminating anti-pig attitudes in Eurasia. Whatever their role in this regard, however, determining the origin of the anti-pig attitudes of pastoralists is a broader problem involving peoples of different language families as well. However the question is ultimately resolved, it does seem relevant that there is little, if any, prejudice against pork, apart from Moslem or other outside influences, in places where pastoralists have had small influence. This includes Western Europe, the Guinea coast and Congo Basin of Africa, and East Asia and the Pacific islands.

The Problem of Egypt.—Egypt presents special problems. One persistent explanation of Egyptian anti-pig feelings is that the pig fell from a position of respect because of the ascendancy of the god Horus over his rival Seth, with whom the pig was associated.[596] Support for this is found in the legend, mentioned above, that Seth, disguised as a pig, attempted to destroy the "eye of Horus," probably the moon, and that Horus avenged himself by establishing pig sacrifice to the moon.[597] The fact that Seth lost status in ancient Egypt, and that at the time of the Greek observers the Egyptians considered both the pig and Seth symbols of evil,[598] lends credence to this hypothesis. If true, anti-pig sentiment may have developed in Egypt because of a religious struggle independent, or largely so, of outside forces.

In seeking further understanding, however, one cannot ignore the remarkable parallels between ancient Egyptians and various peoples in Africa's northeast and elsewhere in thinking about snakes, fish, hippopotami, and pigs. In ancient Egypt, these four were all among the creatures symbolic of Seth, and therefore unacceptable to Horus and held in contempt or sacrificed by people.[599] The harpooning of hippos in religious rites goes back to first-dynasty times in Egypt (Figure 12), and at least from New Kingdom times the hippopotamus was viewed as a manifestation of Seth and was hunted for ritual reasons. The harpooning of Seth as a hippopotamus, which was dismembered and its flesh distributed, was a central feature of the annual ritual drama, in honor of Horus, carried out at Edfu in the third and second centuries B.C.[600] Of special interest in the drama was mention of the impaling of fish by Horus, along with the killing and ritual eating of snakes.[601] The pig was also ritually impaled in ancient Egypt in connection with the cult of Horus, but this may have been a later development. This is in accord with the Horus myth, mentioned above, that when Horus was a child, pigs continued to be offered to him, a practice that later ceased.[602]

It is thus quite conceivable that the Egyptians extended their views of the hippopotamus to the pig, to which it bears a considerable resemblance. It may be no accident that, as we shall see, certain peoples elsewhere in Northeast Africa reject fish as unclean along with hippopotami, pigs, and the pig's wild relatives (bush pig and wart hog). In modern Ethiopia, for example, pork and hippopotamus flesh are generally rejected as unclean food, with the hippo traditionally eaten only by despised hunting groups who were regarded as impure. We will see in the fish chapter that various Cushitic peoples in Ethiopia and adjacent areas of Northeast Africa, also reject fish as food, and some refer to them as dirty water-snakes.[603] I am suggesting that the parallels be-

12. Hunting a hippopotamus in ancient Egypt (from J. Gardner Wilkinson, 1878).

tween ancient Egypt and modern Ethiopia may have culture-historical significance, and may have been transmitted to Egypt from elsewhere in Africa or gone in the other direction.

If one were to speculate on other outside forces that may have contributed to Egyptian anti-pig sentiments, one could not overlook the major political changes that immediately preceded the New Kingdom. Of special note are the Hyksos, those hated Asiatic invaders who ruled Egypt just prior to New Kingdom times, who identified Seth with Baal, their principal Asiatic deity, and elevated him to a respected position in Egypt.[604] By tradition, one of the last Hyksos rulers went even further by seeking to suppress other Egyptian deities and promote the worship of Seth.[605] Whether or not this is true, the Hyksos aroused strong anti-foreign feelings among Egyptians, and, with their overthrow, a strong reaction developed against Seth, as the deity of foreigners.[606] What I am suggesting is that the pig, because of its association with Seth, may also have become a target of special hostility among New Kingdom Egyptians.

An alternative hypothesis is that anti-pig sentiments were enhanced in Egypt because the eighteenth dynasty (1567–1320 B.C.) was a time of Egyptian expansion in Asia, which reached northern Syria and Mesopotamia, and that the Egyptians adopted anti-pig sentiments from Asians, among them Indo-Europeans with whom they had contact.

Curious Efforts to Gain Acceptability for Pork among Hindus, Moslems, and Jews

Turning from the origins of the ban on pork to the contemporary world scene, I would note a curious unwillingness on the part of Westerners to accept the rejection of pork by Moslems, Jews, and Hindus, and an eagerness to get them to eat pork. One reads, for example, of a failed attempt to encourage the use of imported pork in India by stressing that it is one of "the three whites," white being a positive color to Hindus.[607] One of the other whites is milk (cow's milk is indeed pure to Hindus), but, unfortunately, the third is the egg, which, as we shall see, is unclean. Whatever balance of feelings the appeal may have created, it did not overcome the basic impurity of pork. Whiteness was insufficient to offset the excrement-eating habits of an animal associated with untouchables.

An equally interesting example is the controversy that arose in recent decades over the babirusa (*Babirousa babyrussa*), a piglike animal (family Suidae) native to Celebes and the Moluccas. The controversy developed after a study, supported by the U.S. Agency for International Development, included the babirusa among a group of overlooked animals of tropical Asia that offered considerable promise for animal husbandry in tropical regions.[608] The suggestion was that the babirusa's potential as a source of tasty flesh could best be developed by bringing it under domestication. On hearing of the report, however, another researcher objected that the survival of the babirusa was already threatened, and that an effort to capture animals for breeding might in fact lead to extinction of the species.[609] What interests us here, however, is the observation that the babirusa is a rudimentary ruminant whose flesh might be acceptable food to Moslems and Jews. This acceptability is possible because, like common cattle, the animal meets the standard set down in Leviticus: it chews the cud and has a cloven hoof. If, indeed, attempts were made to domesticate the babirusa as an acceptable pig, it would be a development unique in the history of domestication. It would be the only case of an animal domesticated because an ancient religious injunction had made the flesh of a distant relative, in this case the true pig, unacceptable as human food. It would also be a further demonstration of the lengths to which some humans may go to get around prejudices against flesh food.

3

> I yield to none in my worship of the cow. Cow-protection is the gift of
> Hinduism to the world and is one of the most wonderful phenomena in
> human evolution. . . Hinduism will live so long as there are Hindus to
> protect the cow.
>
> —Gandhi, *How to Serve the Cow*

Common cattle were domesticated in southeastern Europe and the
Near East by 6000 B.C. or before. For nearly a century, some scholars
have argued that initial domestication took place for ritual purposes.[1] I
think it likely that this was so, but, in any case, it was not long before
common cattle, in addition to serving major economic uses, were playing an important role in ritual and religion, the bull symbolic of male
gods, and the cow, of mother goddesses (Figures 13 and 14). By classical
times in the Mediterranean and Near East, that role was rich, varied,
and amply expressed in art and sculpture.[2] With the rise of Christianity
and Islam, however, the repudiation of ancient cults and their deities
brought on a striking decline in the religious role of cattle in those regions. Today one must turn to Hindu India, and perhaps to Buddhist
Tibet,[3] to gain full appreciation of how vital a role bovines can play in
ritual life. Hindu India has the world's most important surviving cattle
cult, centered on the cow, and it is directly tied to the rejection of beef
as human food.

The Indian Center of Beef Avoidance

Domesticated common cattle (in this case, the zebu, *Bos indicus*) were
known in Baluchistan, along the western margins of the Indian subcontinent, by the fourth millennium B.C.[4] and possibly much earlier.[5] The
remains of domesticated zebu cattle have also been found in many early

13, 14. Chatal Huyuk shrines, with bull horns and heads (after James Mellaart, 1965).

sites within the Indian subcontinent proper. In those sites, as true at Mehrgarh in Baluchistan, they account for a majority of all animal bones uncovered.[6] The indications are that the keeping of common cattle was a very successful activity, that such cattle played an unusual role in the life of early Indian peoples, and that people ate their flesh.[7]

Today India has a very large population of domesticated bovine animals (195 million in 1989). Most of them are common cattle and water

15. Mithan (*Bos frontalis*).

buffalo, but there are also small numbers of mithan (*Bos frontalis*) in the hills and mountains of the far northeast and east (Figure 15), and yak or yak hybrids in the Himalayas. India's domesticated bovine population is far greater than that of the United States (98 million in 1989) or Europe (125 million), and amounts to over 15 percent of all bovines in the world. Common cattle, which are far more numerous than other bovines, play a vital role in the economic life of India. Oxen are important in plowing and traction. Cow's milk and its products are major elements of diet. Common cattle of all sorts provide dung for household fuel, as well as hides and other useful products. Beef is one of those useful products. However, among Hindus, who number over 700 million people (1994 est.), about 80 percent of India's population, the cow is a sacred animal, and most Hindus not only refuse to eat beef but also take other actions to protect common cattle from harm.

The water buffalo is India's second most numerous bovine. It performs many of the same functions as common cattle. If kept from long exposure to the sun and given an opportunity to cool itself in water, in many ways the water buffalo has been the superior animal. It is able to thrive on coarser feed. It is stronger and better able to plow the heavy soils of irrigated paddies. Under village conditions, buffalo cows commonly yield twice as much milk as do zebu cows. Buffalo milk has nearly double the butterfat content. It commands a higher price in the

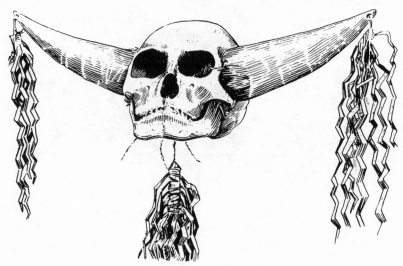

16. Mithan horns on human skull taken by headhunters (after J. H. Hutton, 1921).

open market because it provides more of the ghi (clarified butter) and other dairy products so prominent in Indian diet.

The yak and the mithan are found in hill or mountain areas on the fringes of India, and are unfamiliar animals to most Hindus. Instead, they fit into quite different cultural contexts. The yak is kept mainly by Buddhist mountain people. The mithan, on its part, is principally an animal of tribal people who traditionally did not use it for milking or plowing, but kept it for reasons of prestige and sacrifice (Figure 16).[8]

We will turn later to an examination of the eating or avoidance of water buffalo flesh, but we will first consider the sacred-cow concept, its historical development, and the ways in which it is expressed today in Hindu religion, folk thought, and everyday behavior. We do this because, if one is to appreciate the patterns of beef eating and avoidance in contemporary India, one must understand the socio-religious context in which they developed.

Historical Development of the Sacred-Cow Concept

The Aryans, those remarkable Indo-Europeans who came to have a profound impact on subsequent Indian history, were a pastoral people who did some cultivation. For them, common cattle were a source of

meat and milk; an essential aid in traction, as in pulling wheeled vehicles; and a measure of wealth.[9] In Aryan battles, the winners expected
to obtain additional cattle as booty, and indeed the early Aryan word for
battle translates as "struggle for kine."[10] The Vedic records, the sacred
Aryan literature, also reveal that the ritual role of common cattle, including cows, bulls, and oxen, was of unusual significance.[11] People
took various actions to assure that cows and other common cattle were
healthy and that they increased in number. The bull was honored as
a symbol of power. After man and the stallion, it was at the top of
the hierarchy of sacrificial animals, required for the *sautrāmaṇī,* a major
Vedic group sacrifice which consisted of a bull, a ram, and a male goat.[12]
People sacrificed the bull to powerful Vedic deities, whom they sometimes called bull. Among these was Indra, favorite of the Vedic Indians,
the god of weather and war, who liked beef very much.[13] People considered the cow, on its part, as auspicious and pure, and commonly made
the gift of a cow to a Brahmin prior to his carrying out a rite.[14] For Vedic
Indians, cow's milk and dairy preprations served not only as food, but
in ritual as well. Cow's milk was recommended for consumption by persons getting ready to carry out certain rites. It served as a charm to keep
evil forces away. It was an ingredient in substances used for purposes
of magic. It was given to someone who sought to become wealthy, and
it served in other beneficial ways.[15] At the same time, cows, like bulls
and oxen, were important sacrificial victims, and were also sometimes
killed at weddings or in honor of important guests.[16] Cow's flesh was
eaten on such occasions,[17] and seems to have been fully acceptable food
to kings, priests, and sages. This is demonstrated in the account of
Yājñavalkya, a famous Vedic sage in the areas of ritual and metaphysics,
who admitted to eating beef "provided that it is tender,"[18] a statement
unthinkable for a devout Hindu to make today. A review of evidence on
the cow and other common cattle in the Vedic literature led Sanskrit-
ist W. Norman Brown to observe that, regardless of the ethnic group
or historical period, there seems to be no other sizable body of literature that gives common cattle such prominence.[19] Yet, Brown believes,
however highly cattle were regarded and honored, there is "never . . .
a hint that the animal as a species or the cow for its own sake was held
sacred and inviolable."

    In Jain and Buddhist writings, the concept of ahimsa makes its first
appearance in the sixth and fifth centuries B.C., and it came to occupy

a paramount role in the ethical teachings of those religions. The sixth and fifth centuries B.C. were a time of deep-seated change in India, one in which the role of priestly castes, the Brahmins, was reexamined along with traditional religious beliefs and values. Written accounts reveal that Jains and Buddhists argued for ahimsa and against taking life, although they did not focus solely on the cow. Buddhists did, however, object to indiscriminate slaughter of cows, especially for sacrifice. The Buddha did not prohibit beef, though he did forbid the flesh of humans and certain other animals (including elephant, dog, horse, lion, tiger, panther, bear, hyena, and serpent).[20] Moreover, when King Aśoka made Buddhism the state religion about 250 B.C., he did not specifically prohibit common-cattle slaughter or beef eating, though he declared in his famous rock edicts, "Not to injure living things is good" and "No animal may be slaughtered for sacrifice."[21] Thus, Buddhism took a stand against cruelty and animal sacrifice[22] but did not single out common cattle for special consideration.

Ahimsa—which among present-day Hindus has a special relevance for the cow—is not alluded to in the Vedic literature except in its final works, following 500 B.C., where it is barely mentioned. The earliest evidence of the sacred-cow concept, which was not at first associated with ahimsa, occurs in works written near the beginning of the Christian Era, though it is treated in an uncertain manner. Both concepts, however, gradually gained acceptance among Brahmins.[23] Though the slaughter and eating of common cattle by Hindus continued,[24] many others came to emulate the Brahmins who adhered to the sacred-cow concept, and the early centuries of the Christian Era saw the slow emergence of the modern pattern. The *Mānava Dharma-śāstra* (c. A.D. 200?), for example, listed the slaying of common cattle among the offenses for which penance must be done.[25] By the fourth century A.D., the death penalty was given for killing a cow, and in succeeding centuries the concept of the sacred cow gained widespread acceptance as an essential tenet of the Hindu faith.[26] In the seventh century, the Chinese traveller Hsüang-tsang observed that Indians were forbidden to eat "the flesh of the ox," and that those who did so were despised and scorned and lived apart from others.[27] The legend, from this period, of a Tamil king who decreed the execution of his own son for accidentally killing a calf well illustrates the climate of opinion that may have prevailed by that time.[28]

The Sacred-Cow Concept in Modern India

Turning to the fortunes of the sacred-cow concept in later times, one notes the strong impetus it received from rivalry between Hinduism and Islam following Moslem invasions of the eleventh century. When Europeans arrived in India, they, too, sometimes ran afoul of Indian feelings about the sacred cow. In 1670, for example, a bulldog kept at a European trading establishment at Honnore (Honavar) on India's west coast killed a cow, and an enraged mob responded by killing every European there.[29] Still later, with the struggle against British imperialism, the cow and its treatment became a major political issue for Hindus, for, as shown in the Gandhi quotation at the beginning of this chapter, the inviolability of the cow is central to their faith.

With independence, commitment to the sanctity and inviolability of the cow was so deeply embedded in the minds of the traditional Hindu public that cow protection and a ban on cow slaughter were incorporated into the Constitution of India, to initiate decades of legal controversy often involving Moslems.[30] Cow slaughter remains an emotional issue today. It is banned or restricted in various Indian states, and there are continuing efforts to gain a complete national ban. In addition, various actions have been taken, from an individual to a national level, to favor the cow as a sacred animal.[31] Most Hindus display a curious ambivalence in their advocacy of the sacred-cow concept, sometimes addressing the economic good sense of banning cow slaughter and sometimes appealing to religious sensibilities. Gandhi, for example, wrote, "The motive that actuates cow protection is not 'purely selfish,' though selfish consideration enters into it."[32] A similar view by someone sympathetic to Gandhi's position is even more explicit:

The cow protection ideal set up by Hinduism is essentially different from and transcends the dairy ideal of the West. The latter is based on economic values, the former while duly recognizing the economic aspect of the case, lays stress on the spiritual aspect viz. the idea of penance and self-sacrifice for the relief of martyred innocence which it embodies. Under a dairy ideal, means do not count, even cow slaughter is resorted to for insuring cheap milk supply and getting rid of what are supposed to be uneconomic and superfluous cattle. Under the religious ideal, means are the principal thing—in fact everything. The essence of cow protection according to Hinduism thus does not lie in the mechanical act of "saving" the animal *per se*, . . . but in the self-purification and penance behind the act.[33]

Hindu religious motives are thus seen as having a dynamic quality, one of several factors influencing the cattle economy of India, and the door is left open to the idea that protecting cows may have a negative economic impact. If, Gandhi insists, the protection of cows were motivated merely by selfish (economic) considerations, "the cow would be killed, as in other countries, after it ceased to give full use."[34]

Whatever the explanations Hindus may offer to Westerners about spiritual and economic aspects of the sacred cow (and they are varied and often conflicting), cow symbolism has continued to be important among the public in modern times.[35] As Deryck O. Lodrick has observed, along the highways of India, one sees gaily decorated trucks with the cow and suckling calf painted on their sides. The imprint of the cow and calf on a banner at a political meeting proclaims the speaker to be a member of the Congress Party. One may encounter Hindus, led in a procession by naked *sādhus*, leaving a meeting organized by right-wing political and religious groups in support of a total ban on cow slaughter, loudly saying, *Go hamārī mātā hai!* (The cow is our mother!).

In popular Hinduism, the cow is the favored animal of Krishna, and much of the cow-oriented ritual seen in India today centers around worship of this celebrated deity at festivals such as Gopashtami and Govardhan Puja.[36] In addition to Krishna festivals, the cow and cattle are worshipped on many other occasions (Figures 17 and 18). Some of these involve rituals performed with the cow representing some deity, and others mark ceremonies performed for the welfare of cattle and generally are related to agricultural festivals.[37] The cow, as a sacred being, is also an object of circumambulation (*parikramā* or *pradakshiṇa*), walking around a person or thing, which may benefit the performer or object of the act.[38] In Hindu thinking, the cow possesses abundant *śakti* (divine power, as of a female deity), and the literature is full of illustrations of how caring for a cow, its presence, or even the sight of it brings good fortune and drives away evil or protects against it.[39] In southern India, a cow is sometimes placed in front of a temple, with its head facing outward so that people arriving will see its face.[40] Not only is the sight or presence of a cow pleasing, but also its products are protective and purificatory.[41] Even dust gathered from the hoof print from a cow is beneficial: an effective and strong ingredient in Hindu medicines.[42] Of special relevance in purification are the *pañchagavya,* the "five products of the cow" (cow's milk, curd, ghi, urine, and dung).[43] These products, which have served in similar ways since early times, each have secular uses much as in other parts of the world, but in India they also play

17. Cow decorated for ceremony, Ajmer, India (photo by Deryck O. Lodrick).

a significant role for orthodox Hindus in gaining and maintaining the state of ritual purity they so greatly desire.[44] Individual products of the cow were used in ceremony in earlier times, but the term *"pañchagavya"* first seems to appear in the Sūtra period (c. 500 B.C.—A.D. 100).[45] Since that period was associated with the rise in sanctity of the cow, it seems likely that the two are related.

Perhaps most significant in Hindu everyday life in North India today is behavior relating to *kachchā,* inferior cooked foods, and *pakkā,* superior ones.[46] *Kachchā* foods are usually prepared with water or water and salt, whereas *pakkā* ones are prepared with milk products, usually ghi, or (by extension of attitudes regarding the purity of ghi) vegetable oil. In simplest terms, it is the purity of the cow, imparted through its milk to cooked food, that increases acceptability of *pakkā* foods.[47]

Also of interest among Hindus is a rebirth ceremony involving the sacred cow, more usual in South India than in the north, that was known from early times at least into the nineteenth century. This cere-

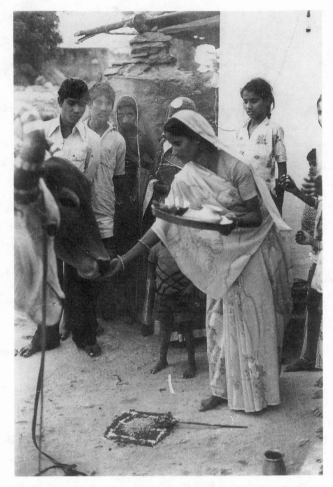

18. Cow worship in a Rajasthani village (photo by Deryck O. Lodrick).

mony, *hiraṇya garbha* (Sanskrit for "golden womb"),[48] has roots in a Vedic concept of the world's creation[49] and sometimes involved a person, commonly a ruler, being reborn by passing through a large cow fashioned of gold. The person undergoing the ceremony was cleansed of pollution or guilt, as from contact with non-Hindus or committing a vile act of some sort. In one case, a ruler underwent the ceremony after betraying a Hindu ally in fighting with Moslem invaders, and after he passed through the cow, the wife of his Brahmin guru took him into her arms, as a nurse would, and put him to her breast and fondled and rocked him while he attempted to weep like an infant.[50]

Among the most touching expressions of sentiment for ahimsa and the cow are India's animal homes. Field research by Lodrick provided for the first time a clear picture of these institutions from a geographic and cultural perspective.[51] Altogether there are said to be about three thousand animal homes in India, which in 1955 were estimated to contain about 600,000 cattle. There are two principal traditional forms of animal homes: *goshalas,* homes for aged and infirm cattle, and *pinjrapoles,* which admit animals of many types, including cows. *Pinjrapoles* are reflections of dedication to ahimsa, a concept to which the Jain religious community is most strongly committed. Thus, today they are overwhelmingly centered in Gujarat, a traditional Jain stronghold. *Goshalas,* by contrast, are in large part reflections of concern with the sacred-cow concept, and are most closely linked with the Hindu community. *Goshalas* are found widely across India, though their greatest numbers are in the north or west. Traditionally *goshalas* were charitable institutions intended to care for aged and infirm cattle, but today most reflect a blending of the religious and economic goals of cow protection and cattle improvement. Prominent in this change are government agencies that have been trying to use *goshalas* as breeding centers and in other ways to raise the quality of Indian cattle and amounts of milk production. Nevertheless one report indicated that about 30 percent of the cattle in *goshalas* have been kept with at best minimal return.

One could go on at considerable length with the ways in which the sacred-cow concept are expressed in modern India. What I have sketched above, however, should suffice. It reveals clearly that we are dealing with a concept rich in the ways it is expressed, one that generates strong feelings, and reaches into many areas of human activity. An appreciation of this will help the reader to understand the matter of beef eating and avoidance in India.

Beef Eating and Avoidance in Modern India

Indian Moslems, Christians, and many tribal peoples do eat beef. Also at variance with general Hindu practice are the low Hindu castes whose members commonly eat beef. These include leather workers, some scavenger castes, and other untouchables.[52] Though certain of them slaughter cattle, they seem to obtain most beef from animals that have died a natural death, which certain untouchables are obliged to remove from the village.[53] Other Hindus have the utmost contempt for them, and even accuse them of poisoning cattle to obtain beef. Thus the purity and ritual position of the untouchables is damaged in not one, but three, ways: they eat beef; they eat carrion; and, allegedly, they murder cows. Untouchables have responded to this situation in various ways. Though they may deny it, some continue to eat beef secretly because it is cheap and is considered strengthening, and because, whether or not they eat beef, they would be condemned for doing so. One South Indian untouchable illustrated the perception of beef as strengthening with a story of a tug-of-war reputedly held in the Indian army "between a team of fifty beefeaters and fifty vegetarians—and the beefeaters, of course, won." Among themselves, moreover, certain South Indian untouchables delight in stories of members of higher castes who are tricked into eating beef, enjoy it, and ask the source of such tasty "mutton."[54] On the other hand, the contempt of other castes has led certain untouchables to give up eating beef in an effort to make themselves more acceptable to the general Hindu community. One reads, in this regard, of the Chamar caste of Kotah State in northwest India abandoning beef eating in the present generation, and expelling members who have persisted in the practice.[55] One also reads of grades among untouchable castes in one area of South India based on whether or not they eat beef, and, among beef eaters, according to whether they eat beef occasionally or regularly, and, for the latter, whether in the form of freshly killed beef, which is less polluting, or carrion, which is more so.[56]

Hindus of other castes are not without blame in the matter of cow slaughter, for many farmers sell cattle in bazaars even though they may suspect that the cattle will ultimately be killed and eaten. In 1992, for example, there were reports of cattle sold in bazaars supplying large-scale cattle smuggling operations by rail and truck in the very heartland of Hinduism, the Ganges Valley.[57] The numbers are astounding: almost five thousand cattle trucks passed daily through one town on their way to slaughterhouses in the port of Calcutta, with frozen beef ultimately reaching consumers in the Near East. The trade has continued, even though more than two hundred police raids have been carried out in the past two years, and even though 850 persons, most of them Hindus, have been arrested in the last six months. The reason for its persistence is that, from the farmer's perspective, it makes economic sense to sell surplus, unneeded cattle, and, from the merchant's perspective, the business is lucrative.

Moslems, largest religious minority in India (1994 est.: 11 percent of India's total population, or nearly 100 million people), find themselves in an unaccustomed position with respect to cow slaughter and beef eating. Instead of being vigorous propagators of avoidance, as they are with pork, they are on the defensive. In deference to Hindus, certain Moslem rulers of India have urged their coreligionists to protect cows, and have passed legislation designed to preserve cattle.[58] In spite of this and actions by Moslem cow-protection societies, most Indian Moslems reject the Hindu view of cattle. In predominantly Moslem sections they do not hesitate to eat beef or to sell old or infirm cattle for slaughter. In Hindu areas, however, Moslems act with greater caution, in some places giving up slaughtering cattle and eating beef in order not to offend their Hindu neighbors. In other places, as in the village of Shamirpet in Hyderabad, they continue to eat beef but slaughter their cattle outside the village, to respect feelings of the Hindu majority and to avoid trouble.[59] Their fears are based on a long series of incidents in which outraged Hindus have severely punished Moslems for their transgressions. In Srinagar in Kashmir, for example, a group of Moslems was imprisoned for years by Hindu rulers for having slaughtered and eaten cattle during a famine.[60] Moslem cattle slaughter continues to create friction with Hindus today, and there is little likelihood that differences will soon be reconciled, though with division of former British India into three states, two Moslem (Pakistan, Bangladesh) and one secular but with a Hindu majority (India), there are more clear-cut regions of beef eating and avoidance.

The behavior of other groups in the subcontinent with respect to cattle slaughter and beef eating has been varied. The Sikhs, whose religion is an offshoot of Hinduism, have a reverence for cattle similar to that of Hindus, and do not eat beef. In fact, they have been among the strongest opponents of cattle slaughter, and hence frequently at odds with Moslems on that score.[61] In Sri Lanka, Sinhalese Buddhists have strong religious objections to killing animals or raising livestock for slaughter, but, despite this, many of them eat beef, which can be readily purchased.[62] I have no specific information on present-day cattle slaughter and beef eating in former Portuguese India, but it is now part of India and subject to its laws with respect to cattle slaughter. However,

19. Killing of a mithan by strangulation (after C. von Fürer-Haimendorf, 1963).

even in former times in Portuguese Damão and Diu, cattle were never sold for slaughter because the population was predominantly Hindu. In former Portuguese Goa, even Christian peasants rarely raised cattle for beef, in this perhaps unwittingly following pre-Christian habit. There was, however, a demand for beef in urban centers, and cattle were smuggled in from India to supply it.[63]

Eating beef has been respectable and fairly common among India's tribal groups (who today number about 8 percent of the total population, or over seventy million people). The Dire of Hyderabad, for example, eat it openly at feasts.[64] The Gadaba sacrifice bulls to gods at every feast, and then distribute the flesh among guests.[65] The mithan-keeping tribal peoples of eastern India sacrificed these animals in interesting and varied ways (Figure 19), and, apart from restrictions applying to women, ate their flesh with relish.[66] There are also reports of other tribal groups rejecting cow slaughter and beef eating, some of them quite strongly. The Reddis of Hyderabad are as strict as any Hindus in their avoidance of flesh of cattle and water buffalo.[67] The Kharias of Chota Nagpur and Central India expel from the tribe a family whose members, whether intentionally or accidentally, kill a cow, calf, or ox, and the family must undergo purification ceremonies to be reinstated.[68] The Kamars of Chhattisgarh in Central India not only expel cattle slaughterers from the tribe, but also reject beef as food.[69] Many Bhils of Central India are of no fixed opinion about killing cows and eating their flesh, yet a man who was guilty of many "cow murders" was said to have contracted leprosy as punishment.[70] It is possible that in some cases such views developed independently of Hindu influence, but Hindus seem to be implicated wherever historical information is available.[71] This is well documented for the Saoras (Sabaras), a Kolarian (Austro-Asiatic) people of Orissa. The Saoras formerly sacrificed cows and bullocks to their deities, among them the god of the dead,[72] goddess of smallpox, and rain goddess. They also killed cows at funerals so that the animals would join the deceased in the afterworld. One Saora deity, a noted cattle thief and beef eater, received cow sacrifices so that people's herds would be safe and their crops fertile. The flesh of sacrificed animals, moreover, was eaten. Yet by the 1950s, because of Hindu influence, the sacrifice of cows and oxen had become very rare among the Saoras, carried out only on extraordinary occasions, and then the killing was sometimes done by non-Saoras. In addition, the Hindu ban on beef was gradually being accepted by Saoras, and taken very seriously by those who rejected beef. In one village where the ban on beef had been accepted, a man had some Dōms (members of a Hindu or Christian caste of scavengers and musicians) sacrifice a cow to the goddess of smallpox, and he could not resist eating beef at the feast that followed. At once, it is said, his stomach became distended, and he died the next day. Many other villagers also fell sick, and, before they became well, sacrifices of other animals were required as well as promises that they would never again eat beef.[73] The Saora case reflects the general pattern of acculturation in India. As tribal groups accept Hindu ways, Hindu attitudes toward cow slaughter and beef eating continue to spread. Some Hindus, who regard the mithan as a relative of common cattle, even urge tribal groups in eastern India to abandon their consumption of mithan flesh.

One group, a curious anomaly, remains apart from the struggle in the Indian subcontinent between traditional views of Hindus and Moslems. This is the Shin, a nominally Moslem people of Dardistan in northwest India, who, unlike all other groups of the subcontinent, treat common cattle with abhorrence. They keep cattle for plowing but avoid them as much as possible, touching a newborn calf, for instance, only with the end of a forked stick.[74] They do not drink cow's milk, eat dairy products, or use cow dung for fuel. This attitude is especially strange in view of Shin history, for they are believed to have been an upper-caste Hindu tribe which was forced to migrate from Kashmir. They might therefore be expected to share either normal Hindu or normal Moslem attitudes toward cattle.

Turning briefly to the water buffalo, one might expect, against the background of its economic usefulness in India, that it would enjoy a respect among Hindus equal to that of common cattle. This, however, is not the case,[75] and, indeed, the water buffalo is viewed quite negatively in Hindu mythology, rites, representations, and religious attitudes.[76] This appears to reflect the water buffalo's fall from grace because the Aryans associated it with Dravidian peoples, as shown in the North Indian folk-saying that Aryans were white people who had white cattle, and Dravidians, dark people with dark cattle (water buffalo). Other non-Aryan groups as well were tied closely to the buffalo, as shown among the Saora tribal people just mentioned, for whom the water buffalo plays a major role in ritual and sacrifice.[77] In Hindu myths, there is a buffalo demon, Mahiṣa, who is commonly slain by the warrior goddess Durgā.[78] Yama, god of the dead, rides on a water buffalo. In the *Śatapatha Brāhmaṇa,* moreover, the wild buffalo is depicted as an impure scapegoat, unsuited to sacrifice.[79]

In general Hindu thinking today, the water buffalo is dirty and the bearer of bad luck, associated with demons, sickness, and death.[80] Despite the prevalence of such views, certain groups have a buffalo god. The buffalo has also been a sacrificial animal, especially among Dravidians in South India. Though such sacrifice has become very rare in the south,[81] it was carried out in connection with blood offerings to female deities, among them Durgā and a host of village goddesses.[82] Village-goddess sacrifice was intended to protect people from the evil such deities can bring, and might be carried out with additional precautions to see that evil was kept away. After a water buffalo was sacrificed to a village goddess, its flesh was eaten and was highly esteemed. Since sacrifice is contrary to Brahminical teaching, Brahmins did not usually participate in such sacrificial rites. Nor did they, or most other Indians of high caste, eat water buffalo flesh.[83] At the same time, the avoidance of water buffalo flesh is not nearly as common among Hindus as that of common cattle, and when tribal peoples or low-caste Hindus seek to enhance their social status by giving up some type of bovine flesh, that of the zebu is always the first to be proscribed.[84] Relevant here is the case of the Saora villagers who gave up cow slaughter and beef eating under Hindu influence, and who, when they violated that ban by eating the flesh of a cow, atoned for it in part by ritually killing a water buffalo.[85]

Southeast Asia

Although India is the Old World center of rejection of cattle slaughter and beef eating, similar attitudes, in part fostered by Buddhism, have also been found in Buddhist Southeast Asia from antiquity to the present day.[86] In Burma, it was illegal in pre-British times to slaughter beef animals or to sell or possess their flesh.[87] In modern Thailand, though cattle and water buffalo are sometimes sacrificed or slaughtered for food, it is against Buddhist tradition, and usually against a man's best interests, since work animals are a symbol of wealth.[88] In ancient Indochina, according to Pierre Gourou, a buffalo was slaughtered for great feasts, though both buffalo and common cattle were too valuable and too useful in agriculture for slaughter on ordinary occasions. Moreover, the authorities issued ordinances to prohibit slaughter of horned animals and trade in horns and hides.[89] Other observers have also indicated a reluctance to eat beef among the Indochinese. John Crawfurd, who was in Cochin China in 1821, reported that people did not use flesh of either cattle or buffaloes as food.[90] John White noted in 1823 that in Annam beef consumption was confined to the Chinese population;[91] and at the end of the nineteenth century, Prince Henri d'Orléans noted that chiefs at Thac-By in Annam regarded beef as coolies' food.[92] In much later times (1960), it was reported that Khmer peasants in Cambodia eat very little beef, in part because, as Buddhists, there are objections to killing animals or raising them for slaughter. They also believe that it is wrong to eat a work companion, and thus in rural areas about the only bovines that are killed are injured or sick animals, old cows, and

heifers, and not by Khmer but by Chinese or Cham butchers.[93] At the
turn of this century, Lucien de Reinach observed an instinctive repugnance for beef in Laotians, which he regarded as a vestige from ancient
times when they were a pastoral people and had prohibitions against
slaughtering oxen for food.[94]

The spread of Western influence in Buddhist areas of Southeast Asia
has encouraged use of beef. Before the Second World War, it was even
being shipped from Thailand to Singapore and Hong Kong.[95] Despite
this, remnants of old attitudes continue to survive here and there. The
people of Thailand, because of Buddhist scruples, will not slaughter
beef animals near their villages.[96] Burmese of a generation ago would
neither kill cattle nor sell beef, although they would sell pork, fowl, and
fish. As a result, all beef butchers in Burmese markets were Indians.[97]
Today Burmese are more ready to forgo beef than any other common
flesh food, and when a Burmese Buddhist wishes as an act of piety to
give up eating flesh of one animal, he generally gives up beef.[98] Such
acts are encouraged by monks and quasi-religious groups, which from
time to time organize campaigns against beef eating.[99]

One departure from strict Buddhist precept is found among the Thai.
Despite their reluctance to slaughter common cattle and water buffalo,
Thai love their own form of bullfighting (also found from Madagascar
to Japan and in ancient Egypt), in which bulls are pitted against each
other rather than against humans. In southern Thailand, where bullocks are raised especially for this purpose, the bullfight is a weekly affair, on which the local government collects an admission tax.[100] Though
bullfighting used to occur in northern Malaya (it is now banned there)
and in South China and may still be found in other parts of Southeast
Asia, it has not been determined how the practice is reconciled with
Buddhist or Moslem belief, or whether it has a historical affinity with
the sacredness of cattle in the area.

Widespread acceptance of Islam in Malaya and Indonesia has almost
completely counteracted whatever ancient reluctance there may have
been to eat beef. In Malaya, for example, people consume beef, though
it is expensive and they can afford it only for special occasions; several
decades ago many cattle and water buffalo were imported each year from
Thailand, both for slaughter and for draft purposes.[101] Indonesians, too,
generally eat beef without prejudice, and according to one informant
it is one of the cheapest foods available. There are indications however

that, in the past, reluctance to eat beef was also present in Malaya. One aboriginal group, for instance, will not touch the flesh of water buffalo.[102] In the last century the Malays preferred the flesh of water buffalo to that of common cattle, an indication, it has been suggested, that in former times they, like Hindus, prohibited beef as food.[103]

In the Mentawei Islands off Sumatra, beef is tabooed and refused by natives.[104] On Bali, a remaining center of Hinduism in Indonesia, in the last century male Brahmins avoided beef.[105] The Dyak tribes of Sarawak, according to one observer, regard the bull and cow as sacred, and will eat neither their flesh nor their dairy products.[106]

Some groups in the Philippines kept water buffaloes for their flesh in pre-European times, though common cattle were not known until after the arrival of Europeans.[107] There is no evidence that people are reluctant to eat flesh of either animal, but beef is scarce and is generally consumed only a few times a year at important feasts.

Tibet, Mongolia, and East Asia

Just as Buddhism seems to have been the vehicle by which Indian feeling against cattle slaughter and beef eating was introduced to Southeast Asia, so it appears to have been an agent by which the feeling penetrated Tibet and Mongolia. Its effect, however, seems to have been minimal. In Tibet, where the hardy yak (*Bos grunniens* or *Poephagus grunniens*) and its hybrids replace water buffalo and common cattle as the most numerous bovine animals,[108] Combe writes that Lamaist law forbids eating "cow" flesh, by which, it seems, he implies something more than normal Buddhist commitment to ahimsa and vegetarianism.[109] At the same time, according to Harrer, the cold of Tibet requires that some meat be eaten.[110] He notes further that in one of Tibet's leading Buddhist institutions, Drebung Monastery near Lhasa, though no killing of animals was permitted, dried yak flesh was supplied by nearby communities. The diet of ordinary Tibetans seems to have been affected little, if at all, by any reluctance to consume flesh in general or beef in particular. As Palmieri notes, most Tibetans like meat, including that of bovines, and try to include some meat in their main meal every day.[111] Indeed, Tibetans consume yak flesh, whether cooked or raw,[112] in larger quantities than any other meat except mutton, and also eat flesh of common cattle and yak–common cattle hybrids.[113]

The only records of widespread group avoidance of flesh of a bovine animal in the Tibetan culture area are along the Himalayan borderlands with India. The Ladakhis of eastern Kashmir, in the region sometimes called Indian Tibet or Western Tibet, are an example; in their case, however, refusal to eat yak flesh is a direct result of Hindu influence and is accompanied by the belief that the yak is sacred.[114] Similar cases of "beef" avoidance, noted by Palmieri, are found among a few other Himalayan peoples.[115] In all cases, however, Hindu rather than Buddhist influence is involved.

As for Mongolia, where the numerous herds of bovine animals in traditional times consisted, on average, of 70 percent common cattle and the rest either yaks or crosses between the two,[116] there are hints of anti-beef feeling that are directly tied to Buddhism. I say "hints" because all we have is Prejevalsky's observation that Lamaist priests would not touch "beef."[117] Among the public, however, Buddhist flesh prohibitions are not strictly followed, and most Mongols eat beef on occasion.

In the past several decades, the pattern of Mongol and Tibetan life has been greatly altered by China and the former Soviet Union. Following the Soviet model, experimental breeding stations were set up in Mongolia,[118] and cattle were raised commercially, which likely increased the availability of beef for many people. At the same time, Buddhism has been on the defensive, and one suspects that beef consumption increased.

In China, water buffalo and common cattle are found widely and are fairly numerous (74.8 million bovines altogether in 1989), though their numbers are less than 40 percent of those in India. The domesticated water buffalo may have been known in Central China already in the fifth or fourth millennium B.C., and at a somewhat later date in sections of North China.[119] Remains of common cattle have been found in sites of the Yang-shao culture (c. 5000–3000 B.C.) in North China, and are believed to have been fully domesticated there following roughly 3000 B.C.[120] So far as we know, there was no reluctance to eat beef in earliest times in China. In Han China (206 B.C.—A.D. 220), for example, beef was a feast food that might also be buried with the dead, and it appears to have been more popular than pork.[121] In T'ang times (A.D. 618–907), however, beef eating declined because of Buddhist opposition, and those who still ate beef were not comfortable about it.[122] Its lack of status probably led to its absence among the dishes served at formal dinners and in restaurants in Sung times (A.D. 960–1279).[123] The status of beef is clear in nineteenth-century China, where common cattle and water buffalo were extolled for their contributions in the human scene, where their fat was unacceptable for use in candles burned before images of gods, and where beef was not among the flesh foods offered to the gods.[124] Pro-cattle sentiments were expressed in religious tracts and posters, with one tract attacking persons who raised beef cattle or consumed beef as more sinful and merciless than predators such as wolves and tigers. Another tract compared cattle slaughter with female infanticide, another reprehensible practice. Chinese folktales were also involved, commonly detailing the punishments experienced by people who slaughtered cattle or ate beef. Such sentiments found their way even into the Ch'ing court, which, according to one account, prohibited beef in the environs of the palace because it was wrong to kill and eat animals that had served humans so faithfully.[125] Nevertheless, royal offerings of cattle to deities at certain annual festivals were permitted, as well as cattle sacrifice in homage to Confucius.

Despite the importance of Buddhism in the decline of beef eating in China, it is not certain that all Chinese anti-beef sentiments derived from India. In fact, some Chinese scholars insist that such sentiments were known in their land before Buddhism arrived, and derived from the usefulness of bovines. Support for the latter argument is seen in the facts that, in places noted for adherence to Confucian teachings, the cow was honored as symbolic of agriculture, and that many conservative Confucian scholars were as disgusted with the idea of eating beef as Moslems were of consuming pork.

Another factor in the reluctance of Chinese to slaughter cattle was that they were symbolic of the social status of the family. From the size of the ox tied near a Chinese farmhouse one could tell how much land the family cultivated and to what social class it belonged; people were proud of their oxen and put their best animals where they would be seen. When marriage arrangements were being made between two families, and the girl's family inquired into the economic position of the prospective husband, investigators were careful to note the size and quality of the ox. If his family was eager for the marriage but did not have a cow or ox, they might have borrowed one from a neighbor or friend to display in front of their house.[126] Out of the close tie between the Chinese farmer and his ox grew his reluctance to part with his animal and his tendency to look down on anyone associated with slaughter of cattle. A farmer who was forced by poverty to sell his animal took as great care in selecting a buyer as if he were finding a husband for his daughter, and was especially concerned that the animal should not fall into the hands of a butcher. The traditional opinion about butchers was that no one could become rich as a professional butcher, that a butcher's soul would be condemned eternally, and that his children, if he had any, would be poor and weak.[127]

As a result, many Chinese refused to become butchers, and, at least in some places, slaughter of cattle became the work of Moslems. China's Moslems are noted for their beef eating. Beef is one of their important flesh foods, and, if left to their own ways, they eat beef without hesitation.

The traditional hesitation of Chinese to eat beef has diminished in modern times, and there has been an increasing demand for this meat in both towns and villages. One modern study found that 80 percent of families of Ting Hsien in Hopeh Province in North China ate beef, though sellers were apparently Moslems from another village.[128] We do not know how effective contact with Westerners may have been in encouraging beef eating, but under communism, cattle population has increased and, given Communists' lack of tolerance for such traditions, reluctance to eat beef has probably been undermined still further.

In the past, Koreans, like Chinese, ate very little beef, for cattle were needed for work and too valuable to be killed, and their slaughter was also regulated by law.[129] Eating beef was permitted only at important festivals, when slaughtering was done by a butcher who was a sort of government official.[130] Even in modern Korea, oxen are too valuable to be killed for food except on rare occasions. Sometimes oxen, which are regarded as members of the family, appear to be better fed than people themselves.[131] Elsewhere on the mainland of northeastern Asia cattle seem to be recent introductions and are not an important source of flesh food. The Manchu of a generation ago had relatively little knowledge of cattle; they did not milk cows; they killed few cattle; and beef was only a supplementary food.[132] Among the Gold tribe of the lower Sungari, cattle also seem to have been introduced recently. Though people used them for plowing, they were in such short supply that on one occasion in the 1930s authorities around Fuchin forbade their slaughter for meat.[133] In northeastern Siberia, Yakut rarely killed their oxen for food, and preferred horsemeat to beef.[134]

Attitudes toward cattle in Japan in the past were similar to those of China and Korea: people did not kill cattle for food, and Japanese considered it wrong to eat beef.[135] Bans on eating meat, including beef, had first appeared in Japan following introduction of Buddhism in the sixth century A.D., and were part of the national food scene from that time onward. When, however, Emperor Meiji moved to modernize and Westernize Japan in the second half of the nineteenth century, he set an example by eating beef. Beef eating thus became symbolic of the nation's new outward-looking perspective. Since eating beef was regarded as the sign of a civilized person, other Japanese came to eat it as well. Initially people ate beef in Western-style restaurants, later in their homes.[136] When Japan obtained control of Korea, Japanese began importing cattle for both work and slaughter, and by the early years of the century there were few important towns in Japan that did not have beef for sale to official and merchant classes.[137] Today beef is a very popular though expensive food. Survivals of ancient attitude occur among some old people who still refuse beef and in assignment of slaughtering to a separate slaughterers' and leather workers' caste, the Eta.

The Near East and the Mediterranean Area

Cow, bull, and calf were important in ceremonial life in the early Near East and Mediterranean, commonly occupying special positions with respect to the gods, and sometimes being deified themselves. In the Avesta, earliest religious record of ancient Iran,[138] for example, there is a holy primeval bull associated with the moon, and sacrifices are made to both as well as to other common cattle.[139] The urine of a bull (or cow or ox) (*gaomaēza* or *gōmēz*), or consecrated urine (*nīrang*), is employed as a purificant.[140] The cow is the personification of the animal world and its protector. It is described as created by the god Ahura Mazdā (Ormazd). It is thus among the "Ahuric" (good) animals, clean and holy.[141] Indeed, cattle of all sorts were highly praised, and constituted the principal form of wealth.[142] There are references to "joy-creating cattle," to "the holy cattle-breeding man," and to the heroic settler on the frontiers of Zoroastrian civilization who "gained cattle" for the Prophet.[143] Cattle also served in ritual and sacrifice, with a thousand oxen mentioned for a single sacrifice.[144] The flesh of common cattle of all sorts was consumed, and there is no evidence of any prejudice against beef.

The bull was also an important figure among the deities, or a companion of deities, in Mesopotamia and adjacent areas. The Sumerians regarded it both as a kindly protector of the home and as a malevolent storm demon; one conception perhaps derived from the character of the domestic animal, the other from that of the wild bull.[145] These concepts apparently were taken over, intermingled, and modified by certain other groups in the area, such as the Semitic Babylonians, who designated their divine bulls by words of Sumerian origin. Perhaps because bulls were associated with the supernatural, perhaps because they symbolized strength, colossal stone or metal statues of them were frequently built at entrances of temples, houses, and gardens as protection from evil spirits. These and other bull figures were often given wings and, in Assyrian times, a human face. There are assertions in Mesopotamian history and legend that, when the figures were destroyed or had departed, the temple they guarded fell to the enemy. Bull worship occurred among the ancient Hebrews, whether introduced from Syria or from Egypt. Aaron, during the absence of Moses, set up a golden bull as an object of worship [146] and a visible manifestation of the god who had brought them from Egypt. In later times Jeroboam I erected images of bulls in sanctuaries of the northern kingdom, Israel. These bulls were then worshipped, which was regarded as a great sin and an affront to Jahweh.[147] The use of oxen or bull figures to support the famous brazen sea that was constructed in Solomon's temple [148] suggests a survival, at least in form, of an ancient belief in the sacredness of bulls. There are hints of a similarly supported sea in a Babylonian temple,[149] from which the Hebrews may have derived their inspiration.

The rise of anthropomorphic gods in western Asia meant that animals alone were no longer objects of worship, though they continued to appear as companions of human deities. The bull, for example, was designated son of the storm god in western Asia, and the storm god was frequently pictured standing on the back of a bull. In the north of Syria, a center of worship of the storm god Hadad, the bull was sacred to the god. When this god was introduced to Rome, where he was known as Jupiter Dolichenus, he was depicted as standing on a bull, with a thunderbolt in one hand and battle ax in the other. In ancient Egypt, from which Israel to some extent derived its religious inspiration, cattle

20. Apis bull (from J. Gardner Wilkinson, 1878).

were among the most important animals consecrated to deities. The bull was worshipped primarily in the delta. Especially famed were the Mnevis bull of Heliopolis, who was associated with the sun-god Re-Atum; and the Apis bull of Memphis (Figure 20), associated with the lunar deity Ptah-Seker-Osiris. There was also the cow goddess Hathor of Momemphis, who was called the Egyptian Venus and is believed to have been associated with the moon (Figure 21). Egyptian bovine gods are thought to have been embodied in live animals, which were cared for and honored, and, at least in later times, when they died might be mummified and ceremonially buried amid great mourning. In some places in Egypt people kept animals which they regarded as sacred but not as incarnations of a god.[150]

In ancient Greece the ox was an attendant or servant of Demeter;[151] and at the ancient seat of Demeter worship at Eleusis near Athens sacred cattle were maintained.[152] In addition, both bulls and cows were sacrificed in Greece, bulls usually to gods and cows to goddesses such as Athena.[153] In Rome, too, bulls and oxen were sacrificed to the gods, bulls being choicest of victims.[154] The bull also played an important role in the myth and ritual of the Roman Mithras, whose cult spread across the Mediterranean world and beyond as far as Roman Britain.[155]

The high status of bovines did not lead to a general cessation of cattle slaughter or beef eating. Indeed, in some cases it may have encouraged the use of cattle as sacrificial animals, as at the Athenian Bouphonia and

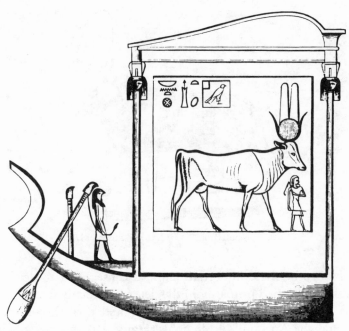

21. Cow of Hathor (from J. Gardner Wilkinson, 1878).

Magnesian Bull Festival, stately annual feasts in which an ox or bull was killed and its flesh eaten (in earliest times, probably in a raw state) by devotees.[156] There seem, however, to have been cases of reluctance to eat the flesh of cows. In ancient Egypt, for example, both cows and bulls were sacred to certain cults; yet, if one accepts the accounts of Herodotus[157] and Porphyry,[158] cows, which were associated with the goddess Hathor-Isis, were venerated more than any other animal, and, at least from the fifth century B.C. to the third century A.D.,[159] were never sacrificed, nor was their flesh eaten, whereas bulls were sacrificed and eaten. Similar practices were reported for the Phoenicians and certain peoples adjoining Egypt. The pastoral tribes of Libya as far as Lake Tritonis, said Herodotus, would not eat cow's flesh, nor would women of Barce and Cyrene. The feeling against cow slaughter and eating, however, must not have been universal in Libya, for people of Marea and Apis, on asking priests of the god Ammon for permission to kill and eat heifers, supported their request with the claim that they were Libyans, not Egyptians.

North of the Mediterranean avoidance of cow's flesh does not seem to have occurred. There did develop, however, an interesting reluctance to slaughter oxen, though they were used for sacrifice to many gods.[160] The ancient Greeks in Attica and the Peloponnesus so respected the ox that they considered it a capital crime to kill one.[161] The ancient Romans once banished a man as if he had been a murderer for killing an ox for insufficient reason.[162] Unlike the Chinese, however, ancient Greeks and Romans did not associate their respect for oxen with feeling against eating beef. Indeed, the flesh of sacrificial cattle was normally consumed after offering deities their share, and, as Varro indicates, oxen were sometimes sold specifically for slaughter.[163]

In the Near East and Mediterranean today, general factors limiting the eating of beef are its scarcity, high cost, and the prestige value and usefulness of cattle.[164] There exist, however, a few strange survivals in the area. In Mesopotamia "the ox" is regarded as a "taboo animal," and in Mosul it is an insult to say that a man eats its flesh.[165] The Mandaeans of Iraq and Iran (if an unclear statement has been properly interpreted) not only regard the killing of water buffalo and common cattle as a crime but also reject flesh of the latter. A Mandaean is quoted as saying that cattle were created for plowing, for draft, and for producing milk, but not for food. Associated with rejection of cattle flesh among Mandaeans is the belief that the bull is sacred to the sun and to life. Nevertheless, the bull does not figure as a Mandaean magical symbol, and the living cow has no special religious importance; nor are milk, cattle dung, or urine believed to possess magical or other special virtues.[166]

Africa South of the Sahara

Archeological and linguistic evidence in recent decades has gradually added to our knowledge of common cattle in sub-Saharan Africa in early times. For firm knowledge of how people view and use common cattle and their products, however, one must rely on written evidence dating mainly from the nineteenth and twentieth centuries. Modern sub-Saharan Africa can be divided roughly into three large areas in terms of the position of cattle: a northern belt stretching more than thirty-five hundred miles across the Sudan from Senegal to Ethiopia; a western region consisting of the rain forest and adjacent savannas of West Africa and the Congo Basin; and an eastern and southern region,

including the savannas and grasslands that extend from the southern
Sudan to the Republic of South Africa and into southwestern Africa.

The northern belt is located between the Sahara Desert to the north
and the zone of tsetse fly and sleeping sickness to the south.[167] It contains both pastoral groups and farmers, and cattle are fairly numerous,
though concentrated in the hands of such pastoral peoples as the Fulani,
who are estimated to own over 90 percent of Nigeria's six million
cattle.[168] People here commonly regard cattle as symbols of wealth, and
possession of them bestows prestige on a man. They are reluctant to
slaughter their cattle, and usually do so only for important feasts and
ceremonies. At the same time, cattle are not as much the center of social
and ceremonial life as in eastern and southern Africa.

In the western region, by contrast, there are few cattle, because of the
presence of tsetse-borne sleeping sickness. It is true that in a few places
resistant strains of cattle exist, such as the Ndama and dwarf breeds of
West Africa, but they are seldom present in large numbers, and where
infestation by tsetse flies is particularly bad, they are absent altogether.
Where cattle are present, people commonly know so little about their
care that they are provided with no accommodations and permitted to
live in a semiwild state. In the southwest Congo region, a traveller who
was given an ox as a gift had to stalk it and shoot it as if it were a
wild beast.[169] The peoples of the western region do not generally rank
cattle high in the prestige structure, but tend to regard them simply
as another source of meat, though a scarce and expensive one. There
are, nevertheless, a few groups in the region who have taken over from
peoples of the Sudan or of East Africa the notion that cattle are prestige animals. Among pagan peoples of the Jos Plateau of Nigeria, for
example, some wealthy men purchase cattle for prestige purposes and
place them in the care of Fulani herdsmen.

The third sub-Saharan region, in eastern and southern Africa, has
dense or fairly dense cattle populations in some places (around Lake
Victoria, in Rwanda-Burundi, Zimbabwe, Angola, Namibia, and the
Republic of South Africa), interspersed with areas with tsetse infestation
and sparse cattle populations. The eastern and southern region is particularly interesting in terms of the position of cattle in society and economy. Indeed, cattle are of such striking importance in the economic,
social, and ceremonial life of various native peoples that the phenomenon has been designated a "cattle complex" by Melville J. Herskovits,[170]

and has attracted much interest among scholars and others. The term "cattle complex," as used by Herskovits, is a culture complex in which there is a dominating element or integrating force that gives meaning to a way of life, and serves to distinguish ethnic groups who share the same integrating force from other ethnic groups who lack it.[171] Most peoples in the cattle-complex region are cultivators, and have a high dietary dependence on agricultural produce. At the same time, cattle are at the heart of the prestige structure of cattle-complex groups, and the central element of society around which life revolves.[172] It is said that the life of the Nandi of Kenya would be a meaningless void without cattle, that the Suk live for their cattle, that the Maasai despise anyone who performs work other than tending cattle,[173] and that the Nuer have a profound contempt for people with few cattle or none.[174] Among many peoples it is only through ownership of cattle, which generally is on an individual basis, that full participation in social life is possible. It has been noted that a man belongs to the lower class if he does not possess cattle, and that without them, he cannot court a wife, offer valuable sacrifices, heal diseases, or attend funerals.[175] Among the Bari of the Sudan, a man who has no cattle may not, when he dies, be given the correct ceremonies;[176] among the Tswana of southern Africa, a man who owns many cattle is respected and influential in tribal affairs;[177] and among the Kikuyu of Kenya, such a man is praised in songs.[178] Conversation is mostly about cattle; epigrams, riddles, and symbolism center on them; and languages contain a wealth of descriptive terms for them.

In their economic role, cattle are sometimes used to purchase grain and other goods and to pay fines and obligations, including those involved in the widespread custom of bride price. This last is, in effect, a contractual arrangement between families of the bride and groom; the groom gives cattle to his in-laws as a guarantee of his good behavior and to recompense them for loss of their daughter.[179] The bride price has serious implications for a man, for, as Harold Schneider has pointed out for the Pakot (Suk of West Suk District) of Kenya, a man must have a bride to establish a viable economic unit.[180] Another custom, which has perhaps equal economic significance, is the lending of cattle. This lending to neighbors, relatives, or friends gains a man their support and incidentally widens distribution of dairy products and cattle, since the borrower keeps the milk of the loaned animal and in some cases is permitted to keep a calf born of loaned cows.

One of the understandable consequences of the importance of cattle in social and economic life of eastern and southern Africa has been an enhancement of cattle raiding. In the past, when the authority of central governments was absent or weak, certain stronger groups, such as the Maasai, accumulated enormous numbers of cattle (four decades ago the Maasai numbered only forty-five thousand people, but owned about one million cattle, in addition to large numbers of goats and sheep).[181] Weaker groups, on the other hand, suffered serious losses. A century ago the Sejeju, Digo, and Giryama of Kenya and Tanzania had large herds of cattle, but within thirty or forty years, as a result of raids by the Maasai, they had hardly any left. Similarly, the Pokomo of Kenya had no cattle because of raids of the Somali and Galla;[182] and a chief of the Teuso of Kamion, Uganda, many years ago reputedly forced his tribe to give up keeping stock because of raids by stronger neighbors.[183] In other cases, small-scale group abandonment of cattle keeping came about when conquering pastoralists refused subject farmers the right to keep cattle. Also, a number of pastoral groups themselves were forced to give up or decrease cattle keeping when they migrated into tsetse-infested regions and their cattle died of sleeping sickness. This was particularly common along the eastern margins of the Congo Basin.

A further interesting aspect of the cattle complex is that people not only are proud of their animals but also display a strong affection for them. The Bari of the Sudan have loving reverence for their cattle;[184] some people among the Hima of Uganda pet and coax their cattle as if they were children and cry over their ailments;[185] and the Turkana of Kenya sing and dance to their cattle in the evening.[186] Some groups go even further, and consider certain things associated with cattle to be holy. The Nandi of Kenya regard milk, dung, and grass as sacred because of their association with cattle;[187] the Ngoni of the Lake Malawi (Nyasa) region look on the cattle corral as a sacred place and therefore suitable for the grave of a great chief.[188] In many groups a man maintains a special tie with one bull or ox, on which his courage and fortune in battle depend. When this animal becomes old and feeble, it is not permitted to die but is ceremonially killed. Occasionally the tie between man and beast has been so strong that the man has committed suicide on the death of his animal.

Many Western observers claim that cattle-complex peoples are extremely inefficient in their use of cattle for subsistence purposes. They point to the unnecessarily large herds of cattle that people accumulate, which has brought on such serious overgrazing and erosion as to present a major threat to the environment and to human well-being. They also point to these cattle peoples' concern with animals' coloring or size and shape of horns[189] rather than with quality or quantity of milk or flesh, and to the practice of keeping cattle alive regardless of size or state of health, and refusing to slaughter them specifically for flesh or to sell them for market. It is true that overgrazing and environmental deterioration are serious, even life-threatening, problems in the region. It is also true that cattle-complex groups traditionally did not breed animals for their flesh or milk, that they are reluctant to kill them, and that most of them eat beef only when an animal dies naturally or is slaughtered for some important ceremonial occasion.[190] There are even instances of cattle peoples refusing to slaughter their animals for food when the group is on the verge of starvation. At the same time, certain scholars have argued that the behavior of cattle-complex peoples is a rational response to dietary need and ecological pressure. Large herds, especially through the custom of lending cattle to relatives and friends, insure the cattle owner against catastrophic loss of all his animals through raids, disease, or drought. The more cattle a man possesses and the more widely they are dispersed, the more likely that some will be left. Moreover, because of the animals' low productivity, large herds are needed to provide a regular supply of milk, meat, and blood for human consumption. In addition to using blood of slaughtered animals, many East African peoples regularly bleed live cattle and use blood, usually mixed with milk, as food. Bleeding is done with either a miniature bow and arrow or a knife, which cuts the jugular vein of the animal and provides a flow of blood that is usually caught in a gourd.

Cattle-complex peoples of Africa, unlike Hindus, do not have a prejudice against beef; there are numerous references to their eating it. Indeed, in some cases cattle have actually been slaughtered primarily for their flesh. The Zulu king formerly fed his troops from the royal herd of cattle,[191] and chieftains among the Chagga of Tanzania have sometimes slaughtered cattle to provide food for corvée labor.[192] The Mbundu of Angola slaughter cattle when pasture is poor and food scarce.[193] The Lozi of Zambia eat beef when other animal products are in short supply, for to them cattle are primarily a food resource, and only secondarily of prestige value.[194] The Pakot of Kenya say frankly that, if it were a question of a person starving or eating his last remaining animal, he would eat the animal.[195] Partly as a result of European influence, various groups now also slaughter or sell their animals commercially.

Another accusation made against cattle-complex peoples is that they tend to gorge themselves at frequent feasts, thus not using efficiently even those animals they are willing to slaughter. On the other hand, as Harold Schneider has pointed out, times of ritual slaughter and feasting often coincide with the time of year when need for flesh is greatest, and that need may in fact determine when ritual slaughter occurs.[196] Indeed, Schneider and others have argued that the cattle-complex peoples also show marked concern for economic considerations in their slaughtering practices. The extent to which this is true is still debatable, but some cattle peoples apparently recognize the importance of cows as producers of milk and bearers of young, and for this reason slaughter steers more often. In the Lake Victoria region bull calves are emasculated and reared only for slaughter.[197] Though the Kikuyu kill a bull on important occasions, it is unusual to kill cows, which are kept for breeding.[198] In trade among the Pakot of Kenya, cows are worth more than steers, and people assert that, while steers with specially trained horns may be most beautiful, cows are more valuable because they provide milk and bear calves.[199]

There can be little criticism of the completeness of use cattle-complex peoples make of cattle products. Treated hides are used for sleeping mats, for hut coverings, for making sandals, and for many other things. Horns are used as containers; urine serves as hair dressing, face wash, and as an ingredient in softening hides and skins. Dung serves as construction material and fuel. Moreover, many groups do not hesitate to eat flesh of diseased animals as long as the disease is not communicable. They also eat many more parts of the animal than most Westerners will, commonly consuming even viscera.

It is probably because of the overwhelming importance of ritual, social, and affectional aspects of cattle in the cattle complex that some Westerners have underestimated the extent to which economic factors are considered by cattle peoples. True, there is much inefficiency in cattle keeping and use. Animals are not bred for milk or meat. Though they eat grass and require care, male and female animals are kept beyond the point of diminishing returns. On the other hand, the end of almost every animal is the pot. When detailed comparative studies are made of the relative efficiency of animal husbandry among cattle-complex peoples and other cattle-herding groups, it may well be found that the former are far more efficient than has generally been acknowledged. In any event, the position of cattle in the cattle complex in eastern and southern Africa, unlike Hindu India, has not led people to abandon beef eating. On the contrary, they eat it freely and relish it.

Origin and Diffusion of the Avoidance of Beef

It remains a matter of controversy why the sacred-cow concept arose, why the killing of cattle was discontinued by Hindus and beef eating completely abandoned except by lowly and despised castes. Some scholars have suggested that the Aryan conquerors of India, who sacrificed and ate cattle, were forced to give up these practices because they were offensive to earlier groups who revered cattle and who composed the bulk of the population.[200] If one looks for a non-Aryan source for the sacred-cow concept, the people of the Indus Valley civilization are prime candidates. The bull and ox are represented on Indus Valley seals and as figurines (Figure 22), and they may have had religious significance. On the other hand, they are relatively rare, and appear less often than the noted Indus Valley "unicorn." In any case, the cow is absent, at least among the figurines, and however one interprets the Indus Valley remains, the evidence does not support the view that the cow was a sacred animal.[201] It has also been argued, in support of non-Aryan roots, that among Hindus of South India, for whom pre-Aryan influences are stronger, the idea of the sacred cow is the most widespread today.[202] On the other hand, if one examines present-day practices of tribal peoples and lower Hindu castes in India, the evidence suggests the opposite. Low castes are the very ones who persist in eating beef, and when they give up the practice it is usually in an attempt to command more respect from castes above them. As for contemporary tribal groups, many, including ones in South India, have slaughtered cattle and eaten beef. Among those who have rejected beef, moreover, Hindu influence is often apparent. W. Norman Brown, in his careful weighing of the historical record, credited the Brahmins with championing the concepts of ahimsa and sanctity of the cow in Hinduism, with the concepts gradually gaining prestige and more widespread acceptance

22. Zebu bull on Indus Valley seal (after John Marshall, 1931).

after "fighting their way against popular resistance or apathy."[203] This suggests that the sacred-cow concept was introduced from above, not forced from below or by groups outside Indo-Aryan society.

Another suggestion is that Hindus renounced the eating of beef, along with all other meat, as a health measure, either because meat decomposes rapidly in a warm climate and is readily subject to external infection by flies and other insects, or because in a hot climate the human stomach is so weakened that beef cannot be digested. Montesquieu, in considering the Hindu ban on beef, went so far as to say that meat is not too tasty in hot climates,[204] which makes one wonder whether he had ever tasted beef curry, beef saté, or any of the other delicious tropical meat dishes that have gained world renown. Somewhat related to the above, but from a different cultural perspective, is the explanation provided by some Hindus who spoke to al-Bīrūnī in the eleventh century. The explanation was an elaborate one involving the hot-and-cold concept as it affected Brahmins: the prevailing high temperatures of India; the coldness of the interior of the human body, and the weakening of Brahmins' ability to digest beef; the necessity for them to strengthen digestion by using betel nut and betel pepper, which are heating; and, ultimately, an incompatibility of their bodily condition with eating beef, which is cold.[205]

A third suggestion, perhaps inspired by accounts of large-scale cattle slaughter in the Vedic records, is that early Hindu lawgivers issued their prohibitions to protect animals against improvident destruction.[206] In the eighteenth century, Montesquieu wrote, in *The Spirit of Laws,*[207] that Indian prohibitions on cow slaughter and beef eating are reasonable and suited to conditions of shortage of feed, high incidence of cattle disease, and low rate of reproduction, which lead to a constant danger that there would be too few animals to do the tilling. Over the two and a half centuries since Montesquieu wrote, similar views by Western writers have appeared repeatedly, with Marvin Harris their most persistent present-day advocate (though he does not cite Montesquieu). Harris has suggested that population increase following 1000 B.C. in the Ganges Valley was accompanied by deforestation, floods, and lengthy droughts. Farms, he contends, grew smaller, and cattle, as plow animals, became increasingly important to peasant survival. As a result, cattle became the main object of the religious ban on meat eating. To kill cattle for their flesh would have endangered a farmer's livelihood. Therefore, Harris concludes, beef was tabooed as a practical matter "for the same reason that pork was tabooed in the Near East: to remove temptation." Harris sees the ban as originating as a practical matter, "the cumulative result of the individual decisions of millions and millions of individual farmers." Those who did not slaughter their cattle were "more likely to hold onto their farms, and to pass them on to their children."[208]

Harris's scenario is out of keeping with W. Norman Brown's observation, mentioned above,[209] that the concept of the sanctity of the cow developed within the socio-religious realm, that of the Aryan Brahmins, and gained popularity because of the influence Brahmins were able to exert. In advancing his views initially, Harris presented no convincing historical evidence, nor has he done so in the three decades since. Yet, in a newer, revised hypothesis, he again expresses faith in the primacy of techno-environmental determinants in the rise of the sacred-cow concept, and characterizes the extended, critical struggle between Buddhists and Brahmins as a response, a religious rivalry "for possession of the stomachs and minds of the Indian people." [210]

Harris's general approach to the sacred-cow question has been criticized by various scholars, including fellow anthropologists. John W. Bennett, a cultural anthropologist, took Harris to task for excluding religion as a factor in the cattle situation of India. Religion, Bennett insisted, can be viewed as a plan for humans to follow, and, in those terms, Hindu actions in support of the sacred cow must be taken into account. The result of Harris's approach, Bennett argues, is that humans do not appear to utilize resources, but that the two are associated in a mechanical system of some type.[211] A decade later, anthropologists Freed and Freed concluded, from a study of cows and water buffaloes in a village setting, that sentiment and opinion have a major impact on human conduct; that the claim that the sacred-cow concept, which is strongly supported by Hindus, has no effect on how they use cattle is lacking in good sense; and that "few students of Indian society any longer take it seriously."[212] In a similar vein, anthropologist and Indologist Gabriella Eichinger Ferro-Luzzi accuses Harris of "simplistically reduc[ing] a complex phenomenon to utilitarian criteria only."[213]

Perhaps the sharpest criticisms of Harris's views about the origin of the sacred-cow concept, in terms of Marxist theory, are those of Diener and associates, who follow what they call "a new evolutionary viewpoint" that focusses on the economic and political constraints that operated in India in the past.[214] Diener observed elsewhere that Harris's interpretation of Marx's theoretical position is a flagrant misrepresentation, Marx having contended in the bulk of his writings that people debate and conflict concerning the practical world, not that the result is always profitable.[215] Thus, says Diener, Harris misuses Marxism in ignoring religion as a socio-political force in the sacred-cow controversy and in focussing on a search for economic returns and environmental influences behind sacred-cow beliefs.

To me, the major question in our search for the origins of the sacred-cow concept is, What occurred in the centuries preceding and following about 500 B.C. that may account for the rise of the sacred-cow concept and the ban on eating beef? Was there, first of all, an increase of population, deforestation, floods, and extended droughts at the time the sacred-cow concept developed? The *Rig-veda*, which looks back to the time when the Aryans first settled in India, indicates that the valleys

of the middle and upper Indus and its tributaries, as well as adjacent
sections of eastern Afghanistan, were the center of Aryan settlement
in India. The Vedic records write of its "seven rivers," *sapta-sindhavah,*
and the Aryans seem to have remained there until about 900 B.C. Later
in the Vedic period, from roughly 900 to 500 B.C., the Aryans migrated eastward and their center of attention shifted from the Punjab to
the Ganges plains. They also penetrated the eastern Ganges Valley and
peninsular India, particularly along its eastern side.

Overpopulation, desiccation, deforestation, and flood have long been
invoked by certain historians, archeologists, climatologists, and earth
scientists to explain the decline of the Indus Valley civilization. Such
claims have been challenged,[216] but, whatever their merit, that decline
occurred about 1700 B.C., over a millennium before the first evidences
of the sacred-cow concept in the Vedic records. It is true that, since the
decline of the Indus Valley civilization, the Thar Desert of western India
has not remained static, and that in Rajputana today it is advancing an
average of a half mile a year. Thus it is possible that there were extended
droughts around 1000 B.C.[217] which stimulated an eastward migration
of the Aryans to better-watered lands. The likelihood of strong pressure
is lessened somewhat by the fact that the initial Aryan heartland in the
Punjab is better endowed than any part of western India in its somewhat higher rainfall and its location at the foot of the Himalayas, whose
heavier precipitation and meltwaters feed its rivers. Even in a severe
drought, the Aryans may still have had water for irrigation, as well as
feed along the riverbanks for their animals. If, nevertheless, drought
had led the Aryans to migrate from the Punjab into the middle Ganges
Valley, the possibility of that drought playing a role in the rise of the
sacred-cow concept remains unlikely, because the first clear evidence of
that concept in the Vedic records is roughly five hundred years after the
Aryan migration appears to have begun.

The question, then, is one of the conditions, environmental and cultural, that the Aryans encountered in the middle Ganges area, their
heartland from 900 B.C. onward, immediately before the first appearance of the sacred-cow concept in their literature. Agrawal and Lal
have noted that, when the Aryans migrated into the Ganges Valley, it
was well-watered and densely forested.[218] Wheeler has suggested that,
if one is to understand the time of Aryan settlement in the Ganges
Valley, one must first replant " 'the dark and pathless forest,' the *mahā-*

vana."[219] Hopkins writes of the luxuriant, almost impenetrable forest in the area south of the Ganges, whose tigers presented a serious risk to humans who entered it.[220] Allchin and Allchin write of the need for steady clearing of the Ganges forests by the Aryan migrants to make way for agriculture.[221] The Ganges Valley seems not to have been an easy place for herdsmen and farmers at that time, and, far from concern about drought in the centuries immediately before the first evidence of the sacred-cow concept, Aryan settlers in the Ganges Valley were pioneers facing the formidable tasks of clearing forest for cultivation, pasture, and settlement, and of dealing with earlier groups who may have opposed them. Involved here was not a mere migration, but one entailing a process of clearing and expansion of plow cultivation that was to continue for millennia.[222]

What, then, were the factors, during the early centuries of Aryan settlement of the Ganges Valley, that may have contributed to the rise of sacred-cow concept? As background, I would note that in the Ganges Valley the coming of iron implements is credited with enabling large-scale clearing and cultivation, as well as a food surplus and development of craft skills and commerce.[223] This seems to have culminated, in the sixth century B.C., in significant changes in the political and socio-cultural realm, especially the rise of cities and large political states. Not to be overlooked in this period was continuing contact with and assimilation of pre-Aryan peoples, and the "great intellectual ferment of the period," with increasing religious turmoil between Brahmins and followers of "new revolutionary philosophers," among them advocates of ahimsa and vegetarianism such as the Buddha and the influential Jain reformer Mahāvīra.[224]

Present evidence indicates that a hypothesis of drought is inappropriate for the Ganges Valley at this time, and thus unsuited as an explanation for the rise of the sacred-cow concept. This strengthens the likelihood that the sacred-cow concept evolved in the socio-cultural realm. Diener and associates have suggested that the prohibition of beef in India derives from deliberate action taken by early Indian states to further their political and economic ends. They note a large-scale sedentarization of agriculture, expansion of trade, and rise of urban states such as Magadha at the very time the sacred-cow concept was gradually being established. They argue that those states fostered the ban on beef as part of a broader effort to provide surpluses for the politically dominant urban elites. According to their hypothesis, cow veneration did not develop because it was beneficial to peasants or as a reflection of an ecological adaptation favorable to them. Instead, it was a state policy imposed on peasants, one that may have had a quite detrimental ecological impact. That the prohibition took a religious form they view as reflecting the close links between the urban elite, the state, and emerging religious ideas and movements.[225] The Diener, Nonini, and Robkin hypothesis will appeal to socio-political determinists who favor class struggle as a vital factor in human history.[226] It also fits with the fact that certain modern governments, concerned not only with urban elites but also with urban unrest and violence, have sought to keep urban food prices low. On the other hand, the hypothesis is strangely at variance with other critical facts. Textual evidence makes it clear that elite groups, especially Brahmins, did indeed favor the ban on beef, but they, not the lower castes, observed the ban most strictly. Indeed, as Eichinger Ferro-Luzzi observes, "while the high castes have been depriving themselves of beef for centuries and millennia, at the beginning of this century many low castes still ate beef and to this day beef eating has not quite disappeared among Harijans."[227]

I, like many Indian and Western scholars, prefer another hypothesis, that—whatever the inputs of environmental, economic, and socio-political factors—the sacred-cow concept evolved mainly because of religious controversy. This hypothesis is in accord with the historical evidence, and, if true, it would be little different from many other changes in thinking and behavior that have occurred through history around the world. One present-day example is the unresolved struggle between pro-life (anti-abortion) advocates, most of whose views are rooted in Christian theology, and pro-choice (pro-abortion) advocates, whose position derives from the secular view that a woman's rights take precedence over those of a fetus. With respect to Hindu India, it is clear that religious influences were important in bringing about radical change in patterns of cow slaughter and beef eating. Among those influences, say Stutley and Stutley, were the ahimsa teachings of Jains and Buddhists, along with the growing beliefs that human life and animal life are the same, and that blood sacrifice is contemptuous.[228] In describing changes in patterns of consuming beef and other flesh foods, Walker writes of "the pressure of indigenous custom and the influence of Buddhism," and of establishment of a prohibition on meat so as to enable Hinduism "to compare more favourably with Buddhism as a religion of kindness" and nonviolence.[229] Ambedkar, champion of the untouchables, followed this line of thought in arguing that the rejection of beef eating had its origin among Brahmins as a stratagem in their extended, centuries-long struggle against Buddhists, when Buddhism was a major critic of Brahminism and of the cattle sacrifice that was an integral part of Brahmin religion. Brahmins, Ambedkar argues, could improve their position in the struggle for men's minds by giving up cattle sacrifice, and they not only did this but also went one step further than most Buddhists and became vegetarians.[230]

The antiquity of the sacred-cow concept, its early ties with ahimsa, and the role of ahimsa and other elements in its ultimate success remain matters of controversy.[231] Brown, however, attributes that success to at least five factors, and documents his position with extracts from the Vedic literature. The five factors include the major role of the cow, its milk, and other products in Vedic sacrificial ritual; the ties of the cow with the mother-goddess cult; the view that a Brahmin's cow, like his other property, is sacred and inviolable; the gradual acceptance of figurative uses of words for the cow as literal; and the concept of ahimsa, which embraced the cow along with other animals. For Brown, ahimsa, which first appeared at the end of the Vedic period, was not alone responsible for the sanctity of the cow in Hinduism, but it provided a moral basis for that sanctity, and played a decisive role in the coalescence of factors that preceded it. Among present-day Hindus, however, the strength of commitment to ahimsa is so great that many people present it as the essential, even sole, element in the cow's sanctity. In the words of Gandhi, "[Behind Hindu efforts to save the cow] lies one thing and that is *ahimsa,* otherwise known as universal compassion. . . The cow to me means the entire sub-human world. . . [Thus] in its finer or spiritual sense the term cow protection means the protection of every living creature . . . [and] a Hindu who protects a cow should protect every animal."[232]

Whatever combination of factors may have contributed to the rise of the sacred-cow concept, textual evidence strongly supports the primacy of religious concerns. Moreover, the theories of Indologists, whatever their weaknesses, have the strength, in the words of Eichinger Ferro-Luzzi, "of seeking the explanation of a spiritual phenomenon in spiritual terms."[233] The concept gained ground during a time of religious turmoil. Before that time, even Brahmins slaughtered cows and ate beef. Buddhists objected to animal slaughter and to the cattle sacrifice of Brahmins. Afterwards, Brahmins no longer followed those practices, but had become leading proponents of ahimsa and the position that society in general should abandon cow slaughter and beef eating. One wonders whether this is what was meant by the Hindus who told eleventh-century Moslem traveller al-Bīrūnī that originally they had been permitted to sacrifice cows and eat their flesh, but that later this had been banned "on account of the weakness of men [Brahmins?], who were too weak to fulfil their duties. . ."[234] In any case, penalties for cattle slaughter became more severe in the early centuries of the Christian Era, a time of struggle between Brahmins and Buddhists; and in India today, the rule against beef eating is observed more rigidly by Brahmins and upper-caste groups than by untouchables.

The limited diffusion of beef avoidance was probably related to failure of strong Indian influence to spread much beyond South and East Asia. It may also relate to the fact that pastoralists, who were among the most vigorous carriers of flesh bans, did not find beef avoidance appealing and did not adopt it.

4   CHICKEN AND EGGS

And there are several things the slaughter of which is very bad, and
the sin is abundant, . . . and . . . of these the sin is most as regards
the cock.

        —Pahlavi texts, Sad Dar 34.3

Rightly or wrongly it is part of my religious conviction that man may
not eat meat, eggs, or the like. There should be a limit even to the
means of keeping ourselves alive. Even for life itself we may not do
certain things.

        —Gandhi, *An Autobiography*

The avoidances of beef and pork are well publicized and their existence
is widely recognized by the public, but even well-informed people are
frequently unaware that there is an equally widespread avoidance of
chickenflesh and eggs in the Old World. Though the avoidance is most
common in Africa, it has been suggested that it is an ancient Oriental
element that was introduced to Africa. This view derives in part from
the fact that the chicken (*Gallus gallus* = *Gallus domesticus*) is descended
from wildfowl of Southeast Asia and India, whether solely from the red
junglefowl (*Gallus gallus*) or from some other species as well.[1] In any
case, we turn first to that region, its place of domestication, and nearby
regions, to see whether the avoidance is or has been present there.[2] Since
the chicken has unusual roles in the economy and society of Southeast
Asia, these will be taken up first to determine their relevance to the use
and avoidance of chickenflesh and eggs.

Southeast Asia, the Pacific Islands, India, Tibet, and Mongolia

A striking aspect of the traditional role of chickens in Southeast Asia
is their importance in sacrifice and divination. Indeed, it is held by

some that chicken domestication was carried out there not for culinary purposes, but for obtaining a ready supply of birds for sacrifice and divination, and that only later did their flesh and eggs become of primary importance. The importance of sacrifice and divination even today may make chickens quite expensive, and not readily available for purchase, as disappointed European travellers, hoping for a chicken dinner, have sometimes reported.

Sometimes divination involves the use of a chicken's intestines or liver, though more often it requires the femora, or thighbones, which have fine perforations. Bamboo splinters are inserted into the perforations, and the angle at which they project is the basis of prophecy. This form of divination was formerly found not only in Southeast Asia but also among minority peoples of South China. It is still practiced among the Lolo, the Karen people of Upper Burma, the Ahom and other Thai tribes, and the Palaung and other tribes of Mon-Khmer stock.[3] For these groups, the cock[4] plays a basic role in myth, in prayers and rituals, and in stories of tribal migration. It is also believed to be a sacred bird, a messenger of the gods and endowed with knowledge of the future and of good and evil. It is primarily for these reasons, and because the cock through its crowing serves as a timepiece, that people keep fowl, not for their flesh or eggs. Among the Palaung, for example, each household has one cock or more and occasionally a hen or two for rearing young. Cocks are kept mainly for their crowing, which helps people keep time, and it is considered good fortune to have a cock that is first to crow and bad fortune to have one that is last. In former times, the Palaung also used the bones of chickens for divination. Now, however, the Palaung are Buddhists and do not kill chickens, and, though cockfighting occurs, the cocks are not permitted to kill one another. Though Palaungs may eat chickenflesh when an animal dies or when a Moslem or Chinese is available to slaughter a chicken, they rarely consume eggs, which most regard as food suited only for sick people.[5] Among the Karen, traditional persons seldom attempt any undertaking, whether great or small, without receiving a favorable omen from chicken bones. Through divination, the Karen believe, they come into direct contact with the powerful unseen forces that dominate the world. If, after a favorable omen, a venture fails, some other force has interfered, and they must win its favor in order to succeed.[6]

A quite different form of divination with chickens is followed by the

Purum Kuki of Manipur when they seek to determine whether a site is appropriate for a new village. On a day chosen because of its auspiciousness (Monday is favored), they go to the proposed site for an answer to their question. A man, while reciting a prayer, strangles a cock with his hands and drops it to the ground, and the omen is based on the position of the bird's legs after it has died. If the right leg rests on the left one, the omen is good; if not, the place is eliminated as a possible village site. A good omen, however, does not conclude the matter, for a second, different sort of omen is required, apparently to confirm the first one.[7] Still another form of divination with chickens is followed by the Lakher in choosing an appropriate village site.[8] Certain village elders take two cocks and go to the site being considered, and stay in a temporary shelter there overnight. One cock is placed on top of the shelter, and the other, beneath. If, in the morning, the top cock crows first and the bottom cock then answers, the omen is favorable. If the sequence is reversed, however, the omen is bad and the site is not used.[9]

The divination complex also involves the use of hen eggs, for eggs are believed to possess supernatural qualities and to be capable of bringing on dreadful consequences, such as injury, sickness, and death.[10] Among some hill tribes of South and Southeast Asia, eggs are simply thrown on the ground and predictions made from the patterns of color that form when the yolks break. The Karen of Burma ascertain the source of sickness by this form of egg divination, the diviner rubbing the sick person with the egg, then breaking the egg into the palm of his hand and carefully examining the yolk for colored streaks and blood, which indicate the cause of the illness.[11] A somewhat similar form of egg divination is found among the Dafla of Arunachal Pradesh in India, but the Daflas use a boiled egg, which they cut in half to examine the yolk.[12] Egg divination among the Khasi of the Assam Hills involves the diviner throwing an egg down on a board as hard as possible, with the omen determined by the position of the shell fragments.[13] A still different sort of egg omen involves puncturing an egg (or eggs) at one end and placing it on a fire. Such divination, with two eggs, is employed by the Purum Kuki, mentioned above, to obtain their confirmatory omen in village-site selection. While the affair is going on, the following prayer is offered: "Oh Eggs! If this site be good for us, you remain well. Oh Eggs! If this site be bad, you also be bad." If, after heating in the fire, the contents of the punctured eggs overflow or remain full to the brim, the omen is favorable. If the eggs are not full or are decayed, the omen is unfavorable and the idea of setting up a village at the site is given up.[14]

Cockfighting (along with other types of animal fighting, whether with elephants, bovines, ducks, quail, crickets, or other animals) is probably more popular in China and Southeast Asia than anywhere else in the world.[15] It is believed to have been a sophisticated offshoot of divination that developed when communities entered contests with each other to determine which was superior. The question was decided by divine judgment through a fight between sacred roosters.[16] It is strange that the tribes in Southeast Asia who consider the cock sacred do not practice cockfighting,[17] and that instead it is restricted to the high civilizations, whether Moslem, Buddhist, or Hindu, some of which have sought to stamp it out.

Even in modern times, cockfighting in Southeast Asia could be so important, as in Indochina in the nineteenth century,[18] as to lead observers to the view that chickens were kept more for that purpose than for food. Cockfighting has been opposed for thousands of years by religions of Indian origin, such as Hinduism and Buddhism, because it is contrary to the concept of nonviolence. Nevertheless, it has persisted to the present day, the object of attack by clergy and devout laymen. Special fighting cocks were bred in some places, and in India, if the seventeenth-century account of John Fryer is to be trusted, there was a breed of fighting cocks as large as turkeys.[19] If a Burmese did not have a specially bred game cock, he at least had an ordinary cock that he used for fighting, and a cock that was not combative enough was in danger of being killed and eaten in a curry.[20]

Whether stimulated by interest in more intricate patterns of thighbone perforations or in more combative cocks, many peoples of Southeast Asia have interbred domesticated and wild fowl. The Palaung encourage interbreeding because the bones of the junglefowl have much more variation in position and number of perforations, and therefore are preferable for divination.[21] The Palaung not only capture wildfowl and cross them with domestic birds, but also bring home the eggs of junglefowl and set them under the village hen for hatching. The domestic chickens of the Angami Naga of Assam resemble the local junglefowl, with which they interbreed occasionally, and must forage like wildfowl, being fed only enough to keep them from straying.[22] In Burma most domestic fowl fly about freely, and are difficult to catch, and in fact are little different from the wildfowl of the nearby forest.[23]

Turning to the eating and avoidance of chicken and eggs, one notes first that many peoples in the region under consideration do make dietary use of chickens and eggs, and that the peoples who employ them in divination and cockfighting do not avoid chickenflesh or eggs for that reason. There are, nevertheless, scattered groups in the region who have been reported to be indifferent or opposed to eating them. The Vedda of Sri Lanka, for example, have a marked antipathy to the flesh of domestic fowl, and most of them do not eat the flesh of domestic or wild fowl. This rejection is apparently of a magico-religious nature, but it cannot readily be explained as a borrowing from Hinduism because it seems equally strong among all Vedda, even those little influenced by Hinduism. In the Himalayas, the Black Kafirs of Chitral, a pagan people, have a taboo against hens, and they consider it revolting to have contact with a hen or egg,[24] but whether this derived from Buddhist or Hindu influence, we do not know. The Sabimba, one group of Orang Laut of Malaya, scrupulously avoid the flesh of fowl as food, though other sections of the tribe relish it.[25] The Batak of Sumatra almost never eat the eggs of their chickens.[26] On Buka and Bougainville in the Solomon Islands, domestic fowl seem to be kept only for the tail feathers of the cocks, which are used on ceremonial occasions as hair ornaments; though people regularly gather and eat the eggs of a small bushfowl when they are almost ready for hatching, they leave the eggs of the domestic fowl alone.[27]

The justification for the indifference or avoidance is seldom stated by the observers, but beliefs associated with sex, fertility, and childbirth are involved in some cases.[28] Similar associations are found in the Western world,[29] but in the West such symbolism, except at Lenten fasts, has not been associated with a general rejection of chickens and eggs as food, as it is among some peoples of India, Southeast Asia, and the Pacific region. In Borneo, certain pagan Dusun view eggs as dirty food deriving directly from a cock's semen.[30] Most aborigines of Malaya have a prejudice against eating eggs, apparently because of fertility beliefs, and some have a prejudice against chickenflesh as well;[31] among the rural Annamese, pregnant women do not eat chickens, which are believed to be toxic to them;[32] and the Isneg Apayao of the Philippines think women will die if they eat chickenflesh after childbirth.[33] Though both men and women among the Sema Naga eat chickens, women are subject to various restrictions: they must not eat chickens that lay in scattered places lest they become unfaithful; and at harvest time women who eat fowl are not permitted to approach the front of the field house where the grain is stored,[34] an observance that is perhaps also related to fertility beliefs. Though it is not indicated specifically, beliefs involving fertility, childbirth, and sex may also be involved in other cases. Among the tribal Kamar of Chhattisgarh in India only men eat fowl;[35] among the Bhumia of Madhya Pradesh, women are never allowed to eat eggs, whether of the hen or any other bird;[36] the Ao Naga prohibit eggs to women, and to girls after they have been tattooed, which is usually shortly before puberty;[37] and the Marquesas Islanders prohibit chicken to women at all times.[38]

Of special interest is the preference, by some groups in Southeast Asia and the Pacific islands, for brooded eggs in which the fetus is well developed. This may be of nutritional importance because, judging from analyses of their food value,[39] such embryonated duck eggs are substantially higher in calcium than ordinary ones. A century ago in Cochin China, people regarded such eggs as a delicacy and consumed them mainly at important feasts. When invitations were sent out for a feast, the hens were set to brood, and ten to twelve days later the eggs were considered ripe enough for the epicure.[40] Other groups in the Malay world share this taste.[41] Adult Bontoc Igorot in the Philippines, though they sometimes feed their infants hard-boiled fresh eggs, themselves prefer to eat eggs that have "something in them"; this preference is widespread in the Philippines,[42] where such eggs often are served as a special delicacy.[43] Indeed, in the Philippines the production and marketing of fertilized eggs is carried out on a fair scale, and has an annual revenue of ten million dollars.[44] The taste for embryonated eggs may have survived from the time before domestication, when people gathered the eggs of wildfowl, many of which contained embryos.

The avoidances of chickens and eggs mentioned thus far are those developing either out of indifference to these foods or out of primitive magico-religious beliefs. In fact, however, it is the major religions of Hinduism and Buddhism that are at the root of most cases of chicken and egg avoidance in the region. In India, for example, members of virtually no respectable Hindu caste will eat chicken, and members of many low castes and tribes in India also reject chicken and eggs.[45] One judges from observations in the former Central Provinces, however, that there may be differences among Hindus in attitudes toward chickens. In one section of that region, people do not regard fowl as unclean, and almost all castes that eat goats will also eat fowl. Yet in its northern districts people abhor fowl for their dirty eating habits, and a man sometimes takes a purificatory bath after touching one.[46]

The best account I have found of Hindu attitudes toward eggs is that of Eichinger Ferro-Luzzi, whose observations deal especially with South India. Eggs, she observes, are dirty because they come from the unclean chicken. She cites an advertisement in an Indian newspaper whose appeal is just the opposite of what one might find in the West, for a food, in this case ice cream, "not contaminated by eggs." Because of the impurity of eggs, she observes, they are infrequently used in ritual and are unsuited to and rarely offered to deities. Indeed, with one exception, Eichinger Ferro-Luzzi found no eggs in any food offerings made to gods in South India.[47] Raw eggs come in for special attention, for they are also considered immature and imperfect, and thus "doubly impure." Though raw eggs are offered to snakes or snake gods in South India,[48] even people who eat eggs are revolted by the thought of consuming a raw egg or a soft-boiled one. This is because raw eggs are more closely tied to killing, and eating them is a greater violation of ahimsa than eating boiled eggs. Prior to the coming of the British, who introduced fried eggs and omelettes, the only way nonvegetarians ate eggs was in egg curry, for which hard-boiled eggs were used. Westernization has led many Indians to adopt the standard English breakfast of fried eggs, but without bacon, and even certain Indian vegetarians have taken up the use of eggs. At the same time, one reads of a Brahmin who became violently ill from seeing eggs being broken and beaten for an omelette.[49]

It has been suggested that Hindus came to avoid chickens and eggs as a negative reaction to their use by Moslems,[50] or that the Hindu dislike of chickens originated in a desire to distinguish between their way of life and that of tribal peoples who use fowl in ceremonial propitiation.[51] I believe, on the contrary, that the rejection derives from Hindu vegetarian beliefs and from the view that the domestic chicken, because of its feeding habits, is an unclean animal. The Kashmiri Pandits, for example, refuse to eat domestic fowl or their eggs because they believe that fowl eat filthy things,[52] but they will eat wildfowl.[53] The people of a Mysore village are concerned with the eating habits of chickens that wander about, in the same way they are disturbed by excrement-eating pigs. Though they are stricter in rejecting pork, they are more likely to avoid chickenflesh than the flesh of sheep or goats.[54] Hindus in general, moreover, do not have the same objection to the flesh of ducks, geese, and wild birds that they have to domestic fowl; and in North India all game birds are considered clean.[55] The attempt of some Americans to encourage the use of vegetarian (i.e., unfertilized) eggs in India thus overcomes the vegetarian objection to killing living creatures, but not the argument that eggs are unclean because of chickens' eating habits.[56] The Ho of Chota Nagpur are an example of a tribal people who have been influenced by the Hindus to give up eating fowl or eggs. Lower-class Ho still eat domestic fowl, but members of the upper classes have accepted Hindu ways; they keep domestic fowl for sacrifice but reject them as food.[57]

Buddhism too has spread the avoidance of chickens and eggs. In Sri Lanka and Southeast Asia the effort has not always been successful; some devout people give up eating one or both, but other Buddhists persist in the practices. Despite religious objections to poultry rearing, some Buddhist villagers in Sri Lanka raise a few hens, mainly for their eggs; there are also objections to eating chickenflesh and eggs, but they are consumed on rare occasions; ordinarily, however, villagers sell their chickens and eggs to Moslem merchants for marketing in larger settlements.[58] On the other hand, in Thailand even Buddhist priests may eat eggs.[59] An early Javanese account (A.D. 1365) written by a Buddhist priest lists "birds" and eggs as acceptable food, as stated by the ancient sacred literature.[60] To the north of India, Buddhism has been somewhat more effective. The Sherdukpen of Arunachal Pradesh, whose religion is a blend of Buddhism and local beliefs, keep chickens solely for trade purposes, for they consume neither the flesh nor the eggs.[61] In Ladakh District in Kashmir the Brogpa, some of whom are Buddhist and some Moslem, are not permitted to raise fowl or to eat eggs.[62] In Tibet, chickenflesh, like pork, may contain dangerous "black pills" because chickens, by eating worms, are guilty of the evil of taking many lives. Chickens are also said to have claws like those of the vultures that play a major role in disposing of dead bodies in that country. Chickens are forbidden to lamas and distasteful to other people, and are seldom eaten.[63] Eggs, apparently because they come from fowl, are also believed to be unclean and harmful,[64] and many Tibetans, including high lamas, avoid eating them. On the other hand, it is said that Buddhist clergy members are permitted to eat them, and in Lhasa even the great lama has been reported as doing so.[65] The Mongols, like the Tibetans, have a great dislike of fowl.[66]

China and East Asia

The chicken is believed to have been introduced to China from the south, but China itself cannot be ruled out as the possible place of chicken domestication. The red junglefowl is found today on Hainan Island and in a narrow strip along China's border with Burma and Indochina, and in early times its distribution may have extended well to the north. Domesticated chickens were found in North China at least by 3000 B.C., and there are suggestions that they were there much earlier, by 6000 B.C. or so.[67]

In traditional China, chickens were occasionally fed, but to a large degree they consumed items that humans could not, such as what was left over from cultivation and food preparation as well as insects and other small creatures.[68] For the province of Fukien, there is even a report of people going to pits where human excrement was kept and scooping out the maggots with nets for feeding chickens and ducks.[69] Chickens, on their part, supplied people with eggs and flesh, as well as excrement for fertilizer. Systems of chicken husbandry seem to have been impressively organized and sophisticated, with certain big cities having incubators and hatcheries.[70]

In traditional China, chickenflesh and eggs were among the important sources of animal protein, and restrictions on eating these foods were found principally among Buddhists, for whom the foods were banned or not ordinarily consumed by monks.[71]

Eggs were expensive in traditional China, so that farmers of modest means tended to sell their eggs instead of eating them. Like various groups in Southeast Asia and Oceania, the Chinese have a liking for fertilized eggs in which the embryo has developed.[72] They have also developed remarkable techniques for processing eggs that enable them to cut down losses from spoilage and lower expenses of handling. Most notable among Chinese preserved eggs are "hundred-year-old eggs" (also known by other names), a treat not appreciated by many Westerners.[73]

Cockfighting (along with other forms of bird fighting) was found in traditional China as well as in Southeast Asia, with the southern city of Canton identified by various observers as especially prominent in this regard. Divination with fowl and eggs also occurred, possibly deriving mainly from Thai peoples.[74]

The position of eggs in China has also been affected by their role as a symbol of fertility. Eggs play an important role in engagement and marriage ceremonies, and one reads of two eggs that have been colored red (for joy and good fortune)[75] being rolled over a bride's breasts and into her lap in an effort to assure her fertility. Eggs may also serve in a ceremonial washing of the bride, and then be offered to wedding guests.[76] Red eggs are commonly found on tables at marriage feasts and in the bridal chamber, and are commonly presented to persons attending. They are of special importance to guests who wish to have children and who may take them along to eat at home.

In the rest of East Asia, the Chinese have been instrumental in encouraging the use of chickens and eggs. Chinese settlers in Inner Mongolia brought chickens with them, and, despite Mongol prejudice against fowl, have continued to use them.[77] In Formosa, people raise chickens for both their eggs and their flesh, which now constitute important sources of animal protein for them.[78] The Atayal aborigines of Formosa obtained chickens from the Chinese in fairly recent times, and now keep them for their flesh, though they do not eat the eggs.[79] For the Manchu, chickens are a sacrificial animal, and both chickenflesh and eggs are important dietary elements.[80] Koreans also keep chickens and eat them and their eggs.[81] The Japanese raise chickens at home and sometimes make pets of them. Because of this, some villagers feel so mean if they consume household chickens that they frequently let them die of old age.[82] The Japanese have no prejudice against eating chickens that are obtained by purchase or gift; but both chickenflesh and eggs are expensive, and in traditional times ordinary people could not afford them often. The only evidence uncovered of prejudice against eggs in Japan is for the Ainu, who are said never to eat them.[83]

West of India

Bones of domesticated chickens were found at Mohenjo-Daro, where the chicken is said to have been completely domesticated by about 2000 B.C.[84] On the other hand, chicken bones were not found at all other Indus Valley sites, and at only a minority of early sites in western India reviewed by P. K. Thomas.[85] It is often assumed that it was from India that the domesticated chicken spread westward to Bactria and Iran, but West and Zhou argue that the domesticated chicken had reached China long before it was known in India, and that its initial westward spread was from China, not India.[86] There is uncertainty about the time of its introduction to the Near East and Europe, but it reached Greece and Italy by the tenth to the eighth century B.C. or earlier, and Britain prior to the Roman conquest.[87] Aristophanes and other Greeks called the cock the Persian bird,[88] and Peters has suggested that the chicken may have reached Europe by two routes, one from the Persians by way of Greece, and the other by way of Scythia to the Teutons and the Celts.[89]

In Zoroastrian Iran, the chicken became involved with religious belief, with the dichotomy of good and evil, light and darkness. As in Southeast Asia, the cock was a herald of the dawn who ushered in the new day with his crowing and dispelled the evil spirits of night.[90] In the Kianian period (c. second millennium B.C. to 700 B.C.) the cock was the most sacred of domestic birds, one that urged people to wake up early and work hard, a way of existence also encouraged by the prophet Zoroaster (Zarathushtra) (c. 628–551 B.C.).[91] The cock's morning crowing was an important part of the daily ritual of the Zoroastrian, who, wherever he settled, took care to get a cock.[92] Making a gift of cocks to the pious was considered a highly meritorious act.[93]

Southeast Asian, Indian, and Zoroastrian ideas and practices spread westward with the chicken. In the Greco-Roman world, for example, the cock was a herald of dawn, associated with the sun, useful in divining and weather forecasting,[94] sacrifice, and cockfighting.[95] The cock was associated with various gods, but, because of its combativeness and courage, it had special ties with Ares, god of war, and other warrior deities, including Athena, who, in her shrine at Elis, was represented with a cock perched on her helmet.[96] The cock's combativeness was regarded as a manifestation of its sexual drive, and may have led to its special association with Dionysus (Bacchus), who was god of not only wine but also vegetation and fertility, and whose symbol was the phallus. As a result, cocks were sometimes depicted with a human phallus instead of a head and neck. Official cockfights were held in the theater of Dionysus at the Acropolis in Athens, and the high priest's chair there bore a representation of a cockfight.[97] In the Greco-Roman world, the cock was also associated with the underworld, and, in the interests of the dead, cocks were sacrificed to deities of the underworld. The cock also symbolized hope for an afterlife, which may explain its appearance with Hades and Persephone, and for the well-known relief at Sparta which depicts a deceased man offering a cock to the underworld deities.[98] In addition, it was commonly represented, particularly on tombstones, with Hermes,[99] who conducted souls of the deceased to the afterworld.[100] In a similar vein, the cock is frequently depicted on cult monuments of rider gods in the Danubian provinces of the Roman Empire in ways suggesting that it was a chthonic creature, but on some monuments it was also associated with the sun and celestial regions, a herald of dawn that also brought light to places of burial and drove off the evil spirits of darkness.[101]

When a person was cured by Asclepius, Greek god of medicine (Greek: Asklepios), he or she was expected to make a sacrifice, with a cock preferred, at one of the god's temples, and to hang up a votive tablet there that included the patient's name, illness, and method of cure.[102] One recalls the last words of Socrates, when the poison he drank began taking effect: "Crito, we owe a cock to Asclepius. Pay it and do not neglect it." [103] Though the meaning of this statement has been a matter of controversy since antiquity,[104] many modern scholars hold that Socrates was alluding to his view that life is a sickness for which death is the remedy, that he expected his soul to be separated from his body and healed by Asclepius, and that he was asking that the customary offering be made to the deity.[105] Thus, it is appropriate that, in a statue in the Roman Forum, Asclepius should be accompanied by a child holding both a cock and a sacrificial knife.[106]

Cocks were kept in the temple of Asclepius in Athens.[107] Cocks and hens were kept in a Greek temple area dedicated to Heracles (Hercules to the Romans) and his wife Hebe. According to Aelian, at the latter temple area large numbers of tame cocks and hens were dedicated to Heracles and Hebe, and were fed at public expense.[108] The divine couple had individual temples, separated by a water channel. Except at the mating season, the cocks remained near the temple of Heracles and were fed there, whereas the hens remained and were fed in the temple of Hebe. The account gives no reason why Heracles was associated with the cock, but one notes that Athena was his guardian deity, and that he was often depicted in early Greek art and poetry with a bow and arrow or club, or as a well-armed warrior.

Gimbutas has presented interesting evidence of the symbolic role of eggs and their use in representations of fertility goddesses in "Old Europe" (before infiltration and acculturation by Indo-Europeans).[109] This, of course, was long before the arrival of the domesticated chicken, but such symbolism relating to hen eggs came to be widespread in the classical world.

In Rome, the egg, symbolic of life and fertility, was used in the rites of Venus and various deities associated with the earth and reproduction. Thus, an egg preceded the religious procession for Ceres, goddess of agriculture. Macrobius also wrote that in the rites of Liber, Roman god of fertility and wine (who was also called Bacchus and identified with Dionysus), eggs were honored, worshipped, and called the symbol of the universe, the beginning of all things.[110] Eggs are represented on Roman sarcophagi, and funerary offerings of eggs, whether real or made of clay or stone, were common in early Greece,[111] perhaps with the wish that the spirit of the departed may have a renewal of life.

Such associations are found widely across Europe. Eggs, for example, are found in burials or in urns near places of burial or cremation in sites in Roman Britain, for, like pomegranates, they symbolized rebirth and the renewal of life.[112] In Sweden and Russia, clay eggs, apparently symbols of immortality, have been uncovered in numerous burial places.[113] Cockfighting became and remains popular in many countries, despite the persistent opposition of Christianity. In Christianity, the cock came to represent Jesus risen from the dead, the Christian hope for a future life,[114] and representations of cockfighting are found in Christian art to encourage the faithful to triumph over their baseness and qualify for eternal life.[115] The cock warns of the approach of day, announcing Jesus's arrival and driving away the spirits of night.[116] Hamlet refers to a cock's crowing dispelling the evil forces,[117] and in northeast Scotland the cock has been thought to have the power to see evil spirits, and has also been viewed as a prophet, its actions being watched for omens of death. In a parallel with Greek practice relating to Asclepius, people of County Galway in modern Ireland, sacrificed a cock to cure a sick cow.[118] One also reads of the "prophetic singing" of the cock in Lithuania,[119] which was regarded as reflecting "the rhythm of nature with its perennial changes and rejuvenations."[120]

Despite the rich cultural and ritual associations of chickens and eggs, the flesh and eggs were not subject to general bans in early western Asia and the Mediterranean area, though members of the clergy or devotees of particular sects sometimes rejected certain forms of them as food. Even the ancient Iranians did not refuse chickenflesh, which was part of their daily food.[121] According to the Pahlavi text quoted at the beginning of this chapter, it was considered wrong to slaughter cocks, but if a cock did not crow, it was proper to do so.[122] In Mithraism, whose deity is of Iranian origin, the cock played a role in iconography, and devotees offered white cocks to Mithras and consumed them in ritual meals, perhaps because of their association with the rising sun and the afterlife or immortality.[123] In ancient Greece, a cock was consecrated to the goddess Maia, mother of Hermes, and initiates in her mysteries abstained from eating domestic birds; so did initiates in Demeter's Eleusinian Mysteries.[124]

As for cases of chickenflesh avoidance elsewhere in Europe, Julius Caesar reported that the Britons considered it wrong to eat chickens, and kept them for amusement or enjoyment.[125] There may be survivals of reluctance to eat chickens even today in Britain, for people of the Faroe Islands are said to be reluctant to eat chickenflesh because its light color resembles that of human flesh.[126] On the Aegean island of Chios, shepherds keep cocks but not hens, for hens produce eggs, and this, say Argenti and Rose in *The Folk-lore of Chios,* brings on illness among their sheep.[127] Eichinger Ferro-Luzzi reports that in several parts of Germany, as well as in Italy and Lithuania, people attribute aphrodisiac qualities to eggs, though she has not heard of prejudice against the chicken.[128]

The antiquity of the chicken in Palestine has long been a matter of uncertainty. Chicken bones were not among those reported in Early Bronze Age sites (c. 3500–2000 B.C.) reviewed by Horwitz and Tchernov.[129] Chickens are not mentioned among the animal representations or bones found in early Palestinian sites reviewed by Bodenheimer.[130] In addition, there are differences of opinion over whether the chicken is mentioned in the Old Testament,[131] and some scholars in the past have favored a late introduction of the chicken to Palestine, perhaps not until a century or two before the beginning of the Christian Era.[132] Early representations of chickens found in Palestine, on the other hand, suggest a much earlier introduction, perhaps for cockfighting. One representation of what appears to be a cock was found on a Hebrew seal uncovered at Tell el-Nasbeh (the ancient Mizpeh?) in levels that date to the eleventh or tenth century B.C. [133] Among the other representations are cocks and hens on pottery fragments found at Gibeon dating from the seventh century B.C., [134] and fighting cocks on seals, found elsewhere, from early in the sixth century B.C. or before. [135] In addition, a few bones of chickens, dating sometime between the mid-twelfth to the early tenth century B.C., have been uncovered at Tel Beer-Sheba; [136] some chicken bones, dated to about the tenth century B.C., have also been identified at the City of David, Jerusalem, [137] and a few, of roughly similar age, at the site of ancient Lachish, and at a site in Jordan. [138] Thus, it seems that chickens were known in Palestine by the beginning of the first millennium B.C., though they do not seem to have played a significant economic role at that time.

On linguistic grounds, some biblical scholars believe that the chicken may have been introduced to Palestine by way of Babylonia, but the Jews, like certain other Mediterranean peoples, considered the chicken a Persian bird, and certain of their beliefs and practices are reminiscent of Persian ones. There is evidence, however, that the chicken was not accepted without question by all Jews, for one reads in rabbinical writings of bans on rearing chickens in Jerusalem or on its Temple Mount, because they scratch the earth and pick up items that are unclean by the Levitican code. [139] In addition, there were objections to selling white cocks to idolaters, [140] apparently so as not to facilitate their use in sacrifice. On the other hand, some writers in the Talmud speak well of cocks for their morning crowing, refer to the chicken as the best of birds, and note the practice of bringing a cock and a hen, symbolic of fertility and reproduction, to a wedding ceremony where the newlyweds were urged to "be fruitful and multiply like chickens." [141] A similar practice is reported among Polish Jews who induce a cock and hen "to fly over the bridal canopy." [142] Despite early objections to sacrifice, by the ninth century A.D. the chicken was used by Babylonian Jews as an atonement offering at the time of Yom Kippur, a practice also found widely among Jews today. The flesh of such chickens may be donated to the poor, or, if eaten by those who make the sacrifice, items equivalent in value may be given to the poor. [143] The chicken has also served the Jews, in one place or another, as a scapegoat in other rites, among them ones intended to remove sin from an individual or drive demons from a newly completed home. [144]

Eggs were consumed by the Jews as everyday food and on ceremonial occasions, in some cases symbolizing mourning and possibly resurrection and, in others, life and fertility.[145] Thus, one reads of a Jewish belief that a childless woman who finds and eats an egg with two yolks will certainly bear children, and that, with similar hopes, a Russian Jewish bride would carry an egg in her bosom when she went to her wedding ceremony.[146]

The information on the chicken in ancient Egypt is confusing, but it seems to have been known there by about 1500–1200 B.C. if not earlier.[147] In those early times, the chicken may have been a mere curiosity, a strange bird imported from abroad, for clear evidence of dietary use is much later. In any case, chickens were too late an arrival in Egypt to be incorporated into the religious pantheon;[148] they were sacrificed in ancient Egypt, but there is no evidence that they were used for purposes of divination or that consumption of their flesh was banned. Nor, though there are strange beliefs about eggs of all sorts in Egypt,[149] have I found anything to indicate that they were banned as food.

Among Moslems, the chicken is looked upon with favor as a bird that crows when evil spirits are near and wakes the faithful for their morning devotions.[150] Most Moslems, like Near Eastern peoples in general, eat fowl and eggs without prejudice.[151] In Arabia, however, chicken and egg avoidance is present here and there. Eggs are viewed as paupers' food;[152] and unsophisticated Arabs look down on poultry and their products, though they are generally available to the traveller.[153] Tribesmen in the Medina area do not eat chicken or eggs;[154] and in some villages in the Tihama lowlands along the Red Sea coast of Saudi Arabia, people keep chickens but never eat their flesh or eggs, both of which are forbidden food. In the village of Darb in the Tihama, a curious crowd gathered to watch eggs being prepared for St. John B. Philby, something they had not seen before.[155] It is interesting that the Tihama has a sizable population of blacks, who may have brought the avoidances with them from Africa. The people of the Qara Mountains, in Dhufar in the Hadhramaut, also refuse chickenflesh and eggs, and would consider it a personal affront to be served eggs.[156]

The attitudes of the above peoples of South Arabia are matched by those held by certain peoples of the Sahara Desert, where chickens are found in practically all oasis settlements and in many pastoralist camps as well. One of these Sahara groups is the Ahaggar Haratin, a black agricultural folk who keep chickens but as a rule eat only the eggs. The Ahaggar Tuareg do not eat either fowl or their eggs, and even in time of famine give them only to children. The Tuareg's black slaves who have recently eaten chickens and eggs are not permitted to use communal drinking vessels. The Moors, the basically white population of the Spanish Sahara and adjacent territory, reject both domestic fowl and their eggs. On the other hand, the Chaamba, a nomadic Arab people, and the Teda of the Tibesti, most of whom are nomadic, do eat chicken and eggs.[157]

There is little evidence of the chicken in sub-Saharan Africa prior to 1000 A.D., but, though it is uncertain just when the chicken was introduced, it may have been well before that date.[158] Nor is it known by what route or agent chickens spread into sub-Saharan Africa: whether via Egypt or elsewhere in North Africa, or more directly from Southeast Asia; whether at the hands of Malaysians (by way of Madagascar) or by Indians, Arabs, or some other ethnic group. It is clear from European accounts, however, that not all African groups had chickens even in the last century, and that some who had them kept them not for food but for purposes and with attitudes surprisingly similar to those of Southeast Asia. This would seem to favor a more direct route of introduction across the Indian Ocean. This possibility is further supported by the fact that in Africa rejection of the flesh and eggs of the domesticated guinea fowl (*Numida meleagris*), which is of African origin, seems to be quite rare, though not altogether absent.[159]

Returning to the chicken, pastoralists among the Nyoro keep a cock to wake them in the morning.[160] In the last century the Pondo reared fowl, but only for feathers and head ornaments.[161] The natives of Uzinza in the Nyanza region of Uganda kept fowl only to sell to travellers or for divining purposes through the use of blood and bones.[162] And the Hangaza of the northern border of Urundi keep chickens for divining purposes but do not eat them or their eggs.[163] The use of chickens in divining has also been reported for the Maji of Ethiopia, the Azande of the Sudan, and the Nyoro. And though the cockfighting complex seems to be absent, the rejection of chickens and eggs as food is found in almost every part of Africa, sometimes applying only to eggs, sometimes to chickens, and sometimes to both.

The feelings associated with the avoidance of chickens and eggs in Africa vary considerably from place to place. Among some groups, such feelings are strong, even violent, whereas among others they are mild. Some groups support their bans with severe sanctions, whereas others have mild sanctions or lack them altogether. The most severe sanctions I have found are those in Ethiopia among the Kafa, who are reputed to have made slaves of women who broke the rule against eating chicken,[164] and among the Walamo, said to have put to death anyone who violated the restrictions on eating fowl, which they regarded as sacred.[165] Among other groups, such as the Mbum Kpau of Chad, the horror women feel about eating chickenflesh is ordinarily sufficient to deter them from doing so.[166] The Galla and Somali in the nineteenth century disdained the flesh of chickens, and today consider eggs to be the excrement of fowls, as do the Kikuyu, Kamba, Teita, Chagga, Nyamwezi, and Rundi.[167] Examples of milder attitudes are those of the Cape Nguni, who consider poultry women's food;[168] the Nuer, whose men think that eating eggs is effeminate;[169] the Mano and Dan of Liberia, who believe that wounds heal up more slowly if one eats eggs;[170] and the Chuka of the Mount Kenya area, whose warriors believe that eating eggs will turn a man "bald and pink, 'like a European.'"[171] Such views have led to quite varied reactions to Europeans who have consumed such foods. Knowing that an American anthropologist ate chicken (and goatflesh), women among the Mbum Kpau of Chad felt sorry for her because she had no children, and they also tried to make certain that she did not include such foods in dishes she served them.[172] Many East African tribes, on the other hand, have been as disgusted to see a European traveller eat eggs as the traveller would have been to see Africans eat garbage.[173] The German explorer Eduard Vogel may have been killed partly because he offended the local populace by eating eggs.[174]

African chicken and egg avoidances take a bewildering diversity of forms. In many places, the avoidance applies to the entire group, but elsewhere it varies with the sex, age, and social position of the individual, and in the case of eggs, with their state of decay and method of preparation. Women are more generally subject to prohibitions than men, and among many groups they do not taste the avoided food for many years. The prohibitions are most common for women of childbearing age, and are based on fear of barrenness or difficult delivery, injury to the unborn child, or lasciviousness. Among the Mbum Kpau of Chad, for example, women express concern with barrenness, suffering and dying when they give birth, and of bearing children who are

sick or abnormal.[175] Among the Tembu and Fingo, Nguni groups of the
Cape region, eggs are believed to have an aphrodisiac effect, driving
women who have eaten them to approach men from other kraals. In
fact when a woman says to a man, "I shall cook eggs for you," it is
recognized as a sexual advance. The Xosa combine two beliefs in their
contention that eggs make a woman not only unable to restrain her
passions but also unable to conceive. And the Yaka of the Congo area
believe that should a woman eat an egg she would become insane, rip
off her clothes, and run away into the bush.[176]

O'Laughlin has written an interesting account of the prohibition of
chicken and goatflesh to women among the Mbum Kpau of Chad in
terms of what she sees as male social and culinary dominance.[177] Among
some African groups, however, the avoidance of chicken and eggs applies to men, as well as to women during their reproductive years;
women outside the reproductive years are free to eat the food, apparently because infertility and sexual injury would not be problems for
them. One such group is the Yao of Malawi, who believe that eggs cause
sterility, with the result that only people not of child-bearing age eat
them.[178] Among the Moru of the Sudan, only children and aged people
eat chickens and eggs.[179] The Mwimbe of Kenya forbid them to adult
men and women.[180] And the Maji of Ethiopia slaughter chickens solely
on ritual occasions, then let only youths eat them.[181]

In view of the widespread fear in Africa that eating chickens and
eggs will destroy fertility or interfere with sexual functions, it is very
interesting to find the belief that eggs can be rendered safe to eat by
some treatment such as cooking, by allowing them to rot, or by permitting them to develop into a recognizable form of life—which recalls
preferences for brooded eggs among certain Southeast Asian groups.

Badly needed is a study of contemporary changes in patterns of consumption of chickens and eggs in Africa. Here I would note only that
such change is taking place. Bridget O'Laughlin, for example, reported
that, when eating at the homes of young professional people and government officials in the Cameroons, chicken was almost always served
as the first course, that all women diners would eat it, and that this indicated their "advanced education and 'modern' orientations." She also
observed that among the Mbum Kpau of Chad a handful of young girls
consume chickenflesh surreptitiously before they are initiated or mar-

ried; and that a generation ago, a man did not eat chickenflesh until his initial child could walk, whereas today such an observance is absent.[182]

Origin of the Avoidances of Chicken and Eggs

The literature is surprisingly deficient in reasoned general hypotheses for the origin of chicken and egg avoidances. Lagercrantz did suggest that the African avoidance of chickens and eggs is an ancient Oriental element which was spread in East Africa by "Hamitic" cattle herders who had no chickens and who despised the subject population who kept them.[183] Indeed, there are surprising parallels between African and Southeast Asian attitudes toward chickens and eggs, and further investigation of possible Oriental links seems justified, especially through studies along the avenues of possible introduction to East Africa.

As for India, which is within the broad geographic area where chicken domestication first took place, there are hypotheses that explain Hindu chicken and egg avoidance in terms of the Hindus' wish to distinguish themselves from Moslems, who eat chickens and eggs freely,[184] or from tribal groups who use fowl in propitiation ceremonies.[185] The evidence I have collected suggests, on the other hand, that Hindu avoidance of chickens and eggs is based primarily on commitment to vegetarianism, as well as concern with scavenging and predation by chickens, which make them impure.

I believe that chicken and egg avoidance in South and Southeast Asia quite likely goes back to remote antiquity. I also believe that in all likelihood the initial basis for the avoidances was a widespread conviction, still prominent in those regions today, that food is more than simply nutrient matter. Food is seen as deriving from a world both mysterious and fraught with danger, and if humans are not careful, malevolent forces in nature can gain access to their bodies by way of food they eat. Among the Orang Asli aborigines of Malaysia, for example, every animal is believed to have a spirit that is potentially damaging to the person who eats its flesh, and the fear of ill effects from eating meat is behind most Orang Asli food taboos. Consuming an animal possessed of a strong spirit can bring on the disease *sawan,* which may involve convulsions, high fever, unconsciousness, and more. Food taboos, moreover, apply especially to persons on whom survival of the group depends, such as pregnant and nursing women, husbands of pregnant women, and children. Old men, and women beyond menopause, on the other hand, observe few, if any, food taboos.[186] I believe that group avoidances of chickens and eggs should be viewed in the context of Orang Asli thinking, that the avoidances may first have developed out of fear that these foods contain elements harmful to the humans who eat them.

I believe further that in establishing the avoidances in question, the basic human concern was with the dangers posed by eggs. My account demonstrates that the identification of eggs, whether of chickens or other creatures, with life and fertility is widespread, if not universal. The recognition that eggs represent developing life and are a harbinger of what is to come may have led early humans to seek signs of the future in them, contributing to the divination complex of Southeast Asia.[187] Though I have presented information on the symbolism of eggs above, I believe it to be of such importance in the matter of chicken and egg avoidance that I would stress it further. The symbolism of eggs is well illustrated in the account of the dedication of a Shaivite temple in western India;[188] first the *linga,* phallic symbol of the deity Shiva, is lowered through a hole in the roof and installed inside the temple, then the hole is filled in, and a metal or stone egg is placed on the temple dome, and finally the temple flag is raised. A similar symbolism, found in parts of South India, involves worship of the snake, a phallic symbol, with offerings of eggs and milk, likely because of their ties with fertility and life.[189]

Eggs are also found in creation stories around the world. Hellbom has collected information on such stories, and has classified them into four types, each with a different geographic distribution. The four types are (1) stories of the cosmic egg or world egg, which concern the creation of the universe, the earth, or heavenly bodies from an egg; (2) stories of the human egg, which deal with the birth of the first human being, or the ancestor of a tribe or people from an egg; (3) stories of the god or hero egg, which focus on the birth of deities or heroes from an egg; and (4) stories of the magic egg, which relate to marvellous things that emerge from an egg, commonly with the assistance of a sorcerer.[190] Such symbolism is found in the Vedic account of a golden egg from which Brahmā, the creator god, was born.[191] In a similar vein is the ancient Egyptian myth of the god Seb and the goddess Nut, who produced a great egg from which emerged the sun-god Rē‹, one of Egypt's most powerful deities, who was also associated with creation.[192]

With the rise of Christianity, the egg was incorporated into its symbolism, especially as a herald of spring and representative of life and resurrection at Easter. In medieval Easter services, colored eggs were put in a reproduction of Christ's tomb, and on occasion clergy members would place eggs on an altar as they said to each other, "Christ is risen."[193] Among Catholics in Eastern Europe gifts of colored, decorated eggs are popular at Easter. Eggs are also prominent in Easter feasts of the East Slavs (Russians, White Russians, Ukrainians), who prepare many festive Easter dishes in an egg form.[194] The Western practice of hunting Easter eggs left by a rabbit is thus not simply a children's game, but also the remnant of a rite of fertility in which both the eggs and rabbit represented fertility.[195] In this regard, one notes the Germans' tradition of taking Easter eggs and burying them in their fields,[196] and similar traditions about eggs in Germany and elsewhere. Among Germans and Slavs, for example, a rich harvest was believed to be assured by smearing a mixture of eggs, bread, and flour on the plow on the Thursday preceding Easter.[197] Traditionally, the Cheremis and Votyak would toss eggs into the air before they began planting their crops, and at other times they would bury an egg in their fields as a gift to the earth mother.[198] To make certain their cereals would grow, Finnish farmers in former times would place an egg in the plowed soil, or put one in their pockets and keep it there during the entire period of sowing.[199] The Zigula (Zeguha) of Africa also place eggs in newly planted fields to assure their fertility.[200] The Yezidis exchange eggs at their spring feast,[201] and in Iran, eggs are considered suitable gifts at the time of the new year, known as the Feast of Red Eggs.[202]

Eggs also play a role in assuring the fertility of humans. In seventeenth-century France, a bride was required to break an egg upon entering her new home to assure her fecundity.[203] In Morocco, an egg is used in magic or medicine to encourage fecundity in a woman, to enhance a man's virility, and to facilitate childbirth; at weddings it both assures the happiness of the newlyweds and aids the bridegroom in consummating the marriage.[204] These customs are paralleled in Iran by the exchange of eggs between bride and groom on completion of the marriage contract, and the giving of colored eggs on New Year's Day because eggs mark "the origin and the beginning of things."[205] Among the Lepchas of Sikkim, one way for a woman to propose marriage is to offer eggs to the man she has chosen, with acceptance of the gift indicating an affirmative answer.[206] There is a Chinese custom of presenting the mother of a newborn child with eggs to eat,[207] to convey the wish that her fertility continue. The meals of mourners among the Jews traditionally included an egg, possibly symbolizing resurrection, as among the Baghdad Jews who gave the mourning family boiled eggs for consumption when they came back from the funeral ceremony.[208]

The egg, as a symbol of life and fertility, may also present dangers to humans. In Iraq, people are reluctant to present an egg to a friend after sunset, for fear that would be giving a life away.[209] There is a report for the fellahin of Upper Egypt of a divorced woman who attempted to make her former husband's other wife barren by magical means which included burying in a tomb an egg and a palm leaf, both inscribed with spells.[210] If the palm leaf represents virility, the intended effect of consigning it together with the egg, symbol of female fertility, to the abode of evil and death is not hard to divine. The account mentions that the spell would no longer be effective if egg and palm leaf were removed from the tomb. The Ibibio of Nigeria have a tradition that the first women on earth, who were barren, were given an egg, symbol of fertility, by Eka Abassi, goddess of heaven, who insisted she would withdraw her gift should human beings eat eggs.[211]

Such fears of injury through eating a fertility symbol in all likelihood were the original basis for rejecting eggs as food, though the rejection has been applied in different ways from place to place: for example, by prohibiting eggs to everyone or to certain prestigious persons, or to those who are in particular danger of loss of fertility. This probably accounts for the more widespread and stringent application of the restrictions to women, who since they bear the young are more vulnerable to the evil influences that affect successful reproduction.[212] In antiquity, the condition of women was far more critical than it is in contemporary Western society, where the marvels of modern medicine offer a good chance of survival even to infants that are premature, deformed, diseased, or otherwise at serious risk. In antiquity, by contrast, high prevailing rates of mortality, even among normal newborns and their mothers, could pose a threat to the very survival of a family and community.

If it were not eggs in themselves but their fertility-inhibiting quality of which people are afraid, it would be understandable if they were to use eggs after the dangerous quality is dissipated. This may account for some groups rejecting fresh eggs but eating ones that are rotten or in which the fetus has begun to develop, or their placing other conditions on the eating of eggs, according to the mode of preparation.[213] The destruction of life in the egg or the transformation of the egg into a recognizable form of animal life, the fetus, may eliminate the fertility-inhibiting quality. One even wonders whether the widespread use of embryonated eggs, for example in Africa, China, and Southeast Asia, may have had its origins in fertility fears associated with fresh eggs.

Though the data presented above are incomplete, further study should provide additional evidence of whether the avoidance of chickens or that of eggs is basic. The literature I have surveyed favors the claims of eggs: many groups eat chicken while restricting the use of eggs, whereas only a few use eggs freely while restricting the eating of fowl.[214] In any case, it is clear that both avoidances have been present since antiquity, that they are associated with fertility beliefs in various places, and that in this context eggs are more significant than chickens. Until more careful studies are completed, it remains a matter of speculation whether the avoidances had single or multiple origins, and how they came to be found so widely in the Old World.

The avoidances are being modified rapidly in Africa today because traditional ways are under pressure, and because, unlike pork among Moslems in Africa, chicken and egg avoidances lack the support of an organized religion there. In South and Southeast Asia, on the other hand, modification of the avoidances is taking place more slowly because they are supported by Buddhism and Hinduism.

That peoples around the world should reject pork, beef, and chicken and eggs may seem strange to most Westerners because such beliefs are not ones the majority of us hold. The next three flesh avoidances we consider—horsemeat, camelflesh, and dogmeat—may seem more normal from an ethnocentric Western perspective, but in fact we are dealing with quite similar phenomena.

5

HORSEFLESH

You say . . . that some have the habit of eating wild horses and very many eat tame horses. This, holy brother, you are in no wise to permit in the future but are to suppress it in every possible way, with the help of Christ, and impose suitable penance upon the offenders. It is a filthy and abominable practice.
—Pope Gregory III, written to Boniface, apostle to the Germans, *The Letters of St. Boniface*

Though some have argued that horses were confined in corrals by Pleistocene hunters in France,[1] the horse is not believed to have been fully domesticated until much later. In contrast with common cattle, sheep, and goats, moreover, its initial domestication seems not to have occurred in the Near East or southeastern Europe. Instead, it was likely domesticated, by 4000 B.C. or earlier, somewhere to the north, in a belt stretching from central Germany and Eastern Europe across Inner Asia,[2] much of this grassland with large populations of wild horses.

Receiving the most attention in recent decades are the horses of Dereivka (fourth millennium B.C.), some of which are thought to have been domesticated. Dereivka is a site of the Early Kurgan culture in the Ukraine that Marija Gimbutas and many others believe to have been Proto-Indo-European, before separate Indo-European groups had emerged.[3] It is of particular interest that, before they seem to have possessed domestic horses, the people of Dereivka lived by hunting wild horses for their flesh. Might the horses of Dereivka have been domesticated primarily for their flesh, "as a low-maintenance food source . . . well adapted to steppe winters, unlike cattle and sheep (also raised and eaten by the Dereivka herders)"?[4] Or, because horse domestication occurred after other domesticated animals elsewhere already served secondary purposes (e.g., packing and traction), might one of these

168

purposes have been more important in horse domestication? Whatever the initial motivation, a review of Early Kurgan evidence makes it clear that the role of horses in providing flesh for human consumption was quite important.[5]

As for riding, some scholars believe that to control herds of horses it is essential to have riders, which implies that horse riding developed at the same time as horse domestication. This fits with evidence of bit wear presented by Anthony and Brown showing that the Dereivka people did ride one of their horses.[6] In addition, at Dereivka and other Early Kurgan sites, horses were killed when people died, with the flesh of such a horse apparently eaten and its head or skull, along with certain bones, buried in the grave.[7] Horse-head scepters made of stone, which were uncovered from Early Kurgan graves, suggest a further ritual role,[8] but overall the evidence from Early Kurgan sites is too scanty to permit more than speculation on such matters.[9] I would, nevertheless, mention a few elements of horse sacrifice that recur widely among later Indo-European peoples: the sacrifice of horses to the most exalted of the gods, especially ones associated with the sun and sky;[10] and the preference for young, white stallions for such sacrifices.

It was not long, a millennium or two at most, before domesticated horses were found widely in neighboring areas, where they served a range of uses, with riding prominent among them.[11] With gradual improvements in the technology of riding and the development of chariots,[12] horse pastoralists, with their great mobility, became unusually formidable fighters.[13] If one accepts Gimbutas's Kurgan hypothesis, it was from the Pontic-Caspian area that warlike Indo-Europeans with horses and chariots infiltrated Europe, bringing with them a religion focussed on bellicose sky gods and the sun instead of on the female deities of the peoples who preceded them.

The traditional Old World center of horsemeat eating was located in the very grasslands where the horse was domesticated. This also developed into a region with many pastoral peoples whose lives centered to an unusual extent on horses, wild and domestic.

Iran, Inner Asia, and Their Borderlands

In a cemetery (mid-second millennium B.C.), believed to have been early Indo-Iranian, along the Sintashta River in the steppe east of the southern Urals, Gening[14] uncovered numerous remains of horses that had been ritually killed.[15] In some cases, an entire horse had been placed in a burial chamber; in another case, the chamber contained horse skulls and legs, together with chariots;[16] and in still another, it contained horse bones along with bones of other animals. For Iran itself, the earliest literary evidence, that of the Avesta, reveals that various deities—especially Ahura Mazdā, the supreme deity, who was associated with the sun, and his aid Mithra, a powerful celestial deity who brought rain and directed the sun's course—are associated with horses and ride chariots pulled by four white horses. Ahura Mazdā is called not just "bright and glorious," but also "shining and swift-horsed."[17] Ten pregnant mares are mentioned as being intended for sacrifice to Ahura Mazdā, and horses were sacrificed to other deities as well, with individual sacrifices described as numbering a hundred or even a thousand horses.[18] Classical sources reveal that horses, identified as white in some accounts, were offered in sacrifice by the Persians, particularly to Ahura Mazdā.[19] The horse was also used in divination, and, indeed, Darius was chosen as Persian king by a horse's neighing. In addition, sacred white horses were sometimes found in royal Persian armies, such as those of Cyrus and Xerxes.[20] As described by Herodotus, the army of Xerxes, while marching on campaign, included the chariot of "Zeus" (Ahura Mazdā), which was pulled by eight white horses and immediately preceded the chariot of the king. Ahura Mazdā's chariot was so sacred that no human was permitted to ride in it, and the charioteer directed the horses with reins while walking behind on foot.[21] The horse also served the Persians as a water spirit,[22] and one reads of a struggle between a black horse, which is evil, and a white horse, which is good, with enriching rains brought on by the white horse's victory.[23] Though sacrifice does not necessarily involve eating flesh of the sacrificed animal, for Iran there are clear references to horsemeat dishes prepared for feasts, to roasted horsemeat served at birthday meals of the wealthy, and to soldiers eating their horses when food was scarce.[24]

The Massagetae, pastoral peoples living north of Persia, also sacrificed horses to the sun-god,[25] and so, apparently, did the Armenians.[26] The Scythians (c. eighth to second century B.C.), those horse pastoralists who entered the Pontic-Caspian area from Inner Asia, sacrificed horses (white ones are mentioned in a few cases) and ate their flesh, as did their conquerors, the Sarmatians.[27] Horse sacrifice or slaughter, accompanied at least in some cases by horseflesh eating, was also reported in later centuries for various Inner Asian peoples.[28] One such report is by Ruy Gonzalez de Clavijo, Spanish ambassador (A.D. 1403–1405) to the court of Tamerlane, who found horseflesh a favorite food at the emperor's court in Samarkand.[29]

Reports from the nineteenth century indicate that the horse served the peoples of Inner Asia for riding, for packing, and for food. Its hide and hair were used for various manufactures, and its milk was made into kumiss and other fermented products. A Kirghiz family of five was likely to own at least fifteen horses, as well as other domestic animals. The Kalmuck (Torgut) of the southern Volga region brought herds of a thousand horses to market in the spring. The Mongols were—and are—dependent on horses, and Mongol shepherds tend their flocks on horseback. The practice of setting aside the best pastures for horses has been responsible periodically for the starvation of many cattle.[30] By some reports, early and modern, Mongols seem to have eaten horseflesh as everyday food; by others, they eat horseflesh on special occasions.[31] Despite attempts by Buddhists to abolish the practice, only pious priests abstain.[32] Mongols are also reported as ritually killing a man's horse at his grave and burying it with him.[33] Though I have uncovered no details of Mongol ritual killing of horses, in 1921 Gryaznov attended a funeral dinner held by Khakassians (Siberian Turkic people) in the Yenisei Valley. The dinner, which was held forty days after the death, ended with the slaughter and consumption of an entire horse by those attending, after which the horse's hide, together with skull and shank bones, was suspended from a birch tree adjacent to the cemetery, on which there were similar remains from earlier funeral dinners.[34]

An extreme example of the importance of horses in Inner Asia is that of the Yakut in the nineteenth and early twentieth centuries. According to Yakut tradition, the horse was given to humans by a benevolent deity, who also saw that they learned how to make kumiss. The Yakut considered it sinful to beat a horse. Their love songs compared the hero to a colt and the heroine to a mare. When a horse died, its bones were not permitted to lie on the ground but were placed on a platform, the manner of disposal used for human bodies. And when a Yakut found a horse's skull he would hang it in a tree out of respect.[35]

The Yakut preferred horseflesh to all other meat, including beef.[36] Their myths pictured kumiss and the flesh of fat mares as foods fit for heroes. They slaughtered an animal for food whenever one could be spared from the herd; and, at feasts, four persons, it is claimed, could handily eat a horse.[37] The favorite dish for the bride to serve to the groom at their wedding was a boiled horse's head with horseflesh sausages.[38] Their fondness for horseflesh led the Yakut to become adept at stealing horses. Because of this, whenever two convoys with horses camped near each other, men were posted to guard the animals. A group that managed to steal a horse would decamp quickly, ride some distance away, slaughter the animal, bury the bones, and hide the flesh in their saddlebags.[39]

South, East, and Southeast Asia

The horse was not among India's earliest domesticated animals but, whenever it was introduced, it seems to have become common in India after the arrival of Indo-European groups.[40] The Vedic records reveal that the Aryans had a high regard for the horse. The horse was an associate of sky deities and symbolic of the morning sun.[41] One example is Varuṇa, a sky, weather, and solar deity equivalent to Ahura Mazdā of the Avestans, who was also the god of horses and possessed numerous white horses. Another is Agni, god of fire, including the sun, who had horses to pull his chariot,[42] and was often referred to as a horse.[43] In addition, there were individual godly horses, including Dadhikrā, the swift winged conqueror of chariots, a vanquishing hero greatly feared by his opponents. The Vedic accounts also present the horse as the noblest of animals, strong, energetic, important in the ritual and everyday life of nobles, and useful in divination. A chariot with horses was a special mark of nobility. As among the ancient Persians, black horses were used in rainmaking, and one reads in the Vedas of a black horse being ritually sprinkled with water in an effort to bring on rain.[44] Rites were carried out in honor of horses used in transport, or in an effort to obtain dependable horses, in which animals were washed, fed, perfumed, and decorated. Other rites were carried out for curing their diseases, or for purifying or protecting horses against evil.[45] In addition, the horse was a sacrificial animal among Vedic Indians.[46]

At Vidarbha in Maharashtra, where evidence of ritual killing of horses and burial of horse skulls and leg bones has been found beneath Iron Age stone circles, cut marks on certain bones suggest that the flesh was eaten.[47] Because skulls and leg bones are the most common horse remains in Early Kurgan burials in the Pontic-Caspian area,[48] because Indo-Europeans identified the horse with the sun, and because stone circles apparently associated with sun worship are found in an Andronovo site in Inner Asia,[49] one wonders whether the Vidarbha remains are those of Aryans.

Horses were too valuable to have provided a regular source of meat to Vedic Indians.[50] There is, moreover, a difference of opinion among scholars about the acceptability of horseflesh as food in that period. Ghurye has observed that at the time of the *Rig-veda,* the flesh of sacrificial horses, and perhaps any horse, was eaten and relished,[51] and this seems borne out by the sections of the *Rig-veda* he cites.[52] Walker has written in general terms that Vedic Indians were very liberal in regard to food acceptability, and consumed horseflesh freely. Yet, when talking about horse sacrifice in ancient India, he implies that not all persons found horseflesh acceptable.[53] In a similar vein, Oldenberg argues that in Vedic times horseflesh was among nonedible items, and that the eating of horseflesh, though enjoyed at times of sacrifice, was exceptional, a priestly ritual affair, not a survival from a time when horseflesh was a normal food.[54] In stronger statements, Keith[55] and Stutley and Stutley[56] cite a reference in the *Taittirīya Saṃhitā* about eating "a human corpse or the corpse of a horse" in connection with a rite, as indicating that horseflesh was "an abhorrent thing . . . not a Vedic dish."[57] For later times, there is clear sentiment against eating horsemeat, and by the Gupta period (early fourth to late fifth century A.D.), the situation seems to have been like that of today, with horseflesh generally avoided by Indian people.[58] This is consistent with al-Bīrūnī's inclusion of horses among animals whose flesh was forbidden to Hindus, above all to Brahmins, in the eleventh century.[59]

Horse eating on a limited scale did, however, continue in connection with the *aśvamedha* (horse sacrifice),[60] which is believed to be derived from an ancient Indo-European fertility rite. A horse (or sometimes as many as a hundred sacrificial horses in one ceremony) was the highly prized offering at the *aśvamedha,* a royal religious rite carried out to assure a king's strength, success, and supremacy, along with the well-being and fertility of his land.[61] There is a story of an Indian king called Sagara who had carried out ninety-nine horse sacrifices, thereby gaining such merit and strength as to lead the god Indra to fear him and seek to prevent still another sacrifice, for if Sagara completed a hundred horse sacrifices, he would have been more powerful than Indra himself.[62] A stallion, preferably white, was required for the *aśvamedha*,[63] which involved, among other things, the symbolic mating of the horse with the queen while those present made obscene remarks. Near the end of the rites, some flesh was ceremonially eaten by clergy and others involved, and what was left was burned. The *aśvamedha* continued to be practiced in later times, with the last one held in the eighteenth century.[64]

What may be survivals of early beliefs and practices involving the horse are still found in India among Hindus and tribal peoples. Around the turn of this century, for example, the maharaja of Mysore had a white horse, without blemish and possessing the proper auspicious marks,[65] that only he could ride and that was used only in religious rites.[66] In addition, various Hindu castes in India believe that the horse is pure and has the power to cleanse and bestow luck. When a cooking pot becomes impure, one way to cleanse it is to have a horse smell it. In northern India, it is considered auspicious to have a horse and rider enter a field of sugar cane; and in the Deccan, people believe that evil spirits will not approach a horse.[67]

Furthermore, some non-Aryan groups in India who originally lacked horses fell under Hindu influence in this regard.[68] Today, certain non-Aryan Hindu deities, such as Dharma of Bengal and Aiyaṇar, Khaṇḍobā, Birobā, and Mhaskobā of southern and/or western India, are associated with a horse or a white horse.[69] A stone horse may be set up in front of their temples, for example at Mhaskobā's principal temple at Vīr in Poona District. In the cult of Khaṇḍobā, devotees at certain festive times may act as if they were the deity's horses, and on occasion the horse itself has been worshipped as the deity.[70]

Though the custom of horse sacrifice is not followed by orthodox Hindus, what some observers regard as a survival of Vedic horse sacrifice is found in the use, by Hindus and tribal peoples, of terra-cotta horses as votive offerings. Such votive horses are especially plentiful among tribes and castes once ruled by the warlike Marāthās and Rājputs.[71] One finds votive horses at the temples of the deities mentioned above, for example large numbers of clay horses at Aiyaṇar's temples in Tamil country. Aiyaṇar, whose worship is not found outside Tamilnadu,[72] is a martial deity and defender of the village. He is believed to ride around it at night with his forbidding army to repel trespassing deities and demons.[73] Clay horses, in red or other colors, may also be set up in fields in South India to drive away evil spirits, or in thanks to Aiyaṇar as guardian of the fields or for curing illness or any other good fortune.[74] It is of interest that no animals of any sort seem to be sacrificed to Aiyaṇar,[75] and that members of the Tamil potter's caste not only make the votive horses, but also serve as hereditary priests in his temples.[76]

As described by Haku Shah for tribal groups of Gujarat, terra-cotta figurines of various kinds serve as offerings, but those of horses are most common.[77] Terra-cotta horses vary in style from one locality to another. They also vary in size, the largest being about three feet or so in height. They may be hollow, solid, or partly solid and partly hollow, with hollow ones having large openings at the mouth, chest, tail, and/ or legs. The tribal people of Gujarat consider the horse a family deity. They also offer terra-cotta horses to ancestral and other deities in the hope of obtaining good crops, human and animal fertility, good health, and other desirable things. The offerings may be made by individuals or groups, and may involve a single figurine or as many as forty or fifty. Terra-cotta horses and other figurines are carried carefully (it is a bad omen if they are damaged), often in procession, to outdoor shrines, the largest of which are in remote locations where a rich assemblage of figurines may accumulate. Chickens and goats may be killed at the time a horse figurine is offered, and the figurine marked with some blood or a dot of bright red powder (likely turmeric). Haku Shah's account does not mention fires being lighted in the figures, but Zeuner pictures a hollow burnt-clay sacrificial horse from India which, according to him, is filled with hay and set afire, the horse's limbs, tail, and mouth serving as flues.[78] In Zeuner's view, this is a survival of ancient times, involving the replacement, for sacrificial purposes, of real horses, because of their high value, with baked-clay ones.

Some tribal people of Gujarat, including the Bhils, also paint horses (among them, copulating horses) on the walls of their houses, usually outside.[79] Rājput Bhils are said to worship a stone horse.[80] Gond tribal people of Kodapen in South India, on their part, honor a horse god at the beginning of the rainy season by worshipping a stone, by offering a pottery image of a horse, and by sacrificing a heifer.[81] Among the Saora of Orissa, tutelary deities ride horses, and people have a taboo against touching horses or horse excrement or eating horseflesh. Some Saora say that this is because horses are vehicles of the gods, but, curiously, the Saora also express contempt for horses.[82] The non-Hindu Garo of eastern India, on their part, kill horses as part of a fertility rite.[83]

Most of South Asia is not good horse country because of monsoon rains, humid heat, and limited pasture,[84] and today India has only a small horse population (955,000 in 1989, compared with 10.5 million for China). Even the limited amount of horseflesh that becomes available is not widely used. It is true that a few untouchable Hindu castes, such as the Mahar of Maharashtra, eat the flesh of dead horses, but other untouchables,[85] as well as Hindus generally, refuse altogether to eat horsemeat. That refusal is supported by stories, such as one about members of the sweeper's caste. According to the story, sweepers, instead of burying a king's dead horse, decided to eat it, and gave a leg to the king's priest, who was executed when the source of the meat was discovered.[86] There also used to be a common belief in India that eating horseflesh caused cramps; and when a sepoy rifleman missed his target in practice, his fellows jokingly accused him of having eaten horsemeat.[87]

Buddha's specific prohibition of horseflesh[88] is paralleled today by its being forbidden in Tibet by Buddhists. Tibetan nomads have such strong feelings against eating horseflesh that they shake with nausea when they hear of Chinese and Mongols doing so.[89] Yet even they are sometimes forced by famine to resort to it; and for one group, the people of Bangba Chugdso, the flesh of wild horses is a staple food.[90]

Wild horses were found in North China and Mongolia in antiquity, but there is no clear evidence that the horse was domesticated there.[91] Instead, the domestic horse may have been introduced but not domesticated in this region. In either case, and despite claims of earlier domesticated horses, 2000 B.C. or so seems the likely date when they first appeared in Kansu in China's northwest. There is also evidence that people of the Shang dynasty, or certain of them, in the North China Plain (eighteenth to twelfth century B.C.) kept domesticated horses and hunted wild ones. They used horses to pull chariots (which were strikingly similar to ancient Western chariots that likely had spread to Shang China). They used them for sacrificial purposes, and they may have eaten their flesh.[92]

Despite the encouragement of horse breeding by subsequent Chinese emperors to counteract the threat of the Hsiung-nu, the Mongols, and other nomadic peoples to the west, horses have not usually been numerous in China Proper. They have played only a minor role in Chinese agriculture,[93] and have provided little for the nation's diet. There are, however, references to the eating of wild or domesticated horses in China from ancient times onward. King Mu of Chou is reported to have taken three hundred horses along for eating on one of his mythical expeditions to the Pearl Swamp.[94] One reads of horsemeat as a favorite food in Han times (206 B.C.—A.D. 220); as obtainable without difficulty in cities in Sung China (A.D. 960–1279); and as regular fare in Ming times (A.D. 1368–1644).[95] In subsequent centuries, horses continued to serve as human food wherever, in terms of availability, that was practical. One notes a general statement about Chinese horsemeat eating in the seventeenth century in Robert Burton's *Anatomy of Melancholy,* which relies on observations by a Jesuit who lived in China for many years; a nineteenth-century account that horsemeat was eaten widely in China by the poor, and that horsemeat butchers were found in all big cities; and scattered references from more recent times as well.[96]

In Japan the Ainu are very fond of horseflesh,[97] though they have few if any horses. Among the Japanese, there were Buddhist objections to the eating of horsemeat along with other types of flesh food. As noted previously for beef, it was during the Meiji era that horsemeat came into more general use, having been placed on sale in Japan in the late 1880s.[98] Today the Japanese eat horsemeat without prejudice, and it is a fairly common ingredient in sukiyaki. The meat is generally obtained from domestic animals which have outlived their usefulness for draft purposes.

Horses are found in small numbers in Southeast Asia, though the region in general is not well suited to them. For mainland Southeast Asian peoples, the eating of horseflesh is absent or, at best, uncommon. Even the Meo of Indochina, who are renowned horse breeders, do not eat horsemeat.[99] For island Southeast Asian groups, too, horseflesh eating is not the rule, though there are reports of it and even of horse sacrifice.[100]

The Near East and Africa

There is considerable uncertainty as to whether, in the records of ancient Mesopotamia, the onager (*Equus hemionus*), horse, or other equids were being represented or mentioned. It is generally believed, however, that the domesticated horse was known in Mesopotamia and elsewhere in Southwest Asia by the third millennium B.C., but that it became common only when Indo-European peoples arrived in the second millennium B.C. [101] One would expect ritual killing and eating of horses to have been prominent among the newly arrived Indo-Europeans, as was true in the Ukraine, the presumed Proto-Indo-European homeland. Among the Hittites, best documented of the Indo-European migrants to Southwest Asia, the horse was used for riding and pulling chariots, and was clearly an important animal. According to one account, horses were fed barley and fodder in contrast with dogs and pigs, which ate garbage. [102] The importance of horses is indicated further by their frequent mention in the legal code: prices of horses; penalties for stealing, killing, or blinding horses; instructions about what to do with horses that are found; and such. [103] The role of horses in religion, sacrifice, and diet, however, is less clear. It is true that the horse was tied to an important deity, Pirwa, and some have thought this association to have come from the Hittites' background as "horse-using Indo-European invaders." [104] It was also included among animals killed at a funerary rite;[105] and bones of horses have been uncovered in Hittite graves, recalling the kurgan burials of the Ukraine and suggesting a possible link to pastoralists there. [106] There is nothing, however, to indicate that the horse was as important in burials as it was to the kurgan peoples, or that it was ritually killed apart from burials. [107] This suggests that despite the fact that Hittite religion had Indo-European elements—apparently including, in earliest times, the deity Sius (Zeus) as a sun-god—it seems to have derived largely from non-Indo-Europeans who preceded the Hittites and constituted the majority population in the heart of their Anatolian realms. [108] In any case, in his study of Hittite food production, Hoffner does not include the horse among animals that provided meat or milk. [109] Whether through Indo-European influence or otherwise, in the fourteenth century B.C. horsemeat was consumed in the vicinity of the city of Nuzi east of Assyria, for which there is a record of a lawsuit involving the theft and eating of a horse. [110]

Though the idolatrous kings of Judah dedicated horses to the sun-god,[111] there is no evidence that they sacrificed or ate them. On the contrary, horsemeat was forbidden to the Hebrews because it failed to meet the Levitican standard of being a cloven-hoofed and cud-chewing animal. One can only speculate on what effect the Hebrew ban may have had on the Prophet Mohammed, for he never ate horseflesh, though he did not declare it unlawful.[112] As a result, there is some doubt among Moslems about the legal status of the practice of eating horseflesh.[113] Abū Ḥanīfah (A.D. 699–767), founder of the Hanifite school of Islamic jurisprudence, declared it unlawful, and apparently it was forbidden to adherents;[114] but other Moslems, particularly in Inner Asia, do not subscribe to this view and continue to eat horsemeat.[115] Nevertheless, the restrictive view has gradually gained support even in Inner Asia. Thus the Tadjik of Turkestan, strict Moslems who live in the midst of horse eaters, refuse horseflesh and mares' milk because of religious prohibitions,[116] as do most Moslems of the Near East.[117]

In pre-European times, horses were found in many sections of sub-Saharan Africa north of the equator, and they played a major role in the military and political history of West Africa.[118] At the same time, horseflesh has never been an important food in sub-Saharan Africa. Indeed, many groups there refuse to eat it, in some cases because of Islamic or European influence and in other cases not. In Ethiopia, both predominantly Moslem groups, such as the Galla, and Christian and pagan peoples, such as the Amhara, Kafa, and Mao, refuse it.[119] In the Republic of the Sudan, the tribes of the Nuba Mountains avoid eating horsemeat; and when some Nuba tribesmen in Orombe (Otoro) ate their horses after the animals had died, their more conservative fellow tribesmen were disgusted.[120] Among the Gonja of Ghana, a people whose country is inhospitable to horses, they are kept only in small numbers, as by major chiefs for prestige purposes, but they are not eaten.[121] Among the Mamprusi of Ghana, where horses were formerly employed in raids and other fighting, the horse is symbolic of the king; horses are instructed "to dance to the same drum-rhythms as royals"; and the king's horse is dressed in leather trappings and used in regular rituals that occur through the year. The killing of horses for food is prohibited among the Mamprusi, though the ban on horseflesh is relaxed when a king chooses a throne name and provides a meal for his princes of meat that is ordinarily avoided.[122] In Nigeria, Moslems strictly forbid horsemeat,[123] and certain pagan or partly Islamized groups there and in nearby areas avoid it. Among the Yoruba of Ife, horseflesh is eaten only by humble folk, who consume horses that have died of disease.[124] The Katab of northern Nigeria do not eat horsemeat.[125] In the Bachit area of northern Nigeria's plateau area, horses are common, but there is a ban on slaughtering and eating them, except in one village. If they are slaughtered at all, it is for ceremonial purposes.[126] A generation ago the pagan Bassa of central Nigeria ate horsemeat, though the custom was being abandoned.[127] At the same time, the Warjawa pagans of northern Nigeria continued to eat it at feasts celebrating the planting and harvesting of crops.[128] Various pagan, or mostly pagan, groups of former French Equatorial Africa who keep horses do not eat their flesh; and in the Cameroons the Kpe people are able to keep horses because their mountain homeland is relatively healthful, but they rarely ride them and do not eat their flesh.[129] The Sotho of southern Africa, who first learned of the horse from European settlers, share their prejudice against horseflesh, though a few people eat it; the Swazi don't eat horseflesh either; and the Pedi not only avoid the flesh but also don't even use the hide.[130]

Europe

If Gimbutas is correct about the Early Kurgan people, horse sacrifice and eating go back to the very roots of the Indo-European experience. This is consistent with abundant evidence from Copper, Bronze, and Iron Age burials and art of peoples believed to be Indo-European, as well as from written records of early Indo-Europeans from Western Europe to Scythia, which bear rich testimony to the sacrifice of horses to deceased persons and to gods, to the special association the horse enjoyed with various deities,[131] and to the eating of horsemeat.

In Europe, horse eating and/or sacrifice were found among early Indo-Europeans in the Ukraine, Russia, Scandinavia, Germany, Great Britain, Ireland, Italy, Greece, and elsewhere. At some times and places, horseflesh was a sacrificial food. At others, it seems to have been an ordinary food. In either case, crushed or fragmented bones and skulls of horses are found in various Bronze Age sites in Central and Eastern Europe, most animals apparently eaten after they were no longer useful for riding, packing, and traction.[132]

In ancient Greek art, the horse is often depicted with champions, heroes, and the honored dead,[133] as befitting an animal that enjoyed great prestige. Statues of horses, some with riders or chariots, were also set up in sanctuaries, especially at Olympia. Zeus was prominent there, and most horse statues were dedicated to him in thanks for victory in races carried out there. Horse statues were also placed in sanctuaries in gratitude for victory in war.[134] Indeed, if one takes into account all representations of horses, whether alone or with riders or chariots, the horse is depicted more often than any other animal in the sanctuaries of Olympian gods studied by Bevan.[135]

Despite the fact that horse representations are commonplace, horses were rare objects of sacrifice or other ritual killing among the Greeks, and literary allusions to these practices[136] usually refer to early times, including the mythical past.[137] Thus, very few horse remains have been uncovered in excavations of ancient Greek shrines,[138] and in Mycenaean times there were only rare cases of horse burial.[139] It has been suggested that horses and horse heads sometimes depicted on funerary reliefs may represent animals that were ritually killed.[140] On the other hand, the horse, unlike the lion, bull, and dog, was not depicted as a free-standing funerary animal, at least during the period from 450 to 300 B.C.[141]

In Greek tradition, various deities were associated with the horse, but none seem to have had stronger associations than Poseidon,[142] god of horses (Figure 23), who was called Hippios and was offered horses in sacrifice. In addition, a few other deities, such as Helios, the sun-god, received horse sacrifices, with white the preferred color for horses sacrificed to the sun.[143] Even as late as the second century A.D., Pausanias mentioned a mountain peak, in the Laconia region of the southeastern Peloponnesus, that was sacred to the sun-god, to whom horses were sacrificed in a manner similar to that of the Persians.[144] Various parallels, especially sacrifice of white horses to the sun-god, has led some authorities to conclude that the custom of horse sacrifice may have been taken over by the Greeks from the Persians or even the Scythians.[145] An alternative view is that horse sacrifice was typical of Indo-Europeans in their ancestral homeland and continued among various peoples, including the Greeks, after they migrated into other areas. Contrary to Scythian and Iranian practice, however, there was a strict ban on eating horseflesh in ancient Greece,[146] though one cannot be certain whether that was observed on all ritual occasions.

Strabo[147] reported that the Veneti (Heneti), an ancient Indo-European people of northeastern Italy[148] noted as traders and horse breeders, sacrificed a white horse in connection with the cult of Diomedes, legendary Greek hero of the Trojan war.[149] In classical Rome, on

23. Poseidon riding a horse (from Lewis R. Farnell, 1896–1909).

the other hand, the white horse, while symbolic of the power of Jupiter, was not sacrificed to him. Indeed, the only Roman horse sacrifice was made to Mars, god of war, at an October festival (Equus October), just as in India the earliest god to receive the *aśvamedha* was Indra, the warlike Vedic god.[150] In Rome, the rites were in the spirit of war. The sacrificial horse was a war horse. It had just won a race, and it was killed with a javelin.[151] As one possible explanation of the sacrifice, Plutarch noted that the horse was "spirited, warlike, and martial," an appropriate sacrifice, with a winner chosen because it brought to Mars "victory and power."[152] Other writers, both ancient and modern, have insisted that the real purpose of the rites was to assure crop fertility.[153] Roman armies on campaign seem to have sacrificed an animal or animals, such as bulls or heifers, both before and after crossing a major river, especially when they were entering enemy territory. Such sacrifices were intended to propitiate the spirit of the river and to divine the success of the military venture.[154] I have, however, found no record of horses being sacrificed in this way by the Roman military. It is true that Caesar, when crossing the Rubicon with his forces, dedicated herds of horses to the river, but he did not kill them. Instead, the horses were free to wander without herders, and not long before Caesar was assassinated, the horses are reputed to have foretold the event by refusing to graze and by weeping abundantly.[155]

In northern Europe, horse killing and eating are well documented for the early Slavs, and for the initial period of Slavic civilization, in Russia and elsewhere, horsemeat is described as a typical food.[156] In one site in the upper Dniester area dating from the Late Bronze Age (c. 1200–750 B.C.), horse bones and bits of fat were found in pots buried in a cemetery, which suggests that horsemeat was provided for the deceased and perhaps also consumed by the bereaved at funerary dinners.[157] Horse skulls and bones or horse-shaped figurines have also been uncovered at Slavic places of burial, sacrifice, or worship dating from prehistoric and early historic times.[158] Sometimes horses were buried with their owners, as in Slavic graves dating from the fifth and sixth centuries A.D. in the Elbe-Saale area of Germany.[159] One also reads of divining with horses among Slavs, and of their war god's white horse that could be ridden only by a high priest.[160]

The Balts, too, shared in good measure the Indo-European high regard for the horse, which was believed to possess supernatural powers. In mythological songs in Lithuania and Latvia, horses are associated with celestial bodies, especially the sun, and are identified as the Sons of God. In early times, horses were sacrificed at seasonal rites in an effort to assure continued fertility and well-being. They were especially honored in springtime, as in traditional Lithuania, where, on St. George's Day (April 23), people bathed and decorated horses.[161] The horse's ability to fertilize also found expression in folklore, folk song, and folk art as a symbol of love and joy (especially the white horse). Skulls of horses were sometimes mounted on poles, fences, or other places to guarantee fecundity, a good harvest, and the well-being of people and their animals, and, because the horse was also protective, to ward off the evil eye, disease, and other ills. In Lithuania, carved horse heads were also found in a variety of places, among them the bedposts of recently married people and the tops of roofs. Such carved horseheads even appeared on the top of tombstones in nineteenth-century Protestant cemeteries.[162]

Among early Germanic peoples, an oft-mentioned association was that between the horse and the deity Odin (Figure 24),[163] to whom

24. Odin riding a horse, depicted on a Swedish helmet, c. A.D. 900 (from O. Montelius, 1888).

horses or white horses were sacrificed and their flesh cooked and eaten. Whether or not Odin was involved is not stated, but Tacitus (c. A.D. 200–276) described German ritual uses of horses quite similar to those of the Persians. According to Tacitus, white horses, which knew the intentions of the gods, were maintained "at public expense in . . . sacred woods and groves." Such horses were not used for work, but on occasion they were yoked to a sacred chariot and, accompanied by priests, kings, and civil officials, their neighing and snorting were listened to for purposes of divination.[164] This recalls reports for early Persia and India. In India, for example, it was considered auspicious when a horse neighed after it saw a Brahmin,[165] and people, for this reason, even made horses sneeze.[166] In Europe, the horse was also associated with other deities, such as Freyr. Its flesh was eaten in sacrificial dinners. There is also abundant evidence of horse burial in Scandinavia and elsewhere among Germanic peoples. The discovery at Trundholm in Denmark of the Bronze Age model of a sun-chariot, which was pulled by a horse, suggests an association of horse and sun. A similar chariot has been found in Sweden, and it has been speculated that there may have been full-sized chariots pulled by horses that were later sacrificed to the sun-god. Whether or not this is so, in later times the horse itself was a symbol of fertility,[167] with a stallion's penis held in particularly high esteem. One reads, in this regard, of a case in Norway, where a white stallion, attended by women, was killed in a rite that included obscene remarks about the horse's penis and about ceremonial castration.[168] In a Norse saga, there is an account (perhaps a caricature of life among peasants living in an outlying area of northern Norway) that confirms the association of the horse's penis with fertility. When a family's draught horse died, they skinned the animal and prepared and ate its flesh. In addition, however, the housewife dried and preserved its penis, which she treated as her god, storing it in a chest and bringing it out every evening and chanting verses over it.[169]

In various prehistoric sites in Ireland, horse bones have been found along with bones of other animals, to confirm the eating of horseflesh there.[170] Some horseflesh may have become available when horses were killed for eating, whereas other horseflesh became available on ritual occasions. An affair of the latter sort is provided in the twelfth-century account by Catholic clergyman Giraldus Cambrensis of the ritual killing and eating of a horse at the coronation of a king in Ulster.[171] First, the candidate's people assembled, and a white mare was brought out.[172] Then the candidate had "bestial intercourse with her before all, professing himself to be a beast also." [173] Then the mare was slaughtered, cut up, and its flesh boiled in water. A bath was prepared from the broth, and the candidate sat in it. He ate horsemeat that was brought to him, and so did the observers. He also drank some of the broth in which he had bathed, not in a vessel or with his hand, but simply by dipping his mouth into it. Completion of the above ceremonies confirmed his royal authority.

The Cambrensis account calls attention to the role of the horse in ritual and religion among early Celtic peoples, and this was true not only in the British Isles but on the mainland of Europe as well. The horse, sometimes depicted in traditions of island Celts as bearer of the

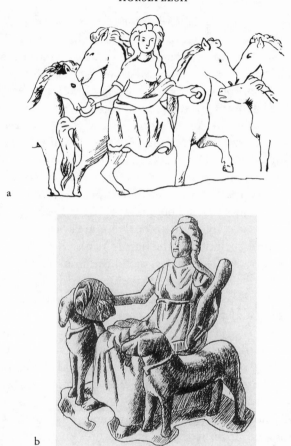

25. The horse goddess Epona (from John Arnott MacCulloch, 1918; see MacCulloch 1916–32): (a) feeding horses (Tyrol); (b) holding a cornucopia and seated between two foals (Wiltshire).

deceased to the afterworld, was associated with such Celtic deities as Rhiannon ("great queen") of Wales, Macha and Édain Echraidhe (*echraidhe* = horse riding) of Ireland, and, perhaps most notably, Epona of Gaul (Figure 25).[174] Epona (*epos* = horse) was adopted as protector of the Roman cavalry, and one finds her not only in Gaul but also widely in the Roman Empire.[175] She is frequently mentioned in inscriptions and depicted on monuments, commonly between two horses facing each other or mounted on a horse (the mounted Epona often held in her hands a cornucopia or other container overflowing with gifts).[176]

Jaan Puhvel has argued that the Gaulish word *"epomeduos"* likely referred to a sacrificial rite involving the horse, and apparently derived from an Indo-European term similar to the Sanskrit *aśvamedha*.[177] Details are available, however, only on early Irish, Roman, and Indian horse sacrifices.[178] Wendy O'Flaherty, in comparing the three, concludes that horse sacrifice in Ireland was "fertile and nourishing," and that in Rome it was essentially martial, whereas in India it was "royal and sacred," with the element of sexual union occurring in horse sacrifice in both Ireland and India.[179]

Christianity and the Decline in Eating Horseflesh

Though, as we have seen, horse sacrifice did occur in Greece and Rome, people there seem to have ignored completely the horse as food, apart from using its products as medicine.[180] Indeed, the Romans were disgusted with the idea of eating horses, and did so only when there was no alternative but starvation.[181] These attitudes seem to have been taken over by the Catholic church, and with the introduction of Christianity to northern Europe, pressure was exerted to eliminate horse eating along with other pagan customs.[182] In some cases, the pressure was subtle: the Penitential of Archbishop Ecbert ruled that horseflesh was not prohibited, but added, in what looks like a hint, that many families would not buy it.[183] In time, however, the strict view prevailed, and the Catholic church made a serious attempt to stamp out the practice. In Ireland in the ninth century, for example, a handbook for use by confessors required that horse eaters do penance for three and a half years.[184] As indicated in the quotation at the beginning of this chapter, Pope Gregory III ordered Boniface, apostle to the Germans, to forbid the eating of horseflesh, which he had tolerated until that time (c. A.D. 732).[185] Boniface did not succeed at once, for he later wrote to Pope Zachary I, who succeeded Gregory, that horse eating remained a barrier to conversion. In any case, all groups that were subsequently converted were also pressured to give up the practice.

The tale of Hakon the Good, tenth-century king of Norway, illustrates the difficulty that could arise between Christians who were taught not to eat horseflesh and pagans who continued to kill horses and eat horsemeat. Hakon was raised in Britain, where he had become a Christian, and when he returned to Norway and became king, he was asked to sacrifice a horse at a fall celebration, as tradition required, for peace

and "good seasons." On the second day of the celebration, he was expected to eat horsemeat, which, as a Christian, he refused to do, along
with rejecting horsemeat broth. A compromise was reached, however,
in which he leaned his head over the cauldron where the horsemeat
had been prepared, and then opened his mouth. The compromise must
not have satisfied his followers, whose well-being depended on the entire ritual being carried out properly. As a result, at a horse sacrifice at
the following Christmas, Hakon ate some horse liver and "drank from
bowls" in honor of the gods, whether mead alone or also broth from the
cauldron in which the horsemeat had been prepared.[186]

Though the Church ultimately won the day in most of Scandinavia
and the rest of Europe, rather than lose the Icelanders, who strongly
resisted change, it granted them an exemption which enabled them
to continue eating horseflesh right up to the present.[187] In addition,
there are indications that horseflesh eating never completely died out
elsewhere. Indeed, it seems to have been eaten even by some Christian
monks, for among the benedictions of Monk Ekkehard (A.D. 980–
1069?) of St. Gall in Switzerland to be given over the food served in the
monastery, there is one referring to the flesh of wild horses.[188] That the
Irish, at least to some extent, continued to eat horseflesh after the introduction of Christianity is attested by various evidence, including the
occurrence, amid the refuse of meals at an archeological site at Ballin-
derry, of horse bones which were split in the same manner as the bones
of other domesticated animals known to have been eaten.[189] Horseflesh
eating also persisted in Denmark, where a horsemeat feast was held in
1520.[190] Robert Burton in *The Anatomy of Melancholy* wrote that young
horses were commonly eaten as "red deer" in Spain, and were supplied
to the navy for food, especially around Málaga.[191] By the seventeenth
century, however, horseflesh had generally come to be regarded as a
low-class food in Europe and not suitable for prestigious gatherings.
It took starvation to bring many Europeans to eat it, and accounts of
sieges show that people killed and ate their horses only after first eating
grass, oats, and even leather jackets.[192]

Attempts to Repopularize Horseflesh

It was in the role of a scarcity food that horsemeat began to assume
importance again in northern Europe. In eighteenth-century France,
a great deal of horsemeat (*viande de cheval, viande chevaline,* or, collo-

26. Horsemeat butchershop in Cahors, France.

quially, *chevaline*) was eaten by the half-starved poor, though the sale of horsemeat was not legal.[193] When Copenhagen was besieged by the English in 1807, the Danes, in desperation, ate their horses, and they continued to do so after the siege and food shortage had ended. The marketing of horseflesh was made legal in Württemberg in 1841, and, in the next dozen years, in Bavaria, Baden, Hannover, Bohemia, Saxony, Austria, Belgium, Switzerland, and Prussia; not long after, it was legalized by Norway and Sweden, and finally, in 1866, by France (Figure 26).[194] Its dietary possibilities had attracted the attention of the European intelligentsia, and serious efforts were made to popularize it. Important individuals, including the eminent French zoologist Isidore Geoffrey St. Hilaire (1805–61), joined the cause of encouraging horseflesh eating, "*hippophagie*." St. Hilaire pointed to the widespread eating of horsemeat in other parts of the world, to its importance among the ancient Germans, to its potential for increasing protein in the diet of the poor, and to its excellent taste. He served a variety of horsemeat dishes in his home to help popularize it. The most effective advocate of horse-meat, however, was Émile Decroix (1821–1901), head veterinarian of the French army and later head of a school of veterinary medicine near Paris.[195] Decroix was involved in publicity of various sorts, such as distributing horsemeat to the poor in Paris and organizing a *banquet hippophagique* which featured horsemeat dishes. That affair, held at the Grand Hotel in 1865, was attended by 135 people. Though certain horsemeat dishes were not as well received, the horse soup was judged good, and the boiled horsemeat and cabbage was acclaimed excellent. The same year, a horsemeat butcher shop (*boucherie hippophagique* or *boucherie chevaline*) was opened in Paris, and it was soon followed by others.

The French campaign stimulated an interest in horsemeat in England;[196] a rise in meat prices following an epidemic among cattle enhanced this interest and led to the holding of horsemeat banquets in England in 1868. The importance of French inspiration is illustrated by the Falstaff Hotel banquet in Ramsgate: the horsemeat was imported from France and prepared by a French cook.[197] English enthusiasts, like their French counterparts, praised horsemeat in public lectures, served horsemeat at public dinners to encourage its use, and even organized the Society for the Propagation of Horse Flesh as an Article of Food. The French word "*chevaline*" came to be used in English for horsemeat and things related to horsemeat (e.g., "chevaline delicacies"). Horsemeat butcher shops were opened in London, too, but Simmonds, writing in 1885, observed that, not only had they not succeeded, but the entire effort to popularize horseflesh in England had completely collapsed.[198]

The campaign to popularize horsemeat nevertheless met with some success on the Continent, especially in France, where in 1876 horsemeat butchers in Paris alone marketed the flesh of over nine thousand horses, mules, and donkeys, amounting to more than 3.7 million pounds.[199] Horsemeat eating has been practiced, however, by only small segments of the French population, for it has continued to symbolize low status and poverty.[200] According to Daniel W. Gade in his excellent article on horsemeat in France, at the beginning of this century horsemeat had enjoyed the reputation of being healthy food, but later many people came to consider it unhealthy. This perspective was encouraged in 1967 by a minor, but highly publicized, discovery of salmonella in horsemeat, after which the Ministry of Education stopped schools from serving it in their cafeterias.[201] There is also a common sentiment that the horse is a human companion and therefore should not be eaten. The result of all this is that horsemeat restaurants are no longer found in Paris, and that one rarely finds horsemeat recipes in French cookbooks.[202]

The supply of horseflesh in France had initially been obtained mainly from domestic sources. However, there was a continuing decline in the number of horses in France since the First World War because of competition from motor vehicles, and the domestic supply of horsemeat decreased and foreign sources of horses and horsemeat, whether in Europe or overseas, came to assume an increasing role. By 1965, one-third of all France's horsemeat came from foreign sources, mainly as chilled meat and live animals; by 1972, the proportion had risen to 68 percent.[203]

Consumption of horsemeat in France is quite low. In 1969, for example, total consumption was about eighty-eight thousand or eighty-nine thousand metric tons, and in 1982, just thirty-seven thousand metric tons.[204] On an annual per capita basis, consumption in 1969 was only one kilogram compared with roughly twenty kilograms or more for both (1) pork and pork products and (2) beef and veal.[205] France's sizable Moslem and Jewish minorities, as one would expect, consume very little if any horsemeat.

How much horsemeat is used in Central and Eastern Europe today is not certain, but in Czechoslovakia in 1932 it amounted to 1 percent of the meat consumed in the entire country.[206] In Moravia during roughly the same period, except at times of scarcity such as wartime, horseflesh was ordinarily eaten only by certain poor people.[207] In the Balkans, Moslems as well as Catholic and Orthodox Christians consider horsemeat unclean food; and the report that horsemeat was marketed for culinary purposes in Italy led people to call that country "an accursed and unclean place."[208] The Poles have strong prejudices against horsemeat, and eat it only in times of dire need.[209] According to a Finnish informant, horseflesh was not eaten in his village a generation ago, and the man responsible for killing aged and crippled horses lived apart from others and was regarded as a pariah. Today, however, horsemeat can be purchased in Finland and is used by some people, though it is still not fully accepted as food and is not found in restaurants.

Calvin W. Schwabe has likened the prejudice of Westerners against horseflesh to that of Hindus against beef and Moslems and Jews against pork. Nevertheless, he considers it likely that in most Americans the taste for horseflesh "is but superficially latent," and, to encourage them, he provides some interesting horsemeat recipes from around the world. One finds among them "Grilled Horsemeat" from Japan, "Piquant Stew" from Peru, "Deep-fried Horsemeat" from Switzerland, and "Spaghetti Sauce Bolognese" (*Salsa alla bolognese*) from Italy.[210] In the United States, the horsemeat cause is not a lost one: it is legal to market it; there are plants for slaughtering horses (in 1973 there were at least six of them, though the flesh was mostly used for pet food or for consumption abroad);[211] horsemeat sold in the United States is subject to federal inspection; it is nutritious, low in fat, and reasonable in price; and some people do buy and consume it. One even reads of a horsemeat shop in Connecticut so successful that fifteen franchises were set up in New England and New York, with four thousand to five thousand pounds of horsemeat in various forms being marketed on a daily basis.

Despite this, the idea of killing and eating horses offends many people, and in 1973 United States senator Richard Schweiker of Pennsylvania even sponsored a bill to ban the sale of horsemeat for consumption by humans. More serious threats have come from direct public action against the practices. This is perhaps best illustrated by the unfortunate case of the Utah Tongans,[212] many of them Mormons who, starting in the mid-1950s, began migrating to Utah from their South Pacific homeland, and by 1983 were a minority of good size, seventy-five hundred in all. Though the horse was not known in Tonga in pre-European times, European missionaries, Tongans say, taught them to like horsemeat. In any case, Tongans have been purchasing horses in Utah for eating, which gives them a bad public image and makes their children the butt of jokes in school. Hearing of the demand for horsemeat among the Tongans, the M & R Packing Company, a Hartford, Connecticut, firm that deals in horsemeat, made arrangements in 1983 to sell horsemeat in Utah through the supermarkets of the Harmon's, Inc., chain. When the first shipment arrived at a Harmon's market in Ogden, Utah, store officials were astonished to find that shoppers quickly bought out their entire supply of horsemeat patties and steaks. When word of Harmon's activities reached the public, however, several people began protesting at one of their stores outside Salt Lake City, and in a short while two hundred horse lovers had volunteered to assist in the picketing. Rethinking the matter, Harmon's quickly dropped their plans for selling horsemeat, and the Tongans were left to continue buying horses in local livestock auctions or obtaining them in other ways. The Utah Tongan case is interesting because it involves a good demand for horsemeat as well as a packer and marketer able and willing to supply it, but one in which public sentiment has interfered with the normal operation of our market economy.

The practice of horsemeat eating in global terms continues to be under pressure from the spread of Western influence (in some cases by means of Christianity) along with that of Islam and, perhaps, religions of Indian origin. Certainly the practice is less common in the Old World today than it was in ancient times, and the groups of horse eaters still found in Asia and Africa for the most part represent survivals, groups which so far have resisted pressures to abandon the practice.

Origin of the Avoidance of Horseflesh

In some cases, prejudice against horseflesh sprang from the reaction of a world religion, such as Christianity, to the sacrifice and eating of horses in pagan religious rites. In others it may derive from the animal's high status and its supposed holy qualities and association with deities. The efforts to reintroduce horseflesh eating in Europe in the last few centuries is a rare example of a counterattack against a flesh prejudice, and today one can get horsemeat in many parts of Europe.[213] In France, which some consider the font of horsemeat eating in modern Europe, however, the practice seems to be on the wane.

6

CAMELFLESH

Camels we have made for the sacrifice of God . . . mention his name
[when you sacrifice camels] and eat of them.

—the Koran 22:35

The Near East and Neighboring Areas

Arabia is the likely place of earliest domestication of the dromedary,
or one-humped camel, with most authorities favoring a date in the third
millennium B.C. or earlier. The Bactrian, or two-humped camel, in
turn, may have been domesticated in Iran or Turkestan at about the
same time or, at most, several centuries earlier or later.[1] From their
places of domestication, the two forms of camel slowly spread, and before the discovery of the New World, domesticated camels of one type
or another were found in a broad belt extending from the Atlantic coast
of the Sahara eastward to Mongolia, northernmost China, and a bit beyond into what today is easternmost Russia.[2] In general, the dromedary
occupied the hot deserts and steppes from Africa to western India, and
the Bactrian, the colder arid lands from the Black Sea eastward. Today
the dromedary is by far the more numerous of the two, 15 million in
1981 compared with 1.4 million Bactrians.[3] Arabia is often singled out
for the importance of dromedaries there, and indeed among Bedouins
it is such an essential animal that, when a man dies, his wife commonly
laments his death by saying, "*Ya gamali, ya gamali . . . jamali rah*"
(I have lost my camel).[4]

H. Epstein has speculated that the camel was domesticated for its
flesh, not for work purposes, though he acknowledges that evidence to
support this is lacking.[5] Whatever the reasons for its domestication, it is
clear that the dromedary camel was sacrificed and eaten, and had strong

194

religious associations among the Arabs long before the rise of Islam. In the ancient city of Palmyra in Syria, a hub of trade and eclectic in its religion and art, deities are commonly depicted as mounted on dromedary camels or standing on their backs, particularly outside the city in places where Arab religious beliefs and practices prevailed. The Arab deity Arṣû is sometimes depicted in flowing Bedouin robes riding on a dromedary, and his twin, 'Azîzû, is also pictured on a dromedary.[6]

In the Avesta, there are references to camels being sacrificed in numbers as large as a thousand,[7] which indicates that such sacrifice was important in ancient Zoroastrian Iran as well.[8] In early Inner Asia, by contrast, the camel played little if any role in sacrifice, the principal sacrificial animals being the horse, common cattle, and sheep.[9]

After the rise of Islam, just as the slaughter and eating of horses in Europe was identified with pagan custom, so the sacrifice and eating of camels came to be associated in the Near East with the religion of the Arabs, as almost an Islamic rite, a sort of profession of the faith (see the quote at the beginning of this chapter). Camels, along with other legally acceptable animals (sheep, goats, and cattle), are sacrificed in Arabia today at one of Islam's two canonical festivals, the Id al-Adha (Sacrificial Feast); along with sheep, goats, and cattle, numerous camels (sixty thousand in 1983, by one estimate) are also sacrificed at the time of the annual pilgrimage (*hajj*) at Mina, a village not far from Mecca, as offerings by various of the two million or so pilgrims.[10] In former times at the Id al-Adha in Isfahan, Iran, a camel was decorated, formally presented to the king, and then taken in a large parade to the place of sacrifice, where it was dispatched by an imperial executioner, and the segments of its body then given to delegates from various professions in the belief that consuming the flesh stimulated one's religious commitment. There was a similar procession and sacrifice at the time of the other Islamic canonical festival, the Id al-Fitr (Festival of Breaking Fast, or Lesser Festival), which follows Ramadan, the month of fasting. After the sacrifice, the flesh was fought over, and part of it was prepared and consumed ritually and part preserved by salting and later given to ill persons as a sanctified food.[11] The common Moslem custom of slaughtering camels on ceremonial occasions is based on the belief that the camel has certain holy qualities.

The holy qualities of the camel are believed to endow its flesh and other products with medicinal value. Camel urine is drunk in Morocco as a remedy for fever, and its flesh is eaten as a cure for boils as well as for general strength.[12] That such beliefs have existed since early times is attested by the Spanish Moslem naturalist and traveller Ibn al-Baytar (Ibn el-Beïthar), who, in the thirteenth century, described the medicinal and magical uses of camel milk, meat, and urine in the Islamic world.[13]

Camelflesh is also widely used in the Near East simply as food, though, even in earlier times, camelflesh was seldom plentiful. In Iran, except on occasions of ceremonial slaughter, Moslems ordinarily ate it only when animals had broken their legs or become sick.[14] In former times, a few young camels were sometimes killed for their meat in Saudi Arabia,[15] but in ordinary times only injured animals were slaughtered. On the rare occasions when the Rwala Bedouin slaughtered a camel, they ate almost every part except the contents of stomach and intestines. The camel's head embellished the platter at a Rwala feast, much as the boar's head did in royal feasts of northwest Europe. The Rwala apparently regarded camelflesh primarily as a food at such feasts; their ravenous manner of eating it seems out of keeping with the notion that this was an act of faith.[16] In 1974, Egypt imported sixty-four thousand camels to slaughter for their flesh,[17] and, though Egyptian fellahin cannot afford to buy much meat, they are very fond of camelflesh[18] and do manage to purchase an occasional piece of it.[19] At Kharga Oasis in Egypt, people used to eat diseased camels, slaughtering them before they died, but the government banned the practice; the Bedouins of Egypt, in turn, both sacrifice and eat camels.[20] In the Sahara Desert, to kill a camel would be to destroy one's capital; therefore camels are eaten only in towns of good size, or for major festivals, or when an animal is so sick or badly hurt that it is not expected to live.[21]

This general pattern of consumption has long prevailed among the Moslem peoples living on the fringes of the Near East, from India and Inner Asia to sub-Saharan Africa: camels are slaughtered mainly for ritual purposes or when they are too old to work effectively.[22] In sub-Saharan Africa, camelflesh is also eaten without prejudice by some non-Moslem groups. It has been reported that camels are now bred for food by the tribes on the shores of Lake Rudolf;[23] that, though the camel is a fairly recent introduction among the Turkana, it is used in bride price payments and other compensation, and its flesh is eaten;[24] and that the Pakot of Kenya sometimes substitute a camel for a steer in a ritual feast, in spite of camels not being so highly esteemed or having the same ritual status.[25] The rejection of camelflesh by the pagan Katab of northern Nigeria[26] may derive from unfamiliarity or in negative reaction to Islamic ways, the latter a rather rare phenomenon among pagan groups of this area.

Though statistics are unreliable, it appears certain that there has been a major decrease in numbers of dromedary camels in several countries in Southwest Asia over the past several decades because of the decline of camel pastoralism.[27] At the same time, FAO statistics indicate that worldwide numbers of dromedaries have increased from 9.5 million in 1948–52 to 15.4 million in 1981, and that numbers of Bactrians have remained steady at or about 1.4 million from 1969–71 to 1981.[28] Whatever the change in numbers from country to country, camelflesh continues to be marketed in the Near East, in some cases by groups that raise camels solely for their flesh, as in the Sudan, Somalia, and northern Kenya, which market a good part of their camelflesh in Egypt and various petroleum-exporting countries.[29] If FAO statistics are correct,[30] these three countries, along with Ethiopia, have nearly 60 percent of all camels in the world (1981). Even the Chaamba nomads of the Sahara started, in about 1940, to raise camels especially for sale to butchers in commercial centers. In some places, moreover, camelflesh is sold on a larger scale, as in Damascus, where a section of the bazaar is devoted to the marketing of camelflesh.[31]

The rejection of camelflesh is found chiefly among non-Moslem peoples of the Near East, for whom it goes back far into the past, but it also occurs to some extent on the margins of the Near East.

In ancient Israel, the camel was known earlier,[32] but was rare before about 1000 B.C., at which time the ancient Hebrews, as farmers, were raided regularly by camel-mounted Midianites from northwest Arabia.[33] From the eighth century B.C. onward, camels were commonplace in southern and southwestern Palestine, where they served household needs and carried trade goods across the Sinai and Arabian deserts.[34] The eighth century was a time of Assyrian military campaigns in Palestine, and in the ruins of a Philistine settlement south of Gaza (at levels dating from 675 to 600 B.C.), both dromedary and Bactrian camels were slaughtered and eaten on a large scale.[35] Though camels were also kept by Hebrews, sometimes in large herds, at least in Mishnaic times (first to the third century A.D.), Jewish camel keepers were considered "mostly wicked."[36] In any case, Hebrews did not eat camelflesh, which was banned by the Levitican code[37] because the camel is not cloven-footed.[38]

A ban on camelflesh was also observed at Haran in ancient Mesopotamia;[39] and it was enforced by the Syrian Christian hermit St. Simeon Stylites (c. A.D. 390–459), who forbade camelflesh to his Saracen converts in an effort to rid them of their heathen ways.[40] In modern times, the meat has been said to be rejected as food by Zoroastrians of Iran,[41] Mandaeans of Iraq and Iran,[42] Nuṣayrīs of Syria,[43] Christian Copts of Egypt,[44] and Jews.[45] In Ethiopia, where camelflesh is an important food for Moslem pastoral peoples, Christians of the highland will not eat it; they regard it as unclean and consider its use a Moslem habit.[46] Some Christian highlanders have maintained their prejudices against the products of the camel even after conquering and settling in areas where camelflesh and milk were mainstays of the local diet. A century ago, the ruling class of the Mansa, a tribe of cultivators living thirty miles northwest of Massawa, kept the prohibition against using camel meat and milk as long as they were Christians, but dropped it when they abandoned Christianity.[47]

Though Moslems themselves have adopted many Hebrew food observances, they claim that the Hebrew prohibition of camelflesh was abrogated by Jesus, whom they recognize as a prophet. Feeling against eating camelflesh has been almost entirely eliminated among converts to Islam, though a few survivals are found. R. Campbell Thompson reported that in Mosul in Iraq it was an insult to say that a man eats camelflesh.[48] In a similar vein, one tribe of Baluchis not only strictly avoid camelflesh, but also in setting up a serious appointment will say, "If I fail in this, may I be made to eat camel's flesh."[49] Robert Graves observed that one group of Indian Moslem soldiers who served with T. E. Lawrence in Arabia during the First World War refused camelflesh as contrary to their beliefs.[50] This attitude is not typical of Moslems in western India, who eat camelflesh without hesitation.[51] It is, however, in keeping with long-established Hindu Indian practice, for already in the Sūtra period (c. 500 B.C.— 100 A.D.) camelflesh and camel milk were singled out as not to be consumed.[52] One also reads in that literature that dreams in which camels were observed were impure.[53] In a similar vein, al-Bīrūnī mentioned camels among creatures that should not be killed for consumption, in particular by Brahmins.[54] In modern times, members of the Balahi caste of untouchables in Nimar District in the Central Provinces of India might kill camels, but they regard their flesh as unclean and do not eat it; even members of the Chamar caste, who eat carrion and the flesh of many types of animals, will not usually touch the carcasses of camels.[55]

In Mongolia, too, there is some reluctance to consume camelflesh. Though Chinese traders in Mongolia eat it, and the Mongols themselves drink camel milk, they do not usually eat the flesh of domestic camels.[56] The status of camel meat is illustrated by the observation that, when Mongol caravan drivers are not given enough meat, they carry camelflesh into the tent, roast it over the fire, and make believe they are eating it so as to embarrass the caravan leader.[57] The Mongol reluctance to eat the flesh of domestic camels is said by Lattimore to derive from the feeling that it would be an insult to the souls of those who have provided humans with a living. The fact that the Mongols have no prejudice against eating the flesh of feral camels (domestic camels that have returned to the wild) seems to support this suggestion. As for the Chinese, I have found scattered reports, for early and modern times,[58] that they have eaten the flesh of camels in regions where these animals were found. Camel hump was a special delicacy eaten in the royal court, and I have found nothing to indicate that the Chinese have been reluctant to consume camelflesh.

Origin of the Avoidance of Camelflesh

The origin of the avoidance of camelflesh is not known. We know only that in the Near East it dates back to pre-Islamic times. It is also clear that with the rise of Islam the rejection of camelflesh by some non-Moslem groups in the Near East was reinforced by negative views of Moslem ways. Camelflesh is thus another interesting example of a flesh food that, like pork, beef, and horseflesh, became embroiled in religious controversy. In this case, however, the use of a flesh, not its avoidance, became symbolic of membership in a major religious group, Islam.

7　DOGFLESH

Ambassadors came to Carthage from Darius, king of Persia, bringing
an edict, by which the Carthaginians were forbidden to offer human
sacrifices, and to eat dogflesh.

　　　　　　　　　　　　　　　　　—Justin, *History of the World*

Domestication of the Dog, and Its Flesh as a Possible Motive

The dog may be the earliest animal to have been domesticated, by
12,000 B.C. if not earlier, and its principal ancestor, in the view of most
zoologists, is the wolf.[1] Oft-repeated assertions, by both specialists and
the public, are that the dog's initial domestication came about because
(1) Paleolithic humans recognized the dog's hunting abilities and tamed
it to assist hunters; and (2) that the dog, accustomed to human hunters
and eating the remains of their kills, was a volunteer responsible for its
own domestication. In a careful review of the evidence, Manwell and
Baker conclude that such beliefs, however reasonable they may appear
to persons of Western background, cannot be proved, that in fact there
are several other possibilities as to why the dog was first domesticated.[2]
One possibility they mention is that the earliest domestication of dogs
was carried out, at least in part, to have a supply of dogflesh ready at
hand for human consumption. This is the same possibility for which
Langkavel, after a thorough survey of dog eating around the world,
argued a century ago: that food was very important in the struggle for
existence of the earliest humans, and that they domesticated the dog to
have its flesh readily available for eating.[3]

Whether or not human liking for dogflesh was responsible for, or
even involved in, the initial domestication of *Canis familiaris,* it is clear
that dog eating is an ancient practice and that, however objectionable

some peoples may find the practice, it has continued to the present day. In view of the persistent shortages of protein discussed earlier, this is fortunate in terms of human nutrition, for dogmeat has about the same amount of protein as and less fat than lean pork.[4]

The Reaction of Westerners to the Killing and Eating of Dogs

Many Westerners have strong negative reactions to the killing and eating of dogs, and there are regular examples of this in the popular press. One is the 1959 case of Andrew O'Meara, a United States Army officer who killed, skinned, and put a stray dog on a spit in Peoria, Illinois, to demonstrate means of military survival to some friends.[5] He was observed, reported to the police, and, since there was no law against dog eating, he was prosecuted under an Illinois statute against cruelty to animals. Somewhat surprisingly, Lieutenant O'Meara pleaded guilty, and was fined the maximum two hundred dollars permitted by the statute. An interesting aspect of the case is that, though O'Meara had killed the dog with a sudden blow, and could have pleaded innocent, he felt public pressure sufficiently to plead guilty and agree to accept the maximum fine. The judge in the case received crank letters and threatening phone calls, one from as far away as Washington, D.C., to make certain that he did what people expected of him.[6]

In 1980 there was a somewhat similar case, this one in California, which led to a public outcry not only in that state but also across the nation. It developed with the discovery that refugees from Indochina (not identified by ethnic group in the newspaper accounts at hand) were trapping and eating animals, including stray dogs and cats, in Golden Gate Park, San Francisco.[7] Many Californians were outraged, and a state senator presented a bill to the Senate Judiciary Committee that would have made it a misdemeanor, punishable by a fine of up to five hundred dollars and a jail term of up to six months, for killing a dog or cat for eating purposes or permitting it to be eaten.[8] A concerned college student in San Francisco wrote to the Catholic priest in charge of the local diocese's aid to Southeast Asian refugees, and asked what his agency was doing to stop them from eating pets. The priest, an enlightened person, responded by observing first that dogflesh is a traditional food of some Southeast Asian refugees. Though he did not condone the trapping of animals in the park, he pointed out that great numbers of dogs and cats are killed every day in Humane Society pounds, and that he saw nothing wrong with making such flesh available to persons whose cultural background enables them to eat it. This response led to the involvement of animal-protection groups and protests to the Catholic archdiocese from the Society for Prevention of Cruelty to Animals, the San Francisco Animal Control and Welfare Commission, and the Animal Protection Institute.[9] These exchanges had the makings of a classic struggle between strongly held but clashing viewpoints—animal rights versus human rights (in this case, the right to eat dogs and cats). In some ways it was reminiscent of the conflict, mentioned in the beef chapter, between Hindus and secularists in India about cow slaughter and beef eating. The San Francisco priest's opinion is not a matter subject to litigation, but, if the case had developed in a different way and the American Civil Liberties Union had become involved, one wonders what the United States Supreme Court might have said about the legality of dog eating.

Despite my use of examples from the United States, strong reactions against dog killing and eating are not peculiarly American, but are shared by other Western cultures. Indeed, in the same year the Golden Gate Park episode stirred emotions in California, there was a heated public exchange on the opposite shores of the Pacific in Hong Kong.[10] In this case, however, it was between a majority Chinese community among whom there was a tradition of dog slaughter and eating, and a minority British community to many of whom those practices were abhorrent. Since the British were the rulers, Hong Kong had a ban on slaughtering and eating dogs since 1950, with violations subject to fines of up to one thousand dollars (H.K.) and six months in jail, not much different from what was being proposed in California. Despite the heavy penalties, the practices of killing dogs and eating their flesh (known euphemistically as fragrant meat or hornless goat) continued in one way or another. The 1980 flare-up came about when an official of the Hong Kong chapter of the Royal Society for the Prevention of Cruelty to Animals (RSPCA) wrote an editorial in the society's annual report suggesting repeal of the ban. His concern was that dog slaughter and eating should be brought into the open, and that government regulation of Chinese dogmeat butchers would assure that dogs were killed in a more humane manner and that acceptable hygienic standards were followed in butchering and marketing the flesh. In addition, it would, of course, have reduced the number of pets that were stolen, something also of concern to British residents. Members of Hong Kong's Chinese community were understandably pleased because of the implication that the British were finally coming to their senses in recognizing the legitimacy of dog eating. That, however, was not altogether the case. Though the *South China Morning Post,* along with many of Hong Kong's Chinese-language newspapers, supported repeal of the ban, other members of the British community were outraged. Several members of the RSPCA resigned from the organization immediately after reading the editorial. Others demanded the resignation of the official who wrote the editorial. In addition, the local newspapers were full of strongly worded letters to the editor for the next two weeks, and there was even a thirty-minute television special in which both sides of the controversy were presented.

It is understandable that Western prejudices have led to a conviction that when people do eat dogflesh they must be starving and desperate. A good example of this is found in the 1982 court case about a recluse in Michigan who pleaded guilty to cruelty to an animal and was sentenced to ninety days in jail, the maximum penalty, for shooting and eating a neighbor's dog. The sentencing judge is quoted as saying that one should not weigh "what a desperate man should eat. If a man is starving, he has a right to do what he has to do. My compassion wasn't for the dog, it was for the man." Yet the account presents strong evidence that the man had repeatedly killed and eaten dogs, as well as cats; and it indicates that, when he was apprehended, he was cooking "dogmeat stew and escalloped potatoes with dog liver." [11] Though this sounds like a meal to which many a dogflesh eater around the world would have welcomed an invitation, the conclusion appears to have been reached, without further questioning, that the Michigan man had eaten dog out of desperation. The possibility that he ate dogflesh because he considered it tasty was simply not raised in the article.

Dog Eating in Various Regions of the Old World

Dog eating was common in the past among Indians of the Americas,[12] and in two areas in the Old World: (1) eastern and southeastern Asia and the Pacific islands, and (2) Africa. We turn first to Asia (China; its neighbors, including Vietnam; India and Southeast Asia outside of Indochina) to determine the importance and context of dog eating there, after which we will do the same for the Pacific region and Africa. Then we will turn to Europe, Southwest Asia, and Iran, where dog eating has not been the usual pattern in historical times. Following that, we will consider the origins of anti-dogflesh feelings.

The Asia-Pacific area was the largest area of dog eating in the Old World. It extended from China northward into Korea and eastern Siberia, southward and southwestward through Southeast Asia at least as far as Assam, and eastward across the Pacific to the Hawaiian Islands. Not all groups in this broad expanse ate dogflesh, and dog eating peoples have been under long-continued pressure to abandon the practice, first from Hindus and Buddhists, subsequently from Moslems and Westerners. Hindus generally look on the dog as unclean, and, in addition, they favor nonviolence and vegetarianism. Buddhists, like Westerners, regard the dog as a friend and protector of the family. They are also opposed to taking life and are committed to vegetarianism, which act against killing dogs and eating them. Moslems, on their part, avoid dogflesh because they consider the dog an unclean animal. Despite pressures from the above groups, some peoples have persisted in eating dogs right up to the present day, perhaps most conspicuously the Chinese.

China

In early North China (c. 6500–3000 B.C.), the dog and the pig were two of the most important domesticated animals. Dogs, apparently domesticated, were also found in Central Chinese sites dating from 5000 to 3000 B.C. [13] Early Chinese written records reveal that dogs not only served in hunting, as guards, and in ritual, but also as a major source of meat. Indeed dogflesh was served at ceremonial dinners and eaten even by kings;[14] and a special breed, the chow, was developed for culinary purposes.[15]

In contemporary China, dogs are sometimes used in hunting. In Inner Mongolia and Manchuria, they may pull sledges. They assist pastoralists with sheep and other herd animals. They may be watchdogs or pets, and in Peking there is even a dog temple, which seems to date from the seventh century A.D., where dog owners would make offerings intended to cure their sick pets. Like pigs and chickens, dogs serve as scavengers who eat things that humans do not. Moreover, their end, among Han Chinese or minorities, may be in the pot.[16]

There are early reports of Mongols eating dogs, a practice also apparently found among certain Turkic peoples who likely even had "professional dealers in dogmeat." [17] I have found no reports of modern Mongols eating dogs, and Moslem Chinese or Tibetans, on their part, consider the eating of dogs repulsive, though for different reasons. The Tibetans, as Buddhists, have a high regard for dogs, and treat them well and even honorably in symbolism and everyday life.[18] They do not raise dogs for their skins, as some other Asian peoples do, and they enjoy calling the Chinese by the epithet dogflesh eaters.[19]

Though Tibetan jibes have had little if any effect, there has been a decline in the acceptability of dogflesh as food among the Chinese in recent centuries. In the last century, Monseigneur Perny visited half of China's provinces and concluded that dogflesh was eaten by poor people everywhere, but that persons who were well-off consumed less dogflesh and then only one or two times a year in the hope that their digestive systems would be aroused.[20] The Cantonese, most numerous group in the southeastern coastal province of Kwangtung, have the reputation of being China's leading dog eaters, as reflected in the Chinese folk saying "Loaves of steamed bread are afraid of dogs; dogs are afraid of people from Kwangtung." There was a successful market in Canton in the sixteenth century where dogs were sold for their flesh. Dogs in cages were also hawked about the city, and there were shops where one could purchase raw or cooked dogflesh.[21]

Nineteenth-century accounts of Canton contain references to much dogflesh eaten, to dogflesh as a strengthening food, to the sale of dogs for their flesh, to dog carcasses displayed in the windows of restaurants specializing in dog and cat dishes, and to respectable persons dining in those restaurants. Today among the Cantonese, however, dog eating is usually practiced only on a small scale (Figure 27) because dogflesh is hot in the hot-cold classification of foods, a strengthening food to be eaten mainly in winter. Indeed on Taiwan people say that when dogmeat is consumed in winter, one can sleep without a quilt because of the warming effect of the meat.[22]

Because its flesh toughens as a dog matures, and because dogs eat all manner of filth, the Chinese came to prefer the flesh of suckling pups and to regard puppy hams as a delicacy. Late in the last century, T. T. Cooper wrote of dog hams as expensive delicacies in China, with most of them coming from the province of Hunan, where they were

27. Dog carcass in a Canton market (photo by Stephen F. Cunha). Reprinted with
permission from *Food in China*. Copyright CRC Press, Inc. Boca Raton, FL.

cured along with pig hams.[23] The reader may be pleased to know that
descriptions of two Chinese processes for making dog ham can be found
in Calvin W. Schwabe's *Unmentionable Cuisine*.[24] The reader will also find
there recipes for two Chinese dog dishes. One is "Stir-fried Dog," made
first by deep-frying chunks of puppy flesh, then stir-frying them in
oil along with typically Chinese ingredients: ginger, garlic, soy sauce,
green onions, bean curd, and dried, salted black beans. The second is

"Red-cooked Dog," made with cut-up puppy flesh sautéed in oil with garlic and ginger, then simmered in soy sauce, along with water, sugar, and two forms of bean curd. When the dish is nearly ready, rice wine is added, and, finally, it is served with lettuce. These sound like fine dishes fit even for a gourmet, and one wonders what French and Italian chefs might have created if cultural prejudice had not denied them the opportunity to experiment with dogflesh.

As with pork eating, the Chinese carried the habit of dog eating with them when they left the mainland: to Taiwan, Southeast Asia, and elsewhere. They have been under pressure in some of those places, however, to abandon the practice of dog eating, and many have given it up. In Taiwan, dogmeat is not sold in markets, but there are certain restaurants that serve it, especially in "fragrant-meat" stew. The police of Taipeh, moreover, have promulgated stringent laws dealing with slaughter of dogs and selling of dogflesh, ostensibly to stop the theft of dogs for sale to restaurants.[25] Those Chinese in foreign areas who persist in eating dogflesh in some cases adopt various expedients to avoid drawing attention to it. In Hong Kong, where dog slaughter and eating are illegal, Chinese gourmets have eaten it only in private, but even so, as we have seen above, there have been flare-ups of controversy. The depth of feeling that can develop is revealed in a letter to the editor once written by a British man which said that any person who eats a dog should be strung up, castrated, and given a deliberate beating. A Chinese responded in a gentle, but convincing, manner that since antiquity his people had considered dogflesh suitable for eating, and suggested that the British perspective illustrated once again that Europeans in Asia were offensive and had no appreciation of local customs.[26]

It is not just Europeans who have acted against dog eating, however. In mainland China, Communist authorities have organized campaigns to reduce the number of dogs by killing them. One such campaign was begun during the germ warfare scare at the time of the Korean War, because, according to official Communist pronouncements, dogs had become infected. Actually the campaign may have been an attempt, in a country chronically short of food, to get rid of an animal that may compete with humans for food.[27] Following 1952, teams of executioners killed large numbers of dogs in every city of China. By 1957 William Kinmond, who travelled extensively in the country, saw evidence of dog life in only one Chinese city, Lanchow, though in the countryside there

were still a few dogs that had evaded the national dragnet. The situation
struck him as so bizarre that he named his book of observations on the
Chinese scene *No Dogs in China*. There was another dog-killing campaign in 1963, when army, police, and Communist Party activists were
all mobilized to kill dogs, and the reasons given on this occasion were
economic as well as hygienic. The argument was that animals that provided nothing useful to humans should be eliminated because they eat
valuable food.[28] Meanwhile, according to one newspaper account, those
dogs not eliminated would be kept in cages and eaten.

Even a government as powerful as that of Communist China, however, was unable to eliminate dogs from their country. Dogs were still
found in China in 1977, especially in rural areas but even in cities such
as Peking, where a small number of restaurants were able to serve dogmeat dishes.[29] By 1987, moreover, the dog population seemed to have
recovered to a considerable degree, and one district in Kwangsi Province was reputed to have over 400,000 dogs, which created a rabies
problem.[30]

China's Neighbors

Much of northern Vietnam was ruled by China for a millennium or
more, and its everyday life has been greatly affected by Chinese ways,
among them the custom of eating dogs. In Annam, many dogs are kept,
and they serve as guards and scavengers that compete with village pigs
for food, and ultimately are used for food themselves. They may also be
killed on ritual occasions, such as times of drought.

Pierre Gourou has pointed out that among the Annamese of the
Tonkin Delta the peasant really enjoys a dog chop and a cup of rice
wine, and that few dogs live to grow old, for they are boiled or roasted
for food when they reach full growth. There is no specialized rearing of
dogs in the Tonkin Delta; trade in dogs, moreover, is carried out on only
a small scale, and they are seldom seen in markets. Annamese peasants
have preferences about the best types of dogs to eat, and they regard
red-haired dogs and black-tongued dogs as tastier than other kinds.
Though considerable dogflesh is consumed fresh, it is also made into
sausages, which can be found for sale in the marketplaces and in towns.
When officials meet for deliberations in a Tonkinese village and must
be provided with a light meal, dogflesh is one of the dishes commonly
given them. It is also customary, when a dog bites someone, for the

officials who arbitrate between victim and owner to eat the offending beast. If the dispute is not settled promptly, they eat other dogs as well, which are provided, of course, by the disputants. Thus when a controversy between villagers seems difficult of solution, peasants remark, "Things are going ill for the dogs."[31]

Dogs are also consumed by certain tribal groups in Vietnam,[32] but in Laos a different situation seems to have prevailed, apparently because of Buddhist strictures. According to a report about Vientiane in the late 1950s, there was a law that banned the killing of dogs, and this led to packs of dogs, many of them crippled, rabid, or mangy, that wandered unmolested in the streets.[33] Among non-Buddhist tribal people of Laos conditions are different, as with the Lamet who use their dogs for sacrifice, and, though adults don't like dogflesh, it is given to children for eating.[34]

Though some Koreans abroad deny that their people eat dogflesh, there are many references to the practice in Korea and even to dogmeat sold in butcher shops.[35] One Korean informant told me that, in considering dog eating in Korea, one must distinguish between dog eating for culinary purposes and dog eating for reasons of health.[36] Koreans, he noted, look on dogmeat as a healthful food appropriate to the warm part of the year, and traditionally they raised dogs for eating in summer; there is even a Korean saying that dogs like the end of summer because they will no longer be eaten. Persons of all social classes, even some of the upper class, may eat dogflesh for reasons of health. Consumption of dogflesh for food, however, was described by Hulbert early in this century as confined to poor people, and my Korean informant told me that this is certainly true of South Korea today, where dogs are eaten by very few people. On the other hand, one cannot ignore reports from the past that the dog was killed in family rituals, that dogmeat was a common food, that Koreans enjoyed it, and that dog sirloins were served to guests on large trenchers—all of which suggest that dog eating was widespread and quite respectable. Whatever the reason for dog eating, Korean families would not normally eat their household dogs, but would sell them to butchers, then buy dogflesh for eating.

Western influence may have stopped some Koreans from eating dogs, and one reads of a Christian Korean who considered it wrong to eat dogflesh because dogs are so intelligent and faithful. Yet dog eating has persisted in Korea, even though there was a campaign in Seoul several years ago to prohibit dog-soup restaurants in order to prevent unfavorable impressions among foreigners who came to the 1988 Summer Olympics. A Western reporter noted that one dogflesh restaurant, though it was required to shut down, set up business in a less-conspicuous location within a few months. The new location was at the back of a building, and could be reached only by going down an alley. Despite this, and despite the lack of a sign to identify it, the restaurant was full at lunchtime, and among the diners were some high government officials.[37]

Buddhist influence in Japan, as in other parts of Southeast and East Asia, helped to protect the dog from being abused or killed. In the late seventeenth century, moreover, matters went to an extreme when one emperor who was born under the sign of the dog took unusual actions to benefit dogs. He decreed that every street maintain a certain number of dogs and provide them with food; he ruled that people who insulted dogs or treated them badly were subject to severe punishment, and if a person killed a dog he could receive capital punishment; huts were required in each street to care for sick dogs; and if a dog died it had to be taken to the crest of a hill or mountain and given a proper burial. The result of all this, according to Kaempfer, was that there were many dogs in the streets of Japan, which were "very troublesome to passengers and travellers."[38] Some of the old sentiment survives in modern Japan, where the dog is a pet and household guard, and where the average person would be shocked at the idea of eating them. Some Japanese did eat dogs during the last war when there was a scarcity of food, and there is also a report that in 1953 one group of Eta, members of the slaughterers' caste, ate dogs when food was scarce. They did not consider dogflesh much different from other kinds of meat; they distributed pieces of cooked dogflesh to family and guests; and they considered it a good day when dogflesh was available, because all members of the family could eat meat. In 1960, when the living standard was appreciably higher, the same group of Eta ate dogs only rarely; at that time pork, beef, and horseflesh were the principal meats consumed.[39] In addition, the Ainu aborigines of Japan both ate dogs and used their skins for winter clothing.[40] This and archeological evidence of dog eating during the Middle Jomon period (c. 3600–2500 B.C.)[41] suggest that dog eating may have been more common in Japan in the past.

There are also groups in northeast Asia who eat dogflesh. The

Chukchee both kill dogs ritually, with such flesh not normally eaten, and slaughter dogs strictly as food or obtain flesh when a dog is killed for its skin. In a time of need in 1901 the Chukchee living near the mouth of the Anadyr River on the Mariinsky coast ate almost all their dogs. Even in times of plenty, however, a Chukchee family at the beginning of this century would slaughter a fat dog and eat its head and intestines; because Russians, Cossacks, and American whalers scoffed at them for this, however, they tended to conceal the fact.[42] The Gilyak, in turn, like dogflesh and eat it whenever possible. They not only eat dogs of their own that become too old for draft purposes, but also sometimes beg Russian settlers for their fat house dogs.[43] The attitudes of certain other northeast Asian peoples toward dogflesh contrast sharply with these. One group of Tungus, for example, noting that they were Christians, expressed contempt for both the Gilyak and the Orochon for eating dogs.[44]

India and Southeast Asia Outside of Indochina

In the Indian subcontinent, dog eating on a regular basis is apparently found today only among tribal peoples in the borderlands between Burma and eastern India-Bangladesh.[45] All dog-eating groups in this region on which I have information are Tibeto-Burman in speech (most are Naga and Chin), and generally they adhere to traditional beliefs and practices and are little affected by Hinduism or Buddhism, though Christianity has made inroads among some of them in recent times. These dog-eating groups may ritually kill and eat dogs so frequently as to pose a supply problem. The Rengma Naga of the Assam Hills minimize that problem by permitting female dogs to breed while eating or disposing of male dogs so that only enough are left for breeding purposes.[46] The Apa Tani of Arunachal Pradesh, who have too few dogs to meet their needs, purchase dogs from neighboring groups. Few Apa Tani dogs are killed solely for eating, however, and instead dogflesh is available mainly at the frequent sacrifices made to deities at times of illness or personal disaster, or in connection with ceremonies carried out by raiding parties.[47] The Adi, in turn, ritually kill dogs at rites to assure the fertility of the land; to prevent summer drought; to make certain there is sunshine during the rainy season; and to help in cases where a woman has a difficult delivery.[48] Dogflesh is believed by many groups to have medicinal value, but people are also fond of dogmeat, and they make efforts to prepare it in tasty ways. Roast dog is a great delicacy, and a well-liked festival dish is puppy stuffed with rice. The puppy is first given an abundance of rice to eat; then, when it can eat no more, it is struck on the head, skinned, roasted, and finally served along with the rice from its stomach.[49] Among the Naga tribes of Manipur, rice prepared in this manner is considered to be the very best, "the most dainty dish which can be set before anyone."[50]

Among the Angami Naga of the Assam Hills, dogs, like pigs, are scavengers and are killed and eaten in large numbers at a rite intended to prevent illness in the coming year, probably because the Angami consider dogflesh strengthening food.[51] Besides ordinary village dogs, some Angami men own hunting dogs, which they treat better and may bury with honors. As an alternative, such a dog may be killed and eaten when it is too old to hunt, but it is never eaten by the man who has trained it or used it in hunting. The Sema Naga have similar beliefs and practices regarding dogs and dogmeat, which they regard as an excellent tonic. Although a man will not eat his hunting dog, he will sell it for food when it is past usefulness. When a Sema man dies, his favorite dog may be slaughtered as his body is being lowered into the grave, so that its soul may accompany his and guard him on the trip to the village of the dead. On the death of a great hunter, it is essential that a dog be killed, for such a hunter's soul is in special danger from those of the numerous animals he has killed. Among some Sema, the flesh of dogs killed at a man's grave is eaten by the person who buries the body; other Sema divide it among those who attend the funeral. The position of dogflesh among the Sema Naga is illustrated by the story of one Sema clan, the Awomi, which amalgamated with some Sangtam who claimed that they belonged to the same clan. One Sema Awomi pointed out that if the Sangtam were really fellow clansmen, they would eat dogflesh. Many of the group did then adopt the practice, though others did not. Today, as a result, the Awomi clan is divided into two groups, those who do and those who do not eat dogmeat.[52]

In Vedic myths in India, the dog plays an important role, often as an associate of deities and faithful companion of humans.[53] One of its associations is with Rudra, who is sometimes called lord of the dogs and whose dogs are wide-mouthed and howling animals who swallow their prey unchewed. Rudra is a many-sided deity, often malevolent, associated with storm and rain, and also a carrier of disease. In addition, however, he is a kindly physician to whom people regularly appeal, for he knows every remedy for curing sickness and disease.[54] Another association, which has persisted to the present, is that between Yama, lord of the dead, and two fierce four-eyed dogs,[55] Śyāma ("dark") and Śabala ("brindled" or "spotted"),[56] sons of Saramā ("swift one"), watchdog of the god Indra, from whom all dogs are believed to have descended. The two dogs guard the way to Yama's realm, and protect the souls of holy spirits from harm.[57] At the same time, an element of fear seems to have been present, for the dead person was urged to run past and outdistance the dogs.[58] In any case, it is likely that the mythical association of dogs with death and the dead helped prepare the way for humans to perceive them as impure.[59]

In the everyday Vedic world, the dog's status was ambivalent. One reads that a greatly respected family was called dog, and that many sages had canine names.[60] That dogs enjoyed a certain respectability is further shown in a litany described in the *Taittirīya Saṃhitā* (third century B.C. or earlier), in which honor was to be given to "hunters, . . . dog-leaders, . . . dogs, and . . . lords of dogs."[61] Yet the dog was also unclean. It was unsuited for sacrifice itself, and it was driven away from a sacrifice.[62] It is true that a "four-eyed dog" was killed at the *aśva-medha* (horse sacrifice), but this was apparently done to eliminate evil spirits that endangered the sacrificer.[63] Elsewhere in the Vedic records, one reads that it is a bad omen to have dogs wandering about in one's house and to hear the sound of dogs.[64] Contact with a dog, moreover, is polluting, and might require washing or bathing.[65] Food and implements touched by a dog are also unclean, and the latter had to be thrown out or cleansed.[66] Brahmins, when eating, should not be observed by a dog.[67] A ceremony is made inauspicious if carried out in sight of a dog;[68] and if a dog moved between a teacher and pupil, the study of the holy scriptures had to be interrupted, as they did when dogs were barking.[69] There were also dog demons who brought on epilepsy in children, and who had to be propitiated.[70] As a final indication of the dog's status, the *Chhāndogya Upanishad* says that those whose earthly behavior is evil are at risk of being reborn as a dog or some other evil creature.[71]

There is little to suggest that dogs were ever eaten on a regular basis by honorable folk in parts of India outside of the east. There is, for example, no evidence of dog eating in prehistoric sites in India, except at Inamgaon in the western Deccan peninsula (c. 1000–700 B.C.).[72]

The *Rig-veda* does contain a reference to a *rishi* (inspired poet or visionary) cooking dog intestines, but it was a case of utter desperation
that made him eat, or think of eating, such unclean flesh.[73] In the
Āpastamba Dharma-sūtra (?500 B.C.—A.D. 200) and *Vasishtha Dharma-
sūtra* (100 B.C.—A.D. 500), dogflesh is among the forms of forbidden
meat. Indeed, should a respectable person ingest dogflesh, he has to
cleanse himself by fasting, eating clarified butter, and undergoing initiation rites again.[74] Though dogflesh was "sometimes recommended for
strength in medical treatises," the philosopher Vātsyāyana (A.D. 400)
wrote, ". . . that does not mean that wise men should eat it."[75]

In the symbolism of post-Vedic Sanskrit literature, the dog is an
antitype of the sacred cow. At one extreme are the Brahmins, who drink
milk of the pure cow and are entirely pure themselves, and at the other
extreme are the untouchables, who eat flesh or milk of the impure dog
and who are altogether impure themselves.[76] At the same time, some
masters have had a high regard for individual dogs, as indicated in the
tale in the *Mahābhārata*[77] of Yudhiṣṭhira, king of the Pāṇḍavas (a group
now believed to be of mixed Aryan or even non-Aryan descent), who
asked the god Indra that his dog be permitted to accompany him into
the celestial realm. Yudhiṣṭhira said, "This dog, O lord, is highly devoted to me. He should go with me. My heart is full of compassion
for him." Indra's response was that the dog be left behind, but when
Yudhiṣṭhira refused, saying that would be an unrighteous act, Indra
relented and praised Yudhiṣṭhira for his loyalty to the animal.[78] There
are also tales of dog eating in the post-Sanskrit literature.[79] On the other
hand, not once are the untouchable "dog cookers,"[80] who are said to
eat dogs, described as actually cooking dogflesh.[81] One wonders, therefore, about their guilt or innocence in this matter, whether certain of
them were, in fact, dog eaters, or whether, because of their low social
status, they were unjustly depicted as consuming a food scorned by
respectable folk.

Early Indian Buddhists, at least to some degree, also considered
the dog unclean, as shown in their characterization of Hindu thinking
about pilgrimage as "a dog swimming in the Ganges [who neverthe-
less] is not considered pure."[82] By implication, even the most sacred of
India's rivers cannot cleanse a dog. There is a case, during the lifetime
of the Buddha, of people eating dogflesh at a time of famine; when
Buddhist monks came asking for alms, people offered some dogflesh to
them, perhaps as a test. When the monks ate the dogflesh, however,

the people were incensed that they should eat the flesh of such repulsive and abhorrent animals. When they took the matter to the Buddha, he agreed, and made it an offense for monks to eat dogflesh.[83]

Today, Hindus generally view the dog as an evil scavenger, an animal of omen,[84] and impure. Indeed, there have been objections by strict Hindus to the practice, found at some temples, of giving to dogs the uncooked food offerings made to the gods.[85] On the other hand, stories of affection for dogs also occur. Brahmins in western India have been reported to interrupt their worship to feed rice or bread to a dog. This was done in the name of Yama's two dogs, mentioned above, with an appeal for their protection in the afterlife.[86] There are also differences in Hindu feeling for dogs, with some persons emphasizing their role as guards of the home and human companions. The Marāthās, those great warriors and advocates of Hinduism, have, as one of their deities, Khaṇḍobā, a pre-Aryan martial god. Khaṇḍobā (*khanda* = sword), who is considered protector of the Deccan and whose worship is common in present-day Maharashtra, had a watchdog who alerted him when his enemies were near. At one time, Khaṇḍobā had the head of a dog. Dogs are believed to be descended from him. Khaṇḍobā came to be identified with Shiva, who often has a hungry black dog as a companion and who was worshipped as a dog until, in the ninth century, this was brought to an end as heresy. Khaṇḍobā's rites still contain hints of his canine background. One reads of the belief that attendants at one of Khaṇḍobā's temples have dog ancestors, and that at his festivals each year they bark, act like dogs, and eat from bowls on the ground. The fertility associations of the god are shown by the fact that couples without children will appeal to him, and that when they bear a daughter she may become a temple servant at his shrine. In keeping with the above, the Marāthās have always loved dogs, and one Marāthā Raja, after his dog saved him from a tiger, presented the dog with an estate, permitted him to use a palanquin, dressed him in fine robes and jewels, and put his own turban on the dog's head. Today Khaṇḍobā is often depicted as accompanied by a dog, and dogs are worshipped weekly and, at the annual celebration of Khaṇḍobā, ritually decorated and fed. Marāthās will not hurt dogs; on the contrary, instances of affection for dogs recur in the literature and in everyday life.[87]

There are also certain places in India and Nepal where dogs are revered because they are associated with other Hindu deities, most notably Bhairava (or one of his contemporary variants, such as Bhairon

28. The Hindu god Bhairava riding on a dog (photo by
David G. White, copyrighted by the University of Chicago
Press; see White, 1991).

or Bhaironath), one of many names used for Shiva. Shiva, as we have
seen, has long had ties with the dog, and, consistent with this, he is a
flesh eater who is sexually potent, a god of what is cruel and terrible
who determines human destiny and death.[88] As Bhairava (*bhairav* = ter-
ror; Figure 28),[89] he is commonly depicted as accompanied by a dog or
riding on a dog. Bhairava is associated with death, and is thought to be
"invisibly present in cemeteries" and to perform a dance in crematoria.[90]
Indeed, in Benares, Yama, lord of the dead, lacks his normal power over
people who die. Instead, Shiva permits those who die in Benares to be
liberated at once, and it is Bhairava who directs the process.[91]

The temples of Bhairava are the only Hindu temples to which dogs are permitted entry, and indeed they are even honored in these temples.[92] In Benares, a center of Shiva worship, there is a noted temple of Bhairon (or Bhairava in some other form), one containing an image of a dog to which people offer representations of dogs made of sugar.[93] The temples of Bhairava are also an exception in Hinduism in that untouchables are permitted to enter them. This came about because the sects responsible for gaining official status for Bhairava in Shaivism were established by untouchables,[94] who commonly oppose the caste system and the priesthood and who may even bar Brahmins from membership.[95]

Though Bhairava is a god of lower ritual status, his local manifestations may be honored even by upper-caste persons.[96] One of these is Bheru Ji, the deity of greatest concern to Rājput women when they think of "possession." Possession by Bheru Ji, moreover, involves sexual intercourse, for he is considered an "insatiably lusty bachelor, . . . who delights in seducing women, especially young virgins." Though Rājput women associate possession by Bheru Ji with persons of low caste, they honor him immediately before they marry "so that he will not violate their virginity."[97] In her discussion of Bheru Ji among Rājput women, Harlan does not mention the dog, but this deity's lust recalls a widespread perception around the world of dogs as unusually addicted to sex.

Kipling suggests that dog eating in modern times may be more common in India than people suspect, and notes that in Hindu poetry low-caste groups are ridiculed as "dog cookers."[98] He also writes that gypsy castes or tribes, such as the Sānsiya of Rajasthan, will occasionally eat dogs,[99] and that there is a folk saying, "When gypsies come in at one end of town, dogs go out the other." Even if there were some basis for such claims, incidents of dog eating among Hindus would be exceptional. The pattern prevailing today is that members of Hindu low castes, like other Hindus, are not dog eaters. Most tribal peoples do not eat dogflesh, and even in eastern India certain tribal groups refuse it.[100] The Dafla, for example, express abhorrence at the very idea of eating dogflesh, though they do sell dogs to their neighbors, the Apa Tani, for eating.[101]

Also rejecting dogflesh in India are the Moslems. Under Moslem influence, pagan Kafirs of the Hindu Kush came to look on the dog as so unclean that when G. S. Robertson visited them in the last century he was forced to tie up his dogs when approached by persons who were ritually clean.[102] The Jains, because of their commitment to nonviolence, will not kill or eat dogs; nor, because of the dog's sanctity to them, will the Parsis, Zoroastrians living mainly in the Bombay area (total population in India today, probably more than 150,000). In early times, every Parsi street had a dog, which served both ritual and guard purposes, and was fed by people. Even today, in front of the large dinner tray used to carry food to a Parsi table is a small plate of food, called a morsel for the dog, which is given to the household dog or street dogs. Until recently, it was also customary for Bombay Parsis to send bread to the towers of silence along with a human corpse, to feed the dogs kept there for use in purification rites of the dead.[103] Against the background of Parsi respect for dogs, it is understandable that, however noble the motive, they object to killing dogs. In the mid-nineteenth century, for example, British authorities, concerned about the numerous rabid dogs in Bombay, issued an order that all stray dogs be shot. This made the Parsis so furious that they rioted and, when the riot was suppressed by troops, they attempted to block supplies from being provided to ships in the Bombay harbor.[104]

In the Burma-Thailand region the practice of dog eating is an ancient one, as shown by evidence from Bang Chiang, a site in northeastern Thailand, dating from roughly 3500 B.C. onward.[105] Today, dog eating is still practiced by some (but by no means all) groups, most of which follow traditional religions[106] and use dogs on much the same basis I have described above. I have found little to indicate anything more than local trade in dogs, though Kingdon-Ward did observe two Lisu tribesmen driving a dozen dogs from China to northeast Burma to sell for their flesh.[107] That this may not have been a one-time affair is suggested by the wooden yokes some of the dogs wore, apparently to facilitate controlling them. In addition, one reads of a dogmeat market in northeastern Thailand at which roughly forty to seventy dogs were killed each day.[108]

Burmese and Thai Buddhists differ from the dog eaters above in refusing to eat dogflesh,[109] sometimes basing their rejection on a specific prohibition by the Buddha.[110] Because of their commitment to nonviolence, they also refuse to kill dogs, even unwanted puppies. As a result, villages occupied by Burmese people traditionally have had large packs of seemingly unattached dogs which serve no function other than those of scavenger and village guard. The dogs of Burma, like scavengers everywhere, have obtained food wherever they can, but they have been in a favored position because they are permitted to consume some of the food given to Buddhist monks during their daily round of begging, as well as offerings left at the pagodas.[111] A similar situation is described for Thailand, where one observer at the turn of the century wrote of the innumerable "pariah dogs . . . with skeleton frames and sunken eyes, many of them in the last stages of disease and decay, [who] snap at the dirtiest bone, or feast on the filthiest rubbish they can find." Buddhist law, he observed, was responsible for permitting such pariahs to live and multiply, their main contribution that of "vigilant and industrious scavengers."[112]

Judging from Tambiah's account of a village in northeastern Thailand, objections to eating dogflesh can go well beyond Buddhist belief. In one way, he reports, villagers consider the dog as an associate and friend. In another, they view it as the most incestuous of animal species, in which parents have sexual intercourse with their offspring.[113] Because this is out of keeping with proper human behavior, villagers treat dogs as if they were debased humans, and one of the worst insults a villager can make is to say to another that a dog had intercourse with his ancestors. Dogs are also considered unclean because they eat excrement. People's refusal to eat dogflesh is thus based on concern with incest and impurity, matters that generate powerful feelings of revulsion, and it is no surprise that villagers do not use dogs for sacrifice, that they ban dogflesh as food, and consider dog eating to be disgusting.

There have been efforts to reduce the numbers of pariah dogs in some places. In Burma, dogs were so numerous and troublesome that the British, on taking control, tried to reduce their number by poisoning and clubbing them. One can imagine how abhorrent this campaign was to Burmese Buddhists from the story of a British assistant resident who, apparently while protecting himself in the Mandalay bazaar, killed a dog with a swift blow of his stick; as a result, he was forced to flee for his life from an incensed mob.[114] Some decades ago, however, the independent Burmese government under General Ne Win undertook a similar effort in Rangoon to reduce the size of the scavenger packs of dogs by leaving poisoned meat out every night for them, but removing the carcasses before daybreak so as not to offend Buddhist feelings.[115] The Burmese were motivated by a desire to clean up their city, not, as the Chinese Communists mentioned previously, by the hope of saving food for humans.

Another interesting rejection of dogflesh in Southeast Asia and neighboring areas is that of groups who, like the Yao of Indochina and South China and in a way reminiscent of the attendants at Khaṇḍobā's temple mentioned above, believe that the dog is their ancestor.[116] There are variations of the legend supporting this, which commonly involve a ruler who was attacked by a rebel or marauder. Unable to contain the enemy forces, he offered a reward to anyone who would eliminate the enemy leader. The reward included the hand of the king's daughter or beautiful girls, much land or half of his kingdom, and, in some cases, gold. A dog named P'an Hu killed the enemy leader, married the ruler's daughter (or the beautiful girls), and their offspring were the tribal ancestors.[117] Legends involving the marriage of a princess and a dog to develop a new tribe occur among many groups in Southeast and East Asia (though not all the groups involved reject dogflesh), and somewhat similar stories are found elsewhere in Eurasia, as well as in Africa and North America.[118] There are even reports of groups in Southeast Asia simulating the appearance of dogs. The men of the Nicobar Islands wear ears attached to a fillet tied around the head, and conceal their genital organs "in a blue bag with a long red point to it, . . . the waist-band . . . arranged to fall down behind in a tail." [119] It is quite conceivable that beliefs in dog ancestry originally developed from totemic observances; various other groups of Southeast Asia regard the dog as a totemic animal and therefore reject its flesh. The Ao Naga, for example, have a dog clan whose members assert that they have canine characteristics and who until recently rejected dogflesh (they now use it as a medicinal).[120] On Sumatra, one clan of Batak regards the dog as its totemic animal and forbids the eating of dogflesh,[121] though other Batak eat it.

The Bauri of Bengal reject dogflesh for a slightly different reason: the dog is their sacred animal and they will neither kill one nor touch its carcass; indeed if a dog has drowned in a tank, people are not permitted to use the water until the uncleanness has been removed by the waters of an entire rainy season. The Bauri claim that they chose the dog as their sacred animal as a counterpart to Brahmin reverence of the cow.[122]

In Malaya and the Malay Archipelago, as in much of Southeast Asia, the pattern of dog eating is quite mixed. There has been a decline in dog eating, encouraged in recent times by Islam and Christianity. It is clear, however, that feeling against eating dogflesh existed at least two centuries before serious Islamic penetration of the area. In the *Nāgarakṛtāgama,* a eulogy written in A.D. 1365 to King Hayam Wuruk of Majapahit in Java, the Buddhist clergyman Prapañca mentions that the holy writings of antiquity forbid dogflesh and decree punishments for violations.[123]

Despite the antiquity and strength of religious antipathy, dog eating survives today in various places, as on Sumatra, Java, Bali, Celebes, the Moluccas, Borneo, and the Philippines—usually among peoples who are not members of the major religions. In Sumatra, the Batak are most often mentioned as dog eaters;[124] about 1930 in the Lake Toba area, where they are found, dogmeat was sold in marketplaces, and at the time of major market days meat stalls were piled high with raw and cooked dogflesh.[125] In addition to purchasing dogflesh in marketplaces, most Batak also fatten dogs for eating. On Java, Chinese settlers eat dogflesh to some extent, as do certain non-Moslem emigrants from Celebes, and, late in the last century, an exceptional Hollander did so, too.[126] On Celebes, the Minahasa and non-Moslem Sadang eat dogs.[127] On Bali, an outlier of Hindu culture, dogflesh is banned, and, though dog eating is still found in some remote villages, most Balinese look on the practice as repugnant. Because of this and because people apparently do not kill surplus animals, Bali has a superabundance of dogs— some household animals, others homeless scavengers that are ill fed and in poor condition[128]—creating a situation reminiscent of Burma and Thailand. On Buru and Aru islands in the Moluccas, men eat dogflesh to aid them in becoming brave and quick in war.[129] On Borneo, some Dyak eat it.[130] The Kenyah, on the other hand, believe that killing a dog will cause a person to go insane, and they do not eat dogflesh.[131] The Klemantan of Borneo are afraid to kill dogs, though one group of them will sometimes slaughter a dog ceremonially, or simply cut off its tail; in the latter event, a person who is taking an oath licks blood from the stump of the tail, an act that makes a solemn and binding oath and is known as consuming the dog.[132]

Alonso de Arellano observed dog eating on Mindanao in 1565,[133] and from that date, the time of first permanent Spanish settlement in the Philippines, until the present, there has been pressure from Christians against dog eating. I have found a report of occasional dog eating, some of it for medicinal purposes, among Tagalog-speaking people in rural areas of Quezon Province on Luzon,[134] but the rest of my information pertains to peoples who adhere to traditional beliefs and practices. In the early 1950s it was noted that dogs could no longer be sold in the public market of Baguio in Luzon, which was frequented by Igorot who came in from the hills to trade. Nevertheless, the dog market continued outside of town, for roast dog is an Igorot favorite.[135] The Bontoc Igorot also eat dogs, but only on ceremonial occasions such as funerals and marriages. The animal is slaughtered, its tail cut off, its hair singed in the fire and sheared, and then its body is cut up and boiled. Since people feed dogs sparingly and give them little attention, Bontoc Igorot dogs are seldom fat when eaten.[136] Apayao men also eat dogs on ceremonial occasions, though women refuse dogmeat.[137] In imitation of certain Igorot, a few Ifugao have also taken over the custom of eating dogmeat,[138] but apparently others of that group, as well as the Ibilao of Luzon,[139] do not eat dogs.

The Pacific Region

In Melanesia, Micronesia, and Australia, dog eating was found among various peoples in the past.[140] The Tasmanian Aborigines had no dogs before the Europeans arrived late in the eighteenth century. The Australian Aborigines hunted the native dog, the dingo, and captured and tamed pups to keep around their camps as companions, camp guards, and aids in hunting, though opinions differ about the dingo's importance in this role. Camp dogs fed themselves as scavengers because most groups did not feed them; nor was their material welfare looked after to any degree. At the same time, Aborigines exhibited great fondness for dogs, and among some groups a woman would even nurse a dingo puppy. The flesh of wild dingoes was eaten when other food was not readily available, but camp dogs, according to Smyth, were not eaten.[141]

In Polynesia, where the dog was present in most places at the time of first European contact,[142] it was one of three domesticated animals, the other two being the pig and the chicken. The dog was commonly fed in one way or another. It served as a companion and pet, scavenger, guard, aid in hunting and war, an offering to deities and spirits, a prestige symbol, and a source of flesh.[143] Its flesh—eaten in Hawaii, Tahiti, Samoa, and New Zealand among other places[144]—was fully acceptable as food, as demonstrated by the facts that on Futuna dogmeat was served to guests, that on New Zealand it was pleasing to the palate and a taboo food eaten by Maori priests, and that on Hawaii it was regarded as a delicacy superior to pork, suitable for offering to the gods and serving to chiefs, even those of the highest rank.[145] On Hawaii, it is said, few dogs reached old age, though ordinary folk seldom obtained dogflesh, and in times of scarcity it was set aside for the sole consumption by chiefs.[146]

European attitudes toward dogs and pigs, both important animals in the region, were puzzling to native peoples. The Hawaiians, for example, kept dogs and pigs as pets that were often fondled and nursed by women,[147] but ultimately they were eaten. Europeans, on the other hand, insisted that the two animals should be treated differently, the dog as a pet whose flesh was not eaten, and the pig as a food animal but not a pet.[148] On one occasion, a group of native Hawaiians, in jest, fastened the head of a pig to the body of a dog, and tricked a foreigner into eating and liking it.[149] Despite the bewilderment of native peoples, eventually European sentiment against dog eating prevailed in Polynesia, and there was a decline in the practice throughout the region. The Maori of New Zealand, for example, abandoned dog eating after European contact.[150] Where it still persists, moreover, it is carried out surreptitiously. For instance, in Samoa and Hawaii, where the practice continues, people today are unwilling to admit to it.[151]

North Africa

I include Egypt here because it is on the African continent, even though, in terms of the position of dogs and dietary use of dogflesh, it has stood apart from the rest of North Africa. It seems from paintings that in ancient Egypt the dog was a companion of people of all classes and a favorite household animal. At Predynastic Hierakonpolis, dogs were often interred in cemeteries,[152] and burials of dogs, presumably respected companions and guardians, have been uncovered at Egyptian sites of varying ages. Herodotus said that on the death of a dog in Egypt, all members of a family would shave their heads and bodies in sorrow, and that a female dog was buried in a consecrated chest.[153] Egyptian mourning on the death of a household dog was noted by Diodorus Siculus as well.[154] Coffins containing mummified dogs have also been uncovered, especially for the Ptolemaic period, at centers of worship for deities to whom they were sacred.[155] On the other hand, Anne Burton

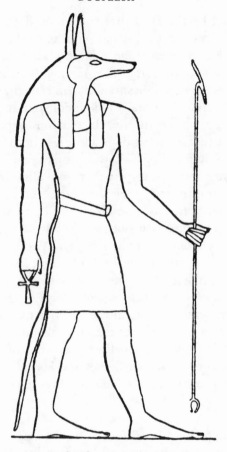

29. Anubis (from A. Erman, 1907).

writes that statements by Greek observers may be exaggerated, and
that, though dogs were treated with fondness by ancient Egyptians,
they appear "not to have been highly regarded." [156]

In seeking an understanding of the dog's ritual position, we face
a serious problem, because ancient Egyptians, and classical Greek
writers as well, seem not to have clearly distinguished among the various kinds of Canidae, whether jackals, wolves, or dogs. Anubis (lord
of embalming, disposal of the dead, and bodyguard and associate of
Isis) (Figure 29) was commonly represented by a recumbent jackal
(Figure 30), [157] and may have originally been conceived of as a jackal. [158]

30. Jackal of Anubis protecting a dead person (from J. Gardner Wilkinson, 1878).

On the other hand, Anubis is described by Greek writers as represented by a dog, having the head of a dog and being called dog. In one account of Anubis, Plutarch wrote that in early times the dog had a place of honor in Egypt over all other animals;[159] and in another, Diodorus Siculus included dogs among Egyptian animals that were worshipped.[160] The Greeks also talked about a separate dog cult and wolf cult in ancient Egypt. According to one view, the dog cult, whose deity was Anubis, was centered on a town the Greeks called Cynopolis (modern Hardaï?),[161] and the wolf cult, whose deity was Wepwawet, was especially important at a place they called Lycopolis (modern Asyût). Opinions differ somewhat among modern scholars, but Anne Burton believes it likely that the ancient Egyptians worshipped only the jackal, and that there were two different aspects of that species, a reclining jackal, Anubis, and a standing jackal, Wepwawet.[162] The cult of Wepwawet remained largely in the Lycopolis area, whereas the cult of Anubis spread throughout Egypt along with the ascendancy of the cult of Isis and Osiris. The wolf seems left out when one considers the animal mummies found near ancient Lycopolis, which were identified as either pariah dogs (*Canis familiaris*) or hybrids of dogs and small jackals (*Canis lupaster*).[163] The find also suggests that dogs were involved in cult activities at Lycopolis, and that there may have been deliberate crossbreeding between canine species. Whatever the links between Anubis,

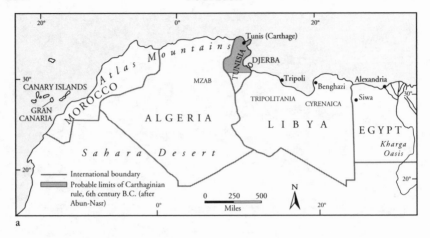

a

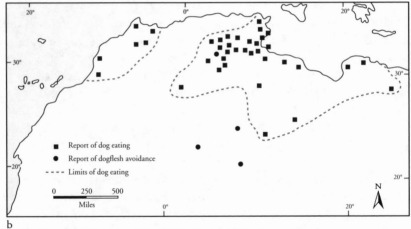

b

31. Maps: (a) Northwest Africa (b) Dog eating in Northwest Africa in recent centuries.

on one hand, and jackals, dogs, and wolves, on the other, there is a tradition that the dog lost its position of primacy among the animals when, after the Persian conqueror Cambyses had slain the sacred bull of Apis in Egypt (c. 525 B.C.), the dog was the only animal to eat its body,[164] degrading itself by such repulsive behavior. Whether the dog's status was lofty or lowly, dogmeat was not a food of the ancient Egyptians, though they did use dog leg, tooth, blood, genitals, liver, and dung as medicines to be applied externally.[165]

In contrast with Egyptian practice, dogmeat was eaten by early Berber peoples from western Egypt across Northwest Africa, and perhaps to the Canary Islands (Figure 31).[166] Often cited in this regard are statements made in classical times by Justin and Pliny. According to Justin, King Darius of Persia sent a message to the Carthaginians asking for assistance in fighting the Greeks and, as shown in the quotation at the beginning of this chapter, he also demanded that the Carthaginians abandon the practices of human sacrifice and consumption of dogflesh.[167] It is not clear whether the account was referring to the Carthaginians themselves or to Berbers under Carthaginian rule, for if the Carthaginians did in fact eat dogs, it would have been a departure from the customs of their Phoenician homeland,[168] and would imply that they took up the practice from native groups after they settled North Africa in the ninth century B.C. As for Pliny, in a description of a Roman expedition beyond the Atlas Mountains in the first century A.D., he mentions a people being called Canarii, who had "their diet in common with the canine race,"[169] a statement which some scholars interpret as indicating that they were dog eaters.

In any case, there is convincing evidence in various medieval Arabic accounts that dog eating was quite widespread in Morocco, Algeria, and Tunisia. Dogs were fattened on dates and sold for consumption by individuals or in butcher shops. People considered dogflesh tasty, and women believed that their characteristic plumpness was brought on by dog eating. Despite the scorn that Moslems have heaped on the practice, and the feeling by some Moslems that dogflesh is impure, dog eating has continued in North Africa into the present century, largely or entirely among Berbers.[170] Some of the places it has been practiced are small, isolated settlements in the interior, including Sahara oases, whereas others have been coastal cities such as Tunis, Tripoli, and Benghazi, which have had dogmeat butcher shops and, certain of them, dog markets as well. No special breeds of dogs have been developed for their flesh in North Africa, and the dogs consumed have seemed to be mostly of a native, pariahlike breed. On the other hand, the greyhoundlike seluki, a hunting dog, has not been eaten, for Moslems of the region view it differently from other dogs: it is given special care, and it is not considered impure but possessed of *baraka* (beneficent force, of divine origin). In North Africa, dogs have sometimes been consumed whole, like a suckling pig in Europe, or they have been cut into smaller pieces (whether fresh, dried, salted, or spiced) that commonly end up in a stew, in one case with fenugreek, garlic, and onion as flavoring.

Of special interest is the occurrence of dog eating in Siwa Oasis in western Egypt, whose inhabitants are Berbers.[171] The natives of the Kharga Oasis of Egypt, who are of mixed Berber and Bedouin stock, probably have also eaten dogs, and dog eating has been reported in Alexandria among many persons from the Maghreb who settled there, as well as among their descendants.[172]

There are indications that some Northwest African dog eaters considered dogflesh simply as a tasty kind of meat. On the other hand, the consumption of dogflesh in the region often had magico-religious and nutritional or medicinal significance. On the island of Djerba (Jerba) and in the Mzab, for example, eating dogflesh was linked especially with a fall celebration.[173] At Siwa and on Djerba it has been eaten by people who wished to become fat;[174] and in Morocco it has been given to small children to strengthen them.[175] It has also widely served as a therapeutic to cure syphilis, to prevent and cure fever,[176] to counteract poison or witchcraft, to cure barrenness in women, and to assure the birth of a son. This medicinal use of dogflesh and the fact that in some places dogs are slaughtered at specified times and by strange methods suggest that the original purpose in eating dogs in North Africa may have been ceremonial or religious. There is also the curious case in Morocco of one Moslem religious order, the Isowa, who assembled annually at the shrine of its founder, where devotees danced and devoured live goats which they tore to pieces. Occasionally the dancers seized a dog wandering about during the affair, tore it to pieces, and ate or pretended to eat it in rage.[177]

What is most surprising about the Northwest African center of dog eating is that it has persisted despite a millennium of pressure from Islam and despite the scorn that settlers and officials from France and Italy, the principal colonial powers of the region, must have heaped on dog eaters. The situation in many ways resembles that of India, where tribal people and low Hindu castes have persisted in eating forms of flesh that have been rejected by members of respectable Hindu castes. It shows that nutritional good sense can sometimes prevail against great odds. Today, however, most Northwest Africans would be as offended, or more so, at the thought of dog eating than any Westerner. The religious revival sweeping the Islamic world today, moreover, offers little hope to the long-suffering dog eater in that region.

Africa South of the Sahara

Dogs, generally of a lean, ill-tempered, mongrel type, are found among almost all modern sub-Saharan African peoples. They serve a few groups as a herding animal and some groups as a companion and aid in hunting. Their primary function, however, is as a scavenger and guardian who consumes the refuse of the village and protects it from predators.

Dog eating in modern sub-Saharan Africa is found mainly in the rain forest and adjacent savannas of West Africa and the Congo Basin, where to some groups it is a preferred form of flesh. The Tallensi of Ghana and the Poto of the Congo area, for example, consider dogmeat a delicacy.[178] Among the Mamprusi of Ghana, the dog is considered part of a hierarchy of animals who serve humans, and the Mamprusi are prohibited from killing them for eating. Though the Mamprusi generally avoid dogflesh, it is eaten in a "courtship stew" provided by a king to his royal lineage, an act which reestablishes ties between the king and his court.[179] In Nigeria, where dog eating is found among various groups (including Yoruba, Ibibio, Efik, Anga, Birom, Kagoro, and others), not all persons within those groups eat dog, but those who do eat it regard it as a special delicacy. Dog eaters in central Nigeria have special names for dog parts, which derive from a perceived resemblance between the dog and a Peugeot 404 station wagon. The dog itself is called 404 station wagon; its head, gearbox or loudspeaker; its legs, 404 wheels; and so forth. The high regard dog eaters have for dogflesh is clearly shown by the fact that, in a meat market near Jos in central Nigeria, sellers of dogflesh attracted more buyers than sellers of any other kind of flesh.[180] The Mittu of the southern Sudan used to like dogflesh so much that soldiers of a slave trader's encampment in Mittu country bred dogs to barter to the Mittu for slaves.[181] When a dog stole a piece of meat from the marketplace of some Ngala people of the Congo area, they seized the animal, cut it open, and thus had not only the stolen meat but also the dog itself, which they prized more.[182] Outside the above center of dog eating, most groups in Africa who eat dogflesh as food do so under extenuating circumstances.[183] The Gogo and Rangi of Tanzania eat it only in time of need.[184] The Mandanda point out that their enemies the Zulu do not like dogflesh and would not steal Mandanda dogs, though they would steal other animals.[185] The Lango of Uganda prescribe eating dogflesh in ordeals or tests of guilt, but only because they consider the dog an unclean animal.[186] There are also nineteenth-century reports of the people of Fazogli, along the Blue Nile in the Sudan, ritually killing and eating a dog at an annual festival, sometimes involving a formal trial of the king, where a dog is substituted for the ruler.[187] In a similar vein, the Koma of southern Ethiopia, at an annual celebration of the new moon, have been reported as killing a dog and presenting its tail to their ruler to eat, thereby extending his position until the next celebration.[188]

Liking for dogflesh has not led Africans in the center of dog eating to develop special breeds of dogs for their flesh,[189] but they employ other means to make the meat tender. Some groups castrate dogs to encourage plumpness.[190] Some fatten them for slaughter, much as we fatten pigs and chickens.[191] Others use methods of slaughter intended to make the flesh tender, such as breaking the dog's legs and leaving it to whimper and cry (many tribes in the Congo Basin do this).[192] There are also reports of people slaughtering dogs by beating them to death; though it is not so stated in the reports, this may be done in the belief that beating makes the flesh tender. It should not be assumed from the above that dog eaters are necessarily indifferent or cruel to dogs. In fact, certain dog eaters, including the Azande of the Sudan,[193] the peoples of the Congo Basin,[194] and the Mbundu of Angola,[195] have considerable affection for their dogs. But this has not lessened their liking for dogflesh any more than East Africans' affection for cattle has diminished their taste for beef.

Dogflesh is also highly regarded by some African groups for its protective and curative qualities. Many Nigerians, for example, have a high regard for the dog's ability to fend off evil magic (*juju*),[196] and for its sexual power, for, as one Nigerian informant observed, "Dog meat dynamizes potency."[197] Love potions may thus be prepared from dog parts. Young women who want to get married may eat puppies, and a childless woman may go to a medicine man who prepares for her a mixture containing the flesh of female dogs. Certain Yoruba who seek sympathy and funds from others for starting a trading venture grind up the head of a dog and use it as an ingredient in a medicinal soap. Some Nigerians also believe dog fat to be effective against fever and syphilis.

The ritual killing of dogs is also common in tropical Africa,[198] and is not limited to dog eaters. It is carried out to make it rain or stop raining, to bind alliances, to make peace, to develop friendships, to make a funerary offering, to keep away disease[199] or cure it, to inaugurate a blacksmith, to initiate a diviner, to celebrate a festival, and for similar reasons. In some cases the dog is eaten for its medicinal or spiritual value; in others it is consumed more as a food; and in still others its body is given away or thrown into the bush for wild animals to devour.

Mention of discarding the body brings us to the restrictions on eating dogflesh that are found in sub-Saharan Africa. Some, like the restrictions on other flesh food, have the goal of preventing ritual contamination, and are directed at individuals who are in particular danger, such as officials, women, and children. The Ibo around Awka in Nigeria require that the "priest of the earth" avoid dogflesh; should a dog even enter the priest's house, it is immediately killed and thrown out.[200] The Tallensi of Ghana regard dogflesh as the food of men, and women neither eat nor cook it.[201] Among the LoDagaa of Ghana, the dog is associated with hunting, an exclusively masculine activity, and men are permitted to eat dogflesh but it is ordinarily prohibited to women.[202] The Afusare of Bauchi in Nigeria, on the other hand, prohibit dogflesh to everyone except the senile.[203]

Some African groups prohibit dogflesh to everyone. Such groups are found within the West and Central African center[204] as well as in the regions of dogflesh rejection.[205] Though some groups may always have rejected dogflesh, others have recently given up the practice of eating it. The Bango of the Congo explain their decision to reject dogmeat by citing a rash of incidents in which dogs ate wounded hunters or travellers.[206] In fact, their rejection of dogflesh, like that of many other peoples, may have resulted from Christian or Moslem influences, which have acted strongly against the practice. In one contrary case, that of the pagan Warjawa of Nigeria, traditional people appear to regard feasts of dogflesh and horseflesh as symbolizing their ancient way of life and as distinguishing themselves from Moslems of their area.[207]

The feelings against eating dogs range from indifference to disgust. The Badjo of the northeast Congo regard the dog as an inferior animal, and only poor people eat its flesh; the Yaka of the Congo fear that the meat will cause illness.[208] The Zulu consider dogflesh repulsive,[209] and the Bongo and Dinka both say that they would rather die of hunger than eat it [210]—attitudes which recall those of Westerners.

Europe

Using evidence from myths and cult images, Gimbutas reconstructed the position of the dog in Old Europe as it was before invasion and settlement by Indo-Europeans.[211] On one hand, the dog was a malevolent creature of the night.[212] On the other, it was a defender against wicked powers. In the former sense, the dog was tied to the moon goddess, her most important animal and one sacrificed to her. Whether obtained in connection with sacrifice, ritual killing, or at other times, there are suggestions that dogflesh was consumed in early Europe at some times and places. In some Neolithic, Bronze Age, and later sites in Central and Eastern Europe, for example, broken, crushed, or charred dog bones and skulls suggest that dogs were eaten, and imply that dog brains were a special delicacy.[213] In at least one site there, some dog bones also bore evidence of roasting, carving, and gnawing.[214] Cut marks, apparently incurred during defleshing, are also found on some dog bones in ancient sites in Britain and Denmark.[215]

Ritual burials of dogs, perhaps associated with their role as guardians, are found in various Copper-Bronze Age cultures in the Ukraine.[216] Dog burials also occur in what are probably the graves of their owners, as at Slavic sites in the Elbe-Saale region of Germany that date from the fifth and sixth centuries A.D.,[217] and at many early Slavic places of sacrifice and worship dating from prehistoric and early historic times.[218] The use of dogs in sacrifice and/or dogs or dog images as grave offerings is also testified to for Germanic peoples and for Roman Gaul.[219] Not to be overlooked in early Europe are other roles of the dog, especially that of a corn spirit able to assure healthy crops and bountiful harvests.[220]

In mainland Greece, Cyprus, and Crete, there are Late Bronze or Early Iron Age burials of dogs with humans in tombs or in cemetery pits adjacent to human burials. Such burials may reflect the affection a master had for his dog, and his need for its companionship or other services in the afterworld.[221] Homer, who provides the earliest literary evidence on Greek dogs, writes of hunting dogs, dogs of shepherds and swineherds, and dogs killed at a funeral, perhaps as an escort for the deceased.[222] He describes dogs as pets that were fed at the table, and expresses a high regard for the dog's loyalty [223] and bravery. On the other hand, Homer, with an ambivalence found in later Greek writing as well, [224] also uses the term "dog" in an insulting way, and writes of dogs as fierce and bloodthirsty, impure scavengers who defile the corpses of warriors killed in battle. [225]

The dog as a carrion eater is a recurrent theme in Greek literature, [226] and as such the dog benefitted humans by removing the impurity of death from their realm, [227] but left the perception of the dog as polluted. The tie to death is well illustrated by Cerberus (Kerberos), the multiple-headed dog that guarded the gate of Hades. [228] The impurity of the dog is clearly shown by its exclusion from certain holy places. Dogs were not permitted to enter the Athenian Acropolis, where the city's principal civil and religious buildings were located, or to enter or be kept on the island of Delos, [229] also a place of great sanctity. They were also banned from certain other sacred islands and places [230] and, in addition, were not normally sacrificed to Olympian gods. [231]

Of all Greek deities, the dog was most closely associated with Artemis, goddess of the hunt (Figure 32), and Hecate, a goddess of sorcery and imposture who haunted the wilds. [232] The two were associated, but Artemis was the more genuinely Hellenic goddess of the wild for whom the dog was mainly an aid in hunting. Though Artemis, like Hecate, was a goddess of childbirth and brought on or cured illnesses, [233] unlike Hecate, Artemis did not assume the form of a dog, nor do dogs seem to have been sacrificed to her. [234]

According to Gimbutas, Hecate was a survivor from pre-Indo-European times and, like Artemis, useful in assuring a proper birth of children, but also a many-sided successor to the Great Goddess, of whom the moon goddess mentioned above was one form. [235] Hecate was associated with night, death, and the underworld, as shown by a representation of her, [236] partly as a dog, consuming the body of a dead man in the underworld. Hecate was mainly a goddess of women who feared her and sought protection of their households against evil influences. When a woman left her house she would pray to Hecate, and images of Hecate as the guardian of gates were set up outside the doors of houses, as well as outside the gates of temples and cities. The dog was Hecate's companion, and she liked to be addressed as dog. Dogs, with puppies commonly mentioned, were regularly offered at crossroads, which were sacred to her. Their flesh, apparently cooked, was a prominent ingredi-

32. Artemis, with dogs, wearing a dress with fish representation (from *Ephemeris Archélogique* [*sic*], as reproduced by William Radcliffe, 1921).

ent in the "meals of Hecate" served to the goddess there.[237] The intent of such offerings was purificatory, to remove evil from the household, or at least restrict the fearful goddess to her crossroads.[238]

Hecate was worshipped throughout the Greek world, and some of the other reports of dog sacrifice,[239] though not always specific, seem to have related to Hecate. Pausanias wrote that, at the Ionian city of Colophon in Asia Minor, people sacrificed a black female puppy to Hecate as "the wayside goddess."[240] And Plutarch observed that dogs were killed in purificatory rites in Boeotia,[241] which was an ancient place of Hecate worship.[242] In addition, there are reports of dogs being ritually killed for other purposes. Young men of Sparta, for example, sacrificed a puppy, representing the bravest of domesticated animals, to the war god Enyalius, bravest of the gods.[243] The Argives killed dogs to help a woman bearing a child, and at a spring sheep festival.[244] The reasons for the latter sacrifice remain a matter of dispute, but Harris Russell proposed that it may have had a practical goal, to reduce the number of dogs that prey on sheep.[245]

Porphyry has written that the Greeks did not eat dogs,[246] and this was certainly the normal pattern in classical times. As to the disposition of dogs that had been killed ritually, Nilsson has observed that Greek rites in which dogs were killed were not sacrifices in the usual sense. Instead, such dogs were scapegoats by means of which the impurity of people and places was removed. When the dogs had taken on the impurity, they were completely destroyed so that the impurity would be eliminated with them.[247] This is in accord with the observation that Greeks would sometimes object to eating foodstuffs as "food for Hecate." [248] On the other hand, there is also evidence that Hecate's food offerings were eaten out of poverty or bravado, and seem to have been regarded favorably by the poor.[249] Aristophanes said that, though intended for the goddess, in fact Hecate's meals were "soon snapped up" by needy travellers.[250] He did not mention the dogflesh in the meals, but it is difficult to imagine it being passed over.

There is other evidence, though much of it is controversial, that certain other people in Greece, at one time and place or another, did consume dogflesh. At Bronze Age Lerna (mostly in levels dating from c. 2200 to 1900 B.C.), near Argos in the Peloponnesus, dog bones show frequent marks of cutting and occasional marks of burning or gnawing, making it likely that dogflesh was eaten.[251] The Greek poet Ananius (sixth century B.C.), in a discussion of the best seasons for eating various sorts of fish and meat, is quoted as saying that it is agreeable to eat female goats and swine in the fall, which is also "the season for the hounds, the hares, and the foxes." [252] Some have taken this to mean that dogflesh was eaten in the fall,[253] whereas others contend that it signifies only that fall was the season for hunting.[254] In a play by Aristophanes (c. 450–380 B.C.),[255] there is talk of punishing a political opponent by making him a seller of sausages of poor quality at the city gates, "there let him dogs'-meat mix with asses' flesh." [256] This may have been an attempt at ridicule by Aristophanes, and, in any case, seems to confirm the fact that dogflesh was not a usual food.[257] Sextus Empiricus (early third century A.D.) wrote that it is possible that dog eating was once accepted among the Greeks,[258] and that, though it was considered wrong by Greeks in his day, some Thracians were reputed to eat dogs.[259]

However unacceptable dogflesh was as a food in Greece, there seems to have been less reluctance to consume dog and puppy flesh or soup in the treatment of various ailments.[260] Of special interest in the dog's medicinal role is the relationship it had with Asclepius, Greek god of medicine.[261] Asclepius, who was a chthonic and mantic deity, concentrated on the health problems of individuals, was addressed as doctor, was identified with the snake and the dog, and was sometimes called by those names.[262] Sacred snakes and dogs were kept at Asclepius shrines for use in healing, and there is a tradition that when the god first came to Athens from Epidaurus, the cult center, he brought sacred dogs with him.[263] In a similar manner, a sacred snake was always dispatched from Epidaurus when a new shrine was being established, and on some occasions the snake escaped to determine the site of a new temple.[264] At Epidaurus, the Asklepieion, which goes back to the sixth century B.C., was set in a grove of trees in the countryside six miles from the port city. It contained a temple of Asclepius and lesser shrines or chapels dedicated to other deities, among them Artemis Hecate (who was also identified with the dog) and Asclepius's wife Epione ("gentle-handed"), whose name was appropriate to the cult (like that of his sister, other wife, or daughters Hygieia, "health"; Iaso, "healing"; and Panakeia, "panacea"). The Asklepieion at Epidaurus also contained places of sacrifice (including a rotunda considered the finest circular structure ever built by the Greeks), gymnasia, a stadium, theater (most beautiful in Greece, according to Pausanias), sacred spring, fountain, baths, hospital, library, and lodgings for staff and visitors.[265] Other Asklepieia, too, were places of healing, commonly health spas[266] with sacred groves of trees, waters for drinking and bathing, shrines, guest houses, and other facilities. In the Asklepieia, a variety of procedures might be followed, among them purification by bathing, burning of incense, or fumigation; diet and fasting, offering, sacrifice, and prayer; healing dreams experienced in a sacred dormitory;[267] and practical things such as exercise, use of lotions and salves, and burning, purging, and surgery. Dogs played an important role in the diagnosis of strange diseases. In such cases, a dog, through contact with an ill person, was thought to contract the disease, and was then killed and examined to determine its nature.[268] In addition, through their licking, dogs served in healing,[269] as in giving sight to the blind and curing tumors and badly infected wounds.[270] For example, on a slab uncovered at Epidaurus, which dates from roughly the third century B.C., one reads of "Thuson of Hermione, a blind boy, [who] had his eyes licked in the day-time by one of the dogs about the temple, and departed cured."[271] Sacrifice was made to a dog figurine in a sanctuary of Asclepius at Piraeus. At the main Asclepius shrine in Athens, sacrificial cakes were offered to the god and his dogs. Sometimes, moreover, dogflesh was apparently provided to patients to eat as medicine.[272]

Greek physicians (Asklepiads, or "sons of Asclepius") in theory were descended from the healing god. Thus it is fitting that Hippocrates (c. 460–377 B.C.),[273] father of Greek medicine, writes of the medicinal qualities of dog and puppy flesh,[274] and that the famous physician Diocles (fourth century B.C.), following the custom of the earliest Greek medical guild,[275] apparently prescribed dogflesh to certain patients.[276]

Faced with a destructive plague from 295 to 293 B.C., Roman officials consulted Apollo and were advised to send representatives to Epidaurus to obtain the assistance of his son, Asclepius. They did this when conditions permitted, and, according to legend, the deity, in the form of a large snake, went with the Romans. When their ship had gone up the Tiber and reached Rome, the snake left the ship and remained on an island (now the Isola Tiberina) which, in antiquity, was sometimes called the Island of Asclepius or the Island of the Epidaurian serpent. The temple of Asclepius (Latin: Aesculapius) was built there, staffed by priests from Epidaurus who had brought sacred snakes and sacred dogs with them. The plague epidemic abated, and the temple, as well as other Asclepius shrines established in Rome, prospered. Ultimately, in Christian times, a hospital and church, San Bartolomeo, were built on the site of the temple, and in present-day Rome, the island remains a center of medicine.[277]

Whatever positive influence the Asclepius cult may have had on Roman views of the dog, they, like the Greeks, harbored quite ambivalent attitudes toward the animal. They considered the dog devilish and unlucky. It served in divination, in warding off or curing human disease and other evils, bringing rain, and in other ways[278] similar to those found in Greece. The Roman Diana, a goddess of fertility, woodlands, and the hunt, was associated with and honored dogs, like the Greek goddess Artemis, with whom she came to be identified.[279] The god Hercules, on his part, considered dogs his enemies, and dogs were never seen in his enclosures.[280] In addition, the priest of Jupiter avoided dogs and neither mentioned nor touched them. Plutarch explained this in terms of the dog's ferocity rather than its impurity. He said that the priest of Jupiter was the embodiment and sacred image of the god, a refuge for petitioners and suppliants, and that, if dogs were present, they might frighten people away.[281]

There is also evidence that certain Romans considered the dog a faithful friend. Pliny (A.D. 23–79), for one, wrote of dogs in terms that would warm the heart of the modern dog lover.[282] Furthermore, the Lares praestites, guardian deities who protected the city of Rome, are depicted as wearing dog skins and being accompanied by a dog.[283] Such associations did not, however, deter Romans from ritually killing puppies or adult dogs, though dogs were at the lower end of the sacrificial hierarchy.[284] Columella wrote of the requirement that a Roman kill a puppy before shearing sheep on a holiday or taking part in sowing, picking grapes, or harvesting or transporting hay on such days.[285] Plutarch and Pliny wrote of a puppy or bitch being sacrificed to the goddess Genita Mana, who presided over childbirth and death, in the interests of the household, perhaps, according to Plutarch, in the hope that none of the family would die.[286] A dog or suckling puppy, along with a sheep, was sacrificed to the deity Robigus at the Robigalia, a spring festival (which corresponds with the Catholic festival of St. Mark's Day, held on the same day as the Robigalia, April 25)[287] to prevent wheat from developing rust (*robigo*).[288] Dogs were also sometimes ritually killed at the Lupercalia, an annual Roman feast of purification.[289] In addition, the Romans crucified dogs once a year, because, by a doubtful tradition, they had failed to alarm the defenders of Rome's Capitoline Hill of a night attack by invading Gauls early in the fourth century B.C.[290]

That the Romans consumed dogflesh is clearly shown by Pliny, who explained the use of suckling pups in sacrifice to the gods, and puppy flesh at feasts for inaugurating priests, in terms of the high regard people had for their flesh.[291] It may be, as Neil suggests, that dog eating in Rome was "a religious survival" and not a secular affair.[292] In either case, one wonders whether the practice brought on significant amounts of trichinosis in humans, for, in modern Italy, studies have found differing incidences of trichinosis in dogs: from none to nearly 24 percent in two groups of dogs examined.[293]

Though dog eating fell into disrepute in Rome and elsewhere in Europe, the associations of the dog with illness, death, and healing— as in the cult of Asclepius—continued. When the dreaded Black Death (plague), which ravaged Europe in the fourteenth century, first appeared in Messina, demons in the form of dogs moved among the population. One account tells of a black dog holding a sword in its paws, gnashing its teeth, attacking people, and destroying their valuables.[294] The dog was also associated with certain Christian saints concerned with sickness and healing. One is St. Roch (Roche) (c. A.D. 1298–1327), a devout, ascetic Frenchman who, during a plague epidemic, is credited with caring for the ill in Italy and with miraculous healing.[295] He himself then became sick, was thrown out of the town of Piacenza, and retreated into a forest, where he would have died if a dog had not been sent with bread each day. The cult of St. Roch, who is appealed to particularly in cases of the plague, spread to various countries in Western Europe as well as overseas. St. Roch is usually depicted as a pilgrim with a wound on his thigh, accompanied by a dog with a loaf of bread in its mouth. On his holy day in August, dogs are taken to his altar to be blessed and fed pastry or other baked goods so that they will be free from rabies during the coming year. Also of note is St. Lazarus, the beggar whose sores were licked by a dog in the biblical parable,[296] and to whom, in later times, dogs were holy.[297] The military and religious Order of St. Lazarus, which was established in Jerusalem in the twelfth century, spread to various European countries, and became particularly important in France. The order focussed on caring for the ill, especially persons with leprosy.[298]

I have found nothing to suggest that dog eating was involved in any of the above, but to some extent it did continue elsewhere in Europe in medical and other contexts. In a glossary of Old Irish, for example, one reads that one way a seer can divine the future is to chew dogflesh. In addition, there is an early Irish folktale about the hero Cúchulainn, who was prohibited from eating the flesh of a dog, and who died after he did so.[299] One also reads that in the mid-sixteenth century the Italian physician Girolamo Cardan treated John Hamilton, Catholic archbishop of St. Andrews in Scotland, with the flesh of puppies.[300] In addition, one finds mention of dog eating in two seventeenth-century accounts: one by Thomas Muffett that puppies were eaten in Corsica in his time,[301] and a second by John Josselyn that the flesh of young spaniel puppies was extolled in seventeenth-century England and France.[302] Though one cannot tell whether or not it had a basis in fact, Gerhart Hauptmann in his play Die Weber, whose setting is Sudetenland in the 1840s, depicted needy weavers eating dogflesh, but not without qualms.[303] In Extremadura in Spain at the present day, dogmeat is a delicacy.[304] It is also eaten in rural Switzerland and other alpine lands, with Schwabe providing information on how the Swiss prepare dried dog meat (Gedörrtes Hundefleisch) and noting that the only cases of human trichinosis in Switzerland in the 1970s came about, not from eating pork, but from undercooked dogflesh.[305] Early in the twentieth century, moreover, J. S. Thomson wrote of dog eating in Germany, where, he said, about eight thousand dogs were killed for dietary purposes in the previous year, fourteen hundred of them in the cities of Kassel (Cassel) and Chemnitz.[306] One reads further that of 42,400 dogs slaughtered at various times between 1904 and 1924 in three German cities (Chemnitz, Breslau, and Munich), from 0.6 to 1.2 percent were found to be infected with *Trichinella*.[307] This was a far higher percentage than found among the four million pigs slaughtered in the three cities during the same period (0.0032–0.0098 percent), and one suspects that some trichinosis must have derived from eating dogflesh.[308] That a certain amount of dog eating also occurs elsewhere is revealed by the fact that several European countries have passed legislation to make sure that dog slaughter and marketing is carried out in a proper manner.[309]

Most Europeans, however, strongly reject the idea of killing and eating dogs, and find it unacceptable that an animal who has served faithfully as a human companion, guardian of the homestead, and hunter's assistant, should meet such a fate. Famine, of course, has sometimes led such people to change their minds, and one reads of dog eating in Russia and the Ukraine during the famine after the First World War,[310] and in Warsaw during the rebellion against the Germans in the Second World War. Certain Europeans overseas, whether out of curiosity or hunger, have also tried dogflesh, as Oviedo and De Soto did in the New World and Captain James Cook's party did on the voyage of the *Endeavour* in 1769.[311] When the Cook expedition arrived in Tahiti, they were short of flesh food, and the natives suggested that they eat dogflesh. Some of the Cook party strongly opposed eating it; others did so, but were not enthusiastic about its taste. Cook himself liked it, judging it sweet and almost as good as English lamb. Acceptance of dogflesh can be a difficult thing for Europeans, but, if they are open-minded and experimental, they are sometimes pleasantly surprised, as shown in the account of T. T. Cooper, a nineteenth-century traveller in China:

While waiting for the return of the coolie, Philip and myself breakfasted at a fine tea shop, the proprietor of which, thinking that his customer was a Mandarin, prepared an elaborate meal, consisting of a number of dishes, and among others, fried dog ham! When this delicacy was put on the table mine host made his appearance, and informed me that I was in luck, for he just then happened to have a dog ham in cut, which he had only received from Chung Ching [Chungking, Szechwan] a few days previous. Though aware that the Chinese considered dog hams a delicacy, I was scarcely prepared to be brought into contact with it; it may be imagined, therefore, that I was somewhat startled when informed that the unclean flesh was actually before me, and, worse still, had positively made my mouth water by its savoury odour. For a few minutes prejudice carried all before it, and I was on the point of ordering away the horrid dish, but as Philip seemed to enjoy it, reason put in an appearance, and argued so strongly against prejudice, making such a strong point of the fact that I was a traveller, seeing and noting everything with an impartial eye, that, in order to prove myself an impartial judge between reason and prejudice, I proceeded with stoical fortitude to taste doggie; one taste led to another, and resulted in a verdict for reason; for in summing up, after a hearty meal, I pronounced the dog ham to be delicious in flavour, well smoked, tender, and juicy. The landlord having heard that the Yang-jen, as that test had discovered me to be, had conquered his prejudice, brought in the ham to show me. It was very small—not much bigger than the leg of a good-sized sucking-pig; the flesh was dark, and the hair had been carefully removed, while the paw had been left, as a stamp of its genuineness,[312] as the proprietor remarked. Dog hams are a just delicacy in China, and as such bring a very high price . . .[313]

Southwest Asia and Iran

In a second-millennium B.C. Indo-Iranian site along the Sintashta River in the trans-Ural steppe, mentioned earlier, ritual killing and burial of dogs occurred, likely because of an association of the dog with the realm of death.[314] Judging from Afshar's excellent study of the dog in Indo-Iranian tradition,[315] among the earliest Indo-Iranians such associations made the dog ritually impure, and it was only later that Zoroastrians reversed the position of the dog to symbolize life and ritual purity. Zoroastrians held the dog to be the most holy of all animals associated with their supreme god Ahura Mazdā.[316] Its principal good attribute, from a Zoroastrian perspective, is that it sleeps little and is ever watchful.[317] It was considered a serious offense if a person failed to feed his dogs, or mistreated or killed them. Even if his dog went mad, the Zoroastrian was required to care for and heal it, if possible.[318]

Their beliefs led the Zoroastrians to some unusual customs, which were found also among other groups influenced by them. One custom involved using dogs in ceremonies to cleanse the living body and purify a corpse.[319] The ceremony for cleansing a corpse (called *sagdid*, "sight of a dog") involves a dog viewing it. It is performed repeatedly while the corpse is still at home. Observers have advanced various explanations for the *sagdid*, some focussing on the eyes of the dog and on the dog's ability to have a beneficial influence on the dead person or to determine whether he or she is actually dead, and others focussing on the respect enjoyed by the dog, the special relationship it has with humans, or its symbolic role.[320] There is also a popular belief among modern Parsis that the dog is intended to guide the soul of the dead in the direction of heaven and to protect it along the way.[321] In addition, Zoroastrians exposed human corpses facing the sun, to be eaten by dogs and vultures,[322] and even today the Parsis do not look with horror at the practice.[323]

Against the above background, it is understandable that Zoroastrians took what action they could to stamp out the practice of dog eating among others, as in the case cited above about Darius and the Carthaginians. It may be significant that in Roman Mithraism, the dog also played a major role in iconography as companion of Mithras and symbolic of the good.[324]

For other parts of ancient Southwest Asia, there is clear evidence of dog sanctity, impurity, or use in ritual. Among the Hittites,[325] dogs served as household guards in addition to being owned by herdsmen and hunters. There were laws relating to damage by dogs and injuries by dogs or to them, with dogs owned by hunters and herdsmen valued more highly than household dogs. As we have seen, the dog, like the pig, was considered a scavenger that fed on garbage, and was mentioned along with the pig as an impure animal to be kept away from temples and temple kitchens. It seems not to have served in rites performed by royalty, nor was it among the animals ordinarily sacrificed to deities. Instead, puppies (in some cases, black puppies are specified) or dog images served in rites of prevention and purification performed by civilians and the army.[326] An image of a small dog was made of tallow and placed at the entrance to the king's palace to drive out evil spirits at night, just as it would keep people out of the courtyard during the daytime. A puppy was mentioned as a scapegoat used to remove evil from the royal palace. There are also references to the killing of puppies to protect against an epidemic and similar dangers. The flesh of animals killed on such occasions seems to have been cast out, burned, or buried, and I have found no evidence that people ate their flesh or made dietary use of dogflesh of any sort,[327] though excrement and body parts of dogs might serve medicinal purposes.[328]

In early Mesopotamia, dogs were companions of hunters and guardians of cattle, sheep, and goats. In Sumer, some dogs seem to have been scavengers, for one proverb mentions a dog (*ur*) eating a pig in the marketplace. Dogs also were fed leftovers of human meals, as well as spoiled food. The Sumerians regarded female dogs as loving to their offspring. Far from being warm associates of humans, however, dogs in general are depicted as vicious, self-centered, disloyal, and greedy in their eating habits.[329] I have found nothing to suggest that they were eaten as food.

The ancient Babylonians also had ambivalent views of the dog. They believed the dog to possess elements of sacredness, and sometimes it was regarded as good, sometimes as evil. Yet the dog was considered an associate of demons and an animal of omen, and thus people observed and interpreted its movements carefully.[330] Though the presence of dogs in the roads was believed essential to the welfare of a place, care was taken lest they defile a person or house.[331] The dog was not included on the lists of sacrifices to major Babylonian deities, and its flesh was banned as food. Indeed, the Babylonians and Assyrians seem to have eaten dogflesh, as true of other unclean foods on occasion, only as a medicine.[332]

One reads of the use of "dog" in personal names in Babylonia or Assyria,[333] which suggests a certain respectability. The Babylonians and Assyrians also had gods who were accompanied by a dog or dogs.[334] The Babylonian god Marduk, for example, was occasionally represented by a dog symbol, and is pictured with four dogs, who were named Iltebu, "the pursuer"; Ukkumu, "the seizer"; Iksuda, "the capturer"; and Akkulu, "the devourer."[335]

In addition, the dog was sacred to the Sumero-Babylonian goddess Bau (Gula in Akkadian) (Figure 33), who came to be identified with Ninisina, whose emblem was the dog and who was sometimes depicted as having the head of a dog. Gula was a goddess of healing and medicine, as indicated in a hymn (c. 1400–700 B.C.) in which she says: "I am a physician, I can heal, I carry around all (healing herbs), I drive away disease, I gird myself with the leather bag containing health-giving incantations, I carry around texts which bring recovery, I give cures to mankind. My pure dressing alleviates the wound, My soft bandage relieves diseases. . . I am merciful, I am compassionate. . . I bring up the dead from the underworld, . . . I am a physician, I am a diviner, I am an exorcist. . ."[336] It has been speculated that Gula's association with dogs may have come about because the licking of dogs was con-

33. Bau/Gula with a dog (from William Hayes Ward, 1910).

sidered cleansing and therapeutic. There is a royal text dating from the
Semitic first dynasty of Isin (2017–1794 B.C.) of the Old Babylonian
period that deals with dedication at Isin of a "dog house" (i.e., temple)
for Ninisina, who was patron goddess of the city. Excavations near the
temple have uncovered clear evidences of a dog cult, among them more
than thirty dog burials, as well as copper pendants with engravings of
dogs; a human being on its knees and embracing a dog; and bronze or
clay dog figurines, one of which bears a prayer "to Gula, lady of life,
great physician. . ."[337] The dogs of Gula were of a particular breed,
and figures of such dogs were buried beneath the threshold of a house,
palace, or temple to keep evil forces away.[338] Oaths were sworn in the

name of Gula's dog, which, on occasion, was referred to as if it were divine.[339] Dogs seem to have served in taking omens,[340] and were ritually killed in connection with her cult,[341] though I have found nothing to suggest that their flesh was eaten. Little is known, however, about Gula's cult,[342] though it continued to be important in Neo-Babylonian times, when an inscription by Nebuchadrezzar II (who ruled from 604 to 562 B.C.) mentions at least three separate chapels or shrines to Gula in a temple complex at Barsip (Borsippa), as well as a Gula temple in nearby Babylon.[343]

Also of interest, at Haran in ancient Mesopotamia (today just north of the Syrian border in southern Turkey), which was the center of a syncretic cult, the dog was a sacred animal that received ritual offerings.[344] In what may be a survival of ancient beliefs, in modern northern Syria the Nuṣayrīs, whose religion derives in part from that of ancient Haran, are reported to worship the dog.[345]

The dog also played a role in healing cults in the eastern Mediterranean region, though the gods involved, their associations with one another, and their use of the dog remain little understood. In Palestine at the ancient coastal community of Ashkelon, a cult center of the goddess Astarte, archeologists have discovered a dog cemetery dating from the fifth century B.C. that is said to be the largest animal cemetery ever uncovered in the ancient world. Altogether over seven hundred dog carcasses have been unearthed, and likely the total number of burials was in the thousands. Sixty to seventy percent of the animals were puppies, but there are no cut marks or other evidence that they were sacrificed, slaughtered, or eaten. Lawrence E. Stager, the archeologist on whose work I rely, suspects that dogs were sacred in an Ashkelon cult, and that, like Gula's dogs at Isin, they were honored by burial near a temple or shrine—though, at the time of writing, none had been found.[346] Stager concludes that in all likelihood the people who buried the dogs were Phoenicians,[347] and that the cult was that of a healing deity, perhaps Resheph-Mukol (Resheph likely means "burning," "fever," "plague"). Stager identifies likely associates and predecessors for Resheph-Mukol among the Canaanites, as well as information on certain of the god's overseas ventures and associations. Mukol, for example, is mentioned as an associate of Astarte in an inscription found at a Phoenician port on Cyprus. At another site on Cyprus, Resheph-Mukol is identified with the Greek Apollo-Amuklos. The tie between

Resheph and Apollo is further revealed in the fact that the Roman city
of Apollonia in coastal Palestine had previously been known as Resheph
(and even today the place is known in Arabic as Arsuf). Also of possible
relevance is S. A. Cook's observation that among modern Palestinians
"even the dog has been known to have a shrine in his honour," and that
in Palestinian folklore, the dog is treated in a way hardly appropriate
to Islam.[348]

Of even more interest is early archeological evidence (sixth century
B.C.?),[349] uncovered in Anatolia at Sardis, capital of Lydia, that puppies
were cut up and prepared in ritual meals. For each of the meals, which
numbered almost thirty altogether, a dinner service was provided, typically a jug shaped like a cooking pot, which contained the puppy
remains, a small wine pitcher, a cup, a dish that may have contained
bread, and an iron knife. The puppy bones contained cut marks of the
sort that come from butchering, removing flesh, or cutting, but it is
uncertain whether or not the dogmeat was actually cooked. It is notable
that the dinners, which were all buried, were found, not in shrines or
elaborate ritual settings, but in unpretentious houses or shops.[350] It has
been suggested by Greenewalt that the "puppy dinners" were offered
to the deity Kandaulas, who was either a hero god or a god of the
underworld.[351] Kandaulas, whose name may have meant "dog choker,"
was identified in a few early fragments with one or both of the Greek
deities Heracles and Hermes, though the nature of the relationship is
unclear.[352] Greenewalt writes of the Sardis material as having "a side
interest as evidence . . . for 'cynophagy,' the eating of dogflesh . . . ,"
and he adds that it is conceivable that the ritual dogflesh, or some of
it, was eaten by devotees.[353] This leads him to the question whether
the Lydian dish *kandaulos,* a rich, elaborate one mentioned in classical
accounts,[354] was named for the deity, and whether, at least at one time,
it contained dogflesh.[355]

Sardis was a multilingual community, with Carian as well as Lydian
residents, and it has been argued by Pedley that the practice of ritual
dog killing may have come to Sardis from Caria or that Carians and Lydians shared a religious heritage in that regard, possibly deriving from
Mesopotamia.[356] Robertson, on the other hand, has identified strong re-
semblances between the Sardis puppy dinners and Hittite practice, and
suggests that they may have been ancient Anatolian practices shared by
Lydians and Hittites or derived from Hittites who moved to Sardis after

the fall of the Hittite Empire. In either case, the argument goes, they were not normal offerings to deities of the sort found in Greece, where devotees consumed the flesh.[357]

Walter Burkert has presented evidence that knowledge of Gula reached the Greeks in the seventh century B.C., and may have influenced the cult of Asclepius and possibly that of Apollo.[358] Starting late in the sixth century B.C., representations of dogs, of several breeds, became common on grave stelae or monuments in Greece, and freestanding dog figures also served to mark places of burial.[359] The popularity of the dog motif at that time is explained by influences from the East,[360] and one suspects that the cults of Gula and other healing deities were involved.

Apollo, among other things, was a god of pestilence, and was often called the leading healing god. As Apollo Maleatas, he directed the healing temple at the Asclepius cult center at Epidaurus, and was honored there, but it was his son, Asclepius, who dealt actively with sick people on a personal basis. Like the Vedic Rudra, Apollo might cause, forestall, or terminate disease and pestilence, and is credited with assisting in ending a plague epidemic in Greece in the fifth century B.C.[361] As we have seen, Asclepius had special ties with the dog, and overlooking the Asclepius cult center at Epidaurus, was a temple of Apollo Maleatas on Mt. Kynortion ("dog ascent" or "dog altar"). There is a tradition that this Apollo temple had been built on the ruins of one dedicated to an earlier deity (the hunter Maleatas?) who was associated with the dog, and it was assumed that this led to Asclepius's tie with the dog at Epidaurus.[362] Apollo seems to have had ties with another dog deity on the Greek island of Anaphe, where the local Apollo was called by a term that does not sound Greek and is nearly the same as one applied to Gula in Mesopotamia.[363] One notes further that the Lycians and Carians of southwest Asia Minor claimed that they were descended "from the dog Apollo,"[364] and that dog and puppy sacrifice was popular in Caria and made to more than one deity.[365]

One judges from Old Testament accounts that dogs were kept among the ancient Hebrews mainly by herdsmen and farmers as guards. Dogs also congregated in pariah packs and prowled about the streets, living as scavengers and commonly consuming flesh not acceptable for humans, such as animal carcasses and even human bodies.[366] Such pariah dogs were considered treacherous, dangerous, and unclean, and the term "dog" when applied to a human was a matter of disdain, insult, or self-reproach.[367] Indeed, rabbinical scholar Eliezer ben Hyrcanus (first to second century A.D.) said that a person who breeds dogs is like one who breeds swine, meaning that he is cursed.[368] Contrasting views were also found in the rabbinical literature,[369] but overall the dog remained in a lowly position, as shown by use of the term "dog" for wicked heathen because they were ceremonially unclean. Even Jesus used this expression on occasion.[370] Also in the New Testament, the term "dog" is sometimes applied in a figurative sense to refer to those who did not appreciate what is sacred,[371] to those who introduced untrue doctrines cynically,[372] or to a sinner who repeated his sins.[373] There are allusions to the ritual killing of dogs in Isaiah,[374] which indicates that this practice was known, likely among the ancient Canaanites. As for dogflesh, the Hebrews refused to eat it. Even though the dog is not mentioned in the dietary prohibitions of Leviticus or Deuteronomy, it falls into the banned category of animals that walk on all four paws.[375]

Turning to Islam, one finds quite ambivalent attitudes toward dogs. It has often been noted that Moslem peoples have a certain respect and affection for dogs, especially for pets. The killing of a dog can arouse considerable feeling. In the Islamic world generally, it is considered a good act for a person to feed a dog and give it drink.[376] In Palestine, people say that it is better to feed a dog than to feed a human, meaning that the dog is grateful and will not forget the kindness, whereas the human may.[377] In Morocco, greyhounds are believed to be possessed by a good spirit. In Tangier and among the Ait Waryager, people believe that a house in which a greyhound lives is not molested by spirits.[378] In Andjra, a good hunting dog is respected and prayed for. When it dies, its body, unlike those of ordinary dogs, is buried or hidden.[379]

On the other hand, Moslems have long had strong feelings that dogs are unclean. Some have claimed that this view was incorporated into the Islamic faith because of the Prophet's dislike of dogs. According to one Islamic tradition, Mohammed ordered that all the dogs of Medina, especially ones of a certain dark color, be killed.[380] By another tradition, he said that if a dog should drink from a container, it must be washed seven times, the first time with earth.[381] On the other hand, Orientalist Ignaz Goldziher has presented evidence that in Arabia at the time of Mohammed the dog was not yet impure, that dogs entered mosques without profaning them, had good qualities, including the ability to see demons, and were even regarded with a certain affection. Goldziher argues further that the dog became impure later, when Islam was being established in Iran, in negative reaction to the unusually high regard in which the dog was held by Zoroastrians.[382] Afshar, in his study of the dog in Indo-Iranian tradition, agrees that "the Persian contribution," an exaggerated Islamic reaction to Zoroastrian ways, led the dog to join the pig as one of Islam's most impure animals.[383] On the other hand, Afshar also stresses the importance of Judaism as background to Islamic thinking about the dog.[384]

Whatever the origins of the negative perception of the dog, at And-jra in modern Morocco people believe that, if a dog were to eat from a vessel or lick it, it would break unless washed seven times in hot water. The Ait Waryager require that the washing be with water that has been made pure by putting seven stones in it. Moroccans also believe that a man who kills a dog becomes polluted, that the meat of any animal he slaughters is unfit to eat, and that he should not be permitted to perform certain religious sacrifices.[385] In Palestine early in this century, strict Moslems, especially members of the Shāfiʿī school, regarded dogs as so dirty that, if a wet dog shook itself forty steps from the place where they were at prayer, they stopped the proceedings, performed certain ablutions, and started their prayers over.[386] Because of such attitudes, most dogs are neglected, noisy pariahs in Arab towns,[387] and are kept from entering the mosques.

As for dog eating, there is no specific Koranic prohibition against the practice. Yet, outside North Africa, I have found only one reference to the consumption of dogflesh in the modern Near East.[388] Indeed, Moslems have been active in eliminating dog eating among converts, especially in North Africa, along the fringes of the West African area of dog eating, and in the Malay world.

Of particular interest in the history of dog-human relations is the case of Iran. We have seen that ancient Zoroastrians had an unusually high regard for the dog. With the acceptance of Islam, however, its position changed drastically; the dog became satanic and ritually impure; and today its status in Iran is little different from that found in the rest of the Islamic world.[389] Though Iranians are fond of dogs they keep as pets, and though huntsmen are proud of their greyhounds and pointers, most dogs are pariahs, wandering half starved through the streets.[390] Some Iranians believe that, whereas humans are the noblest of creatures, the dog is the lowliest. On the other hand, it is said that a grateful dog is better than a thankless man, and that, if a man has one of the seven qualities a dog possesses, he will go to heaven. It is also believed that any person who sheds the blood of a dog will die.[391] Even Zoroastrians in Iran have adopted such Moslem views, and have forgotten their former high regard for the dog.[392] Dogflesh continues to be rejected in Iran, but for quite different reasons from those when Iran was a Zoroastrian land.

Hindus and Buddhists also disapprove of the eating of dogflesh and have taken action in South, Southeast, and East Asia against the practice. By far the most effective anti-dog force in the last few centuries, however, has been the Europeans who ruled a vast colonial empire and had enormous impact in many areas of native life. As a result of the action of these powerful groups, there has been a considerable decrease in the number of dog-eating peoples in the Old World and a reduction in the size of the area in which the practice is common. The forces arrayed against it are so numerous and their influence so pervasive that, unless a new champion appears, dog eating seems likely to continue its precipitous decline.

Origins of Anti-Dogflesh Feelings

It is clear that since antiquity the position of the dog in human societies has been ambiguous, "honored and despised, loved and hated, petted and kicked,"[393] and that these perceptions, singly or in combination, have contributed to the rejection of dogflesh as human food. One of the most powerful factors in this regard is familiarity, which is common between humans and their pets. It may develop between hunters and their dogs, and herdsmen and their dogs. Intimacy makes it difficult if not impossible for humans to eat such dogs, and it may not only affect an individual and his or her dogs, but also lead an entire people to reject the flesh of all dogs. I hasten to add that this path has not been followed by all peoples. Intimacy between a human and an individual dog does not necessarily lead that person or his or her group to avoid all dogflesh. Among dog-eating groups, it is not uncommon for people to avoid eating animals with which they have been closely associated, but to sell them, knowing what fate awaits them, when they are too old to be useful. An owner may experience guilt from selling a dog, but this is less painful than if he had killed it and eaten its flesh. A human is even less disturbed by buying someone else's dog for killing and eating, and still less disturbed by buying the flesh of a dog slaughtered by someone else. None of this, however, rules out the possibility that some peoples followed the first path, that of rejecting the flesh of all dogs.

A persistent theme in the literature—from ancient India, Mesopotamia, Anatolia, Greece, and elsewhere—is that the dog, like the pig, is an unclean scavenger that, given an opportunity, will eat even human corpses. As Anna S. Meigs has observed, the very thought of consuming carrion-eating animals, such as dogs and vultures, brings on disgust reactions in humans because people associate carrion with decay, which, in turn, pollutes the carrion eaters.[394] Such concerns did not lead all peoples to reject dogflesh, but it is clear that they were in the minds of many dog eaters. This is, in part, why the Chinese and various other dog eaters prefer puppy flesh to that of adult dogs. It is not just its tenderness, but also that puppies—particularly milk-fed puppies—have not had the opportunity to feed on carrion and other disgusting substances. At some times and places, as is well documented in the Vedic literature, such feelings were critical in fostering strong feelings against both dogs as unclean animals and dogflesh as unacceptable food.

The dog's carrion-eating propensities established a widespread early perception that the dog was associated with death, disease, and spirits or deities that brought on death and disease and might also prevent or cure them. Such associations were behind much of the ritual killing of dogs in the ancient world. They also led the dog to a role in medical cults, such as those of Gula and Asclepius. Though in such contexts the dog gained a certain sanctity, its basic impurity and the unacceptability of its flesh usually remained.

One cannot always separate the view of the dog as a creature that eats impure foods from one that it is a predator that kills other creatures. In religions of Indian origin, such as Buddhism, Hinduism, and Jainism, the dirty eating habits of dogs are clearly of great concern, but also of importance is commitment to the sanctity of all life. One cannot dismiss ahimsa concerns in weighing the origins of dogflesh rejection in India, and perhaps elsewhere as well. Nor can one dismiss the view that dogflesh rejection developed among some people, such as the Zoroastrians, because of the dog's association with particular deities who gave it sanctity and protection.

The eater of dogflesh faces certain risks of disease, among them trichinosis and hydatid disease. Hydatid disease, which is found in various parts of the world, can be transmitted by handling dog feces or intestine, and involves transmission of a tapeworm (*Echinococcus granulosus* or closely related species), a parasite that grows like a tumor in various human organs and can lead to the death of its human host.[395] I have mentioned the trichinosis danger above. Despite Westerners' readiness to explain Hebrew pork rejection in terms of fear of trichinosis, however, there has, to my knowledge, been no suggestion that the rejection of dogflesh can be explained in such terms.[396] Nor, to my knowledge, has a champion emerged to advance an explanation of dogflesh rejection in terms of environmental deterioration and techno-environmental change. Some highly imaginative cultural materialist may yet propose such a hypothesis, but my view is that the dirty eating habits of the dog, on one hand, and its close association with humans, on the other, are the main reasons so many of the world's peoples, ancient and modern, have rejected dogflesh as food.

8

FISH

Speak not to me with a mouth that eats fish.
—Somali nomad taunt, from R. F. Burton's
First Footsteps in East Africa

Background

Fishing and fish eating are characteristic of the overwhelming majority of peoples in the Old World. Their importance is minor in some places. In others, such as Portugal and Japan, fish is so important a dietary element as to make it difficult to imagine how people could survive without it. Fishing is carried out in oceans and seas, rivers and streams, lakes, ponds, marshes, and elsewhere. Fish may be processed and traded to distant areas, sometimes in forms unfamiliar to most Westerners (for example, the fermented fish pastes and sauces of Southeast Asia). Some peoples have, over many centuries, developed impressive trade networks to distant lands to obtain piscine delicacies, with Chinese efforts to obtain shark's fin and bêche-de-mer (sea slug) particularly impressive.[1] However, it is not the above matters that concern us here, but departures from the fish-eating norm, the practices of peoples who, for one reason or another, reject fishing and fish eating.

Such ichthyophobia occurred at the time of first European contact among the Tasmanian Aborigines. The Aborigines were hunters and gatherers, most of whom lived in coastal areas of an island that had an abundant fish resource in the seas nearby. Yet, though they consumed crayfish, shellfish, and sea mammals, they looked on scaled fish with abhorrence and refused to eat them.[2] There is evidence that at one time such fish had been a major food of Tasmanian Aborigines, and that roughly 3,800 to 3,500 years ago they stopped eating them. Archeologist Rhys Jones, who has considered the matter, failed to find reasonable explanations for Tasmanian cessation of fish eating in terms of changes in technology or ecology, and he was led to a cultural explanation: that fish came to be avoided because of a deliberate "intellectual decision" on the Aborigines' part that persisted for thousands of years even though it was maladaptive in economic terms.[3] The reasons for the origin of the Tasmanian fish avoidance remain controversial.[4] Whatever they may have been, we are dealing with an isolated case quite different from the situation in Asia and Africa, where fish avoidance has extended across large regions and involved many ethnic groups.

Before turning to fish avoidance in Africa and Asia, however, I would note that widespread fish avoidance in traditional times was by no means restricted to the Old World. It was common, as well, in the American Southwest. Some peoples of the Southwest (Zuni, Hopi) refused to eat fish because water was sacred to them, and because they believed that fish, like all creatures living in water, partook of that sanctity.[5] Many Navajo and Apache of the Southwest also rejected fish as food, though fish were of considerable dietary importance to most of their northern Athapascan relatives.[6] For this reason, it has been argued that the Navajo and Apache became fish avoiders only in imitation of the Pueblo Indians, and after they moved into the Southwest several centuries ago. It has also been suggested that the ban on fish may have led to the loss of Athaspascan words for fish in the Southwest.[7]

Whatever the origins of Navajo fish avoidance, early observers report that Navajos were afraid to eat all water creatures, among them snails, turtles,[8] clams, eels, and waterfowl. Some persons went further in refusing to come into contact with fish or even eat candy made in the form of a fish. Some Navajos explained their fear by observing that such creatures were "people of the water." That is, they were children or retainees of the water monster who lives in the ocean but also rules the waters of the land. To eat water creatures, Navajos insisted, would incur the monster's wrath and punishment.[9] One even reads of a Navajo who underwent purification ceremonies to remove the pollution that came from being wet with water that had contained fish.[10] This practice is reminiscent of the ritual purification a Hindu may undergo after doing violence to a cow or eating beef.

Contact with Hispanic and Anglo-American peoples has led the Navajo and other Southwest Indians to give up their traditional rejection of fish. Thus, today tinned fish such as sardines are commonplace in trading posts in Navajo country. Frozen fish are popular, too, though some individuals, especially elderly ones, remain disinclined either to fish or to eat fish.[11]

Fish Avoidance in Africa

As in the American Southwest, fish avoidance in Africa is found particularly among peoples who live in arid and semiarid regions (Figure 34).[12] This account, therefore, concentrates on those regions. We will first consider fish avoidance among the ancient Egyptians, then, in succession, among Nubians, Berbers, Cushites, and native peoples of eastern and southern Africa.

Ancient Egyptians

The ancient Egyptians seem to have been more concerned with animals, both domesticated and wild, than any other people of the ancient Mediterranean and Near East. Their concern derived from the concept of *maat,* under which the natural world, including animals, was considered divine and permanent. This contrasted with the human world, which was constantly changing and often subject to anarchy.[13] It was because of this view that the ancient Egyptians incorporated animals into cult activities, and that several fishes, particularly the oxyrhynchus (*Mormyrus* spp.) (Figure 35), lepidotus or Nile barbel (*Barbus bynni*), and, to a lesser degree, the Nile perch (*Lates niloticus*), became sacred.[14] There were centers of worship of such sacred fish. One was the community the Greeks called Latopolis (modern Isna), where *Lates niloticus* was sacred and where numerous latus fish mummies have been uncovered. Another was Oxyrhynchus (now El Bahnasa), where *Mormyrus* was revered and bronze models of it have been found.[15]

In such communities and the districts surrounding them, the flesh of the sacred fish was forbidden food.[16] They were not necessarily avoided in neighboring districts, however, a situation that sometimes led to controversy. One example, mentioned by Plutarch, involved the people of Oxyrhynchus, who were offended that the residents of nearby Cynopolis ate the sacred fish of the Oxyrhynchites. Their response was ritually to kill and eat a dog, which was sacred to the Cynopolites, an act that led to fighting and considerable damage.[17]

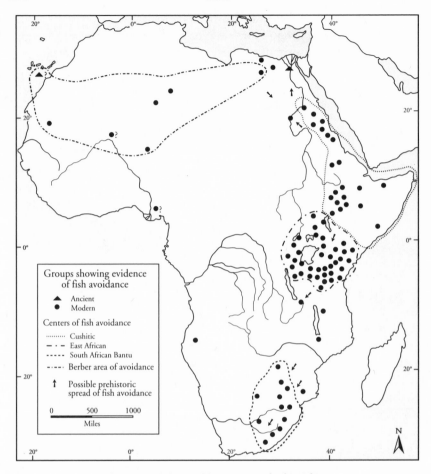

34. Map: Avoidance of fish as human food in Africa.

Returning to the avoidance of fish in general, we see that for most people in ancient Egypt fish was a highly regarded food (Figure 36).[18] Fish remains and fishing implements are found in Predynastic Egyptian sites (before c. 3100 B.C.). Representations of fish and fishing are common in temples and tombs in Old Kingdom (c. 2686–2181 B.C.) and

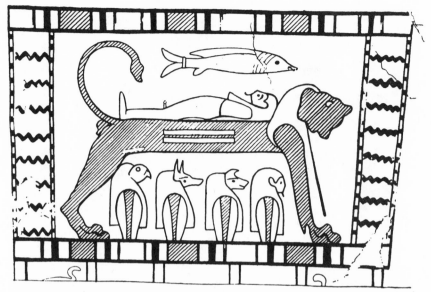

35. Oxyrhynchus fish in ancient Egyptian funerary scene (from Ahmad Kamal, *Annales du Service des Antiquités de l'Égypte*, 1908).

New Kingdom (c. 1570–1085 B.C.) times. On the other hand, fish were rejected as unclean food and not usually eaten by Old Kingdom nobles. Fish were not mentioned in the longer offering lists in Old Kingdom times. They were not offered to the dead, and indeed a person who ate fish was not allowed to enter a funerary chapel.[19] In addition, the ancient Egyptian word for abomination was depicted by a fish sign, and likely represented the lepidotus, the fish most widely considered to be sacred.[20]

The rejection of fish declined in later times, and there are indications that certain pharaohs even made fish offerings to deities.[21] In the times of Herodotus (c. 484–425 B.C.) and Plutarch (c. A.D. 46–119), fish was consumed by most lay Egyptians, though it was banned to priests.[22] One explanation given was that in the struggle between the deities Seth and Horus, the associates of Seth turned themselves into fish to avoid the wrath of Horus.[23] This is why, in a sacrament once a year on the ninth day of the month Thoth, ordinary people prepared and ate fish outside their front doors. Priests, on their part, burned fish outside their doors, but did not eat them.[24] The association of fish with Seth is

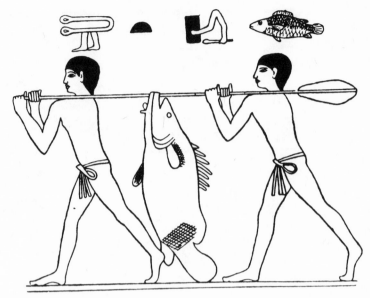

36. Ancient Egyptian men carrying a large fish (from W. M. Flinders Petrie, 1892).

also clearly shown at the annual festival held at Edfu, when, in honor of Horus, worshippers crushed fish beneath their feet.[25]

We do not know whether ancient Egyptian priests came to reject fish as food because of its association with Seth. Nor do we know whether the rejection reported by Herodotus and Plutarch was a survival from Old Kingdom times. As for Old Kingdom nobles' rejection of fish, Bates has argued that this came about because of an increase of cattle herding or the ascendancy in the Nile Valley of a powerful group of cattle owners who rejected fish on religious grounds.[26] This raises the question whether Egyptian fish avoidance was of Egyptian origin or whether it derived from non-Egyptian peoples, especially Nubians, Berbers, or Cushites among whom the avoidance was also found.

Nubians

The Nubians are an agricultural people who live along the Nile in southern Egypt and the northern Sudan. They are of mixed Negroid-Caucasoid background, and their language is related to those of the Nilotes to the South. Through much of history, however, they have been greatly influenced by Egyptian culture and religion.

Nubia has long been an impoverished land, from which men migrated to Egypt and elsewhere to find work, commonly leaving their wives and children behind. Despite their poverty, however, Nubians failed to make as full use of the Nile fish resource as they might have. In the early years of the nineteenth century, Burckhardt reported that the Nubians even lacked fishing equipment. The only exceptions were at the first and second cataracts of the Nile, where fish were sometimes captured in nets.[27] A few decades later, Pückler-Muskau made similar observations, that in the areas of the Nile south of Aswan where he travelled, Nubians failed to make use of the rich fish resource.[28] Early in this century, Schäfer was surprised that his boatmen in northern Nubia failed to supplement their diet by fishing.[29] Though he did observe fishing at Dongola, the fishing tribes and castes at Dongola seemed not to be true Nubians.[30]

Stimulated by my interest in the matter, K. W. Butzer, working with an expedition to Nubia in the 1960s, reported that at Elephantine, Nubians had no strong general prejudice against fishing or fish eating, but they were vague about the latter. They claimed that they did catch and eat fish, but Butzer found good evidence to the contrary, and concluded that their claims were based on their wish that the questioners regard them favorably.[31]

One recalls, in regard to Nubian fish avoidance, the inscription carved on a basalt block at a temple that Nubian king Piankhi (c. 730 B.C.) built at Jebel Barkal (Napata). The inscription reveals that Piankhi, conqueror of Egypt, refused to permit into his palace those Egyptian nobles who were uncircumcised and were fish eaters. The reason given on the inscription is that fish eating is "held in abomination in the royal house."[32] Some scholars think that the Piankhi inscription may simply reflect general Nubian views that prevailed at the time. Others have suggested that Piankhi's Nubian dynasty was of Libyan (Berber) origin. If so, one wonders whether his views may have been of Libyan origin or, as an alternative, survivals of the views that occurred in old Egypt along its southern borders in conservative Nubia.

Berbers

Fishing and fish eating are the rule in contemporary North Africa west of Egypt, with fishing locally important along the shores of the Mediterranean and the Atlantic, where it is carried out by Europeans and indigenous groups. It is also practiced in the interior wherever conditions are suitable, as along rivers of the Atlas Mountains, though fish consumption here is lower than in coastal areas. Even in the heart of the Sahara Desert, however, fish are not completely absent, and fishing is practiced to some extent.

Where fish avoidance occurs in the region, it is usually found among Berbers, its original inhabitants but now a minority. When one finds Arabs who reject fish as food, Berber ancestry is suspected. The Arabic-speaking Awlad ʿAli of western Egypt, for example, have contempt for fish,[33] but they are said to be a mixed Berber-Arab people. Fish avoidance is also reported for most Moors,[34] the Caucasoid people of Mauretania and adjacent areas, who are mainly pastoral. The majority of Moors speak Arabic, but scattered groups speak Berber, which is taken as evidence that the Arabic-speaking Moors are of mixed Berber-Arab origin. It seems likely that their fish avoidance derives from their Berber ancestors.

That fish avoidance among Berbers is not a recent phenomenon is clearly shown by the ban on fish among members of the ascetic medieval Berber religion (eighth to twelfth century A.D.) of the Barghawāṭah, who lived in eastern Morocco.[35] In modern times, the best-known Berber fish avoiders are Tuareg peoples (Ahaggar, Ajjer, and eastern Iwllemmeden Tuareg). These are pastoral groups who migrated into the Sahara under pressure from the Moslem Arabs who invaded North Africa. Though certain Tuareg groups, under Islamic influence, no longer avoid fish, others persist in their traditional views. The literature provides few explanations of Tuareg fish avoidance, most saying only that fish is banned, taboo, or "taboo for no apparent reason."[36] In any case, the matter was one that could generate strong feelings. Among the northern Tuareg (Ahaggar and Ajjer) in the middle of the last century, for example, nobles not only refused to eat fish themselves but also were displeased when others did so. Thus, their black slaves were not allowed to use the common drinking vessels for a while after they had eaten fish.[37]

Other Berber groups reported to have avoided fish are certain ancient Guanche inhabitants of the Canary Islands (those of Las Palmas), and the natives of Siwa Oasis in western Egypt. At the time of initial European contact, the Guanche of Las Palmas not only failed to eat fish but also lacked knowledge of how to capture them.[38] Late in the last century, the Berber inhabitants of Siwa Oasis, though their lakes contained abundant small fish, did not eat them at all, though Arabs who came to Siwa did fry and eat them.[39] Even as late as the 1930s, Cline was able to say the same thing, that the Siwans eat no native fish.[40]

Like the Arabs, the Teda, a black people of Nilo-Saharan speech whose country centers on the Tibesti, seem to lack any prejudice against eating fish. One reads of women and children catching small fry in pools of water and eating them. One also reads that southern Teda are unusually fond of dried fish brought in from the Sudan.[41] Nor is fish avoidance found among the Fulani of West Africa, who are believed by some to be of ancient Saharan origin. The same is true of the Nilotes of the southern Sudan. Indeed, in that region, the only fish avoiders I have uncovered are the Didinga,[42] who may have become so through contact with Cushites of southwestern Ethiopia.

Cushites from South Coastal Egypt to Somalia

This area of fish avoidance is in Northeast Africa from the southern Red Sea coast of Egypt through Eritrea and Ethiopia to Somalia, a region that in some places (coastal areas bordering the Red Sea and Indian Ocean, and inland regions with streams, rivers, and lakes) is blessed with abundant fish. Neither the Amhara nor any other Semitic people of Ethiopia appear to avoid fish. Instead fish avoidance seems to be limited to certain Cushitic peoples. These dark-skinned Caucasoids have lived in Northeast Africa since great antiquity, long before the early invasions of Ethiopia by Semites from South Arabia (c. 1000–400 B.C.) and the Arab invasions of Egypt and the Sudan that began in the seventh century A.D.

Fish avoidance is well documented for the northernmost Cushites, the Beja nomads (Ababda, Bisharin, Amarar, Hadendowa, Beni Amer) found from southern Egypt to Eritrea. Most of them are said to be contemptuous of fishermen and to avoid fish even at times of severe food shortage.[43] Despite this, there are certain fish-eating Beja living along the shores of the Red Sea. The latter are believed to be descendants of the ichthyophagi ("fish eaters"),[44] primitive fish-dependent peoples reported in antiquity by Strabo,[45] Diodorus Siculus,[46] and Pausanias[47] as living along the Red Sea.[48]

Fish avoidance has also been reported among a few remnant groups of agricultural Cushites (Agau of Sahalla, Qemant) in northern highland Ethiopia.[49] It is also found among various Cushites (Galla, Sidamo, Walamo, Kafa, Somali, and other peoples) in southern Ethiopia and Somalia. Such avoidance, however, is by no means universal among these groups.

Cushitic fish-avoiding peoples vary in their attitudes toward fishing and fish eating. Among some, feelings are quite mild, as with a group of Agau we visited in northern Ethiopia. When asked about their failure to make use of the fish in a nearby river, a tributary of the Nile, Agau men initially claimed ignorance, politely insisting that they did not know how to catch fish. If they had the needed skills, they claimed, they would catch fish and eat them. Further inquiry revealed another minor objection, that fish are bony and difficult to eat. Other observers have reported stronger objections among other Cushitic groups. Among these are the Haruro (Western Sidamo) living on an island in Lake Margherita, a south Ethiopian Rift Valley lake rich in fish. One evening, according to R. N. D. Read, a group of Haruro men watched him closely when he was preparing fish for his companions. In an effort to film their reaction, suddenly and with no warning he offered a piece of fish to one of the Haruro. The man smiled and the other Haruro men laughed. Then, "shaking his head and finger from side to side [the man] muttered something which when translated would surely mean . . . 'Uh! uh! . . . you can't fool me! I wouldn't touch THAT!'"[50] A more specific Haruro objection is that, if a person were to eat fish, his teeth would fall out.[51] Other Cushitic peoples say that fish are dirty water snakes and that fish eating is shameful, as shown in the Somali taunt quoted at the beginning of this chapter.[52] A. Fischer reported that for certain Galla the smell of fish was very unpleasant. He also observed, ". . . a member of this tribe would fly into a great rage if one touched him after handling a fish."[53] An extreme case is that of the Walamo, who in the past even put to death persons who broke their fish taboo.[54]

Among Cushites where fish avoidance occurs, fishing and fish eating may be practiced by some classes or in some districts. Such persons are not, however, considered respectable by others, who commonly look on fish as a low-class food and regard fishermen with scorn and refer to them in derogatory ways. Among the Kafa, for example, fishing is not done by true Kafa, but by a caste of pariah hunters, the Manjo.[55]

Indigenous Peoples of Eastern and Southern Africa

Much of East Africa is arid or semiarid, yet it enjoys an abundant fish resource in some places, most notably its great lakes, rivers, and the Indian Ocean. Some groups make good use of this fish resource, whereas others refuse to catch or eat fish.

George P. Murdock believes that Cushites are responsible for introducing the custom of fish avoidance to East Africa, and for encouraging other ethnic groups to adopt it there.[56] Whether or not he is correct, all the Southern Cushites of Tanzania on whom I have information (Fiome, Iraqw, Burungi, Alawa) are reported as avoiding fish. So do certain East African Nilotes and Bantu, but only, Murdock argues, groups from areas where Cushites seem to have lived in early times.

My search has uncovered fish avoidance among various Nilotic peoples of East Africa, among them the Maasai, Turkana, and Suk. Fish are found in almost all the larger streams in Maasai country. Yet Maasai are reported as having a dread of fish, which they despise and refuse to catch or eat.[57] Even when rinderpest reduced their herds drastically late in the nineteenth century, Maasai persisted in refusing to eat fish as long as they still had cattle.[58] It is true that, at one time or another, certain Maasai lost so many cattle that they were forced to settle down and become farmers, and that such peoples usually became fish eaters. The Maasai who remained pastoralists, however, looked on such fish-eating groups with scorn.[59]

One finds similar reports for Turkana pastoral groups living near Lake Rudolf in Kenya, who, even though the lake has abundant edible fish, look on it as a food of last resort.[60] There are Turkana who fish in the lake, but they live apart from, and are looked down on by, the pastoralists.[61] In a similar manner, the Suk have contempt for fishing and leave this activity primarily to the poor. Indeed, there is a Suk saying that, if a well-to-do man does eat fish, his cows will no longer give milk.[62]

Fish avoidance is also found among the Hima and Tussi,[63] pastoral Bantu-speaking groups believed to be of Nilotic origin, as well as among Bantu speakers in various parts of East Africa. One traditional explanation of Bantu fish avoiders is that fish are too much like snakes and lizards, and thus unfit to eat. Some Nandi even call them lizards.[64] If a Kikuyu does eat fish, he is considered ceremonially impure.[65] Though Nyoro cultivators practice fishing and eat fish, fish are forbid-

den to Nyoro pastoralists, who will not even permit them in their cattle
kraals.[66] The strength of feeling some Bantu have about fish eating is
clearly demonstrated in the account of a Kamba manservant who, after
long employment by Europeans, had taken up fish eating. Just as he
and his European employer were ready to partake of a fish dinner, the
servant's wife arrived. She had not seen her husband for over a week,
and had walked for more than an hour to reach the camp. Yet she was so
offended at seeing him about to eat fish that she turned around at once
and left without speaking.[67]

It may be significant that in East Africa fish avoidance is found no
farther south than Tanzania, at the southern margins of Cushitic and
Nilotic settlement. This may be related to the fact that pastoralists,
who are conspicuous among East African fish avoiders, were impeded
by tsetse-fly belts in Tanzania and beyond in their attempts to migrate
southward. As a result, Bantu groups of Zambia and northern Mozam-
bique were protected from pastoral dominance, and nearly all of them
make dietary use of fish.

The same can be said of the Bantu of the Congo Basin and of peoples
of West Africa. There is, however, another center of fish avoidance
in southern Africa. The origins of this center are unknown, whether
fish avoidance developed independently in southern Africa or whether
it was introduced. In either case, no general avoidance of fish occurs
among the earliest inhabitants of southern Africa, Bushmen hunters
and gatherers. It also seems to be quite rare among their linguistic relatives, the Hottentots, a herding people.[68] For this reason, in seeking an
explanation of fish avoidance in this part of Africa, it seems best to focus
on the Bantu, among whom the trait is more common.

Fish avoidance was found among many Bantu groups in southern
Africa, among them the Zulu, Xosa, Swazi, Tswana, Ndebele, and
others. Among some ethnic groups, all people avoided fish. Among
other groups, the trait was observed only in certain areas, or by just
one sex, or by certain clans, castes, or classes. As one early nineteenth-
century observer wrote about the Bantu ("Kaffirs") of southern Africa,
"They have as great an antipathy to fish as to swine's flesh." He added
that they "would as soon think of sitting down to a dish of snakes as
to partake of any of the inhabitants of the deep."[69] As in East Africa,
these fish avoiders insisted that fish were unclean water snakes, and they
considered it disgusting and demeaning to eat fish. Certain southern

Tswana, for example, abhorred persons who ate fish.[70] The very touch of fish was too much for some, as among native household servants who gave up their jobs rather than cook fish for Europeans who employed them.[71] A fish avoider among fish-eating peoples might persist in his avoidance, and present it as a mark of distinction. Webster cites such a case, of a Zulu boy who lived among the Thonga, but, unlike them, rejected fish, and, as a result, claimed a higher social status.[72]

In modern times, European influence has led many Bantu in southern African to abandon their anti-fish stance, but this has not been true everywhere. In the 1930s, one observer reported that among the Venda, young boys often caught and ate fish. At the same time, it remained an unpopular food that old men and women refused and would not allow people to bring near their houses.[73] Among the Tswana around Gaberones, southeast Botswana, in the 1970s, fish avoidance persisted, but it was declining, at least in urban areas.[74] This came about for various reasons. Reservoirs near Gaberones had been stocked with fish. The government encouraged fishing, and even brought in some fishermen from the Okavango area of northern Botswana to instruct local people in fishing techniques and fish preparation. In addition, patients, without being informed beforehand, were given fish to eat as part as of their hospital diet. Canned fish, moreover, became available in shops, and in forms (for example, chunks or fillets) quite different from an entire fresh fish.

Returning to the question of the origin of fish avoidance among the Bantu in southern Africa, scholars have noted that they share various culture traits with cattle-herding peoples of East Africa to the north. One suspects, therefore, that fish avoidance may have been introduced from East Africa at some unknown date by cattle-herding groups who managed to bypass or penetrate the tsetse belts without losing all their animals.

Southwest Asia and the Greeks and Romans

Frobenius and von Wilm as well as Lagercrantz regarded African fish avoidance as a "Hamitic" culture trait,[75] presumably introduced to Africa from Asia at some ancient date. Despite this, to my knowledge neither they nor any other scholar has looked seriously at fish avoidance in Southwest Asia or in Asia as a whole.

Southwest Asia

Arabia is the land deserving of first consideration because it is immediately across the Red Sea from the lands of the Cushitic fish avoiders. Fishing and fish eating are well documented for various coastal areas of the Arabian Peninsula. In addition, camels, cows, other livestock, and even dogs may be fed fish heads or fish, whether fresh or sun dried.[76] As in Judaism, in Islam a fish meal symbolizes immortality,[77] and fish are mentioned in the Koran as suitable food for Moslems on pilgrimage.[78] There is no Moslem ban on fish eating among Arabs, though particular species may be rejected as well as fish not captured and killed in accordance with Islamic precepts. According to Niebuhr, the writings of early Moslem theologians say that, to be pure, fish should be captured by net or by hand when stranded by a receding tide.[79] Despite this, fish are also taken by other means by Arab Moslems today, though people do not always agree on the qualities that make a fish acceptable.

Even Bedouin Arabs have been reported as eating fish or practicing fishing,[80] and I have found only a few reports suggesting that some Arabians may be reluctant to eat fish. One of these said simply that Bedouins far in the desert eat fish, but "reluctantly and only in case of necessity."[81] The second, by Cheesman in the 1920s, said that camel herders, when offered a gift of uncooked cod, refused it, saying that they would rather eat snake. Cheesman adds that the herders had never seen fish before, and were uncertain about its permissibility for Moslems. Later, however, they were presented with cooked fish, and, after some argument, they ate it, and in succeeding days they would always ask for more fish.[82] Such reactions seem to reflect unfamiliarity rather than strong antipathy to fish of the sort found among the Cushites of Africa.

In other parts of Southwest Asia as well, the position of fish is quite different from that among the Cushites. In antiquity, fishing and fish use were widespread, and in many places, fish were of considerable dietary importance and played a rich and varied symbolic and ritual role.[83] The heartland of the Hittites[84] was in the interior, not on the coast, yet, though Hittite texts contain few references to fishermen, fish, including river fish and sea fish, were familiar to them. It seems that a certain amount of fishing was done in Hittite country and that, even if they were not consumed on a regular basis, fish played a role in diet.[85] They were eaten fresh or dried, and were even used in bread. Fish were also included in a good number of rituals, sometimes apparently as offerings.

In Mesopotamia, the Tigris and Euphrates rivers contained an abundance of fish in antiquity. Fish were also caught in streams, marshes, ponds, and even the sea. Fish are frequently represented in art,[86] as by Assyrian sculptors who depicted their waters as full of fishes of various types. There were also commercial fishermen in Mesopotamia, and fish were eaten and appear to have been important in diet.[87] That fish were fully acceptable as food is suggested by the fact that, in Sumer, they were served on the table of a king.[88]

It may be that in antiquity, as is true among certain modern peoples of Southwest Asia, fish, because of their fecundity, symbolized life. This would explain their being included among grave offerings at Ur,[89] and their use in later times in funerary rites as symbols of rebirth.[90] If so, they would have been especially appropriate in rites for mother goddesses, whose principal function was to assure human fertility and well-being. In keeping with this, major temples in Mesopotamia employed fishermen who were charged with obtaining fish as food for deities and temple staff, and this was a respectable activity (Figure 37). Nearly all deities received a basket of fish among their offerings. A few (some associated with water, some with fertility), moreover, received fish in prodigious amounts as the sole offering. In early Babylonian times, the goddess Ninni received fish sacrifices. She is described as wearing a fish cloak and fish sandals and carrying a fish scepter. She also sat on a throne of fish while she travelled on a happy ship laden with blessings, to which a multitude of fish came to honor her and make way for her vessel.[91] In Babylonia and Assyria, gods or priests are sometimes depicted as wearing fish dress[92] on what may be ritual occasions (Figure 38).

In Mesopotamia, impurity in humans was believed to have been brought on by sins committed or by spells cast by a sorcerer. This, in turn, enabled demons to take possession of the person and bring on disease and other problems. Thus, the main goal of many Mesopotamian rituals was to exorcise demons, to return them to their proper realms. This was done in a variety of ways, but birds were commonly used to carry away such evil, and fish also sometimes served. This is well illustrated in the prayer "May a bird take my sin up to the sky; may a fish take my sin down to the abyss!" In one such rite, carried out in connec-

37. Babylonian hero carrying fish (from Léon Heuzey,
Revue d'Assyriologie et d'archéologie orientale, 1904).

tion with "the evil of a creaking beam," "dust from the beam is put on a
live fish," which was probably returned to the river, serving as a "scape-
fish" to eliminate the evil. Whatever happened to the fish, because it
was impure, it was almost certainly disposed of in some manner and
not eaten.[93]

In Sumer and elsewhere in Mesopotamia there were restrictions on
the use of animals and vegetables in connection with rituals of one
sort or another, and on particular days of the year. Fish, along with
garlic, leeks, dates, pork, and beef, was among the foods that were
frequently banned, though apparently it could be consumed freely on
normal occasions.[94] Oppenheim has suggested that at one time fish
bans in Mesopotamia may have gone beyond this. He notes that,
whereas in early Mesopotamian literature many kinds of fishes are mentioned, in documents that follow the Kassite period (c. 1600–1157 B.C.)
fishing and fish eating are seldom mentioned. When fishes are identified, moreover, they are referred to by a generic term, with names of
specific fishes absent except in accounts relating to lexicography. It is
possible, Oppenheim speculates, that this reflects the development of
a popular (rather than a cultic) taboo on fish.[95] If such a taboo had, in
fact, developed, one might suspect the Kassites of having had a hand
in this. On the other hand, there is repeated mention of fish trade
in Neo-Babylonian and Neo-Assyrian times (first millennium B.C.),
which shows that fish continued to play a major role in human diet.[96]

38. Assyrian fish gods at the tree of life (from William Hayes Ward, 1910).

In classical accounts, the association of fish and religious cults in Southwest Asia is more clearly documented. Of special importance are repeated references to the Syrian goddess Atargatis.[97] Atargatis was mainly a goddess of fertility and life-giving water, and was tied to such Near Eastern fertility goddesses as Ishtar of Babylonia and Assyria and Astarte/Derketo of the Phoenicians and Philistines.[98] The temple of Atargatis at the cult center of Hierapolis (not far from present-day Aleppo) was described by Lucian (who was born in the Roman province of Syria in the second century A.D.).[99] It was, Lucian said, the largest and wealthiest in Syria. It was also an object of pilgrimage through-out western Asia. Lucian wrote that near the temple of Atargatis at Hierapolis, there was a lake (pond?) of great depth in which lived sacred fish which grew to large size, and where devotees swam in the waters daily while "performing their acts of adoration."[100] Ponds containing sacred fish were also found at all other temples of Atargatis,[101] as well as at shrines of the closely related fish-tailed Phoenician goddess Astarte.[102] That the sanctity of fish in Syria goes back much earlier is shown by Xenophon (c. 431–350 B.C.), who wrote of a river there full of large, quite tame fish that people regarded as deities and did not permit any-one to harm.[103] Athenaeus quoted the historian Mnaseas (c. 140 B.C.) as writing that, whenever devotees of Atargatis prayed to her, they would make "offerings of fish made of silver or gold."[104]

Mnaseas also observed that, though ordinary people were legally banned from eating real fish, they were required to bring fish to Atargatis, who liked to eat them. Her priests, he went on, daily presented the deity with such fish, attractively prepared and served, which, after being offered to the deity, were consumed by the priests. Burkert[105] writes that for Syrians every meal of fish was a controlled sacred act, and Cumont[106] describes Atargatis's meals as "mystic repasts [in which] priests and initiates consumed the forbidden food in the belief that they were absorbing the flesh of the divinity herself."[107] Diodorus Siculus (first century B.C.) wrote that Syrians in his day viewed fish themselves as gods and did not eat them.[108] The Attic poet Menander (342–292 B.C.) asserted that, whenever Syrians eat fish, their feet and stomachs swell, upon which they don sackcloth, sit on a dung pile along the road, and propitiate the goddess by humiliating themselves.[109] Even in the first century A.D., according to Plutarch, punishments were feared by the superstitious.[110] Atargatis, it was said, would chew through a violator's shins, and bring on body sores and dissolve his liver. At about the same time, the Roman poet Ovid (43 B.C.—A.D. 17) wrote that careful Syrians considered it a sin to serve fish, and would not foul their mouths with them.[111]

It is interesting that even in modern times, sacred bodies of water, whose fish are not to be caught and eaten, are found in the homeland of Atargatis. At Urfa (the ancient Edessa) in southeastern Turkey, an ancient pond dedicated to Atargatis, now adjacent to a mosque, still contains sacred fish in great numbers. Today, however, the pond is called Abraham's pond, and the fish, Abraham's fish. Fishing is prohibited there, and it is held that anyone who eats the sacred fish will die immediately. Urfa is only about eighty miles northeast of the ruins of the cult center at Hierapolis. Near Aintab (ancient Doliché) in Syria, perhaps ten miles from Hierapolis, is another pond that contains many fish that one is forbidden to catch. In addition, such inviolable fish are reported at other places in Syria, as well as in Lebanon, Turkey, and elsewhere in the region.[112] Of particular interest are accounts of the Yezidis, members of a syncretic religious cult of Kurdistan and nearby areas whose beliefs resemble those of old Assyrian and Iranian religions as well as Manichaeism and Nestorian Christianity. In the mid-nineteenth century, Badger reported that the Yezidis regarded nearly all fountains and springs as sanctified.[113] In addition, fish, because of their association with water, were called *moobârak,* "blessed," a word also used for other sacred things. Thus, only a few Yezidis of the low class ever ate any food that came from the waters.[114]

There are also certain reports by nineteenth-century travellers in Turkey that Turks did not consume fish even in times of scarcity. Travellers also noted that people had a prejudice against fish, and considered them unhealthy and the cause of illness.[115] Some travellers, after they became ill on eating certain fish in Turkey, concluded that fears of illness have a basis in fact. One is tempted to speculate, however, that such attitudes may represent an ancient survival, perhaps not of Atargatis and her cult, but of attitudes brought from Inner Asia, where, as we shall see, certain modern Turkic-speaking peoples reject fish.

Greeks and Romans

Returning to ancient times, one sees that Syrian merchants, mercenaries, and slaves are credited with spreading the cult of Atargatis to Egypt and Greece by the third century B.C.[116] One reads of Ashtaroth, who may have been Astarte (a goddess related to Atargatis), worshipped at Memphis in Egypt, and of one of the Rameses kings naming a son "loved of Ashtaroth."[117] Asherah (= Tanit), a goddess whose name apparently was synonymous with Astarte by the third century B.C.,[118] may have been carried to Greece by Phoenicians long before.[119] The persistence of the Atargatis cult is demonstrated by Apuleius, who, in a second-century A.D. tale set in Greece, writes of one of her itinerant priests.[120] In the Greek world, Atargatis was commonly seen as a manifestation of Aphrodite.[121] In addition, her worship there was often merged with that of Astarte, who also assimilated to Aphrodite.[122] As for the ban on fish, it appears to have been softened among the Greeks, for at Delos such a ban was observed for only three days prior to participation in cult activities of a Syrian deity, perhaps Atargatis.[123]

Asherah/Tanit and the related Astarte was also carried to Carthage, and Astarte reached Italy long before Roman rule extended to the eastern Mediterranean. Tablets, with inscriptions in both Etruscan and Punic, dating from about 500 B.C., were uncovered in 1964 during excavations of a sanctuary at Pyrgi. This is the harbor of Caere (the modern Cerveteri), an Etruscan city in western Italy not far from Rome. The Punic account indicates that the sanctuary had been dedicated to Astarte by the ruler of Caere, Thefarie Velianas, and it expresses his strong devotion to her.[124] One of the Etruscan inscriptions, in turn, is translated as "This is the temple (shrine?) and this is the place of the statue dedicated to Uni-Astarte" by Thefarie Velianas,[125] the local deity Uni (Etruscan homologue of the Roman Juno) being linked to Astarte. It has been suggested that the ruler in question may have been supported by the Carthaginians or that they imposed his rule on Caere.[126] In any case, one can only speculate on how much of Astarte's cult, as it was known in Asia, had been adopted. Even more speculative is the question of what impact, if any, the cult may have had on fish use among the Etruscans of Caere.

A statue of Atargatis herself has been identified in the ruins of a Syrian sanctuary in Rome,[127] and there are indications of a cult reminiscent of that of Atargatis elsewhere in Roman Europe. I am referring to the Rider cult of the Danubian provinces of the Roman Empire (including modern Bulgaria, Romania, Yugoslavia, and Hungary). That cult, whose name derives from a male god who rides horseback, also had a Great Goddess, whose most important religious symbol was the fish. On Danubian monuments, fish are usually depicted on a table, really a tripod, in front of the goddess, and, in one instance, on an altar. Fish (in several cases, dolphins) were among the altar foods provided in a banquet for a triad of deities, including the goddess and two equestrian deities. They were also part of "the sacred foods served to initiates" at a banquet.[128] Dölger has argued that the Great Goddess was the principal deity of the Danubian Rider cult. He has also argued that she was Atargatis, though assimilated with other deities having comparable traits.[129] Tudor, on the other hand, insists that there is no evidence that the Danubian goddess, like Atargatis, was associated with sacred bodies of water, and no documentary or archeological evidence for her origin in Asia. As a result, one can only guess as to what fish prohibitions, if any, her devotees were expected to observe.

There were also similarities between the worship of Atargatis and Cybele, mother goddess of Anatolia, whose worship reached Rome in 214 B.C. There, Cybele was known as the Great Idaean Mother of the Gods, and was usually worshipped with the god Attis. The Roman emperor Julian, in a hymn to Cybele composed in A.D. 362 at Pessinus, her cult center in Galatia, sought to explain the symbolic meaning of cult beliefs and practices. Julian wrote of various foods, including fish, that were banned during the spring rites of Attis involving castration. He noted, ". . . the use of all kinds of fish is forbidden." He also advanced reasons "we ought to abstain from fish, at all times if possible, but above all during the sacred rites." [130] In Rome, too, a ban involving food and drink, including fish, was observed during the spring rites; though some devotees would have favored a permanent ban, [131] I have uncovered no mention of a general fish avoidance among followers of Attis and Cybele in the Roman Empire (the cult reached not just Greece, Italy, and North Africa, but also more distant parts of the empire, among them Spain, Gaul, and Britain). Even without Cybele, there seems to have been a significant force against fish eating emanating from Southwest Asia to affect other parts of the Roman Empire as well.

The Levitican code of the ancient Hebrews [132] banned the eating of fish that lacked fins and scales. [133] Fish with fins and scales, [134] on the other hand, could be eaten, and, whether fresh or salted, in the Old Testament they were favorite foods, and in the Talmud, delicacies. [135] In addition, fish formed a significant part of Hebrew diet. [136] In Talmudic times, if not earlier, there were professional fishermen on inland waters, such as the Sea of Galilee, as well as along the Mediterranean coast. In Old Testament times, fish sellers from Tyre in Phoenicia are mentioned as being in Jerusalem. That city also had the Fish Gate, [137] which took its name either from the Tyrians or a nearby fish market. The Palestinian port of Acre on the Mediterranean seems to have been a major fish emporium in Talmudic times. Indeed, the expression "carrying fish to Acre" had a meaning similar to the English "carrying coals to Newcastle." [138]

As for the role of fish in Hebrew ritual and religion, ancient and modern, one notes that the Hebrews did not sacrifice fish, [139] and that the Bible banned the use of their likenesses along with other idols. [140] At the same time, it was believed that Jehovah created and blessed fish. [141] They were eaten on Friday night to honor the forthcoming Sabbath; the more observant a Hebrew, the more likely this was to be so. [142] The Hebrews, especially persons who observed the law, are described as little fishes. [143] Fish also symbolized fertility and were prescribed for pregnant women as leading them to have graceful children. [144] Such symbolism has continued among Jews into modern times, as in Bosnia, where Sephardic Jews conduct a "fish dance" at their wedding rites. In Morocco, the final day of the wedding feast is called fish day because, on that day, the bridegroom sends fish to his bride. [145] In what may have double symbolism, an Oriental Jewish bride would step over fish roe in the hope that she would bear children.[146] Fish were also symbols of good luck, protective against the evil eye,[147] and were viewed as food of the fortunate in heaven. They enjoyed a further symbolic role deriving from the great legendary sea creature Leviathan,[148] on which the blessed would dine with the coming of the Messiah, to represent the resurgence of the nation.[149] The eating of fish on Friday evening, according to some, anticipated and symbolized that banquet. In this connection, rabbis assured the faithful that the Leviathan had fins and scales, and that its flesh was kosher.[150]

It has been argued that the Christians took over the fish symbol in Syria, perhaps as a device to counter pagan cults such as that of Atargatis. It has also been noted, however, that there are parallels between Christian and Jewish fish symbolism, some of which Christians seem to have adopted from the Jews.[151] That Christ's initial disciples were fishermen from the Sea of Galilee makes it even more understandable that the fish became symbolic of Christ as the Messiah in early Christianity. It also explains why, like bread, fish was served in the Eucharist to represent his body and the future bliss his followers would enjoy. The fish also came to be a symbol for Christ's disciples and converts, who, in contrast with Jesus, and like the Hebrews mentioned above, were "little fishes."[152] On early Christian lamps, one sometimes finds a newly baptized person dressed in fish clothing (Figure 39).[153] This is in keeping with Christ's instruction, "Except a man be born of water and of the Spirit, he cannot enter into the kingdom of God."[154] Somewhat later came the awareness of an acrostic relationship with the Greek word for fish, whose letters were the same as the first letters of the words for Jesus Christ, Son of God, Saviour.[155]

Of special interest, from my perspective, is the fact that fish were permissible food during Christian fasts on Friday (day of Christ's crucifixion) and during Lent. This fact made fish critical in Lenten diet, when flesh was not permitted, thereby creating a large demand for fish in the Christian world. As Pierre Deffontaines has noted, however, there were striking differences in availability of fish from one European country and region to another. Some, especially in the interior, simply did not have a large enough fish resource to meet demand. This encouraged long-distance trade in fish, much of it dried or salted cod. Cod fishermen left for the fishing grounds off Iceland and Newfoundland in September, and returned before Lent. Important, too, were the special

39. Early Christian lamp with new convert in fish dress (from Raffaele Garrucci, 1872–81).

needs for fish on Fridays, which had a striking effect on the weekly rhythm of economic activity. European fishermen worked particularly hard on Wednesdays and Thursdays to catch fish for Friday consumption. Fish were carried on special trains, sometimes in two sections, that ran each week from coastal ports to interior cities such as Paris and Basel. Problems of supply were especially serious for interior areas, and this encouraged the establishment of fish ponds there. Deffontaines notes that many monasteries, whose fasts were more numerous and rigorously observed, were set up near lakes or marshes, and were leaders in pond-fish cultivation.[156] From whatever perspective one views the situation, the conclusion is inescapable that Christianity has been a strongly positive force in encouraging fish consumption.

Returning to the classical Greek world, fish sacrifice was quite rare, and normally fish were eaten without such rites.[157] On the other hand, there were various waters, usually associated with deities of water and fertility, whose fish were inviolable to the public, as in ancient Southwest Asia. Pausanias wrote that people were afraid to catch fish in a lake at Aegiae, which, on its shore, had a temple of Poseidon (god of the sea, rivers, and other fresh waters; patron of fishermen) and was named after him. The fear was that persons who caught fish there would turn into fish.[158] Pausanias also wrote of a spring at Pharae whose waters were sacred to Hermes (who, among other things, was a god of fertility), and whose fish, which were dedicated to him, were not caught.[159] Pausanias described the fish in certain coastal waters near Eleusis as sacred to the fertility goddesses Demeter and her daughter Persephone/Kore,[160] and said that only their priests were permitted to catch fish there.[161] Diodorus Siculus, in turn, wrote that at Syracuse, the Greek city in Sicily, there was a fountain sacred to Artemis (goddess of the wild, perhaps originally a mother goddess), and that its many large fish were holy, not to be caught and eaten by humans.[162] Persons who did eat them in desperate times of war were severely punished. Among these were rebelling slaves who should have known better than to eat forbidden fish, because they were under the leadership of Eunus, a prophet of Atargatis who could have told them of the risks involved.

Certain Greek deities also seem to have had broader concerns relating to fish. The mythical Nestor is quoted by Plutarch as saying that the priests of Neptune (Poseidon), who was considered the first father, never eat fish because humans and fish both originated in liquids.[163] Plutarch also wrote of Poseidon's priests at Leptis rejecting all sea foods, and of Aphrodite, who had been born in the sea, having a kinship with all sea creatures, which, therefore, are sacred and which she does not like to be slaughtered.[164] In addition, devotees of one cult or another would not eat fish of one or more species temporarily, as was the case with persons being initiated in the Eleusinian Mysteries.[165]

Also interesting in the classical Greek world were vegetarians, whether individuals or groups, who included fish among avoided flesh foods. One such group consisted of women known as Bees (Melissai), devotees of Demeter who lived a clean, virtuous life, and ate only vegetarian food.[166] A second group was the Orphics, a mystical cult claiming inspiration from Orpheus, mythical hero and singer. Orpheus had said that it was murder to kill a living creature. He also said that, if humans are to return to their former state in closer association with the gods, animal sacrifice and flesh food must be rejected. Because Greek life was based on such murder, the Orphics renounced and were marginal participants in that life. They lived as wandering beggar priests and fortune tellers, ascetics who consumed no meat, eggs, beans, or wine.[167] Perhaps most noteworthy and explicit in their fish avoidance, however, were the Pythagoreans, a philosophical and religious society (sixth century B.C. to fourth century A.D.) established among Greeks in southern Italy, but later dispersed widely in the Greek world. Little is known of Pythagoras with certainty, and one is forced to approach his thinking from the perceptions of others who may have lived long after his time. Pythagoras emerges as a reformer committed to striving for high moral standing. He believed in friendship, generosity, piety, marital fidelity, and a simple life and avoidance of excess, including excess of food and drink. He opposed killing, including animal sacrifice, and suggested that sacrifices to the gods be modest personal items such as cakes, honey, and incense. He also believed in the soul's immortality, in reward and retribution after death, and in reincarnation of the soul in humans or other animals. He was convinced that there was a strong bond between humans and other animals, or at least animals that might possess souls. Because of this, he held that humans should behave with justice toward them. In keeping with the above, he was a vegetarian who convinced many to live on raw vegetables and water, and to give up eating flesh, including fish, as well as beans.[168] Certain classical observers suspected that Pythagoras's fish avoidance may have derived from Egypt, with whose seers he had exchanged ideas and whose practices he imitated.[169] Another possibility is that fish avoidance, like other Pythagorean rules, derived from the practices of other cults or the "popular magico-religious beliefs that lay behind the cult rules."[170] In any case, Pythagoreans adhered more strictly to the ban on fish than to ones on other sorts of flesh. Various explanations for this were advanced, including one that Pythagoreans were especially reluctant to kill fish, unlike many other animals, because fish did not compete with humans in any way and caused them no harm.[171]

Though fish may have occupied a special place in their thinking, Pythagorean rejection of fish seems nevertheless to have been part of a general avoidance of flesh. It also appears to have derived from objections to taking life and from the view that animals have souls. Marcel Detienne has argued, however, that one must go beyond these views if one is to understand Pythagorean behavior. He notes that there were differences in strictness among Pythagoreans. The less strict would eat certain kinds of flesh, and were interested in reforming society rather than rejecting it. On the other hand, the most committed Pythagoreans, known as the Pure, ate no flesh food at all, made no flesh offerings, and avoided contact with all hunters and butchers. The actions of the latter group thus involved a deliberate renunciation of the world and its ways. This included the animal sacrifice so central to the politico-religious life of their day.[172] Their behavior, as a result, was a political as well as a moral statement. However strictly Pythagoreans and other vegetarians may have followed such restrictions,[173] this did not deter other classical Greeks from fishing, or prevent fish from being important in their diet, particularly in coastal areas.[174]

Before leaving our consideration of ancient Greece, I feel compelled to bring up the puzzle of Homer, who may have lived in the ninth or eighth century B.C. In his great epics, the *Iliad* and *Odyssey,* Homer looks back to still earlier times. Various ancient writers have observed that Homer pictures the waters surrounding Greece as rich in fish and looks on fish as "an element of prosperity," yet he never presents anyone eating fish.[175] Moreover, there are passages in the *Odyssey* suggesting that Homer's heroes fished only when driven to it by hunger.[176] This evidence has been interpreted in various ways by ancient and modern observers. Meleager of Gadara (third century B.C.) wrote that Homer was born in Syria and argued that he had simply followed the custom of his native land in describing his heroes as abstaining from fish.[177] Others have suggested that, although fishing was practiced and fish were eaten in Homeric Greece, there were class differences in the acceptability of fish as food, with the upper classes rejecting them. It has also been argued, on linguistic grounds, that the heroes' attitudes reflect ones held in the ancient Indo-European homeland from which the Greeks came. In that homeland, the argument goes, there were few sizable bodies of water, and fishing was alien to their pastoral way of life.[178]

The last two suggestions can be questioned: whether in fact the heroes' attitudes were typical of upper-class Greeks in Homer's time, and whether they reflected conditions in the early Indo-European homeland. If that homeland was in the Pontic-Caspian region, as many authorities believe, fishing has been an activity of people living there since antiquity.[179] Whether this was so among all early Indo-Europeans, including pastoral groups of Inner Asia, is an unanswered question.[180] In our search for further evidence of fish avoidance, we now turn eastward to the arid and semiarid lands from Turkestan to the western margins of the Indian subcontinent.

Iran, Turkestan, Afghanistan, and Pakistan

Fish in Iran are obtained from the Persian Gulf and the Gulf of Oman, as well as the Caspian Sea and other interior waters. The interior waters include even qanats, those great tunnels excavated for irrigation purposes, which are capable of providing a good supply of fish.[181] In ancient Iran, fish were eaten as ordinary food or in connection with sacrifice.[182] The early literature, moreover, contains abundant evidence of ichthyophagi, groups with an unusual dietary and economic dependence on fish who lived in coastal Iran. Various classical writers reported such groups along the shores of what today are southeastern Iran and Pakistan, or in the islands of the Persian Gulf.[183] Modern European observers reported similar groups along the entire length of the Persian Gulf from Basra to Hormuz.[184]

Iran has long had religious groups strongly committed to vegetarianism, for example, the Manichaeans and the most learned of the Magi.[185] I have failed, however, to uncover any ancient or modern evidence there of an avoidance centering on fishes of all kinds, though there may have been bans on catching and eating the fish of certain streams, ponds, or tanks, commonly at mosques or other holy places.[186] At a mosque at Kumishah (near Isfahan), there are waters containing fish considered to belong to the Prophet Mohammed, and at one time they had gold rings on their noses and fins.[187] This is a striking parallel with Lucian's observation of a sacred fish in the lake of Atargatis at ancient Hierapolis. That fish, Lucian said, was "ornamented with gold," and had a gold pattern on its rear fin apparently to show that it was dedicated to her temple.[188]

In the arid regions stretching from Turkestan to Afghanistan and Pakistan, fishing and fish eating are also widespread, and in many places fish are of considerable dietary importance. Fishing has been important, for example, on the banks of the Oxus River and in the Aral Sea, and along the Makran Coast and coastal Sind of what today is Pakistan. The Makran Coast was included among the lands of the ancient ichthyophagi, and indeed the very word "Makran" is said to derive from a Persian word meaning "fish eaters."[189]

At the same time, there have been clear indications of fish avoidance from place to place in the region. In Turkestan among the Kazakh, Kirghiz, and Turkomans—Turkic peoples of pastoral nomadic tradition—fish are said to have been little valued. They were scorned, avoided, or rarely consumed other than by certain poor peoples living along rivers or lakes.[190] This fits with the travellers' observations, cited above, of nineteenth-century views of fish in Turkey. That this is not a recent development is shown by the thirteenth-century account of Friar William of Rubrouck, who wrote of Tatars living in the Ukraine whose land contained waters rich in fish, but who didn't even know how to catch them. He found this in striking contrast with the importance of fishing among Ruthenians living in a nearby village on the river Don.[191] One writer has observed that Turkomans believe that eating fish brings on fever.[192] Another reported that the oasis dwellers in the Emirate of Bukhara, most of whom were Uzbek (Turkic) Moslems, considered fish eating to be *makruh* (disapproved of from a religious perspective but not a punishable act).[193]

As for Afghanistan and Pakistan, one reads in certain Baluchistan district gazetteers dating from early in this century of Brahui, members of the only surviving group of Dravidians in Pakistan, scorning fish and dates when they first came to the Makran Coast. These gazetteers also mention tribesmen in interior Baluchistan, most of them Afghans, who did not consume fish.[194] Such behavior is confirmed by other early and modern reports of other Afghan tribes who do not appear to eat fish even though their rivers have fish in them.[195] In addition, most Hazara, a Persian-speaking (Indo-European) people of Mongol affinities in Afghanistan, seldom fish, and seem to have a "traditional aversion" to consuming fish.[196] In contrast with the above, I have uncovered two references to inviolate sacred fish in Afghanistan.[197]

Also of note are the nineteenth-century Kafirs ("unbelievers"), those conservative, pagan, Indo-European (Dardic) groups whose descendants still live in the Hindu Kush region of Afghanistan and what today is Pakistan. The rivers of Kafiristan were rich in fish, yet the Kafirs detested them and could not be made to eat them because they eat "dirt" and are unclean.[198] One observer reported the Kafirs shuddered at the very idea of eating fish, much as Westerners might react to that of eating rats. A second possible case of fish avoidance in Pakistan is that of another Dardic group, the people of Gilgit in general or at least the Shin of Gilgit. Ordinary folk in the Gilgit Valley, according to one account, eat fish when they can obtain it, but rulers and upper classes reject it, saying that it has a vile smell.[199] Another account says that before they adopted Islam, the Shins viewed fish with abhorrence, implying that fish avoidance was more general.[200]

It is of special interest that fish avoidance in the region from Turkestan to Pakistan occurs among peoples of quite different linguistic affiliations, among them: Dravidian, that language family confined largely to peninsular India; Indo-European; and Turkic. We are thus not dealing with a characteristic found among a single ethnic or linguistic group, but one that occurs across a broad region.

India

In Vedic India, the fish (*matsya*) was conspicuous in mythology as a symbol of fertility, and was capable of bringing good luck and fertility to humans.[201] This perception of fish continues today among Hindus and other groups in India. Representations of fish may be found on houses to protect against evil forces, and are sometimes also found on the walls of Hindu temples.[202]

Because of their association with fertility, fish have played a role in marriage rites since antiquity. Thus, in the *Baudhāyana Gṛihya-sūtra* (500–100 B.C.?), one reads of a newly married couple catching a fish in a cloth. After asking a religious student what the future holds, they are told "children and cattle,"[203] and then they make an offering of the fish "for longevity and prestige."[204] Of special interest, the offering is made at the root of a fig tree of a species (*Ficus glomerata*) that served in various rites of "masculine significance,"[205] perhaps in the hope for male offspring. In addition, the offering is intended for herons, symbolic of deceit and betrayal,[206] perhaps to make sure that they would not interfere in the natural course of things. In modern times, fish play a role in Hindu marriage rites in ways remarkably similar to those of the past.[207] Among the Holeya, a caste of field workers and village servants of Kanara, South India, for example, a newly married couple goes to a river or tank, where, using their wedding mat, they scoop up some fish, which they release after kissing them.[208] In some instances, the couple may take one fish home, and place its scales on their foreheads as a guarantee of fertility.[209] In one case, after the fish had been caught in a cloth, the bridegroom was asked, "Did you see a cow or a son?" He, apparently with hopes of having many children, pointed to the fish, symbolic of fertility, and replied, "Yes, they are here." Similar marriage rites are reported for other castes of South India, though some, such as the Shivalli Brahmins of South Kanara, may only pretend to catch the fish.[210] If a suitable body of water is not close at hand, Brahmins of Kanara make a fish of wheat flour, drop it into a container of water, then remove it and place some of the paste on their foreheads.[211] In Bengal, Hindu rites of marriage invariably involve fish. In East Bengal, a pair of fish is dispatched, along with other gifts, to the house of the bride or groom before the pair is wed.[212] Fish are considered an auspicious gift, and may express the hope that the couple, like fish, will have many offspring. When the bride enters her husband's home for the first time, with one hand she holds her husband's hand, and in her other hand she carries a fish. During the first several days after the wedding, moreover, the bride and groom are expected to eat fish daily. If, for some reason, they do not do so, it is a sign that the bride will be an early widow.[213]

The status of fish among Hindus is further enhanced by the belief that fish are manifestations of the supernatural force of a river or stream, and related to the human dead whose ashes have been consigned to their waters and whose souls may enter fish.[214] The latter belief, in transmigration of souls, might bring on a temporary local ban on fishing,[215] but not a permanent one.

We turn from a general background on fish symbolism and status in India to fish use and avoidance in ancient times. In sites of the Indus Valley civilization (c. 2500–1700 B.C.), there are remains of fish in homes and among offerings to the dead, as well as representations of nets on potsherds. In addition, net sinkers and fish hooks have been uncovered. All this attests to the fact that fishing was a regular activity of the Indus Valley people, and that fish was a significant dietary element. In Indus Valley levels at the site of Balakot along the seacoast, indications are that fishing was intensive (fish bones accounted for nearly half of all bones uncovered), and it is thought that fish may have been traded to interior communities.[216] Indeed, several fish uncovered at the interior city of Harappa were almost six feet long.

Fish signs are prominent in Indus Valley script, and some Indus communities had baths whose waters are believed to have served in ritual purification. However, in the absence of an accepted decipherment of Indus Valley script and lack of other literary evidence, it is impossible to tell what the ritual position of water and fish may have been.[217]

There has been speculation about fish use and avoidance among the Indo-European Aryans, those pastoral people who entered India from the northwest sometime in the second millennium B.C. The *Rig-veda* mentions fish once,[218] but there is nothing to indicate that the Aryans ate it. In part because of this, some Indologists have supposed that the early Aryans had an aversion to fish, that fish eating was not in favor with them. At the same time, many words for fishermen occur in the *Yajur-veda* (700–300 B.C.?), which leads Prakash to infer that by then the Aryans were consuming fish.[219] Their acceptability as food is shown, moreover, in the Gṛihya-sūtras, rules relating to household behavior (c. 700/600–100 B.C.), in which fish are offered to Brahmins attending ceremonies, and included among the first solid food a father gives an infant son whom he wishes to be quick (like a fish).[220] It is data of this sort that have led certain writers to conclude that fish were widely consumed in Vedic India.[221]

At the same time, the view that fish should not be eaten has long been found among Hindus, especially Brahmins, as well as members of other religions of Indian origin. The Jains, however, seem to be the only religious or ethnic group in India to abstain strictly from fishing and fish eating. Their abstention is based entirely on commitment to ahimsa, for they do not view fish or any other animal species as sacred (except, possibly, for the snake).

Hindus, who, as we have seen, compose 80 percent of India's population, share the Jain commitment to ahimsa and vegetarianism. Unlike Jainism, however, Hinduism has not eliminated fish eating among its adherents, and members of most Hindu castes will eat fish of one sort or another. Fish are usually rejected as food, however, by Brahmins and members of certain other castes (*jatis*) of high ritual status or ones seeking such status.[222] Their objections may be on the grounds of ahimsa and vegetarianism, or because fish are considered disgusting creatures like snakes. Some Hindus also say that a fish eater is at risk of ritual pollution because fishermen, who are of low caste, have touched them. Such views may extend even to the use of fish meal as fertilizer, a practice to which devout Hindus sometimes object.[223] In some cases, however, dietary need has overcome whatever reluctance to eat fish a caste may have. One sees this reflected in a song of the Nayar caste, who formed the aristocracy along the Malabar Coast in South India: "Then there is a kind of banana of the sea (fish). And the Nayars cannot live without it."[224]

There are even reports of certain Brahmin castes (Bengali Brahmins, Oriya Brahmins, Brahmins of certain parts of Bihar, Saraswat Brahmins of northern India, and Kashmiri Pandits) eating fish.[225] Such behavior is perhaps most readily understood for Bengali Brahmins, for their homeland has a very dense population, a persistent shortage of animal protein, and an abundance of fish in its many deltaic waterways and ponds as well as in the sea. Despite the temptation such abundance presented, there were restrictions in ancient times against Bengali Brahmins eating fish, and, though restrictions seem to have eased, even today some strict Brahmins still refuse to do so.[226] Bengali commentators have found fish eating difficult to reconcile with Hindu sacred writings.[227] This means that Bengali Brahmins who do eat fish, as well as members of certain other castes, have been troubled about the effect fish eating may have on both their ritual purity and social standing. One method employed to avoid guilt is to call fish the flower of water, implying that they are not flesh but vegetable food.[228] Another way is to claim that the fish they eat are cleansed by the waters of the holy Ganges in which they live.[229] Despite this, shame remains, and devout Bengali Hindu widows are reported as giving up fish eating in an apparent effort to gain merit.[230] One also finds such feelings among other Bengali castes. One such caste is the Kaibartta, who for a long time consisted of two caste sections, one that lived by agriculture and the other by fishing. In time, the agricultural Kaibarttas, whose occupation was a respectable one, banned all intermarriage with the fishing Kaibarttas, whose occupation was despised. In addition, the agricultural Kaibarttas gained recognition as a separate caste under a new name, the Mahishya.[231]

In addition to caste being a factor in the acceptability of fish among Hindus, there are local and regional differences. In fact, anthropologist J. H. Hutton has said that differences in the acceptability of fish by locality may well exceed those by caste status. In support of this, he notes that the majority of respectable castes in Bengal eat fish, whereas in arid Rajasthan in western India the very thought of consuming fish is disgusting. He also observes that in Assam, traders from Rajasthan refuse to allow fish to be carried on their trucks. One was even overheard as saying that hauling fish for human consumption "was as bad as carrying snakes."[232]

Hindu fish avoidance is related not only to a person's caste and place of origin, but also to his or her sect affiliation. Various sects or subsects encourage fish avoidance, but Vaishnavism (worship of the deity Vishnu as well as Rama and Krishna, his principal incarnations)—as part of its strong commitment to vegetarianism in general—is mentioned most frequently.[233] It would be wrong for an adherent of Vaishnavism either to eat fish or to offer fish to Vishnu or his leading incarnations.[234] One reads, for example, of a poor boy in South India who took fish curry to offer to Krishna, and was belittled and reprimanded for it.[235] That such feelings can also affect others is shown by the case of some Bengalis who settled in Uttar Pradesh at Brindaban, a templed community sacred because of its importance in Krishna lore. The Bengalis were so affected by the sanctity of the place that they eliminated fish from their diet.[236]

It is interesting that in South India, where fish is a staple food among coastal peoples, in most places people do not offer it even to non-Vedic deities. This appears to be independent of Sanskritization, and Eichinger Ferro-Luzzi suggests that it may be based on the fact that the "cold blood of fish would not suit the temper of blood-relishing village deities." One group of fishermen in coastal Andhra Pradesh told her, on the other hand, that they did not offer fish because it is smelly, and that its presence would keep people from focussing on the gods.[237] In the same vein, in Tamilnad among a group of fishermen and other non-Brahmins who offered fish curry to the gods, dried fish, rather than fresh fish, was preferred.[238]

Despite the Bengali Brahmin justification of their fish eating in terms of fish being purified by waters of the sacred Ganges, other Hindus have a different view of the matter, insisting that fish living in sacred waters should not be eaten. Such sacred waters may be rivers or streams, lakes, ponds, tanks (artificial bodies of water often associated with temples),[239] or waters of other kinds. As we have seen, the view that fish living in such waters are themselves sacred is widespread in Eurasia, and in India, too, it goes far back in history. The Great Bath at Mohenjo-daro, ancient Indus Valley city, is believed by some to have been the predecessor of the ritual tanks of later India.[240] Three centuries before the beginning of the Christian Era, Megasthenes, Greek ambassador to the Indian court of Chandragupta, reported attractive palace tanks that contained "fish of enormous size but quite tame."[241] The literature on modern India contains numerous references, from various parts of the subcontinent, to sacred fish, often in places with special ties to Vaishnavism or Shaivism. Hardwar, "the gate of Hari" (= Krishna), a city located where the Ganges enters the plains, is one place where sacred fish are found. So is Mathura, place of Krishna's birth on the Jumna River, and Benares, holy city of Shiva along the middle Ganges.[242] Brahmins strongly resent any effort to fish in such holy places, and instead of fishing, one sees people feeding fish. To gain religious merit, devout Hindus at such places may make thousands of flour balls, wrap them in bark or paper on which the name Rama is written, and then cast them into the water for fish to eat. When a fish eats the balls in the name of Rama, the donor's salvation is assured.[243]

Tanks and ponds containing sacred fish are also numerous. In Poona District alone, there were reported to be about twenty-seven sacred bodies of water of this sort.[244] Such fish are revered, protected, and fed, whether by individuals who bring food for that purpose, and thereby gain merit, or from temple funds or ceremonial food offerings. One reads of fish of special sanctity having rings of gold attached to their fins.[245] With such treatment, fish usually become numerous, large, and very tame. As a result, fish may be called at times of feeding, as by voice or dinner gong, and they may come boldly up to a person and take food from his or her hand.[246] The feeding and protection of sacred fish are a touching manifestation of religious belief, but where Hindus avoid eating all fish, the avoidance seems to derive from their regional origins and caste and sectarian affiliations.

Among the other religions of modern India, those of Moslems, Parsis, and Christians were introduced from abroad and, with respect to fish, differ strikingly from Jain, Buddhist, and Hindu thinking. Most Moslems, though they may refuse fish of certain kinds,[247] have no general objections to fishing or fish eating. They may even invent ingenious explanations to permit them to eat fish not killed with the proper Islamic benediction.[248] At an official level, the government of the Islamic Republic of Pakistan made a deliberate effort in the 1950s, later abandoned, to encourage fish consumption (and reduce the slaughter of livestock) by establishing two meatless days a week. There are, it is true, sacred waters at mosques and elsewhere whose fish are not eaten. There are also some Indian Moslems who reject all fish, as through coercion by Hindu vegetarians,[249] but these are an exception rather than the rule.

The Parsis, an ethnic and religious minority concentrated in the area of Bombay, are descendants of Persian Zoroastrian immigrants who left their homeland after the Moslem conquest. For them, fish are fully acceptable as food, auspicious items exchanged on such joyful occasions as marriage.[250]

Fish are also consumed by Indian Christians and tribal people. S. T. Moses, a Hindu writing of South Indian Christians, calls them immoderate in their consumption of fish, noting with surprise that even the most pious Christians eat fish on Fridays and during Lent.[251] Among tribal people in India, fishing is generally a respected occupation and fish an acceptable food. For the Lakher of eastern India, fish symbolize purity and good health, and are prepared and served when a house is dedicated.[252] The mythology of some Bhil tribal people of Gujarat contains many references to fishing, an activity in which even their gods participate;[253] and the Purum of Manipur in eastern India make offerings of fish to certain deities.[254] Though fish are not plentiful in the country of the Saora of Orissa, they kill and eat them for various ritual purposes, such as assuring a good crop.[255] Fishermen may be concerned with water deities. This is so among the Khasis of Assam, certain of whose chiefs sacrifice goats to the river goddess before fishermen begin their annual fishing in the river Punatit.[256] Where one finds pressure against fishing and fish eating among tribal peoples, however, it can usually be traced to the great religions of Indian origin. The Meithei of Manipur, who have accepted Vaishnavite Hinduism, are one example of this. Though they have not been able to stop eating fish, the Meithei are not supposed to practice fishing.[257] The Sherdukpen, a tribal people of Arunachal Pradesh who have been influenced by Buddhism, continue to practice fishing and eat fish, but their lamas can eat only fish that have been killed by others.[258]

Buddhism and the Spread of Opposition to Fishing and Fish Eating

The case of the Sherdukpen calls attention to the fact that Buddhism, though now of minor importance in India itself (1994 est.: six million adherents, 0.7 percent of India's population), has not only shared the vegetarian commitment of the Jains and Hindus, but has also been a leader in spreading vegetarianism, including the rejection of fish, to foreign peoples.

In India among early Buddhists, as in early Europe[259] and western Asia, the fish symbolized fertility. In Zimmer's words, it represented "the breeding force of the sea, the fecundity of the waters out of which come organisms without number, procreative and self-engendering."[260] Because of the fish's dietary importance, the fish symbol, like the cornucopia, also represented abundance and plenty, and was often depicted on Buddhist altars. In a strikingly different way, fish also symbolized *matsya-nyāya,* "the law of the fish," the sort of life without moral restraints that is found among creatures living in the waters.[261] Against the background of Buddhist commitment to ahimsa, one might expect an awareness of the predatory role of fish to influence its use as food.

Buddha (who died about 500 B.C.) did not forbid fish to his monks. Instead, they were expected to adhere to the rule of the "threefold-pure," under which a monk was not to eat fish that he saw, heard, or suspected to have been caught in order to feed him.[262] There seems, however, to have been a controversy among the Buddhist clergy members as to whether such restrictions sufficed, whether they should eat fish under any circumstances. Devadatta, whose campaign for greater strictness was mentioned previously, is said to have urged that the order adopt five further rules of behavior, including one requiring monks to avoid fish throughout their lives.[263] The Buddha's rejection of that proposal meant that, ever since, members of the Buddhist clergy have been permitted to eat fish, but only if the fish were obtained in accordance with the rule of the threefold-pure.

The controversy over the acceptability of fishing and fish eating among Buddhists has, however, persisted over the millennia since. This is well demonstrated in the many Buddhist sculptures showing fishermen being hooked and pulled toward a fiery furnace.[264] On the other hand, fish have continued to be consumed by Buddhists. Even during the reign of the Mauryan emperor Aśoka (third century B.C.), one of India's greatest rulers, there seems to have been no general ban on fish eating. The emperor was committed to ahimsa, and he stopped royal hunters and fishermen from carrying out their normal activities. In addition, there were general bans on molesting or eating certain kinds of fish. There were also restrictions on fishing and selling fish on certain days. These, however, are explained in terms of maintaining the fish resource and providing a steady supply of fish, which were an important commodity and were regularly eaten in Mauryan times.[265]

In present-day Buddhist Sri Lanka (Ceylon), Sinhalese in general make known their dislike of eating fish.[266] They may also object to certain methods of fishing as cruel. Virtually all Kandian Sinhalese, for example, regard it as wrong to fish with a hook. Some believe it disgraceful for a female of any age to catch fish.[267] At the same time, fishing and fish eating continue among the Sinhalese, and fish prepared with onions, salt, and chili peppers is a favorite dish.[268] In modern India, there is a Buddhist movement among low-caste Hindus who become Buddhist converts in an effort to raise their social status. New Buddhists, however, remain fish eaters, as they were before conversion.[269]

In Buddhist Tibet, or West Tibet (Ladakh), on the other hand, there are clear manifestations of anti-fish sentiments, some of which are of Buddhist inspiration, whereas others may be survivals of pre-Buddhist Tibetan religious beliefs. Some travellers in Tibet have observed that fish are infrequently eaten, that some Tibetans do not eat them at all, that they are taboo or unacceptable as food, or that fishing is banned by religion.[270] Other travellers indicate more specifically the Buddhist associations of the bans: that lamas are not permitted to eat fish; that the ban derives from the Dalai Lama, supreme Tibetan religious authority; that the ban on fishing springs from Buddhist reluctance to take life; and that people are convinced that fish contain impurities which, if consumed, will send one to hell.[271]

Though Tibetans insist that it is a sin to take the life of any living creature, the sin increases with the number of lives destroyed. This makes fishing particularly offensive, for it commonly involves taking many lives, whereas the slaughter of a yak involves just a single life. Killing fish is also offensive because they are unable to cry out for help or mercy, leading to the Tibetan saying "To kill the tongueless fish is an unforgivable sin."[272] Somewhat different are the objections that fish eat human corpses cast into a river and that human souls may enter fish, making eating them an act little different from cannibalism,[273] and that fish are unclean, sinful creatures little different from snakes and frogs.[274] There is also fear that fishing may anger local deities, who might flood a river and obstruct passage of a caravan, or create a hailstorm to injure the caravan's livestock.[275]

It is understandable that lamas and devout Buddhist laymen not only refuse to fish or eat fish, but also sometimes try to stop others from doing so. A lama once told me that if he saw someone fishing he might chide that person, or he might overlook the violation. Fish may also be liberated by Buddhists in an effort to gain merit. For example, a lama from Darjeeling travels frequently to the town of Siliguri thirty miles away to release live fish in a river in the interests of devout Buddhists. In one case, a Tibetan woman purchased fish in Siliguri, had them carried downstream to prevent fishermen from catching them again, after which they were blessed by a lama before they were liberated in the river.[276] The Tibetan woman's intent was to eliminate sins committed by her long dead mother, but fish liberation may also be made in the interests of the living.[277] One reads, for example, of a lama who, in order to help a sick person, negotiated the release of five hundred fish at a fishing village. Then he had the sick person repeat this prayer: "By virtue of my having ransomed the lives of these animals, let health, longevity, prosperity, and happiness perpetually accrue to me."[278]

Despite such sentiments, many ordinary Tibetan men (women less often) persist in fishing and fish eating. This fits with Palmieri's observation that, despite their Buddhist commitment to ahimsa, very few Tibetans reject meat as food.[279] Fish eating is reported even in Lhasa, Tibet's capital and the Dalai Lama's traditional headquarters. A group of Tibetan monks told me, however, that fish are served, not in Tibetan restaurants in Lhasa, but in Chinese restaurants, and then eaten largely by Chinese diners. There is, however, one place in Tibet where the ban has been eased. This is in a desert lacking in agriculture and pasture, where no food is available other than fish in a river.[280] Despite its permissibility, such fishing leads others to hold people of that region in low regard, much like butchers, who also take life.[281] A Tibetan nomad once told me that, in his district, fishing was carried out mainly by poor men, but not by better-off men or by women. To avoid offending their women, fishermen would sneak cooking utensils from their houses, and cook and eat their fish away from home. Then, they would cleanse the utensils thoroughly before returning them.

There is abundant evidence that among Mongols, too, many people in traditional times looked down on fishing, and rejected fish as food.[282] This situation, which, according to Lattimore, derived from the needs of a nomadic way of life, has, however, been greatly changed in recent decades.[283] North of Mongolia in Siberia, on the other hand, there seems to have been no general avoidance of fish. Groups there practice fishing and eat fish according to local availability and dietary need.

Before turning to the Buddhist lands of Southeast and East Asia, I would first emphasize the importance of fish in many parts of the region. The dietary staples in much of Southeast Asia are rice and fish, often in fermented or dried, salted forms, obtained from the sea or inland fisheries. This is illustrated in Thailand by the saying "rice on the land and fish in the water." It is also illustrated by the facts that virtually all market stalls and village stores have dried fish for sale, and that peasant families eat fish of some sort at every meal.[284] In Burma, too, no market, large or small, would be complete without a section devoted to the sale of fish and fish products.[285] In Cambodia, where the Tonle Sap has unusually rich fish resources, nearly all rural folk participate in fishing, whether as a full- or part-time activity.[286] There and elsewhere in Indochina, not only are fish a dietary essential, but the liking for fish is a culture trait shared by all peoples.[287] In East Asia, the Japanese and Koreans are noted for their fishing activities and the variety and importance of fish in their diets. The fishing activities of the Chinese are less well known, but since ancient times they have used an impressive range of fishes. They have employed a broad range of fishing methods. They have been world leaders in fish farming. Indeed, in some coastal regions per capita fish consumption may be comparable to that of Japan. Even where fish consumption is low, this reflects cost and availability, for most Chinese relish fish.[288] One could go on to document the importance of fish and fishing in modern Southeast and East Asia, but the general pattern would be the same.

Nevertheless, Buddhism has been active in spreading the views of fish and fishing described for India and Tibet. During periods of heat and drought, when the water of ponds and tanks has almost dried up, Burmese may collect live fish in jars of water and carry them to a river for liberation, a highly meritorious act.[289] Along the Irawaddy River, Buddhist pilgrims may also catch tame fish and place gold leaf on the heads, as they do on statues in their pagodas.[290] Burmese Buddhists express scorn for fishermen, regard them as outcasts from respectable society, and expect that fishermen will ultimately suffer punishment for their sin of taking life.[291] In Thai cosmology, a special place is designated for the punishment of persons who kill fish or support the practice.[292] Thus, special efforts are taken to avoid guilt for killing fish. Thai fishermen pretend that fish are not killed by removing them from the water. Thai fish eaters, on their part, may insist that they bear no responsibility for such killing either. In Thailand at the Songkran Festival, held at the time of the traditional new year, live fish, whether purchased or caught specially for the occasion, are freed to gain merit, and in some places, processions of girls in festive dress carry bowls of fish to the river for release on this joyous occasion.[293] It is clear, however, that efforts to avoid guilt have not been altogether successful. When Thai people reach old age, they are expected to become complete vegetarians, giving up fish as well as meat in an effort not to take life any longer. This fits with the Thai view that fishing by elderly persons is "pitiful and wrong."[294] Yet, despite the above, the Thai royal family is reported as granting fishing rights to the highest bidder.[295] Even Buddhist clergy are permitted to eat fish as long as the fish are provided in a way that does not violate the rule of the threefold-pure.

The Buddhist fight against fishing and fish eating in East Asia is yet to be told, but Buddhist thought has affected even lands as strongly dependent on fishing as coastal China, Korea, and Japan. In seventh-century Japan, for example, Emperor Temmu, apparently to reduce cruelty to animals, set down regulations as to methods of fishing. In the following century, Emperor Shōmu took additional actions, such as ordering the liberation of cormorants used by fishermen,[296] an act intended both to stop their use in fishing and to gain merit from their liberation.[297] Despite such manifestations of Buddhist belief, there was no general ban on fishing and fish eating in Japan, though, as we have seen, there were Buddhist bans on meat, including beef. It is true that because of the greater number of lives lost, some Buddhists consider it a greater violation of ahimsa to kill fish than to kill oxen. Yet the Japanese failed to ban fishing, and, in at least one case, sought to extend the permissibility of fish to meat. The case, reported by Chamberlain early in this century, involved displaying the term "mountain whale" above certain restaurants in Japan to indicate that they had venison for sale. The logic, he pointed out, was this: "A whale is a fish. Fish may be eaten. Therefore, if you call venison 'mountain whale,' you may eat . . . it. . . ." In any case, Chamberlain contends, Buddhist failure to ban fish in Japan appears to have been a "concession to human frailty."[298] Indeed, it is hard to imagine how the Japanese, one of the world's premier fishing peoples, could have survived such a ban.

The first Indian Buddhist monks to arrive in China (around the beginning of the first century A.D.) were committed to ahimsa and vegetarianism. Since that time, Confucianist and Taoist views of vegetarianism have been influenced by Buddhism. The Buddhist religion,

40. Cormorant fishing in China (photo by Stephen F. Cunha). Reprinted with permission from *Food in China*. Copyright CRC Press, Inc. Boca Raton, FL.

however, has remained the nation's most vigorous advocate of those practices, whether through direct action by laymen and clergy or by royal decrees.[299] In A.D. 691, for example, the empress Wu, a devoted Buddhist, raised Buddhism above Taoism, and promulgated various laws to enhance it, including a ban on all fishing and slaughter of animals. In a similar vein, there was a persistent but unsuccessful effort by Buddhists to ban cormorant fishing (Figure 40).[300] One notes also the Buddhist practices of liberating animals and of feeding fish, birds, and other creatures at their temples in China. Sometimes animals were kept at Buddhist temples or monasteries, as, for example, fish and turtles in ponds where people could gain merit by feeding them.[301] Buddhist religious tracts, in turn, decried the killing of animals and eating of flesh in ways little different from those found in Hindu tracts in India.[302]

Chinese vegetarian cuisine has had a strong association with Buddhism, and was stimulated by the example of temple and monastery food. Pilgrims travelling to distant temples and monasteries would normally eat only vegetarian fare, and near temples one usually found several vegetarian restaurants. Within temples and monasteries, Buddhist monks and nuns would eat only vegetarian dishes, and visitors, too, would partake of such fare. In the Peking area, people would go to Buddhist temples or monasteries for vegetarian meals, though urban restaurants, on request, also served them.[303] In some locales, people could also get vegetarian dishes at restaurants that specialized in them. Nevertheless, the ties with Buddhism have led many vegetarian dishes in China to bear names like "Buddha's Delight" and "Lo-han Grand Vegetarian Ensemble" (Lo-han are the lesser Buddhist temple gods). Chinese vegetarians became masters at preparing flavorful analogues, usually made of cereals and bean curd, that resemble fish or other flesh foods. Such analogues could bear such a close resemblance to flesh as to raise serious doubts about their nature and acceptability.

Understanding the everyday conduct of traditional Chinese in terms of philosophy and religion is difficult, because people spoke of the three belief systems of Confucianism, Taoism, and Buddhism as though they personified the concept of religion, with people commonly taking part in rites and accepting aspects of more than one of the movements. This has led to notable differences from one person to another in views of, and commitment to, vegetarianism. Despite this, many Chinese believe that it is wrong for a religious devotee to consume flesh. Such expectations were perhaps most marked for Buddhist clergy, with a list of items banned or usually avoided by Chinese Buddhist monks in the first half of this century,[304] including not only meat but also fish[305] and certain other food items. In a similar vein, Gould-Martin, on the basis of fieldwork and literary evidence, writes of a Chinese vegetarian diet called *su*, which is followed by Buddhists, and is based on ahimsa concerns as well as on Taoist wishes to attain immortality.[306] A *su* diet excludes meat, fish, dairy products, onions, garlic,[307] leeks, and alcoholic beverages. Vegetarianism might also be imposed at times of crisis, such as drought. In addition, many Chinese, at various times in their lives, made vows not to eat flesh. Such vows might have been made to a deity along with specific pleas, such as for longevity, wealth, good health, and male children. They might also have been made as part of a religious initiation, or in connection with the vegetarian associations found among both Buddhists and Taoists. Vows to avoid flesh were usually of limited duration, observed only at stated times or occasions. Vows for lifetime abstinence from flesh were far less common, made only by clergy and devout lay people, the latter more often women, especially widows.

Whether or not Hinduism, once found widely in Southeast Asia, acted in a way similar to Buddhism with respect to fish and fishing, I do not know. Bali is one place where Hinduism has persisted among an indigenous people. The attitudes toward fishing and fish eating there require further investigation, but Covarrubias sketched a situation quite different from the prevailing one in Southeast Asia. The Balinese, he observed, view the mountains, along with the lakes and rivers found there, as the places in which their deities reside. Thus they represent everything that is sacred and healthy, and provide fertility to the land. The sea, on the other hand, is a place fraught with peril from coral reefs, sharks, poisonous fish, and other creatures. Even more to be feared, however, are evil spirits that live there. Balinese in general cannot swim and rarely go into the sea, except to bathe along the coast. As for fishing, it is usually carried out on a small scale, and the majority of Balinese rarely eat fish. In the words of Covarrubias, "They are one of the rare island peoples in the world who turn their eyes not outward to the waters, but upward to the mountain tops." Whether or not this is related at all to their Hindu beliefs, he does not say.[308]

Conclusion

Among modern African fish avoiders, whether in the Sahara or Northeast, East, or South (southern) Africa, the pervasive explanation is that fish are unclean water snakes, and that it is disgusting and degrading to eat them. In Africa, the Cushites of the Ethiopia region may be central to understanding the distribution of fish avoidance. The trait is widespread among Cushites there. If Murdock is correct, they may have spread the trait to the Bantu and Nilotic peoples of East Africa. From that region, it may have been carried to southern Africa by cattle herders, perhaps in the first millennium A.D. Along the northern margins of Cushite occupance, however, their role in spreading fish avoidance is less clear. Indeed, there are early evidences of the avoidance among Nubians, Egyptians, and Berbers that may have an independent origin. One is struck, however, by the prominence of fish avoidance in arid and semiarid regions and among groups of pastoral tradition, and the virtual absence of a general fish avoidance in tropical rain forest areas. Among pastoralists who avoid fish, moreover, it is usually impoverished individuals and groups who consume fish, an act that confirms their lowly social status and assures its continuation. Pastoralist scorn for fish and fishing has been made easier by the steady supply of protein they obtain from the milk and meat of their herds. They have been, moreover, in an excellent position, because of their physical vigor, fighting ability, and military conquests, to encourage at least some agricultural peoples to avoid fish as food.

As for India, the major font of fish avoidance in modern Asia, three principal explanations of the rejection of fishing and fish eating are invoked. One, little different from those advanced by modern African fish avoiders, is that fish are impure creatures like snakes. A second Indian explanation for avoiding fish, absent in the American Southwest and Africa, is that it is wrong for humans to take the life of any living creature and to eat its flesh. One also finds in India the concept of sacred water, and the view that fish living in such waters, as at Benares, are also sacred and not to be eaten. Though observance of this rule seems not to have contributed to a general avoidance of fish in India, in the American Southwest, where, in the past, all water was considered sacred, all fish, along with all water creatures, were sanctified and not to be eaten.

To me, it is striking that the rejection of fish because of their impurity is the explanation found most widely in Africa and Asia. It is also notable that such fish rejection occurs principally in arid and semiarid sections of Asia and Africa, and that everywhere groups of pastoral tradition are prominent among fish avoiders. One suspects that, whether or not they were the first to reject fishes of all kinds as human food, pastoral groups were prominent in the dissemination of this practice. The rejection of fish because of ahimsa considerations, on the other hand, is very likely of Indian origin. Though fish are not rejected by all the adherents of religions of Indian origin, these religions, particularly Buddhism, were the means by which the avoidance was introduced to fish-dependent lands in Southeast and East Asia. One seems to be dealing with a culture trait, avoidance of fish as human food, that may have had multiple origins and that over many millennia in Asia came to have rich and varied socio-religious associations and patterns of observance.

9 CONCLUSION

Naturally a religious phenomenon is not purely religious; it also has a social aspect, a historical aspect . . . Yet no full understanding of religious matters is attained by resolving them into something else . . . It is a mistake to degrade religion into a political epiphenomenon . . . To a religious historian, the action in the foreground is not merely a reflection of the background.

—H. te Velde, *Seth, God of Confusion*

Purity is for man, next to life, the greatest good . . .

—the Vendidad 5.21

Do Avoidances of Flesh Foods Derive Primarily from Economic, Nutritional, and Health Considerations?

Many Westerners, if they are asked about our foodways (our cultural attitudes and patterns of behavior toward food) as they relate to flesh food, are quick to say that the types of flesh we eat are ultimately based on availability, cost, taste, nutritional value, and health considerations. Such persons ignore the fact that we, like other peoples in the world, in fact reject the majority of flesh foods readily available to us. Restrictions on the use of flesh foods, moreover, are usually more common than those on plant foods.[1] Edmund Leach has categorized the living creatures available to the English into those seen as edible or inedible; very few indeed fall into the edible category, and, even among these, many are consciously or unconsciously banned. This is because use of living creatures for food among the English, like all other ethnic groups, is influenced by "rules, prejudices, and conventions," many of which were established for unknown reasons in the distant past.[2] The result is that only after a potentially edible creature passes the cultural barriers to acceptability do factors like taste, availability, cost, and nutritional value come into consideration. Thus the food customs of the English, like those of other Western peoples, make no more sense—in terms of utilizing flesh that is available, cheap, tasty, nutritious, and without undue danger to our health—than do those of non-Western peoples. It is as questionable, in these terms, for Westerners to reject grasshoppers, dogflesh, and horsemeat as human food as for Hindus to reject beef or Africans to reject chicken and eggs.[3] Why we should continue to reject such flesh foods will become clear as we proceed, and here I would note only that such rejections derive from human cultures, and that it is far easier for a people to adopt a ban on a flesh food than to discard one. This is in part because once a ban is adopted it tends to be reinforced by strong feelings of disgust. Eating disgusting flesh may bring on nausea and vomiting; and, though this may be sufficient for people to dislike and avoid such flesh,[4] the bans may gain further support from religious sanctions.

Strength of Feeling Associated with Flesh-Food Avoidances

Some negative group attitudes toward the acceptability of flesh food are conscious and explicit, like those surrounding pork in the Islamic world. All Moslems are aware that the pig is unclean and pork unacceptable as food, and many Moslems openly express loathing for them. Other attitudes of this sort may not be as apparent, and people may even be unaware of them unless something, such as observing someone eating unacceptable flesh or threatening to do so, brings them to the surface. Consider the case of two young biologists in the United States who were engaged to be married. On a field trip, a caterpillar fell on the young woman's blouse and frightened her. Her fiancé removed it, laughed at her fright, and, apparently to demonstrate that her fear was groundless, swallowed the creature. Far from soothing her, his act so shocked the young woman that she broke their engagement. Another person might have overlooked such a violation or made light of it. Or the issue might have been evaded by pretending that the flesh was of a different and acceptable kind. We have seen that Moslem Iranians may permit a native cook who is preparing ham or bacon for a European to save face by simply calling the meat nightingale's flesh rather than pork.

Rather than overlooking the matter or providing an easy way out for a violator, people may express strong feelings of disgust when they see unacceptable flesh being prepared or eaten. Such strong responses are far less likely if a violation involves a food of plant origin, though the violator may be considered odd, made the object of ridicule, and lose social status. The Amhara of northern Ethiopia, for example, have traditionally associated eating the false stems of the bananalike *Ensete* plant, an excellent carbohydrate food, with ethnic groups whom they look down upon, but an Amhara simply loses status with his group by eating it, nothing more.[5]

The strength of feeling that can be associated with unacceptable foods of animal origin, however, is often of a different order of magnitude, for, as Tambiah has observed, animals are forceful vehicles in which ideas that are "highly emotionally charged" may be incorporated.[6] This is superbly demonstrated in the blunder that set off the Sepoy Rebellion of 1857–58, which rocked British rule in India. An already precarious situation, involving the Indian regiments, was fanned into violent mutiny by the rumor (later shown to have had some foundation) that the new Enfield rifle cartridges, which Hindu and Moslem sepoys had to place in their mouths to uncap, were greased with fat from cows and pigs. The one animal was sacred to Hindus, and the other, defiling to Moslems. Examples of strong individual reactions abound as well. Marston Bates tells of a French lady who, at a dinner party in South America, ate a dish that she found delicious. From subsequent talk, she suddenly realized that the iguana she had eaten was a lizard, and she became violently ill.[7] The explorer Prejevalsky reported that one of his Mongol guides nearly turned sick on seeing his European companions eat boiled duck, which like other types of fowl he considered unclean; in this case, the observation of others consuming it was enough to produce a reaction.[8] Mere mention can also have such an effect, which seems to have been Shakespeare's intent by including in the witches' broth for Macbeth a strange and revolting collection of products almost entirely of animal origin:

> FIRST WITCH   Round about the cauldron go;
> In the poison'd entrails throw.
> Toad, that under cold stone
> Days and nights hast thirty-one

Swelter'd venom sleeping got,
Boil thou first i' th' charmed pot.
. . .

SECOND WITCH   Fillet of a fenny snake,
In the cauldron boil and bake;
Eye of newt and toe of frog,
Wool of bat and tongue of dog,
Adder's fork and blind-worm's sting,
Lizard's leg and howlet's wing.
For a charm of pow'rful trouble,
Like a hell-broth boil and bubble.
. . .

THIRD WITCH   Scale of dragon, tooth of wolf,
Witches' mummy, maw and gulf
Of the ravin'd salt-sea shark,
Root of hemlock digg'd i' th' dark,
Liver of blaspheming Jew,
Gall of goat, and slips of yew
Sliver'd in the moon's eclipse,
Nose of Turk and Tartar's lips,
Finger of birth-strangled babe
Ditch-deliver'd by a drab,
Make the gruel thick and slab.
Add thereto a tiger's chaudron,
For th' ingredients of our cauldron.
. . .

SECOND WITCH   Cool it with a baboon's blood,
Then the charm is firm and good.[9]

Group Sanctions against Violation of Bans on Flesh Food

In many societies, conforming to bans of particular flesh foods is of utmost importance, and strong sanctions may be applied to violators. An Ethiopian Christian who ate camelflesh, which was regarded as a Moslem food, was once subject to excommunication; an orthodox Moslem or Jew who eats pork is likely to be ruled out of his group; and an upper-caste Hindu who eats beef is despised by his caste and deprived of his caste affiliation, a dangerous situation in rural India, where one's life is tied so closely to those of caste members. Where flesh-food avoidances are tied to established religions, as in the above examples, they tend to be strongly held and particularly difficult to modify. As Porphyry noted about the ancient Syrian avoidance of fish, the Jewish avoidance of pork, and the Phoenician and Egyptian avoidance of the flesh of cows, though many rulers have tried to change these ways, adherents would rather die than violate the rules that ban the eating of these animals.[10] Such strength of feeling should not lead one to overlook the fact that individuals may vary in their observance of bans on flesh food. This is because, as Laderman has observed,[11] food ideology, like other systems of belief, is subject to interpretation, justification, and change. There are ways of evasion and procedures for handling clear violations of the bans, the intent of which is to maintain the integrity of the food system while minimizing social and religious disharmony.

Ways in Which Bans on Flesh Food Are Observed

Flesh-food bans, besides differing in the strength of feeling associated with them and the severity of the sanctions supporting them, vary in the ways in which they are observed. Thus, prohibition of a flesh food may not pertain throughout the year but only at certain times, as during mourning, illness, on religious fast days, or other specific occasions of limited duration. It may relate only to the cooking or eating of a food together with other foods of one type or another. Some peoples of East Africa, for example, will not eat meat together with milk, a custom curiously like Orthodox Jewish observance.[12] Among the Maasai, this custom applies to all members of society, of whatever sex or age. Even among Maasai warriors, whose ideal diet—which they follow as much as possible—consists solely of meat, milk, and blood, the prohibition against eating meat and milk together is very strong.[13] A similar form of avoidance is found among certain Eskimo groups, who will not mix sea foods with land foods. There is also the case of the Nambikwara Indians of Brazil, who have many domesticated animals suitable for eating, yet keep them simply as pets, sharing their food with them, and playing and talking with them, but not even eating the eggs laid by their hens. The native peoples of the Amazon Basin are noted for their liking for pets, and their behavior may be viewed with great sympathy by many vegetarians and animal-rights advocates, but to the rest of us, it appears strange to keep all animals solely for affectional purposes.

A flesh ban may affect only particular segments of society, whether clans, castes, classes, or age, sex, or status groups. Persons whose services are vital to the successful functioning of the group, especially shamans and priests, are most often singled out. Malinowski has noted a Trobriand belief that, if a magician breaks the food avoidances associated with his magic, a crop failure will follow. Other bans may apply to specific age or sex groups, such as infants, children, women, or men. Among certain Australian Aborigines such flesh restrictions are gradually removed as children get older. The Binbinga, for example, forbid the newly initiated boy to eat snake, female kangaroo, wallaby, and a considerable list of other flesh foods. When, however, his whiskers are grown and he has made certain formal offerings of the foods to some old men who have a special connection with them, he is free to eat them. A Warramunga tribesman, on the other hand, is usually middle-aged before he is permitted to eat "wild turkey" (bustard or megapode?) and emu.[14]

The manner in which an animal dies often determines whether its flesh is acceptable. For some peoples the flesh of animals that die a natural death may constitute the bulk of the meat consumed, whereas other groups reject such flesh. Many groups prohibit the flesh of animals killed by predators. The Chukchee used to refuse the flesh of reindeer killed by wolves for fear they would become easy marks for their enemies. Other groups go still further, prohibiting the flesh of all animals not killed according to ritual observances. Most familiar, perhaps, are the provisions of that sort followed by Orthodox Jews, but ritual observances are also found among other groups, such as Moslems, who may refuse to eat even fish and locusts if they have not been killed in the proper manner or with the appropriate benediction. It was a special problem to us when on mule trip in Ethiopia, for accompanying us were Christians, Moslems, and one Jew (Falasha), and none of these groups would eat the flesh of animals killed by the others. Observance of a group's traditional means of slaughter is necessary to assure not only the well-being of the persons who eat the meat, but also the continued success and survival of the group. In one New Guinea village, when the traditional way of ritually killing pigs by deliberately cruel methods was forbidden, the people begged for permission to kill one pig by the traditional method, arguing that unless the mango trees heard the squeals they would not bear fruit.

Some restrictions against flesh food involve the condition of the flesh. Decayed flesh or that of diseased animals is often rejected, although there are groups who do not hesitate to eat such meat. Other restrictions apply only to particular parts of animals or to certain organs believed harmful to humans. There are restrictions, too, that apply to the flesh of all wild animals, that of all domesticated animals, or that of domesticated animals raised by members of other ethnic groups or other clans or villages. We have seen that the Murut of Borneo will eat only home-raised pigs and not those of neighboring villages. A final form of restriction is the one of primary focus in this study, that which affects an entire animal species.

Inequalities in the Distribution of Flesh

Differences in wealth and status often lead to differences in the distribution of available flesh food. In many Pacific islands and in the Northern Territories of Ghana, chiefs and other officials are singled out for preferential treatment in the distribution of flesh. Elsewhere members of prestigious groups have preferential status. All-male cult groups among the Lele of the Kasai region of Zaire have prior rights to hunt certain animals or to eat specific parts of them. Only a few small animals such as birds, squirrels, and monkeys are left for ordinary people to hunt and consume at will.[15] Among other peoples, older men are given special treatment when flesh food is divided. The Nuba of the Sudan treat their old men as privileged guests at feasts; when the flesh of game is available, a large share of it is presented to them as a matter of politeness or because they need it for various rituals.[16] On Alor in Indonesia, flesh food is viewed as the property of the men. At feasts, the principal times when meat is available, it is distributed to households according to the men in them; the men share it with their dependents, the women and children. The system of distribution thus reinforces the prestige of men in society.[17]

One should not, however, conclude that male prestige is the sole factor involved in restricting women's consumption of animal protein. Ellen M. Rosenberg, drawing on data from various parts of the world on sexual differences in diet, especially in regard to meat, places the matter in a broader perspective. While acknowledging that dietary restrictions of women may indeed by related to a society's prestige structure and may be supported by taboo, she argues that they are rooted in a desire to control population size. If a group wants to limit its population, according to Rosenberg, women, and on occasion children, will be subject to dietary restrictions, especially ones relating to animal protein. If, on the other hand, the group desires a larger population, the diet of women will be supplemented. Eichinger Ferro-Luzzi suggests a quite different reason for sexual differences in consumption of meat. She notes that in certain Hindu households where meat is eaten the husband usually eats meat, but the wife does not. This, however, is in a society where vegetarian principles are honored, where meat is not a prestige food, and where the husband's eating of meat is not a reflection of his status. On the contrary, the wife's refusal of meat enhances the regard in which she is held because it is based on her stronger commitment to "purity and hence her greater refinement." [18]

At the same time, denial situations are so common in the Old World as to contribute to the lack of an adequate supply of protein to many women, although as bearers of the young they are in particular need of it. In aboriginal Hawaii and other Pacific islands, as we have seen, women may be forbidden the flesh of pigs and chickens; and many peoples of Africa forbid chickenflesh and eggs to women but not to men. The Ngongo, a subtribe of the Kuba of the Congo area, go so far as to prohibit the flesh of all domestic animals to women. Even where women are not prohibited a flesh food, they may be discriminated against in the division of the meat. The Chukchee of Siberia carry this to great lengths: the Chukchee woman skins the slaughtered reindeer, cuts up the flesh and prepares it, and in return receives the leftovers and the bones after her husband has selected and eaten the choice parts himself. The Chukchee have a saying, "Being women, eat crumbs," which portrays the position not only of their women but also of women among various other Old World peoples. In addition to the restrictions on eating flesh food that apply to women generally, others apply under certain circumstances, as during pregnancy, nursing, menstruation, or during the child-bearing ages. Many groups, on the other hand, have customs that offset these restrictions and provide women with special flesh supplements or rights. The Hadza, hunters and gatherers of Tanzania, for example, share their meat with persons who ask for it, and there is a special obligation to give meat to pregnant women. [19]

Origin of Group Bans on Flesh Foods

Psychological Background

All bans on flesh food that we have considered reflect the human cultures in which they are found, including human perceptions of the animals in question, an animal's social and economic role, its relations with humans and gods, its ritual purity or impurity, and similar matters. Understanding a person's culture is thus a first step to understanding his or her behavior in accepting or rejecting flesh foods. The food behavior of individuals and groups is also rooted in psychology which, at least in part, is shared with other animal species. Before proceeding with culture-historical aspects of the flesh bans in question, therefore, it seems essential that I provide a brief background from a psychological perspective.

Fortunately, we now have available a series of studies, carried out by psychologist Paul Rozin and associates, which makes our task much easier.[20] These, in my opinion, are the most important contributions to our understanding of the psychological basis of group rejection of flesh foods in the three decades since *Eat Not This Flesh* first appeared. Perhaps most basic in Rozin's thinking is what he calls "the omnivore's dilemma," which involves humans along with other omnivores. The omnivore has the capability of consuming a broader range of foods than the carnivore or herbivore. This presents omnivores with a distinct survival advantage, but at the same time involves substantially greater risks because of the vast array of potential foods, many of which may be dangerous to health and well-being. The risk is increased because potentially harmful substances are ingested, taken into the animal's very body to become part of it. Humans, like other omnivores, are therefore faced with a dilemma—the need to try new foods in order to obtain adequate nutrition, and the danger new foods pose. One result is what Rozin calls neophobia, fear of unfamiliar foods. That such fears have been with humans since antiquity is shown in an Assyrian dream book: "If [in his dream] he [a person] eats meat he knows: peace of mind. If he eats meat he does not know: no peace of mind."[21] It is fortunate for human evolution and survival that neophobia has not kept humans from trying new foods, but it is a factor that we must take into account in considering flesh-food bans from a culture-historical perspective.

Neophobia may be a spontaneous response, as in the case of a man and woman who saw fields of artichokes in California for the first time. They were invited to try the artichokes, but answered with finality, "Oh no! We never eat strange foods." [22] Neophobia may also involve more deliberation. In either case, it seems to be the basis for the widespread rejection of the flesh of unfamiliar animals around the world, as among certain Guiana Indians who reject the flesh of animals, such as oxen, sheep, and goats, that had been introduced from abroad and were not native to their country. Though the Indians will eat such animals when no other food is available, they will do so only after a medicine man or old woman has blown on the flesh, apparently to expel the spirit of the animal.

One concern of a potential flesh eater is that by ingesting flesh he or she takes on undesirable qualities of the animal or part of the animal eaten. This is one aspect of the belief in what Rozin and his associates call "you are what you eat." [23] Flesh, blood, or organs of animals, on the other hand, may be deliberately consumed to obtain their desirable qualities. One reads, for example, that among various groups in eastern Africa people eat the flesh, heart, or blood of a lion or leopard to make them strong and brave like those animals. [24] Certain American Indian peoples ate dogflesh before a battle to gain the dog's courage. [25] In Nigeria, some people use roasted or fried dogs' eyes as an ingredient in a powder intended to improve their eyesight. [26] Such powders are used by many diviners and night watchmen, but there are also risks for a fearful user, who may start barking like a dog. [27] In this book, our greatest concern is with fear of undesirable qualities as it leads people to reject the flesh of entire species of animals. Examples of this are the avoidance of hare or deer lest a person become timid, or tortoises lest he or she lose swiftness and become heavy and stupid. [28] Also relevant is the case of the peccary, that wild, piglike animal of the New World. According to R. A. Donkin, several Indian groups who hunted wild animals had selective bans on peccary flesh, including ones followed by particular individuals, such as pregnant women, and others observed by an entire group. [29] Such bans seem to have been based on peoples' fears that they would take on undesirable qualities of the peccary by eating it, or risk other dangers from doing so. It is clear that people in many parts of the world, ancient and modern, have refused to eat pork for similar reasons, fear that they would take on undesirable characteristics of the pig, or that they would become piglike. Take, for example, the reaction of certain Carib Indians to pigs when pigs were first introduced to their land. Instead of welcoming pigs as a tasty new source of protein, they refused to eat pork out of concern that pigs have small eyes.[30] In a similar vein, pregnant mothers among certain groups in tropical Africa in traditional times were not permitted to eat the flesh of the tree hyrax (*Dendrohyrax arboreus*) lest their children, like the hyrax, have only three fingers; the scaly anteater (*Manis tricuspis*) is also avoided out of fear that, because the anteater curls up, the mother will have a difficult delivery.[31] Pregnant women among the Mbum Kpau of Chad refuse to eat snakes lest they bear snakelike children, or fish with bony heads or antelope with twisted horns lest their children be deformed.[32] Pregnant Chinese women may also avoid mutton and lamb out of fear that the child will be an epileptic; this is based on similarities in Chinese words for lamb or mutton and epilepsy, for the latter means literally "mad lamb" or "lamb in convulsions."[33]

That this is a fundamental and persistent belief among Westerners, too, is demonstrated in the literature,[34] and in the results of a questionnaire, intended to elicit responses in a subtle way, administered to American college students by Rozin and his associates.[35] Each student was first provided with a brief description of one of two cultures, with data on hunting and food habits included among other information on social organization and other things. The two cultures were identical except that the people of one hunted boars for their tusks, but ate only turtles; and those of the second culture hunted turtles for their shells, but ate only boars. After reading the descriptions provided them, students were asked to rate individuals from the two cultures in various categories, with the result that a very significant number of the students rated boar eaters as more like boars (i.e., able to run faster than turtle eaters), and turtle eaters more like turtles.

Belief in "you are what you eat" may derive from the "law of contact or contagion" proposed by Sir James G. Frazer in *The Golden Bough* as a form of sympathetic magic (though it occurs beyond the realm of what may narrowly be defined as magic).[36] The law of contact or contagion involves an individual having contact with someone or something, and, as a result, taking on the essence of that person or thing. Contact may have beneficial results for an individual, as when a Catholic touches the robe of the Pope, or a Hindu has contact with the sacred cow or its products, or contact may have bad effects. The same is true when a person has contact through eating flesh. As it applies to the flesh avoidances considered in this book, the law of contact or contagion usually involves a person becoming polluted by eating the flesh of an unclean animal, or by contact with the animal or a person associated with it.

Concern with purity and pollution, whether or not these involved animals and their flesh, has, for most peoples and periods of history, been a matter of highest priority, for one cannot approach the gods and receive their blessing if one is impure.[37] That purity was essential to the ancient Greeks is shown by the facts that Homer, in his account of Hector coming home from battle, saw that Hector did not offer a libation to Zeus before he washed his hands, and that Hesiod, too, insisted that a person who brought a sacrifice to the gods "be pure and clean."[38]

In the modern world, concern with contagion continues to be widespread, though there are differences from culture to culture in the strength of feeling it generates and in the ways for dealing with it. Some of the most interesting examples are found in Hindu India, where many individuals are vitally concerned with maintaining their ritual purity. The pure Hindu must constantly be on guard, for, by contact with an impure person, it is the pure one who becomes polluted, not the impure one who is purified.[39] Pollution may be permanent or temporary, voluntary or involuntary, external or internal. External pollution can perhaps best be visualized as "touch" pollution, since it involves mere contact with polluting agents. Internal pollution, on the other hand, involves penetration of the body by pollutants, including impure foods, and is by far the more serious of the two and the more difficult to eliminate.

The temporary pollution of Hindus may be removed by performing various acts or ceremonies, and by cleansing with purificatory agents. Of all such agents, fire is the most powerful,[40] and may be used in various ways.[41] Sun, Ganges water, and the "five products of the cow" mentioned in the beef chapter are also among the major agents. In any case, Hindus make serious efforts to avoid pollution, and in village India, members of unclean castes, such as the sweepers who remove village refuse, may not be permitted to take water from the community well. From a civil rights perspective, many Westerners may be irate at what they perceive as unacceptable social discrimination, but from the Hindu perspective it is a proper act carried out by villagers committed to one of their highest religious goals, maintaining a state of ritual purity. It is because this view has been so widespread and pervasive in the world since antiquity that I chose the quotation, from an ancient Iranian source, at the start of this chapter.

A second law of sympathetic magic advanced by Frazer is "the law of similarity,"[42] which states that things resembling each other do, in fact, share basic qualities. I would cite several cases in which the law of similarity has extended the ban on the flesh of one animal or food to another perceived to resemble it. One is the rejection of monkey flesh as food in a northeastern Thailand village because the monkey is believed to have descended from humans, and eating it would be like cannibalism.[43] Another is the throwing away of tuna in many coastal Hindu Indian villages because of the red color of its flesh,[44] apparently because it is similar to that of meat. Among other examples in India, the Satnāmis, a Hindu sect, extend their ban on meat to eggplant, because eggplant is believed to turn into meat,[45] apparently a reference to its consistency when cooked and eaten. Members of the Baniya caste, in turn, extend their meat prohibition to carrots, turnips, onions, and red pulse because they are reddish in color and thus resemble flesh.[46] Even a name similar to that of a forbidden domestic animal may lead to rejection, as in the extension of the Hindu ban on eating the flesh of the sacred cow to *Boselaphus tragocamelus,* a wild antelope whose name, *nilgai,* means "blue cow." In a similar vein, one of the major reasons given by women in Tamilnad for rejecting eggs during pregnancy is that they fear the disease *muccadaippan,* which makes breathing difficult and brings on pneumonialike symptoms. They do this because the first part of the name for the disease, *mucc,* means "egg," and the second part, *adaippan,* signifies "a stoppage or blocking," which would cause breathing problems.[47]

Returning to the question of why flesh foods, rather than plant foods, are almost exclusively the objects of disgust, Angyal advanced a hypothesis five decades ago that has stood up quite well over the years. He argued that disgust derives from a primitive dread of being contaminated or debased, and is generated principally by waste products of the human and animal body, which in a broad sense includes anything coming from the body. There is both a fear of coming into contact with the object of disgust and, even more, of ingesting it.[48] Edmund Leach has argued further that emissions came to be unclean because they are not part of the human body but are at its very edge, neither in nor out, thus ambiguous and subject to strong taboos.[49]

Angyal sees support for his hypothesis in the more general acceptability of the flesh of herbivorous animals than that of carnivores, for, though herbivores may be regarded as disgusting, that quality is enhanced in carnivores by the disgusting things they may consume.[50] The same could be said of omnivores, and indeed, among the land animals we have considered in this book, the two most widely regarded as disgusting (pig, dog) are both omnivores.

Angyal's observation that disgust reactions relate almost exclusively to substances of animal origin has been confirmed by Rozin and Fallon.[51] In a study of American students who were given questionnaires and interviews, these researchers found that students expressed disgust for virtually all reptiles and amphibians and most birds and mammals, as well as for bodily secretions and excretions and a good number of organs (among them, eyes, heart, intestines) of species that provide other flesh acceptable as food.

Why animals and not plants? Rozin and Fallon explain this in terms of human recognition of their similarity to other animals, which increases the likelihood that a person who eats an animal's flesh will take on its physical and psychological characteristics. Also of significance, they suspect, is the fact that animals produce feces, a special focus of disgust reactions.

One can find rich support for this in the historical and ethnographic record. The ancient Greeks, according to R. Parker, used the term "dung eater" in the sense of a person "who will stop at nothing." Like "temple robber," "murderer," and "mother sleeper," "dung eater" was an insult that referred to one of "the most degraded and polluting acts."[52] No Greek, of course, would eat dung, and indeed Greeks commonly singled out excrement-eating animals in their flesh rejections, because the person who ate such flesh became a dung eater himself. Because there are many excrement-eating animals, the Greeks could not rule out the flesh of all of them. At the same time, according to Parker, it may have been no accident that, in Hippocrates's *Sacred Disease,* the men who treated the illness by purification advised their patients to reject the meat of various animals often accused of eating excrement and other filth, among them dogs and pigs.[53]

In a similar vein are reports from modern South India that the purity of meat, except for beef, is directly tied to the "dietary purity" of the animal from which it comes.[54] Thus, the flesh of goats is cleaner than that of pigs because the goat feeds on vegetation outside the settlement, whereas the pig is a village scavenger that eats leftover foods (polluted by saliva) and even human excrement. Even lower in purity, however, is the flesh of crows, which is eaten by the caste of lowest status, and dogflesh, an unthinkably debased food.[55]

Not to be overlooked among bodily products is saliva. The Hua, a highland people of New Guinea, out of fear for their health, avoid the polluting saliva of certain categories of people. A Hua should not share a knife with such persons. He should not drink water from the same cup or bamboo drinking tube. Nor should he eat dishes that have been partly consumed by such persons.[56] Hindus have similar concerns and practices relating to the use and disposal of eating and drinking implements and vessels.[57] For a Hindu, saliva, even his own, is one of the most impure substances, and partly responsible for the dirtiness of human "leavings" and their unacceptability as food.[58] This is well illustrated in a Tamil story about the god Shiva. The god, masquerading as a human, goes to a restaurant as the guest of one of his followers. On their table is some coffee that had been spilled by a diner who preceded them. Observing a fly struggle to get out of the spilled coffee, Shiva, apparently in the spirit of ahimsa, assists the fly with his finger, whereupon his follower condemns Shiva because the coffee had been made impure by saliva.[59] In South India today, what remains from a person's meal may be eaten by his or her spouse or by a young child. Otherwise, it is thrown out or given to an untouchable.[60] One reads of South Indian untouchables who themselves refuse to eat food left on a plantain leaf (from which food is eaten) by a member of some other caste, and who take great pleasure in recounting a story that emphasizes their superiority over another group, perhaps a mythical one, whose members will eat such leavings. Interestingly, the name by which they call the latter group means literally "saliva untouchables."[61]

Human leavings are never offered to Hindu gods,[62] but the leavings of food offered to high gods are considered differently, as long as the food has been offered in a proper manner by a Brahmin.[63] Indeed, a worshipper is considered blessed if he or she later consumes such consecrated food (*prasāda*).[64] On the other hand, in South India, should a human taste such food before it is offered to the deity, it becomes irretrievably polluted. Pollution, by extension, may be applied even to foods that humans have not tasted, for example an entire bunch of bananas of which one has been eaten.[65] Saliva, as I have mentioned, is also a factor in the impurity of one of the animals considered in this book, for Hindu aversion to the dog is partly based on its penchant for licking its master.[66]

Anna S. Meigs has argued that the disgust people feel for bodily emissions is one aspect of a broader concern with keeping unwanted rotting or dying substances (as well as their carriers and symbols)[67] from gaining access to their bodies.[68] In keeping with her view is the widespread disgust that people, since antiquity, have had for carrion eating, especially when it involves human corpses. The ancient Hebrews feared having their bodies eaten by dogs,[69] and, as we have seen, in ancient Greece the dog's eating of human corpses seems to have been a factor in its impurity. The ancient Greeks not only rejected dogflesh as food, but they were also disinclined to eat any animal that ate carrion. One such animal, most banned of all fish, was the red mullet, which was believed to have a special liking for polluted items, and would consume human corpses as well as dead fish.[70] Among modern Hindus, untouchables who remove and handle human bodies or animal carcasses, and who eat the flesh of dead animals or may once have done so, are burdened with permanent pollution.[71] As we have seen, untouchables who eat beef, the flesh of the sacred cow, get an added dose of impurity.[72] Because of similar concerns with death, along the Malabar Coast of India, people abstain from fishing after a ruler dies, for fear of eating the fish inhabited by his soul.[73] The Malabar abstention is a temporary one, but the ancient Pythagoreans of the Greek world seem to have had a continuing ban on fish and other flesh foods partly because of their belief in the transmigration of souls.

Other Explanations of Flesh-Food Bans

Explanations of group flesh avoidance, of course, must go well beyond those presented above. Quite prominent, for example, is the belief, held by vegetarians, that killing animals and eating flesh is morally wrong. A lama in Darjeeling, when talking to Deryck Lodrick, singled out three sinful animals not fit for eating, and all three (pig, hen, fish) commonly kill other living creatures. Sometimes related to this belief, and sometimes not, is concern with fear of punishment or retribution in the afterlife for killing an animal. It is for this reason that when a great Sema Naga hunter dies, a dog is slain to accompany him on his journey to the land of the dead and to protect him from the spirits of the animals he has killed. Such fear commonly extends beyond the killer to the person who eats an animal's flesh, and precautions are taken by flesh eaters to eliminate such guilt. One means of doing this, followed by the Palaung of Burma, who are Buddhists, is to eat only the flesh of animals that have died from natural causes or have been killed by members of other ethnic groups who have no objections to slaughtering animals.[74] Another way is to assign slaughter to professional butchers. This is the case in many Buddhist countries, where household animals are commonly given to butchers who are non-Buddhists and who are looked down upon because of their professional activities. Professional butchers in Tibet, for example, have been the most despised of classes, regarded as professional sinners because they violate the Buddhist precept against taking life.[75] The ancient Guanche of the Canary Islands did not allow their professional butchers to enter the homes of other people, to handle their property, or to associate with anyone but those of their own calling.[76] Even in classical Greece, where the official view was that animals should serve the needs of humans, the Pythagoreans viewed the *mageiros* (butcher-cook-sacrificer), like the hunter, as a murderer.[77] The Bemba of Zambia consider the hereditary official who kills most of the animals used for ritualistic purposes at the principal chief's court a daring fellow for performing such dangerous work. For his own protection, he undergoes purification ceremonies after the slaughter.[78] Quite similar to this is the notion that food touched by a murderer is contaminated, that the spirit of death is in it. In 1771, Samuel Hearne, observing a group of Copper Indians, noted that those who had killed some Eskimos were regarded as unclean, were prohibited from cooking food for others or for themselves, and ate only from their own dishes.[79]

Some of the hypotheses advanced to explain flesh-food avoidance, unlike those above, emphasize not fear but affection. It is widely observed, for example, that humans reject the flesh of animals with which they are particularly familiar. In our society, children often cannot bear to eat the flesh of a chicken that has been raised for the pot but has become a pet; the young Clarence Darrow was so shocked at the "murder" of his pet that he refused from then on to eat chickenflesh of any sort. This reluctance to slaughter or eat familiar animals exists in many parts of the world. Among the Bari of the Sudan, when a man's favorite ox grows old and is ceremonially killed, his friends eat the flesh, but the owner himself sits grief-stricken in his hut. It was because of such sentiments that members of the Donner party, caught in the snows of the Sierra Nevadas in 1846–47 and faced with starvation, distributed the flesh of their dead companions in such a way that people would not eat members of their immediate families. Similar sentiments may be involved in Phraan Muan, a village in northeastern Thailand, where Tambiah was told that water buffalo and common cattle raised by a family at home should not be killed in their family or household rituals, nor should village animals be killed in collective rituals of that community. Instead, animals needed for such purposes should be obtained elsewhere, those for family rituals from other families or villages, those for village rituals from other villages. If this practice were not followed, people said, bad things would happen to their common cattle or water buffalo. They would have small numbers of offspring; they would be difficult to raise; and they would suffer from disease and death.[80]

Two types of rejection are present in the above examples: individuals' rejection of the flesh of a particular animal associated with them, and group rejection of the flesh of an entire class of animals because of close contact in daily activities. Such association, it should be noted, does not necessarily lead either the individual or the group to reject the flesh of animals of an entire species. A person or group may suffer feelings of guilt at permitting the slaughter of such animals, and then seek ways to assuage its conscience. It is common, for example, for an individual to grieve when a pet is slaughtered. It is said that Indian women of the Quito area of Ecuador are so fond of their fowl that they neither sell nor slaughter them. Yet, when a traveller staying with them finds it necessary to kill a chicken for food, the landlady, despite shrieks, tears, and wringing of hands, will afterwards quietly accept payment for the animal. It does, however, appear quite possible that familiarity with animals, particularly in functional relationships and as pets, led one group or another to reject flesh of an entire species of animals.

Related to the above is the notion that some flesh avoidances were instituted to prevent the destruction of animals useful to humans. The view that the ox that tills the ground should not be slaughtered is still found in many places, such as Greece, China, and Korea; and though this view derives in part from a desire to preserve useful animals, it is also motivated by affection for a companion, friend, and member of the family. One finds similar views among other groups, for example the Gold tribe of Manchuria in the 1930s, and the Burmese after the

Second World War. In the case of horses, however, most Asian horse peoples, who are more dependent on horses than anyone else, have not prohibited the eating of horseflesh. On the contrary, they use it extensively.

Still another explanation for the origin of particular avoidances is that they were developed by a favored group in an effort to keep the best foods for themselves. We have seen above that the mechanism for such a development exists in many places. Thus it is quite possible that the self-interest of a favored group, whether of old or prestigious men, members of particular societies or age classes, persons politically dominant, or whatever else, has led to the institution of a food avoidance which at first applied to other members of the society but gradually came to apply even to the self-designated elite.

Of the flesh foods on which we have focussed in this book, the application of the chicken and egg avoidance to women of child-bearing age has been viewed by some observers as deriving from masculine selfishness. Whatever effect the avoidance may have on the distribution and availability of animal protein to the two sexes, I believe that the chicken and egg avoidance was brought on initially, among tribal peoples of southern Asia and Africa, by human concerns about the dangers of eating eggs, to which women were especially vulnerable. In most parts of the world, eggs are associated with sexuality, fertility, reproduction, and life. Those associations have affected the way eggs are used, for example as aphrodisiacs by people in certain European countries. They have also led to eggs being viewed as improper food for some high-status persons with special needs to remain pure, such as Christian clergy or Christian laymen at Lent. In Europe, on the other hand, such associations did not lead to a general avoidance of eggs or the flesh of fowl that produce them. Some non-European peoples, however, have rejected eggs altogether as human food or banned them to certain segments of society, especially women of child-bearing age. However appealing the male selfishness theme may be in the eyes of women's rights activists in the West, in the lack of any supporting evidence it is a dubious procedure to extend such views to ancient peoples in distant parts of the world. On the basis of the evidence, I am not inclined to the position that the prohibition of chickens and eggs to women is a masculine plot. Instead I think that most men love, like, or at least appreciate their mothers, wives, and daughters, and that, if certain of those women were expected to avoid eggs and chickenflesh, it was likely for reasons other than masculine dietary greediness. In this regard, one notes that among some peoples men, too, were not allowed to eat chicken and eggs; and that, among many, children and old women— before or after the time in the life cycle these foods were considered a threat to their fertility and their offspring—were permitted to eat them freely. The chicken and egg avoidances also fit well with other dietary restrictions observed by pregnant women and nursing mothers around the world, which are designed principally to assure the well-being of mothers and their newborn. As described in a Vietnamese village by G. C. Hickey,[81] once clear symptoms of pregnancy develop, a woman starts following a pattern of behavior and observing food avoidances to minimize the stresses of pregnancy and to assure the birth of a child that is not defective. For alcohol is viewed as bad for pregnant women, and if she eats unclean meat, for example beef and dogflesh, the child could be an imbecile.

I believe that bans on women eating chickenflesh and eggs came into force not by men imposing them on women, but by a general consensus in which women participated, and indeed had the greatest stake. If I am correct, the decision was shared by men and women, and rested in a desire to assure the survival and good health of mother and child, and the continued existence of the family and society in general. It was based, moreover, on a perception of the egg as a symbol of sex, fertility, and life that was shared by peoples all over the world. In the case of egg avoiders, however, things seem to have been taken a step further and in a different direction from the one in which most peoples had taken them. The decision could have gone the other way, with pregnant women required to eat eggs rather than avoid them. Among the Chinese, we have seen that the view of eggs as fertility symbols is expressed in a rich variety of ways, and that eggs are among the foods prescribed for pregnant women. When a Chinese mother gives birth, moreover, friends and relatives bring her gifts of eggs, which may be numerous and contribute substantially to meeting her special nutritional needs during this time of bodily stress.[82]

Of particular interest among the flesh avoidances we have considered is the case of fish. The avoidance of fish among Buddhists and Hindus is clearly tied to the concept of nonviolence, in which the taking of life of all sorts, including that of fish, is considered wrong. Similar views occurred elsewhere in the Old World, as among the ancient Pythago-reans. In addition, however, are the views that fish in certain sacred waters are not to be eaten, or that fish, sometimes in common with other creatures that live in water, are unclean. In both of the last two cases of fish rejection, the perception of fish is related to the medium in which they live. This is paralleled by the traditional rejection of fish and all other water creatures by certain Indian groups of the American Southwest, which, according to certain Navajos, is based on fear of a water monster who rules the waters of the land.

Another group of explanations, in favor because they fit with present-day Western views, are hygienic in nature, that an avoidance comes about because people want to preserve their health. Though hygienic explanations have been used to account for the rejection of several flesh foods, the best-known of these hypotheses relate to the rejection of pork by the ancient Hebrews. As I have shown, however, there is no convincing evidence that the Hebrews or any other Near Eastern group gave up eating pork for fear of disease. In the trichinosis hypothesis, one of the most popular present-day explanations of Hebrew pork avoid-ance, we seem to be dealing with what Mary Douglas calls "medical materialism," which, she argues convincingly, has plagued studies of comparative religion and led observers to seek hygienic explanations for even the most unusual rites of antiquity. In her words, ". . . it is one thing to point out the side benefits of ritual actions, and another thing to be content with using the by-products as a sufficient explanation. Even if some of Moses's dietary rules were hygienically beneficial it is a pity to treat him as an enlightened public health administrator rather than as a spiritual leader."[83]

Despite the questionable applicability of hygienic explanations to the pork avoidance of the Near East, one cannot dismiss concerns with dirt and pollution in the origin of this and other flesh avoidances. Such con-cerns are found among all peoples, ancient and modern, primitive and advanced, non-Western and Western. Indeed, Douglas has argued that contemporary Western views of dirt and pollution and those of other peoples reflect cultural systems, and that pollution behavior around the world differs only in detail. In Western thinking, according to Douglas, the avoidance of dirt is an issue not of religion but of aesthetics and a hygiene controlled by awareness of disease-causing organisms. If, she contends, we eliminate such hygienic notions from our thinking, we are left with the old view of dirt, common to peoples in various parts of the world, as inappropriate matter or "matter out of place," matter that fails to fit into ordered systems of thought and behavior. In this concern with order, she insists, there is no particular difference between primitive and modern peoples, except that systems are more comprehensive and operate more strongly in primitive cultures, whereas in modern cultures they are disconnected, distinct segments of life. Douglas also sees "no clear-cut distinction between sacred and secular" in matters of dirt and pollution, for "the same principle applies throughout."[84] One may conclude from her writings that, if one is to understand avoidances of flesh foods in a particular culture, one must view them in terms of that culture's systems of thought and behavior, whether secular or sacred. We have found that, among many groups, the sacred is strongly involved in flesh avoidances, among them beef and pork. Therefore, I would add that, if Westerners are to gain proper insights into origins of such avoidances around the world, they should make a special effort to avoid focussing narrowly on pathogenic organisms.

The totemic relationship that may exist between an animal and a primitive group, whether tribe, clan, lineage, or other unit, is commonly said to have arisen because in the past the animal helped the group in some way. The observances connected with the totemic animal take a great variety of forms, but usually the group shows honor and affection for the totem and places restrictions on killing it. Though some groups permit unrestricted use of a totemic animal's flesh, most have strong restrictions, either forbidding it altogether or permitting only sacramental consumption. The Selkup Samoyed, for example, never kill or eat their totemic animal, however predatory it may be; this would be the equivalent of cannibalism. Among most of the northern tribes of central Australia a man is not permitted to kill or eat his totem or that of his father or his father's father. Instead he is responsible for increasing its number. However, the Arunta perform special ceremonies in which men eat the flesh of their totem in order to bring about such an increase.[85] Though some groups do not insist that a wife follow her husband's totemic avoidances, others expect her to observe them at all times or at least on particular occasions. In the Northern Territories of Ghana, a wife customarily observes her husband's totemic food avoidances either when nursing her infants or throughout her child-bearing period. This is because people believe that food is transformed into milk, and that the child would be violating the avoidance if the mother ate flesh forbidden to her husband's group.

The process of identification which may contribute to rejection of the flesh of a totemic animal may, among some more advanced peoples, lead to rejection of the flesh of an animal associated with a god or goddess, viewed as an embodiment of the deity, or regarded as a deity in its own right. The Zoroastrians, for example, divided all animals into two classes: those that belong to Ahura Mazdā, their supreme deity, and those that belong to Ahriman, his evil opponent. To kill an animal belonging to Ahura Mazdā was regarded as a sin, and to kill one of Ahriman's was a pious act. Severe penalties were imposed on anyone who killed a dog, most sacred of all animals belonging to Ahura Mazdā. These observances were so important to the Zoroastrians that, as we have seen, they tried to introduce them among the peoples with whom they came into contact.

One of the things that has struck me, in my search for origins of group avoidances of flesh foods, is the importance of foods and food animals in identifying groups of people. This is well demonstrated in the amusement of the classical Greek poet Anaxandrides in addressing his Egyptian contemporaries about their food habits, as quoted at the end of my introductory chapter.[86] In a similar vein, when the Tibetans of the Kansu-Tibetan border hear about other groups, they ask: "Is their mouth the same as ours, or is it like the mouth of the Moslems, or do they have some other mouth?"[87] Rozin and Fallon have observed that the mouth provides entry to the human body, is the principal route by which pollution enters the gastrointestinal tract, and is the final point of defense against such entry; it represents the boundary between an individual and the outside world.[88] In the sense used by the Tibetans, the word for mouth assumes a broader meaning in distinguishing ethnic groups as well. From this, it is a simple step to refer, usually in a derogatory sense, to other groups in terms of a food they consume. Strabo, in a manner common among classical Greek writers, makes repeated use of foods, usually ones of animal origin, in identifying peoples living south of Egypt or along the Red Sea, among them Chelonophagi ("turtle eaters"), Elephantophagi ("elephant eaters"), Struthophagi ("bird eaters"), Acridophagi ("locust eaters"), Rhizophagi ("root eaters"), and Spermophagi ("seed eaters").[89] We have observed that the followers of Tamerlane called the emperor of China the pig emperor, just as a recent newspaper reports that conservative Moslem Malays revile the Chinese as "pork eaters."

The Chinese themselves have made use of such allusions in referring to persons of other ethnic groups or to other Chinese. Outsiders, for example, refer to people of a village in Shantung as sweet-potato eaters, an offensive term because sweet potatoes are inferior food, and using them, a mark of poverty.[90] Certain traditional Chinese, who view milk as a disgusting bodily secretion, unclean, like urine, say that Europeans have a butter smell about them.[91] The Japanese, in turn, add that people influenced by foreigners have a butter odor about them.[92] One can think of many similar examples in the Western world. One should not overlook the fact that American troops in the First World War referred to the British, French, and Germans, respectively, as Limeys, Frogs, and Krauts—all because of foods they identified with the peoples in question. In a similar vein, the Palaung of Burma, who never eat frogs, may, when angry at a Shan (who do eat frogs), refer to him contemptuously as frog eater.[93] In a like manner, the Mbala of Central Africa, who reject frogs as food, refer to their neighbors, the Huana, as froggies because Huana women eat them.[94] What I am suggesting here is that, from this sort of identification of a flesh food with an alien group, it is reasonable to expect, in some cases, that the food in question is rejected simply because of the association.

We should not leave the question of the origins of flesh-food avoidances without stressing that many of these developed so long ago, before the earliest written records, that we will never know with certainty what factors led to their development. I have dealt with the techno-environmental determinism of Marvin Harris elsewhere,[95] and here I would say only that, as an effort to explain the origins of flesh avoidances, it appears contrived and rooted in prior commitment to a particular theory. This is in agreement with Andrew P. Vayda's observation that Harris went wrong in two senses: (1) his confidence that "general formulas, laws, or prescription[s]" can explain developments in human society, and (2) his "monism," commitment to a single principle that has operated everywhere through history, "one key to unlock all doors."[96] We are, after all, dealing with food avoidances of considerable number, with peoples of widely contrasting cultural backgrounds, and often with peoples in the distant past. A broad range of factors, often in combination, has been involved in the development of flesh-food avoidances. Religion, moreover, is not the least of these, but has been a powerful determinant in its own right. This is in agreement with te Velde's observation, quoted at the beginning of this chapter, that religion can be an important element in human life, and that one should not make it into something else of a nonreligious nature.[97]

To gain a proper understanding of flesh bans, it is incumbent that one maintain as open a mind as possible, for it is almost certain that they came about by many distinct paths, including some of which we are still unaware. Keeping an open mind is particularly difficult for Americans, for most of us are secularists and materialists who live in a culture of culinary deprivation, with many of us considering flesh, like other food, as something to be consumed in haste, a bodily necessity but little more. Things are quite different among many of the world's peoples today, and they have been for most peoples through history. For such peoples, food has had far richer and more interesting social and cultural associations that, if ignored, may seriously impede our understanding. Compare, for example, the present-day American reluctance to eat eggs, out of concern with cholesterol, with the appeal of the director of the World Jain Mission, one that emphasizes divine intent, purity and impurity, cruelty to animals, and a range of benefits from not eating eggs:

Since nature has not provided eggs as edible articles of food, rather they are meant for procreation, they cannot be the natural diet of human beings. Their origin and growth are from filthy substances, which man abhors even to touch. Their eating involves cruelty and robbery . . . Please commit not the sin of killing. We appeal to our friends to correct their eating habits by turning to natural foods and by abandoning the habit of eating meat and eggs. By showing mercy to animals, [including] chickens[,] they will gain mercy and will be happy and healthy.[98]

Factors Involved in Changing Foodways, Including Those Relating to Flesh Food

Like other aspects of human culture, flesh avoidances may change with the passage of time. They may also be diffused to other cultures and reinterpreted by them. That diffusion has been a major way in which flesh avoidances have spread is suggested by present-day patterns of distribution. It would be impossible to understand the present-day occurrence of pork avoidance in the Old World without referring to Islam, its major agent of diffusion. Nor could one appreciate attitudes toward beef in East and Southeast Asia without considering Buddhism. I would contend that one of the most profitable approaches to the history of flesh-food bans is to seek an understanding of the contending food ideologies and their interaction over time. On the other hand, flesh avoidances may also develop independently in different places, ultimately to develop patterns of distribution that present difficult and even insoluble problems to the culture historian.

Another question is how established flesh avoidances come to change, for example how a flesh that once was rejected as food comes to be accepted. Because change everywhere tends to follow similar patterns, certain types of individuals are more likely to be found among the agents of dietary change and others among the agents resisting it. Older people, for example, are more thoroughly imbued with the traditional foodways of a group and tend to resist change, as do country folk and those in the group who benefit in status or in some other way from maintaining an avoidance.

Among those active in bringing about abandonment of traditional foodways are persons who have had broader experience with food, such as educated persons, traders, and well-travelled persons. That experience is an important factor in this regard is supported by Stefansson's observation that, among dogs and humans, individuals accustomed to a variety of foods take more readily to a new food than individuals used to a restricted diet. People of an intellectual bent, he asserts, are more willing to try new foods because of a sense of adventure[99]—a statement perhaps borne out by the tradition of experimentation with strange foods on college campuses in the United States.[100]

In addition, infants and young children are more willing than adults to try new foods. Indeed many children in the initial two years of life will put all sorts of things in their mouths that adults find disgusting. Though this tendency decreases rapidly after that time, most children under age eight, though they may reject such items, do not fully understand or express the disgust reactions found in adults.[101] Ultimately, however, the child's reaction changes, showing a strong correlation with that of its parents in the foods regarded as contaminating and disgusting,[102] and with others of its culture, as well.

The importance of age in willingness to experiment with new flesh foods occurs in other species as well, as shown by Stefansson's experience with dog teams in the Arctic: the older a dog, the longer it persisted in refusing types of flesh that were unfamiliar. Among humans, moreover, children are also permitted greater deviation from group foodways. Thus, in terms of both inclination and freedom from strictures, they seem to be in a far better position to try new foods. In some cases around the world, they are further encouraged in such deviation by food shortage and the discrimination they so commonly experience in gaining full access to the family food supply. Cora DuBois has pointed out that the child of Alor, who is given no food between morning and evening meals, soon learns to forage for itself by scraping remnants for the cooking pot; collecting insects, which are spurned by adults; and raiding the fields for fruit and vegetables.[103] Among the Tallensi of Ghana, young children will seek and consume creatures such as toads and snakes, which are disgusting to older children and adults.[104] This resourcefulness is duplicated among other groups in the Third World. Indeed, any study of food among Third World peoples would be incomplete without considering the myriad of tidbits obtained and eaten by children away from home. The question remains whether children in fact play much of a role in gaining acceptability of new flesh foods, for as they get older they are increasingly subject to the food restrictions of their groups. In East Africa, little girls, who are permitted great liberty in eating when they are young, are gradually subjected to the food avoidances of the group. The beginning of these restrictions is a sad time for them, when some of their favorite foods may be forbidden.[105]

Though the role of mothers and other women in changing foodways needs more careful study, the traditional pattern has been that women side with the forces resisting change. Among the Yukaghir of Siberia, for example, contact with the Yakut led some people to eat new flesh foods, including beef and horseflesh. Yukaghir women, however, displayed an aversion to this "alien food," and when horsemeat was cooking, some Yukaghir women would even leave the house because they could not stand the smell.[106] Another example is that of the Japanese in Hawaii. In the 1940s, when most Hawaiian Japanese had come to eat beef and pork, many old women continued to abhor the idea, which in Japan had been discouraged by Buddhist teachings.[107]

Traditional foodways tend to be maintained unless modified by disruptive factors of some sort. Perhaps the most common mode of change, as Jitsuichi Masuoka has pointed out, is through the disorganization of traditional institutions that accompanies culture contact and culture

change, and which is more pronounced in urban than in rural areas.[108]
Differences in the availability of food, changes in traditional tastes for
food, disruption of customary sanctions, and shifts in the social status
of individuals are often involved in the process.

The introduction of new types of flesh food may be facilitated by an
awareness of what Elisabeth Rozin calls "flavor principles."[109] These are
the combinations of spices and other flavorings that differ from culture
to culture, and that give cuisines a special quality. From this perspective, Italians would recognize, feel familiar with, and more readily
accept food prepared with tomatoes,[110] olive oil, garlic, and herbs. In
Rozin's words, "Be it dromedary hump or acorn meal, its culinary identification will ultimately be determined by the way it is flavored."[111] My
view is that, if (and this is an emphatic "if") there is no strong feeling of disgust associated with eating a particular type of flesh and no
powerful institutional support for rejecting it, a promising avenue for
gaining its acceptance is by use of dishes flavored appropriately. Under
the right conditions, sweet-and-sour horsemeat should be more favorably received by the Cantonese, and camel teriyaki by the Japanese. It
would, however, be folly to expect a favorable reaction by offering beef
curry to traditional Hindus, or dog souvlaki to Greeks.

In gaining acceptability for a new or rejected flesh food by significant
numbers of people in a society, perhaps the most important thing is that
the time be right. That, as we have seen, was the case in the nineteenth
century with the coming of the Meiji Era to Japan, when the Emperor
Meiji set a public example by abandoning the ancient Buddhist rejection of beef, and beef eating came to symbolize Japan's openness to the
Western world.

Lacking such official sanction, a promising way of introducing a
flesh is by means of a foreign cuisine that enjoys high standing. The
reader will recall that in nineteenth-century England, the Society for
the Propagation of Horse Flesh as an Article of Food brought in French
chefs to prepare horsemeat at banquets, and that some English enthusiasts called it *chevaline* rather than horsemeat. Though their efforts were
not ultimately successful, one must admit that *"chevaline frites"* was a
much more likely prospect for gaining culinary acceptance than "fried
horsemeat."

In recent decades, socio-cultural change in the United States has led
to a new interest in ethnic cuisine, and, at least among some segments

of society, to a certain openness to new foods, including flesh foods. Despite the furor in Utah about Tongan immigrants who eat horse-flesh and that in San Francisco over dog eating among Southeast Asian refugees, the time may be right for efforts at gaining a limited accep-tance of certain new flesh foods. For me, the most interesting example of such an effort is that of Calvin W. Schwabe, who has travelled and resided in many parts of the world. Schwabe first wrote his delightful book *Unmentionable Cuisine,* which presented convincing arguments for Westerners to try new types of flesh foods, and provided recipes for flesh, collected from throughout the world, that were not regularly con-sumed in the United States. Among the recipes, one finds "Red-cooked Dog" and "Dog Ham" from China, "Poached Eel in White Wine" (*An-guille à la bonne femme*) and "Octopus in the Style of Provence" (*Poulpe provençale*) from France, "Deep-fried Horsemeat" (*Fondue bourguignonne*) from Switzerland, and a host of similarly exotic dishes. Schwabe ar-gues that, in the United States, many readily available flesh foods are simply not used; that people's bias and lack of knowledge are important contributors to this waste; and that if such foods were consumed our nutritional well-being would be improved and our culinary enjoyment enhanced. In addition, Schwabe participated in an annual affair at a Berkeley, California, restaurant attended by open-minded chefs, who were served some of his exotic dishes and who went home with new insights, even if they did not become active advocates of unmentionable cuisine. In downtown Mexico City, there is an even rarer phenome-non—an "innovative" restaurant, Fonda Don Chon, that serves Aztec dishes and bills itself as "the cathedral of pre-Hispanic food." Among the unusual foods it may serve are parrots, snakes, rats, armadillo, iguana, fried worms, ants' eggs, toasted crickets, and corn fungus, which attract open-minded people, Mexicans and foreigners, who want to try and judge such fare.

Notes
References
Index

NOTES

Chapter 1. Introduction

1. Orr and Gilks, 1931.
2. Maynard and Swen, 1956: 411–12.
3. S. D. Gamble, 1933: 100–101.
4. Nietschmann, 1973: 108–10.
5. Hyndman, 1983–84: 289–91.
6. Woodburn, 1968: 52.
7. A. I. Richards, 1939: 42, 57–58, 63, 65.
8. Douglas, 1955: 5.
9. de Garine and Pagezy, 1990: 43.
10. de Garine and Pagezy, 1990: 43–44; de Garine, 1991: 64.
11. For a historical review of vegetarianism in India, see Alsdorf, 1961.
12. Jains believe that animals have a close affinity to human beings and that, like humans, they may make religious vows and may be rewarded or punished in subsequent reincarnations for good and bad actions in this life. This likeness explains, at least in part, the Jain view that all life should be preserved, that animals should not be killed (Jaini, 1987: 174, 176).
13. For example, by the World Jain Mission: *How healthy are eggs? (with medical opinions against egg-eating)*, by Davidson and Gross, 1960; and *Right food*, by Talbot, 1956.
14. Eichinger Ferro-Luzzi, 1977a: 361–62, who notes that Hindus, by contrast, consider honey to be an unusually pure substance because it is not made by humans. Because of this, honey serves in Hindu ritual, and in anointing and washing representations of Hindu deities.

15. Walker, 1968, 1: 495.

16. Westermarck, 1924, 2: 498–99.

17. For the animals that may be kept in *pinjrapoles*, see Lodrick, 1981: 16, 19–22, 68–69, 82–86, 163, 204, 261–62.

18. Lodrick, 1981: 17.

19. Godbole, 1936: facing page 72.

20. Simoons, 1970: 557–58.

21. Eichinger Ferro-Luzzi, 1977a: 363, 373; Eichinger Ferro-Luzzi, 1985b: 491.

22. Harper, 1959: 227–28.

23. In Tamilnadu, too, all gods of high status are vegetarian and receive vegetarian offerings (Eichinger Ferro-Luzzi, 1977a: 362–65, 373; Eichinger Ferro-Luzzi, 1981: 243, 245–46, 260–62, 263; Eichinger Ferro-Luzzi, 1985b: 499–500).

For food behavior, including vegetarianism, of supernatural beings and their devotees in North India, see Khare, 1976: 92–111.

24. Vegetarian commitment even influences the god or goddess a Hindu may worship, as in South India, where upper-caste vegetarians will not normally worship meat-eating deities. On the other hand, Eichinger Ferro-Luzzi (1981: 251–52) has described an interesting procedure followed by some Telugu Brahmins to enable them to worship a "powerful blood-thirsty village goddess" without violating their vegetarian principles.

25. For Jain influences on the young Gandhi, see Hay, 1970.

26. Hay, 1969: 307–8.

27. Gandhi, 1949: 3–4.

28. Eichinger Ferro-Luzzi, 1981: 242; Eichinger Ferro-Luzzi, 1985b: 496.

29. Eichinger Ferro-Luzzi, 1981: 242; Eichinger Ferro-Luzzi, 1990: 42.

30. Eichinger Ferro-Luzzi, 1977b: 548.

31. Despite the widespread unacceptability of alcoholic beverages as offerings to high gods in India (Eichinger Ferro-Luzzi, 1977a: 365–66), when Rājputs "open a bottle of whiskey, they often tip a little on the ground in an offering to the mother goddess before they drink. They say '*Jai Mata-ji*' as they do this—'Long live the Mother (Goddess)' " (Deryck O. Lodrick, pers. comm.).

32. One Rājput, citing a poem similar in sentiment, is quoted as saying: "Rajputs are very lusty, Sahib. It is because of their food and their drink. It makes them so that they have to have their lust, poor fellows" (Carstairs, 1957: 188). In South India, fish and eggs, along with meat, are among the most characteristic "passion-raising," or *rājasik*, foods (Eichinger Ferro-Luzzi, 1977b: 544).

33. Carstairs, 1957: 87, 109–10, 118, 165, 188; Harlan, 1992: 127 and n.

34. Khare, 1966: 234; Khare, 1970: 103.

35. Liu, 1937: 134–35.

36. Porphyry *On abstinence from animal food* 4.16.

37. Bliss, 1912: 80.

38. Harnack and Conybeare, 1910–11: 574; Burkitt, 1925: 45.

39. Porphyry *On abstinence from animal food* 4.2.

40. Ritson, 1802: 3, 52–53, 57, 86, 102, 124, 146.

41. The proper definition and use of the word "sacrifice" are matters of continuing scholarly controversy (see, for example, Ruel, 1990). In my use of the word, I follow Joseph Henninger (1987a, b) insofar as possible, though the literature is not always sufficiently detailed to enable us to distinguish sacrifice from similar phenomena. "Sacrifice," which I consider synonymous with "offering," is a ritual act involving a gift— for us usually an animal or its products—to honor or propitiate a supernatural being, whether a deity, spirit, demon, or, after death, a human thought to have superhuman powers. Animal sacrifice differs from other forms of ritual killing that do not involve a supernatural being, as is true when an animal is killed to accompany the spirit of a dead person to the afterworld. Though it may not be sanctified, the flesh of such animals, or some of it, is commonly eaten by the survivors, as at a funeral feast. Animal sacrifice also differs from "eliminatory rites," in which scapegoats—commonly but not necessarily animals—are loaded with the sin, evil, and misfortune of a community and then driven out or killed.

Henninger notes that "sacrifice" derives ultimately from the Latin "*sacer*" (holy) and "*facere*" (to make), and that this implies a ritual act of the highest order in which the offering becomes sanctified. As a result, sacrifices are commonly suitable for consumption by, and are beneficial for, humans. Though not all offerings are considered sanctified and proper human food, by definition a scapegoat is burdened with unwanted, undesirable things, and its flesh is normally regarded as impure, not suitable for people to eat.

42. Detienne, 1989a: 17–18. For interesting background on sacrifice, hunting, and funerary rituals, especially among the ancient Greeks, see Burkert, 1983a: 1–82.

43. Simoons, 1954, 1970, 1991: 454–63.

44. Athenaeus *Deipnosophists* 7.299.

Chapter 2. Pork

1. Bökönyi, 1974: 208; Flannery, 1983: 164, 181–83; Reed and Perkins, 1984: 19; Epstein and Bichard, 1984: 146–51.

2. For which, see especially H. Epstein, 1971b, 2: 349–56; Flannery, 1983: 171–81; Stampfli, 1983: 445–47; Epstein and Bichard, 1984: 147–49; Horwitz and Tchernov, 1989, 2: 283, 288; Hesse, 1990: 208, 211, 215–16.

3. Hecker, 1982: 63–64; Epstein and Bichard, 1984: 148; Reed and Perkins, 1984: 19; Hassan, 1984: 221; Hassan, 1988: 148, 156; Redding, 1991: 21.

4. See, for example, Hayes, 1965: 112, 122, 130; Darby et al., 1977, 1: 172–73.

The terms "Lower Egypt" and "Upper Egypt" are used here in the ancient sense. Lower Egypt includes the Nile Delta and its borders, with the province (nome) of Memphis its southernmost unit. Upper Egypt includes the rest of Egypt's Nile Valley south of 30° north latitude. Since Roman times, however, it has been common to divide the country into three sections: Lower, Middle, and Upper Egypt. When used in the latter sense today, Lower Egypt would be identical with ancient Lower Egypt, whereas Middle and Upper Egypt would be parts of ancient Upper Egypt. To avoid confusion, I follow the ancient division throughout.

5. Kees, 1961: 37, 91–92.

6. The relations between, and associations of, Horus and Seth in Egyptian history and prehistory have long been matters of scholarly controversy, for which see Griffiths, 1960: 130–48; and te Velde, 1977.

7. One of these is Neolithic Merimde-Benisalame, where pigs accounted for 41 percent of all domesticated animals that were eaten (von den Driesch and Boessneck, 1985: Table 2; Boessneck, 1988: 15). The other is Old Kingdom Kom el-Hisn, where they accounted for over half (Wenke, 1985: 9; Redding, 1991: 21).

8. Predynastic Naqada (Hassan, 1984: 221; F. Hassan, pers. comm.); New Kingdom Tell el-Amarna and other sites (Hecker, 1982: 62, 63–64); Predynastic Hierakonpolis (McArdle, 1982: 117, 119); Old Kingdom–Middle Kingdom Elephantine (Boessneck and von den Driesch, 1982: 21, 50, 90–91, 114–15); and New Kingdom el-Hibeh (Redding, 1984: 41–42, 44).

9. Hawass et al., 1988.

10. For which, see Hakker-Orion, 1975; Yakar, 1985, 2: 374; Stampfli, 1983: 446; Horwitz and Tchernov, 1989, 2: 283, 288; Hesse, 1990: 208, 211; Miller, 1990: 134.

11. Hecker, 1982: 61–62.

12. Redding, 1991: 21. Redding, however, suggests that whereas pigs were important from the Neolithic through Old Kingdom times, their importance appears to have declined subsequently for reasons mentioned in a note below.

13. Coffin Texts, Spell 157, trans. in Faulkner, 1973–78, 1: 135–36.

14. For the Egyptians, the eye of Horus was not merely a part of his body. It symbolized the sovereignty of their nation (Griffiths, 1980: 179, 211). It also represented the moon, a natural phenomenon, as well as divine life and power, from which energy in general derived. Thus, an affliction of the eye brought on not just blindness but also inertia and inaction. In the case quoted, the sight of a black pig causes the eye to rage and cease functioning, which leads Horus to become unconscious (Gonda, 1969b: 7; te Velde, 1977: 46–47).

15. Coffin Texts, Spell 158, trans. in Faulkner, 1973–78, 1: 136–37.

16. te Velde, 1977: 81–98.

17. Pyramid Texts, trans. in Faulkner, 1969.

18. Some have thought that the Seth animal, which was represented in various forms by the ancient Egyptians, was a real one, whether a long-snouted mouse, dog, donkey, camel, giraffe, okapi, pig, or some other creature. Others have thought it to be a mythical creature of some sort, with te Velde concluding that it appears to be "an imaginary animal related to the griffin" (1977: 13–26).

The word for Seth animal, which is found in the Pyramid Texts (Section 1935, trans. in Faulkner, 1969: 280), is a word also used for the domestic pig (Newberry, 1928: 217). Some scholars, such as Newberry, have assumed that where the word occurs, the domestic pig is intended, though, as te Velde (1977: 21) has observed, the word also means "destiny."

In another questionable translation, Barguet (1967: 149, cited by Darby et al., 1977, 1: 208 n29) has suggested that in the Pyramid Texts, Section 1268, Horus is "blinded by a pig." Faulkner's rendering (1969: 201, 202 n10) of that section, however, is that Horus is called "Blind of . . .", and he gives the meaning of the word following "Blind of" as "unknown."

19. te Velde, 1977: 79.

20. See, for example, te Velde, 1977: 7–12; Hornung, 1982: 103, 109; and Griffiths, 1980: 122.

21. Griffiths, 1960: 31–33.

22. Book of the Dead, Spell 112, trans. in Budge, 1960: 337, and Faulkner, 1985: 108–9.

23. Some have also cited as evidence of anti-pig sentiment in the Book of the Dead a curious statement about a spell (Rubric to Spell 125, trans. in Faulkner, 1985: 34): that the "written procedure" is to be drawn "on a clear floor of ochre overlaid with earth upon which no swine or small cattle have trodden." Like Budge (1904, 2: 369), however, I find it difficult to explain why the pig was singled out in the statement.

24. Budge, 1904, 1: 189n, 190; Darby et al., 1977, 1: 175.

25. Redding (1991: 23–25, 29 n1) has suggested that in ancient Egypt, when human population and demand for grain increased following Old Kingdom times, the economics of pig husbandry, as compared with that of common cattle, sheep, and goats, may have changed, with a resulting decline in numbers of pigs. In support of this view, however, Redding presents data for only five sites of Old Kingdom and later times, and acknowledges that his data are insufficient and that some evidence is not in agreement with his suggestion. Of further concern in the Redding hypothesis is evidence presented by Diener and Robkin (1978: 498) that the keeping of pigs and the keeping of cattle are complementary and usually not economic alternatives. I also wonder whether an increase in human population in Egypt would have led to an overall decline in pig population. In China, which has undergone a striking population increase since antiquity, pig populations appear to be higher today than they ever were. This is not to say that the importance of the pig did not fluctuate over time in Egypt, for in different Neolithic levels at Merimde-Benisalame, pig bones, as a percentage of those of all domesticated food animals, varied from 18 to 53. At Merimde-Benisalame, however, much lower percentages of pig bones were found in the earliest levels (I, II: 31 percent) than in the latest (IV, V: 52 percent) (Boessneck, 1988: 15, 16).

26. Paton, 1925: 17, 29.

27. Darby et al., 1977, 1: 180–85.

28. For this scene, its meaning, and controversy over the animal's identity, see Darby et al., 1977, 1: 181–84. Some observers believe the animal to be a dog, but, after a point-by-point examination of the representation, H. M. Hecker and Dexter Perkins, Jr., conclude that it "is clearly a pig or piglet" (Hecker, 1982: 60).

29. Gardiner, 1923: 22.

30. Darby et al., 1977, 1: 180–85.

31. Newberry, 1928: 211. Dating for dynastic Egypt is based on Hayes, 1970.

32. Newberry, 1928: 211; Kees, 1961: 92.

33. For additional evidence of tolerance of pigs in early New Kingdom dynasties, see Darby et al., 1977, 1: 186–90.

34. Lesko, 1987: 178.

35. te Velde, 1977: 118–21; Lesko, 1987: 178.

36. te Velde (1977: 135–38) has presented interesting information on the use of Seth in personal Egyptian names, which also suggests that the god enjoyed favor in New Kingdom times. The use of Seth in personal names (servant of Seth, worshipper of Seth, chosen of Seth, Seth gives salvation, Seth rules, etc.) did not occur in Old Kingdom times, rarely in Middle Kingdom times, but often in New Kingdom times.

37. Hornung, 1982: 220. Gardiner (1961: 250–51) has noted additional complications in Sethos's position: that the Abydos temple in question, which was among the most beautiful in the ancient world, was a national shrine dedicated to Osiris and other gods; and that Sethos, whose name identified him with the god who killed Osiris, may have built the temple at the latter's sacred city to assuage the feelings of Osiris's powerful priests.

38. te Velde, 1977: 138.

39. Herodotus *History* 2.47.

40. For an argument that Herodotus's statement about the pig was too extreme, see Dawson, 1928: 599–608.

41. Aelian (*On the characteristics of animals* 10.16) wrote that pigs were abhorrent to the sun and moon, and that Egyptians sacrificed them at no time but the annual lunar festival. Plutarch (*Isis and Osiris* 5.8), in turn, said that Egyptians regarded the pig as unclean and that priests would not eat pork, though the pig was sacrificed and eaten once a year, when the moon was full, presumably in honor of Osiris (Griffiths, 1970: 281). Though the above seems to confirm that the pig had a lowly status, a papyrus from late in the second century B.C. indicates that swineherds enjoyed a standing as great as that of other rural workers (Darby et al., 1977, 1: 190), and Aristides, Clemens, and Cyril all believed the pig to be sacred to the Egyptians (Newberry, 1928: 213).

42. Préaux, 1939: 221–23; Darby et al., 1977, 1: 190–94.

43. Leviticus 11:7–8; Deuteronomy 14:8.

44. Proverbs 11:22.

45. Feliks et al., 1971–72: 506. See, for example, Shabbath 129a.

46. Casanowicz and Hirsch, 1907: 609; Feliks et al., 1971–72: 506–7.

47. Isaiah 65:3–4; 66:3, 17.

48. 1 Maccabees 1:44–48, 50; 2 Maccabees 7:1–40; Diodorus Siculus *Library of history* 34–35.1.3–4. For a summary account of pig sacrifice in Palestine and the ancient Near East, see de Vaux, 1971: 252–69; for classical references to pig sacrifice there and elsewhere, see Chwolsohn, 1856, 2: 306. For Hebrew sacrificial practices in general compared with those of Canaanites, Mesopotamians, and Arabs, see de Vaux, 1961: 433–41.

49. 2 Maccabees 6: 18–31; 4 Maccabees 5: 1–30.

50. Sir William Smith, 1893, 3: 1393; J. D. Davis, 1944: 585.

51. Matthew 8:28–34; Mark 5:1–20; Luke 8:26–33.

52. Questions have been raised about the cultic role of the Tell el-Farʿah structure (Hesse, 1990: 209, citing P. Wapnish).

53. de Vaux, 1956: 130–31; de Vaux, 1967: 375; de Vaux, 1971: 252–53.

54. H. O. Thompson, 1970: 5, 140, 143. See Goldwasser, 1992, for another relic

of Seth (1320–1280 B.C.?), found at what may have been an Egyptian post in Canaan.

55. S. A. Cook, 1908: 47–48; Macalister, 1912, 2: 8, 378–80; W. C. Wood, 1916: 243.

56. de Vaux, 1971: 254–55.

57. de Vaux, 1971: 256.

58. Hesse, 1990: 198–99, 209, 214–15, 217, 218, 219, 220. For a review that reaches different conclusions, and presents some additional evidence, see von Rohr Sauer, 1968: 205–7.

59. Ancient Ugarit is usually called Canaanite, but some think it more proper to designate it Northwest Semitic. In part, this is because of the confusion that exists between two ancient Semitic peoples, the Phoenicians and Canaanites. The names Phoenicia and Phoenician derive from ancient Greek terms, the first applying to coastal areas of the eastern Mediterranean that are now part of Lebanon and nearby sections of Syria and Palestine, and the second to the Semitic people living there. Some scholars say that the Phoenicians called themselves Canaanites, but others doubt this. In any case, the relationship between the two peoples is uncertain, and the precise meaning of "Canaanite" and "Phoenician" is not always clear. We generally use the term "Canaanite" to refer to the Semitic people who were the principal ethnic group in early historical Palestine, but who extended to the north, and who were known by that name to the ancient Hebrews. We use "Phoenician," in turn, in the Greek sense, for the coastal Semitic people whose homeland was mainly in present-day Lebanon, merchants and seafarers whose activities led them to establish colonies far across the Mediterranean world, whether directly or through their descendants, the Carthaginians.

60. J. Gray, 1957: 49–50n; Noth, 1960a: 78. Though one text at Ugarit (c. 1400–1300 B.C.) mentions the "eight swine" or "eight swineherds" of Baal, most active deity of Canaan and central to its fertility cult, the exact tie between the pig and Baal remains unclear.

61. This is in agreement with the discovery of pig bones in two Middle Bronze Age tombs at Sasa in Palestine (Horwitz, 1987: 253).

62. Sources for my discussion of the Hittites include Hrozný, 1922: 67–71, 149, 151; Hrozný, 1953: 144, 149; Goetze and Sturtevant, 1938: 5, 11, 17, 98–101; Goetze, 1962: 34; Gurney, 1940: 101–2; Gurney, 1990: 66, 125, 126; and Gurney, pers. comm.; Masson, 1950: 6, 8–9; Hoffner, 1967: 180, 183; Hoffner, 1974: 64–65, 70, 71, 81, 120, 208, 219; Kümmel, 1967: 152; Friedrich, 1971: 43, 45 and n, 81, 102, 115 and n; Macqueen, 1975: 77, 137; Moyer, 1983: 29–33, 37–38; and D. P. Wright, 1987: 59, 104–6.

63. Hittite rites for removing evil did not usually involve demons of any sort (D. P. Wright, 1987: 261–63).

64. D. P. Wright, 1987: 104–6, who provides interesting parallels to this in Hebrew and Hindu practice.

65. Hoffner, 1967: 180, 183.

66. Jensen, 1886; Maspero, 1901: 560; Handcock, 1912: 19; Van Buren, 1939: 78–81; Salonen, 1974.

67. At Abu Salabikh in southern Mesopotamia, street deposits, dated to about

2500 B.C., contain milk teeth of young pigs, which suggests that they may have been permitted to run free in the streets to feed on waste and garbage (Miller, 1990: 126, citing an unpublished manuscript by S. Payne). There are also texts, including one found at the Sumerian city of Ur (Salonen, 1974: 8; van der Toorn, 1985: 173 n339), indicating that barley was fed to pigs.

68. Kramer, 1981: 130.

69. Kramer, 1963: 110; Salonen, 1974: 6, 7.

70. van der Toorn, 1985: 33.

71. Gordon, 1959: 132, 291, 292.

72. van der Toorn, 1985: 171–72 n314. Van der Toorn (p. 34) notes that Teshrī-tum was originally the first month of the year, a time of considerable religious activity directed toward earning the goodwill of deities for the year to come. Avoiding certain foods, he adds, appears to have been a way of assuring the worthiness of persons participating in the rites of the new year.

73. Limet, 1987: 137.

74. Gordon, 1959: 143, 144, 305; Saggs, 1962: 176. Pig fat and skin were also used by the Sumerians and Akkadians (Kramer, 1963: 110; Salonen, 1974: 9, 10).

75. Mallowan, 1965: 64. Curiously, however, the pig is not included in M. W. Green's article (1980) on animal husbandry in early Uruk.

76. Hilzheimer, 1941: 48.

77. Van Buren, 1939: 41.

78. There are few, if any, references to pigs in the Drehem tablets translated by Nesbit (1966); Keiser (1971); and S. T. Kang (1972).

79. Keiser, 1971: 58–59.

80. Sayce, 1902: 358.

81. Stampfli, 1983: 446, 449.

82. T. J. Meek, 1935: xlviii, li, lii.

83. Jensen, 1886; Jastrow, 1898: 398; R. C. Thompson, 1903–4, 2: xlvi–xlvii.

84. Ungnad, 1908: 534; Handcock, 1912: 19–20.

85. In Babylonia and Assyria, two categories of medical experts are mentioned, the āšipu (magical expert), and asû (physician). The magical expert was a learned person, steeped in tradition, whose powers derived from deities, and who spoke for them. Though sometimes the magical expert might anoint a sick person and carry out cleansing rites, his main focus was on external forces that brought on sickness. His cure derived from incantation, ritual, figurines, amulets, and such. The physician, who sometimes competed and sometimes cooperated with the magical expert, might also employ incantations, for example to the healing goddess Gula, for strengthening his efforts. However, he focussed mainly on natural causes of illness, on the body of the ill person, on washing and rubbing, on collecting and administering medicines, on bandages, and on other hands-on treatments (Ritter, 1965).

86. R. C. Thompson, 1903–4, 1: lii; 2: xxxi, xxxiii–xxxiv, 17–21; Delaporte, 1970: 164; Waida, 1987b: 326. Other products of the pig (fat, excrement) also served as medicine in Babylonia and Assyria (Jastrow, 1917: 247).

87. R. C. Thompson, 1903–4, 2: xxxiii–xxxiv, 17–21.

88. Salonen 1974: 3; Waida, 1987b: 326.
89. Van Buren, 1939: 81: Salonen, 1974: 3.
90. Simoons and Baldwin, 1982.
91. Salonen, 1974: 3.
92. Sauer, 1952: 30–32.
93. Salonen, 1974: 3, citing B. Brentjes. For another Mesopotamian fertility goddess associated with young pigs, see Salonen, 1974: 4.
94. Salonen, 1974: 5, 6.
95. Delaporte, 1970: 164.
96. de Vaux, 1971: 256–57.
97. Xenophon *Anabasis* 2.2.
98. Xenophon *Anabasis* 4.4, 6; 5.2.
99. In a similar vein, Sayce (1887: 83; 1902: 466–67) wrote of the avoidance of the word for domestic pig on Semitic Babylonian and Assyrian inscriptions, and of the absence of the wild boar on Babylonian offering lists to the gods, which, in his view, reflected their impurity. Other early conjectures on the role of the pig in Mesopotamia are sometimes confusing (e.g., Peters, 1897–98, 2: 131; Jastrow, 1898: 661–62).
100. Saggs, 1984: 168.
101. Olmstead, 1968: 558.
102. Saggs, 1965: 175.
103. Lambert, 1960: 215; van der Toorn, 1985: 34.
104. For more information on Utu, see Frymer-Kensky, 1987.
105. van der Toorn, 1985: 35, 173 n335, citing A. L. Oppenheim.
106. See, in this regard, Noth, 1960a: 78–79.
107. Chwolsohn, 1856, 2: 42, 445; W. R. Smith, 1914: 290.
108. W. C. Wood, 1916: 243.
109. Porphyry *On abstinence from animal food* 1.14. Maurice Dunand (1964: 18), in his account of Byblos, wrote that though the pig was among the domesticated animals kept in Neolithic times, it had become rare in the Chalcolithic period, was "never to re-appear in this country . . . [and] was later to become prohibited on religious grounds."
110. Lucian *Syrian Goddess* 54.
111. N. Robertson, 1982b: 328.
112. Strabo *Geography* 12.8.9.
113. Diodorus Siculus *Library of history* 5.62.4–5.
114. Julian *Orations* 177 B–C.
115. Pausanias *Description of Greece* 7.17.9–10.
116. Frazer (1935, 5: 264–65) suggests that this myth may have been invented later to explain a preexisting practice. For other variants of this story, see N. Robertson, 1982b: 325.
117. Vickery, 1936: 61.
118. Hippocrates *Regimen* Appendix. 18.
119. Artemidorus Daldianus *Interpretation of dreams* 1.70.
120. Paulus Aegineta *Seven books* 1.84.

121. Pliny *Natural history* 8.210; 28.136.
122. Martial *Epigrams* 13.41.
123. Paulus Aegineta *Seven books* 1.84.
124. Toynbee, 1973: 131–32.
125. Toynbee, 1973: 132.
126. Alcock, 1980: 63, citing Cicero *The Laws* 2.22.
127. For Greek and Roman deities to whom pigs were offered, see Mayrhofer-Passler, 1953: 192–93, 198–99. For a brief description and explanation of animal sacrifice among the ancient Greeks, see Burkert, 1985: 55–59. For excellent, perceptive, many-sided accounts of Greek sacrifice, see Detienne and Vernant, 1989. Such animal sacrifice has not ended in Greece even today, as shown in Stella Georgoudi's fascinating study (1989) on the slaughter of animals in Greece in connection with popular worship of saints in the Orthodox church.
128. Livy (1.24, trans. in B. O. Foster et al., 1949–63) writes, for example, of a pig ritually killed by the Romans at ceremonies marking the conclusion of a treaty.
129. Cato (*On agriculture* 139) mentions a sacrifice of the private sort in saying that, before thinning a grove of trees, a farmer should sacrifice a pig to the deity of the place to win its favor.
130. Pigs were also sacrificed to deities by other ancient Italians, as shown on bronze tablets (300–100 B.C.) found at Iguvium in Umbria (Poultney, 1959: passim).
131. Dumézil, 1970, 1: 149, 167, 231, 237–40; 2: 554; and Puhvel, 1978: 360–61, 362. Scenes believed to represent the *suovetaurilia* have been found in sites in Roman Britain (Henig, 1984: 86).
132. von Rohr Sauer, 1968: 203.
133. Gonda, 1969a: 132. For a review of perceptions of the pig in Europe and its role in fertility, see Gonda, 1969a: 129–31. Such fertility associations may have led to the custom, found in Greece and Italy, of a bride and groom sacrificing a swine together, and to that of painting "the posts of the entrance to the bridal chamber . . . with swine's blood" (von Rohr Sauer, 1968: 203).
134. Dumézil, 1970, 1: 240, 370, 375–77; 2: 554–55, 559.
135. Gimbutas, 1982: 211–15.
136. Detienne, 1989a: 3, 8, 11.
137. Harrison (1955: 153) also says that the pig was the most common sacrificial animal in Greece, whereas Burkert (1985: 55) writes that the pig was the third most common, after sheep and goats.
138. Frazer, 1935, 7: 74; Nilsson, 1949: 86.
139. Nilsson, 1940: 24.
140. For information on the association of swine with various Olympian deities, on representations of swine in their sanctuaries, and on the sacrifice of pigs and wild boars in ancient Greece, see Bevan, 1986, 1: 67–81.
141. Frazer, 1935, 8: 16; Burkert, 1985: 13; Bevan, 1986, 1: 72–73.
142. For pig sacrifice and the myth of Kore, see Burkert, 1983a: 256–64.
143. For northern European parallels to the Thesmophoria, see Frazer, 1935, 8: 20–21.

144. Simon, 1983: 17–18; Burkert, 1985: 13.

145. For which, see Frazer et al., 1910–11: 838–40; Nilsson, 1940: 24–26, 49; Nilsson, 1949: 91–92; Harrison, 1955: 150–62; Burkert, 1985: 242–46; and Detienne, 1989b. For the Thesmophoria along with other Demeter festivals, see Simon, 1983: 17–37.

146. In the fifth century B.C., Aristophanes even wrote a play about the affair, *Thesmophoriazusae* (women celebrating the festival of the goddess Demeter).

147. On the exclusion of men, see Nilsson, 1940: 24; Burkert, 1985: 242; and Detienne, 1989b: 143–44; for a contrary view, see Simon, 1983: 29. According to Detienne (1989b: 143–44), the literature suggests that in some cases a man, a butcher (*mageiros*), carried out the actual killing, but left shortly afterwards and did not participate in the remainder of the ceremony.

148. Various writers have said that the flesh of pigs killed at the Thesmophoria was not consumed, but Detienne (1989b: 133–35) presents convincing evidence to the contrary. Since flesh of the pig was eaten, R. Parker (1983: 283) suggests, the ceremony "did not serve for purification in any strict sense."

149. Frazer, 1935, 8: 16, 19–20. Farnell (1896–1909, 3: 90–93), while agreeing with Frazer's observations in general, disputes his view that the pig represented Demeter symbolically.

150. Burkert, 1985: 242–43, 244; Detienne, 1989b: 133, 244 n33.

151. Harrison, 1955: 153.

152. Athenaeus *Deipnosophists* 9.375–76.

153. Farnell, 1896–1909, 3: 289–305; Burkert, 1985: 177–78.

154. The worship of Cybele was introduced to Rome in 204 B.C., and with it, Frazer believes, the worship of Attis. Her introduction was in fulfillment of a prophecy that, if the Phrygian goddess were brought to Italy, the foreign invader (Hannibal) would be expelled. The Romans sent emissaries to Phrygia to the sacred city of Pessinus, where they received a black stone that embodied the goddess. The stone was carried back to Rome, where it was received with awe and enthusiasm (Frazer, 1935, 5: 265–66; Julian *Orations* 159 C-161 B).

155. Vermaseren, 1977: 115.

156. Frazer, 1935, 8: 23.

157. In keeping with this, Artemidorus Daldianus noted that a woman who dreamt that she received the gift of a pig's head from her lover started to dislike him and ultimately broke up with him, for the pig "does not enjoy the favors of Aphrodite" (*Interpretation of dreams* 5.80).

158. There are reports of such sacrifice at a few places (Starkie, 1909: 165; A. H. Sommerstein in Aristophanes, 1980: 196; N. Robertson, 1982b: 327).

159. Farnell, 1896–1909, 2: 646–47; W. R. Smith, 1914: 290–91; Frazer, 1935, 8: 23; and N. Robertson, 1982b: 327. Aphrodite seems not to have been among the earliest deities of the Greeks, and some scholars hold that she came from Asia. The question has also been raised whether she may have arrived in Greece together with Adonis (Burkert, 1985: 176–77).

160. For details of this controversy, see Wenham, 1979: 181–85.

161. Katsh, 1954: 122.

162. Koran 2:172; 5:3; 6:146; 16:115.

163. Diener and Robkin, 1978: 501.

164. For criticisms and a defense of the hypothesis, see Diener and Robkin, 1978: 509–35. For an attempt to evaluate archeological evidence from early Palestine in these terms, which I find quite unconvincing, see Hesse, 1990: 200–201, 209, 212, 219–20.

165. Macalister (1912, 2: 8) writes, however, of the belief among Arabs of Palestine that a wild boar's tusk is highly effective against the evil eye. Noting the occurrence of such tusks in his excavations of ancient Gezer, he suggests that this belief is likely an ancient one.

166. Rushdy, 1911: 163.

167. H. Epstein, 1971b, 2: 330.

168. Bökönyi, 1974: 207.

169. Moslem antipathy to the pig has contributed to its unimportance in some sections of Bosnia, Herzegovina, and western Serbia (Great Britain Admiralty, Naval Intelligence Division, 1944–45, 3: 110–11).

170. Rushdy, 1911: 163; Darby et al., 1977, 1: 200–201.

That the early Copts considered pigs acceptable is suggested by the fact that St. Menas, an important Coptic saint, kept pigs. With the Moslem Arab conquest of Egypt (A.D. 641), however, pig keeping and pork eating by Copts experienced a decline. By the end of the eighteenth century, domestic pigs were almost entirely absent in Egypt (Darby et al., 1977, 1: 200–201), and in the nineteenth century it was observed that Egyptians "almost universally" avoided pork, not because it was banned, but because they thought the animal was dirty (E. W. Lane, 1908: 547).

In modern times, Egypt's small numbers of pigs (ninety-four thousand in 1989)—dwarfed by the numbers of sheep and goats, bovines, and donkeys—are said to be concentrated in areas where Copts are numerous, such as the provinces of Qena, Asyut, and Minya, and within town and city limits, especially Cairo, Alexandria, Port Said, and Ismailiya. In the town of El Bayadiya, just south of Luxor in Upper Egypt, free-ranging pigs are owned by many families, and move unattended along the streets. Pigs are kept in Egypt not only by Copts, but also, in some communities in Upper Egypt, by Greek merchants, who sell them in Cairo and Alexandria for consumption by "Christians, foreign residents, and tourists" (Newberry, 1928: 212; Towne and Wentworth, 1950: 61; Besançon, 1957: 255; von Rohr Sauer, 1968: 202; Darby et al., 1977, 1: 209; I. Shaw, 1984: 52). The domestic production of pork (estimated at two thousand metric tons in 1989), at least in the late 1950s was too small to meet demand, requiring that much additional pork be imported (Platt and Hefny, 1958: 188).

171. Dussaud, 1900: 94.

172. Layard, 1849, 1: 301.

173. Drower, 1937: 47.

174. Fisher, 1950: 204; Simmons et al., 1954: 113, 151.

175. Guys, 1863: 167.

176. Zucker, 1972.

177. Zucker, 1972.

178. *New York Times,* July 20, 1985, 1, p. 2.

179. "Pigheaded protest," *Time,* December 3, 1990, p. 79; Marcus, 1993.

180. Gruner, 1930: 220.

181. Paulus Aegineta *Seven books* 1.84.

182. Moslem groups that have been reported as eating the flesh of wild pigs include the Nimadi hunters of Mauretania (Marty, 1930: 121–23); certain groups in Morocco, Algeria, and Tunisia (Doutté, 1905: 42–44); the Egyptian Bedouin and many fellahin of one province (before the wild boar became extinct in Egypt) (Lane, 1908: 299; G. W. Murray, 1935: 89–90); the Rwala Bedouin (Musil, 1928: 28, 395); the Baluchi of Bampur (Phillott, 1907: 341); and the Moro of Mindanao. Other Moslem groups, such as the people of Pemba (Craster, 1913: 283–84), the Iranians (E. C. Sykes, 1910: 241), and the Afghans (Fox, 1943: 118), have refused such flesh as unclean.

183. In addition to survivals of the use of pork for food among Moslems, there is a perhaps more general medicinal use of the flesh of the wild boar. In Morocco, for instance, certain people eat the liver of the wild boar to gain the animal's strength. They also believe the flesh of the boar to be bracing for children, to be a remedy for syphilis, and to make a man insensitive to pain.

184. Deffontaines, 1948: 373.

185. de Planhol, 1959: 58.

186. For information on the two Mediterranean systems of pig keeping (in woodlands or at home), see Clutton-Brock, 1981: 74–75.

187. Coon, 1931: 41. For additional information on Berber pig keeping and pork eating, see Murdock, 1958: MW 14, Zekara; and Murdock, 1959: 116.

188. Coon, 1931: 60.

189. For percentages of common cattle, pigs, and sheep and/or goats in Neolithic sites in various parts of Europe, see Milisauskas, 1978: 61, 67–68, 72–75, 82–83, 134–39, 143, 146–47, 190–91, 196–97; in Neolithic England, see Grigson, 1982: 306–8; in Neolithic Serbia, see Greenfield, 1986: 105, 118, 278, 284, 361; and in Neolithic north-central Europe, see Bogucki, 1988: 60–61, 131–32, 154, 159; Bogucki, 1989: 123, 125, 127, 130.

190. Milisauskas, 1978: 71; Clutton-Brock, 1981: 72. For notes on the forest feeding of pigs in medieval Europe, see Parain 1944: 162, 167 (general); Briard, 1979: 106–7 (Germany); and Ernle, 1961: 16–17 (England); for forest feeding of pigs in Europe at other early times and places, see Grigson, 1982 (Neolithic England); Clutton-Brock, 1976: 378 (Anglo-Saxon England); and Greenfield, 1984: 50–51 (Bronze Age central Balkans).

191. Motz, 1982: 202.

192. Hull, 1928: 144–49; Gonda, 1969a: 129–30.

193. Tacitus *Germany* 45.

194. Jahn, 1884: 105–6; Turville-Petre, 1964: 82, 107, 109, 125, 156, 165–69, 175–79, 224, 255; Gelling and Davidson, 1969: 164–66; Motz, 1982: 200–203. For

a comparison of Freyja with the goddesses Anat, Ishtar, and Inanna of antiquity, see Motz, 1982.

195. Gelling and Davidson, 1969: 164–65; Branston, 1974: 150–51.

196. Farbridge, 1908–26: 133.

197. Similar uses of the heads of swine at Christmas are found among other Scandinavian peoples, as well as among the Germans, Slavs, and English (Mayrhofer-Passler, 1953: 192).

198. Gelling and Davidson, 1969: 165, citing Nilsson. For additional information on the yule boar and other customs relating to pigs and crop fertility in Germany and Scandinavia, see Frazer, 1935, 7: 298–303.

199. MacCulloch, 1911: 24–25, 117, 210–12; Hull, 1928: 143–49; Ross, 1967: 308–21, 357; Gelling and Davidson, 1969: 164–65; Rhys, 1972: 501–4; Ní Chatháin, 1979–80; Alcock, 1980: 63; MacCana, 1987: 157.

200. Ní Chatháin, 1979–80: 210–11.

201. MacCulloch, 1911: 210. The early Celts of Galatia in Asia Minor also rejected pork (MacCulloch, 1911: 210), but this is less surprising, since much of Asia Minor was anti-pig country.

202. Hull, 1928: 144.

203. Gregor, 1881: 129–30.

204. In certain areas of the Balkans, even Christians gave up pork eating (de Planhol, 1959: 57), apparently because of Moslem influence.

205. Blair, 1956: 66.

206. There are questions as to whether the Sudanese pigs are wild or feral (domestic animals that have returned to the wild). There have also been suggestions that wild *Sus* are found in sub-Saharan West Africa, a view that H. Epstein rejects (1971b, 2: 327–29).

207. It has also been suggested that pigs were introduced to the Sudan from Southeast Asia by way of East Africa, or that they were domesticated in the Sudan from the wild Sennar pig (*Sus sennaarensis*). Both of these possibilities are considered highly unlikely by H. Epstein (1971b, 2: 347–49). On the other hand, Kroll (1928: 185) has noted the similarity of the domestic pigs of Sennar to local wild pigs, so, at the very least, there appears to have been interbreeding with wild *Sus sennaarensis*.

208. These statements are confirmed by several observations: (1) Pigs were kept in the Nubian kingdoms which bordered Egypt on its southern marches and which were strongly influenced by Egyptian civilization. (2) Today pigs of types apparently unrelated to those of modern Europe are found in the steppe region of the Sudan: in Sennar (Bruce, 1790, 4: 421; Hartmann, 1883: 31; Hahn, 1896: 217; Seligman and Seligman, 1932: 413); among the Kadullu, Ingassana, and Berta (Cerulli, 1956: 17, 18); and among the pagan people of the southern Nuba Mountains (Seligman and Seligman, 1932: 368). (3) In the case of Sennar, pigs were present for almost two centuries before intimate contact with Europeans developed. (4) There is a tradition among one group in the Nuba Mountains that when their ancestor emerged onto the earth from a rock he was accompanied by pigs (Seligman and Seligman, 1932: 393), which suggests that the pig may indeed be an ancient domesticate among

them. (5) Pigs have also been reported among pagan groups farther south along the Sudan-Ethiopian border: among the Gumuz living around Hulgizi near the Blue Nile (Cheesman, 1936: 371); among the Maban, who live south of the Gumuz near Kurmuk; and in many villages of the Koma, a group of border tribes living still farther south and not far from the Jokau River, a tributary of the Sobat (Corfield, 1938: 151; Cerulli, 1956: 18).

209. When James Bruce (1790, 4: 306–7) and his hunting companions in Christian Ethiopia killed five wild boars, even Bruce chose not to eat the flesh out of fear that this would offend the Ethiopians.

210. The use and rejection of hippopotamus flesh in Africa needs further investigation. For notes on its use and avoidance in Ethiopia and elsewhere in the continent, see Simoons, 1958.

211. Paulitschke, 1893: 228–29; Murdock, 1959: 325.

212. Budge, 1928, 1: 105; R. Herzog, 1957: 152.

213. In becoming Moslem and adopting the Islamic ban on pork, African peoples may justify the ban in a traditional manner. Each matrilineal clan among the Gonja of Ghana, for example, observed a prohibition of some sort, in some cases because of a service rendered by an animal in the past. Following that tradition, Moslem Gonja explain their ban on pork by saying that the pig had once assisted one of their ancestors named Mohammed (Goody, 1982: 82).

214. H. Epstein, 1971b, 2: 332.

215. Crowfoot, 1925: 125; Nadel, 1947: 60.

216. In the 1880s, it is said, the Gumuz tribe of the Sudan-Ethiopia border possessed many pigs (Cerulli, 1956: 18). Though some members of the group in the south may still keep pigs, the people living in the border region west of Lake Tana—who have considerable contact with both Islam and Ethiopian Christianity—have none at all today (personal observation).

217. Some (i.e., Murdock, 1959: 266–67; H. Epstein, 1971b, 2: 346–47) have raised the possibility that the pig had spread to the Senegambia area of West Africa in pre-European times. The more common view, however, is that Europeans are responsible for introducing the domestic pig to both West and Central Africa and East and South (southern) Africa. This is supported by European tradition; by the unquestioned present-day role of Europeans in diffusing pig keeping; by the spotty distribution of domestic pigs in tropical Africa; by their similarity to domestic pigs of the Iberian Peninsula; and by the fact that many peoples use the same name for the domestic pig and the wild bush pig (*Potamochoerus*), which suggests that they simply applied the name for a familiar wild animal to a newly introduced domestic one.

218. Because of Islamic influence, pigs are absent, or pork is rejected, or both, among many West African groups, such as the Nupe (Nadel, 1951: 203), Bolewa of Bauchi (Temple, 1922: 68), and Yoruba. Moslem influence was also evident among the Ashanti of the Gold Coast a century ago, for William Hutchinson, British resident at Kumasi, reported that a "Moorish Shereef" made a great fuss when he discovered pork in a boy's room (Bowdich, 1819: 412).

219. In the Nubian provinces of the Sudan, for example, "Arab hunters" ate the

flesh of wild boars when food was scarce (S. W. Baker, 1867: 166). Unfortunately we cannot be certain whether the "wild boars" were bush pigs or wart hogs. In Ethiopia, Mansfield Parkyns (1868: 208) noted, some Moslems ate the flesh of the wild swine. Nathaniel Pearce (1831, 2: 253) reported that an Ethiopian ate with him the meat of a wild hog, apparently a wart hog, because he was ill and the meat had medicinal value. In Begemder and Semyen in northwestern Ethiopia, people say that they never use the blood or flesh of the bush pig for medicinal purposes, but here and there the flesh of the wart hog is so used (personal observation). The Kafa of southwest Ethiopia consider the flesh of wild swine unclean, whereas their neighbors the Janjero eat it (Huntingford, 1955: 109, 138). The Xosa of the Republic of South Africa also eat "the wild hog," though they refuse domestic swine (Westermarck, 1924, 2: 327–28).

220. Among the groups reported in this century as still not eating pork are the Barabaig of Tanzania (Huntingford, 1953b: 96), the Yao of Malawi (Stannus, 1922: 347), and the Lemba of southern Africa (Stayt, 1931: 44).

Of other tribes in southern Africa: (1) The Zulu formerly did not regard pigs as fit for human consumption, but today pig sties are frequent in their kraals (Bryant, 1949: 290, 343). (2) In former times the Ngoni did not eat pork, though they may do so now (Earthy, 1933: 38). (3) Though pigs are kept by the southern Sotho (Basuto), and their flesh and fat are prized, some still refuse to eat them because of their dirty scavenging habits (Ashton, 1952: 135). (4) Some Thonga refuse to eat pork, apparently because it is a recent introduction with which they are unaccustomed (Junod, 1913, 2: 52, 66).

In Madagascar, some groups keep pigs and others do not. Thus, the Hova, a plateau people who have strong Malaysian elements in their culture and are Malay in physical appearance, keep them; the Sakalava, plains people and cattle herders who are black African in appearance, do not (C. Keller, 1901: 130). Among the Bara of southern Madagascar, another plains group of cattle herders, the pig is regarded as impure. It was introduced by European example to Betsileo people who descended from the central plateau, and the Bara have begun to raise them, though they remain of little importance (Faublée, 1942: 184–85). The Tanala are cultivators, but many groups of them consider the pig unclean because it eats excrement and other filth; they not only refuse to kill or eat pigs but also will not permit pork to be cooked in their pots or allow it in the village. Some Tanala explain their avoidance of pork by pointing out that the pig in the past did a good deed to their group (Linton, 1933: 230–31), an explanation that seems totemic in nature.

221. For notes on human use of the bush pig in Africa, see Simoons, 1953.

222. Meadow, 1975: 278–80, 282; Meadow, 1983: 370, 393; Voigt, 1983: 278.

223. Flannery, 1983: 170–76; S. J. M. Davis, 1984: 270, 274.

224. Zeder, 1984: 287, 289.

225. Meadow, 1985–88.

226. Yasht 10.70.127, trans. in Darmesteter and Mills, 1880–87.

227. S. J. M. Davis, 1984: 270.

228. Dhalla, 1922: 260.

229. Dhalla, 1922: 375.

230. I say this because a bas-relief dating from that period depicts a royal pig hunt

in a marshy area, with the dead pigs not just left there but carried off by elephants, presumably for a banquet (Reed, 1965: 7–12).

231. Pahlavi texts, Dēnkard 8.41.13, 18; Epistles of Mānūškīhar 1.8.3; Shāyast lā-shāyast 2.58, trans. in West, 1880–97; also West, 1880–97, 5: 260n; 18: 311n.

232. Nweeya, 1910: 241.

233. E. C. Sykes, 1910: 72, 240–41.

234. This belief was also recorded among Turkoman along the eastern shores of the Caspian Sea just north of Iran (Vámbéry, 1864: 72–73).

235. Phillott, 1907: 341; E. C. Sykes, 1910: 241. In Baghdad, too, a wild boar is sometimes kept in the stable (Phillott, 1907: 341), and the practice is also reported for Egypt (H. Epstein, 1971b, 2: 330) and Morocco (Westermarck, 1926, 2: 314–15).

236. Herodotus *History* 4.63.

237. Minns, 1913: 49.

238. Featherman, 1885–91, 4: 537.

239. Westermarck, 1924, 2: 326–27; Paine, 1957: 117n.

240. K. Donner, 1926: 26.

241. Great Britain Admiralty, n.d.: 169.

242. Lattimore, 1941: 220.

243. Krader, 1955: 312, 315.

244. Sauer, 1952: 28, 31–32; Clutton-Brock, 1981: 76; Reed and Perkins, 1984: 19.

245. Hemmer, 1978.

246. Groves, 1981: 61.

247. Chang, 1986: 100, 102.

248. *Recent archaeological discoveries in the People's Republic of China,* 1984: 9–11; Chang, 1986: 90–91, 93.

249. Gibson, 1935: 342, 346–47; Sowerby, 1935: 234–37; Creel, 1937a: 182–83, 242–43; Creel, 1937b: 43, 78–79, 81, 200; Li, 1957: 21–23.

250. Maynard and Swen, 1956: 413. Not only was the pig's flesh consumed, but also in some parts of China it was customary to cook pig ribs in a sweet and sour sauce of sugar and vinegar, which made the calcium in the bones digestible. This provided an invaluable source of calcium for pregnant women (Winfield, 1948: 72–73).

251. Gerard, 1952: 260–61.

252. Ekvall, 1939: 23.

253. L. H. D. Buxton, 1929: 51–52.

254. Lattimore, 1929: 227–28.

255. Banister, 1987: 17.

256. Broomhall, 1910: 226, 244–45, 281.

257. Bell, 1928: 53.

258. Cammann, 1951: 35.

259. Yamasaki, 1900: 233; Stanford University, 1956: 259.

260. Shirokogoroff, 1924: 132–33.

261. Griffis, 1882: 267; Hulbert, 1906: 20; Heydrich, 1931: 42; Osgood, 1951: 31, 77.

262. Groot, 1951: 75.

263. Beardsley et al., 1959: 107.

264. Bernatzik, 1954, 2: 154–55.

265. Clason, 1977: 260–61.

266. Badam, 1984: 347; Rissman, 1989: 16–17. For a contrary view, see Epstein and Bichard, 1984: 147.

267. J. Marshall, 1931, 1: 27, 28; Nath, 1979: 324; Allchin and Allchin, 1982: 191. In the recent excavation of a mound at Harappa, very few pig bones were reported in a standardized count (15, not identified as to state of domestication), as compared with bones of sheep and/or goats (346) and bovines (345) (Meadow, 1991: 101).

268. *Rig-veda* 1.61.7; 1.88.5; 1.114.5; 1.121.11–12; 8.29.4; 8.66.8–10; 10.67.7; 10.86.4; 10.99.6, trans. in R. T. H. Griffith, 1963; Macdonell, 1897: 67, 75, 151; Macdonell and Keith, 1967, 2: 245, 461.

269. Gonda, 1969a: 135–45.

270. Macdonell and Keith, 1967, 2: 145–47.

271. Prakash, 1961: 15–18.

272. Punekar, 1959: 6–7.

273. Oldenberg, 1988: 200–201.

274. *Śatapatha Brāhmaṇa* 12.4.1.4, trans. in Eggeling, 1882–1900.

275. *Vaikhānasa Gṛihya-sūtra* 6.1, cited by Gonda, 1980: 281.

276. *Mānava Dharma-śāstra* 3.239, trans. in Bühler, 1886.

277. *Vishnu Smṛti* 81.7, trans. in Jolly, 1900.

278. Banerji, 1980: 116.

279. *Mānava Gṛihya-sūtra* 2.14.11, cited by Gonda, 1980: 102.

280. *Āpastamba Dharma-sūtra* 1.5.17.27–29, and 1.7.21.14–15, trans. in Bühler, 1896.

281. *Vasishṭha Dharma-sūtra* (23.30, trans. in Bühler, 1882); *Baudhāyana Dharma-sūtra* (1.5.12.3, trans. in Bühler, 1882); and *Gautama Dharma-sūtra* (17.29, trans. in Bühler, 1896). Banerji (1980: 154) indicates that similar statements also appear in writings of *Kālidāsa*, among them the *Abhijñāna-śakuntalā*.

282. *Chhāndogya Upanishad* 5.14–20, trans. in Bühler, 1886.

283. In describing Brahmin funeral practices in western India, Margaret Stevenson (1920: 165–66) writes of the deceased's smaller sins (*upa-pātaka*) which are morally demeaning and require forgiveness. Among them is the eating of banned items such as garlic or onions, along with lying, cheating, refusal to give alms to worthy persons, smoking, and other behavior unbecoming of a Brahmin.

284. *Chhāndogya Upanishad* 5.10.7, trans. in Vol. 4 of Swami Nikhilananda, 1949–59.

285. It has long been a matter of controversy whether the food in question (*sūkara-maddava; sūkara* = "relating to swine") was a pork tidbit or something for which pigs had a great liking. For more on the controversy, see Wasson, 1982, who, himself, believes that the food was likely an underground fungus.

286. *Jātakas* 50, 186, 283, 388, 541, 544, trans. in Cowell, 1973.

287. Rao, 1974: 231, 233.

288. Aelian *On the characteristics of animals* 3.3; 16.37. Ctesias himself did not visit

India, and his account derives from accounts of Indians in Persia and from Persians who had visited India.

289. Prakash, 1961: 176.

290. Prakash, 1961: 210–11.

291. Lawrence, 1895: 117; J. Marshall, 1931, 1: 74; S. Fuchs, 1950: 357; Hutton, 1963: 77; Walker, 1968, 1: 48.

292. Tod, 1983, 1: 451–52; Walker, 1968, 1: 48.

293. Walker, 1968, 1: 48.

294. Walker, 1968, 1: 47; 2: 575; Stutley, 1985: 88.

295. Stutley, 1985: 86.

296. That the keeping of pigs and eating of pork by members of some low castes is the pattern throughout Hindu India is attested by numerous specific and general references in the literature: Russell, 1916, 4: 8; G. W. Briggs, 1920: 45; Blunt, 1931: 94–96; Bhagwat, 1944: 89–91; Desai, 1945: 117; M. Singh, 1947, 91; Hutton, 1963: 78; B. S. Cohn, 1955: 73; Dube, 1955: 176; Srinivas, 1955: 20; Wiser, 1955: 318, 346; University of California, 1956, 1: 149–50. Though one cannot be certain that they were Hindu (since other religions in India also have castes), one notes that B. C. Allen (1912: 102) wrote of pigs as conspicuous near "the sweepers' lines in Dacca" (East Bengal is a predominantly Moslem area).

297. Srinivas, 1955: 9, 21, 26.

298. S. Fuchs, 1950: 357.

299. B. Cohn, 1955: 73.

300. Gondal, 1948: 22.

301. Eichinger Ferro-Luzzi (1977a: 362–63) has observed that, though belief in blood sacrifice remains strong in South India, animal sacrifice is decreasing there, and that sacrifice of pigs is now very rare. She found just a single case of pig sacrifice in South Canara, in which the animal was offered to a demon. On blood as an offering to village deities and as food for Hindus, see Eichinger Ferro-Luzzi, 1977a: 362; Eichinger Ferro-Luzzi, 1981: 249.

302. Whitehead, 1916: 17–20; Thurston, 1912: 165, 189, 201, 211, 305.

303. Bhagwat, 1944: 89–91. After sacrificial rites for the terrible Nadividhi Sakti, the goddess is asked to leave the village, and, in some places in South India, people attempt to keep her from coming back by burying four piglets alive, with only their heads above ground, one at each corner of the village (Elmore, 1915: 42–44).

304. Whitehead, 1916: 17–20.

305. Kinsley, 1986: 146. For notes on pig sacrifice among Hindus outside of South India, see Bhagwat, 1944: 90; M. Singh, 1947: 116; B. Cohn, 1955: 58; and Lodrick, 1992.

306. For brief accounts of Śākta cults in India, see Walker, 1968, 2: 336–38; and Stutley, 1985: 47–48, 120–23.

307. Gonda (1970: 68) notes that, while Hindus do not hesitate to eat food offerings made to Vishnu, they view ones made to Shiva with contempt. One wonders how much of this can be attributed to Shiva's wives and their blood sacrifices.

308. Walker, 1968, 1: 50.

309. R. V. Russell, 1916, 4: 8–13; Hivale, 1944: 100–101; Verrier Elwin in Hivale, 1944: 115–16; R. P. Das, 1987: 246.

310. R. V. Russell, 1916, 4: 8–13.

311. Food offered to a god becomes *prasāda,* or sanctified and thought to result in salvation (Gonda, 1970: 74).

312. Eichinger Ferro-Luzzi, 1981: 252.

313. Lodrick, 1992: 142–44, 152.

314. Elmore, 1915: 46–47.

315. Such facts do not appear to deter those who would think the worst of other ethnic groups, as shown in a story published in 1985 in a Teheran newspaper. In the Teheran case, however, the animal was the dog, and the villains were Zionists, who were accused of attempting to "corrupt Moslem children" by means of the dog. The story alleged that Zionists, who control the media, were doing this by means of television cartoons that show the dog as a "delightful, playful, intelligent animal that is fun to pet and play with" (Afshar, 1990: 54–55).

316. Slater, 1918: 131; Ayyar, 1926: 239–40.

317. Roy, 1960: 157.

318. Fürer-Haimendorf and Fürer-Haimendorf, 1948: 353.

319. Fürer-Haimendorf, 1943, 2: 97–98, 100.

320. Elwin, 1955: 114, 126, 192, 194, 241, 255, 281, 294, 305, 322–23, 338.

321. Bhagwat, 1944: 92–94; Hivale, 1944: 100–101.

322. Bhagwat, 1944: 91–92, 95–99.

323. Roy, 1960: 157.

324. Elwin, 1955: 523.

325. Fürer-Haimendorf, 1943, 2: 97–98.

326. S. Fuchs, 1960: 70.

327. D. N. Majumdar, 1937: 26.

328. Sopher, 1959: 7.

329. Wijesekera, 1965: 143.

330. de Reinach, 1901, 1: 406; League of Nations, 1937: 78; Andrus, 1943: 31.

331. Gourou, 1936: 427.

332. Simoons, 1991: 3–5, 513–15.

333. Delvert, 1961: 154–59.

334. On Alor, however, pigs are controlled by the men, for they are regarded as currency (C. DuBois, 1944: 22) and figure in the prestige structure, as they do in the Pacific islands.

335. de Young, 1955: 98.

336. H. I. Marshall, 1922: 64–65.

337. Ferrars and Ferrars, 1901: 150.

338. Frazer, 1935, 2: 107.

339. H. I. Marshall, 1922: 284.

340. Lévy-Bruhl, 1923: 186.

341. Frazer, 1935, 1: 382.

342. Featherman, 1885–91, 2: 402; Burkill, 1935, 2: 1724; Covarrubias, 1942: 41, 103–4; Mr. Dyatmoko, Jogjakarta, pers. comm.

343. E. Young, 1898: 111; Graham, 1924, 1: 156–57; V. Thompson, 1941: 333–34; Andrus, 1947: 54; de Young, 1955: 98; Tambiah, 1969: 438.

344. This has not led all Thais to reject pig sacrifice, as shown in the village of Phraan Muan, where sacrifice of pigs and other animals is carried out, not in connection with Buddhism, but for propitiating evil spirits and guardian spirits of the village (Tambiah, 1969: 439).

345. Burkill, 1935, 2: 1725; W. E. Maxwell, 1881: 22; R. R. Wheeler, 1928: 255; V. Thompson, 1943: 59; Cole, 1945: 121.

346. Cole, 1945: 196–97; Ewing, 1963: 60–61.

347. Evans, 1923: 15; Rutter, 1929: 75.

348. Teston and Percheron, 1931: 389; LeBar et al., 1964: 247, 248.

349. See, for example, LeBar, 1972–75: passim.

350. Raffles, 1817, 1: 49; Mr. Dyatmoko, Jogjakarta, pers. comm.

351. O. J. A. Collet, 1925: 216.

352. Ormeling, 1957: 113–14.

353. Ratzel, 1896–98, 2: 306.

354. Best, 1924, 2: 354; P. H. Buck, 1932: 83; P. H. Buck, 1938a: 310–12; P. H. Buck, 1944: 15–16; Beaglehole and Beaglehole, 1938: 106.

355. P. H. Buck, 1938a: 194–95.

356. Curiously the Maori word for pig, "*poaka*," which is derived from the English word "pork," is very similar to the original Polynesian word for pig, "*puaka*" (P. H. Buck, 1950b: 110–11).

357. Rivers, 1914: 333; Raymond Firth, 1930: 107.

358. S. H. Malcolm, 1952: 5, 36.

359. Smyth, 1878, 1: 237.

360. Frazer, 1935, 8: 296.

361. Frazer, 1935, 8: 33.

362. Seligman, 1910: 680.

363. Seligman, 1910: 681.

364. A. B. Lewis, 1932: 52.

365. Burrows, 1949, 18; Spiro, 1949: 7.

366. Mead, 1930: 48–49.

367. P. H. Buck, 1930: 119, 323; Grattan, 1948: 55.

368. Malinowski, 1935, 1: 46–47.

369. Herskovits, 1952: 429–30.

370. P. H. Buck, 1944: 15–16.

371. Beaglehole and Beaglehole, 1938: 106.

372. P. H. Buck, 1944: 15–16.
At Nukahiva in the Marquesas Islands a stone image of a pig's head was found buried with some human bodies (Ratzel, 1896–98, 1: 306); it may have been a symbol of rank of a chief or another important person. On Nias Island off Sumatra, the pig's head is the portion presented to the leading chief who is at hand (Loeb, 1935: 133).

In the southeast Solomons, pigs are associated with chiefs because of the latter's right to hold feasts (Ivens, 1927: 241–42). In the Marquesas Islands, the chief can taboo the slaughter of pigs to guarantee an adequate supply for a future feast (Herskovits, 1952: 275). The people of Vanikoro, or La Pérouse Island, eat pork mainly at the homes of chiefs, who apparently consider its use a privilege of their rank (Featherman, 1885–91, 2: 94).

373. Featherman, 1885–91, 2: 47.

374. Webster, 1942: 118.

375. Webster, 1942: 118.

376. Steiner, 1956: 88.

377. Malynicz, 1970; Vayda, 1972.

378. Leroy, 1978–79: 183–84.

379. Among the Wola of New Guinea, more than 40 percent of all disputes (for example, over domestic affairs, slander, sex offenses, land rights, and theft) are about pigs, for which see Sillitoe, 1980–81 ("Pigs in disputes").

380. Leroy, 1978–79: 209.

381. Frazer, 1935, 1: 339.

382. Strathern, 1971.

383. J. R. Baker, 1929: 30; Deacon, 1934: 16–17; Harrisson, 1937: 25.

384. Harrisson, 1937: 25.

385. Harrisson, 1937: 24–35.

386. Williams, 1936: 224–25.

387. Seligman, 1910: 681–82.

388. Watson, 1965: 65.

389. Rubel and Rosman, 1978.

390. Linton, 1955: 98.

391. Vayda et al., 1961: 71–72.

392. For a more detailed description of the four explanations, see Wenham, 1979: 166–71.

393. Porphyry On abstinence from animal food 1.14.

394. In Psalms (80:13), one reads of wild boars of the woods, apparently a reference to the brush along the banks of the Jordan River from which boars ventured forth to damage grape vines and other crops.

395. I use "trichinosis" to refer to infection with nematodes of the genus *Trichinella,* because the term has been in use for well over a century and is more familiar to the general reader than "trichinellosis," the term now being encouraged.

396. R. Campbell Thompson (1903–4, 2: xlvi–xlviii), in writing of ancient Mesopotamian bans on various foods, among them pork, beef, fish, and dates, on particular days, suggests that "the element of hygiene probably enters largely into these restrictions." That view is not in accord with the observation, mentioned above, that in Sumer the avoidance of certain foods at the time of the new year seems to have been intended to assure a person's ritual purity so as to enable participation in rites. If, however, rapid decay of flesh had been a problem in ancient Mesopotamia, it is difficult to see how a ban on pork for a few days would have been an effective solution.

397. Aelian (A.D. 170–235), for example, explained the Egyptian view, that the pig is impure and pork not to be eaten, in such terms, as deriving from the pig's "sheer gluttony" which leads it to eat human bodies and even its own young. "Sober men,"

he added, "are accustomed to prefer those animals which are of a gentler nature and have some sense of restraint and reverence" (*On the characteristics of animals* 10. 16).

398. Maimonides *Guide for the perplexed* 3.48, trans. in Friedländer, 1956: 370–71.

399. For which, see Novak, 1976: 40–46.

400. One may question why the chicken, which may be as dirty in its eating habits as the pig, was not included in the Levitican ban. This may be because the chicken, to which there is no certain reference in the Old Testament, may not have been known, or at least was not a common household animal, in Israel at the time the Levitican bans were established.

401. Gould, 1970b: 3–4; Kozar, 1970: 423–24.

402. The role of rats in transmitting the parasite to pigs is a matter of controversy. Infection of rats with *Trichinella* is widespread and serious, but in one study of farm pigs (Hanbury et al., 1986) pig cannibalism, rather than rats, was identified as the means by which trichinosis was transmitted.

403. Kozar, 1970: 423–24; Yamashita, 1970: 460. On the two cycles, see W. C. Campbell, 1983a: 426–34.

404. For most of the time since its discovery in 1835, it was thought that there was a single *Trichinella* species, *T. spiralis*. Now additional forms have been identified, whether species, subspecies, varieties, or geographic strains. The principal villain in the Near East, however, seems to be the original form discovered by James Paget in England (now sometimes *Trichinella spiralis spiralis*), which is the most widespread form, one to which pigs have a high susceptibility. A second form that occurs in the Near East is *T. spiralis nelsoni,* or *T. nelsoni,* to which pigs have low susceptibility (Dick, 1983; W. C. Campbell et al., 1988: 9–10, 15–17; W. C. Campbell, 1991: 83, 92–97). For a recent revision of the taxonomy of the genus *Trichinella,* in which five related species are proposed, see Pozio and La Rosa, 1991; Pozio, La Rosa, Murell, and Lichtenfels, 1992; and Pozio, La Rosa, Rossi, and Murell, 1992.

405. W. C. Campbell, 1991: 97.

406. What appears to have been a cyst of *Trichinella spiralis* was found in the mummy of an Egyptian weaver named Nakht, who lived in the twelfth century B.C. This oft-cited, earliest-known case of human trichinosis, it is claimed, was "definitely pork-related" (Millet et al., 1980: 80, 84). One can, however, first question whether the cyst was *Trichinella* or some other parasite, such as *Echinococcus granulosis,* which is endemic in modern Egypt. If the cyst was *Trichinella,* one could still object to Millet and his associates' certainty that Nakht's infection was pork related. While it is true that trichinosis is found among pigs in modern Egypt (Azab et al., 1988; W. C. Campbell et al., 1988: 61–62; W. C. Campbell, 1991: 84–86), there are many carriers of *Trichinella,* almost all of them carnivores or omnivores, but, in rare cases, even herbivores (Gould, 1945: 65–72; W. C. Campbell, 1983a; Kim, 1983; W. C. Campbell et al., 1988: 19–21, 30–33). Thus, it is not uncommon for *Trichinella* infections in humans to derive from carriers other than the pig. Wild animals are important reservoirs of the disease, and at some times and places in the world human trichinosis has derived largely from wild animals (e.g., Alaska, 86–100 percent from bear and walrus; Khabarovsk area of the former Soviet Union, 82 percent from bear;

Slovakia, 96 percent from bear and wild boar: Bessonov, 1985: 258; Ramisz, 1985: 192; W. C. Campbell et al., 1988: 30). Of the wild animals in which infections of *Trichinella* have been reported in Egypt or elsewhere in Africa (for which, see Nelson, 1970: 480–87; Kim, 1983: 486–88; W. C. Campbell, 1983a: 436–41; W. C. Campbell, 1991: 84–92), moreover, a few seem to have been eaten on occasion as food or medicine in ancient Egypt (hyena, hippopotamus, hare: Darby et al., 1977, 1: 252, 257, 260–61).

There is also a possibility, however remote, that human trichinosis infection in the Nile Valley could have come from other domesticated animals. Among the possible carriers are dogs, which, at least around piggeries and the abattoir of Alexandria, have high levels of *Trichinella* infection (Selim et al., 1981; Barakat et al., 1982). Though it remains uncertain what the role of dog eating may be in human trichinosis (Nelson, 1970: 486; W. C. Campbell, 1991: 90), in general in the Old World today, it appears that *Trichinella* are found in a higher percentage of dogs than pigs (Kozar, 1962: 25, 29, 36–37, 40–41, 44–45, 48–49, and passim). It is true that there is very little to suggest that dogflesh was ever eaten by the Egyptians themselves (Darby et al., 1977, 1: 251–52), but there are reports of dog eating among modern people of Berber stock in western Egypt. Such groups were likely dog eaters in antiquity, and, when they migrated to the Nile Valley, they could have continued their dog eating, as some Berbers are reported to do in Egypt today.

Another possible candidate, strange as it may seem, is the camel. In a shop in modern Cairo a young German tourist bought a salted, air-dried, flesh delicacy called pastyrma (*basterma*) which was said to be camelflesh (it is usually made from beef). When eaten at a party in Germany, the flesh brought on an outbreak of trichinosis (Bommer et al., 1985). There are two important questions about the incident: whether the flesh was indeed camelflesh, and whether the camel can, in fact, be the carrier of encysted larvae of *Trichinella*. There is an additional question about the camel as a carrier in antiquity. The consensus of scholarly opinion is that the time of Nakht was before camels had become part of Egyptian economic life. Nor is there any evidence of camel eating in Egypt before the Arab invasion (Darby et al., 1977, 1: 254). If those who espouse an earlier presence of camels in Egypt are correct, however, the matter would have to be reconsidered. In any case, the possibility of transmission by camelflesh cannot be ruled out until the results of further investigation are available. Such transmission would be no stranger than the outbreaks of human trichinosis in France and Italy brought on by consumption of horsemeat (W. C. Campbell, 1983a: 435–36; Bommer et al., 1985: 316; Ancelle et al., 1988; W. C. Campbell et al., 1988: 30–31; Pozio, Cappelli, et al., 1988; de Carneri and di Matteo, 1989).

407. One recent study suggests that, in Turkey, trichinosis is very rare in both domestic and wild swine. Not a single animal among 535 domestic pigs examined (1979–83) for *Trichinella spiralis* in the Istanbul abattoir was infected. Nor were *Trichinella* found in any of six hundred samples of meat products (among them sausage, salami, ham) that were examined. Of 1,165 wild boars tested, *T. spiralis* was found in 2 animals, with 3 and 0.8 larvae per gram in the 2 infected animals (Nazli and Inal, 1987).

Of 4,950 carcasses of wild boars from north-central Iran, only 2 were found on examination to be infected with *T. spiralis.* Of over 21,000 wild-boar carcasses, mainly from the east Caspian region, only 5 were infected (Kim, 1983: 483).

Before the 1970s, examination of pigs in Egyptian abattoirs failed to turn up any evidence of trichinosis infection. Since that time, however, it has become clear that high or very high percentages of infection are found in Egyptian domestic pigs. In one study, using direct microscopic examination, 4.5 percent of over 40,000 pigs killed at the Cairo slaughterhouse in 1975–76 were found to be infected (Kim, 1983: 486; W. C. Campbell, 1991: 84–85). A study of 250 pigs in Cairo carried out at the Cairo abattoir a decade or so later (Azab et al., 1988: 383–84) found 4 percent infected when microscopic examination was used, but 35.6 percent when using an indirect method, the immunofluorescent antibody test (IFAT).

Lebanon seems to have the highest percentages of infected domestic pigs in the region today, ranging from 15 to 30 percent of carcasses examined (Kim, 1983: 482).

408. Kim, 1983: 482–83.

409. Yamashita, 1970: 457; Schwabe, 1984b: 547; Blondheim et al., 1984. By contrast, in Thailand between 1962 and mid-1983 there were 67 outbreaks of human trichinosis which involved nearly 2,800 people and resulted in 85 deaths (Dissamarn and Indrakamhang, 1985).

410. Another group of Bedouins who obtained the head of that wild boar but cooked it thoroughly were unaffected—an example of the importance of thorough cooking (Steele, 1970: 495; Yamashita, 1970: 457).

411. Yamashita, 1970: 457.

412. Eisenman and Einat, 1992.

413. Azab et al., 1988: 384; W. C. Campbell, 1991: 84–86.

414. W. C. Campbell, 1983b: 3–18.

415. Kim, 1983: 481.

416. The trichinosis situation in the United States is believed to have been so bad because garbage feeding of swine was prevalent, though, curiously, grain-fed swine are not altogether free of *Trichinella* infection either (W. C. Campbell, 1983a: 435; W. C. Campbell et al., 1988: 26–27). Whatever the source of the pork that people ate, studies between 1931 and 1950 disclosed an average incidence of human trichinosis at autopsy of 16 percent in the United States (W. J. Zimmermann, 1970: 379; Kim, 1983: 454–55). With better detection techniques, the percentage of infection might have run as high as 25–30 percent (Belding, 1958: 145).

Some ethnic groups living in the United States, moreover, had much higher incidences than average. Though human trichinosis was very rare in Germany and Italy by the 1930s, one survey done from 1936 to 1941 found trichinosis in 28 percent of German-Americans and 29 percent of Italian-Americans—these high incidences reflecting both the popularity of pork and pork products and the consumption of American-produced pork (Kim, 1983: 455; Schwabe, 1984b: 547). Members of other ethnic groups may have had similar problems with American pork. Two epidemics of trichinosis were reported in the early 1970s among Thai immigrants living in New York City who used uncooked but fermented American pork in preparing certain of their traditional dishes (W. C. Campbell et al., 1988: 33).

417. The outbreak in one German village was not typical of most cases. Of its

population of 2,000, 337 people became sick, and 101, nearly a third, died (Steele, 1970: 494).

418. Belding, 1958: 145.

419. Pawlowski, 1983: 372–77.

420. Gould, 1945: 237–38.

421. Virchow, n.d.: 30, 39; Gould, 1945: 14.

422. Gould, 1970a: 270; Pawlowski, 1983: 369.

423. Virchow, n.d.: 30–31.

424. The situation in the United States has improved markedly in recent decades, largely because of laws against feeding raw garbage to pigs or against all garbage feeding. The number of infected people was estimated to have declined from nearly 16 million in 1940 to 4.4 million in 1970 (Schwabe, 1984b: 551). The problem thus has become less serious but has not gone away completely. Nor has the trend been consistently downward. In terms of annual cases of human trichinosis reported, in the 1940s there were 400 per year, which declined to 57 per year from 1982 to 1986, only to have the decline reverse sharply in 1990, when there were two large outbreaks involving 106 people (McAuley et al., 1991).

425. Gould, 1945: 15–16, 19, 56, 284–85. For the story of the vain attempts to get a system of inspection established in the United States, see Schwabe, 1984b: 549–52.

426. From 1861 to 1890, over 12,500 cases of human trichinosis were reported in Germany (about 5 percent of them fatal). By contrast, 10 outbreaks, involving about 2,000 cases, were reported from the end of the Second World War until late 1991. At Bitburg in 1982, for example, an outbreak involved 402 cases, 193 of them with acute trichinosis of whom over 40 percent still had symptoms six months later (Remig and Froscher, 1987). The principal sources of infection in Germany have been illegally slaughtered pigs, minced pork and sausage (some of which was of unknown origin), and flesh of wild boars that had not been inspected (Hinz, 1991).

427. Virchow, n.d.: 39.

428. Chandler, 1955: 396.

429. See, for example, the statements by noted biblical archeologist William F. Albright (1968: 176–81) and pathologist and trichinosis authority S. E. Gould (1970b: 3–4). Not all authorities on trichinosis, however, agree with Gould, for example W. C. Campbell (1983b: 3–4), who writes that it is not known "whether or not [trichinosis] was a factor in the Mosaic proscription of pork consumption."

430. Calvin W. Schwabe, pers. comm.

431. Quoted by J. Cohn, 1973: 17–18.

432. Harmer, n.d.: 181–83.

433. Coon, 1951: 346.

434. Harris, 1972, 1973, 1974: 35–45; Harris, 1978: 193–208; Harris, 1985: 67–87.

435. Harris, 1972: 36.

The view that the tastiness of pork actually contributed to its being forbidden to Hebrews was advanced in the first century A.D. by Philo, Jewish theologian and philosopher of Alexandria (*On the special laws* 4.95–112, trans. in Colson and Whitaker, 1929–62, 8: 65–77). Philo's hypothesis, however, was an unusual blending of moral, symbolic, and hygienic factors. He believed that Moses established the food bans to encourage moderation, charity, and, above all, reverence and obedience to God. Moses set a path of self-control and simple contentedness for his people that was neither strict austerity nor fancy living but something halfway between the two. According to Philo, the animals Moses chose to ban were ones with the choicest and fattest flesh (the pig, Philo held, had the tastiest flesh of all land animals), ones that, because they were so tempting, could lead to overindulgence. Overindulgence was considered a wrong that places both the soul and body at considerable risk, the risk to the body being upset and sickness. Philo also noted that the banned animals were either carnivores or animals of other sorts that symbolized undesirable moral characteristics. It was thus proper for a civilized person to avoid their flesh.

436. Diener and Robkin, 1978: 496–98.

437. According to early Jewish and Christian tradition, Moses was the actual author of all five books of Moses (Genesis, Exodus, Leviticus, Numbers, Deuteronomy). Most present-day biblical scholars, however, accept four major sources for these books, which are referred to as J, E, P, and D. Of the two books where the prohibitions on flesh food are elaborated, Deuteronomy is a complex document drawn from various sources, and most modern scholars believe that it was composed some time during the seventh century B.C. (Weinfeld and Rabinowitz, 1971–72: 238, 243; Weinfeld et al., 1971–72: 1576–77; J. A. Thompson, 1974: 47–68: Sarna, 1987: 158–59). Its section on pure and impure animals (Deuteronomy 14:3–21) is similar to that in Leviticus (Leviticus 11), and is believed to have been borrowed from P, "the Priestly Source" (Weinfeld and Rabinowitz, 1971–72: 248). Leviticus, in turn, falls entirely within P, and may have been composed by a group of scholarly priests over a period of centuries, no earlier than the tenth to eighth century B.C., with the book in final form perhaps by the seventh century B.C. (Weinfeld and Rabinowitz, 1971–72: 243). It is believed, however, that these books drew on earlier material, including oral tradition, some of which may go back to the time of Moses. There are, at the other end of the time span, questions of dating and later revision. This means that in seeking to explain the origins of the flesh bans in Leviticus and Deuteronomy, we seem to be dealing with a time period from roughly 1300 to 400 B.C.

For more on oral and written tradition and the books of Moses, see Roland de Vaux's "Reflections on the present state of Pentateuchal criticism" (1971: 31–48).

438. Numbers 13:23–27.

439. Deuteronomy 8:7–9.

440. Deuteronomy 11:11–12, 14–15.

441. Lemche, 1988: 109–10.

442. For excellent general accounts of the Canaanites and their land or agriculture, see D. C. Hopkins, 1985; and Lemche, 1991.

443. As Clason and Clutton-Brock (1982: 145) have observed, in preagricultural times in the Levant, which was well populated with lions and other predators, sheep and goats were not swift enough to escape pursuit. On the other hand, their nimble-

ness and aggressiveness in grazing and browsing suited them to craggy mountain country where feed was sparse and predators relatively few. The principal wild animals hunted for food in the Levant in preagricultural times were gazelle, able to survive there because they were swift, wary, and wide-ranging. When goats and sheep were domesticated and introduced to the lowlands, they were able to avoid destruction because herdsmen protected them from predators, which, over time, became far fewer or even extinct. However useful sheep and goats were to humans, their aggressive feeding habits had the unfortunate effect of bringing on a serious degradation of vegetation that has continued to the present day.

444. Horwitz and Tchernov, 1989, 2: 280–81.

445. Horwitz and Tchernov, 1989, 2: 281–88.

446. They were completely absent or amounted to less than 1 percent of animals in two southern sites, likely because of lower precipitation.

447. Hesse, 1990: 211.

448. Pigs are said to have accounted for only a small percentage of domesticated animals in Early Bronze Age Anatolia (estimated, at one site, at 7 percent of all domesticated animals). As in Palestine, sheep and goats were in the majority, and common cattle accounted for a third of all domesticated animals (Yakar, 1985, 2: 374). This contrasts sharply with the Bronze Age situation in the woodlands of the central Balkans (Serbia), where, judging from bones uncovered in eight sites, domesticated pigs constituted from 21 to 59 percent of all animals, wild or domesticated. They were the most numerous domesticated animal in four of the sites, whereas common cattle were in three, and sheep and goats, in one (Greenfield, 1986, 2: 361).

449. For which, see Hesse, 1990: 195, 206–220.

450. Hesse, 1990: 208.

451. Levy, 1986: 104; Grigson, 1987: 231–32, Table 7-2.

452. Hesse, 1990: 211.

453. The latter site, Tell el Hayyat, is not far from the Jordan River, a habitat especially well-suited for swine.

454. For reviews of one or more of these hypotheses, see Lemche, 1985: 1–79; Ahlström, 1986: 5–9; Fritz, 1987; Finkelstein, 1988a, 1990; Stiebing, 1989: 149–65; Zerfal, 1991; Frendo, 1992; and Silberman, 1992. For a weighing of the various hypotheses against recent archeological evidence, see especially Finkelstein, 1988b: 295–314.

Various writers have raised the possibility that climatic variations or fluctuations, including extended drought, may have played a role in this. Commonly cited are two studies (Weiss, 1982; Neumann and Parpola, 1987) that suggest that there may have been an extended drought in the eastern Mediterranean at the end of the Bronze Age that led to striking political changes and human migrations. The first study, however, does not present any paleo-environmental evidence for this, nor does it deal with Palestine. The second study does consider paleo-environmental evidence, but it focusses on Assyria and Babylonia, and touches on Palestine only in mentioning two studies that provide inconclusive results. Also cited in support of an extended dry period in Palestine following 1300 B.C. is evidence drawn from places (i.e., sub-

Saharan Africa, the Himalayas of India) so distant from Palestine and affected by such different patterns of atmospheric circulation, as to lead one to question their relevance to Hebrew settlement in the hills of Canaan.

The idea that climatic shifts, especially drought followed by famine, are responsible for major historical events, nevertheless, has great appeal for certain scholars. In the case of Canaan, W. H. Stiebing (1989: 182–87, 190–95) may be the strongest advocate of the view that extended drought, famine, and political unrest in the eastern Mediterranean was the major factor leading Canaanite farmers and seminomads to "become stateless brigands or fleeing refugees" following about 1300 B.C., and to settle in the hill country when drought abated following 1150 B.C. Israel Finkelstein (1988a: 44; 1990: 685) has also written of the possibility that extended drought played a role both in shifts in political and economic power in Canaan at the end of the Bronze Age and in sedentarization of pastoral groups there.

The end of the Bronze Age, one should note, does not seem to have been one of major climatic change in Palestine. Liphschitz and Waisel (cited by D. C. Hopkins, 1985: 100) have used dendroarcheological evidence to demonstrate that in Palestine over the past four or five thousand years there have been "no drastic changes in the composition of . . . vegetation . . . and, therefore . . . [no] extreme ecological or climatic changes." Goldberg and Yosef (1982: 404) have observed that the transition to the arid climate of the present day occurred from roughly 3000 to 2400 B.C. in the Early Bronze Age; and D. C. Hopkins (1985: 99–108), after a review of the evidence, concluded that at the start of the Early Iron Age the climate of highland Canaan was the same as it is today. Finkelstein (1988a: 44), despite the views mentioned above, has observed that there is "no evidence of any climatic change" in Palestine in Iron Age I. Lemche (1985: 423–24), in turn, believes it certain that droughts did occur in the second millennium B.C., but he observes that the climate problem is hard to deal with because of a lack of concrete data, and knows of no sources that demonstrate that a drought-induced famine occurred in Palestine between 1500 and 1000 B.C. This fits with Dando's observations that, though famines are noted in ancient Palestine (nine altogether in Old Testament times), in only one of the nine is drought mentioned as the primary determinant (Dando, 1983: 238, 242). Moreover, neither that famine (in the mid-ninth century B.C.) nor any other is reported in the Bible for the start of the Iron Age.

As a geographer aware of the damage done to the reputation of his discipline by the incautious statements of Ellsworth Huntington and other environmental determinists several decades ago, I am especially hesitant, without more convincing paleo-environmental evidence from Palestine itself, to invoke climatic variations as a major factor in Hebrew settlement of the hills of Canaan.

455. See "Opening the highland frontier" in Stager, 1985: 3ff.; as well as Borowski, 1987: 6, 15; Finkelstein, 1988b: 324–35; and Broshi and Finkelstein, 1992: 55.

456. Stager, 1985: 4.

457. D. C. Hopkins, 1985: 112–14; Esse, 1991: 7.

458. Van Zeist and Bottema, 1982: 284, 289, 319. Dendroarcheological research has also determined that, with few exceptions, the natural vegetation surviving in

various regions of Israel today includes the same species that existed in the Early Bronze Age II and III (c. 3100–2200 B.C.), which implies that "the same macroclimate that prevails today existed in EB II and III" (Liphschitz et al., 1989, 2: 265–66). One possible conclusion to be drawn from this is that, in seeking to explain the reduction in woody vegetation in Palestine prior to and following the time of Moses, it may be best to focus less on climatic fluctuations than on other factors, particularly the role of humans and their herd animals. This is in accord with Currid's study (1984: 6–7) of deforestation in the foothills of Palestine, which assigns the primary role to human factors.

459. Albright, 1933: 130.
460. Weitz, 1971–72: 787.
461. Aharoni, 1982: 158.
462. Liphschitz and Waisel, 1986: 153–54.
463. Zerfal, 1991: 32–33.
464. Currid, 1984: 3–6; D. C. Hopkins, 1985: 114–15; Stager, 1985: 4–5, 15. For orchards and vineyards in Iron Age Israel, see Borowski, 1987: 101–33.
465. For which, see Reifenberg, 1955: 28; Baly, 1957: 93–94, 181, 191, 220, 227–28; and Baly, 1963: 48, 49, 60–62, 68, 76, 79, 82, 84.
466. Noth, 1966: 34.
467. Hyvernat and Hirsch, 1907: 433.
468. Bertholet, 1926: 25; Baly, 1957: 83–84, 93; D. C. Hopkins, 1985: 118.
469. Bertholet, 1926: 26; Noth, 1966: 34; Rowton, 1967: 266–67, 276–77; D. C. Hopkins, 1987: 180.
470. For notes on sacred trees and groves in Palestine, see de Vaux, 1961: 278–79; and Zohary, 1962: 71–72.
471. Feliks, 1971–72d: 221 and map on p. 224; Feliks, 1971–72e: 1294.
472. Feliks, 1971–72e: 1293.
473. Feliks, 1971–72e: 1293–94.
474. Pigs are generally considered unsuited to transhumant migrations, and I have found nothing to indicate that they were involved in transhumance in early Palestine. At the same time, pigs can be driven, though not without difficulty (Grigson, 1982: 299), and the possibility of transhumant pig herding in early Palestine should not be ruled out.
475. Weitz, 1971–72: 787, who, along with Hyvernat and Hirsch (1907: 433–34), also identifies other biblical and modern forests.
476. Hyvernat and Hirsch, 1907: 434.
477. See, for example, Parsons, 1962a, and Humbert, 1980: 75–77, 82–87, and passim (modern Spain); Silbert, 1966, 2: 684–701 (modern Portugal); and Diener and Robkin, 1978: 498 (on the general mobility of pigs).
478. Great Britain Admiralty, Naval Intelligence Division, 1944–45, 3: 110–11; Halpern, 1958: 24–25, 27, 54. Pigs raised in this way in the former Yugoslavia are able to eat not only the flesh of their dead fellows but also the carcasses of wild animals, and in one study a fairly high percentage of them (nearly 22 percent) were found to be infected with *Trichinella*. The intensity of infection in the animals, however, was

extremely low (0.02–0.16 larvae per gram of diaphragm sample), and thus their flesh was less dangerous to humans. A far smaller percentage (1.2 percent) of pigs raised on small private farms in Yugoslavia, on the other hand, were found to be infected, but their intensity of infection was far higher (0.76–6,450 larvae per gram) (W. C. Campbell et al., 1988: 28). The high percentage of *Trichinella* infection in grazing pigs was confirmed in a survey in the same area five years later (Marinculic et al., 1991).

479. See, for example, Aharoni, 1982: 158, 159; Borowski, 1987: 6, 15–16.

480. Joshua 17:17–18.

481. Zohary, 1962: 71. D. C. Hopkins (1987: 181) suggests that in the Early Iron Age fire was likely far more important than the ax in clearing for cultivation. Like Zohary, he also says that, whatever means of clearing was employed, the task of removing stumps and roots was far more difficult than the felling of trees.

In the centuries following the time of Moses, some wood was even exported. This is revealed in the Papyrus Golishef (eleventh century B.C.), which shows that wood from the forests on Mt. Carmel was shipped to Egypt by way of the port of Dor (now Tantura) in Palestine, and that such trade had been carried out in the past (Bertholet, 1926: 25–26; Zohary, 1962: 72). Though some timber was still found in the Carmel region in the 1920s, a trade like that of the Papyrus Golishef was simply unthinkable. On the contrary, timber was so rare in Palestine in the 1920s that "all strong planks and beams [had] to be imported" (Bertholet, 1926: 26). Nor can the Papyrus Golishef be cited as evidence that woody vegetation was abundant in ancient Palestine. That it was not is clearly shown by the fact that the ancient Hebrews had to import wood regularly, especially timber of particular kinds from Lebanon.

482. The final destruction of the coastal oak forest on the Sharon Plain, which had been mentioned by Richard the Lion-Heart and later was described as one of the most extensive and attractive oak forests of the area, came about during the First World War when the Turkish army cut trees to provide fuel for their locomotives. The use of wood for making charcoal has also been important in Palestine. Despite the availability of fuels of other sorts, charcoal continued to serve as a household and commercial fuel in Palestine until the 1950s (Taylor, n.d.: 34, Bertholet, 1926: 26; Zohary, 1962: 92, 209–10).

483. Taylor, n.d.: 33–43; Reifenberg, 1955: 29–31; Zohary, 1962: 209–10; Weitz, 1971–72: 787–78; D. C. Hopkins, 1985: 115–17.

484. Taylor, n.d.: 27–32; Reifenberg, 1947: 146–47; D. C. Hopkins, 1985: 116–17.

485. D. C. Hopkins, 1985: 117–20.

486. Grigson, 1982: 299–300.

487. One might have expected the Hebrews to be responsible husbandmen concerned with maintaining in good condition the land God had given them, and that, even though economic necessity led them to clear trees and brush, they would do so with caution and with environmental preservation in mind (for a view of this sort, see Chapter 5, "Ancient Israel and the natural environment," in J. D. Hughes, 1975). Michael Zohary (1962: 211–12) points out, however, that even though both Hebrews and Arabs had great respect for trees—as symbols of godliness and the power of

God—and preserved sacred trees and sacred woods, this seems not to have been incompatible with the extensive forest destruction they carried out.

488. Bodenheimer, 1960: 173, quoting Taylor; Reifenberg, 1955: 98; Weitz, 1971–72: 788.

489. Taylor, n.d.: 27.

490. Murphey, 1951: 124; Furon, 1958; Mikesell, 1960: 447.

491. de Planhol, 1959: 58–59.

492. In regions of greater aridity, the percentage of sheep and goats was overwhelming. In Early Iron Age levels at Tel Beer-Sheba, an important center in the northern Negev Desert, for example, they accounted for 78 percent of all animal bones uncovered, compared with 13 percent for common cattle, and a mere 0.23 percent for pigs (Hellwing, 1984: 106, 108, 110, 114).

493. Reifenberg, 1947: 147.

494. Hesse, 1990: 214–18. It is likely for this reason that one finds no mention of pigs in Borowski's account (1987) of Iron Age agriculture in Israel, or in Finkelstein's survey (1988b: 121–39) of early Ephraim and its contrasting environments.

495. Hesse, 1990: 217–18. In all but one level at the three Philistine sites, percentages of pigs ranged from 4 to 19. In levels at the other Palestinian sites (fourteen sites altogether), those percentages, with two exceptions, ranged from 0 to 1.5. That certain early Hebrews kept pigs is borne out by literary evidence (Shipley et al., 1899–1903, 4: 4824–26; Casanowicz and Hirsch, 1907: 609; Feliks et al., 1971–72: 506–7).

496. Reed and Perkins, 1984: 19.

497. Mesopotamia: Saggs, 1984: 168; D. P. Wright, 1987: 257, citing Contenau; Egypt: Hoffman, 1974; Miller, 1990.

498. Diener and Robkin, 1978: 497–98.

499. Feliks, 1962: 23.

500. Redding, 1981: 245.

501. Diener and Robkin, 1978: 498, citing Thesiger.

502. H. Epstein, 1971b, 2: 326.

503. Grigson, 1982: 299.

504. For further evidence of the versatility of the pig in its feeding, see Diener and Robkin, 1978: 498.

505. H. Epstein, 1971b, 2: 357.

506. J. L. Buck, 1956: 246.

507. Hesse, 1986: 17, 21, 25.

508. Richard Redding (1991: 22) has noted that wild and feral swine in Europe have a special liking for cultivated plants, and he cites studies which show that from 30 to 90 percent of their diet was made up of field crops. He observes further that in Iran fields of grain are planted by Bakhtiari pastoralists in valleys and left unprotected when they go on their seasonal migrations (except to set up "scare pigs" in the fields), and that the Bakhtiari regularly complain about the damage done by wild swine. From this, Redding makes a general statement, apparently embracing domestic pigs as well, that pigs "prefer the same plants" as humans, and, even more critically, that

they "compete directly with humans." I reach a quite different conclusion: that, *if permitted to do so,* pigs, like goats, sheep, common cattle, deer, *and a host of other animals, wild and domestic,* would compete directly with humans by raiding crops. The need to protect crops from animal crop-robbers is not one involving pigs alone. Nor is it unique to the Near East. On the contrary, it is one that cultivators face throughout the world, and they handle the problem in a variety of ways depending on its severity (for some interesting methods of pig control in New Guinea, see Sillitoe, 1980–81: 258ff.). The Bakhtiari case suggests that the damage done by wild swine is insufficient for the pastoralists to take greater precautions than they do now. In lowland Ethiopia we have often observed fields of sorghum planted in dry stream beds by seminomads who, after planting, left with their herd animals on migrations. They protected their sorghum by setting up thick thorn-brush fences, which seemed quite effective as deterrents to would-be animal crop-robbers. The Bakhtiari could do the same.

509. Hoffner, 1967: 183.

510. As we have seen, there are reports from Mesopotamia of barley being fed to domestic pigs. In addition, barley was sometimes used for fattening wild boars for slaughter (Salonen, 1974: 5, 6). In ancient Egypt, moreover, pig keeping had developed beyond scavenging, as is shown by the ancient pig farm uncovered in a village, dated to the fourteenth century B.C., near the ancient city of el-Amarna (Shaw, 1984: 49–53; Kemp, 1987: 40; Kemp, 1989: 255–56). The pig farm was an impressive affair with substantial pens, and the pigs were usually slaughtered in their first or second year of life. Special places were set aside for the purpose of slaughtering, and they had been covered with white plaster. Pork, in turn, was salted and packed in pottery containers, and likely was produced not only for home use but also for marketing in the main city. The pigs, it is said, were grain fed, but they may also have consumed garbage, whether from rubbish heaps found nearby or by scavenging about the village part of the time.

511. Ernle, 1961: 17.

512. S. T. Kang, 1973: 287.

513. Hoffman, 1974: 44.

514. Miller, 1990.

515. Diener and Robkin, 1978: 498–99.

516. Miller provides an excellent example of this, citing W. Willcocks, an irrigation specialist working in rural India in the late nineteenth century. According to Willcocks, "We built a village some distance from the works for the workmen and, to ensure proper sanitation, we had a trench dug round it about a quarter of a mile from the outermost houses. Within the line of this trench nothing was allowed. We had begun to engage a gang of labourers to bury everything offensive with earth, in accordance with the Mosaic Regulations in the wilderness, when four men turned up in the office and asked to be allowed to divide the circumference into four quarters, and each of them would take his quarter and feed his pigs there. They were given permission, and we had no further worry for a long time."

517. Haynes and El-Hakim, 1979: 102–5.

518. Miller, 1990: 126.

519. G. E. Wright, 1964, 2: 304–5.

520. Hellwing and Adjeman, 1986: 145–46, 151.

521. Hesse, 1990: 215.

522. Shabbath 155b, and Berakoth 55a, cited by Casanowicz and Hirsch, 1907: 609, and Feliks et al., 1971–72: 506–7.

523. Hesse, 1990: 218.

524. D. N. Freedman, 1976: 99–100.

525. For a brief summary of this legislation as of two decades ago, see Feliks et al., 1971–72: 507.

526. Zucker, 1972.

527. These figures are roughly comparable to those reported elsewhere in Egypt for that period (Janssen, 1975: 10, 165–67, 177–78, 265–71, 525–27).

528. Hecker, 1982: 62.

529. Hesse, 1990: 212.

530. See, for example, de Garine, 1976: 151–55; and Eichinger Ferro-Luzzi, 1985b: 484–86.

531. Diener and Robkin, 1978, and the commentaries that follow the article.

532. Milgrom, 1971–72: 142.

533. Leviticus 11:45.

534. Stein, 1957: 150–52; I. Epstein, 1959: 24–25; Werblowsky and Wigoder, 1966: 116; Klein, 1979: 303–4; Novak, 1987: 272–73.

535. For a comparison of views of impurity, and its elimination, in the Bible and in Mesopotamian and Hittite literature, see D. P. Wright, 1987; for views of purity and impurity in early Israel and Mesopotamia, including the role of food prohibitions and dietary rules, see van der Toorn, 1985: 27–39; for purity and impurity among the ancient Greeks, see R. Parker, 1983; and among ancient Persians, Choksy, 1986.

536. Klein, 1979: 303.

537. Werblowsky and Wigoder, 1966: 116.

538. Stein, 1957: 145–46, 152; Novak, 1987: 272. Presenting a special problem, as Jacob Neusner (1973) has observed, are the significant changes in Hebrew views of purity that have occurred from one time to another. This means that, in seeking the origins of the Hebrew ban on pork, one must exercise great caution and unusual persistence.

539. Douglas, 1966: 41–57 (Chapter 3: "The abominations of Leviticus"). For a weighing of Douglas's views of purity in general against the historical record, see Neusner, 1973: 119–30; for Douglas's views on the matter, see Neusner, 1973: 137–42.

540. Douglas, 1972: 71–79; Douglas, 1973: 60–64; Douglas, 1975: 261–73, 282–89, 304–9.

541. Douglas, 1975: 304.

542. Douglas, 1975: 272.

543. Douglas, 1973: 60–63.

544. Soler, 1979.

545. Leviticus 20:24–26.

546. Soler, 1979: 30.

547. For example, Noth, 1965: 89–96; and Wenham, 1979: 168–81.

548. Milgrom, 1971–72: 142.

549. de Vaux, 1971: 47.

550. Neusner, 1973: 130.

551. In the Late Bronze Age, according to Ahlström (1986: 4), Egypt dominated Canaan, and there were Egyptian military and administrative centers both in the Sinai and along the south coast (e.g., Gaza, Beth-shan).

552. Craigie, 1976: 231.

553. There is abundant documentation for the contrasting human attitudes toward the flesh of domestic pigs and wild boars. Among the Hindus of a Mysore village, for example, the domestic pig, which wanders around the village eating human excrement, among other things, is an impure animal whose flesh is avoided by all but the lowest castes. Some persons who reject the flesh of the domestic pig, however, do not hesitate to eat that of the wild boar (Srinivas, 1955: 20).

554. Århem, 1989.

555. Lattimore, 1941: 220.

556. Lattimore, 1941: 220.

557. Clavijo, 1859: 134.

558. Albright, 1939.

559. Alt, 1967; Noth, 1960b: 68–80; Aharoni, 1982: 153–80.

560. Mendenhall, 1962; Gottwald, 1979.

561. For a discussion of 'Apiru, the meaning of the term and the character of the people called by this name, see Lemche, 1985: 421–22; Ahlström, 1986: 13–14; Stiebing, 1989: 53–54, 157.

562. Finkelstein, 1988a, 1988b: 336–56; Finkelstein, 1990.

563. Zerfal, 1991.

564. Joseph A. Callaway (1985: 33, 43) is an exception. He accepts Alt's view of infiltration of the highlands, but argues against the early Hebrews being nomads. Instead, he contends, they were "primarily farmers and secondarily herders of small cattle" who came from lowland Canaanite territories to the west. Their background, he contends, "was in agriculturally-based sedentary village life rather than that of nomads or even semi-nomads."

565. Finkelstein, 1988b: 330–35. This changed rapidly in succeeding centuries, but even as of 1000 B.C. the total area of "Israelite" settlement in Palestine is estimated to have had a population of only sixty-five thousand people (Broshi and Finkelstein, 1992: 55).

566. Mendenhall, 1962: 67, 73–79.

567. W. M. Ramsay, 1890: 32–33.

568. Gurney (1940: 101), on the other hand, did point out the possible role of the Hittites in the matter.

569. Moyer, 1983: 32–33, 37–38.

570. Hrozný, 1953: 112–13, 232–33; Ghirshman, 1977: 3–9, 27–28.

571. Ahlström, 1986: 3–4.

572. Ghirshman, 1977: 20–44, including Fig. 5.

573. It is unclear why this might have been so, but Shamash was not only the sun-god and god of justice but also the best diviner among the gods. He was called the lord of divination and lord of visions, and was a healing god called upon to eliminate sickness and extend life (Jayne, 1962: 99–100, 102, 108–9, 111, 127). May it be that, because the pig was associated with evil, illness-causing, underworld beings such as Lamashtu, it was the natural enemy of Shamash, whose name was invoked by exorcists seeking to drive out the evil beings that possessed the body of a sick person?

574. Hrozný, 1953: 234–35.

575. Carnoy, 1908–26: 568–70.

576. L. B. Paton, 1908–26c: 180.

577. The Hyksos, "shepherd-kings" who seem to have been Semites from the Syria-Palestine area, ruled in Egypt from about 1674 to 1567 B.C., and may have been part of those migrations. Little is known about them, however, and I have found nothing to connect them with anti-pig feeling. On the contrary, their special ties with Seth, mentioned above, may well have led the pig to enjoy a respectable status and role in ritual. Also of possible significance is the abundant evidence of anti-pig feeling in Egypt in the centuries following the Hyksos period. For the origin of the Hyksos, their possible identity with northern peoples, and their use of horses and chariots, see Van Seters, 1966: 181–95.

578. Albright, 1957: 205; 1966: 8, 13, and passim. The Hurrians, who belonged to a now-extinct language group, neither Semitic nor Indo-European, were an impor-tant people in northern Mesopotamia and eastern Anatolia in the second millennium B.C., and seem to have constituted the majority population in the Mitanni kingdom and parts of the Hittite realms.

579. Albright, 1957: 205; see also de Vaux, 1961: 222–25.

580. The location of that homeland has long been a matter of controversy. Many authorities, however, place it in the grasslands of the Pontic-Caspian region from the Dnieper eastward to the Volga. There are numerous pitfalls in seeking to determine the origin and spread of language groups such as the Indo-Europeans, and in trying to establish links between that spread and changes in the archeological record. Never-theless, scholars have been undeterred by the uncertainties entailed, as revealed in the rich literature and controversy about Indo-European origins published over the past century. Even in recent decades, scholars have published studies that have reached quite different conclusions. To mention just a few of the more recent of these, Marija Gimbutas (1956: 79–80, 89–92; 1961, 1977, 1980, 1986, 1989: xx–xxi) has for de-cades argued for a homeland in the Pontic-Caspian steppe. Lothar Kilian (1983) has envisaged a homeland embracing a broad belt across northern Europe from Scandi-navia to the Urals. Tomas Gamkrelidze and Vyachislav Ivanov (1984, 1985a,b) speak of a homeland in Armenia and nearby areas, and Colin Renfrew (1987), in Anatolia. In a careful weighing of the evidence, J. P. Mallory (1989) dismisses, on linguistic and archeological grounds, the notion of an Anatolian homeland. He also argues against the idea of a homeland as broad as all northern Europe or one as narrow as Arme-nia. Instead, Mallory reaches a conclusion similar to that championed by Gimbutas,

placing the Indo-European homeland in the Pontic-Caspian region from the Dnieper eastward to the Volga. He suggests that Proto-Indo-European likely evolved from about 4500 to 2500 B.C. among hunting-fishing communities confined to main river valleys; that those communities adopted farming and stock raising during that period; that common cattle were especially important, though their food animals were varied (sheep and/or goats, common cattle, pig, horse); and that dairying, including the manufacture of butter and possibly cheese, was practiced. For other recent reviews of the Indo-European problem, see Anthony, 1986, 1991a. For a review of certain recent works favoring the origin of the Indo-Europeans in Anatolia or just to the east, see Crossland, 1992, who is inclined toward some version of the Gimbutas hypothesis. For a view more critical of the Gimbutas hypothesis, see Drews, 1988: 25–35.

581. Mallory, 1982: 211; Mallory, 1989: 118–19. Hamp (1987) has suggested that various words relating to pigs and pig keeping among Celtic languages in Europe (and possibly Germanic ones as well) derive from pre-Indo-European peoples who preceded the Celts.

582. Gimbutas, 1970: 157, 171, 190; Gimbutas, 1986: 307; Telegin, 1986: 82, 84, 87, 88, 163; Mallory, 1989: 118–19, 187, 217.

583. Matyushin, 1986: 138, 139, 140–41, 142, 143, 144–45.

584. Shnirelman, 1992: 130–31, 133–34.

585. For maps of the distribution of Proto-Indo-Europeans in their homeland (4500–3500 B.C.), in the final period of Proto-Indo-European linguistic unity and early expansion (3500–3000 B.C.), and of Indo-Europeans after linguistic differentiation and widespread expansion into Inner Asia (3000–2500 B.C.), see Anthony, 1991a: 209, 211, 213.

586. Mallory, 1989: 217, 228.

587. In three Middle Bronze Age Kurgan graves excavated at Vardzia in eastern Georgia, pig bones seem to have been found in only one, and altogether, among the many bones uncovered, there were only two pig bones (Tsitsishvili, 1975: 431–32).

588. Mallory, 1989: 228. Like the Iranians, the Andronovo people also seem to have worshipped the sun. For this and a summary of Andronovo culture, see Levin and Potapov, 1964: 45–48.

589. Gening, 1979: 17–20.

590. Mallory, 1989: 228.

591. Epstein and Bichard, 1984: 147–48.

592. Levin and Potapov, 1964: 43–45; Matyushin, 1986: 148; Mallory, 1989: 223–26. Gryaznov (1969: 46–51) agrees with most of the above, but suggests that the Afanasievo people were also cultivators on a modest scale, and that they lived a sedentary life in their small settlements.

593. Levin and Potapov, 1964: 48–50; Phillips, 1965: 43–45; Gryaznov, 1969: 97–130.

594. Dumézil, 1970, 1: 149, 167, 231, 237–40; 2: 554; Puhvel, 1978; Mallory, 1989: 133–34.

595. Puhvel, 1978: 354.

596. D. Paton, 1925: 17, 29.

597. Wilkinson, 1878, 3: 298–99; Farbridge, 1908–26: 133; Gaillard, 1934: 115; Griffiths, 1960: 31–33, 109; Griffiths, 1970: 281.

598. Wilkinson, 1878, 3: 143, 298–99. On the demonization of Seth, see te Velde, 1977: 138–51.

599. te Velde, 1977: 26.

600. According to Darby and associates (1977, 1: 256–57), hippopotamus hunters in ancient Egypt "at least knew the taste of the flesh of their victim; or perhaps shared [it] in a ritualistic feast." For more on the hippopotamus in ancient Egypt, see Keller, 1963, 1: 406–7; and Darby et al., 1977, 1: 256–57.

601. Griffiths, 1960: 46–47, 89, 105, 134; A. Burton, 1972: 135; Fairman, 1974: 20, 27–35, and passim. Neither ancient nor modern Egyptians have eaten snakes as food (Darby et al., 1977, 1: 411–12). As we shall see in the chapter on fish, moreover, the snake is rejected as food by many sub-Saharan African peoples. Such rejection is found even among certain hunting and gathering groups, for example the Hadza of Tanzania (Woodburn, 1968: 52) and the !Kung Bushmen of Botswana (Lee, 1968: 35).

602. Hornung, 1982: 144, citing Münster.

603. In a parallel from Angola, some Kuvale explain their refusal to eat hippo flesh by saying that, because the hippo lives in water, it is a fish, and they never eat fish (Wentzel, 1961: 351–53).

604. Griffiths, 1960: 128; Van Seters, 1966: 171–80; H. O. Thompson, 1970: 130–31; te Velde, 1977: 118–21, 126–28.

605. F. L. Griffith, 1910–11: 176.

606. See te Velde, 1977: chapter 5 ("Seth the foreigner").

607. Eichinger Ferro-Luzzi, 1977a: 361.

608. *Little-known Asian animals with a promising economic future*, 1983: 89–94.

609. Germani, 1985.

Chapter 3. Beef

1. Hahn, 1896; Boettger, 1958: 33ff.; Isaac, 1962; 1970: 105–9; Simoons and Simoons, 1968: 244–58.

2. Malten, 1928; Conrad, 1959; Bevan, 1986, 1: 82–99; Gimbutas, 1989; Walsh, 1989; Schwabe, 1993. The same was true of Celtic, Baltic, and Germanic peoples, for which see Gimbutas, 1958: 43–45; Ross, 1967: 302–8; and Gelling and Davidson, 1969: 163–64.

3. The role of bovines in Hinduism in India is fairly well known, but their role in Tibetan religion is not. The best account I have found of bovines (yaks and yak hybrids) in Tibetan religion (Buddhist and pre-Buddhist) is that of Richard Palmieri (1976: 183–249), which reveals a rich and varied religious role quite different from that of Hindu India.

4. Epstein and Mason, 1984: 14–15.

5. Finds at the Baluchistan site of Mehrgarh (which may have been occupied from roughly 7000? to 2500 B.C.) have led to the suggestion that common cattle may have

been present nearly as early there as in the Near East. Whether or not this was so, the size of common cattle diminished significantly in the earliest levels of Mehrgarh (a sign that the process of domestication had begun?), and the percentage of bones from common cattle increased from 4 in earliest levels to 65 in later ones (Meadow, 1984).

6. Badam, 1984: 343; Meadow, 1984: 329; P. K. Thomas, 1984: 358.

7. Allchin, 1969: 321; P. K. Thomas, 1984: 357–58.

8. Simoons and Simoons, 1968.

9. W. N. Brown, 1957: 30; Gonda, 1980: 98–100. For an interesting perspective on warriors, priests, and cattle among the Aryans and other Indo-Iranians, see Lincoln, 1981: 49–162.

10. Childe, 1926: 83; W. N. Brown, 1957: 30.

11. W. N. Brown, 1957: 30–31; Walker, 1968, 1: 255.

12. Puhvel, 1978: 354, 357, who also provides information on the bull in the hierarchy of sacrificial animals of other early Indo-European peoples.

13. Macdonell, 1897: 54–66, 88–100; Walker, 1968, 1: 255. For more on the bull in Vedic religion and sacrifice, see Ghurye, 1979: 38–45.

14. Gonda, 1980: 278, 282, 337.

15. Gonda, 1980: 182–83.

16. Some Vedic feasts rivalled those of ancient Germans in the number of animals slaughtered and quantity of alcohol consumed (Sanjana, 1946: 106). In that great epic the *Mahābhārata*, Rantideva, a pious and charitable ruler, slaughtered two thousand cattle and other animals each day to feed the beggars and Brahmins who gathered in his kingdom (Walker, 1968, 1: 142).

17. For occasions in Vedic India when cows and other common cattle were killed and eaten, see W. N. Brown, 1957: 31–32 and passim; Walker, 1968, 1: 255–56; and Gonda, 1980: 11, 19, 45, 99–100, 157, 159, 172, 185, 187, 338, 339, 384, 406, 433, 435, 436–37, 450, and 453.

18. *Śatapatha Brāhmaṇa* 3.1.2.21, trans. in Eggeling, 1882–1900.

19. W. N. Brown, 1957: 30–35, 39.

20. *Mahāvagga* 6.23.9–15, trans. in Davids and Oldenberg, 1881–85.

21. Davids, 1903: 294–95; Ambedkar, 1948: 98–99.

22. The Buddha was pushed in the direction of a more general prohibition of flesh food by Devadatta and his supporters, but this apparently did not involve beef to any greater extent than other flesh foods. Resisting pressures for a more general prohibition, the Buddha expounded his famous principle permitting three pure kinds of flesh, a principle which has often been described as "unseen, unheard, and unsuspected": fish and meat were permitted if the monk did not see the animal killed or hear the slaughter or suspect that it was done on his account (*Mahāvagga* 6.31.14, trans. in Davids and Oldenberg, 1881–85; and *Kullavagga* 7.3.14–15, trans. in Davids and Oldenberg, 1881–85). In keeping with this principle, the *Pātimokkha*, one of the oldest Buddhist textbooks, declared that no monk should, when he is not sick, request for his own use and eat fish and flesh (*Pātimokkha, Pākittiyā Dhammā* 39, trans. in Davids and Oldenberg, 1881–85).

Followers of Buddha divided into two groups with respect to use of flesh food:

those who believed in the gradual acceptance of Buddha's teachings and who adhered to the threefold-pure system described above, and those who believed in immediate acceptance of the higher truths expounded late in Buddha's ministry, and who demanded a more thorough self-denial; some of the latter were so strict that they abstained not only from all types of flesh food but from milk and milk products as well (Watters, 1904–5, 1: 54–57).

23. W. N. Brown, 1957: 35–39.

24. In a similar way, the progress of ahimsa is not always clear or direct, for Walker (1968, 1: 279) observes that the eating of meat was repeatedly sanctioned even in the Purāṇas, which are relatively late (starting in the sixth century A.D.). For the ambivalence toward ahimsa and meat eating in the Epics, see Hopkins, 1969: 377–79.

25. Mānava Dharma-śāstra 11.60.109–17, trans. in Bühler, 1886.

26. W. N. Brown, 1957: 39; Walker, 1968, 1: 255–57.

27. Watters, 1904–5, 1: 178; Beal, 1958, 2: 143. All meats, including beef, were believed by the practitioners of Ayurvedic medicine to have pharmaceutical qualities. In the case of beef, that use seems to have been influenced by the rise of the sacred-cow concept, for which see F. Zimmermann, 1987: 185–86 ("Reverence for the bovine").

28. Basham, 1954: 120.

29. The considerable gap in cultural understanding is revealed by the monument erected to the Englishmen killed at Honnore, which noted that "they were sacrificed to the fury of a mad priesthood, and an infuriated mob" (Crooke, 1906: 144).

30. Sathe, 1967; Simoons, 1973.

31. Hoffpauir, 1977; Freed and Freed, 1981: 487–88.

32. Gandhi, 1954: 5.

33. Gandhi, 1954: 85–86.

34. Gandhi, 1954: 5.

35. Parel, 1969; Freitag, 1980; A. A. Yang, 1980; Simoons and Lodrick, 1981: 123–25.

36. Lodrick, 1987, 1991, 1992.

37. Simoons and Lodrick, 1981: 127; Lodrick, 1991, 1992.

38. Simoons and Lodrick, 1981: 128–29.

39. Simoons and Lodrick, 1981: 129–30.

40. Thurston, 1912: 58.

41. Of special interest in this regard is the observation (Eichinger Ferro-Luzzi, 1987: 100) that even though cow dung is a powerful purificant to Hindus because it comes from the sacred cow, this has not raised the ritual status of the low-caste groups who make a living from collecting, processing, and selling cow dung.

42. Walker, 1968, 1: 257.

43. The number five is a frequently used number in Vedic accounts which, among other things, symbolizes completeness (Gonda, 1980: 37), and in that sense it is quite appropriate that for purificatory purposes there be "five products of the cow."

44. The products of the cow may also provide omens. In southern India, for example, people say that if a cow urinates when it is being purchased, it is a very good sign, but if it passes dung, it is a bad sign (Thurston, 1912: 58–59).

45. *Vasishṭha Dharma-sūtra* 27.14, and *Baudhāyana Dharma-sūtra,* 4.5.14, trans. in Bühler, 1882; Gonda, 1965: 425. See also "the *pañchagavya* in history" in Simoons, 1974b: 29–30.

In later Vedic texts, the *pañchagavya* was used as a purificant in much the same manner as today: in purifying a corpse or living person, in cleansing a house by sprinkling it about, and in similar ways (Gonda, 1970: 83, 84; Gonda, 1980: 47, 114, 185, 188). In a traditional Brahmin funeral ceremony in western India, the son of a deceased, after asking forgiveness for his father's sins, will sip the *pañchagavya* for purposes of purification, though in modern times he may use *pañchamṛita* (milk curd, clarified butter, sugar, and honey). Then he will bathe ritually, after which the *pañchagavya* is smeared on his body (M. Stevenson, 1920: 166).

46. South India lacks a precise equivalent to the *kachchā-pakkā* food classification, but similar views exist about the purity of cow's milk and impurity of water and water-cooked food (Eichinger Ferro-Luzzi, 1977a: 359–60; Eichinger Ferro-Luzzi, 1981: 246–47; Eichinger Ferro-Luzzi, 1985b: 494–95).

47. For more on *kachchā* and *pakkā* foods, see Blunt, 1931: 89–90; Mayer, 1960: 33–40; Marriott, 1968; L. Dumont, 1970: 84–89, 142–43, 145–46, 304–5; Simoons, 1974b: 24–26; Khare, 1976: 12, 17–26, and passim; Simoons and Lodrick, 1981: 131.

48. For which, see Simoons and Lodrick, 1981: 131–32.

49. *Rig-veda* 10.121.

50. Gonda (1965: 322) writes of such a rite in early times in which a royal participant was cleansed over a vessel of gold that contained water mixed with *pañchagavya,* and who was then left to meditate on the Hiraṇyagarbha. The intent of the ceremony, according to Gonda, was to enable the man to gain "the indestructability of gold and participate in immortality." As described in recent centuries, the ceremony varied significantly in character, and the vessel in form and composition, but the stated intent was purification and rebirth; for which see Simoons and Lodrick, 1981: 131–32.

51. Lodrick, 1981.

52. Blunt, 1931: 95–96; B. Cohn, 1955: 72; Hutton, 1963: 78.

Of special interest is the myth, advanced by certain untouchables, that implicates the cow in the origin of their lowly status. According to that myth, the first untouchable was a Brahmin who encountered a cow stuck in the mud. He pulled on its tail in an effort to help it free itself, but instead, the cow died. Because he had touched a dead cow, the Brahmin was polluted, and his older brothers expelled him from their caste to make him the first untouchable (Moffatt, 1979: 16). For a similar myth, see Kolenda, 1964: 75. For a different myth explaining the origin of an untouchable caste in South India through improper cooking of beef, accusations of theft, and outcasteing, see Moffatt, 1979: 120–22.

53. See, for example, Moffatt, 1979: 193–94.

54. Moffatt, 1979: 119.

55. Gondal, 1948: 22, 25. For abandonment of beef eating by another Chamar group, see B. Cohn, 1955: 72–73.

56. Moffatt, 1979: 140–41, 157, 164–65, 180–82.

57. Awasthi, 1992.

58. Sundara Ram, 1927: 122–23.
59. Dube, 1955: 67, 176.
60. A. Durand, 1900: 160.
61. Sundara Ram, 1927: 96–97, 100–101, 103, 119; Gangulee, 1939: 207.
62. Wijesekera, 1965: 114, 141.
63. Sopher, 1959: 7.
64. Fürer-Haimendorf, 1943, 2: 329.
65. Golish, 1954: 49.
66. Simoons and Simoons, 1968: 194–96.
67. Fürer-Haimendorf, 1943, 2: 96.
68. S. C. Roy and R. C. Roy, 1937: 186–87.
69. Dube, 1951: vi, 48, 134.
70. Koppers and Jungblut, 1942–45: 657.
71. The Munda of Chota Nagpur (D. N. Majumdar, 1937: 26) and some Syn-teng of Assam (Gurdon, 1904: 58) have given up eating beef, apparently as a result of Hindu influence. The Toda, a small South Indian group of pastoralists, maintain buffalo herds, and in the past slaughtered and ate buffalo calves, if only ceremonially. Though there is one report of their slaughtering buffaloes ceremonially not long ago, they have adopted the idea from their Hindu neighbors that slaughtering and eating buffalo is disgraceful (Breeks, 1873: 9–10; W. E. Marshall, 1873: 130; Rivers, 1906: 274–75, 290; Golish, 1954: 16–17).
72. On one occasion, sacrifice to the god of the dead, Ettang-Jambusum, was made to save the life of a young boy he was believed to have seized and crippled. Sacrifices were also made to this deity because, when he seized a man's soul, he beat it; when a cow was offered to him, however, the pain was less severe (Elwin, 1955: 101).
73. Elwin, 1955: 9, 92, 101, 108, 110, 169–70, 191, 222, 337, 355, 510, 522–23, 527.
74. Drew, 1875: 428; Leitner, 1893, Appendix 6: 1.
75. Crooke, 1896, 2: 236ff.
76. Hoffpauir, 1977, 1982; Hiltebeitel, 1978b.
77. Elwin, 1955: 101, 188, 194, 229, 268, 271, 275, 285, 295, 304–5, 364–65, 383–84.
78. For early literary references or temple depictions of Durgā as slayer of the demon buffalo, see Harle, 1963: 238, 243.
79. Hoffpauir, 1977, 1982; Hiltebeitel, 1978b. On the basis of Indus Valley seals depicting water buffaloes, it has been suggested that the wild buffalo symbolized a terrible god already in those times, a view Gonda (1965: 87) considers speculative.
80. Hoffpauir, 1982: 227. Eichinger Ferro-Luzzi (1985b: 494) has presented an interesting example, in stories from a South Indian district, of the contrasting ways in which people view the water buffalo and cow in terms of life and death. In one story, water buffalo's milk is poured into the mouth of a dying person to hasten death and avoid extending the person's agony. This, Eichinger Ferro-Luzzi observes, relates to the belief "that the buffalo is the vehicle of the god of death." The second story is of a boy who is advised by an aunt that he can save the life of his mother, who is very ill, by pouring cow's milk into her mouth. He is too disturbed to do this correctly, and his

mother dies. The point is made, however: cow's milk has restorative, life-sustaining qualities, just the opposite of water buffalo's milk.

81. Eichinger Ferro-Luzzi, 1977a: 363, who attributes this to the buffalo having been placed in the same category as the sacred cow.

82. Fawcett, 1890: 268–69, 273, 276–77, 279–80, 281–82, and passim; Elmore, 1915: 38–39, 43–44; Whitehead, 1916: 18–19; Shulman, 1976: 128–29; Hoffpauir, 1982: 226; Kinsley, 1986: 112, 114, 146, 205–8. For such sacrifice among the Rājputs, see Harlan, 1992: 61–63, 88.

83. In the eleventh century, on the other hand, al-Bīrūnī included the water buffalo among animals whose flesh was not banned to Hindus, apparently even Brahmins (E. C. Sachau, 1971: 151).

84. Hoffpauir, 1982: 226–27.

85. Elwin, 1955: 522.

86. Though common cattle in India outnumber water buffalo by a ratio of 3.5 to 1, in most of mainland Southeast Asia the number of water buffalo is far higher, and in Burma they outnumber common cattle. Since people in Southeast Asia generally have similar attitudes toward both animals, and since many writers on the region use the word "beef" to refer to the flesh of both animals, the two types of flesh will not be distinguished in this section.

87. Fielding Hall, 1917: 230; Tambiah, 1969: 437–38.

88. Landon, 1939: 92.

89. Gourou, 1936: 428–29.

90. Crawfurd, 1830, 2: 268–69.

91. J. White, 1823: 253.

92. d'Orléans, 1894: 123.

93. Delvert, 1961: 154–55.

94. de Reinach, 1901, 1: 403–4.

95. V. Thompson, 1941: 332–33.

96. de Young, 1955: 91–92.

97. Fielding Hall, 1917: 229.

98. Mi Mi Khaing, 1946: 86.

99. C. J. Richards, 1945: 42.

100. Landon, 1939: 92.

101. Grist, 1936: 309, 311; Rosemary Firth, 1943: 71–72.

102. Williams-Hunt, 1952: 94.

103. W. E. Maxwell, 1881: 22.

104. Loeb, 1935: 166.

105. Featherman, 1885–91, 2: 402.

106. Roth, 1896, 1: 388.

107. Kroeber, 1943: 84.

108. In Tibet, common cattle are kept principally by farmers. Nomads ordinarily keep only one bull for crossbreeding with their yak cows (Combe, 1926: 126). Crossbred animals, or *dzo*, are more docile than yaks, and females give more milk than do yak cows (Bell, 1928: 53–54).

109. Combe, 1926: 127–28. Unfortunately it is not clear whether by "cow"

Combe refers in a general sense to all bovine animals, to adult females of all bovine species, to common cattle as a group, or to adult female common cattle.

110. Harrer, 1954: 246.

111. Palmieri, 1976: 117–21, 126–28.

112. Roasted, broiled, or fried meat is considered impure by Tibetan Buddhists, and bovine flesh is normally boiled or eaten uncooked, whether fresh or in a preserved form (Palmieri, 1976: 128).

113. Bell, 1928: 53–54.

114. H. Ramsay, 1890: 306.

115. Palmieri, 1976: 128–30.

116. Friters, 1949: 14.

117. Prejevalsky, 1876, 1: 56.

118. Friters, 1949: 14.

119. Chow, 1984; Chang, 1986: 279.

120. Simoons, 1991: 302.

121. Yü, 1977: 56–58, 67, 74.

122. E. N. Anderson, 1988: 54.

123. Freeman, 1977: 164.

124. Doolittle, 1865, 2: 186–91.

125. Der Ling, 1914: 40.

126. M. C. Yang, 1945: 48–49.

127. M. C. Yang, 1945: 47–48.

128. S. D. Gamble, 1954: 281.

129. Griffis, 1882: 267, 269–70; Hulbert, 1906: 270–71.

130. Griffis, 1882: 269–70.

131. Osgood, 1951: 77.

132. Shirokogoroff, 1924: 130–31.

133. Lattimore, 1933: 31.

134. Galitzin, 1856: 148; Bush, 1871: 180; Lansdell, 1882: 301.

135. The Ainu of northern Japan, however, had no reluctance to consume beef and were fond of all parts of bullocks, including entrails (Batchelor, 1901: 108).

136. Kunio, 1957: 40; Oiso, 1976: 38–40, 47.

137. Keir, 1914: 817.

138. The Avesta was collected and standardized from the third to the seventh century A.D., but its parts derive from different periods, some perhaps as early as the beginning of the sixth century B.C. For a translation of the Avesta, see Darmesteter and Mills, 1880–87.

139. Vendidad 21.1; Sīrōzah 1.12; Sīrōzah 2.12; Yasht 7 ("Hymn to the Moon"); Yasna 39.1; and Gāh 4.6 (all trans. in Darmesteter and Mills, 1880–87); Darmesteter and Mills, 1880–87, 4: 224n.

140. Vendidad 19.21–22, etc., trans. in Darmesteter and Mills, 1880–87; Darmesteter and Mills, 1880–87, 4: lxxxvi, lxxxviii; A. V. W. Jackson, 1928: 197–98; Haug, 1978: 285–86; Modi, 1979: 54, 66–67, 74, 134; Choksy, 1986: 184–85. For higher Zoroastrian purificatory rites, the consecrated urine of an uncastrated bull

or uncastrated white bull was required. In modern times, Parsis keep a sacred white bull at each of their main fire-temples to obtain its urine and hair, both of which have ritual uses. Such white bulls are stabled in or near temple grounds, do not serve ordinary domestic needs, and when one dies, a replacement is carefully selected, purified, and consecrated (Modi, 1979: 254–59; M. Boyce, pers. comm.). For a summary of Zoroastrian purificatory use of bovine urine, ancient and modern, and contemporary Hindu purificatory use of cow urine, see Simoons, 1974b: 27–28, and 33 n1. For a more general account of purity and pollution in Zoroastrianism, see Choksy, 1986.

141. Sīrōzah 1.14; and Yasna 11.1 (all trans. in Darmesteter and Mills, 1880–87); Darmesteter and Mills, 1880–87, 23: 110. For Zoroastrians, all animals were originally either "Ahuric" (good), or "daēvic" (evil), for which see Choksy, 1986: 177.

142. Gāthās 48.5; Yasna 10.20; Vendidad 21.1; and Yasht 9 ("Gōs Yasht," or Cow Hymn) (all trans. in Darmesteter and Mills, 1880–87); Darmesteter and Mills, 1880–87, 31: 45n, 391.

143. Gāthās 50.2; Vispered 1.9; and Vispered 2.11 (all trans. in Darmesteter and Mills, 1880–87); Darmesteter and Mills, 1880–87, 4: 224n; 31: 170.

144. Vendidad 22.4, 11, 17; and Yasht 8.58 (both trans. in Darmesteter and Mills, 1880–87); Darmesteter and Mills, 1880–87, 31: 349n.

145. Sayce, 1908–26: 888.

146. Exodus 32:1–7.

147. 1 Kings 12:28–33; 2 Kings 10:29; Hosea 8:5–6; 10:5.

148. 1 Kings 7:25; 2 Chronicles 4:4; Jeremiah 52:20.

149. Sayce, 1908–26: 888.

150. Plutarch *Isis and Osiris* 33; Strabo *Geography* 17.1.22, 31; Wilkinson, 1878, 3: 86–94, 115–18, 305–8; Budge, 1904, 1: 24–26, 428–37; 2: 195–201, 346–53; Petrie, 1908–26: 244; W. R. Smith, 1914: 302; Griffiths, 1970: 425; A. Burton, 1972: 240–41, 242.

151. Varro *On farming* 2.5.4; Columella *On agriculture* 6.7.

152. Varro, 1912: 183 n1.

153. Pausanias *Description of Greece* 2.11.7; 2.35.6–7; 4.32.3; 5.16.2–3; 7.22.11; 8.19.2; 9.3.8; 10.9.3–4; Daly, 1950.

154. Pliny *Natural history* 8.183; Varro *On farming* 2.5.10–11, and 1912: 189 n3.

155. Vermaseren, 1963: 67–74 and passim; Henig, 1984: 97–109. Mithras was of Iranian origin, but there is a scholarly controversy over the Roman cult and the degree to which it had Iranian roots. For a brief summary of the controversy, see Afshar, 1990: 184–87.

156. Yerkes, 1952: 68–80.

157. Herodotus *History* 2.18, 41; 4.186.

158. Porphyry *On abstinence from animal food* 2.11.

159. Egyptian records show, however, that cows did serve as sacrificial animals at least in some periods of Egyptian history (Darby et al., 1977, 1: 143).

160. See Bevan (1986, 1: 82–99) for information on ancient Greek sacrifice of common cattle, as well as on their association with various Olympian deities and representations of cattle in their sanctuaries.

161. Varro *On farming* 2.5.4; Columella *On agriculture* 6. Preface. 7.
162. Pliny *Natural history* 8. 180.
163. Varro *On farming* 2.5.11.
164. The Koran specifically permits beef to the faithful (5:1; 6:143–45).
165. R. C. Thompson, 1908:210.
166. Drower, 1937: 37–38, 47–48.

It has been claimed that, among the Druse of Lebanon, there were modern survivals of worship of the sacred calf. This is doubtful, but, if true, it is inconspicuous and limited to small numbers of people (Guys, 1863: 146–59). There is nothing to suggest that beef avoidance is found among the Druse.

167. Deshler, 1963.
168. Great Britain Colonial Office, 1953: 32.
169. Johnston, 1910, 2: 623.
170. Herskovits, 1926. Though Herskovits designated it the "cattle complex in East Africa," he and other scholars recognize that the complex extends beyond East Africa into southern and southwestern Africa. For a recent view of the "cattle complex" from the perspective of ecology, war, and religion, see Lincoln, 1981: 13–48 ("The cattle cycle in East Africa" and "East Africa: Priestly cycle and warrior cycle").
171. For a discussion of the use of the concept of culture complex in anthropology, and a brief statement on the cattle complex of eastern and southern Africa, see Herskovits, 1948: 176–82, 195–97.
172. For an interesting weighing of the proposition that cattle are capital, and East African pastoralists are capitalists, see Hart and Sperling, 1987.
173. Huntingford, 1953b: 20–21, 80, 107. See also Århem, 1989: 12–15.
174. Evans-Pritchard, 1940: 16.
175. Ratzel, 1896–98, 2: 414.
176. Huntingford, 1953a: 27–28.
177. Schapera, 1953: 23.
178. Middleton, 1953: 19–20.
179. Herskovits, 1952: 174.
180. Schneider, 1957: 286–87.
181. Great Britain Colonial Office, 1953: 9.
182. Prins, 1952: 15, 56–57.
183. Gulliver and Gulliver, 1953: 98.
184. Huntingford, 1953a: 27.
185. Westermarck, 1924, 2: 494.
186. Gulliver and Gulliver, 1953: 59.
187. Huntingford, 1953b: 20.
188. Tew, 1950: 103.
189. Some cattle peoples, such as the Nuer of the Sudan (Huffman, 1931: 11–12), regard long, wide-spreading horns as most desirable, a preference that may have led to development and preservation of such exceptionally long-horned breeds as the Galla or Sanga cattle. Also noteworthy is the custom—known in ancient Egypt and Nubia as well as parts of modern East Africa, the Sudan, and Ethiopia—of training the horns

of cattle in unnatural directions. This is not a simple procedure, but one that may require several bouts of painful surgery. The Nandi and the Suk of Kenya prefer one horn trained forward and the other backward, and it is a social necessity for a Nandi man to possess such an animal at some time during his life (Huntingford, 1953b: 20–21, 80). The Dinka of the Sudan have a special name, *muor cien,* for bulls with trained horns. These are highly valued display animals, and an owner may "groom and sing to them hour upon hour" (Schwabe, 1984a: 143). Certain *muor cien* may also be dedicated to ancestral spirits, upon which they become holy animals. For more on such animals, their selection and role in ritual among the Dinka, see Schwabe (1984a), who also reviews the surgical procedure followed by the Dinka, sketches the modern occurrence of cattle with trained horns in Africa, and considers pictorial and literary evidence of the trait in ancient Egypt and Nubia.

190. Among the Tanala of Madagascar, people associate the eating of beef so closely with funeral ceremonies that a dream of cutting or eating beef is considered a bad omen foretelling a funeral (Linton, 1933: 49).

191. Ratzel, 1896–98, 2: 415.

192. Gutmann, 1926: 378–79.

193. Hambly, 1934: 154.

194. Herskovits, 1952: 295.

195. Schneider, 1957: 293.

196. Schneider, 1957: 289, 295.

197. Hambly, 1937, 1: 349.

198. Routledge, 1910: 50.

199. Schneider, 1957: 287–88, 292–93.

200. S. K. Das, 1953: 239–40; Hutton, 1963: 227–28.

201. W. N. Brown, 1957: 29.

202. S. K. Das, 1953: 239.

203. W. N. Brown, 1957: 38.

204. Montesquieu, *The spirit of laws,* Book 24, chapter 24.

205. E. C. Sachau, 1971: 152.

206. Kipling, 1891: 117.

207. Montesquieu, *The spirit of laws,* Book 24, chapter 24.

208. Harris, 1978: 218–23.

209. W. N. Brown, 1957.

210. Harris, 1985: 51–57.

211. Bennett, 1967, 1971.

212. Freed and Freed, 1981: 489. For a fuller range of objections to Harris's views of the sacred cow in India, see also Simoons, 1979; Freed and Freed, 1981; Westen, 1984; and the "Comments" following those articles. For interesting rejoinders to a specific argument of Harris's, that Hindu farmers unknowingly allow unwanted calves to starve, and that differences in survival rates of male and female calves in Kerala necessarily derive from human intervention, see D. W. Murray, 1986; and Sebring, 1987.

213. Eichinger Ferro-Luzzi, 1987: 101–2.

214. Diener et al., 1978. For a further elaboration of that perspective, see Diener et al., 1980.

215. Paul Diener, pers. comm.

216. For reviews of the evidence, see Raikes and Dyson, 1961; Bryson and Baerreis, 1967; Bryson and Murray, 1977: 107–14; Seth, 1978.

217. On the grounds of studies of pollen in lake sediment in four Rajasthan lakes, Seth (1978: 287) infers significantly more arid conditions at about 1000 B.C. than before that date.

218. Agrawal, 1971: 224–28; Agrawal, 1982: 263; Lal, 1984: 14–16.

219. M. Wheeler, 1959: 118, 122.

220. Hopkins, 1901: 230–31.

221. Allchin and Allchin, 1982: 315–16.

222. F. Zimmermann, 1987: 44–45.

223. R. S. Sharma, 1974; Agrawal, 1982: 240, 251–56, 263; and Lal, 1984: 55.

224. Agrawal, 1982: 263.

225. Diener et al., 1978.

226. Eichinger Ferro-Luzzi, 1987: 102.

227. Eichinger Ferro-Luzzi, 1987: 102.

228. Stutley and Stutley, 1977: 176.

229. Walker, 1968, 1: 280.

230. Ambedkar, 1948: 116–21.

231. On this, see W. N. Brown, 1957: 39–47; Alsdorf, 1961; L. Dumont, 1970: 146–51, 305–6; Lodrick, 1981: 53–56; Eichinger Ferro-Luzzi, 1985a, 1987: 99–104.

232. Gandhi, 1954: 3, 5, 6, 32.

233. Eichinger Ferro-Luzzi, 1987: 101.

234. E. C. Sachau, 1971: 139, 152.

Chapter 4. Chicken and Eggs

1. Crawford, 1984: 298–300.

2. Outstanding studies of domesticated fowl from a cultural and historical perspective are all too rare, and I feel called upon to call special attention to two recent ones on the muscovy duck (Donkin, 1989) and guinea fowl (Donkin, 1991).

3. Laufer, 1927: 254.

4. In his article on domestication, Berthold Laufer (1927) uses the terms "cock," "fowl," and "chicken" without distinction. The context suggests he means that the bones of both hens and cocks were important in divination, but that the cock occupied a somewhat more exalted position, that perhaps only cocks, not chickens in general, were sacred—although this is not clear. Laufer says specifically, however, that cocks were kept as timekeepers.

5. Milne, 1924: 192–93, 270–73.

6. H. I. Marshall, 1922: 281–82, 285.

7. T. C. Das, 1945: 41.

8. N. E. Parry, 1932: 61.

9. I have not heard, for any Southeast Asian people, of divination with chickens resembling one used by the early Romans. If, after being presented with feed, chickens ate heartily, with food falling from their beaks, it was a favorable omen to the Romans; if they refused to eat, it was unfavorable (Frazer, 1929, 4: 330; Dumézil, 1970, 1: 121; 2: 599).

10. Bertrand, 1958: 153.

11. H. I. Marshall, 1922: 284–85.

12. Shukla, 1959: 99.

13. Bertrand, 1958: 153–54.

14. T. C. Das, 1945: 41. A similar form of divination is employed by Lakher men of the Lushai Hills in India when trying to determine whether it is safe to carry out a raid (N. E. Parry, 1932: 209); for punctured-egg divination among the Thadou Kuki, see W. Shaw, 1929: 83.

15. For the history of cockfighting among Chinese and English, and a comparison of their poetry on cockfighting, see Cutter, 1989. For an interesting account of cockfighting in Bali, see Geertz, 1972. For cockfighting and machismo in Andalusia, Spain, see Marvin, 1984. For a recent, well-publicized, and costly case involving the law and cockfighting in Ohio, see James, 1992.

16. Laufer, 1927; Crawford, 1984: 300.

17. Laufer, 1927: 255.

18. Crawfurd, 1830, 2: 269.

19. Fryer, 1909–15, 20: 68–69.

20. Scott, 1910: 84.

21. Laufer, 1927: 254.

22. Hutton, 1969: 83.

23. Scott, 1910: 136–37.

24. Schomberg, 1938: 78.

25. Skeat and Blagden, 1906, 1: 131, 134–35.

26. Loeb, 1935: 24.

27. Blackwood, 1935: 284.

28. We don't know whether it is because of such beliefs that some groups apply such restrictions to prestigious persons. Among the Angami Naga, for example, chickenflesh is the most common meat, but both chickenflesh and eggs are prohibited to religious officials responsible for ceremonies and to others of high social status (Hutton, 1969: 91, 232, 339). Among the Kedah Semang, a similar situation prevails, with medicine men rarely eating the flesh of fowl (Skeat and Blagden, 1906, 2: 226).

29. See Newall, 1971: passim.

30. Rutter, 1929: 75.

31. Williams-Hunt, 1952: 94; Evans, 1923: 182.

32. Dê, 1951: 4.

33. Vanoverbergh, 1936–38: 94.

34. Hutton, 1968: 65, 95, 242.

35. Dube, 1951: 49.

36. S. Fuchs, 1960: 70, 119.
37. W. C. Smith, 1925: 33, 113.
38. Webster, 1942: 118.
39. Leung et al., 1973: 111.
40. Crawfurd, 1830, 1: 408.
41. Ratzel, 1896–98, 1: 432; Renner, 1944: 73.
42. Jenks, 1905: 143.
43. Verrill, 1946: 211.
44. Schwabe, 1979: 399.
45. Blunt, 1931: 95, 96; Srinivas, 1955: 20; Hutton, 1963: 77; G. Eichinger Ferro-Luzzi, pers. comm. There are certain Brahmins in eastern Uttar Pradesh who, even though they will eat meat on occasion, reject eggs altogether (L. Dumont, 1970: 141).
46. Hiralal, 1925: 64.
47. Eichinger Ferro-Luzzi, 1977a: 364–65, 373; Eichinger Ferro-Luzzi, 1981: 249–50.
48. Eichinger Ferro-Luzzi, 1977b: 547–48; Eichinger Ferro-Luzzi, 1987: 87.
49. J. A. Dubois, 1906: 282.
50. Cornell University, 1956, 1: 190.
51. Gangulee, 1939: 199. There is clear evidence that the ban was in effect at least by the eleventh century, when al-Bīrūnī included "tame poultry" and eggs of all sorts among items forbidden, in particular to Brahmins (E. C. Sachau, 1971: 151).
52. In a similar vein, a tract against egg eating published by the Jains (Davidson and Gross, c. 1960) includes material on the diseases of chickens that may be transmitted to a person eating eggs.
53. Lawrence, 1895: 254; Modi, 1913–16: 480–81; Biscoe, 1922: 265.
54. Srinivas, 1955: 20.
55. Blunt, 1931: 95; Gangulee, 1939: 199.
56. This, however, is only one factor influencing the use and avoidance of eggs by Tamil women at puberty, during pregnancy, and after giving birth, for which see Eichinger Ferro-Luzzi, 1973a: 170–71; Eichinger Ferro-Luzzi, 1973b: 260; and Eichinger Ferro-Luzzi, 1974: 10.
57. D. N. Majumdar, 1937: 26, 32.
58. Wijesekera, 1965: 72, 115, 143.
59. Le May, 1930: 147.
60. Nāgarakṛtāgama 89, trans. in Kern, 1918.
61. R. R. P. Sharma, 1961: 27.
62. Heber and Heber, 1926: 96.
Though Moslems in India generally do eat fowl and eggs, in the upper Indus Valley a nominally Moslem group, the Shin of Dardistan, have a horror of fowl and will neither touch nor eat them. In districts where the Shin were in a majority in the last century, chickens seemed to be absent (Drew, 1875: 428; Biddulph, 1880: 37–38; Imperial Gazetteer of India, 1909b: 108).

63. McGovern, 1924: 273–74; Bell, 1928: 53–54, 233–34; Ekvall, 1939: 60; Waddell, 1939: 225.

64. Combe, 1926: 128; Bell, 1928: 233–34.

65. Ekvall, 1939: 60; Bell, 1946: 181; Kawaguchi, 1909: 605; McGovern, 1924: 273–74.

66. Westermarck, 1924, 2: 325.

67. Chow, 1984: 364; Chang, 1986: 93; West and Zhou, 1988: 515, 517, 524–25, 528.

68. Dean, 1980: 52.

69. J. P. Maxwell, 1921: 378.

70. Alsop, 1918: 188–89; Holmes, 1948: 25.

71. Liu En-lan, 1937: 134–35; Welch, 1967: 112.

72. Duval et al., 1885.

73. For Chinese ways of making hundred-year-old eggs, see Simoons, 1991: 364.

74. Eberhard, 1968: 432.

75. The color red is not only a symbol of joy and good fortune in China, but it is also protective against evil spirits.

76. Eberhard, 1968: 421.

77. See, for example, Cammann, 1951: 35.

78. Yamasaki, 1900: 233; Stanford University, 1956: 259.

79. Wiedfeldt, 1914: 9, 18, 133.

80. Shirokogoroff, 1924: 133.

81. Griffis, 1882: 267; Saunderson, 1894: 307–8; Van Buskirk, 1923: 1; Osgood, 1951: 77–78.

82. Norbeck, 1954: 72; Beardsley et al., 1959: 201.

83. Webster, 1942: 333.

84. Zeuner, 1963: 444.

85. P. K. Thomas, 1984: 356.

86. West and Zhou, 1988: 517.

87. Gandert, 1975: 362–65; Crawford, 1984: 301–2. There are, however, much earlier claims of domesticated chickens in Greece and other parts of Europe, for example a single individual in strata at Lerna in the Peloponnesus that date from roughly 2000 B.C. (Gejvall, 1969: 48, 49, 58). For a summary of archeological evidence of the chicken in Europe, see West and Zhou, 1988: 520–23, 525, 528.

88. Aristophanes, The birds 483; D. W. Thompson, 1966: 34.

89. Peters, 1913: 377–86.

90. Darmesteter and Mills, 1880–87, 4: 193n.

91. Dhalla, 1922: 185.

92. Hehn, 1885: 241–42.

93. Dhalla, 1922: 185.

94. The Arabs in modern Palestine have a rain-making procession in which a cock is induced to crow, thereby asking God for rain (Goodenough, 1953–58, 8: 68, citing I. Scheftelowitz).

95. Aelian *On the characteristics of animals* 7.7; Pausanias *Description of Greece* 5.25. 9; Peters, 1913: 381; Goodenough, 1953–68, 8: 60–62; D. W. Thompson, 1966: 34–36, 38–39, 41, 42; Lonsdale, 1979: 155; Waida, 1987a: 551.

One surprising parallel is the use of garlic on fighting birds, apparently to stimulate and give them strength. In ancient Greece, garlic was rubbed on fighting cocks, and in modern India it is "administered to wounded or fainting birds" (D. W. Thompson, 1966: 35; Lonsdale, 1979: 155).

96. Pausanias *Description of Greece* 6.26.3.

97. D. W. Thompson, 1966: 35; Waida, 1987a: 551.

98. Goodenough, 1953–68, 8: 67.

99. For more on the cock, Asclepius, and other Greek deities and cults, see Olivieri, 1924.

The cock was also associated with Mercury, as shown in a mosaic from the Danube area in Roman times pictured in Zeuner, 1963: 453. At Uley in Roman Britain at a temple dedicated to Mercury, chicken bones, presumably remains of sacrificial feasts, have been uncovered in significant numbers (Ross, 1967: 158; Henig, 1984: 131).

100. Waida, 1987a: 551. For more on representations of the cock on tombstones in the Greco-Roman world, see Goodenough, 1953–68, 8: 64–67, and passim.

101. Tudor, 1969–76, 2: 216–19.

102. *Encyclopaedia Britannica*, 1910–11a: 276. The cock was also sacrificed to Asclepius in a festival at the city of Epidaurus in the Peloponnesus, center of the cult (Jayne, 1962: 296). Nearly every sizable community in the Greek world had an Asclepius shrine. The cult also became popular in Rome, where the god was called Aesculapius, and the ruins of more than two hundred shrines have been found across the Greco-Roman world. Because Asclepius was popular, and a serious rival of Christ, Christian writers singled him out for harsh criticism, and Christian authorities targeted his temples for destruction (Edelstein and Edelstein, 1945, 2: 132–35, 255–57; Jayne, 1962: 471–72 and passim; Meier, 1987: 464–65). For an excellent account of the contrasts between the two gods, see "Asclepius and Christ" in Edelstein and Edelstein, 1945, 2: 132–38.

103. Plato *Phaedo* 118.

104. Edelstein and Edelstein, 1945, 2: 130–31; Goodenough, 1953–68, 8: 67.

105. Edelstein and Edelstein, 1945, 2: 189–90, who also provide information on other acceptable offerings, animal and otherwise.

106. Kerényi, 1959: 59.

107. D. W. Thompson, 1966: 41, citing Aelian *Varia historia* 2.28.

108. Aelian *On the characteristics of animals* 17.46, citing Mnaseas.

109. Gimbutas, 1982: 101–7, 163–68.

110. Macrobius *Saturnalia* 7.16.8.

111. Kurtz and Boardman, 1971: 77.

112. Alcock, 1980: 56; Henig, 1984: 193–94.

113. Eliade, 1958: 415.

114. Goodenough, 1953–68, 8: 67; Waida, 1987a: 552. In early Christian art, the

cock often appeared with Peter, Christ's foremost disciple (for a reference to examples, see Goodenough, 1953–68, 8: 61). This is in keeping with Christ's prediction that Peter would deny him thrice before the cock crowed, but it may also relate to Peter being among those who saw and acknowledged the risen Christ.

115. Goodenough, 1953–68, 8: 67; Waida, 1987a: 552.

116. Goodenough, 1953–68, 8: 67.

117. *Hamlet* 1.1.149–55.

118. D. W. Thompson, 1966: 41.

119. Gimbutas, 1958: 41.

120. Gregor, 1881: 140–41.

121. Sad Dar 73.3, trans. in West, 1880–97. If a chicken ate "dead matter," however, neither its flesh nor eggs could be eaten for an entire year (Dhalla, 1922: 187).

122. Sad Dar 34.3–4, trans. in West, 1880–97.

123. Vermaseren, 1963: 49–50, 51, 72; Waida, 1987a.

124. Porphyry *On abstinence from animal food* 4.16.

125. Caesar *Gallic War* 5.12.

126. Deffontaines, 1948: 373.

127. Argenti and Rose, 1949: 113. One wonders whether there may be more to the acceptability of the cock than this account suggests.

128. G. Eichinger Ferro-Luzzi, pers. comm.

129. Horwitz and Tchernov, 1989.

130. Bodenheimer, 1960.

131. Cheyne, 1899–1903; Ginzberg et al., 1907; Peters, 1913; Driver, 1955: 133–34; Feliks, 1971–72b.

132. E.g., Peters, 1913: 364–70, 396.

133. Feliks, 1971–72b: 418; Ussishkin, 1978: 88–89.

134. J. B. Pritchard, 1961: 20, Fig. 47.

135. Taran, 1975.

136. Hellwing, 1984: 106, 110.

137. L. K. Horwitz, pers. comm.

138. Ussishkin, 1978: 88–89; West and Zhou, 1988: 520, citing I. Drori, and Boessneck and von den Driesch.

139. Baba Ḳamma 82b; Ginzberg et al., 1907: 139.

140. ʿAbodah Zarah 1.14a.

141. Baba Meziʿa 86b; Giṭṭin 57a; Zeuner, 1963: 447–48; Feliks, 1962: 59; Feliks, 1971–72b.

142. Goodenough, 1953–68, 8: 68 n370, citing I. Scheftelowitz.

143. For the consumption of offerings made in lay sacrifices, as given in the Bible and early rabbinical texts, see D. P. Wright, 1987: 237–42.

144. Ginzberg et al., 1907: 139; Peters, 1913: 371; Goodenough, 1953–58, 8: 68; Waida, 1987a: 552.

145. For the symbolism of cocks among the Jews, see Goodenough, 1953–68, 8: 68–70. For eggs and egg symbolism among the Jews, see Jacobs and Schechter, 1907.

146. Jacobs and Schechter, 1907.

147. Coltherd, 1966: 219, 220, 222; Darby et al., 1977, 1: 301; Crawford, 1984: 301; Boessneck, 1988: 90–91.

148. Coltherd, 1966: 221.

149. Darby et al., 1977, 1: 309, 331–33.

150. Waida, 1987a: 552.

151. Though the Mandaeans of Iraq and Iran eat chickens and eggs, elements of impurity cling to them. Eggs, for example, are never consumed as part of a ritual meal. Nor do novice priests eat them during the sixty-day time of purity when they are being consecrated (Drower, 1937: 48, 155).

152. Graves, 1927: 172–73.

153. Philby, 1952: 642.

154. B. Thomas, 1932: 59.

155. Philby, 1952: 642, 656–57, 661.

156. B. Thomas, 1932: 59, 79.

157. L. C. Briggs, 1958: 41, 90, 134–36.

158. MacDonald, 1992: 306–7.

159. Donkin, 1991: 67–68.

160. Roscoe, 1923: 198, 210.

161. Steedman, 1835, 1:254.

162. Speke, 1908: 44.

163. Trant, 1954: 704.

164. Huntingford, 1955: 109.

165. Cerulli, 1956: 100, 113.

166. O'Laughlin, 1974: 302.

167. Salt, 1814: 179; Paulitschke, 1893: 157, 229; Lagercrantz, 1950: 41–42.

168. Schapera and Goodwin, 1950: 133–34.

169. Huffman, 1931: 14.

170. E. Donner, 1939: 122.

171. Orde Brown, 1925: 99.

172. O'Laughlin, 1974: 302.

173. Sumner, 1906: 339.

174. Lagercrantz, 1950: 44.

175. O'Laughlin, 1974: 302. In a study of the food taboos of pregnant women—160 of them black, and 40 white—in South Carolina, 6 women expressed concern that eating eggs would damage their infants (Bartholomew and Poston, 1970: 16). Though the six women were not identified as to race, one wonders whether they were black and whether we may be dealing with survivals of views widely held in Africa.

176. Torday and Joyce, 1906: 51.

177. O'Laughlin, 1974.

178. Stannus, 1922: 348; Tew, 1950: 8.

179. Nalder, 1937: 177; Baxter and Butt, 1953: 109.

180. Trant, 1954: 704.

181. Cerulli, 1956: 94.

182. O'Laughlin, 1974: 301–2 and n.

183. Lagercrantz, 1950: 42–44.

184. Cornell University, 1956, 1: 190.

185. Gangulee, 1939: 199.

186. Bolton, 1972: 791–93. Christine Wilson (1973:267) mentions other restrictions followed by husbands of pregnant Malay women. That restrictions should apply to husbands of pregnant women is not strange, for husbands are commonly involved in the pregnancies of their wives and in their food cravings and aversions, with the husbands themselves often exhibiting symptoms (Dickens and Trethowan, 1971: 265–67).

187. Probably related to this is the practice, common in ancient Rome (Pliny *Natural history* 10.154) and still found in parts of contemporary America, of divining the sex of the unborn child through the use of eggs.

188. M. Stevenson, 1920: 408–9.

189. Eichinger Ferro-Luzzi, 1977b: 547; Eichinger Ferro-Luzzi, 1987: 87–88, 89, 90–92. For more on the snake in Hindu thinking and practice, see Eichinger Ferro-Luzzi, 1987: 84–92.

190. Hellbom, 1963.

191. Gonda, 1965: 147.

192. The goddess Nut could also grant a dead human the ability "to rise in a renewed body," and representations of the deity along with appeals to her are often found on Egyptian coffins (Budge, 1904, 2: 95, 107, 110–11).

193. Forlong, 1906, 2: 11–13; Newall, 1987.

194. Blair, 1956: 76.

195. M. Leach, 1949–50, 1: 335.

196. Eliade, 1958: 415.

197. M. Leach, 1949–50, 1: 341.

198. Eliade, 1958: 415–16.

199. Eliade, 1958: 415.

200. Lagercrantz, 1950: 44.

201. Drower, 1956: 8, 37–38.

202. Eliade, 1958: 414.

203. M. Leach, 1949–50, 1: 341.

204. Westermarck, 1926, 1: 581; 2: 311. Among the Navajo of Arizona, a similar perception prevails, but with different results: eggs may be avoided by women as a means of birth control, in the belief that consuming eggs "will make them have babies all the time" (Bailey, 1940: 276–77).

205. Massé, 1938: 48, 153.

206. Waddell, 1899: 86–87. There is a story about a young woman of a good Sikkim family who, on her first visit to Darjeeling, was so taken by a European man she met, that she decided she would like to marry him. So, when she offered him eggs and he accepted them, she immediately asked him to wed her at once, only to be told

that he was already married and that it was not customary for European men to have more than one wife (Waddell, 1899: 87).

207. Hutson, 1921: 2; Adolph, 1956: 69.

208. Jacobs and Schechter, 1907; Drower, 1956: 8, 38.

209. The Mandaeans of Iraq and Iran think a death will occur in the household if an egg is given away after dark (Drower, 1937: 48).

210. Blackman, 1927: 108.

211. Lagercrantz, 1950: 42.

212. It is true that some groups, such as the Beni subtribe of the Nupe in Nigeria, are as afraid that eating eggs will make men sterile as they are that eggs will make women barren (Nadel, 1951: 204). I suspect, however, that this is an extension to men of fertility concerns that were originally of primary relevance for women.

213. The Bantu of North Kavirondo, for example, eat only hard-boiled eggs, and consider both soft-boiled and fried eggs disgusting (Wagner, 1949–56, 2: 66). The Luba of the Congo area will eat boiled or fried eggs, but only after the hen has sat on them and they have proved sterile (Lagercrantz, 1950: 41). The Lendu of Zaire reserve fresh eggs for old people (Baxter and Butt, 1953: 126). This may not be a question of honoring old people with food of special value, but one of their being beyond child-bearing age and the risks of infertility.

214. The Yao of Malawi, for example, eat fowl, but only children and old people eat eggs. The Ndebele of Zimbabwe eat chicken frequently, but never eggs. The Nupe of Nigeria prefer chicken to all other food, but do not market eggs and in certain sections do not eat them. The Moru of the Sudan keep chickens and eat them, but only very old men and women eat eggs. Among the Teso of Uganda, men eat chicken but rarely eggs; women, though they are sometimes forbidden chickenflesh, are always forbidden eggs unless they are past child bearing. Among the Bantu of North Kavirondo in Kenya, who traditionally prohibit women, especially those of child-bearing age, from eating either chicken or eggs, a few Christian women have been persuaded to eat chickenflesh—but they still refuse eggs. In Asia, the Malayan aborigines keep chickens and eat them, but most groups do not eat eggs, and people may be gravely offended if asked for them. The Khasi of Assam, in turn, consider chickenflesh a favorite food, but never touch fowl's eggs.

I have found just two groups, both in the Sudan, who use eggs while restricting the use of chickens. Among the Kakwa, except for one section, men and women eat eggs, but young women will eat chicken only after they have had a number of children. Among the Nyangbara, men and women eat eggs, but women do not eat chicken.

Chapter 5. Horseflesh

1. Bahn, 1984.

2. Some have suggested that horses were domesticated independently in various parts of Europe (Piggott, 1983: 87–89; Clutton-Brock, 1992: 11, 55–56). Others have suggested that horses were domesticated earlier in the North Pontic–southern Urals area. Mallory (pp. 180–82 in Telegin, 1986) and Anthony (1991b: 254–55)

have discussed the finds (seventh millennium B.C. and later) of possible earlier horses in the southern Urals and north Caspian area.

3. This section is based on Bibikova, 1969; Gimbutas, 1970: 157–58, 169–70, 190; H. Epstein, 1971b, 2: 501; Bökönyi, 1974: 22–23, 238–49; Bökönyi, 1978: 22–25; Bökönyi, 1984: 166–68; Bökönyi, 1987: 136–38; Nobis, 1974: 221–23; Mallory, 1981, 1989: 197–202; Telegin, 1986: 82–87; Anthony and Brown, 1989, 1991; Anthony, 1991a; Clutton-Brock, 1992: 55–56. Levine (1990: 728–29, 731–39), on the other hand, was unconvinced by evidence presented for domestication of the Dereivka horses. Instead, she argued that evidence strongly suggests intensified horse hunting, possibly with the assistance of certain tamed or domesticated animals.

4. Anthony and Brown, 1991: 32.

5. Bibikova, 1969; Mallory, 1981: 215; Levine, 1990: 738–39; Anthony, 1991b: 261–65; Anthony and Brown, 1991: 32.

6. The most convincing evidences for horse riding, of course, are representations of mounted horsemen. H. Epstein (1971b, 2: 510), in reviewing that evidence, found that, with a few questionable exceptions, there are no such representations before 1500 B.C. Renfrew (1987: 137–38), writing more recently, noted that such representations date only from early in the second millennium B.C., though he acknowledged that horse riding may have somewhat preceded this. In any case, there remains a significant gap between the time of horse domestication and earliest representations of mounted horsemen. Approaching the question from quite a different point of view, Anthony and Brown (1989: 114n; 1991) examined teeth of horses found in early sites in the Ukraine (Upper Paleolithic to Iron Age) for bit wear, and concluded that a bit was used on the "cult stallion," one of the horses at Dereivka. By implication, that horse was ridden, and riding of horses evolved along with horse domestication.

7. Burial of an entire horse was very uncommon in graves of Early Kurgan times. Evidence, though it is quite scanty, also suggests that horses were buried with males and children, but not with females.

8. Maringer (1981: 179) suggests that these graves indicate that the horse was worshipped as a sacred animal.

9. Mallory, 1981: 214–23.

10. For archeological evidence of weather and solar deities in Kurgan culture, see Gimbutas, 1970: 170–75. As for linguistic evidence of an early solar deity, Mallory (1989: 129) notes the similarities in names for the sun deity, whether a god or goddess, among various Indo-European languages: Sanskrit: Surya; Gaulish: Sulis; Germanic: Sol; Lithuanian: Saule; and Slavic: Tsar Solnitse.

11. Anthony, 1991a: 204–17; Anthony, 1991b: 265–67, 273; Clutton-Brock, 1992: 56. Though wheeled vehicles were known by late in the third millennium B.C., indications are that initially—in the Near East and in the Pontic-Caspian grasslands—oxen (or, in the Near East, donkeys and onagers) were used to pull them, not horses (Anthony, 1991a: 205–6; Clutton-Brock, 1992: 12, 68–70).

12. Khazanov, 1984: 91–94.

13. For interesting observations on these Inner Asian fighters, their reputation, training, discipline, horsemanship, and more, see Sinor, 1981.

14. Gening, 1979.

15. For the horse in the hierarchy of sacrificial animals among Indo-Iranians and other Indo-Europeans, see Puhvel, 1978: 354, 356–57, 359.

16. Chariot burial was widespread; for references, see Piggott, 1983: 10, 23, 92, 96, 140, 148, 149, 158, 184, 194, 199–207, 228, 232, 242.

17. Sīrōzah 1.1; Yasht 2.1; 5.11–13; 6.1; 10.67–68, 125 (both trans. in Darmesteter and Mills, 1880–87).

18. Gāthās 44.18; Vendidad 22.3, 10, 16; Yasht 5.21, trans. in Darmesteter and Mills, 1880–87.

19. Herodotus *History* 7.113; Xenophon *Cyropaedia* 8.3.12, 24; Ovid *Fasti* 1.385; Pausanias *Description of Greece* 3.20.4; Philostratus *Life of Apollonius of Tyana* 1.31.

20. Tacitus, 1889: 300n.

21. Herodotus *History* 7.40.

22. For this, and more on the horse and horse symbolism in ancient Iran, also see Dhalla, 1922: 182–84, 368, and passim.

23. O'Flaherty, 1980: 165; O'Flaherty, 1987: 463. In a similar vein, the medieval Slavs dedicated a white horse to the god of light and a black horse to the evil one.

24. Herodotus *History* 1.133; Modi, 1911–34, 1: 84, 95; Dhalla, 1922: 134, 222.

25. Herodotus *History* 1.216; Strabo *Geography* 11.8.6.

26. Xenophon *Anabasis* 4.5.34–36.

27. Lucian *Scythian* 2; Herodotus *History* 4.61; Strabo *Geography* 7.4.6; Pausanias *Description of Greece* 1.21.6; Minns, 1913: 49, 85, 86. For an account of animal sacrifice among the Scythians, see Hartog, 1989.

28. Boyle, 1963: 204–7, 207n; Boyle, 1965: 148n, 149.

29. Clavijo, 1859: 134, 139, 142.

30. Ratzel, 1896–98, 3: 329.

31. Prejevalsky, 1876, 1: 56; J. H. Gray, 1878, 2: 174; Howey, 1923: 201; Friters, 1949: 17; Boyle, 1963: 201; Schwabe, 1979: 157.

32. Hehn, 1885: 36. There are reports of horseflesh being eaten in Kashgar (Forsyth, 1875: 74) and among Uzbeks (Lockhart, 1871: 160–61); Altai Tatars (Great Britain Admiralty, n.d.: 143), Karachai Tatars (Great Britain Admiralty, n.d., 199), Bashkir (Langkavel, 1888: 51), Shors (Levin and Potapov, 1964: 458), Horse Tungus (Horse Evenks) (Levin and Potapov, 1964: 636), pagan tribes of Chuvash of the Volga region in southeast Russia (Featherman, 1885–91, 4: 515–16; MacCulloch, 1916–32, 4: 46), Cheremis of Perm (Molotov) (MacCulloch, 1916–32, 4: 55, 57), Crimean and Nogay Tatars (Featherman, 1885–91, 4: 212, 222), Kirghiz (Featherman, 1885–91, 4: 255–56), Minusinsk Tatars (Featherman, 1885–91, 4: 228), and Lapps (Featherman, 1885–91, 4: 447).

33. Kler, 1947: 24.

34. Gryaznov, 1969: 91.

35. Jochelson, 1906: 262–63.

36. Sarytschew, 1806: 9; Dobell, 1830, 1: 307; Erman, 1850: 299, 309; Lansdell, 1882: 301.

37. Lansdell, 1882: 301.

38. Lansdell, 1882: 301.

39. Dobell, 1830, 1: 307.

40. O'Flaherty, 1980: 245; Badam, 1984: 347–48; P. K. Thomas, 1984: 358; P. K. Thomas, 1989: 109–10; Rissman, 1989: 19.

41. For sun worship in ancient India, see Pandey, 1971, and for the horse and horse sacrifice in such worship, pp. 11, 27–28, 33–34, 36–37, 66–67.

42. Initially, Indian gods are presented as transported in chariots, and only later, in a secondary sense, as riding horses (Gonda, 1965: 113–14).

43. For the association of the horse, chariot, and these and other Vedic gods, see Gonda, 1965: 72–81. For the horse and Vishnu, a lesser deity in early times but later a leading deity with solar associations, see Gonda, 1969a: 147–50.

44. The black color of the horses was believed to encourage black clouds and rain. Other black things were also used in Vedic rain-making rites, among them black cows, milk of black cows, black rams, black honey, black rice, and black clothes. On this and other means of rain making in Vedic India, see Gonda, 1980: 44, 398–99.

45. Macdonell, 1897: 148–49; Walker, 1968, 1: 12–13, 437, 457–59; 2: 552–53; Gonda, 1980: 28, 100–101, 110, 123, 134, 243, 271, 287, 317, 332, 338, 398, 407, 411, 425–26, 437.

46. For more on the horse in ritual, sacrifice, and legend in ancient India, see Ghurye, 1979: 46–63; and O'Flaherty, 1980: 154–64, 174–85, 213–37.

47. P. K. Thomas, 1989: 110.

48. Mallory, 1981: 213.

49. Levin and Potapov, 1964: 47.

50. Judging from the Vedic literature, horse sacrifice was infrequent, and the usual sacrificial animals, and presumably the most common meat animals, were sheep, goats, and common cattle (Macdonell and Keith, 1967, 2: 147–48; Oldenberg, 1988: 200–201).

51. Ghurye, 1979: 52.

52. In the sections in question (*Rig-veda* 1.162.5, 12–13, 18–19), priests ate the flesh of the sacrificed animal (O'Flaherty, 1981: 92 n5).

53. Walker, 1968, 1: 278, 457–58.

54. Oldenberg, 1988: 201, 205, 251, 278 n147.

55. Keith, 1914, 2: 581n.

56. Stutley and Stutley, 1977: 24.

57. *Taittirīya Saṃhitā* 7.2. 10, trans. in Keith, 1914.

58. Prakash, 1961: 176, 210.

59. E. C. Sachau, 1971: 151.

60. For details of the *aśvamedha,* see P.-É. Dumont, 1927 and 1948; Bhawe, 1939; Puhvel, 1970: 160–62; Walker, 1968, 1: 458–59; Stutley and Stutley, 1977: 24–27; Ghurye, 1979: 54–55; and Oldenberg, 1988: 250–51. For parallels between the *aśvamedha* and Roman and/or Irish horse sacrifices, see Dumézil, 1970, 1: 224–27; Puhvel, 1970: 160–64; and O'Flaherty, 1987: 464. For the relationship between horse sacrifice and human sacrifice *(puruṣamedha)* in ancient India, see Wyatt, 1989.

61. Crooke, 1896, 2: 204; Geldner, 1908–26.

62. M. Stevenson, 1920: 297–98.

63. However, al-Bīrūnī's account of the *aśvamedha* involved a mare that was ultimately sacrificed and eaten by Brahmins (E. C. Sachau, 1971: 139).

64. Walker, 1968, 1: 458–59. Because of the growing force of ahimsa, a king is praised in the *Rāmāyaṇa* because no animals were killed at an *aśvamedha* (E. W. Hopkins, 1969: 377).

65. When purchasing a horse, many present-day Indians look for auspicious and inauspicious marks and colors, for which see Crooke, 1906: 255–56. For auspicious and inauspicious marks of horses in the Sanskrit literature, see Banerji, 1980: 114–16, 117, 118–19.

66. Thurston, 1912: 62.

67. Crooke, 1896, 2: 207.

68. Gonda, 1965: 112.

69. R. P. Das, 1983: 685; R. P. Das, 1987: 246; Sontheimer, 1989: 196–97.

70. Sontheimer, 1989: 196–97.

71. Sontheimer, 1989: 197.

72. Kjaerholm, 1990: 72–73.

73. Gonda, 1965: 113; Kjaerholm, 1990: 72–73.

74. Thurston, 1912: 166–67.

75. Walldén, 1990: 89.

76. Kjaerholm, 1990: 73.

77. Shah, 1985. This is the best account I have found of the manufacture and use of such terra-cotta horses, and it contains many good illustrations. In confirmation of Shah's observations, others have noted that the Bhils of western India (one of the tribal groups considered by Shah) venerate the horse more than any other animal, use clay horses as votive objects, and place clay horses and riders beneath village trees (Hutton, 1963: 21; O'Flaherty, 1980: 261).

78. Zeuner, 1963: 332.

79. For which, see Shah, 1985: 17 and 149.

80. Crooke, 1896, 2: 208.

81. Crooke, 1896, 2: 208.

82. Elwin, 1955: 150, 404, 436, 522, 526.

83. Hutton, 1963: 230.

84. Indians have had to import horses in considerable numbers through much of their history, in early times from Bactria and Parthia, in later times from Iran and Arabia (Crooke, 1906: 253–54; Leshnik, 1978).

85. M. Stevenson, 1930: 6; G. W. Briggs, 1920: 45; S. Fuchs, 1950: 357.

86. O'Flaherty, 1980: 261, citing Crooke.

87. Crooke, 1896, 2: 207.

88. *Mahāvagga* 6.23.11, trans. in Davids and Oldenberg, 1881–85.

89. Hermanns, 1949: 163.

90. Combe, 1926: 127–28, 163.

91. For the possibility that horses were domesticated in early North China, see Olsen, 1984.

92. Sowerby, 1935: 234, 237; Gibson, 1935: 344; Creel, 1937a: 182–83, 191, 193; Creel, 1937b: 76, 149–54, 200; Ho, 1975: 355–57; Bökönyi, 1984: 166, 167; Chang, 1980: 143; Chang, 1986: 58, 282, 317, 363; Chow, 1984: 364–65; Chow, 1989: 105; E. N. Anderson, 1988: 20; Clutton-Brock, 1992: 102–5.

93. L. H. D. Buxton, 1929: 81; Yetts, 1934.

94. Eberhard, 1942: 16.

95. Freeman, 1977: 149, 154; Mote, 1977: 201; Yü, 1977: 58.

96. Robert Burton, 1948: 201; J. H. Gray, 1878, 2: 174; Raveret-Wattel, 1884: 607; Simmonds, 1885: 98; A. H. Smith, 1894: 21; E. N. Anderson, 1988: 144. Horse liver, however, was considered poisonous and was avoided by the early Chinese (E. H. Schafer, 1977: 131–32; Yü, 1977: 58; E. N. Anderson, 1988: 144).

97. Batchelor, 1901: 198.

98. Kunio, 1957: 40.

99. Abadie, 1924: 158, 159.

100. Horse sacrifice, possibly of ancient Indian inspiration, is reported for back areas of Sumatra (Hutton, 1963: 230). Horseflesh, in turn, was the preferred flesh of the Batta of Sumatra early in the nineteenth century. In order to obtain flesh of high quality, the Batta devoted special care and feed to horses (Marsden, 1811: 381). On Java at the same period, the slaughter of horses, except for diseased or maimed animals, was banned, but horseflesh was highly valued by ordinary folk (Raffles, 1817, 1: 96). Among the Belu people of central Timor, horse sacrifice is unknown, and horses are hardly ever slaughtered, for their flesh is eaten only by poor people (Vroklage, 1952, 1: 150). In the Philippines, the Bukidnon of Mindanao eat the flesh of decrepit horses (Cole, 1956: 56); the Bisayans of Barrio Caticugan on Negros eat horseflesh, but will kill horses only when they are very old, injured, or sickly (Hart, 1954: 427); the Igorot of Luzon keep horses and use them for food (Ratzel, 1896–98, 1: 431; Jenks, 1905: 107–8); and the Ifugao of Luzon eat horseflesh (Barton, 1922: 416).

101. Van Buren, 1939: 28–34; Hrozný, 1953: 42, 101, 112–13; Zeuner, 1963: 315–19; Zarins, 1978; Bökönyi, 1984: 166–68; Wilford, 1993. For the history of the horse and other equids in ancient Southwest Asia and Egypt, see Clutton-Brock, 1992: 80–95.

102. Goetze, 1962: 33–34.

103. Friedrich, 1971: 37, 39, 41, 43, 69, 71, 73, 79, 81.

104. Macqueen, 1975: 120.

105. Gurney, 1977: 61.

106. Macqueen, 1975: 137.

107. Puhvel, 1970: 171.

108. Macqueen, 1975: 119–20; Gurney, 1977: 10.

109. Hoffner, 1974: 120–21.

110. Saggs, 1962: 176.

111. 2 Kings 23:11; Frazer, 1929, 2: 166. For the occurrence of practices relating to horses, chariot, and the sun-god among neighboring peoples, and their introduction to Rome, see McKay, 1973.

112. Philby, 1928: 45.

113. T. P. Hughes, 1885: 130.

114. Niebuhr, 1889: 59; Herklots, 1921: 315.

115. The Persian doctor Avicenna (A.D. 980–1037) included horseflesh in his classification of foodstuffs, and mentioned that it was very nutritious (Gruner, 1930: 219). In modern Iran, horsemeat is recorded as a remedy for colic (Massé, 1938: 341).

116. Jochelson, 1928: 112.

117. In Egypt, for example, there is no evidence that horsemeat was ever eaten (Darby et al., 1977, 1: 237). On the other hand, the Asyr Arabs not far from the birthplace of Islam were reported by Burckhardt (1830: 138) to eat horsemeat.

118. Goody, 1971: 34–37, 47–48, 66–72; Elbl, 1991.

119. Huntingford, 1955: 109; Cerulli, 1956: 19.

120. Nadel, 1947: 189.

121. Goody, 1982: 50.

122. S. D. Brown, 1992: 86–87.

123. C. K. Meek, 1925, 1: 136; Gunn, 1956: 28.

124. Bascom, 1951: 42.

125. Gunn, 1956: 71.

126. Gunn, 1953: 80 and n.

127. Temple, 1922: 46.

128. Gunn, 1956: 28.

129. Ardener, 1956: 47–48; Murdock, 1958: F110 (Bua), F131 (Sokoro), and F132 (Somrai).

130. Ashton, 1939: 161; Beemer, 1939: 219; Quin, 1959: 103.

131. Koppers, 1936. For a recent survey of this evidence, including that from art, see Maringer, 1981. For notes and sources on the horse in the myth and religion of the ancient Celts, including the horse goddess Epona, see MacCulloch, 1911: 213–215; and O'Flaherty, 1980: 152–54, 167–74, 185–90. For the horse in sacrifice, myth, ritual, and symbolism among the Greeks, see O'Flaherty, 1980: 190–202; and among other Indo-Europeans, O'Flaherty, 1980: 165–66, 202–4.

132. Bökönyi, 1974: 248–49; Greenfield, 1986, 1: 133–34, 200.

133. C. Vermeule, 1972: 57.

134. Bevan, 1986, 1: 194.

135. Bevan, 1986, 1: 201. If one considers only unaccompanied animals, common cattle were more numerous than horses.

136. Among them, Aristophanes Lysistrata 191–92; Festus De verborum significatu, p. 190 in the Lindsay edition; Pausanias Description of Greece 3.20.4; 3.20.9; 8.7.2; Plutarch Pelopidas 22; and Sextus Empiricus Outlines of Pyrrhonism 3.221. For further references, see Stengel, 1880.

137. Henderson (1987: 92n) makes a stronger statement in this regard, that horse sacrifice in Greece was "restricted either to extraordinary incidents or to legendary times." It may even be that certain early Greeks looked down on the ritual killing of horses. In the Iliad (21.132), for example, Achilles, after slaying the Trojan Lycaon, commented on the fact that Lycaon had killed horses by casting them live into a river. Though Achilles himself cast four horses onto a funeral pyre (Iliad 23.171–72), the

question remains whether, as a Greek, he did not quite approve of such behavior (A. T. Murray, in his translation of Homer's *Iliad*, 2: 419n).

138. Bevan, 1986, 1: 200–201.

139. Kurtz and Boardman, 1971: 30; E. Vermeule, 1979: 60–61. For more on horse burials in early Greece and Cyprus, see E. Vermeule, 1979: 58–62 (general and Marathon), and Karageorghis, 1969: 27, 52–54, 55, 57, 75, 129, and passim (Salamis on Cyprus).

140. Bevan, 1986, 1: 194–95.

141. C. Vermeule, 1972: 56, 57. For more on the association of horses with death in ancient Greece, see Malten, 1914.

142. For Poseidon and his special ties with the horse, see Farnell, 1896–1909, 4: 20ff.; Malten, 1914: 179–82 and passim; Detienne and Vernant, 1978: 187–213; O'Flaherty, 1980: 190–93; Bevan, 1986, 1: 195–96, 209–10; and Bremmer, 1987. For the ties of the horse with other Greek deities, see Malten, 1914; and Bevan, 1986, 1: 196–200, 204–13. For other Indo-European deities associated with the horse, see Puhvel, 1970: 164ff.

143. See Bevan, 1986, 1: 200, for evidence of horse sacrifice in shrines of Olympian deities. As among the Iranians, a black horse was inauspicious to the Greeks (Koppers, 1936: 360).

144. Pausanias *Description of Greece* 3.20.4.

145. Stengel, 1880: 182–83; Burkert, 1985: 13.

146. Koppers, 1936: 292.

147. Strabo *Geography* 5.1.9.

148. The name of the city of Venice derives from the Veneti.

149. Tradition holds that the Veneti came to northern Italy from Thrace, from which they brought the worship of Diomedes.

150. Puhvel, 1978: 359.

151. Dumézil, 1970: 1: 154–55, 278.

152. Plutarch *Roman Questions* 97.

153. Frazer, 1929, 3: 344–45; Frazer, 1935, 8: 42–44; Laing, 1963: 55–56. Polybius (*Histories* 12.4b–c) mentions another explanation, in terms of the Trojan horse, which he regards as foolish.

154. Frazer, 1929, 4: 96–97.

155. Suetonius *Lives of the Caesars* 1.81.2.

156. Blair, 1956; 15.

157. Gimbutas, 1971: 36. For later associations of the horse with death in northern Europe, see Malten, 1914: 233–35.

158. Gimbutas, 1971: 43, 44, 158–59.

159. Müller, 1984: 190–91.

160. Gimbutas, 1971: 154, 160–61. In her book on the Slavs, Gimbutas does not mention an association between the horse and sun, but she presents interesting information showing the prominence of sun worship (1971: 164–65).

161. For rites involving the bathing of horses in Vedic India, see Gonda, 1980: 123, 317, 333, 426.

162. Gimbutas, 1958: 18, 41–43.

163. E.g., O. Keller, 1963, 1: 247–48, 253–54.

164. Tacitus *Germany* 10.

165. Banerji, 1980: 116.

166. On the other hand, the Vedic Indians considered it a bad omen for a human to sneeze. If one did so often, it was recommended that he or she touch water to pass the evil on to enemies (Gonda, 1980: 411).

167. Turville-Petre, 1964: 56, 167–68; Gelling and Davidson, 1969: frontispiece, 14–16, 19–21, 90–92, 99, 167–72; Briard, 1979: 128–29. In Scandinavia, hundreds of horses have been uncovered in graves, which implies, as well, a close link between horses and death (Lepiksaar, 1962: 116–17; Turville-Petre, 1964: 56–57).

168. O'Flaherty, 1987: 463.

169. Turville-Petre, 1964: 256–57.

170. Ní Chatháin, 1991: 123.

171. Howey, 1923: 190; Gelling and Davidson, 1969: 91–92; O'Flaherty, 1980: 152; Giraldus Cambrensis, 1982: 109–10.

172. Sacrifice of white stallions was most widespread among Indo-Europeans, but the sacrifice of white mares was found in Ireland and Greece (O'Flaherty, 1980: 165).

173. Giraldus Cambrensis, 1982: 110.

174. For these and other Indo-European goddesses and heroines who are associated with, or represented as, horses, see Dexter, 1990.

175. For Epona in cults of the Danubian provinces of the Roman Empire, see Tudor, 1969–76, 2: 104, 106, 142–44, 281.

176. Tudor, 1969–76, 2: 142–43; Le Roux and Guyonvarc'h, 1987; MacCana, 1987: 157.

177. Puhvel, 1955.

178. For a summary of these, see Dexter, 1990: 293–94.

179. O'Flaherty, 1987: 464. Sexual union, whether of a king with a mare or a queen with a stallion, occurred in the myth and ritual of certain other Indo-European peoples as well. For recurrent themes about the horse (including ones involving sacrifice) in the myth and ritual of Indo-European peoples, see O'Flaherty, 1980: 150, Chart 2.

180. Porphyry *On abstinence from animal food* 1.14; André, 1961: 136.

181. Toynbee, 1973: 185. They did, however, prepare a horsemeat bouillon, which they gave as a remedy to pigs (Pliny *Natural history* 28.265).

182. The actions of other Christian churches with regard to horsemeat need investigation. For whatever reasons, there was a notable decline in eating horseflesh among the East Slavs since antiquity, and by medieval times, its use as food "was something out of the ordinary" (Blair, 1956: 15–16). In the Caucasus area, Armenians and Georgians refuse to eat horseflesh, a refusal, it is said, that may derive from the influence of Christianity (Boyle, 1963: 201n).

183. *The Times* (London), January 25, 1868, p. 6.

184. Ní Chatháin, 1991: 124. Ní Chatháin notes, however, that there are frag-

ments that suggest that even the pagan Irish had "cultic restrictions" on eating horseflesh.

185. Boniface, 1940: 58.

186. Gelling and Davidson, 1969: 91, 168–69.

187. Hehn, 1885: 37; Simmonds, 1885: 101; Howey, 1923: 72; Gelling and Davidson, 1969: 91.

188. Hehn, 1885: 37.

189. De Paor and De Paor, 1958: 89.

190. Graves, 1957: 74.

191. Robert Burton, 1948: 201.

192. Graves, 1957: 74.

193. Fernie, 1899: 250–51; Drummond and Wilbraham, 1940: 364.

194. Simmonds, 1885: 100–101; Gade, 1976: 2.

195. Gade, 1976: 3.

196. The prevailing attitude of the English people toward eating horsemeat is shown in the observation (Fernie, 1899: 250) that the people of Cleckheaton, West Yorkshire, who formerly ate horseflesh (called kicker), were disapprovingly referred to as kicker eaters.

197. The Times (London), February 11, 1868, p. 7.

198. Simmonds, 1885: 104; Drummond and Wilbraham, 1940: 364–65.

199. Simmonds, 1885: 103.

200. One suspects that for some people it may sometimes also symbolize a degree of emancipation from societal norms, as is true of certain university groups in the United States. One notes, in this regard, that the Harvard Faculty Club served horsemeat during the Second World War (M. Bates, 1957–58: 452); and that in the 1950s, horsemeat was sold on a small scale to individual students by a department at the University of California, Berkeley.

201. Gade, 1976: 9.

202. Gade, 1976: 9.

203. Gade, 1976: 6.

204. Rossier, 1984.

205. Gade, 1976: 9.

206. Reich, 1935: 211.

207. Hugh Iltis, pers. comm.

208. Durham, 1928: 292. In the pork chapter, I mentioned that recent outbreaks of trichinosis in Italy came from horsemeat consumption. Indeed, a few years ago it was estimated that 43 percent of all human trichinosis reported in Italy derived from imported horsemeat (de Carneri and di Matteo, 1989).

209. Alicja Iwanska, pers. comm.

210. Schwabe, 1979: 157–65.

211. In the mid-1970s, horseflesh exported by Texas slaughterhouses to Europe went mainly to Germany, France, and Belgium.

212. Psarras, 1983; Wells, 1983: 1.

213. Schwabe, 1979: 157.

Chapter 6. Camelflesh

1. Masson and Sarianidi, 1972: 109, Plate 36; Bulliet, 1975; Compagnoni and Tosi, 1978: 98–102; I. L. Mason, 1984a: 108–9; I. L. Mason, 1984b: 21–23, 26; Grigson et al., 1989: 360; Zarins, 1989: 144–49. The evidence for such early dates for domesticated camels in Arabia is circumstantial, not based on acceptably dated remains in archeological sites, and a decade ago Mason (1984b: 22) was still able to write that "the first direct evidence of the domesticated dromedary in south Arabia (Hadhramaut) is for the sixth century B.C." The mandible of a camel, presumably a dromedary, found at Sihi along the Red Sea coast of Saudi Arabia, has since been dated to roughly 7200–7100 B.C., which makes it the earliest camel remains of any sort in Arabia to have been dated with certainty (Grigson et al., 1989). Unfortunately, however, there was no way to determine whether the mandible or other camel remains from the site were from wild or domesticated animals.

2. For maps of the distribution of dromedary and Bactrian camels in Eurasia and Africa, and data on camel populations of individual countries, see I. L. Mason, 1984a: 112, 113; I. L. Mason, 1984b: 28, 29.

Many uncertainties remain about the historical spread of dromedary and Bactrian camels, among them the antiquity of camel keeping in Israel, Egypt, and other lands surrounding Arabia. For Egypt, many authorities (i.e., Zeuner, 1963: 349–54; Mason, 1984b: 23, 25; Boessneck, 1988: 83) believe that, though the dromedary was known in antiquity and though dromedaries (and perhaps Bactrians) were brought to the Nile Valley by foreign invaders and traders, it was not until quite late, in Ptolemaic or Roman times, that the dromedary was integrated into Egyptian economic life. There are, however, many uncertainties, as well as suggestions that the camel played a significant role in Egypt in earlier times (see, for example, Ripinsky, 1975, 1985). The recent discovery (Rowly-Conwy, 1988) of domesticated camel remains, dating to the early centuries of the first millennium B.C., at Qaṣr Ibrîm in Nubia, about ninety miles south of Aswan, lends support to the latter view.

The history of the camel in India, too, is little understood. Camels appear to have been known in eastern Iran and Baluchistan by the third or second millennium B.C. (Meadow, 1985–88: 907–8, 910; J. G. Shaffer, 1985–88: 1323–25). Camel bones have also been reported in various Indus Valley sites, and some authorities believe that domesticated dromedaries and/or Bactrians were kept by the Indus Valley people (Badam, 1984: 349; P. K. Thomas, 1984: 356, 357; Meadow, 1985–88: 908; J. G. Shaffer, 1985–88: 1323–24; Rissman, 1989: 18–19).

Some (Bulliet, 1975: 153–55, 188; Bulliet, 1978: 1; Meadow, 1985–88: 908) believe that the Bactrian was the earlier of the two domestic forms in India. It has been argued further (J. G. Shaffer, 1985–88: 1323–26) that use of the camel, probably the Bactrian, may have been a significant element in lowering the cost of land transport and stimulating trade among Indus Valley people. The Bactrian was also known to the Aryans at the time of the *Rig-veda*, but apparently was never important to them. Ultimately, moreover, it was replaced by the dromedary, possibly because of the migration of Baluchi camel herders into the region.

China presents additional uncertainty, for Chinese writings contain no mention of domesticated Bactrians before the fourth century B.C. (E. H. Schafer, 1950: 174–77), and this would be an unusually late appearance there.

3. I. L. Mason, 1984a: 108–10, 112, 113.

4. Mahmoud, 1984.

5. H. Epstein, 1971b, 2: 574.

6. Indeed, in artistic representations at Palmyra only deities are depicted as mounted on camels until about A.D. 100, when humans are also shown in that way (Colledge, 1976: 26, 43, 49, 55, 160).

7. Gāthās 44.18; Vendidad 22.3, 10, 16 (both trans. in Darmesteter and Mills, 1880–87).

8. The second part of the prophet Zoroaster's name ("ushtra," from the Old Iranian Zarathushtra) means "camel."

9. Roux, 1959: 51–54.

10. Brooke, 1987.

11. Crooke, 1906: 77; Massé, 1938: 143. In spite of the close association of camel sacrifice and Islam, we must look beyond Islam for the origin of the practice, for it was already common in pre-Islamic Arabia (Gaudefroy-Demombynes, 1908–26; Henninger, 1948: 10; H. Epstein, 1971b, 2: 572).

12. Westermarck, 1926, 2: 290, 291.

13. Ibn el-Beïthar, 1877: 292, 368–70.

14. E. C. Sykes, 1910: 245.

15. Twitchell, 1953: 20.

16. Musil, 1928: 97; Raswan, 1947: 77.

17. R. T. Wilson, 1984: 158.

18. Apparently the camel was not eaten in Egypt prior to the Arab invasion (Darby et al., 1977, 1: 254).

19. A. E. Robinson, 1936: 55; Platt and Hefny, 1958: 189.

20. Hrdlička, 1912: 12; G. W. Murray, 1935: 105–6.

21. L. C. Briggs, 1958: 32; L. C. Briggs, 1967: 18.

22. The eating of camelflesh is reported for Moslems in Afghanistan (J. A. Robinson, 1935: 18), Baluchistan (*Baluchistan District Gazetteer Series,* 1906–8, 3: 78), and for Inner Asian Moslems (Lattimore, 1929: 161); the Kirghiz consider it a valuable food (Featherman, 1885–91, 4: 257); and the Turkomans of Turkestan regard it as a dainty (Jochelson, 1928: 94–95). Along the western frontiers of the Indian subcontinent, Moslem tribes regularly consume camelflesh (Crooke, 1906: 77). In the Sudan, the Kababish slaughter camels for food on important ceremonial occasions such as weddings (Seligman and Seligman, 1918: 151; Hambly, 1937, 1: 383), and the people of Kordofan eat camelflesh on ceremonial occasions (Hambly, 1935: 471). In Nigeria, camels are both ritually killed and slaughtered for food (A. E. Robinson, 1936: 56), but the flesh is forbidden to Hausa women when they are pregnant because it is believed to injure the unborn child or to make the woman barren afterward (C. K. Meek, 1925, 1: 136). The camel has long been known in Northeast Africa and has gradually spread southward, until today it is found at least as far south as the arid

parts of Kenya. As early as 1330 Ibn Batuta described the Somali town of Berbera as filthy with the blood of camels that people slaughtered for food (A. E. Robinson, 1936: 56), and among the Somali of today the flesh is a highly prized staple (I. M. Lewis, 1955: 68, 74).

23. A. E. Robinson, 1936: 65.

24. Gulliver and Gulliver, 1953: 60.

25. Schneider, 1957: 291.

26. Gunn, 1956: 71.

27. For this decline, which was dramatic in Iran, Syria, Turkey, and Iraq (50–95 percent declines), see Bulliet, 1975: 264; and I. L. Mason, 1984a: 113. For the case for and against the camel as an efficient producer of flesh, see Bulliet, 1975: 264–68. For the qualities, digestibility, and nutritional value of camelflesh and its products and the economics of camelflesh production, see R. T. Wilson, 1984: 158–61; and Shalash, 1984: 231–47.

28. I. L. Mason, 1984a: 113.

29. I. L. Mason, 1984a: 112.

30. I. L. Mason, 1984a: 113.

31. Mahmoud, 1984.

32. Barnett, 1985: 17–18.

33. Hakker-Orien, 1984.

34. Barnett, 1985: 28.

35. Wapnish, 1984: 171, 174.

36. Feliks, 1971–72a.

37. Leviticus 11:4; Deuteronomy 14:7.

38. Actually it is cloven-footed, though this cannot be seen on the surface because of the pads that cover its feet (Feliks, 1971–72a: 72).

39. Dussaud, 1900: 94.

40. W. R. Smith, 1908: 367; W. R. Smith, 1914: 283.

41. Nweeya, 1910: 241.

42. Drower, 1937: 47–48.

43. Dussaud, 1900: 94.

44. Lane, 1908: 547; A. E. Robinson, 1936: 55.

45. Leviticus 11:4; L. C. Briggs, 1958: 132–33; L. C. Briggs, 1967: 240.

46. Parkyns, 1868: 291–92; Reale Società Geografica Italiana, 1936: 256.

47. Trimingham, 1952: 162–63.

48. R. C. Thompson, 1908: 210.

49. Crooke, 1906: 77.

50. Graves, 1927: 280.

51. Crooke, 1906: 77.

52. *Āpastamba Dharma-sūtra* 1.5.17.23, 29 and *Gautama Dharma-sūtra* 17.24, trans. in Bühler, 1896; *Vasishṭha Dharma-sūtra* 14.40, and *Baudhāyana Dharma-sūtra* 1.5.12.11, trans. in Bühler, 1882.

53. *Mānava Gṛihya-sūtra* 2.14.11, cited by Gonda, 1980: 102.

54. E. C. Sachau, 1971: 151.

55. S. Fuchs, 1950: 357; G. W. Briggs, 1920: 45.

56. Prejevalsky, 1876, 1: 56, 129; Lattimore, 1929: 160, 162.

57. Lattimore, 1929: 162.

58. A. H. Smith, 1894: 21; Freeman, 1977: 154; Mote, 1977: 201; E. H. Schafer, 1977: 99, 117.

7. Dogflesh

1. Clutton-Brock, 1984: 203–4; Reed and Perkins, 1984: 12; Benecke, 1987.

2. Manwell and Baker, 1984.

3. Langkavel, 1881, 1898: 652–53.

4. Leung et al., 1973: 104, 107.

5. *Wisconsin State Journal,* August 11, 1959, p. 3.

6. Judge Charles W. Iben, pers. comm.

7. *Los Angeles Times,* August 14, 1980, Part I, p. 1.

8. "New bill to ban people from eating dogs," *Daily Democrat* (Woodland–Davis, California), February 9, 1981, p. 4.

9. "Eat-a-dog advocate skewered," *Sacramento Bee,* April 18, 1981, p. A3.

10. Mathews, 1980.

11. "Recluse jailed for eating dog," *Sacramento Bee,* December 2, 1982, p. A12.

12. Langkavel, 1881: 658; Cox, 1957: passim; Driver and Massey, 1957: 181–82.

13. Chang, 1986: 93, 113, 201, 211.

14. Creel, 1937a: 76–77; Erkes, 1943: 204–5, 211–13; Veith, 1949: 206; Chang, 1977: 29; Chang, 1980: 143; E. N. Anderson, 1988: 20, 32.

15. Verrill, 1946: 208.

16. Collier, 1921: 20–28 and passim; Bourke-Borrowes, 1931; Powell, 1945: 178; H. Epstein, 1971a: 125–45 passim; E. N. Anderson, 1988: 102.

17. Tryjarski, 1979: 304–5, who also presents other interesting material on various aspects of the dog among Turkic peoples, including its sanctity and place in myth, ritual, sacrifice, language, and iconography.

18. For more on the dog in Tibetan religious life, see Hummel, 1955–58, 1959–61.

19. Ekvall, 1963: 163, 165.

20. Raveret-Wattel, 1884: 607.

21. Boxer, 1953: 134.

22. Wayne Fogg, pers. comm.

23. T. T. Cooper, 1871: 432.

24. Schwabe, 1979: 172, 175.

25. *China Post,* January 27, 1960.

26. Mathews, 1980.

27. Kinmond, 1957: 163–65.

28. "Chinese Reds reported slaughtering dogs," *Wisconsin State Journal,* July 7,

1963, section 4, p. 3. Similar thinking occurred in the former Soviet Union in 1982, when a tax of as much as $300 annually was imposed on "'nonproductive' meat-eating dogs" (*U.S. News and World Report,* November 2, 1981, p. 38).

29. Munro, 1977.

30. "Disease risk from more dogs," *China Daily* (Beijing), April 25, 1987, p. 3.

31. Gourou, 1936: 426–27.

32. Massy, 1890: 355; Abadie, 1924: 40. The Bahnar and Man, however, do not eat dogs, the latter because of belief in a dog ancestor—a matter we will consider later (Abadie, 1924: 114; LeBar et al., 1964: 136).

33. *New York Times,* September 16, 1959, 1, p. 5.

34. Izikowitz, 1951: 204.

35. Griffis, 1882: 267–69; Saunderson, 1894: 308; Hulbert, 1906: 21, 26; Keir, 1914: 817; Y. Kang, 1931: 107–8; Osgood, 1951: 77–78.

36. Dr. Chan Myun Lee, pers. comm.

37. Schiffman, 1985.

38. Kaempfer, 1906, 1: 196–99.

39. John D. Donoghue, pers. comm.

40. Langkavel, 1881: 659; Jochelson, 1905–8: 519–20; Shinichirō, 1960: 13, 14.

41. Chard, 1974: 131.

42. Langkavel, 1898: 671; Bogoras, 1904–9: 101.

43. Seeland, 1882: 110; Hawes, 1903: 259.

44. Hawes, 1903: 259.

45. In the borderlands between Burma and India-Bangladesh, dog eating has been reported for the Ao, Angami, Rengma, Gallong, Lhota, and Sema Naga, and the Naga tribes of Manipur (T. C. Hodson, 1911: 59–60; S. N. Majumdar, 1924: 57; W. C. Smith, 1925: 32, 110; Mills, 1937: 94; Elwin, 1959: 285; Srivastava, 1962: 34; Hutton, 1968: 69, 104, 123; Hutton, 1969: 81–82, 204, 395–96); for the Khumi, Lakher (men only), Lushai, Thadou, and certain other Chin groups (G. E. Fryer, 1875: 45; Carey and Tuck, 1896: 179, 180, 181; Crooke, 1906: 145; *Imperial Gazetteer of India,* 1909a: 464–65; Shakespear, 1912: 32, 36; W. Shaw, 1929: 86; N. E. Parry, 1932: 83–84, 167; C. J. Richards, 1945: 52; McCall, 1949: 56); as well as for the Garo (Featherman, 1885–91, 4: 82; Gurdon, 1904: 58; Gurdon, 1907: 51), Adi (Elwin, 1959: 285), and Apa Tani (Fürer-Haimendorf, 1946: 43).

46. Mills, 1937: 94.

47. Fürer-Haimendorf, 1946: 43.

48. S. Roy, 1960: 160.

49. Crooke, 1906: 145; R. H. S. Hutchinson, 1906: 23.

50. Hodson, 1911: 60.

51. Hutton, 1969: 81, 204. The Angami also have medicinal uses for dogs. One "antidote for poison is to pluck out the eyes of a living dog and swallow them," and a remedy for dog bite is to apply burnt dog hair and ashes (Hutton, 1969: 100).

52. Hutton, 1968: 69, 71, 104, 123.

53. E. W. Hopkins, 1894: 154–56; Walker, 1968, 1: 288–89; Stutley and Stutley, 1977: 293–94.

54. Macdonell, 1897: 74–77; Macdonell and Keith, 1967, 2: 406; Walker, 1968, 2: 313–14.

55. Indian scholars have commonly taken this to mean a dog with marks around its eyes that suggest a second set of eyes. Other meanings, among them "sharp-eyed" or "eyes that see in all directions," have also been suggested (Bloomfield, 1905: 30–31; Gonda, 1969b: 71 n18; D. G. White, 1988–89: 284–85).

56. In the *Rig-veda,* there is no evidence for this name meaning "brindled" or "spotted." Instead, the two dogs appear to have been distinguished as "dark" and "light," the former, judging from myths of other Indo-European peoples, the dog of death, the latter the dog of life (Bloomfield, 1905: 31–35; Schlerath, 1954: 36; Lincoln, 1979: 274–75; D. G. White, 1988–89: 285–86).

57. Macdonell, 1897: 173; M. Stevenson, 1920: 193; Walker, 1968, 2: 614; Gonda, 1969b: 70–71; Stutley and Stutley, 1977: 269.

58. *Rig-veda* 10.14.10, trans. in R. T. H. Griffith, 1963. For support of the view that Yama's dogs could be ill-disposed, see Bloomfield, 1905: 13–14; and Afshar, 1990: 35 and n. This is reflected in efforts to obtain their goodwill. One reads for early times of a house rite in which Yama's dogs are offered a cake to assure their protection (Bloomfield, 1905: 13–14), and, for modern times, rice balls to keep them from barking at or interfering with those who carry "the sacrifice to the [ancestors] in the other world" (Walker, 1968, 1: 288–89).

59. In this regard, Vedic Indian perceptions were quite different from those of Zoroastrians, for whom the dog played an important role in death ritual, yet remained a pure and sacred creature. For the contrasting position of Yama's dogs in Vedic India and Zoroastrian Iran, see Afshar, 1990: 33–40. For contrasts between Yama's dogs and the Greek Kerberos (Cerberus), see Bloomfield, 1905. For the duality in Indo-European perceptions of the dog, on one hand with death (i.e., Cerberus) and on the other with life and healing (Asclepius), see Schlerath, 1954. For more on the associations of the dog and death, see Bernolles, 1968; and Lurker, 1969, 1983, and 1987. For linguistic evidence on Indo-European hellhounds and the meaning and origin of their names, see Lincoln, 1979.

60. Walker, 1968, 1: 289.

61. *Taittirīya Saṃhitā* 4.5.4, trans. in Keith, 1914.

62. *Rig-veda* 9.101.1, trans. in R. T. H. Griffith, 1963; *Śatapatha Brāhmaṇa* 12.4.1.4, trans. in Eggeling, 1882–1900; Macdonell and Keith, 1967, 2: 406; Oldenberg, 1988: 200–201.

63. *Śatapatha Brāhmaṇa* 13.1.2.9, trans. in Eggeling, 1882–1900; *Taittirīya Saṃhitā* 7.4.15, trans. in Keith, 1914; Keith, 1914, 1: cxxxiv; 2: 612 n8; Gonda, 1969b: 71. For the meaning of the killing of dogs in connection with the *aśvamedha,* see Gonda, 1969b: 71; D. G. White, 1988–89; and Wyatt, 1989: 1, 8n.

64. *Atharva-veda Pariśiṣṭa* 61.1.8; *Jaiminīya Gṛihya-sūtra* 2.7, cited by Gonda, 1980: 101.

65. *Baudhāyana Dharma-sūtra* 1.5.11.36, 39, trans. in Bühler, 1882; *Gautama Dharma-sūtra* 14.29.31–32, trans. in Bühler, 1896.

66. *Āgniveśya Gṛihya-sūtra* 2.7.8, and *Mānava Gṛihya-sūtra* 2.9.10, cited by

Gonda, 1980: 171, 341. Yet, in what appears to differ with this, animals killed by dogs are clean (Gonda, 1980: 284).

67. *Mānava Dharma-śāstra* 3.239, trans. in Bühler, 1886.

68. *Vishnu Smṛti* 81.6–7, trans. in Jolly, 1900.

69. *Mānava Dharma-śāstra* 4.126, trans. in Bühler, 1886; *Yājñavalkya Smṛti* 1.147, and *Āpastamba Dharma-sūtra* 1.10.19, cited by Gonda, 1980: 88, 101.

70. *Āpastamba Gṛihya-sūtra* 7.18.1–2, and *Hiraṇyakeśi Gṛihya-sūtra* 2.2.7, trans. in Oldenberg and Müller, 1892.

71. *Chhāndogya Upanishad* 5.10.7, trans. in Nikhilananda, 1949–59, 4.

72. Badam, 1984: 343; P. K. Thomas, 1984: 358; P. K. Thomas, 1989: 108–9.

73. *Rig-veda* 4.18.13, trans. in R. T. H. Griffith, 1963; R. T. H. Griffith, 1963, 1: 418n.

74. *Āpastamba Dharma-sūtra* 1.7.21.14–15, trans. in Bühler, 1896; and *Vasishṭha Dharma-sūtra* 23.30, trans. in Bühler, 1882.

75. Walker, 1968, 1: 279.

76. D. G. White, 1991: 72–73, 109–10, 246. For more on the standing of "dog cookers" in Hindu mythology, see D. G. White, 1992.

77. *Mahābhārata* 95, trans. by Narasimhan, 1965.

78. Stutley and Stutley, 1977: 294.

79. D. G. White, 1991: 75–78, 83, 84, 86, 247 n15, 250.

80. For an excellent discussion of "dog cookers" and similar terms used in Indian literature for untouchables and other impure groups, see D. G. White, 1991: 71–113. Use of this term is not new, as shown by the statement in one Vedic account (*Śānkhāyana Gṛihya-sūtra* 2.14.22, cited by Gonda, 1980: 101) of the need for offerings to dogs and "persons who cook dogs . . ." in the *vaiśvadeva* sacrifice, which was made to several gods at one time. Presumably the persons who cook dogs are low-caste people who were included in this broad-based sacrifice, though on other occasions they may have been left out.

81. D. G. White, 1991: 187.

82. For this and contrasting Indian Buddhist views of the dog, see D. G. White, 1991: 112–13.

83. *Mahāvagga* 6.23.12, trans. in Davids and Oldenberg, 1881–85.

84. Thurston (1912: 25, 57) has collected several good and bad omens that a dog may provide in southern India. If a dog on a house roof barks when the weather is dry, it indicates that an epidemic is at hand, or, in the wet season, that there will be abundant rainfall. When a person starts out on a trip, it is good luck if a dog crosses his path from right to left; if a dog lies down and wags its tail, some misfortune will befall the traveller; and if a dog scratches himself the traveller will become sick.

85. M. Stevenson, 1920: 385n.

86. M. Stevenson, 1920: 192, 238.

87. Crooke, 1906: 148; R. V. Russell, 1916, 4: 204–5; Hutton, 1963: 20; Walker, 1968, 1: 49, 548; 2: 408; Sontheimer, 1989: 197, 199.

88. E. Herzog, 1967: 52; Walker, 1968, 2: 407–8.

89. Thanks are due to D. G. White for this figure, a Benares folk-art representation of Bhairava riding a dog.

90. Gonda, 1970: 117, 132.

91. D. G. White, 1991: 102.

92. D. G. White, 1991: 102–3.

93. Crooke, 1896, 2: 218, 219; Crooke, 1906: 146–47, 148; M. Leach, 1961: 11, 175; Walker, 1968, 1: 289. I have not determined the range of appeals that are made to Bhairava. In southern India, however, the sounds made by children ill with whooping cough are considered a kind of barking brought on by Bhairava's disfavor. To propitiate Bhairava in such cases, people flatten and smooth an old coin, cut an image of a dog on it, and tie it to the ill child's waist as a charm (Thurston, 1912: 196).

94. Bhairava's occurrence in Sanskrit literature cannot be dated prior to the seventh century A.D. (D. G. White, 1991: 257).

95. D. G. White, 1991: 102.

96. Bhairava has been called an example of a low form of a "good-bad" Hindu deity. This is clearly shown in the fact that in North India his leavings are not eaten by members of respectable castes, but by a priest of low caste "or by such animals as cats and dogs or other nocturnal visitors" (Khare, 1976: 96, 97).

97. Harlan, 1992: 47, 66–67.

98. Kipling, 1891: 271.

99. Crooke (1906: 145) also mentions dog eating by the Sānsiya and other gypsy tribes.

100. Among Indian tribal peoples reported as not eating dogs are the Bhil of Rajputana (Erskine, 1908: 234), Chenchu of Hyderabad (Fürer-Haimendorf, 1943, 1: 70), Bhumia of Madhya Pradesh (S. Fuchs, 1960: 70), Santal of Bihar (Biswas, 1956: 38), Saora of Orissa (Elwin, 1955: 522), Lepcha of Sikkim (Hermanns, 1954: 80), Purum of Manipur (T. C. Das, 1945: 67), Bodo (Kachari) and Dhimal (Featherman, 1885–91, 4: 26), and in Assam, the Khasi (Gurdon, 1904: 58; Gurdon, 1907: 51), Synteng (Gurdon, 1904: 58), and Lynngam (Gurdon, 1907: 195).

101. Elwin, 1959: 182; Fürer-Haimendorf, 1946: 43.

102. Crooke, 1906: 148.

103. Modi, 1979: 429–30.

104. Kaikini, 1951: 39.

105. Higham et al., 1980: 159.

106. Among the groups in Burma for whom dog eating is reported, are the Akha and Maru, who are Tibeto-Burman in speech (Scott and Hardiman, 1900: 589; Crooke, 1906: 146; Scott, 1906: 94, 100; *Imperial Gazetteer of India*, 1908, 1: 46; Davies, 1909: 397; O. G. Young, 1961: 7–8), and the Wa, nominal Buddhists who are Mon-Khmer in speech and are said to fatten dogs for eating (Scott and Hardiman, 1900: 506; Risley, 1903: 219; Crooke, 1906: 146; Scott, 1906: 100; LeBar et al., 1964: 131). Minority peoples of Burma and Thailand reported as not eating dogs include the Palaung (Milne, 1924: 195; LeBar et al., 1964: 123) and southern Karen tribes (F. Mason, 1868: 129), most of whom are Buddhists; and the Kachin (though they do sacrifice dogs) (LeBar et al., 1964: 14), Yumbri, and Lisu (LeBar et al., 1964: 29, 133), most of whom are not Buddhists.

107. Kingdon-Ward, 1949: 218.

108. W. C. Campbell et al., 1988: 65.

109. Ferrars and Ferrars, 1901: 89; *Imperial Gazetteer of India,* 1908, 1: 46; C. J. Richards, 1945: 52; Tambiah, 1969: 433, 436, 455.

110. *Mahāvagga* 6.23.12, trans. in Davids and Oldenberg, 1881–85.

111. Scott, 1910: 83; Fielding Hall, 1917: 244; C. J. Richards, 1945: 41–42.

112. E. Young, 1898: 21.

113. Tambiah, 1969: 435, 436, 439, 455.

114. Scott, 1910: 83, 542–43.

115. *Wall Street Journal,* July 23, 1959, p. 9.

116. Abadie, 1924: 115; C. H. Liu, 1932, 1941; M. Leach, 1961: 46–51; LeBar et al., 1964: 85, 88; Eberhard, 1968: 43–50, 461–63; Eberhard, 1982: 81; de Beauclair, 1970: 6. The dog-ancestor story is not restricted to Southeast Asia. For its distribution in Asia, see C. H. Liu, 1941. For references to myths of dog ancestry elsewhere in the world, see N. W. Thomas, 1908–26: 512.

117. Baudesson, 1919: 105–6; D. G. White, 1991: 142–56.

118. Langkavel, 1898: 673–74; Koppers, 1930; Kretschmar, 1938, 1: 170–92, 212; M. Leach, 1961: 46–51; D. G. White, 1991: 114–39 passim.

119. Hutton, 1963: 255n.

120. Hutton, 1963: 255.

121. Frazer, 1935, 11: 222–23.

122. Crooke, 1896, 2: 222.

123. *Nāgarakṛtāgama* 89, trans. in Kern, 1918.

124. Marsden, 1811: 381; Langkavel, 1881: 659; Featherman, 1885–91, 2: 321; Hahn, 1896: 71; Loeb, 1935: 24–25; Moore, 1930: 210; Mr. Dyatmoko, pers. comm.

125. Moore, 1930: 210.

126. Hahn, 1896: 71; Mr. Dyatmoko, pers. comm.

127. Kennedy, 1953: 37, 43, 128, 130; Mr. Dyatmoko, pers. comm.

128. Covarrubias, 1942: 41–42, 104.

129. Frazer, 1935, 8: 145.

130. Langkavel, 1881: 659; Ratzel, 1896–98, 1: 431; Roth, 1896, 1: 390, 425.

131. Hose and McDougall, 1912, 2: 70–71.

132. Hose and McDougall, 1912, 2: 80.

133. Lessa, 1975: 194, 196.

134. Rola-Bustrillos, 1961: 41, 70, 72.

135. G. A. Malcolm, 1951: 57.

136. Jenks, 1905: 110–11, 140, 142–43.

137. Vanoverbergh, 1936–38: 206; L. L. Wilson, 1947: 11.

138. Barton, 1922: 416.

139. Jenks, 1905: 142.

140. In Melanesia and Micronesia dog eating has been reported among certain groups on New Guinea (Turner, 1878: 482; Seligman, 1910: 230, 257, 450, 454, 455; Rappaport, 1968: 56; Titcomb, 1969: 60–73 passim); for Rossel Island, southeast of New Guinea (Armstrong, 1928: 19); for the Biara of New Britain (Featherman, 1885–91, 2: 47); in inland New Ireland (Titcomb, 1969: 59); on one of the Fiji Islands (L. Thompson, 1940: 141); and in the Caroline and Gilbert islands (Burrows,

1949: 18; Titcomb, 1969: 49–51). It is said, moreover, that though the Papuans of the Trans-Fly region of New Guinea regard the eating of dogs with abhorrence, certain groups of them—the Kaunje and Gambadi—formerly ate dogflesh (Williams, 1936: 420).

141. Smyth, 1878, 1: 147–49; Basedow, 1925: 118; Meggitt, 1965: 13–19; Abbie, 1969: 71–72.

142. At the time of European arrival, dogs were absent in some places, though in a few they seem to have been present earlier. Dogs were not present, by early European accounts, on Easter Island, Tonga, Manihiki, Tongareva, Pukapuka, Rakahanga, Mangareva, Rapa, or in the Cook and Marquesas islands (P. H. Buck, 1932: 83; P. H. Buck, 1938a: 194; P. H. Buck, 1938b: 155, 175, 189, 212, 310, 312; Luomala, 1960: 193–94; Titcomb, 1969: 32–33, 34, 36–37, 38, 40).

143. For other uses of dogs, see Luomala, 1960; and Titcomb, 1969.

144. J. Cook, 1784, 3: 141; J. Cook, 1955: 102–3, 121–22, 262, 506; W. T. Pritchard, 1866: 126; Corney, 1915: 287–88; P. H. Buck, 1930: 127; Burrows, 1936: 133; Burrows, 1949: 18; Luomala, 1960: 190 and passim; Titcomb, 1969: 6–14, 18–20, 23, and passim.

145. Tregear, 1904: 105, 167, 172; Titcomb, 1969: 8, 18–20, 40, 44–45.

146. Titcomb, 1969: 23–24.

147. Three explanations have been advanced to explain the proclivity that women in Polynesia have for nursing their puppies, and it is likely that all three are involved in one place or another: simple affection for the animals; desire for a supply of tender, tasty milk-fed flesh; and relief from discomfort when a woman has excess milk, as when her child has died (Simoons and Baldwin, 1982: 429–30).

148. Titcomb, 1969: 8.

149. Titcomb, 1969: 7.

150. P. H. Buck, 1950b: 110–11.

151. W. T. Pritchard, 1866: 126; P. H. Buck, 1930: 127; Schwabe, 1979: 168–69.

152. McArdle, 1982: 119.

153. Herodotus *History* 2.66–67.

154. Diodorus Siculus *Library of history* 1.84.1–2.

155. Tooley, 1988: 210–11.

156. A. Burton, 1972: 241–42.

157. The jackal may have become a deity associated with the dead because jackals prowled about places of embalming and burial in Egypt, and seemed to be protecting the dead (A. Burton, 1972: 254).

158. Griffiths, 1970: 317, 467; A. Burton, 1972: 254; Murphy, 1990: 110n.

159. Plutarch *Isis and Osiris* 44.

160. Diodorus Siculus *Library of history* 1.83.1.

161. Strabo *Geography* 17.1.40; Murphy, 1990: 110 n. For more on dog sanctity in ancient Egypt, see O. Keller, 1963, 1: 145–46.

162. For a somewhat different interpretation of the evidence, see Budge, 1904, 2: 366–67.

163. A. Burton, 1972: 254, 259.

164. Plutarch *Isis and Osiris* 44.

165. Darby et al., 1977, 1: 251–52.

166. Murdock (1959: 114) writes of the now-extinct Guanche of the Canary Islands as dog eaters. It has even been suggested that the island Gran Canaria may have been so named because its people formerly ate dogs, or because the dog was a cult animal there. Hooton (1925: 56), on other hand, says that there is no evidence that the people of Gran Canaria ate dogs at the time of first European contact.

167. Justin *History* 19.1.

168. At a Punic cemetery (fifth century B.C. and later) on the island of Motya, Sicily, cremated bones of human babies, along with those of puppies and other young domesticated animals, have been uncovered, each individual buried in a jar. The killing of human infants, often the firstborn, was at one time a normal practice in Carthage, and it is suggested that, on Motya, all the cremated bones, including those of puppies, may be those of sacrificial victims offered to deities (Whitaker, 1921: 131, 257–60). There is nothing in the report, however, to suggest that the flesh of the puppies was eaten.

169. Pliny *Natural history* 5.14–15.

170. For more detail on the North African center of dog eating, see Simoons, 1981.

171. O. Bates, 1914: 177; Westermarck, 1926, 2: 306–7.

172. Lane, 1908: 299; Hrdlička, 1912: 12.

173. L. C. Briggs, 1958: 40.

174. Bertholon, 1897: 561; O. Bates, 1914: 177.

175. Westermarck, 1926, 2: 306–7.

176. Canard, 1952: 299.

177. Frazer, 1935, 7: 22.

178. Lindeman, 1906; Fortes and Fortes, 1936: 249.

179. S. D. Brown, 1992: 86, 87.

180. Ojoade, 1990: 218.

181. Schweinfurth, 1873, 1: 393–94.

182. Johnston, 1910, 2: 614–15.

183. Exceptions are the Sango of Tanzania (Kroll, 1928: 193), who apparently slaughter dogs for their flesh, and the Berta of the Ethiopian borderlands, who will eat any kind of flesh, including dogs (Cerulli, 1956: 19).

184. Kroll, 1928: 193.

185. Ratzel, 1896–98, 2: 415.

186. Driberg, 1923: 96.

187. Evans-Pritchard, 1932: 44–46; Frazer, 1935, 4: 16–17.

188. Cerulli, 1956: 26, 33.

189. Bowdich (1819: 429), however, wrote of what may be an exception, that the Paämway (Mpongwe?) of Gabon early in the nineteenth century raised a breed of large dogs for eating.

190. Castrating dogs has been reported for the Ekoi, Banjangi, Yaunde, Bunda, Chewa (Kroll, 1928: 192), and for the Kuanyama Ambo (Loeb, 1962: 173).

191. Fattening dogs has been reported for the Azande (Casati, 1891: 213–14; R. G. Anderson, 1911: 274), the people of the western upper Congo Basin (Johnston, 1910, 2: 614–15), and the Luchazi of Zambia and Angola (McCulloch, 1951: 62).

192. Kroll, 1928: 192–93.

193. Junker, 1891: 305.

194. Johnston, 1895: 294.

195. Hambly, 1934: 155.

196. This seems to relate to the belief that there is a tie between dogs and spirits, that dogs see spirits and bark at them (Ojoade, 1990: 219–20).

197. This paragraph is based on J. O. Ojoade's interesting account (1990) of Nigerian cultural attitudes relating to the dog. The quote is taken from pp. 219–20 of that account.

198. The Tallensi of Ghana ritually kill dogs on special occasions such as the new year festival (Fortes and Fortes, 1936: 249). The Baghirmi people of Chad slaughter them when peace is established (Dornan, 1933: 631). The Yoruba of Nigeria sacrifice a dog twice a year to Ogun, patron of blacksmiths and god of war, and then hang the dog's head, symbol of the sacrifice, conspicuously in a blacksmith's shop (Hambly, 1935: 408, 465). The Tiv of Nigeria sometimes ritually kill a dog, and then give the body to the Utange, a bush tribe, to eat, for the Tiv themselves are not dog eaters (East, 1939: 274). Among the Mbundu of Angola, after a youth has served his apprenticeship and is about to be inaugurated as a blacksmith, a dog is slaughtered and its blood spread on his tools in order to consecrate them (Hambly, 1935: 407). The Ambo of southern Angola and Namibia kill a dog in ceremonies involving witchcraft, sickness, or misfortune of any sort; some of the flesh of the animal is eaten by the patient and the rest by his relatives (Dornan, 1933: 632). And the Shona of Zimbabwe ritually kill a specially fed black dog at the time of sowing to encourage rain to fall on the crops (Dornan, 1933: 631).

199. Dornan, 1933: 630.

200. Frazer, 1935, 10: 4.

201. Fortes and Fortes, 1936: 272.

202. The banning of dogflesh to LoDagaa women may be another effort to confirm the fact that hunting, with which the dog is tied, is the exclusive realm of men. In the same spirit, LoDagaa men are not permitted to have sexual relations with women before hunting, which is intended to keep them from being unmanly when confronted with danger (Goody, 1982: 71).

203. Gunn, 1953: 66.

204. Among the Lange of the southwest Congo, for example, only the western groups eat dogflesh; hence they are known as the Baschilambua, or dog people (Kroll, 1928: 193). There are further references to group avoidance of dogflesh for the Birom of the Bachit area (Gunn, 1953: 80), the Bolewa (Temple, 1922: 68), the Katab (Gunn, 1956: 70–71), and the Tiv in Nigeria (East, 1939: 274); the Sokoro and Bua of the Sudan borderlands (Nachtigal, 1874: 324, 329); the Kpe of the Cameroons (Ardener, 1956: 47–48); the Bubi of Fernando Po (Kroll, 1928: 193); the Kongo and

Songo (Kroll, 1928: 193), and Bango (Bobango) and Soko (Comhaire-Sylvain, 1950: 61) of the Congo Basin and Angola; and apparently the Twa (Batwa) Pygmies of the northwestern Luba country (Johnston, 1910, 2: 507).

205. The Bantu-speaking tribes of southern Africa, for example, never eat or sacrifice dogs (Dornan, 1933: 632; Schapera and Goodwin, 1950: 141). The Tanala of Madagascar consider the idea of eating dogs disgusting (Linton, 1933: 48). The Nandi of Kenya kill dogs on special occasions, but throw them into the bush rather than eat them (Dornan, 1933: 631). In Uganda the Karamojon, Jie, and Dodos prohibit dogs as food (Gulliver and Gulliver, 1953: 35), and the Lendu, who live nearby in Zaire, never eat dogflesh (Baxter and Butt, 1953: 126). In Ethiopia, dogflesh is strongly rejected by Semites, Cushites, and most other groups; in the Sudan, the Nuba (Nadel, 1947: 189), Bongo (Peschel, 1906: 159), and Dinka do not eat it.

206. Comhaire-Sylvain, 1950: 61.

207. Gunn, 1956: 28.

208. Kroll, 1928: 193.

209. Bryant, 1949: 290.

210. Schweinfurth, 1873, 1: 158–59.

211. Gimbutas, 1982: 169–71.

212. For the devil in dog form in the folk traditions of Germany, with supporting evidence from French, Italian, and Celtic sources, see Woods, 1959.

213. Boessneck et al., 1963: 33; Bökönyi, 1974: 320; Bökönyi, 1975: 168; Clason, 1979: 47; Greenfield, 1986, 1: 106, 133, 211–12.

214. Clason, 1980: 150.

215. Harcourt, 1974: 168, 171–72; Brothwell and Brothwell, 1969: 40, citing M. Degerbøl. For other places Central and Western Europe (Switzerland, Bavaria, Sweden, and elsewhere), where dogs also seem to have been eaten in prehistoric times, see Lepiksaar, 1962: 116, 122; Gejvall, 1969: 18; and Greenewalt, 1978: 31n.

216. Telegin, 1986: 23, 26, 29.

217. Müller, 1984: 191.

218. Gimbutas, 1971: 158–59.

219. Jahn, 1884: 134–36 and passim; Jenkins, 1957: 62; Lepiksaar, 1962: 116, 117; M. Paul, 1981: 59–78 and passim.

220. For indications of such a role in Romano-Gaulish religion, see Jenkins, 1957: 70–71.

221. Scholz, 1937: 37; Lilja, 1976: 16–17; E. Vermeule, 1979: 58–59, 61–62. Day, 1984, provides information on dog burials at other periods of Greek prehistory and history.

222. For an excellent survey of the dog in classical antiquity, see O. Keller, 1963, 1: 91–151. For guard dogs, hunting dogs, and house dogs in ancient Greek myth, religion, and everyday life, see Mainoldi, 1984: 59–80, 113–120, 143–60, and passim.

223. Oft-cited in this regard is the account of Odysseus's loyal dog Argos, who recognizes his master after he was away for twenty years, after which it dies (Homer *Odyssey* 17.290–327).

224. For which, see Lilja, 1976: esp. 126–29; Lonsdale, 1979: 149–52; Mainoldi, 1984: esp. 213–14.

225. Lilja, 1976: 13–36; Day, 1984: 29.

226. For carrion-eating dogs in Greek literature, see Mainoldi, 1984: 104–9; 176–80.

227. E. Vermeule, 1979: 108–9.

228. For more on Cerberus, see Bloomfield, 1905; and Scholz, 1937: 33–36. On the associations of the dog with death in Greek myths and rites, see Malten, 1914: 236–37; and Mainoldi, 1984: 37–51.

229. Strabo *Geography* 10.5.5; Plutarch *Roman questions* 111; Mainoldi, 1984: 51–52.

230. R. Parker, 1983: 357.

231. The Olympian Ares, god of war, to whom the dog was sacred, is said to have received offerings of puppies at Sparta, but under the name of Enyalius, to be mentioned below.

232. On the association of the dog with Artemis, Hecate, and other Greek deities, see Mainoldi, 1984: 46–51, 59, 154–56, and passim; and Bevan, 1986, 1: 115–30.

233. Jayne, 1962: 223, 224, 311–13.

234. Farnell, 1896–1909, 2: 507–8; Bevan, 1986, 1: 118–19. Genetyllis, another Greek goddess who was likened to Hecate or Artemis and was associated with child-birth, did sometimes receive sacrifices in the interests of an uncomplicated delivery (Jayne, 1962: 323).

235. Gimbutas, 1982: 196–99.

236. E. Vermeule, 1979: 108–9.

237. Plutarch *Roman questions* 52, 68; Farnell, 1896–1909, 2: 501–19; Frazer, 1929, 2: 168–69; Dornan, 1933: 630; Scholz, 1937: 40–43; Nilsson, 1940: 80, 111; M. Leach, 1961: 18–19, 21–22, 183–84, 276; Jayne, 1962: 326; Lilja, 1976: 65, 80, 101, 103, 127; R. Parker, 1983: 30 and n; Bevan, 1986, 1: 116, 118–19.

238. Jayne, 1962: 326; R. Parker, 1983: 30.

239. For more on the dog in sacrifice among early Greeks, or Greeks and Romans, see Cirilli, 1912; Scholz, 1937; Pedley, 1974: 98–99; Day, 1984: 25–28; and Zaganiaris, 1975.

240. Pausanias *Description of Greece* 3.14.9–10.

241. Plutarch *Roman questions* 111.

242. Farnell, 1896–1909, 2: 507n.

243. Plutarch *Roman questions* 111; Pausanias *Description of Greece* 3.14.9–10.

244. Plutarch *Roman questions* 52; Athenaeus *Deipnosophists* 3.56; Day, 1984: 28.

245. H. L. Russell, 1955.

246. Porphyry *On abstinence from animal food* 1.14.

247. Nilsson, 1949: 86, 87. See also Mainoldi, 1984: 52. For purificatory killing of dogs in ancient Greece, see Mainoldi, 1984: 51–59. For sources on the inedibility of flesh used in purificatory rites, see R. Parker, 1983: 283 n11.

248. R. Parker, 1983: 360.

249. Aristophanes *Plutus* 594; Lucian *Dialogues of the dead* 1; R. Parker, 1983: 30

n65. Merlin (1971: 87), without citing sources, writes that it was customary in Athens to set out meals for Hecate at the end of each month at a crossroads, that the dishes, which contained onions, eggs, and dogflesh, "were scrambled for by the beggars, and the Cynics, and he who partook of this repast was held in abomination."

250. B. B. Rogers, pp. 418–19 in Vol. 3 of his translation of Aristophanes's *Plutus*. See also A. M. Harmon, 1960: 15n.

251. Gejvall, 1969: 15, 16, 17–18, 53, 59. This is about the time the earliest Indo-European Greeks are believed to have arrived in the Peloponnesus, and one wonders whether the apparent decline in dog eating following that time (Gejvall, 1969: 15, Table 10; Day, 1984: 29) was associated with their arrival.

252. Quoted by Athenaeus *Deipnosophists* 7.282.

253. O. Keller, 1963, 1: 142.

254. Lilja, 1976: 46–47.

255. Aristophanes *Knights* 1398.

256. Donkey's flesh was sold and eaten in at least some periods in ancient Greece. For references to this, see Neil, 1966: 182n.

257. Lilja, 1976: 47, 72. The ridicule may have been directed at Hippocrates, Aristophanes's contemporary, who, as mentioned below, recommended dogflesh for medicinal purposes. For more Greek humor about dog eating, see Lilja, 1976: 84.

258. Sextus Empiricus *Outlines of Pyrrhonism* 3.225.

259. Thrace, that region of the Balkans to the north and east of Greece, is, according to Farnell (1896–1909, 2: 507–8), the probable homeland of Hecate.

260. Mainoldi, 1984: 171–75. One use of puppy flesh mentioned by Mainoldi was for treating feminine sterility.

261. Another healing deity associated with dogs was Hephaestus, Greek god of fire and metallurgy (often confused with the Roman Vulcan), who was believed capable of curing snake bite, hemorrhage, and delusion. Hephaestus was initially a god of Anatolia and nearby islands. He had special ties with Lemnos, where the principal town was called Hephaestia, and the famed Lemnian fire (burning natural gas?) was credited to him. Hephaestus practiced healing on Lemnos, and medicinal earth, believed effective against the bite of poisonous snakes and infected wounds, was the island's most noted product in antiquity, and once was marketed widely in Western Europe as *terra sigillata*. Of special interest, in ancient and modern times, is the annual ceremony associated with the digging of this earth. In antiquity, a priestess directed the ceremony, whereas early in this century Christian and Moslem officials shared the honor (Farnell, 1896–1909, 5: 374–90; *Encyclopaedia Britannica,* 1910–11b; Sikes, 1910–11; M. Leach, 1961: 25; Jayne, 1962: 327–28; Burkert, 1983a: 194).

In antiquity, Hephaestus also had an altar at Olympia, a temple in Athens (Pausanias *Description of Greece* 1.14.6; 5.14.6), and another temple at Etna, near the volcano in Sicily. According to Aelian (*On the characteristics of animals* 11.3), the temple area at Etna included a perpetual fire, a sacred grove of trees, and sacred dogs that greeted people affectionately if they came with good hearts and in a proper manner. If, however, a criminal approached, the dogs attacked him, and they also drove away persons coming "from the bed of debauchery." It is clear that the sacred dogs were seen as preserving the purity and integrity of the temple, but Aelian says nothing of a possible medicinal role.

Aelian (*On the characteristics of animals* 11.20) also mentions sacred dogs at a temple of Adranus, a local god in Sicily whom the Greeks identified with Hephaestus, and the Romans, with Vulcan. The dogs of the temple, which were of unusual beauty and size, numbered over a thousand, and performed a function similar to those of Hephaestus at Etna.

Serapis (Sarapis), the Greco-Egyptian god of the sun, fertility, and healing, is also represented with a dog, but his dog was Cerberus, the dog of Greek mythology, who accompanied him when he served in a medical capacity (Van Hoorn, 1953: 110). For the cult of Serapis and its similarities and ties with that of Asclepius, see Jayne, 1962: 346–48; and Meier, 1967: 45–49.

262. Jayne, 1962: 240–303; Meier, 1967: 23–41; Meier, 1987; Fuhr, 1977: 140–42, 145. For the association of the snake with death and healing among certain other peoples, see Schwabe, 1993.

263. Jayne, 1962: 285.

264. Jayne, 1962: 255–56; Meier, 1967: 17; Meier, 1987: 463.

265. Kerényi, 1959: 18–46; Jayne, 1962: 247, 261–68; Meier, 1967: 36–37; Meier, 1987: 464.

266. According to Meier (1987: 464), Asklepieia never "degenerated into mere spas for pleasure."

267. For the procedure followed by an arriving guest, see Jayne, 1962: 276–92; and Meier, 1987: 464. For information on, and an evaluation of, temple medicine, see Edelstein and Edelstein, 1945, 2: 139–80. For more on incubation, or dream healing, in the Asclepius cult, see Edelstein and Edelstein, 1945, 2: 145–58; and Meier, 1967: 53–72. Healing dreams were of various sorts, but when an ill person dreamed of a dog, it was believed certain that he would soon recover (Lonsdale, 1979: 150). There was also skepticism about and ridicule of such faith healing in antiquity, for which see Merriam, 1884: 304, 306–7.

268. Scholz, 1937: 13.

269. In Asclepius's cult, snakes were also used to cure by licking. For the miraculous cure of a man's ulcerated toe by the tongue of a snake, recorded on a slab uncovered at Epidaurus, see Merriam, 1884: 304.

270. Merriam, 1885: 286; Edelstein and Edelstein, 1945, 2: 153; Kerényi, 1959: 32–33; Jayne, 1962: 230, 283, 285, 411; Fuhr, 1977: 142, 143–44; Frazer, pp. 250–51 in Vol. 3 of his translation of Pausanias's *Description of Greece*. For dog licking in treating patients in Europe and elsewhere, see Gaidoz, 1884; in Mesopotamia and among the Hittites, see Collins, 1990: 214–15.

The contrasting perceptions of dog licking and purity need further investigation. Schlerath (1954: 35) has speculated that the widespread view among Indo-European peoples that it is therapeutic for dogs to lick wounds may derive from their early role in eating human corpses, a cleansing ritual-act that released the soul. Among Hindus, on the other hand, saliva of any sort is abhorred, and the dog is considered impure in part because of its habit of licking its master (Walker, 1968, 2: 341).

271. Merriam, 1884: 304.

272. Frazer, pp. 250–51 in Vol. 3 of his translation of Pausanias's *Description of Greece*. For more on the dog in the Asclepius cult, see Reinach, 1884; Scholz, 1937: 46–49; M. Leach, 1961: 24, 137, 176–77, 182–83, 275; Jayne, 1962: 230, 283, 285, 411–12; and Fuhr, 1977: 140–42.

273. Hippocrates *Regimen* 2.46.

274. The ties of Greek physicians with Apollo in his healing aspect and with Asclepius can be illustrated in many ways. Especially interesting is a brief story, attributed to Hippocrates, about an annual festival of physicians, called Lifting of the Staff, on Kos in the Dodecanese Islands. According to Kerényi (1959: 52, 54), the festival involved pilgrimage to a grove of sacred cypress trees on the island. The staff, symbolic of healing power, had likely come from a tree in the sacred grove, and the festival may have involved returning it to its roots in Apollo and Asclepius. After the death of Hippocrates, Kerényi observes, an Asclepius center was built on Kos at a cypress grove sacred to Apollo.

275. Sextus Empiricus *Outlines of Pyrrhonism* 3.224–25.

276. For more on Greek consumption of dogflesh for medicinal purposes, see Mainoldi, 1984: 171–75; on the practice among Greeks and Romans, see Scholz, 1937: 9–10.

277. Kerényi, 1959: 3–17; Jayne, 1962: 464–74; Meier, 1967: 17–19; Meier, 1987: 465.

278. Burriss, 1935; Rose, 1974: 206n.

279. Statius *Silvae* 3.1.52–59; Frazer, 1929, 2: 256; 3: 71–72; Scholz, 1937: 55–56.

280. Plutarch *Roman questions* 90. See our mention below on Heracles (Hercules) and the dog in Lydia.

281. Plutarch *Roman questions* 111.

282. Pliny *Natural history* 8.142–47.

283. Plutarch *Roman questions* 51; Scholz, 1937: 57.

284. Puhvel, 1978: 359. There is also clear evidence of early dog sacrifice among non-Romans in Italy. I am alluding to instructions in the ancient Umbrian dialect on bronze tablets (300–100 B.C.?), found near the town of Iguvium (now Gubbio), that explain how the sacrifice of a puppy or dog to Hondus Jovius, an infernal deity, was to be carried out. The dog was to be unblemished and owned by the temple. It was to be cut up, the sacrificial pieces roasted on spits. Other pieces, as well as the drippings caught in roasting pans, were reserved for special purposes. When the sacrifice of the dog had been completed, what was left of it was to be buried at the altar (Poultney, 1959: 176–89). Though nothing is said about eating the flesh, one wonders, on the basis of Roman practice, whether some of it was eaten by priests or other worshippers.

285. Columella *On agriculture* 2.21.4.

286. Pliny *Natural history* 29.57–58; Plutarch *Roman questions* 52; Scholz, 1937: 56–57.

287. The celebration of St. Mark's Day, like the Robigalia, included a procession and the offering of prayers for the crops (Frazer, 1929, 3: 410–11; Laing, 1963: 44–45).

288. Ovid *Fasti* 4.905–42; Columella *On agriculture* 10.342–44; Varro *On farming* 1.1.6; Frazer, 1929, 3: 406–11; Dumézil, 1970, 1: 158. In one place, Frazer (1935, 7: 261) writes that the intent of the spring puppy sacrifice was to prevent "the supposed blighting influence of the Dog-Star." If this were true, the Robigalia would be an early case of belief in "dog days," a time when, by tradition, the influence of the Dog Star makes dogs go mad and brings all sorts of evils to humans. Long observes (1984: 263n), however, that the sacrifice was not made to the Dog Star but to Robigus, and that the timing of the Robigalia had nothing to do with the Dog Star (Sirius), whose rise, by tradition, brings on the dog days in July or August (or, in the past, September). For an interesting account of the "dog days" of Western tradition, and how they may relate to dogs, disease, death, Hecate, and Asclepius, see Long, 1984.

289. Plutarch *Roman questions* 68, 111; Plutarch *Romulus* 21.8; Dierauer, 1910; Dumézil, 1970, 2: 346–50; Schilling, 1987. The Lupercalia was among the most popular of all Roman festivals. It survived until A.D. 494, longer than any other pagan festival, when it was banned by Pope Gelasius I (Laing, 1963: 40).

290. Pliny *Natural history* 29.57; Aelian *On the characteristics of animals* 12.33. By the same tradition, the attack was thwarted by the defenders after they had been alerted by the cackling of geese. For this reason, geese were honored by the Romans (Aelian *On the characteristics of animals* 12.33; Pliny *Natural history* 10.51; 29.57; Frazer, 1929, 2: 175–76; 4: 140–41). In time, Roman and Greek views and practices relating to the dog came to be richly represented in Romano-Gaulish religion, for which see Jenkins, 1957.

291. Pliny *Natural history* 29.58. Pliny (*Natural history* 29.58) observed that dog blood also served the Romans as an antidote for arrow poisons.

292. Neil, 1966: 182n.

293. Kozar, 1970: 431–32; Schwabe, 1984b: 547.

294. D. G. White, 1991: 68.

295. Delehaye, 1910–11; M. Leach, 1961: 258–59; Fuhr, 1977: 143.

296. Luke 16:20–25.

297. Fuhr, 1977: 142–43.

298. *Encyclopaedia Britannica*, 1910–11c; M. Leach, 1961: 256–57. For other saints who have ties with dogs, whether in medicinal or other contexts, see "Dogs and saints," pp. 254–64, in M. Leach, 1961.

299. Stokes, 1898: 254–55; Mayrhofer-Passler, 1953: 195; Ross, 1967: 340, 341.

300. Neil, 1966: 182n.

301. Muffet, 1655: 78.

302. Josselyn, 1672: 19.

303. Hauptmann, 1951: 28–29.

304. James J. Parsons, pers. comm.; Brenan, 1957: 94.

305. Schwabe, 1979: 172–73; Schwabe, 1984b: 143. For a reference to other outbreaks of human trichinosis in Switzerland brought on by eating the flesh of dog and mink rather than pork, see Kozar, 1970: 425.

306. J. S. Thomson, 1909: 107.

307. Gould, 1945: 70.

308. For one such German report, see Steele, 1970: 494, citing F. S. Billings.

309. Schwabe, 1984b: 143.

310. Sorokin, 1942: 77; Fedenko, 1951: 41.

311. G. M. Allen, 1919–20: 461, 490; J. Cook, 1955: 102–3, 121–22, 262, 506.

312. A similar stamp of genuineness somewhat surprised us when we recently encountered it at a fishmonger's stall in a Canton marketplace. To demonstrate that a fish is truly fresh, it was carefully eviscerated and put on display to potential buyers so as to reveal its still-beating heart, a certification that it had been alive not long before.

313. T. T. Cooper, 1871: 431–32.

314. Gening, 1979: 20, 25–26.

315. Afshar, 1990: 3.

316. See the Vendidad 13 ("The Dog") (trans. in Darmesteter and Mills, 1880–87), for Ahura Mazdā's rules relating to the dog.

317. On the functions of the dog as portrayed in Iranian narrative literature (stray animal, helper, guard or watchdog, hunting aid, foster mother, and human substitute), see Afshar, 1990: 61–172.

318. N. W. Thomas, 1908–26: 512; Dhalla, 1922: 58, 120–21, 178–81; Westermarck, 1924, 2: 501.

319. Dādistan ī Denig 17.20, trans. in West, 1880–97; A. V. Jackson, 1928: 101; Modi, 1979: 135–40.

320. Modi, 1979: 58–61, 66; Afshar, 1990: 43–45.

321. Crooke, 1906: 147.

322. Vendidad 6.44–51; 8.10, trans. in Darmesteter and Mills, 1880–87; Herodotus History 1.142; Haug, 1978: 240.

323. The practice is also found among the Tibetans, who even bred and trained dogs especially to devour corpses, and regarded this as the most honorable disposition of the body, reserved for monks and important people (Crooke, 1896, 2: 219). The custom of feeding human corpses to dogs is also reported elsewhere in Eurasia and Africa (Langkavel, 1898: 661–63; N. W. Thomas, 1908–26: 512; Schwabe, 1978: 58–59), but in most cases it seems to have been restricted to the poor and the disgraced. Reports of dogs devouring live people also appear in various classical accounts, including a report by Onesicritus (c. 325 B.C.) for the Bactrians, who threw persons disabled by disease and old age to the dogs to be eaten (Strabo Geography 11.11.3). Apparently the custom was supported by considerable strength of feeling, for Stasanor, one of Alexander's prefects, nearly lost his power by attempting to destroy it (Porphyry On abstinence from animal food 4.21). For the role of other predators in disposal of the dead, see E. Vermeule, 1979: 46, 108–9.

324. Vermaseren, 1963: 32, 69–70; L. A. Campbell, 1968: 12–15, 196; Tudor, 1969–76, 2: 226; Afshar, 1990: 187.

325. My discussion of the dog among the Hittites is based on Hrozný, 1922: 69, 71, 149; Masson, 1950: 5–9, 17–25; Goetze, 1962: 34; Kümmel, 1967: 150–68 passim; Friedrich, 1971: 45, 102, 115 and n; Hoffner, 1974: 64, 70, 71, 72, 73, 120; Macqueen, 1975: 137; Gurney, 1977: 50, 53; Gurney, 1990: 125, 126, 136; Moyer, 1983: 29–33; D. P. Wright, 1987: 59–60 and passim; and Collins, 1990.

326. For the full range of ways in which puppies served in Hittite ritual, see Collins, 1990.

327. A single incomplete text indicates that a puppy used in ritual was cut up and may have been devoured by barbarians (?), but, since such consumption is otherwise unknown in Hittite texts, Collins (1990: 213) views this interpretation unconvincing.

328. Collins, 1990: 216.

329. Gordon, 1959: 259, 287, 293, 455; Kramer, 1981: 124–25.

330. Such views were also found among the early Akkadians of northern Mesopotamia, as shown on a tablet: "(If) a blue dog enters a palace, that palace will be burned. (If) a yellow dog enters a palace, exit from that palace will be baneful. (If) a spotted dog enters a palace, that palace will give its peace to the enemy. (If) a dog goes into the palace and kills someone, that palace is deprived of peace. (If) a dog goes to a palace and lies down on a bed, that palace none with his hand will take. (If) a dog goes to a palace and lies down on the throne, that palace will be burned" (G. Smith, 1884: 18, 20, 21).

331. Jastrow, 1898: 398–99, 661–62. Water also became impure through contact with a dog (van der Toorn, 1985: 172 n336). Rites were carried out in Mesopotamia to avoid impending evil from a dog urinating on a man or moaning and howling inside a house. These rites involved getting the evil into a dog figurine made of clay, a substitute for the man, which was cast into a river. The last lines of the final incantation at the river, as reconstructed, clearly reveal the intent: "Carry that dog to the depths. Do not release it! Take it down to your depths. Remove the evil of the dog from my body! Give me happiness and health!" (D. P. Wright, 1987: 69–72, 255).

332. Sayce, 1887: 83n, 84, 287–88; Sayce, 1902: 466–67; Jastrow, 1917: 247. For mention or references to use of dog excrement as medicine in Mesopotamia, see Jastrow, 1917: 247; Collins, 1990: 216 n25.

333. R. C. Thompson, 1903–4, 2: xlvii.

334. For their identity, see Fuhr, 1977: 137.

335. The names led Sayce (1887: 288) to suspect that the dogs may originally have been destructive creatures of a deity dealing in death.

336. Lambert, 1967: 121, 129.

337. "Excavations in Iraq 1972–73," *Iraq* (35, 1973): 192; A. Shaffer, 1974: 251–53; Boessneck, 1977: 102; Fuhr, 1977: 135–37; Livingstone, 1988.

338. Van Buren, 1939: 17–18.

339. Livingstone, 1988: 58.

340. For the Sumerian text commemorating dedication of the statue of an omen (?) dog to the goddess under the name Nintinugga (Nin-din-dug = lady who restores life), see Ali, 1966.

341. Burkert, 1983b: 118.

342. In certain early Mesopotamian scenes, a dog is depicted beneath a couch on which two humanlike figures are having sexual intercourse. It has been speculated that the scene may represent a ritual marriage of deities, and that the dog symbolized Gula (Henri Frankfort, cited by Pope, 1972: 185–89), which, if true, may mean that the animal enjoyed a sexual and fertility symbolism as well.

343. Jastrow, 1910–11. There is speculation that in Palmyra, a goddess depicted with a dog at her feet, who is usually thought to be Astarte, may actually have been of Babylonian origin (Will, 1985: 50, 53–55).

344. W. R. Smith, 1914: 291; Dornan, 1933: 630.

345. W. R. Smith, 1914: 291.

346. Stager, 1991, who provides references to other studies that relate to the role of dogs in healing cults.

347. This recalls the stele found at Citium, a city on Cyprus, which had a Phoenician inscription listing persons (masons, architects, scribes, etc.) associated with a shrine of Astarte. The list includes the word *"klbm"* (dogs; Hebrew: *kelabim*), which Reinach (1884) interprets as referring to sacred dogs of the temple, similar to those of Asclepius at Epidaurus.

348. S. A. Cook, 1908: 22.

349. The sixth century B.C. date, tentatively advanced by Greenewalt, has been questioned by Robertson (Greenewalt, 1978: 28–30; N. Robertson, 1982a: 123 and n3).

350. Pedley, 1974: 97–98; Greenewalt, 1978: 1, 4, 10–19, 24–26, 31–38; N. Robertson, 1982a: 122–23.

351. Greenewalt, 1978: 40–55.

352. For a weighing of evidence regarding this matter, see Pedley, 1974: 98; Greenewalt, 1978: 45–52; and N. Robertson, 1982a: 132–37.

353. Greenewalt, 1978: 1, 54 and n.

354. For details on *kandaulos,* see Greenewalt, 1978: 52–54. Classical authors differed as to the ingredients of the dish, which was a stew, but one suggested that it was made of fatty broth, boiled meat, cheese, bread crumbs, and anise (or dill) (Athenaeus *Deipnosophists* 12.516d).

355. Though it is indeed speculative to suggest that the dish *kandaulos* and the ritual dinners were related, such speculation may, in time, bring rewards. For this reason, I do not agree with N. Robertson's (1982a: 124) summary dismissal of the question.

356. Pedley, 1974: 97, 98–99. Pedley, Greenewalt (1978: 31n, 40–54), and N. Robertson (1982a: 124, 129–32 and passim) provide interesting information on ancient ritual killing of dogs in the region.

357. N. Robertson, 1982a: 124, 127–32, 137–40.

358. Burkert, 1983b: 118–19. Most important among the evidence are three Babylonian bronze figurines, found in the temple complex of Hera on Samos, of a man praying with a large dog behind him. Since Hera was the goddess of marriage and the lives of women, the healing abilities of Gula would have been quite relevant to Hera's cult.

359. Kurtz and Boardman, 1971: 135–36, 238; C. Vermeule, 1972: 56, 57; Day, 1984: 29 and n. Representations of Cerberus are also common on Greek sarcophagi— as well as on vase paintings and statues—where a scene is set in, or a theme is related to, Hades (Bloomfield, 1905: 3).

Representations of the dog are also found on grave markers in the Roman world, as at Bonn in Roman Gaul (Jenkins, 1957: 62–63).

360. Day, 1984: 29 n43.

361. Kerényi, 1959: 26–30; Jayne, 1962: 224–25, 242–44, 265, 306–10; Burkert, 1983b: 118; Burkert, 1985: 147, 267.

362. Edelstein and Edelstein, 1945, 2: 227; Kerényi, 1959: 27–30; Jayne, 1962: 308.

363. Burkert, 1983b: 118. If Apollo was indeed influenced by the cult of Gula, one wonders why dogs, as we shall see, were excluded from Delos, Apollo's birthplace and sacred island.

364. Dornan, 1933: 630.

365. Pedley, 1974: 99.

366. For summaries of biblical and rabbinical references to the dog, see Kohler and Schechter, 1907; and Feliks, 1971–72c.

367. 1 Samuel 17:43; 24:14; 2 Samuel 3:8; 2 Kings 8:13; Job 30:1; Isaiah 56:10, 11.

368. Baba Ḳamma 83a.

369. That dogs are mentioned in the rabbinical literature as receiving food at weddings and funerals (Pope, 1972: 184) suggests a somewhat different perspective of them.

370. Matthew 15:26; Mark 7:27.

371. Matthew 7:6.

372. Philistines 3:2.

373. 2 Peter 2:22; Proverbs 26:11.

374. Isaiah 66:3.

375. Leviticus 11:27.

376. W. R. Smith, 1914: 292.

377. Hanauer, 1935: 195–96.

378. This may be related to the common Moslem view (Budge, 1904, 1: 19) that a dog is able to see the angel of death, and that when it does, it will howl.

379. Westermarck, 1926, 2: 103, 308.

380. Goldziher, 1901: 17–18. In Islam, black dogs came to symbolize sensuality or the devil (Lurker, 1987: 396).

381. T. P. Hughes, 1885: 91.

382. Goldziher, 1901.

383. Afshar, 1990: 47–55.

384. Long before the time of Mohammed, Pliny (*Natural history* 6.155–56) wrote that no dogs were admitted into the interior of Sygaros, an island off the southern coast of Arabia, and that they wandered about on the seashore until they died. This recalls the Greek refusal to permit dogs on Delos, and one wonders whether their exclusion from Sygaros may have been based on their impurity.

385. Westermarck, 1926, 2: 303–4.

386. Hanauer, 1935: 194.

387. Doughty, 1888, 1: 337–38; Cheesman, 1926: 108.

388. de Planhol, 1959: 59.

389. Dhalla, 1922: 367; Afshar, 1990: 4–5. The factors involved in this decline are presented in Afshar, 1990: 46–55.

390. E. C. Sykes, 1910: 247–48.

391. Massé, 1938: 196.

392. P. M. Sykes, 1906: 758.

393. Merriam, 1885: 289.

394. Meigs, 1978: 316.

395. Dolman, 1957: 53–55; Schwabe, 1984b: 214–18, 362–73, 419–28, 442–44, 472–84.

396. If one were to develop such a hypothesis, China, the Old World's leading center of dog eating, would be a good place to start. *Trichinella* have been reported in dogs in China, and one study in southern Manchuria before the Second World War found the percentage of *Trichinella*-infected dogs to be very high (20.8 percent) (Kozar, 1962: 25–26; Yamashita, 1970: 459; Kim, 1983: 485–86; W. C. Campbell et al., 1988: 66). That there was an outbreak of human trichinosis in Manchuria in 1984 from eating dogflesh (W. C. Campbell et al., 1988: 66) indicates that, at least in that region, it poses a significant health danger. At the same time, trichinosis among the Chinese in general seems to be relatively rare, presumably because of the very low average meat consumption, and because meat is commonly cut into small pieces before cooking at high temperatures, which facilitates destruction of the parasite.

One also wonders about trichinosis among dog eaters in Southeast Asia and elsewhere. In a dogflesh market in northeastern Thailand, the diaphragms of 421 dogs were examined for larvae of *Trichinella*. Seven (1.7 percent) were found to be infected, with from five to nine larvae per gram of flesh (W. C. Campbell et al., 1988: 65). Though outbreaks of human trichinosis have occurred in northern Thailand nearly every year from 1962 to 1991, surveys (Dissamarn and Indrakamhang, 1985; Khamboonruang, 1991) suggest that infection came mainly from pigs, domestic and wild. It was cautioned, however, that the eating of infected dogflesh might, in time, lead to a public-health problem.

Chapter 8. Fish

1. Simoons, 1991: 431–32, 434–36.

2. Roth, 1890: 75, 101; Jones, 1978: 15–21.

3. Jones, 1978: 42–47; Colley and Jones, 1989: 336–37.

4. For references relating to the controversy, see Colley and Jones, 1989: 336–37.

5. On water and water symbolism around the world, see Eliade, 1958: 188–215.

6. Fish taboos were found among Athapascans of the Pacific coast, though they are described as relatively mild (Landar, 1960: 76n).

7. Landar, 1960.

8. Bans on turtleflesh around the world have not attracted much attention. James J. Parsons (1962b: 9) found that sea turtles are not eaten as human food by most coastal peoples of Southeast Asia, which suggests that the matter deserves more study.

9. Matthews, 1897: 239; Matthews, 1898: 105–6, 111; Bailey, 1940: 276–77; Newcomb, 1940: 20, 57; Reichard, 1963: 588–89.

10. Matthews, 1897: 239; Matthews, 1898: 105–6.

11. Simoons et al., 1979: 68–69.

12. Despite its widespread occurrence, African avoidance of fish has been considered by relatively few scholars. In their *Atlas Africanus,* Leo Frobenius and Ritter von

Wilm (1921–31, 1:5) did provide a useful map of the distribution of fish avoidance in the continent, but unfortunately provided no documentation. Sture Lagercrantz (1953), on the other hand, published a carefully documented, though short, article on the occurrence and manifestations of fish avoidance among African peoples. In addition, I wrote a somewhat lengthier article on the subject (Simoons, 1974c) two decades ago. If needed, the reader can obtain more detail from my article and that of Lagercrantz.

13. Petrie, 1908–26: 245; Aldred, 1961: 189–91; Frankfort, 1961: 13–14.

14. Kees, 1933: 58–59. For representations of these and other fish of ancient Egypt, see Boessneck, 1988: 124–33.

15. Budge, 1904, 2: 382–83; Radcliffe, 1921: 325–26; Bertin, 1954: 38–39; Darby et al., 1977, 1: 392.

16. Kees, 1933: 59; Bertin, 1954: 38.

17. Plutarch *Isis and Osiris* 72.

18. Erman, 1894: 238–39; Kees, 1933: 60–61; Darby et al., 1977, 1: 337–404.

19. Radcliffe, 1921: 324; Kees, 1941: 63; Kees, 1961: 92; Griffiths, 1970: 277.

20. Neumann, 1969: 71n.

21. For an excellent, more detailed account of ancient Egyptian dietary use of fish and the role of fish in religion, see Darby et al., 1977, 1: 380–402.

22. Herodotus *History* 2.37, 77; Plutarch *Isis and Osiris* 7.

23. Budge, 1895: 329; Bertin, 1954: 37.

24. Plutarch *Isis and Osiris* 7.

25. Kees, 1933: 59; Lagercrantz, 1953: 4; Kees, 1961: 92.

26. Bates, 1917: 216.

27. Burckhardt, 1819: 25.

28. Pückler-Muskau, 1844, 3: 8.

29. Schäfer, 1917: 138.

30. R. Herzog, 1957: 153.

31. K. W. Butzer, pers. comm.

32. Breasted, 1906–7, 4: 443; Budge, 1907, 2: 25–26; Montet, 1958: 59.

33. G. W. Murray, 1935: 92; L. E. Grivetti, pers. comm.

34. Arnaud, 1906: 149.

35. Stillman, 1987: 110.

36. L. C. Briggs, 1958: 135; L. C. Briggs, 1967: 245.

37. Duveyrier, 1864: 401, 402.

38. A. C. Cook, 1900: 454.

39. von Grünau, 1899: 276.

40. Cline, 1936: 28.

41. Cline, 1950: 29; L. C. Briggs, 1958: 134.

42. Seligman and Seligman, 1932: 363; Nalder, 1937: 58; Cerulli, 1956: 73; Murdock, 1958: FJ 10, Didinga; Murdock, 1959: 335.

43. A. Paul, 1954: 12.

44. A. Paul, 1954: 12, 35–36.

45. Strabo *Geography* 16.4.4, 7, 13.

46. Diodorus Siculus *Library of history* 3. 15–17.

47. Pausanias *Description of Greece* 1.33.4.

48. Modern cave-dwelling ichthyophagi on the Red Sea shore of Arabia are mentioned by Richard Burton, 1893, 1: 221.

49. Bruce, 1790, 4: 275; Simoons, 1960: 158; Gamst, 1969: 80.

50. R. N. D. Read, pers. comm., May 14, 1962.

51. D. Buxton, 1950: 107–8; Read, 1962: 521, and pers. comm.

52. Richard Burton, 1894, 1: 109.

53. Cited by Lagercrantz, 1953: 4.

54. Cerulli, 1956: 100.

55. Huntingford, 1955: 110.

56. Murdock, 1959: 199.

57. Merker, 1904: 33–34; Baumann and Westermann, 1948: 257; Maguire, 1948: 14; Huntingford, 1953b: 109; Murdock, 1958: FL12, Masai.

58. Hollis, 1904: 319; H. Fuchs, 1910: 125.

59. Huntingford, 1953b: 110. For more on Maasai perceptions of such groups, see Århem, 1989: 13.

60. Gulliver and Gulliver, 1953: 62; Kimble, 1960, 1: 266.

61. Worthington and Worthington, 1933: 140–41. For more on the ties between fishing and pastoral groups in the Lake Rudolf area, see Sobania, 1988.

62. Beech, 1911: 10–11; Huntingford, 1953b: 82.

63. Cunningham, 1905: 8; Mors, 1953: 91–92; Claudine and Jan Vansina, pers. comm.

64. Huntingford, 1927: 438.

65. Routledge and Routledge, 1910: 50; Middleton, 1953: 19.

66. Roscoe, 1915: 77.

67. Lindblom, 1920: 332.

68. Reports of fish eating among Hottentots are numerous (for example, Theal, 1910: 77; Vedder, 1928: 128; Westermarck, 1924, 2: 325; and Schapera, 1930: 179, 238, 300–301, 304), and Fritsch (1868: 339) wrote that aversion to fish did not occur among Hottentots in any way. That this may be too strong a statement is suggested by one report (Featherman, 1885–91, 1: 539) that the Nama Hottentots of the Orange River area, out of fear of toxicity, ate no fish.

69. Kay, 1834: 115.

70. J. G. Wood, 1870: 375.

71. Fritsch, 1868: 338.

72. Webster, 1942: 333–34.

73. Stayt, 1931: 47.

74. L. E. Grivetti, pers. comm.

75. Frobenius and von Wilm, 1921–31, 1: 5; Lagercrantz, 1953: 8.

76. Oil may also be extracted from fish, and fish may serve as fertilizer (W. H. Ingrams, 1936: 60–61; Inayatullah, 1942: 95; Worthington, 1946: 119; Dickson 1949: 160; D. Ingrams, 1949: 133, 157; Faroughy, 1951: 38; Lebkicher et al., 1952: 112; Belgrave, 1953: 53).

77. Goodenough, 1953–68, 5: 48.

78. Koran 5:96.

79. Niebuhr, 1889: 59. See Donaldson (1938: 191) for information on the acceptable ways of catching fish in Iran.

80. Ratzel (1896–98, 3: 211) writes of a group of Bedouin fishermen, the Tuals, who lived near Jeddah; and E. Epstein (1938: 602), of Bedouins of the Awazim tribe who settled down to become fishermen in Kuwait.

81. Lebkicher et al., 1952: 112.

82. Cheesman, 1926: 37.

83. See Dunnigan, 1987, for an excellent short account of fish symbolism around the world.

84. The word "Hittite" may be used for at least four different groups (Moyer, 1983: 19 n1). In this book, I use the term to refer to the Indo-European people believed to have entered Anatolia early in the second millennium B.C., who formed an empire there that lasted until roughly 1200 B.C.

85. Hoffner, 1967: 181–82; Hoffner, 1974: 124–25.

86. Van Buren, 1939: 104–8.

87. Ellison, 1981: 35; Ellison, 1983: 147–48; Limet, 1987: 137.

88. Limet, 1987: 137.

89. Ellison et al., 1978: 175–76.

90. In Christian funerary painting, for example, fish symbolize resurrection and rebirth (Dunnigan, 1987: 347). Such thinking may also be involved in the practice of modern Mandaeans, a cult of ancient origins found in Iraq and Iran, who consume fish ritually at meals for the deceased (Drower, 1956: 8).

91. Van Buren, 1948: 102–3, 110.

92. For references to such representations, see Langdon, 1989: 192 n62.

93. D. P. Wright, 1987: 61, 81, 248–61.

94. R. C. Thompson, 1903–4, 2: xlvii–xlviii; van der Toorn, 1985: 33–35, 171–72.

95. Oppenheim, 1956: 271–72.

96. Saggs, 1962: 175; Saggs, 1965: 175; van der Toorn, 1985: 34, 35.

97. For myths on the past of Atargatis and how she became a goddess, see Burkert, 1983a: 204–5, 206.

98. When Assyrian forces invaded southern Palestine late in the seventh century B.C., they carried away statues of deities from certain defeated cities. As depicted on an Assyrian relief at Nimrud, two goddesses were among those deported, possibly from the Philistine city of Gaza (Barnett, 1985: 20–28). Though they cannot be identified with certainty, one wonders whether Derketo/Astarte/Atargatis was among them.

99. Lucian *Syrian Goddess* 10.

100. Lucian *Syrian Goddess* 14, 45–46.

101. Drijvers, 1980: 79.

102. Macalister, 1965: 95.

103. Xenophon *Anabasis* 1.4.9.

104. Athenaeus *Deipnosophists* 8.346.

105. Burkert, 1983a: 206.

106. Cumont, 1956: 117.

107. In a similar vein in ancient Greece, devotees of Aphrodite, to whom Astarte was assimilated, ate fish on Friday, holy day of the goddess, in an effort to share in her fecundity (Dunnigan, 1987: 346). For further references to sacred meals involving the eating of fish, see Cumont, 1956: 246 n37.

108. Diodorus Siculus *Library of history* 2.4.3.

109. Menander *The principal fragments* 544K, trans. F. G. Allinson in Menander, 1951: 343.

110. Plutarch *On superstition* 10.

111. Ovid *Fasti* 2.473–74.

112. J. Fryer, 1909–15, 20: 238n; Strong on pp. 52–54 in his translation of Lucian *Syrian Goddess;* Cumont, 1956: 245–46; and, specifically on Edessa (Urfa), E. Sachau, 1883: 196–97; and Drijvers, 1980: 79–80. For an account of the cult of Atargatis, see Drijvers, 1980: 76–121; and for photographs of the modern pond and sacred fish at Urfa, see Warkworth, 1898, plate opposite p. 242; and Drijvers, 1980: Plates 2 and 3.

113. Badger, 1852, 1: 117. See also I. Joseph, 1919: 80 (ban on fish in a Yezidi sacred book), and O. H. Parry 1895: 363.

114. For sacred waters and sacred fish among Celtic peoples (the salmon and trout were especially honored), see MacCulloch, 1911: chapter 11 (esp. pp. 186–87) and p. 220; and Ross, 1967: 20–33, 350–51.

115. W. M. Ramsay, 1897: 288–90; Cumont, 1956: 245–46.

116. Martin, 1987: 81.

117. Petrie, 1908–26: 250.

118. Carter, 1987: 382–83 and n.

119. I base this statement on evidence found at the Shrine of Ortheia in Sparta presented in Jane Burr Carter's interesting article "The Masks of Ortheia." As Carter tells it (1987: 355, 359, 374–83), such masks are virtually absent in other Greek shrines of comparable age (seventh and sixth centuries B.C.). On the other hand, prototypes have been found in Cyprus, and, mostly in shrines involving a female fertility deity and her consort, in adjacent western Asia and Babylonia. Carter has suggested that Ortheia may be the Greek name for the Phoenician goddess Asherah/Tanit, who, in turn, is related to other Semitic goddesses such as Ishtar and Astarte, as well as to the Sumerian Inanna. Carter notes that Asherah/Tanit was a goddess of the sea, that in Ugaritic texts Asherah was called Lady of the Sea, and that she may have been brought to Sparta by Phoenician settlers. Carter points out that Ortheia of Sparta had an affinity for animals, and that, to her devotees, she could affect animal and human fertility. We note that water creatures make up a significant portion of the votive animals of the goddess: fish, dolphins, geese or ducks, frogs, turtles, and crabs. Despite this, one can only guess what the role of fish and fish eating may have been among Ortheia's devotees.

My appetite for speculation has been whetted further by Susan Langdon's fine study (1989) of a common art motif, the "horse leader," which occurs on Argive vase painting dating from the eighth century B.C. The motif includes a single man leading or holding one or two horses, which usually have a fish (less commonly a water bird) placed beneath, framed by the horse's body and legs. The horse leader occurs elsewhere in Greek art, but the combination of the horse leader with fish or water bird is exclusively Argive. What Langdon has done is identify a horse-leader–fish–goat motif on a pot uncovered at Ugarit (now Ras Shamra) in Syria dating nearly five centuries earlier. The Ugarit pot, apparently of Mycenaean manufacture, may have been commissioned by a citizen of Ugarit who selected motifs of local significance. Also found at Ugarit was the fragment of a pot, which may have formed a matched pair with the horse-leader pot, on which a man is depicted as sacrificing a fish at an altar. This strongly suggests religious associations for the horse-leader pot as well, likely with the deity Asherah. Langdon does not interpret this as suggesting that the cult of the goddess may have spread from Syria to the Argos area by the eighth century B.C., and indeed, as Eugene N. Lane (pers. comm.) observes, in the absence of concrete evidence, one should be quite wary of viewing the spread of the horse-leader motif from Ugarit to the Peloponnesus as "anything except an artistic motif." I feel obliged, nevertheless, to raise the question of whether more may have been involved, possibly even a special perception of fish and fish eating.

120. Apuleius *Metamorphoses* 8.24. Apuleius's characterization of the priest is unkind, and completely lacking in charity: "a pervert . . . one of those common people from the dregs of society who walk through the city streets and towns banging their cymbals and rattles, carrying the Syrian goddess around with them and forcing her to beg. . ."

121. In keeping with this view is the tale of Aphrodite and her ties to the Euphrates River. According to this tale, an egg fell from heaven into the river. Fishermen retrieved it. It was then hatched by doves, and Aphrodite emerged (Burkert, 1983a: 206).

122. Carter, 1987: 383. Such assimilation can lead to confusion for modern readers. When Artemidorus Daldianus (second century A.D.) wrote that Syrian devotees of Astarte did not eat fish (*Interpretation of dreams* 1.8), one presumes he used Astarte as the equivalent of Atargatis. For brief accounts of Astarte and/or Atargatis, see L. B. Paton, 1908–26a,b; and Martin, 1987: 81–83.

123. Sokolowski, 1962: 108–9; R. Parker, 1983: 359.

124. Dumézil, 1970, 2: 680–81.

125. Scullard, 1967: 103.

126. Pallottino, 1975: 90; Grant, 1980: 152–54.

127. Vermaseren, 1963: 122–23.

128. Tudor, 1969–76, 2: 100, 102–3, 104–6, 108–9, 145–46, 208–16.

129. Dölger, 1920–28, 1: 130ff., and 2: 437ff.

130. Julian *Orations* 176 B–C.

131. Vermaseren, 1977: 114–15, 204 nn647–49.

132. Leviticus 11:9–12; Deuteronomy 14:9–10.

133. William F. Albright (1968: 178–79) presented a hygienic explanation for the

Hebrew ban on fish without fins or scales. He argued that such fish, which tend to be mud burrowers, have significantly more parasites than free-swimming fish, and that when the Hebrews lived in exile in the Nile Valley of Egypt they suffered far more from parasitic diseases than native Egyptians, who were better able to tolerate parasites. He concludes that Hebrew awareness of the danger seems to have led them to ban such fish. For further consideration of hygienic explanations of Hebrew flesh bans, see my chapter on pigs and pork.

134. Eels, of which there are many species, possess continuous dorsal and anal fins, but lack pelvic fins. In addition, they usually have no scales, or they have rudimentary scales covered with skin. As a questionable form of fish, the eel was specifically banned and eel eating punished in the Talmud ('Abodah Zarah 39a; Pesaḥim 24a; 'Erubin 28a).

135. Hirsch, 1907: 403.

136. In Talmudic times, the cooking or eating of fish together with meat was banned because such mixing was seen as injurious to health and as possibly leading to leprosy (Pesaḥim 76b). The linking of leprosy and fish eating was not restricted to the Jews, but seems to have been quite widespread. The matter deserves more attention, and here I would note only that the belief that leprosy developed because of the consumption of putrified or diseased fish, or certain of them, or that it could be treated by giving up fish eating was found among Old World groups as distant from one another as the Gilyak of Siberia (Czaplicka, 1914: 308) and peoples of Western Europe ("Hawaiian leprosy," *Transactions of the Medical Society of the State of California during the Years 1880–81*, pp. 282–83; Creighton, 1899–1903: 2766; Newman, 1946: 48).

137. Zephaniah 1:10; Nehemiah 3:3, and 13:16; 2 Chronicles 33:14.

138. Hirsch, 1907: 404.

139. W. R. Smith, 1914: 219; Bodenheimer, 1960: 213.

140. Deuteronomy 4:15–18. We do not know whether or not this had anything to do with the fish deities of neighboring peoples.

141. Genesis 1:20–22.

142. Goodenough, 1953–68, 5: 42.

143. Goodenough, 1953–68, 5: 33–34.

144. Kethuboth 61a.

145. Goodenough, 1953–68, 5: 50.

146. Jacobs and Schechter, 1907: 54.

147. *Encyclopaedia Judaica*, 1971–72: 1328.

148. The Leviathan, though often called fish in various biblical accounts, seems to resemble a whale, serpent, or crocodile.

149. Goodenough, 1953–68, 5: 35–38; *Encyclopaedia Judaica*, 1971–72: 1327; Dunnigan, 1987: 346.

150. Goodenough, 1953–68, 5: 37, 48.

151. Goodenough, 1953–68, 5: 31–53.

152. Goodenough, 1953–68, 5: 32, 34–35.

153. For a representation of such a lamp, see J. Campbell, 1968: 14.

154. John 3:5.

155. J. Gamble, 1908–26: 138; Baum, 1956: 267–69; J. Campbell, 1968: 12–14; Dunnigan, 1987.

156. Deffontaines, 1948: 378–81.

157. Athenaeus (*Deipnosophists* 7.297); Burkert (1985: 55, 368 n4); and Detienne (1989a: 221 n8) cite a few exceptions. One is the tuna, sacrificed to Poseidon, at a rite called thynnaion, when there was a good catch during the tuna season. Another is the eel. J.-L. Durand writes of the tuna and eel as the only fishes mentioned in a blood ritual in which the victim is consumed. The tuna's acceptability for such sacrifice derives from its abundant blood, which is essential in a sacrificial rite. As Durand observes (1989: 127–28), ". . . a fish that bleeds is fit to die for the gods." It was also fit to eat.

158. Pausanias *Description of Greece* 3.21.5. See Burkert (1983a: 208–12) for more on fish, fishermen, and sacrifice to the gods in Greece. See Bevan (1986, 1: 131–37, 143–45) for information on Greek Olympian deities associated with fish, fish offerings to them, and fish representations in their sanctuaries.

159. Pausanias *Description of Greece* 7.22.4.

160. Pausanias *Description of Greece* 1.38.1.

161. Porphyry (*On abstinence from animal food* 4.16) also noted that in the Eleusinian Mysteries, in which Demeter and her daughter were paramount, fish, along with certain other foods, were banned to the initiated.

162. Diodorus Siculus *Library of history* 5.3.5–6; 34/35.9.

163. Plutarch *Symposiacs* 8.8.4.

164. Plutarch *Whether land or sea animals are cleverer* 35. For additional references to the avoidance of fish by some priests of Poseidon, see R. Parker, 1983: 358n.

165. R. Parker, 1983: 358–59, 360–61, 362–63.

166. Detienne, 1989b: 145.

167. Burkert, 1985: 296–99, 301–2; Detienne, 1989a: 5–8; Vernant, 1989: 50–51.

168. Diogenes Laërtius, "Life of Pythagoras," 8.1–26, in his *Lives and opinions of eminent philosophers;* Guthrie, 1962–81, 1: 166–67, 181–82, 184–95, and elsewhere; de Vogel, 1966: 3–4, 130–31, 138–39, 150–52, 177, 181, 186, 192, 232; Philip, 1966: 147–48, 151–56. According to Diogenes Laërtius (third century A.D.), Pythagoras banned beans among his followers because beans were flatulent and possessed animal qualities. Pythagoras also said that if beans were not eaten, a person's stomach would remain in better condition and that his dreams would be "gentle and free from agitation" (*Lives and opinions of eminent philosophers,* "Life of Pythagoras," 8.18). Other explanations of the ban have been advanced as well, including the fact that beans look like human testicles (Guthrie, 1962–81, 1: 184–85, 187, 189; Darby et al., 1977, 2: 682–85; Murphy, 1990: 113 n180). In modern times, some have suggested that the ban may have derived from awareness of the link between consumption of the broad bean or horse bean (*Vicia faba*) and favism, a hereditary disorder known in Greece (R. Parker, 1983: 364–65). Whatever the true reason, such bans on beans were also found among other Greeks and elsewhere in the classical world, as in Egypt and Rome (Herodotus *History* 2.37; Plutarch *Symposiacs* 8.8.2; Plutarch *Isis and*

Osiris 5; Diodorus Siculus *Library of history* 1.89.4; Pliny *Natural history* 18.117–19; Guthrie, 1962–81, 1: 185n; Murphy, 1990: 113 n180).

169. Plutarch *Symposiacs* 8.8.2.

170. R. Parker, 1983: 359.

171. Plutarch *Symposiacs* 8.8.

172. Detienne, 1989a: 5–6.

173. See Athenaeus *Deipnosophists* 4.160–61, for Pythagorean dietary practices as dealt with by Antiphanes (fourth century B.C.) and Alexis (c. 375–275 B.C.), noted comedy writers of Athens.

I have not been able to determine whether or not Oric Bates (1917: 211) was referring to the Pythagoreans when he observed that fish avoidance occurred in some parts of ancient Italy.

174. Vickery, 1936: 74–79. For the impressive range of fish and fish dishes consumed by the ancient Greeks, see Athenaeus *Deipnosophists* 3.85–93.

175. E.g., Plutarch *Symposiacs* 8.8.3; Athenaeus *Deipnosophists* 1.9.

176. Homer *Odyssey* 4.363–70; 12.329–34.

177. Athenaeus *Deipnosophists* 4.157.

178. Schrader, 1890: 117–18, 317; Rose, 1925: 141–42.

179. Gimbutas, 1970: 160; Mallory, 1983, 1989: 189, 190, 198, 200; Telegin, 1986: 87, 88.

180. In much later times, the pastoral Scythians ate fish and so did the Massagetae, pastoralists who lived north of Iran.

181. Bosworth, 1963: 156.

182. Dhalla, 1922: 188.

183. Diodorus Siculus *Library of history* 3.15; Philostratus *Life of Apollonius of Tyana* 3.55; Strabo *Geography* 15.2.2; Arrian *Indica* 26–31; Plutarch *Life of Alexander* 66.

184. Ouseley, 1819–23, 1: 227–29.

185. Porphyry *On abstinence from animal food* 4.16.

186. Ferrier, 1857: 44; Curzon, 1892, 2: 62–63; Le Strange, 1905: 240; J. Fryer, 1909–15, 20: 238n.

187. Curzon, 1892, 2: 62–63; J. Fryer, 1909–15, 20: 238n.

188. Lucian *Syrian goddess* 45.

189. McCrindle, 1896: 397; Modi, 1926: 437.

190. Levchine, 1840: 322, 418; Zaleskie, 1865: 30; O'Donovan, 1883, 2: 328, and 4: 212; Featherman, 1885–91, 4: 255–56, 258; Olufsen, 1911: 457; Bacon, 1966: 32, 52.

191. Rockhill, 1900: 96–97.

192. O'Donovan, 1883: 328.

193. Olufsen, 1911: 457.

194. *Baluchistan District Gazetteer Series,* 1906–8, 2: 117; 5: 84; 7: 127.

195. Raverty, 1888: 213; J. A. Robinson, 1935: 18.

196. Ferdinand, 1959: 32.

197. One is for Mukkur, a village sixty miles from Ghazni in eastern Afghanistan. At Mukkur, there was a shrine dedicated to a Moslem saint and, adjacent to it, a pool

whose abundant trout were sacred, were unmolested, and were tame and grew very large in size (Bellew, 1862: 196–97). The second is for Sarchama, on the upper Kabul River, where there are specially constructed rock-lined tanks, linked to an Islamic cult, where there is no fishing (Clarke Brooke, pers. comm.).

198. Elphinstone, 1842, 2: 379; Raverty, 1859: 334–35; Fosberry, 1868–69: 192; G. S. Robertson, 1896: 68.

199. Schomberg, 1935: 188.

200. Muhammad, 1905: 94.

201. Walker, 1968, 1: 47–48; Gonda, 1980: 103.

202. Moses, 1922–23: 551; Karmarkar, 1944: 195, 197.

203. For references to other forms of divination involving fish in the Vedic litera-ture, see Gonda, 1980: 104, 255.

204. *Baudhāyana Gṛihya-sūtra* 1.8.6ff., cited by Gonda, 1980: 103–4.

205. Walker, 1968, 1: 358.

206. Walker, 1968: 1: 155.

207. Crooke, 1906: 222; T. C. Das, 1931: 284–86; C. Chakravarty, 1932: 192.

208. Thurston, 1909, 2: 330.

209. Moses, 1922–23: 554.

210. Thurston, 1909, 2: 306; 4: 87; 5: 202, 203; Crooke, 1906: 222.

211. Crooke, 1906: 222.

212. The use of fish in marriage rites in India is not restricted to Hindus. Among the Ao Naga, a tribal people of Assam, for example, a young man, in making a proposal of marriage, catches some fish, and gives them to an old man to carry to the house of his intended bride. He follows the old man there, and the two men are given a drink. Though there is no talk of marriage, the fish are left with the parents, and on the following morning the young man returns and they give him a meal. If the parents eat the fish he brought the previous day, it signals their agreement to the marriage, the starting point for further arrangements (Mills, 1926: 270–71). Fish also serve in marriage ceremonies in other countries in southern and eastern Asia. Among the Palaung of Burma, for example, fish are part of the gift made by the bridegroom (Milne, 1924: 154). In China, Samuel Kidd (1831: 332) writes of a wedding cere-mony that ends with ritual offerings of fish and water plants, which confirm a wife's submission to her spouse.

213. T. C. Das, 1931: 284–85.

214. Crooke, 1906: 221; Crooke, 1908–26a: 9.

215. Similar beliefs occur among the Gonds, a tribal people of Central India, with quite different results. According to Crooke (1906: 221–22), the Gonds go to the river after a funeral, then shout the name of the deceased, catch a fish in which they believe the human soul to be, bring it home, and then may eat the fish in the expectation that the dead person "will be born again as a child in the family."

216. Belcher, 1991; Meadow, 1991: 89.

217. One deity depicted on an Indus Valley seal was identified by John Mar-shall (1931, 1: 52–56), excavator of Mohenjo-Daro, as a proto-Shiva. The identity of that Indus deity with Shiva, however, has been questioned, with much recent opin-

ion against an identification with Shiva (Sullivan, 1964; Srinivasan, 1975–76, 1984; Hiltebeitel, 1978a; Ghurye, 1979: 157; Hopkins and Hiltebeitel, 1987: 221–22).

218. *Rig-veda* 10.68.8; in R. T. H. Griffith, 1963.

219. Prakash, 1961: 16.

220. Gonda, 1980: 104, 120, 376, 450.

221. Walker, 1968, 1: 278; Banerji, 1980: 98. In the eleventh century, moreover, al-Bīrūnī included fish among creatures that were permitted to be killed for consumption by Hindus, apparently even by Brahmins (E. C. Sachau, 1971: 151).

222. In Tamilnad, members of the Chetti (bankers, merchants, etc.) and Vellala (cultivators) castes are reputed to avoid eating fish. Whether or not this is altogether true, it does reveal an orientation toward the Brahminical ideal (Sopher, 1957: 14), which contributes to the maintenance or enhancement of a group's ritual status.

223. N. K. Panikkar, pers. comm.

224. Panikkar, 1918: 287. Indian fish eaters do not eat all kinds of fish, however. Many will not eat fish that lack scales, such as eels. Many view tuna as inferior because of its red-colored flesh (because it resembles meat?), and indeed many fishermen simply discard tuna they catch (N. K. Panikkar, pers. comm.). There are also notable differences in preferences for freshwater fish versus saltwater fish, with inland peoples in India and Pakistan usually favoring freshwater fish and coastal peoples usually favoring saltwater types. David Sopher (1957: 14–15) observed that along India's east coast, many fine beds of oysters remained unexploited; that, except in one area, squid were not eaten; that eels and lobsters were unpopular; and that only poor people consumed sharks and skates. The unpopularity of sharks in India has proved beneficial to the Chinese, who regard shark's fin as a great delicacy and have obtained large amounts of such fins from India (Simoons, 1991: 431–32).

Unfortunately virtually nothing has been done to map the geographic patterns of rejection of individual fish species, or of fishes of particular types, such as the fish without fins or scales banned in Leviticus (9:9–12). It is clear, however, that the ban on fish without scales is quite widespread, occurring not only in the Near East among such groups as Jews, Moslems, and Mandaeans (Drower, 1937: 48), but also among Moslems elsewhere, many Hindu Indians, and such widely scattered African peoples as the Bajas of the Cameroons (Deffontaines, 1948: 369) and Cape Hottentots of southern Africa (Schapera, 1930: 240).

225. Blunt, 1931: 95; *Report on the marketing of fish in the Indian Union,* 1951: 63; Sopher, 1957: 14; Walker, 1968, 1: 280; L. Dumont, 1970: 141; N. K. Panikkar, pers. comm.

226. T. Chakravarty, 1959: 38–43.

227. C. Chakravarty, 1932: 191.

228. N. K. Panikkar, pers. comm.

229. Deffontaines, 1948: 371. For the purificatory role of the Ganges in Hinduism, see "The Ganges and the sacrality of rivers," pp. 187–96 in Kinsley, 1986.

230. T. C. Das, 1931: 276; C. Chakravarty, 1932: 191; T. Chakravarty, 1959: 43.

231. Hutton, 1963: 51–52.

232. Hutton, 1963: 77.

233. *Report on the marketing of fish in India,* 1946: 42; *Report on the marketing of fish in the Indian Union,* 1951: 63; K. N. Sharma, 1961: 46ff.; Farquhar, 1967: 177–78. The history of fish avoidance among Hindu cults is a subject that needs study.

234. T. C. Das, 1931: 276, 277; C. Chakravarty, 1932; K. N. Sharma, 1961: 48. The fish is the first of Vishnu's reincarnations, and he often came to earth in that form (Crooke, 1896, 1: 156, 254; Walker, 1968, 1: 47–48; 2: 544–45, 575; Gonda, 1969a: 125), but I do not know what effect, if any, this may have on Vaishnavite fish avoidance.

235. Eichinger Ferro-Luzzi, 1985b: 499–500.

236. Drake-Brockman, 1911: 21.

237. Eichinger Ferro-Luzzi, 1977a: 364.

238. For use and avoidance of fish by Tamil women at times of puberty, pregnancy, and after childbirth, see Eichinger Ferro-Luzzi, 1973a: 170; Eichinger Ferro-Luzzi, 1973b: 260; and Eichinger Ferro-Luzzi, 1974: 9.

239. For places where fish are sacred, see Crooke, 1896, 2: 253–54; and Crooke, 1906: 222–23. Any tank or pond in which water derives from a holy source or is associated with a sacred place is itself sacred for religious purposes. For information on sacred waters and water spirits and deities in India, see Crooke, 1908–26b.

240. Marshall, 1931, 1: 75; Parpola et al., 1970: 10–11.

241. M. Wheeler, 1959: 176–77.

242. Hamilton, 1815: 561; Crooke, 1896, 2: 253; Crooke, 1906: 222; Frazer, 1939: 84.

243. Crooke, 1908–26a: 9; Karmarkar, 1944: 197.

244. T. C. Das, 1932: 98.

245. Crooke, 1906: 222.

246. Moses, 1922–23: 549, 551, 552, 553.

247. One example is the ban on eating shellfish, which is shared with Moslems elsewhere.

248. Moses, 1922–23: 549.

249. For one devout Hindu's objections to such coercion, and his perspective on ahimsa, fishing, and fish eating, see Gandhi, 1950: 215, 216.

250. Modi, 1911–34, 5: 85, 121.

251. Moses, 1922–23: 550.

252. N. E. Parry, 1932: 66.

253. Naik, 1956: 89.

254. T. C. Das, 1945: 68.

255. Elwin, 1955: 47, 193–94, 308–9.

256. Gurdon, 1914: 114–15.

257. L. I. Singh, 1961: 55; LeBar et al., 1964: 52.

258. R. R. P. Sharma, 1961: 27, 37, 38.

259. For the fish as sex and fertility symbol in prehistoric Europe, see Gimbutas, 1982: 107–11.

260. Zimmer, 1969: 131.

261. Zimmer, 1969: 119. The law of the fish was not restricted to Buddhists, as

shown in the work of the famous Flemish painter Pieter Bruegel, and embodied in the saying "The big ones eat the little ones."

262. *Mahāvagga* 6.31.14, trans. in Davids and Oldenberg, 1881–85.

263. Fish avoidance is included among the five points listed in the Pali-language Vinaya texts (*Kullavagga* 7.3.14, trans. in Davids and Oldenberg, 1881–85), an early work found in Sri Lanka that sets down rules governing the life of Buddhist monks. This work is considered truer to ancient Buddhist tradition than the *Dulva,* the canon law written in Tibetan, in which fish avoidance is not found among the five rules proposed by Devadatta (Rockhill, 1884: 87–88).

264. Moses, 1922–23: 550.

265. Thapar, 1961: 71–72.

266. Wijesekera, 1965: 115.

267. H. Parker, 1909: 51–52.

268. Wijesekera, 1965: 114; Raghavan, 1961: 40–42.

269. N. K. Panikkar, pers. comm.

270. Sherring, 1906: 304; Heber and Heber, 1926: 96; Hermanns, 1949: 58; Tucci, 1956: 166.

271. S. C. Das, 1902: 141; Bell, 1931: 75–76; Waddell, 1939: 225; Harrer, 1954: 178–79.

272. Duncan, 1964: 243. The inability of fish to cry out is invoked to explain bans on fish eating elsewhere, too. There is, for example, a folk belief in Serbia that a pregnant woman should not eat fish lest her child be a mute (Petrowitsch, 1878: 349). Similar to this is the ancient Greek explanation that Pythagoreans avoided fish because fish are unable to speak. In the latter case, however, the avoidance was based on the Pythagoreans' great respect for silence (Plutarch *Symposiacs* 8.8.1).

273. Duncan, 1964: 243.

274. Combe, 1926: 128; Bell, 1928: 233; Lodrick, 1981: 256.

275. Duncan, 1964: 81.

276. Lodrick, 1981: 256 n10.

277. According to a lama in Darjeeling, Tibetans also go to butchers and purchase other animals, among them cows, goats, and hens, to prevent their slaughter (Deryck Lodrick, pers. comm.).

278. Monier-Williams, 1964: 364.

279. Palmieri, 1976: 117–18.

280. Harrer, 1954: 178–79.

281. For the low status of professional butchers in Tibet, see Palmieri, 1976: 121–23.

282. Prejevalsky, 1876, 1: 56; Riasanovsky, 1937: 16; Perlin, 1941: 46; Schram, 1954: 113–14; Thiel, 1958: 323; Lattimore, 1962: 25, 49.

283. Lattimore, 1962: 49.

284. de Young, 1955: 100.

285. Khin, 1948: 73; de Young, 1955: 100.

286. Steinberg et al., 1959: 26, 209.

287. Gourou, 1945: 402.

288. Simoons, 1991: 337–39.

289. Monier-Williams, 1964: 364.

290. Crooke, 1906: 223.

291. Fielding Hall, 1917: 230.

292. Graham, 1924, 2: 38.

293. Anuman-Rajadhon, 1953: 21–22.

294. Hauck et al., 1958: 43.

295. V. Thompson, 1941: 713.

296. Fishing with cormorants is common in both Japan and China. For brief accounts of cormorant fishing in Japan, see Hornell, 1950: 31–33; and L. E. Joseph, 1986. For cormorant fishing in China, see Gudger, 1926; Laufer, 1931; and Simoons, 1991: 340–42. The monograph by Laufer is the most thorough scholarly study ever done of the history and geography of cormorant fishing.

297. De Visser, 1935, 1: 205, 208–9; 2: 449, 648.

298. Chamberlain, 1905: 177.

299. Simoons, 1991: 31–37.

300. Laufer, 1931: 225–26.

301. Latourette, 1964: 544.

302. Still to be investigated is the occurrence of fish avoidance among non-Han minority groups in China. Almost all of them, it seems, are fish eaters, though for Taiwan I have found one report that certain coastal tribes do not eat fish (Wirth, 1897: 364), and another that the Yami ban fishing at certain times of the year (Del Re, n.d.: 30).

303. K. H. C. Lo, 1971: 25–26; K. H. C. Lo, 1979: 106–7.

304. Welch, 1967: 112.

305. Chinese people in general may avoid fish of one type or another. Salmon and tuna, along with other fishes that are tough and oily, strong in taste, and unpleasant in smell, are disdained by the Chinese. This is perhaps best illustrated by E. N. Anderson's encounter with Chinese who, in talking about a tuna-packing factory, described it as an excellent opportunity to sell to naive Westerners fish suited only for fertilizer.

Another example is squid, which, because it does not have red blood, tears, or emotion, is regarded as lacking in food value, and may, as a result, not be consumed. In San Francisco, pregnant Chinese women may be reluctant to eat squid or octopus out of a fear that their children be born with multiple arms or legs. Most shellfish, including shrimp, are among the foods banned to women during pregnancy and after birth, for they are considered hot in the hot-cold system of the Chinese, as well as being wet and poisonous. Another explanation of the avoidance of shrimp, as well as shellfish and certain other creatures, is that they have rough or scaly bodies, or because infants may develop allergies. Such motherly concerns have occurred widely around the world. In ancient Greece, for example, some persons believed that, if a pregnant woman had a dream that she was giving birth to a fish, her infant, like a fish, would be unable to speak; others contended, however, that such a dream meant that, like a fish out of water, her infant would be stillborn or survive for just a little while (Artemidorus Daldianus *Interpretation of dreams* 2. 18).

Returning to the Chinese, we find that the boat people of Hong Kong consider certain sea creatures (for example, sawfish, sturgeon, and whales) to be sacred, and try not to catch them. If such creatures are inadvertently captured alive, they are freed; if dead, they are carried to a temple to serve as offerings (E. N. Anderson, 1969). On the other hand, large fish, along with other creatures that are unusual in appearance or behavior, impressive, or have great strength or ability to harm, may be viewed as strengthening and restoring, and consumed for that reason (Anderson and Anderson, 1968: 25; Anderson and Anderson, 1977: 369; E. N. Anderson, 1988: 141, 147, 192–94; Simoons, 1991: 25–26, 339, 349–50, 357).

306. Gould-Martin, 1978: 40.

307. For information on garlic and onions as unacceptable food in the Old World, see van der Toorn, 1985: 33–34, 171–72; and Simoons, 1991: 157–58, 174–75.

308. Covarrubias, 1942: 10.

Chapter 9. Conclusion

1. Among the Wopkaimin of New Guinea, for example, fully eighty-seven of ninety-one restricted foods are of animal origin (Hyndman, 1983–84: 291).

2. E. Leach, 1964: 31–33, 40–42.

3. One can only speculate on the nutritional implications of such avoidances, but to me the Pythagorean rejection not only of meat and fish, but also of beans, seems a likely path to protein deficiency.

4. For nausea in the development of food dislikes among humans, see Pelchat and Rozin, 1982.

5. As suggested to me by R. Gordon Wasson, mushrooms are an exception to this generalization, for they are foods of plant origin toward which humans may have strong feelings of rejection. Quite likely this derives from the association of mushrooms with decayed matter, which, along with items that have spoiled (Meigs, 1978: 312–14, 316; Rozin and Fallon, 1987: 28), commonly brings on disgust reactions in humans. For differences in attitudes toward mushrooms among European peoples, see Wasson and Wasson, 1957. The Wassons identified an area of "mycophobes," mushroom haters, around the North Sea, especially in England, and one of "mycophiles," mushroom lovers, in Eastern Europe, particularly Russia. In the former area, the Wassons found that mushrooms were burdened by a negative literary tradition of fear and disgust, and that wild mushrooms were little used. By contrast, people in the area of mycophilia exhibited love for, interest in, and knowledge of wild mushrooms. Seasonal expeditions are organized in Russia to collect mushrooms in woods and forests, and a naughty child might be punished by being denied the privilege of going mushrooming. Indeed, Russians hunt wild mushrooms for eating in the fall with such enthusiasm that foreign observers speak of the phenomenon as mushroom fever.

6. Tambiah, 1969: 457.

7. M. Bates, 1957–58: 452.

8. Prejevalsky, 1876, 1: 56.

9. Shakespeare *Macbeth* 4.1.4–38.

10. Porphyry *On abstinence from animal food* 2.61.

11. Laderman, 1984: 547, 553.

12. The custom of not eating milk and meat together is found in other parts of Africa as well. For information on the distribution and possible origins of the custom, see Grivetti, 1980.

13. Århem, 1989: 1–2, 5, 6, 7. As described by Joseph Thomson (1885: 430–31), before starting on a meat diet, Maasai warriors would take a powerful purgative to make certain their stomachs contained no trace of milk.

14. Spencer and Gillen, 1904: 611–14.

15. M. Douglas, 1955: 23–26.

16. Nadel, 1947: 518.

17. C. DuBois, 1944: 57–58. Deserving further attention are the changes that have occurred over time in the social status of men and women as they have contributed to sexual differences in meat consumption. Such differences likely already existed among some hunting and gathering peoples in preagricultural times, but they may have become more pronounced with the coming of agriculture and animal husbandry. One notes, in this regard, Gina Bari Kolata's observations about certain !Kung Bushmen of southern Africa. When the !Kung live as nomadic hunters and gatherers, women contribute, through their collecting activities, 50 percent or more of the food supply of the band, and they also enjoy sexual equality. When !Kung settle down and participate in the agriculture and animal husbandry of their Bantu neighbors, however, the contribution of women to the food supply decreases, and they become increasingly subservient (Kolata, 1974).

18. Rosenberg, 1973: 16–24; Eichinger Ferro-Luzzi, 1985b: 486–88. In the Hindu case, the husband's superior status is reflected in other ways detailed by Eichinger Ferro-Luzzi in an interesting account of the hierarchy of food consumption in families.

19. Woodburn, 1968: 53.

20. For a recent summary of Rozin's work and views, see Rozin, 1990b.

21. Oppenheim, 1956: 271.

22. Townsend, 1928: 65.

23. Nemeroff and Rozin, 1989; Rozin, 1990b: 101–2.

24. Frazer, 1935, 8: 141–42.

25. M. Leach, 1961: 294.

26. This is similar to the practice, among tribal groups of Gujarat, of attempting to heal one's eye by offering an eye made of clay to the family god, to heal one's hand by offering a clay hand, and to heal one's entire body by offering a human figure of clay (Shah, 1985: 15).

27. Ojoade, 1990: 219.

28. Frazer, 1935, 8: 139.

29. Donkin, 1985: 83–86.

30. Frazer, 1935, 8: 139.

31. de Garine and Hladik, 1990: 93.

32. O'Laughlin, 1974: 302n.

33. Ling et al., 1975: 131; Tan and Wheeler, 1983: 44; Wheeler and Tan, 1983: 53, 54.

34. See, for example, Frazer, 1935, 8: 146–47.

35. Rozin, 1988a: 150.

36. Frazer, 1935, 1: 52–54, 174–219.

37. For sources on the concern with purity and impurity among various ancient peoples, see note 535 in the chapter on pork.

38. Nilsson, 1949: 83.

39. H. N. C. Stevenson, 1954: 50ff.

40. Mathur, 1964: 100.

41. Walker, 1968, 2: 259.

42. Frazer, 1935, 1: 52–174.

43. Tambiah, 1969: 441, 456.

44. N. K. Panikkar, pers. comm.

45. Crooke, 1885.

46. *Indian Notes and Queries*, 1886.

47. Eichinger Ferro-Luzzi, 1973b: 260.

48. Angyal, 1941: 401–3, 408–9.

49. E. Leach, 1964.

50. This matter requires further ethnographic investigation, but it is clear that not all human groups have such qualms. The Hadza of Tanzania, for example, do reject the flesh of certain animals (e.g., lizard and snake), but will eat that of predators or scavengers such as the lion and leopard, jackal, hyena, and vulture (Woodburn, 1968: 52).

51. Rozin and Fallon, 1987.

52. R. Parker, 1983: 360–63.

53. Hippocrates *Sacred Disease* 2.1–20.

54. Moffatt, 1979: 114–15. See also Srinivas, 1955: 20. For other ways in which concern with the impurity of feces affects behavior among members of a Brahmin caste in South India, see Harper, 1964: 169.

55. Concern with the purity of flesh foods is particularly important among Tamil women at puberty and after giving birth, as with certain new mothers who avoid chickenflesh because of the scavenging habits of chickens. The fear is that impurity will be passed on to an infant by means of the milk of its mother (Eichinger Ferro-Luzzi, 1973a: 165, 169–70; Eichinger Ferro-Luzzi, 1974: 9, 14–15).

56. Meigs, 1978: 306, 310.

57. Walker, 1968, 2: 341; and Harper, 1964: 156. Walker and Harper also note interesting nonfood manifestations of Hindu concern with the impurity of saliva. Prominent among them are the ritual rinsing of one's mouth intended to get rid of saliva, the widespread practice of clearing one's throat and spitting from time to time, of smoking cigarettes or *bīdis* (leaf-wrapped tobacco) through one's hand so that they do not come into direct contact with one's lips, and the strong dislike of wind instruments because the mouthpiece, wet with saliva, regularly touches one's lips.

58. Walker, 1968, 2: 341; Khare, 1976: 105, 108–9; Eichinger Ferro-Luzzi, 1977a: 357–59; Eichinger Ferro-Luzzi, 1981: 254; Eichinger Ferro-Luzzi, 1985b: 493. Exceptions to the taboo on saliva and leavings (for children and lovers) are mentioned by Ramanujan (1992: 236–37).

59. By Putumaippitan, cited by Eichinger Ferro-Luzzi, 1985b: 493.

60. Eichinger Ferro-Luzzi, 1977a: 357–58.

61. Harper, 1964: 158 and n.

62. In South India, the sole ritual offering of leavings known to Eichinger Ferro-Luzzi (1977a: 358–59) involves food offerings intended for the ancestors. Because the ancestors are associated with death, their food offerings, unlike the *prasāda* of the higher gods, are impure. Thus, families ordinarily offer them ritually to crows, whether initially or afterwards. This is quite appropriate, for crows are also associated with death and are impure animals, and in everyday life they are "the most voracious devourers of leavings." Curiously at odds with the above, however, is the practice of feeding the ancestors' food to cows (Eichinger Ferro-Luzzi, 1981: 262), an animal whose purity exceeds that of any human.

63. For interesting observations on bodily fluids and emanations of Hindu gods, see Eichinger Ferro-Luzzi, 1987: 30–34. Because of the high ritual status of gods, their bodily fluids and emanations, however much people may want to overlook certain of them, are pure. Eichinger Ferro-Luzzi does, however, cite one case in which the general impurity of emanations seems to have influenced the writer of a myth. In the myth in question, Vishnu was building a tank at Benares, but it was holy water rather than sweat that exuded from his body to fill the tank.

64. For *prasāda*, the leavings of a deity, and their use in North India, see Khare, 1976: 98–105. For more on this subject, see Moreno, 1992.

65. Eichinger Ferro-Luzzi, 1977a: 357–58; Eichinger Ferro-Luzzi, 1985b: 498–99.

66. Walker, 1968, 2: 341.

67. Emissions and other impure substances are not always unwanted, for, as we have seen, they may be sought out for ritual, medicinal, and other uses. See also E. Leach, 1964; and Meigs, 1978: 313–14.

68. Meigs, 1978: 312–14, 316–17.

69. For references to this, see Schwabe, 1993.

70. R. Parker, 1983: 360–63.

71. For an excellent account of death and the impurity of untouchables in Gujarat, see Randeria, 1990.

72. Srinivas, 1955: 20.

73. Hutton, 1963: 255.

74. Milne, 1924: 192–93.

75. Waddell, 1939: 567–68; Bell, 1928: 218; MacDonald, 1929: 177.

76. Westermarck, 1924, 2: 493.

77. Detienne, 1989a: 8–9, 12.

78. A. I. Richards, 1939: 64–65.

79. Hearne, 1795: 204–6.

80. Tambiah, 1969: 437–38. Tambiah likens the rules against ritually killing such household animals to the prohibitions involving sex and marriage within the family.

81. Hickey, 1960: 164–65.

82. Though classifications of foods as hot and cold (more appropriately heating and cooling) are ancient and widespread in the Old World and of considerable interest

to dieticians, nutritionists, and students of human culture, it has not been determined whether chickenflesh and eggs and other flesh foods are each classified in the same way by various peoples across substantial parts of the Old World. To determine this would be a study in its own right, and here I would note only similarities in hot-cold classifications of peoples as distant from each other as Malays and Gujaratis, both of whom classify eggs and chicken, like meat, alcohol, and most spices, as hot (Laderman, 1983: 45; Pool 1987: 390). For background on hot and cold foods in North India, see Khare, 1976: 82–86. For an excellent collection of recent articles on manifestations of the hot-cold food concept around the world, edited by Lenore Manderson, see the special issue of *Social Science and Medicine* (25, no. 4, 1987) entitled "Hot-cold food and medical theories: Cross-cultural perspectives."

83. Douglas, 1966: 29.
84. Douglas, 1966: 34–40.
85. Spencer and Gillen, 1904: 164, 166, 283, 291.
86. Athenaeus *Deipnosophists* 7.299.
87. Ekvall, 1939: 60.
88. Rozin and Fallon, 1987: 26.
89. Strabo *Geography* 16.4.7–14.
90. M. C. Yang, 1945: 32–35.
91. Headland, 1914: 174.
92. Browning, 1986: 1.
93. Milne, 1924: 195.
94. A Huana man, if observed eating a frog, would be laughed at contemptuously (Torday and Joyce, 1905: 403).
95. See also de Garine, 1991: 57.
96. Vayda, 1987: 507–8.
97. te Velde, 1977: 74–80.
98. Dr. Kamta Prasad Jain, quoted in Davidson and Gross, 1960: 8.
99. Stefansson, 1920: 543.
100. Differences among college students need further investigation, for Otis (1984) found a significant positive correlation between age and willingness to try new foods in her study of forty-two college students who were from seventeen to fifty years old. One possible explanation, she suggests, is that older university students tend to be especially "curious and adventurous."
101. Rozin and Fallon, 1987: 33–35; Rozin, 1988b: 182.
102. Rozin, 1988b: 169.
103. C. DuBois, 1941: 276.
104. Fortes and Fortes, 1936.
105. Trant, 1954: 704.
106. Jochelson, 1926: 417.
107. Masuoka, 1945: 763.
108. Masuoka, 1945: 759.
109. Rozin, 1982, 1983.
110. Spices and flavorings, of course, have histories of their own. The tomato

arrived in Italy only after discovery of the New World, yet now it is an essential component in a flavor principle identified with Italy. Equally striking is the case of chili peppers, also of New World origin, which have become essential elements in various other cuisines around the world. This came about despite the fact that, as Rozin and Schiller (1980; and Rozin, 1990a) have noted, infant humans initially reject chili, and develop a liking and preference for it only after years of exposure.

111. Rozin, 1982: 197.

REFERENCES

Abadie, Maurice. 1924. *Les Races du Haut-Tonkin de Phong-Tho à Lang-Son.* Paris: Société d'éditions géographiques, maritimes et coloniales.

Abbie, A. A. 1969. *The original Australians.* London: Frederick Muller.

Adolph, William H. 1956. "What early man discovered about food." *Harper's Magazine* 1: 67–70.

Aelian. 1958–59. *On the characteristics of animals.* 3 vols. Trans. A. F. Scholfield. Loeb Classical Library. London: William Heinemann; Cambridge, Mass.: Harvard University Press.

Afshar, Mahasti Ziai. 1990. *The immortal hound: The genesis and transformation of a symbol in Indo-Iranian traditions.* Harvard Dissertations in Folklore and Oral Tradition. New York and London: Garland Publishing.

Agrawal, D. P. 1971. *The Copper Bronze Age in India.* New Delhi: Munshiram Manoharlal.

Agrawal, D. P. 1982. *The archaeology of India.* Scandinavian Institute of Asian Studies, Monograph Series, 46. London and Malmö: Curzon.

Aharoni, Yohanan. 1982. *The archaeology of the land of Israel.* Trans. Anson F. Rainey. Philadelphia: Westminster.

Ahlström, Gösta W. 1986. *Who were the Israelites?* Winona Lake, Ind.: Eisenbrauns.

Albright, William Foxwell. 1933. *The archaeology of Palestine and the Bible.* Second edition. New York: Fleming H. Revell.

Albright, William Foxwell. 1939. "The Israelite conquest of Canaan in the light of archaeology." *Bulletin of the American Schools of Oriental Research* 74: 11–23.

Albright, William Foxwell. 1957. *From the Stone Age to Christianity.* Second edition. Garden City, N.Y.: Doubleday.

437

Albright, William Foxwell. 1966. "The Amarna letters from Palestine"; "Syria, the Philistines and Phoenicia." Fascicle 51, consisting of Chapters 20 and 33 of Vol. 2 of *The Cambridge Ancient History.* Revised edition. Cambridge: Cambridge University Press.

Albright, William Foxwell. 1968. *Yahweh and the gods of Canaan.* Garden City, N.Y.: Doubleday.

Alcock, Joan P. 1980. "Classical religious belief and burial practice in Roman Britain." *Archaeological Journal* 137: 50–85.

Aldred, Cyril. 1961. *The Egyptians.* New York: Frederick A. Praeger.

Ali, Fadhil A. 1966. "Dedication of a dog to Nintinugga." *Archiv Orientální* 34: 289–92.

Allchin, Bridget, and Raymond Allchin. 1982. *The rise of civilization in India and Pakistan.* Cambridge, London, New York: Cambridge University Press.

Allchin, F. R. 1969. "Early domestic animals in India and Pakistan." Pp. 317–22 in Peter J. Ucko and G. W. Dimbleby (eds.), *The domestication and exploitation of plants and animals.* Chicago: Aldine.

Allen, B. C. 1912. *Dacca.* Eastern Bengal District Gazetteers, 5. Allahabad: Pioneer.

Allen, Glover M. 1919–20. "Dogs of the American aborigines." *Bulletin of the Museum of Comparative Zoology at Harvard* 63: 431–517.

Alsdorf, Ludwig. 1961. "Beiträge zur Geschichte von Vegetarismus und Rinderverehrung in Indien." *Akademie der Wissenschaften und der Literatur, Mainz; Abhandlungen, Geistes- und Socialwissenschaften Klasse* 1961: 559–625.

Alsop, Gulielma F. 1918. *My Chinese days.* Boston: Little, Brown.

Alt, Albrecht. 1967. "The settlement of the Israelites in Palestine." Pp. 173–221 in his *Essays on Old Testament history and religion.* Trans. R. A. Wilson. Garden City, N.Y.: Doubleday.

Ambedkar, B. R. 1948. *The untouchables.* New Delhi: Amrit Book Company.

Ancelle, T., J. Dupouy-Camet, M. E. Bougnoux, V. Fourestie, H. Petit, G. Mougeot, J. P. Nozais, and J. Lapierre. 1988. "Two outbreaks of trichinosis caused by horsemeat in France in 1985." *American Journal of Epidemiology* 127: 1302–11.

Anderson, Eugene N., Jr. 1969. "Sacred Fish." *Man* (n.s.) 4: 443–49.

Anderson, Eugene N., Jr. 1988. *The food of China.* New Haven and London: Yale University Press.

Anderson, Eugene N., Jr., and Marja L. Anderson. 1968. "Folk medicine in rural Hong Kong." *Ethnoiatria* 2: 22–28.

Anderson, Eugene N., Jr., and Marja L. Anderson. 1977. "Modern China: South." Pp. 319–82 in K. C. Chang (ed.), *Food in Chinese culture: Anthropological and historical perspectives.* New Haven: Yale University Press.

Anderson, R. G. 1911. "Some tribal customs in their relation to medicine and morals of the Nyam-nyam and Gour people inhabiting the eastern Bahr-el-Ghazal." *Fourth Report of the Wellcome Tropical Research Laboratories at the Gordon Memorial College, Khartoum.* B: 239–77. London: Ballière, Tindall, and Cox.

André, Jacques. 1961. *L'Alimentation et la cuisine à Rome.* Paris: Librairie C. Klincksieck.

Andrus, J. Russell. 1943. *Preliminary survey of the economy of French Indochina.* Washington, D.C.: Bureau of Foreign and Domestic Commerce, Far Eastern Unit.

Andrus, J. Russell. 1947. *Burmese economic life.* Stanford: Stanford University Press.

Angyal, A. 1941. "Disgust and related aversions." *Journal of Abnormal and Social Psychology* 36: 393–412.

Anthony, David W. 1986. "The 'Kurgan culture,' Indo-European origins, and the domestication of the horse: A reconsideration." *Current Anthropology* 27: 291–313.

Anthony, David W. 1991a. "The archaeology of Indo-European origins." *Journal of Indo-European Studies* 19: 193–222.

Anthony, David W. 1991b. "The domestication of the horse." Pp. 250–77 in Vol. 2 of Richard H. Meadow and Hans-Peter Uerpmann (eds.), *Equids in the ancient world.* Wiesbaden: Dr. Ludwig Reichert.

Anthony, David W., and Dorcas R. Brown. 1989. "Looking a gift horse in the mouth: Identification of the earliest bitted equids and the microscopic analysis of wear." Pp. 98–116 in Pam J. Crabtree, Douglas Campana, and Kathleen Ryan (eds.), *Early animal domestication and its cultural context.* MASCA Research Papers in Science and Archaeology, Special Supplement to Vol. 6. Philadelphia: MASCA, The University Museum of Archaeology and Anthropology, University of Pennsylvania.

Anthony, David W., and Dorcas R. Brown. 1991. "The origins of horseback riding." *Antiquity* 65: 22–38.

Anuman-Rajadhon, P. 1953. *Loy Krathong and Songkran Festival.* Thailand Culture Series, 5. Bangkok: National Culture Institute.

Apuleius. 1989. *Metamorphoses.* 2 vols. Ed. and trans. J. Arthur Hanson. Loeb Classical Library. London and Cambridge, Mass.: Harvard University Press.

Ardener, Edwin. 1956. *Coastal Bantu of the Cameroons.* Ethnographic Survey of Africa. Western Africa, Part 11. London: International African Institute.

Argenti, Philip P., and H. J. Rose. 1949. *The folk-lore of Chios.* 2 vols. Cambridge: Cambridge University Press.

Århem, Kaj. 1989. "Maasai food symbolism: The cultural connotations of milk, meat, and blood in the pastoral Maasai diet." *Anthropos* 84: 1–23.

Aristophanes. 1911. *The Lysistrata.* Trans. Benjamin Bickley Rogers as *The Lysistrata of Aristophanes.* London: G. Bell and Sons.

Aristophanes. 1930. *The Knights.* Trans. Benjamin Bickley Rogers as *The Knights of Aristophanes.* London: G. Bell and Sons.

Aristophanes. 1955. *The Plutus.* Pp. 364–467 in Vol. 3 of *Aristophanes,* trans. Benjamin Bickley Rogers. Loeb Classical Library. London: William Heinemann; Cambridge, Mass.: Harvard University Press.

Aristophanes. 1957. *The Birds.* Trans. Dudley Fitts. New York: Harcourt, Brace.

Aristophanes. 1980. *The Acharnians.* Vol. 1 of *The Comedies of Aristophanes,* trans. Alan H. Sommerstein. Warminster, Wilts, England: Aris and Phillips.

Armstrong, W. E. 1928. *Rossel Island.* Cambridge: Cambridge University Press.

Arnaud, Robert. 1906. "Chasseurs et pêcheurs du Tagant et du Hodh." *La Géographie* 13: 148–49.

Arrian. 1983. *Indica.* Pp. 305–433 in Vol. 2 of *Arrian,* trans. P. A. Brunt. Loeb

Classical Library. London: William Heinemann; Cambridge, Mass.: Harvard University Press.

Artemidorus Daldianus. 1975. *The interpretation of dreams, Oneirocritica.* Trans. Robert J. White. Park Ridge, N.J.: Noyes.

Ashton, Edmund Hugh. 1939. "A sociological sketch of Sotho diet." *Transactions of the Royal Society of South Africa* 27: 147–214.

Ashton, Edmund Hugh. 1952. *The Basuto.* London: Oxford University Press.

Athenaeus. 1854. *The Deipnosophists.* 3 vols. Trans. C. D. Yonge. London: Henry G. Bohn.

Awasthi, Dilip. 1992. "Cattle-trading: Making a killing." *India Today,* North American Special Edition (July 31): 42–43.

Ayyar, L. K. Anantakrishna. 1926. *Anthropology of the Syrian Christians.* Ernakulam: Cochin Government Press.

Azab, M. E., T. M. Morsy, T. M. Abdel-Aal, E. H. Safar, S. S. Makaram, H. M. El Hady, and A. A. Kamel. 1988. "Current prevalence of trichinosis in pigs in Egypt." *Journal of the Egyptian Society of Parasitology* 18: 383–90.

Bacon, Elizabeth E. 1966. *Central Asians under Russian rule.* Ithaca, N.Y.: Cornell University Press.

Badam, G. L. 1984. "Holocene faunal material from India with special reference to domesticated animals." Pp. 339–53 in Juliet Clutton-Brock and Caroline Grigson (eds.), *Animals and archaeology.* Vol. 3, *Early herders and their flocks.* BAR International Series, 202. Oxford: British Archaeological Reports.

Badger, George Percy. 1852. *The Nestorians and their rituals.* 2 vols. London: Joseph Masters.

Bahn, Paul G. 1984. "Preneolithic control of animals in western Europe: The faunal evidence." Pp. 27–34 in Caroline Grigson and Juliet Clutton-Brock (eds.), *Animals and archaeology.* Vol. 4, *Husbandry in Europe.* BAR International Series, 227. Oxford: British Archaeological Reports.

Bailey, Flora. 1940. "Navaho foods and cooking methods." *American Anthropologist* 42: 270–90.

Baker, John R. 1929. *Man and animals in the New Hebrides.* London: George Routledge and Sons.

Baker, Samuel W. 1867. *The Nile tributaries of Abyssinia.* Philadelphia: J. B. Lippincott.

Baluchistan District Gazetteer Series. 1906–8. 9 vols. Bombay: Government of India Press.

Baly, Denis. 1957. *The geography of the Bible. A study in historical geography.* New York, Evanston, and London: Harper and Row.

Baly, Denis. 1963. *Geographical companion to the Bible.* New York, Toronto, London: McGraw-Hill.

Banerji, Sures Chandra. 1980. *Flora and fauna in Sanskrit literature.* Calcutta: Naya Prokash.

Banister, Judith. 1987. *China's changing population.* Stanford: Stanford University Press.

Barakat, R. M., M. F. El-Sawy, M. K. Selim, and A. Rashwan. 1982. "Trichinosis in some carnivores and rodents from Alexandria, Egypt." *Journal of the Egyptian Society of Parasitology* 12: 445–51.

Barnett, R. D. 1985. "Lachish, Ashkelon and the camel: A discussion of its use in southern Palestine." Pp. 15–30 in Jonathan N. Tubb (ed.), *Palestine in the Bronze and Iron Ages: Papers in honour of Olga Tufnell.* Occasional Publications, 11. London: Institute of Archaeology.

Barguet, Paul (ed.). 1967. *Le Livre des morts des anciens Égyptiens.* Paris: Éditions du Cerf.

Bartholomew, Mary Jo, and Frances E. Poston. 1970. "Effect of food taboos on prenatal nutrition." *Journal of Nutrition Education* 2: 15–17.

Barton, Roy Franklin. 1922. "Ifugao economics." *University of California Publications in American Archaeology and Ethnology* 15, 5: 385–446.

Bascom, William R. 1951. "Yoruba food." *Africa* 21: 41–53.

Basedow, Herbert. 1925. *The Australian Aboriginal.* Adelaide: F. W. Preece and Sons.

Basham, Arthur L. 1954. *The wonder that was India.* London: Sidgwick and Jackson.

Batchelor, John. 1901. *The Ainu and their folk-lore.* London: Religious Tract Society.

Bates, Marston. 1957–58. "Man, food, and sex." *American Scholar* 27: 449–58.

Bates, Oric. 1914. *The eastern Libyans.* London: Macmillan.

Bates, Oric. 1917. "Ancient Egyptian fishing." *Harvard African Studies* 1: 199–271.

Baudesson, Henry. 1919. *Indo-China and its primitive people.* London: Hutchinson.

Baum, Julius. 1956. "Symbolic representations of the Eucharist." Pp. 261–73 in Joseph Campbell (ed.), *The mysteries.* Papers from the Eranos Yearbooks. Bollingen Series, 30, 2. New York: Bollingen Foundation.

Baumann, H., and D. Westermann. 1948. *Les Peuples et les civilisations de l'Afrique suivi de les langues et l'éducation.* Trans. into French by L. Homburger. Paris: Payot.

Baxter, P. T. W., and Audrey Butt. 1953. *The Azande, and related peoples of the Anglo-Egyptian Sudan and Belgian Congo.* Ethnographic Survey of Africa. East Central Africa, Part 9. London: International African Institute.

Beaglehole, Ernest, and Pearl Beaglehole. 1938. *Ethnology of Pukapuka.* Bernice P. Bishop Museum, Bull. 150. Honolulu.

Beal, Samuel. 1958. *Chinese accounts of India.* 4 vols. Calcutta: Susil Gupta.

Beardsley, Richard K., J. W. Hall, and R. E. Ward. 1959. *Village Japan.* Chicago: University of Chicago Press.

Beck, J. Walter. 1970. "Trichinosis in domesticated and experimental animals." Pp. 61–80 in Sylvester E. Gould (ed.), *Trichinosis in man and animals.* Springfield, Ill.: Charles C. Thomas.

Beech, Mervin Worcester Howard. 1911. *The Suk, their language and folklore.* Oxford: Clarendon.

Beemer, Hilda. 1939. "Notes on the diet of the Swazi in the Protectorate." *Bantu Studies* 13: 199–236.

Belcher, William R. 1991. "Fish resources in an early urban context at Harappa." Pp. 107–20 in Richard H. Meadow (ed.), *Harappa excavations 1986–1990: A multidisciplinary approach to third millennium urbanism.* Monographs in World Archaeology, 3. Madison, Wis.: Prehistory Press.

Belding, David Lawrence. 1958. *Basic clinical parasitology.* New York: Appleton-Century-Crofts.

Belgrave, James H. D. 1953. *Welcome to Bahrain.* Stourbridge, England: Published privately.

Bell, Charles. 1928. *The people of Tibet.* Oxford: Clarendon.

Bell, Charles. 1931. *The religion of Tibet.* Oxford: Clarendon.

Bell, Charles. 1946. *Portrait of the Dalai Lama.* London: Collins.

Bellew, H. W. 1862. *Journal of a political mission to Afghanistan in 1857.* London: Smith, Elder.

Benecke, Norbert. 1987. "Studies on early dog remains from northern Europe." *Journal of Archaeological Science* 14: 31–49.

Bennett, John W. 1967. "On the cultural ecology of Indian cattle." *Current Anthropology* 8: 251–52.

Bennett, John W. 1971. "Comments" [on Alan Heston's "An approach to the sacred cow of India"]. *Current Anthropology* 12: 197–98.

Bernatzik, Hugo A. 1954. *Die neue grosse Völkerkunde.* 3 vols. Frankfurt: Herkul G.M.B.H.

Bernolles, Jacques. 1968. "À la poursuite du Chien de la Mort d'Asie steppique en Occident et en Afrique noire." *Revue de l'historie des religions* 173: 43–84.

Bertholet, Alfred. 1926. *A history of Hebrew civilization.* Trans. A. K. Dallas. London, Calcutta, Sydney: George G. Harrap.

Bertholon, L. 1897. "Ethnologie de l'île de Gerba." Part 2 of "Exploration anthropologique de l'île de Gerba." *L'Anthropologie* 8: 539–83.

Bertin, Léon. 1954. "Les Poissons du Nil au temps des pharaons." *La Revue française de l'élite européenne* 54: 35–40.

Bertrand, Gabrielle. 1958. *Secret lands where women reign.* London: Robert Hale Limited.

Besançon, Jacques. 1957. *L'Homme et le Nil.* Third edition. Géographie humaine, 28. Paris: Gallimard.

Bessonov, A. S. 1985. "Trichinellosis in the USSR, 1979–1983." Pp. 256–62 in Charles W. Kim, E. Joost Ruitenberg, and Jacob S. Teppema (eds.), *Trichinellosis.* Proceedings of the Sixth International Conference on Trichinellosis, July 8–12, 1984. Albany: State University of New York Press.

Best, Elsdon. 1924. *The Maori.* Vol. 2. Wellington, New Zealand: Board of Maori Ethnological Research.

Bevan, Elinor. 1986. *Representations of animals in sanctuaries of Artemis and other Olympian deities.* 2 parts. BAR International Series, 315. Oxford: British Archaeological Reports.

Bhagwat, Durga. 1944. "A pig festival in the Central Provinces." *Man in India* 24: 89–99.

Bhawe, Shrikrishna. 1939. *Die Yajus des Aśvamedha; Versuch einer Rekonstruktion dieses Abschnittes des Yajurveda auf Grund der Überlieferung seiner fünf Schulen.* Bonner orientalistiche Studien, 25. Stuttgart: W. Kohlhammer.

Bibikova, V. I. 1969. "Do istorii domestykatsii konja na pivdennomu skhodi Evropy." *Arkheologija* (Kiev) 22: 55–66. (Trans. in Telegin, 1986: 163–80.)

Biddulph, J. 1880. *Tribes of the Hindoo Kush*. Calcutta: Office of the Superintendent of Government Printing.

Biscoe, C. E. Tyndale. 1922. *Kashmir in sunlight and shade*. London: Seeley, Service.

Biswas, P. C. 1956. *Santals of the Santal Parganas*. Delhi: Bharatiya Adimjati Sevak Sangh.

Blackman, Winifred S. 1927. *The fellahin of Upper Egypt*. London: George G. Harrap.

Blackwood, Beatrice. 1935. *Both sides of Buka Passage*. Oxford: Clarendon.

Blair, Russell. 1956. "The food habits of the East Slavs." Unpublished Ph.D. dissertation, University of Pennsylvania.

Bliss, Frederick Jones. 1912. *The religions of modern Syria and Palestine*. New York: Charles Scribner's Sons.

Blondheim, D. S., R. Klein, G. Ben-Dror, and G. Schick. 1984. "Trichinosis in southern Lebanon." *Israel Journal of Medical Science* 20: 141–44.

Bloomfield, Maurice. 1905. *Cerberus, the dog of Hades: The history of an idea*. Chicago: Open Court; London: Kegan Paul, Trench, Trübner.

Blunt, E. A. H. 1931. *The caste system of northern India*. London: Oxford University Press.

Bodenheimer, F. S. 1960. *Animal and man in Bible lands*. Collection de travaux de l'Académie internationale d'histoire des sciences, 10. Leiden: E. J. Brill.

Boessneck, J. 1977. "Die Hundeskelette von Išān Baḥrīyāt (Isin) aus der Zeit um 1000 v. Chr." Pp. 97–109 in B. Hrouda (ed.), *Isin—Išān Baḥrīyāt I*. Bayerische Akademie der Wissenschaften, Philosophisch-Historische Klasse, Abhandlungen, Neue Folge, 79. Munich: Bayerische Akademie der Wissenschaften.

Boessneck, J. 1988. *Die Tierwelt des Alten Ägypten*. Munich: C. H. Beck.

Boessneck, Joachim, and Angela von den Driesch. 1982. *Studien an subfossilen Tierknochen aus Ägypten*. Münchner Ägyptologische Studien, 40. Munich and Berlin: Deutscher Kunstverlag.

Boessneck, Joachim, J.-P. Jéquier, and H. R. Stampfli. 1963. *Seeberg, Burgäschisee-Sud; Die Tierreste*. Acta Bernensia, 2, 3. Bern: Stämpfli und Cie.

Boettger, Caesar Rudolf. 1958. *Die Haustiere Afrikas*. Jena: Gustav Fischer.

Bogoras, Waldemar. 1904–9. *The Chukchee: Material culture, religion, social organization*. American Museum of Natural History, Memoirs, 11. Leiden: E. J. Brill; New York: G. E. Stechert.

Bogucki, Peter. 1988. *Forest farmers and stockherders: Early agriculture and its consequences in North-Central Europe*. Cambridge, New York, New Rochelle, Melbourne, Sydney: Cambridge University Press.

Bogucki, Peter. 1989. "The exploitation of domestic animals in Neolithic Central Europe." Pp. 118–34 in Pam J. Crabtree, Douglas Campana, and Kathleen Ryan (eds.), *Early animal domestication and its cultural context*. MASCA Research Papers in Science and Archaeology, Special Supplement to Vol. 6. Philadelphia: MASCA, The University Museum of Archaeology and Anthropology, University of Pennsylvania.

Bökönyi, Sándor. 1974. *History of domestic mammals in Central and Eastern Europe*. Budapest: Akadémiai Kladó.

Bökönyi, Sándor. 1975. "Vlasac: An early site of dog domestication." Pp. 167–78 in A. T. Clason (ed.), *Archaeozoological studies*. Amsterdam and Oxford: North-Holland; New York: American Elsevier.

Bökönyi, Sándor. 1978. "The earliest waves of domestic horses in east Europe." *Journal of Indo-European Studies* 6: 17–64.

Bökönyi, Sándor. 1984. "Horse." Pp. 162–73 in Ian L. Mason (ed.), *Evolution of domesticated animals*. London and New York: Longman.

Bökönyi, Sándor. 1987. "Horses and sheep in east Europe in the Copper and Bronze Ages." Pp. 136–44 in Susan Nacev Skomal and Edgar G. Polomé (eds.), *Proto-Indo-European: The archaeology of a linguistic problem. Studies in honor of Marija Gimbutas*. Washington, D.C.: Institute for the Study of Man.

Bolton, J. M. 1972. "Food taboos among the Orang Asli in West Malaysia: A potential nutritional hazard." *American Journal of Clinical Nutrition* 25: 789–99.

Bommer, W., H. Kaiser, W. Mannweiler, H. Mergerian, and G. Pottkämper. 1985. "An outbreak of trichinellosis in northern Germany caused by imported air-dried meat from Egypt." Pp. 314–17 in Charles W. Kim et al. (eds.), *Trichinellosis*. Proceedings of the Sixth International Conference on Trichinellosis, July 8–12, 1984. Albany: State University of New York Press.

Boniface. 1940. *The letters of St. Boniface*. Trans. Ephraim Emerton. New York: Columbia University Press.

Borowski, Oded. 1987. *Agriculture in Iron Age Israel*. Winona Lake, Ind.: Eisenbrauns.

Bosworth, Clifford Edmund. 1963. *The Ghaznavids; their empire in Afghanistan and eastern Iran, 944–1040*. Edinburgh: University Press.

Bourke-Borrowes, D. 1931. "The dog temple at Peking." *Journal of the Royal Central Asian Society* 18: 256–57.

Bowdich, Thomas Edward. 1819. *Mission from Cape Coast Castle to Ashantee*. London: John Murray.

Boxer, C. R. 1953. *South China in the sixteenth century*. Hakluyt Society Works, second series, 106. London: Hakluyt Society.

Boyle, John Andrew. 1963. "Kirakos of Ganjak on the Mongols." *Central Asiatic Journal* 8: 199–214.

Boyle, John Andrew. 1965. "A form of horse sacrifice amongst the 13th- and 14th-century Mongols." *Central Asiatic Journal* 10: 145–50.

Branston, Brian. 1974. *The lost gods of England*. New York: Oxford University Press.

Breasted, James Henry. 1906–7. *Ancient records of Egypt*. 5 vols. Chicago: University of Chicago Press.

Breeks, James Wilkinson. 1873. *An account of the primitive tribes and monuments of the Nilagiris*. London: India Museum.

Bremmer, Jan. 1987. "Poseidon." Pp. 457–58 in Vol. 11 of Mircea Eliade (ed.), *The encyclopedia of religion*. 16 vols. New York: Macmillan; London: Collier Macmillan.

Brenan, Gerald. 1957. *South from Granada*. New York: Farrar, Straus and Cudahy.

Briard, Jacques. 1979. *The Bronze Age in barbarian Europe*. Trans. Mary Turton. London, Boston, and Henley: Routledge and Kegan Paul.

Briggs, George W. 1920. *The Chamars*. Calcutta: Association Press.

Briggs, Lloyd Cabot. 1958. *The living races of the Sahara Desert*. Harvard University, Peabody Museum of American Archaeology and Ethnology, Papers, Vol. 28, No. 2. Cambridge, Mass.

Briggs, Lloyd Cabot. 1967. *Tribes of the Sahara*. Cambridge, Mass.: Harvard University Press.

Brooke, Clarke. 1987. "Sacred slaughter: The sacrificing of animals at the Hajj and Id al-Adha." *Journal of Cultural Geography* 7, 2 (Spring/Summer): 67–88.

Broomhall, Marshall. 1910. *Islam in China*. London: Morgan and Scott, and China Inland Mission.

Broshi, Magen, and Israel Finkelstein. 1992. "The population of Palestine in Iron Age II." *Bulletin of the American Schools of Oriental Research* 287: 47–60.

Brothwell, Don, and Patricia Brothwell. 1969. *Food in antiquity: A survey of the diet of early peoples*. New York and Washington, D.C.: Frederick A. Praeger.

Brown, Susan Drucker. 1992. "Horse, dog, and donkey: The making of a Mamprusi king." *Man* (n.s.) 27: 71–90.

Brown, W. Norman. 1957. "The sanctity of the cow in Hinduism." *Madras University Journal* 28: 29–49.

Browning, E. S. 1986. "Unhappy returns: After living abroad, Japanese find it hard to adjust back home." *Wall Street Journal* (Western edition), May 6, pp. 1, 24.

Bruce, James. 1790. *Travels to discover the source of the Nile, in the years 1768, 1769, 1770, 1771, 1772, and 1773*. 5 vols. London: G. G. J. and J. Robinson.

Bryant, Alfred T. 1949. *The Zulu people*. Pietermaritzburg: Shuter and Shooter.

Bryson, Reid A., and David A. Baerreis. 1967. "Possibilities of major climatic modification and their implications: Northwest India, a case for study." *Bulletin of the American Meterological Society* 48: 136–42.

Bryson, Reid A., and Thomas J. Murray. 1977. *Climates of hunger: Mankind and the world's changing weather*. Madison and London: University of Wisconsin Press.

Buck, John Lossing. 1930. *Chinese farm economy: A study of 2866 farms in seventeen localities and seven provinces in China*. Chicago: University of Chicago Press.

Buck, John Lossing. 1956. "Livestock and fertility maintenance." Pp. 245–66 in John Lossing Buck (ed.), *Land utilization in China*. Facsimile reprint of the 1937 edition published by the University of Nanking. New York: Council on Economic and Cultural Affairs.

Buck, Peter H. 1930. *Samoan material culture*. Bernice P. Bishop Museum, Bull. 75. Honolulu.

Buck, Peter H. 1932. *Ethnology of Manihiki and Rakahanga*. Bernice P. Bishop Museum, Bull. 99. Honolulu.

Buck, Peter H. 1938a. *Ethnology of Mangareva*. Bernice P. Bishop Museum, Bull. 157. Honolulu.

Buck, Peter H. 1938b. *Vikings of the sunrise*. New York: Frederick A. Stokes.

Buck, Peter H. 1944. *Arts and crafts of the Cook Islands*. Bernice P. Bishop Museum, Bull. 179. Honolulu.

Buck, Peter H. 1950a. *Material culture of Kapingamarangi*. Bernice P. Bishop Museum, Bull. 200. Honolulu.

Buck, Peter H. 1950b. *The coming of the Maori*. Wellington: Maori Purposes Fund Board.

Budge, E. A. Wallis. 1895. *The Book of the Dead: The Papyrus of Ani in the British Museum*. London: British Museum.

Budge, E. A. Wallis. 1904. *The gods of the Egyptians*. 2 vols. London: Methuen; Chicago: Open Court.

Budge, E. A. Wallis. 1907. *The Egyptian Sûdân*. 2 vols. London: Trübner.

Budge, E. A. Wallis. 1928. *A history of Ethiopia*. 2 vols. London: Methuen.

Budge, E. A. Wallis. 1960. *The Book of the Dead*. English translation of the chapters, hymns, etc., of the Theban recension. Second edition. 3 vols. in one. London: Routledge and Kegan Paul.

Bühler, George (trans.). 1882. *The sacred laws of the Âryas, as taught in the schools of Âpastamba, Gautama, Vâsishtha, and Baudhâyana*. Part 2, *Vâsishtha and Baudhâyana*. Vol. 14 of *The sacred books of the East*, ed. F. Max Müller. Oxford: Clarendon.

Bühler, George (trans.). 1886. *The laws of Manu*. Vol. 25 of *The sacred books of the East*, ed. F. Max Müller. Oxford: Clarendon.

Bühler, George (trans.). 1896. *The sacred laws of the Âryas, as taught in the schools of Âpastamba, Gautama, Vâsishtha, and Baudhâyana*. Part 1, *Âpastamba and Gautama*. Vol. 2 of *The sacred books of the East*, ed. F. Max Müller. Second edition. Oxford: Clarendon.

Bulfinch, Thomas. 1898. *The age of fable, or beauties of mythology*. New, revised, and enlarged edition, ed. J. Loughran Scott. Philadelphia: David McKay.

Bulliet, Richard W. 1975. *The camel and the wheel*. Cambridge, Mass.: Harvard University Press.

Bulliet, Richard W. 1978. "Camels, horses, and harnessing in South Asia." Pp. 1–2 in Franklin C. Southworth (ed.), *Symbols, subsistence and social structure: The ecology of man and animal in South Asia*. Philadelphia: South Asia Regional Studies, University of Pennsylvania.

Burckhardt, John Lewis. 1819. *Travels in Nubia*. London: John Murray.

Burckhardt, John Lewis. 1830. *Notes on the Bedouins and Wahábys*. London: Henry Colburn and Richard Bentley.

Burkert, Walter. 1983a. *Homo necans: The anthropology of ancient Greek sacrificial ritual and myth*. Trans. Peter Bing. Berkeley, Los Angeles, London: University of California Press.

Burkert, Walter. 1983b. "Itinerant diviners and magicians: A neglected element in cultural contacts." Pp. 115–19 in Robin Hägg (ed.), *The Greek renaissance of the eighth century B.C.: Tradition and innovation*. Stockholm: Svenska Institutet i Athen.

Burkert, Walter. 1985. *Greek religion*. Trans. John Raffan. Cambridge, Mass.: Harvard University Press.

Burkill, I. H. 1935. *A dictionary of the economic products of the Malay Peninsula*. 2 vols. London: Crown Agents for the Colonies.

Burkitt, F. C. 1925. *The religion of the Manichees*. Cambridge: Cambridge University Press.

Burriss, Eli Edward. 1935. "The place of the dog in superstition as revealed in Latin literature." *Classical Philology* 30: 32–42.

Burrows, Edwin Grant. 1936. *Ethnology of Futuna*. Bernice P. Bishop Museum, Bull. 138. Honolulu.

Burrows, Edwin Grant. 1949. "The people of Ifalik: A little-disturbed atoll culture." Unpublished manuscript submitted as a final report, Coordinated Investigation of Micronesian Anthropology. Washington, D.C.: Pacific Science Board, National Research Council.

Burton, Anne. 1972. *Diodorus Siculus*. Book 1, *A commentary*. Études préliminaires aux religions orientales dans l'empire romain, 29. Leiden: E. J. Brill.

Burton, Richard F. 1893. *Personal narrative of a pilgrimage to Al-Madinah and Meccah*. 2 vols. Memorial edition. London: Tylston and Edwards.

Burton, Richard F. 1894. *First footsteps in East Africa*. 2 vols. London: Tylston and Edwards.

Burton, Robert. 1948. *The anatomy of melancholy*. New York: Tudor.

Bush, Richard J. 1871. *Reindeer, dogs, and snow-shoes: A journal of Siberian travel and explorations*. New York: Harper and Brothers.

Buxton, David. 1950. *Travels in Ethiopia*. New York: Medill McBride.

Buxton, Leonard Halford Dudley. 1929. *China, the land and the people: A human geography*. Oxford: Clarendon.

Caesar, Julius. 1952. *The Gallic War*. Trans. H. J. Edwards. Loeb Classical Library. London: William Heinemann; Cambridge, Mass.: Harvard University Press.

Callaway, Joseph A. 1985. "A new perspective on the hill country settlement of Canaan in Iron Age I." Pp. 31–49 in Jonathan N. Tubb (ed.), *Palestine in the Bronze and Iron Ages: Papers in honour of Olga Tufnell*. Occasional Publications, 11. London: Institute of Archaeology.

Cammann, Schuyler. 1951. *The land of the camel: Tents and temples of Inner Mongolia*. New York: Ronald.

Campbell, Joseph. 1968. *The masks of god: Creative mythology*. New York: Viking.

Campbell, Leroy A. 1968. *Mithraic iconography and ideology*. Études préliminaires aux religions orientales dans l'empire romain, 11. Leiden: E. J. Brill.

Campbell, William C. 1983a. "Epidemiology I: Modes of transmission." Pp. 425–44 in William C. Campbell (ed.), *Trichinella and trichinosis*. New York and London: Plenum.

Campbell, William C. 1983b. "Historical introduction." Pp. 1–30 in William C. Campbell (ed.), *Trichinella and trichinosis*. New York and London: Plenum.

Campbell, William C. 1991. "*Trichinella* in Africa and the *nelsoni* affair." Pp. 83–100 in C. N. L. Macpherson and P. S. Craig (eds.), *Parasitic helminths and zoonoses in Africa*. London: Unwin Hyman.

Campbell, William C., R. B. Griffiths, A. Mantovani, et al. 1988. *Guidelines on surveillance, prevention and control of trichinellosis*. Rome: Isituto superiore di Sanità, WHO Collaborating Centre for Research and Training in Veterinary Public Health.

Canard, Marius. 1952. "L'autobiographie d'un chambellan du Mahdî 'Obeidallâh le Fâṭimide." *Hespéris* 39: 279–329.

Carey, Bertram S., and H. N. Tuck. 1896. *The Chin Hills: A history of the people, our dealings with them, their customs and manners, and a gazetteer of their country*. Vol. 1. Rangoon: Superintendent, Government Printing.

Carnoy, A. J. 1908–26. "Ormazd." Pp. 566–70 in Vol. 9 of James Hastings (ed.), *Encyclopaedia of religion and ethics.* 13 vols. Edinburgh: T and T. Clark.

Carstairs, G. Morris. 1957. *The twice-born: A study of a community of high-caste Hindus.* London: Hogarth Press.

Carter, Jane Burr. 1987. "The masks of Ortheia." *American Journal of Archaeology* 91: 355–83.

Casanowicz, I. M., and Emil G. Hirsch. 1907. "Swine." P. 609 in Vol. 11 of Isidore Singer (ed.), *The Jewish encyclopedia.* 12 vols. New York and London: Funk and Wagnalls.

Casati, Gaetano. 1891. *Ten years in Equatoria and the return with Emin Pasha.* Vol. 1. London and New York: Frederick Warne.

Cato. 1934. *On agriculture.* Pp. 1–156 in *Cato and Varro, De re rustica,* trans. William D. Hooper and H. B. Ash. Loeb Classical Library. London: William Heinemann; Cambridge, Mass.: Harvard University Press.

Cerulli, Ernesta. 1956. *Peoples of south-west Ethiopia and its borderland.* Ethnographic Survey of Africa. North-eastern Africa, Part 3. London: International African Institute.

Chakravarty, Chintaharan. 1932. "Cultural significance of fish in Bengal." *Man in India* 12: 191–92.

Chakravarty, Taponath. 1959. *Food and drink in ancient Bengal.* Calcutta: Firma K. L. Mukhopadhyay.

Chamberlain, Basil Hall. 1905. *Things Japanese.* Fifth edition. London: John Murray.

Chandler, Asa Crawford. 1955. *Introduction to parasitology.* Ninth edition. New York: John Wiley and Sons.

Chang, Kwang-chih. 1977. "Ancient China." Pp. 23–52 in K. C. Chang (ed.), *Food in Chinese culture: Anthropological and historical perspectives.* New Haven and London: Yale University Press.

Chang, Kwang-chih. 1980. *Shang civilization.* New Haven and London: Yale University Press.

Chang, Kwang-chih. 1986. *The archaeology of ancient China.* Fourth edition. New Haven and London: Yale University Press.

Chard, Chester S. 1974. *Northeast Asia in prehistory.* Madison: University of Wisconsin Press.

Cheesman, R. E. 1926. *In unknown Arabia.* London: Macmillan.

Cheesman, R. E. 1936. *Lake Tana and the Blue Nile.* London: Macmillan.

Cheyne, T. K. 1899–1903. "Cock." Cols. 855–56 in Vol. 1 of T. K. Cheyne and J. Sutherland Black (eds.), *Encyclopaedia Biblica.* 4 vols. New York: Macmillan.

Childe, V. Gordon. 1926. *The Aryans.* New York: Alfred A. Knopf.

Choksy, Jamsheed Kairshasp. 1986. "Purity and pollution in Zoroastrianism." *Mankind Quarterly* 27: 167–91.

Chow Ben-shun. 1984. "Animal domestication in Neolithic China." Pp. 363–69 in Juliet Clutton-Brock and Caroline Grigson (eds.), *Animals and archaeology.* Vol. 3, *Early herders and their flocks.* BAR International Series, 202. Oxford: British Archaeological Reports.

Chow Ben-shun. 1989. "The domestic horse of the pre-Ch'in period on China." Pp. 105–7 in Juliet Clutton-Brock (ed.), *The walking larder: Patterns of domestication, pastoralism, and predation*. London, Boston, Sydney, Wellington: Unwin Hyman.

Chwolsohn, D. 1856. *Die Ssabier und der Ssabismus*. 2 vols. St. Petersburg: Buchdruckerei der Kaiserlichen Akademie der Wissenschaften.

Cicero, Marcus Tullius. 1970. *The laws*. Pp. 287–519 in *De re publica. De legibus*. Trans. Clinton Walker Keyes. Loeb Classical Library. Cambridge, Mass.: Harvard University Press.

Cirilli, René. 1912. "Le sacrifice du chien." *Revue anthropologique* 22: 325–34.

Clason, A. T. 1977. "Wild and domestic animals in prehistoric and historic India." *Eastern Anthropologist* 30: 241–89.

Clason, A. T. 1979. "The farmers of Gomolava in the Vinča and La Tène Period." *Palaeohistoria* 21: 41–81.

Clason, A. T. 1980. "Padina and Starčevo: Game, fish, and cattle." *Palaeohistoria* 22: 141–73.

Clason, A. T., and J. Clutton-Brock. 1982. "The impact of domestic animals on the vegetation during the first phases of animal husbandry in the Mediterranean and Near East." Pp. 145–48 in John L. Bintliff and Willem van Zeist (eds.), *Palaeoclimates, palaeoenvironments and human communities in the eastern Mediterranean region in later prehistory*. 2 parts. BAR International Series, 133 (i). Oxford: British Archaeological Reports.

Clavijo, Ruy Gonzalez de. 1859. *Narrative of the embassy of Ruy Gonzalez de Clavijo to the court of Timour, at Samarcand, A.D. 1403–6*. Trans. C. R. Markham. Hakluyt Society Works, 26. London: Hakluyt Society.

Cline, Walter. 1936. *Notes on the people of Siwah and El Garah in the Libyan Desert*. General Series in Anthropology, 4. Menasha, Wis.: George Banta.

Cline, Walter. 1950. *The Teda of Tibesti, Borku, and Kawar in the eastern Sahara*. General Series in Anthropology, 12. Menasha, Wis.: George Banta.

Clutton-Brock, Juliet. 1976. "The animal resource." Pp. 373–92 in David M. Wilson (ed.), *The archaeology of Anglo-Saxon England*. London: Methuen.

Clutton-Brock, Juliet. 1981. *Domesticated animals from early times*. Austin: University of Texas Press; London: British Museum (Natural History).

Clutton-Brock, Juliet. 1984. "Dog." Pp. 198–211 in Ian L. Mason (ed.), *Evolution of domesticated animals*. London and New York: Longman.

Clutton-Brock, Juliet. 1992. *Horse power: A history of the horse and donkey in human societies*. Cambridge, Mass.: Harvard University Press.

Cohn, Bernard S. 1955. "The changing status of a depressed caste." Pp. 53–77 in McKim Marriott (ed.), *Village India*. American Anthropological Association Memoirs, 83. Menasha, Wis.: American Anthropological Association.

Cohn, Jacob. 1973. *The royal table: An outline of the dietary laws of Israel*. Jerusalem and New York: Feldheim Publishers.

Cole, Fay-Cooper. 1945. *The peoples of Malaysia*. New York: D. Van Nostrand.

Cole, Fay-Cooper. 1956. "The Bukidnon of Mindanao." *Chicago Natural History Museum, Fieldiana: Anthropology* 46: 1–140.

Colledge, Malcolm A. R. 1976. *The art of Palmyra*. Boulder: Westview.

Collet, Octave J. A. 1925. *Terres et peuples de Sumatra*. Amsterdam: Société d'Édition 'Elsevier.'

Colley, Sarah M., and Rhys Jones. 1989. "Rocky Cape revisited—new light on pre-historic Tasmanian fishing." Pp. 336–46 in Juliet Clutton-Brock (ed.), *The walking larder: Patterns of domestication, pastoralism, and predation*. London, Boston, Sydney, Wellington: Unwin Hyman.

Collier, V. W. F. 1921. *Dogs of China and Japan in nature and art*. New York: Frederick A. Stokes.

Collignon, Maxime. 1901. *Manual of mythology, in relation to Greek art*. Trans. and enlarged by Jane E. Harrison. Second edition. London: H. Grevel; Philadelphia: J. B. Lippincott.

Collins, Billie Jean. 1990. "The puppy in Hittite ritual." *Journal of Cuneiform Studies* 42: 211–26.

Colson, F. H., and G. H. Whitaker (trans.). 1929–62. *Philo*. 10 vols. Loeb Classical Library. London: William Heinemann; Cambridge, Mass.: Harvard University Press.

Coltherd, J. B. 1966. "The domestic fowl in ancient Egypt." *Ibis* 108: 217–23.

Columella. 1941–55. *On agriculture*. 3 vols. Trans. H. B. Ash, E. S. Forster, and E. H. Heffner. Loeb Classical Library. London: William Heinemann; Cambridge, Mass.: Harvard University Press.

Combe, G. A. 1926. *A Tibetan on Tibet*. London: T. Fisher Unwin.

Comhaire-Sylvain, Suzanne. 1950. *Food and leisure among the African youth of Leopoldville (Belgian Congo)*. Communications from the School of African Studies, University of Capetown, n.s., 25. Capetown: University of Capetown.

Compagnoni, Bruno, and Maurizio Tosi. 1978. "The camel: Its distribution and state of domestication in the Middle East during the third millennium B.C. in light of finds from Shahr-i Sokhta." Pp. 91–103 in Richard H. Meadow and Melinda A. Zeder (eds.), *Approaches to faunal analysis in the Middle East*. Peabody Museum Bulletin 2. Cambridge, Mass.: Peabody Museum of Archaeology and Ethnology, Harvard University.

Conrad, Jack Randolph. 1959. *The horn and the sword: The history of the bull as symbol of power and fertility*. London: MacGibbon and Kee.

Cook, Alice Carter. 1900. "The aborigines of the Canary Islands." *American Anthropologist* 2: 451–93.

Cook, James. 1784. *A voyage to the Pacific Ocean*. 3 vols. London: G. Nicol and T. Cadell.

Cook, James. 1955. *The journals of Captain James Cook on his voyages of discovery*. Vol. 1, *The Voyage of the Endeavour, 1768–1771*. Hakluyt Society Extra Series, 34. Cambridge: Cambridge University Press.

Cook, Stanley A. 1908. *The religion of ancient Palestine in the second millennium B.C.* London: Archibald Constable.

Coon, Carleton Stevens. 1931. *Tribes of the Rif*. Harvard African Studies, 9. Cambridge, Mass.: Harvard University Press.

Coon, Carleton Stevens. 1951. *Caravan*. New York: Henry Holt.

Cooper, T. T. 1871. *Travels of a pioneer of commerce in pigtail and petticoats.* London: John Murray.

Corfield, F. D. 1938. "The Koma." *Sudan Notes and Records* 21: 123–65.

Cornell University. 1956. *India: A sociological background.* 2 vols. Subcontractor's Monograph HRAF-44, Cornell-8. New Haven: Human Relations Area Files.

Corney, Bolton Glanvill (trans.). 1915. *The quest and occupation of Tahiti by emissaries of Spain during the years 1772–1776,* Vol. 2. Hakluyt Society Works, series 2, 36. London: Hakluyt Society.

Covarrubias, Miguel. 1942. *Island of Bali.* New York: Alfred A. Knopf.

Cowell, E. B. (ed.). 1973. *The Jātakas, or stories of the Buddha's former births.* 6 vols. Trans. from the Pāli by various persons. London: Pali Text Society.

Cox, Ross. 1957. *The Columbia River.* Norman: University of Oklahoma Press.

Craigie, Peter C. 1976. *The book of Deuteronomy.* New International Commentary on the Old Testament. Grand Rapids, Mich.: William B. Eerdmans.

Craster, J. E. E. 1913. *Pemba, the spice island of Zanzibar.* London: T. Fisher Unwin.

Crawford, R. D. 1984a. "Domestic fowl." Pp. 298–311 in Ian L. Mason (ed.), *Evolution of domesticated animals.* London and New York: Longman.

Crawfurd, John. 1830. *Journal of an embassy from the Governor-General of India to the courts of Siam and Cochin China.* 2 vols. London: Henry Colburn and Richard Bentley.

Creel, Herrlee Glessner. 1937a. *Studies in early Chinese culture.* Baltimore: Waverly.

Creel, Herrlee Glessner. 1937b. *The birth of China.* New York: Frederick Ungar.

Creighton, C. 1899–1903. "Leprosy, leper." Cols. 2763–68 in Vol. 3 of T. K. Cheyne and J. Sutherland Black (eds.), *Encyclopaedia Biblica.* 4 vols. New York: Macmillan.

Crooke, William. 1885. "Egg-plant—potatoes—onions—unlucky." *Panjab Notes and Queries* 3, 27 (December): 41.

Crooke, William. 1896. *The popular religion and folk-lore of northern India.* 2 vols. London: Archibald Constable.

Crooke, William. 1906. *Things Indian, being discursive notes on various subjects connected with India.* New York: Charles Scribner's Sons.

Crooke, William. 1908–26a. "Dravidians (North India)." Pp. 1–21 in Vol. 5 of James Hastings (ed.), *Encyclopaedia of religion and ethics.* 13 vols. Edinburgh: T. and T. Clark.

Crooke, William. 1908–26b. "Water, water-gods (Indian)." Pp. 716–19 in Vol. 12 of James Hastings (ed.), *Encyclopaedia of religion and ethics.* 13 vols. Edinburgh: T. and T. Clark.

Crossland, Ronald. 1992. "When specialists collide: Archaeology and Indo-European linguistics." *Antiquity* 66: 251–54.

Crowfoot, J. W. 1925. "Further notes on pottery." *Sudan Notes and Records* 8: 125–36.

Cumont, Franz. 1956. *Oriental religions in Roman paganism.* New York: Dover Publications.

Cunningham, J. F. 1905. *Uganda and its peoples.* London: Hutchinson.

Currid, John D. 1984. "The deforestation of the foothills of Palestine." *Palestine Exploration Quarterly* 116: 1–11.

Curzon, George N. 1892. *Persia and the Persian question*. 2 vols. London: Longmans, Green.

Cutter, Robert Joe. 1989. "Brocade and blood: The cockfight in Chinese and English poetry." *Journal of the American Oriental Society* 109: 1–16.

Czaplicka, Mary Antoinette. 1914. *Aboriginal Siberia: A study in social anthropology*. Oxford: Clarendon.

Daly, Lloyd W. 1950. "The cow in Greek art and cult." *American Journal of Archaeology* 54: 261.

Dando, William A. 1983. "Biblical famines, 1850 B.C.—A.D. 46: Insights for modern mankind." *Ecology of Food and Nutrition* 13: 231–49.

Darby, William J., Paul Ghalioungui, and Louis Grivetti. 1977. *Food: The gift of Osiris*. 2 vols. London, New York, San Francisco: Academic Press.

Darmesteter, James, and L. H. Mills (trans.). 1880–87. *The Zend-Avesta*. Vols. 4, 23, and 31 of *The sacred books of the East,* ed. F. Max Müller. Oxford: Clarendon.

Das, Rahul Peter. 1983. "Some remarks on the Bengali deity Dharma, its cult and study." *Anthropos* 78: 661–700.

Das, Rahul Peter. 1987. "More remarks on the Bengali deity Dharma, its cult and study." *Anthropos* 82: 244–51.

Das, S. K. 1953. "A study in folk cattle rites." *Man in India* 33: 232–41.

Das, Sarat Chandra. 1902. *Journey to Lhasa and central Tibet*. London: John Murray.

Das, Tarak Chandra. 1931. "The cultural significance of fish in Bengal." *Man in India* 11: 275–303.

Das, Tarak Chandra. 1932. "The cultural significance of fish in Bengal." *Man in India* 12: 96–115.

Das, Tarak Chandra. 1945. *The Purums: An Old Kuki tribe of Manipur*. Anthropological Papers, 7. Calcutta: University of Calcutta.

Davids, Thomas W. Rhys. 1903. *Buddhist India*. New York: G. P. Putnam's Sons.

Davids, Thomas W. Rhys, and Hermann Oldenberg (trans.). 1881–85. *Vinaya texts*. Vols. 13, 17, and 20 of *The sacred books of the East,* ed. by F. Max Müller. Oxford: Clarendon.

Davidson, Irving, and Robert Gross. c. 1960?. *How healthy are eggs? (with medical opinions against egg-eating)*. Tract no. 93. Fourth edition. Aliganj, Uttar Pradesh: World Jain Mission.

Davies, H. R. 1909. *Yün-nan: The link between India and the Yangtze*. Cambridge: Cambridge University Press.

Davis, John D. 1944. *The Westminster dictionary of the Bible*. Revised and rewritten H. S. Gehman. Philadelphia: Westminster.

Davis, Simon J. M. 1984. "The advent of milk and wool production in western Iran: Some speculations." Pp. 265–78 in Juliet Clutton-Brock and Caroline Grigson (eds.), *Animals and archaeology*. Vol. 3, *Early herders and their flocks*. BAR International Series, 202. Oxford: British Archaeological Reports.

Dawson, Warren R. 1928. "The pig in ancient Egypt: A commentary on two passages of Herodotus." *Journal of the Royal Asiatic Society of Great Britain and Ireland,* 597–608.

Day, Leslie Preston. 1984. "Dog burials in the Greek world." *American Journal of Archaeology* 88: 21–32.

Dê, Tranh Dinh. 1951. "Notes on birth and reproduction in Vietnam." Unpublished manuscript by M. Coughlin in the Human Relations Area Files.

Deacon, Arthur Bernard. 1934. *Malekula*. London: George Routledge and Sons.

Dean, William F. 1980. "Poultry production." Pp. 52–64 in J. A. Hoefer and P. J. Tsuchitani (eds.), *Animal agriculture in China*. Committee on Scholarly Communication with the People's Republic of China, Report 11. Washington, D.C.: National Academy Press.

de Beauclair, Inez. 1970. *Tribal cultures of southwest China*. Asian Folklore and Social Life Monographs, 2. Taipei: Orient Cultural Service.

Debysingh, Molly. 1970. "Poultry and Cultural Distributions in India." Unpublished Ph.D. dissertation in geography, Syracuse University. Also University Microfilms, 1971, 71–21, 518.

de Carneri, I., and L. di Matteo. 1989. "Epidemiologia delle trichinellosi in Italia e nei paesi confinanti." *Annali dell Istituto superiore di Sanità* (Rome) 25: 625–33.

Deffontaines, Pierre. 1948. *Géographie et religions*. Second edition. Paris: Gallimard.

de Garine, Igor. 1976. "Food, tradition and prestige." Pp. 150–73 in Dwain N. Walcher, Norman Kretchmer, and Henry L. Barnett (eds.), *Food, man, and society*. New York and London: Plenum.

de Garine, Igor. 1991. "Ecological success in perspective." *Journal of Human Ecology*, Special Issue, 1: 55–72.

de Garine, Igor, and Claude Marcel Hladik. 1990. "Nutritional concepts: Perception, food prohibitions and prescriptions." Pp. 92–94 in Claude Marcel Hladik, Serge Bahuchet, and Igor de Garine (eds.), *Food and nutrition in the African rain forest*. Paris: UNESCO/MAB.

de Garine, Igor, and Hélène Pagezy. 1990. "Seasonal hunger or 'craving for meat.'" Pp. 43–44 in Claude Marcel Hladik, Serge Bahuchet, and Igor de Garine (eds.), *Food and nutrition in the African rain forest*. Paris: UNESCO/MAB.

Delaporte, L. 1970. *Mesopotamia: The Babylonian and Assyrian civilization*. Trans. V. Gordon Childe. New York: Barnes and Noble.

Delehaye, Hippolyte. 1910–11. "St. Roch." P. 425 in Vol. 23 of *The Encyclopaedia Britannica*. Eleventh edition. 29 vols. New York: Encyclopaedia Britannica.

Del Re, Arundel. N.d. *Creation myths of Formosan natives*. Tokyo: Hokuseido.

Delvert, Jean. 1961. *Le Paysan cambodgien*. Le Monde d'outre-mer passé et présent, Études, 10. Paris and The Hague: Mouton.

De Paor, Máire, and Liam De Paor. 1958. *Early Christian Ireland*. New York: Frederick A. Praeger.

de Planhol, Xavier. 1959. *The world of Islam*. Ithaca, N.Y.: Cornell University Press.

de Reinach, Lucien. 1901. *Le Laos*. 2 vols. Paris: A. Charles, Librairie-Éditeur.

Der Ling, Princess. 1914. *Two years in the Forbidden City*. New York: Moffat, Yard.

Desai, Madhukar N. 1945. *The life and living in the rural Karnatak*. Sirsi, N. Kanara: Anand Publishers.

Deshler, Walter. 1963. "Cattle in Africa: Distribution, types, and problems." *Geographical Review* 53: 52–58.

Detienne, Marcel. 1989a. "Culinary practices and the spirit of sacrifice." Pp. 1–20 and 221–24 in Marcel Detienne and Jean-Pierre Vernant (eds.), *The cuisine of sacrifice among the Greeks,* trans. Paula Wissing. Chicago and London: University of Chicago Press.

Detienne, Marcel. 1989b. "The violence of wellborn ladies: Women in the Thesmophoria." Pp. 129–47 and 242–49 in Marcel Detienne and Jean-Pierre Vernant (eds.), *The cuisine of sacrifice among the Greeks,* trans. Paula Wissing. Chicago and London: University of Chicago Press.

Detienne, Marcel, and Jean-Pierre Vernant. 1978. *Cunning intelligence in Greek culture and society.* Trans. Janet Lloyd. Hassocks, Sussex: Harvester Press; Atlantic Highlands, N.J.: Humanities Press.

Detienne, Marcel, and Jean-Pierre Vernant. 1989. *The cuisine of sacrifice among the Greeks.* Trans. Paula Wissing. Chicago and London: University of Chicago Press.

de Vaux, Roland. 1956. "The excavations at Tell el-Farʿah and the site of ancient Tirzeh." *Palestine Exploration Quarterly* 88: 125–40.

de Vaux, Roland. 1961. *Ancient Israel: Its life and institutions.* Trans. John McHugh. New York, Toronto, London: McGraw-Hill.

de Vaux, Roland. 1967. "Tirzah." Pp. 371–83 in D. Winton Thomas (ed.), *Archaeology and Old Testament study.* Oxford: Clarendon.

de Vaux, Roland. 1971. *The Bible and the ancient Near East.* Trans. Damian McHugh. Garden City, N.Y.: Doubleday.

de Visser, M. W. 1935. *Ancient Buddhism in Japan.* 2 vols. Leiden: E. J. Brill.

de Vogel, C. J. 1966. *Pythagoras and early Pythagoreanism.* Assen: Van Gorcum.

de Young, John E. 1955. *Village life in modern Thailand.* Berkeley and Los Angeles: University of California Press.

Dexter, Miriam Robbins. 1990. "The hippomorphic goddess and her offspring." *Journal of Indo-European Studies* 18: 285–307.

Dhalla, Maneckji Nusservanji. 1922. *Zoroastrian civilization.* New York: Oxford University Press.

Dick, Terry A. 1983. "Species, and infraspecific variation." Pp. 31–73 in William C. Campbell (ed.), *Trichinella and trichinosis.* New York and London: Plenum.

Dickens, G., and W. H. Trethowan. 1971. "Cravings and aversions during pregnancy." *Journal of Psychosomatic Research* 15: 259–68.

Dickson, H. R. P. 1949. *The Arab of the desert.* London: George Allen and Unwin.

Diener, Paul, and Eugene E. Robkin. 1978. "Ecology, evolution, and the search for cultural origins: The question of Islamic pig prohibition." *Current Anthropology* 19: 493–540.

Diener, Paul, Donald Nonini, and Eugene E. Robkin. 1978. "The dialectics of the sacred cow: Ecological adaptation vs. political appropriation in the origins of India's cattle complex." *Dialectical Anthropology* 3: 221–41.

Diener, Paul, Donald Nonini, and Eugene E. Robkin. 1980. "Ecology and evolution in cultural anthropology." *Man* (n.s.) 15: 1–31.

Dierauer, U. 1910. "Lupercalia." *Archiv für Religionswissenschaft* 13: 481–508.

Diodorus Siculus. 1933–67. *The library of history.* 10 vols. Trans. C. H. Oldfather. Loeb Classical Library. London: William Heinemann; Cambridge, Mass.: Harvard University Press.

Diogenes Laërtius. 1891. *The lives and opinions of eminent philosophers.* Trans. C. D. Yonge. London: George Bell and Sons.

Dissamarn, R., and P. Indrakamhang. 1985. "Trichinosis in Thailand during 1962–1983." *International Journal of Zoonoses* 12: 257–66.

Dobell, Peter. 1830. *Travels in Kamchatka and Siberia; with a narrative of a residence in China.* 2 vols. London: Henry Colburn and Richard Bentley.

Dölger, Franz Josef. 1920–28. *IXOYC. Der heilige Fisch in den antiken Religionen und im Christentum.* 4 vols. Münster in Westfalen: Aschendorffschen Verlagsbuchhandlungen.

Dolman, C. E. 1957. "The epidemiology of meat-borne diseases." Pp. 11–108 in *Meat hygiene.* WHO Monograph Series, 33. Geneva: World Health Organization.

Donaldson, Bess Allen. 1938. *The wild rue: A study of Muhammadan magic and folk-lore in Iran.* London: Luzac.

Donkin, R. A. 1985. *The peccary—with observations on the introduction of pigs to the New World.* Transactions of the American Philosophical Society, 75, Part 5. Philadelphia: American Philosophical Society.

Donkin, R. A. 1989. *The muscovy duck, Cairina moschata domestica: Origins, dispersal, and associated aspects of the geography of domestication.* Rotterdam: Brookfield.

Donkin, R. A. 1991. *Meleagrides, an historical and ethnogeographical study of the guinea fowl.* London: Ethnographica.

Donner, Etta. 1939. *Hinterland Liberia.* London and Glasgow: Blackie and Son Limited.

Donner, Kai. 1926. *Bei den Samojeden in Sibirien.* Stuttgart: Strecker und Schröder.

Donoghue, John D. 1957. "An Eta community in Japan: The social persistence of outcaste groups." *American Anthropologist* 59: 1000–1017.

Doolittle, Justus. 1865. *Social life of the Chinese.* 2 vols. New York: Harper and Brothers.

d'Orléans, Prince Henri. 1894. *Around Tonkin and Siam.* London: Chapman and Hall.

Dornan, S. S. 1933. "Dog sacrifice among the Bantu." *South African Journal of Science* 30: 628–32.

Doughty, Charles Montagu. 1888. *Travels in Arabia deserta.* 2 vols. Cambridge: Cambridge University Press.

Douglas, Mary. 1955. "The Lele of Kasai." Pp. 1–26 in C. Daryll Forde (ed.), *African worlds.* London: International African Institute.

Douglas, Mary. 1966. *Purity and danger: An analysis of concepts of pollution and taboo.* New York and Washington, D.C.: Frederick A. Praeger.

Douglas, Mary. 1972. "Deciphering a meal." *Daedalus. Journal of the American Academy of Arts and Sciences* 101: 61–81.

Douglas, Mary. 1973. *Natural symbols; explorations in cosmology.* Second edition. London: Barrie and Jenkins.

Douglas, Mary. 1975. *Implicit meanings: Essays in anthropology.* London and Boston: Routledge and Kegan Paul.

Doutté, E. 1905. *Merrâkech.* Paris: Comité du Maroc.

Drake-Brockman, D. L. 1911. *Muttra: A gazetteer.* Vol. 7, District Gazetteers of the United Provinces of Agra and Oudh. Allahabad: Superintendent, Government Press, United Provinces.

Drew, Frederic. 1875. *The Jummoo and Kashmir Territories: A geographical account.* London: Edward Stanford.

Drews, Robert. 1988. *The coming of the Greeks; Indo-European conquests in the Aegean and the Near East.* Princeton: Princeton University Press.

Driberg, Jack Herbert. 1923. *The Lango.* London: T. Fisher Unwin.

Drijvers, H. J. W. 1980. *Cults and beliefs at Edessa.* Études préliminaires aux religions orientales dans l'empire romain, 82. Leiden: E. J. Brill.

Driver, G. R. 1955. "Birds in the Old Testament. II. Birds in life." *Palestine Exploration Quarterly* 87: 129–40.

Driver, Harold E., and William C. Massey. 1957. *Comparative studies of North American Indians.* Transactions of the American Philosophical Society, 47, Part 2. Philadelphia: American Philosophical Society.

Drower, Ethel S. 1937. *The Mandaeans of Iraq and Iran. Their cults, customs, magic, legends, and folklore.* Oxford: Clarendon.

Drower, Ethel S. 1956. *Water into wine. A study of ritual idiom in the Middle East.* London: John Murray.

Drummond, J. C., and Anne Wilbraham. 1940. *The Englishman's food.* London: Jonathan Cape.

Dube, S. C. 1951. *The Kamar.* Lucknow: Universal Publishers.

Dube, S. C. 1955. *Indian village.* Ithaca, N.Y.: Cornell University Press.

DuBois, Cora. 1941. "Attitudes toward food and hunger in Alor." Pp. 272–81 in Leslie Spier, A. I. Hallowell, and S. S. Newman (eds.), *Language, culture, and personality.* Menasha, Wis.: Sapir Memorial Publication Fund.

DuBois, Cora. 1944. *The people of Alor.* Minneapolis: University of Minnesota Press.

Dubois, J. A. 1906. *Hindu manners, customs, and ceremonies.* Oxford: Clarendon.

Dumarest, André. 1935. *La Formation des classes sociales en pays Annamite.* Lyon: P. Ferréol.

Dumézil, Georges. 1970. *Archaic Roman religion.* 2 vols. Trans. Philip Krapp. Chicago and London: University of Chicago Press.

Dumont, Louis. 1970. *Homo hierarchicus: An essay on the caste system.* Trans. Mark Sainsbury. Chicago: University of Chicago Press.

Dumont, Paul-Émile. 1927. *L'Aśvamedha: Description du sacrifice solennel du cheval dans le culte védique d'après les textes du Yajurveda blanc.* Paris: P. Geuthner.

Dumont, Paul-Émile. 1948. "The horse-sacrifice in the Taittirīya-Brāhmaṇa." *Proceedings of the American Philosophical Society* 92: 447–503.

Dunand, Maurice. 1964. *Byblos, its history, ruins, and legends.* Trans. H. Tabet. Beirut: Librairie Adrien-Maisonneuve.

Duncan, M. H. 1964. *The Yangtze and the yak.* London: Mitre.

Dunnigan, Ann. 1987. "Fish." Pp. 346–47 in Vol. 5 of Mircea Eliade (ed.), *The encyclopedia of religion*. 16 vols. New York: Macmillan; London: Collier Macmillan.

Durand, Algernon. 1900. *The making of a frontier*. London: John Murray.

Durand, Jean-Louis. 1989. "Ritual as instrumentality." Pp. 119–28 and 240–42 in Marcel Detienne and Jean-Pierre Vernant (eds.), *The cuisine of sacrifice among the Greeks*, trans. Paula Wissing. Chicago and London: University of Chicago Press.

Durham, M. Edith. 1928. *Some tribal origins, laws and customs of the Balkans*. London: George Allen and Unwin.

Dussaud, René. 1900. *Histoire et religion des Nosairîs*. Bibliothèque de l'École des hautes études, sciences philologiques et historiques, 129. Paris: Librairie Émile Bouillon.

Dutt, Romesh C. 1893. *A history of civilisation in ancient India*. 2 vols. London: Kegan Paul, Trench, Trübner.

Duval, Mathias, et al. 1885. "Sur les oeufs pourris comme aliment en Chine." *Bulletin de la Société d'anthropologie de Paris* 8 (sér. 3): 299–303.

Duveyrier, Henri. 1864. *Les Touareg du nord*. Paris: Challamel Ainé.

Earthy, Emily Dora. 1933. *Valenge women*. London: International Institute of African Languages and Cultures.

East, Rupert (ed.). 1939. *Akiga's story: The Tiv tribe as seen by one of its members*. London: International Institute of African Languages and Cultures.

Eberhard, Wolfram. 1942. *Lokalkulturen im alten China*. Leiden: E. J. Brill.

Eberhard, Wolfram. 1968. *The local cultures of South and East China*. Trans. Alide Eberhard. Leiden: E. J. Brill.

Eberhard, Wolfram. 1982. *China's minorities: Yesterday and today*. Belmont, Calif.: Wadsworth.

Edelstein, Emma J., and Ludwig Edelstein. 1945. *Asclepius: A collection and interpretation of the testimonies*. 2 vols. Baltimore: Johns Hopkins University Press.

Eggeling, Julius (trans.). 1882–1900. *The Śatapatha-Brāhmaṇa according to the text of the Mādhyandina School*. Vols. 12, 26, 41, 43, and 44 of *The sacred books of the East*, ed. F. Max Müller. Oxford: Clarendon.

Eichinger Ferro-Luzzi, Gabriella. 1973a. "Food avoidances at puberty and menstruation in Tamilnad: An anthropological study." *Ecology of Food and Nutrition* 2: 163–72.

Eichinger Ferro-Luzzi, Gabriella. 1973. "Food avoidances of pregnant women in Tamilnad." *Ecology of Food and Nutrition* 2: 259–66.

Eichinger Ferro-Luzzi, Gabriella. 1974. "Food avoidances during the puerperium and lactation in Tamilnad." *Ecology of Food and Nutrition* 3: 7–13.

Eichinger Ferro-Luzzi, Gabriella. 1977a. "The foods disliked by the gods in South India." *Annali dell'Istituto orientale di Napoli* 37: 357–73.

Eichinger Ferro-Luzzi, Gabriella. 1977b. "The logic of South Indian food offerings." *Anthropos* 72: 529–56.

Eichinger Ferro-Luzzi, Gabriella. 1981. "The food of the gods versus human food in South India." *L'Uomo* 5: 239–65.

Eichinger Ferro-Luzzi, Gabriella. 1985a. "Divieti alimentari e sacralità del bovino in India." *L'Uomo* 9: 161–70.

Eichinger Ferro-Luzzi, Gabriella. 1985b. "The cultural uses of food in modern Tamil literature." *Annali dell'Istituto universitario orientale* 45: 483–502.

Eichinger Ferro-Luzzi, Gabriella. 1987. *The self-milking cow and the bleeding lingam: Criss-cross of motifs in Indian temple legends.* Wiesbaden: Otto Harrassowitz.

Eichinger Ferro-Luzzi, Gabriella. 1990. "Food is good to laugh: A Tamil comic view of food." *Food and Foodways* 4: 39–52.

Eisenman, A., and R. Einat. 1992. ["A family outbreak of trichinosis in Israel"]. *Harefuah* (Tel Aviv) 122: 702–4 (in Hebrew).

Ekvall, Robert B. 1939. *Cultural relations on the Kansu-Tibetan border.* University of Chicago Publications in Anthropology, Occasional Papers, 1. Chicago: University of Chicago Press.

Ekvall, Robert B. 1963. "Role of the dog in Tibetan nomadic society." *Central Asiatic Journal* 8: 163–73.

Elbl, Ivana. 1991. "The horse in fifteenth-century Senegambia." *International Journal of African Historical Studies* 24: 85–110.

Eliade, Mircea. 1958. *Patterns in comparative religion.* Trans. Rosemary Sheed. London and New York: Sheed and Ward.

Eliade, Mircea, and Lawrence E. Sullivan. 1987. "Hierophany." Pp. 313–17 in Vol. 6 of Mircea Eliade (ed.), *The encyclopedia of religion.* 16 vols. New York: Macmillan; London: Collier Macmillan.

Ellison, Rosemary. 1981. "Diet in Mesopotamia: The evidence of the barley ration texts." *Iraq* 43: 35–45.

Ellison, Rosemary. 1983. "Some thoughts on the diet of Mesopotamia from c. 3000–600 B.C." *Iraq* 45: 146–50.

Ellison, Rosemary, Jane Renfrew, Don Brothwell, and Nigel Seeley. 1978. "Some food offerings from Ur, excavated by Sir Leonard Woolley, and previously unpublished." *Journal of Archaeological Science* 5: 167–77.

Elmore, Wilber Theodore. 1915. *Dravidian gods in modern Hinduism: A study of the local and village deities of southern India.* Lincoln: University Studies of the University of Nebraska.

Elphinstone, M. 1842. *An account of the kingdom of Caubul, and its dependencies in Persia, Tartary, and India.* New and revised edition. London: Richard Bentley.

Elwin, Verrier. 1955. *The religion of an Indian tribe.* London: Oxford University Press.

Elwin, Verrier. 1959. *India's north-east frontier in the nineteenth century.* London: Oxford University Press.

Encyclopaedia Britannica. 1910–11a. "Aesculapius." P. 276 in Vol. 1. Eleventh edition. 29 vols. New York: Encyclopaedia Britannica.

Encyclopaedia Britannica. 1910–11b. "Lemnos." Pp. 412–13 in Vol. 16. Eleventh edition. 29 vols. New York: Encyclopaedia Britannica.

Encyclopaedia Britannica. 1910–11c. "Order of St. Lazarus." P. 314 in Vol. 16. Eleventh edition. 29 vols. New York: Encyclopaedia Britannica.

Encyclopaedia Judaica. 1971–72. "Fish and fishing." Cols. 1326–28 in Vol. 6. 16 vols. Jerusalem: Keter Publishing House; New York: Macmillan.

Epstein, Eliahu. 1938. "Kuwait." *Journal of the Royal Central Asian Society* 25: 595–603.

Epstein, H. 1971a. *Domestic animals of China*. New York: Africana Publishing Corporation.

Epstein, H. 1971b. *The origin of the domestic animals of Africa*. 2 vols. Revised in collaboration with I. L. Mason. New York, London, Munich: Africana Publishing Corporation.

Epstein, H., and M. Bichard. 1984. "Pig." Pp. 145–62 in Ian L. Mason (ed.), *Evolution of domesticated animals*. London and New York: Longman.

Epstein, H., and I. L. Mason. 1984. "Cattle." Pp. 6–27 in Ian L. Mason (ed.), *Evolution of domesticated animals*. London and New York: Longman.

Epstein, Isidore. 1959. *Judaism: A historical presentation*. Harmondsworth, England; Baltimore, Md.; Ringwood, Australia: Penguin.

Erkes, Eduard. 1943. "Der Hund im alten China." *T'oung Pao* 37: 186–225.

Erman, Adolf. 1894. *Life in ancient Egypt*. London: Macmillan.

Erman, Adolf. 1907. *A handbook of Egyptian religion*. Trans. A. S. Griffith. London: Constable.

Erman, Adolph. 1850. *Travels in Siberia: Including excursions northwards, down the Obi, to the polar circle, and southwards, to the Chinese frontier*. Vol. 2. Philadelphia: Lea and Blanchard.

Ernle, Lord. 1961. *English farming past and present*. Sixth edition. Chicago: Quadrangle.

Erskine, K. D. (comp.). 1908. *The Mewar Residency, Text*. Rajputana Gazetteers, 2-A. Ajmer: Scottish Mission Industries.

Espinosa, Friar Alonso de. 1907. *The Guanches of Tenerife, the holy image of Our Lady of Candelaria, and the Spanish conquest and settlement*. Trans. and ed. Sir C. Markham. Hakluyt Society Works, series 2, no. 21. London: Hakluyt Society.

Esse, Douglas L. 1991. *Subsistence, trade, and social change in Early Bronze Age Palestine*. Studies in Ancient Oriental Civilization, 50. Chicago: Oriental Institute of the University of Chicago.

Evans, Ivor H. N. 1923. *Studies in religion, folk-lore, and custom in British North Borneo and the Malay Peninsula*. Cambridge: Cambridge University Press.

Evans-Pritchard, E. E. 1932. "Ethnological observations in Dar Fung." *Sudan Notes and Records* 15: 1–61.

Evans-Pritchard, E. E. 1940. *The Nuer*. Oxford: Clarendon.

Ewing, J. Franklin. 1963. "Food and drink among the Tawsug with comparative notes from other Philippine and nearby groups." *Anthropological Quarterly* 36: 60–70.

Fairman, H. W. (trans. and ed.). 1974. *The triumph of Horus: An ancient Egyptian sacred drama*. Berkeley and Los Angeles: University of California Press.

Farbridge, Maurice H. 1908–26. "Swine." Pp. 132–34 in Vol. 12 of James Hastings (ed.), *Encyclopaedia of religion and ethics*. 13 vols. Edinburgh: T. and T. Clark.

Farnell, Lewis Richard. 1896–1909. *The cults of the Greek states*. 5 vols. Oxford: Clarendon.

Faroughy, Abbas. 1951. *The Bahrein islands (750–1951)*. New York: Verry, Fisher.

Farquhar, J. N. 1967. *Modern religious movements in India*. First Indian edition. Delhi: Munshiram Manoharlal.

Faublée, J. 1942. "L'Alimentation des Bara (Sud de Madagascar)." *Journal de la Société des africanistes* 12: 157–201.

Faulkner, Raymond O. (trans. and ed.). 1969. *The ancient Egyptian Pyramid Texts.* Oxford: Clarendon.

Faulkner, Raymond O. (trans. and ed.). 1973–78. *The ancient Egyptian Coffin Texts.* 3 vols. Warminster, England: Aris and Phillips.

Faulkner, Raymond O. (trans. and ed.) 1985. *The ancient Egyptian Book of the Dead.* Revised edition. New York: Macmillan.

Faust, Ernest Carroll. 1955. *Animal agents and vectors of human disease.* Philadelphia: Lea and Febiger.

Fawcett, F. 1890. "On some festivals to village goddesses." *Journal of the Anthropological Society of Bombay* 2: 264–82.

Featherman, A. 1885–91. *Social history of the races of mankind.* 4 vols. London: Trübner.

Fedenko, Panas. 1951. *Ukraine, the struggle for freedom.* Augsburg, Germany: Free Ukraine.

Feliks, Jehuda. 1962. *The animal world of the Bible.* Tel-Aviv: "Sinai" Bookstore and Publishing.

Feliks, Jehuda. 1971–72a. "Camel." Cols. 72–73 in Vol. 5 of *Encyclopaedia Judaica.* 16 vols. Jerusalem: Keter Publishing House; New York: Macmillan.

Feliks, Jehuda. 1971–72b. "Chicken." Col. 418 in Vol. 5 of *Encyclopaedia Judaica.* 16 vols. Jerusalem: Keter Publishing House; New York: Macmillan.

Feliks, Jehuda. 1971–72c. "Dog." Col. 152 in Vol. 6 of *Encyclopaedia Judaica.* 16 vols. Jerusalem: Keter Publishing House; New York: Macmillan.

Feliks, Jehuda. 1971–72d. "Flora and fauna." Cols. 220–25 in Vol. 9 of *Encyclopaedia Judaica.* 16 vols. Jerusalem: Keter Publishing House; New York: Macmillan.

Feliks, Jehuda. 1971–72e. "Oak." Cols. 1293–94 in Vol. 12 of *Encyclopaedia Judaica.* 16 vols. Jerusalem: Keter Publishing House; New York: Macmillan.

Feliks, Jehuda, et al. 1971–72. "Pig." Cols. 506–8 in Vol. 13 of *Encyclopaedia Judaica.* 16 vols. Jerusalem: Keter Publishing House; New York: Macmillan.

Ferdinand, Klaus. 1959. *Preliminary notes on Hazāra culture (The Danish Scientific Mission to Afghanistan 1953–55).* Historisk-filosofiske Meddelelser, Det Kongelige Danske Videnskabernes Selskab, bind 37, no. 5. Copenhagen.

Fernie, William T. 1899. *Animal simples approved for modern uses of cure.* Bristol: John Wright.

Ferrars, Max, and Bertha Ferrars. 1901. *Burma.* London: Sampson Low, Marston; New York: E. P. Dutton.

Ferrier, J. P. 1857. *Caravan journeys and wanderings in Persia, Afghanistan, Turkistan, and Beloochistan.* London: John Murray.

Festus, Sextus Pompeius. 1913. *Sexti Pompei Festi: De verborum significatu quae supersunt cum Pauli epitome.* Ed. Wallace M. Lindsay. Leipzig: B. G. Teubner.

Fielding Hall, Harold. 1917. *The soul of a people.* London: Macmillan.

Finkelstein, Israel. 1988a. "Searching for Israelite origins." *Biblical Archaeology Review* 14, 5 (September/October): 34–45, 58.

Finkelstein, Israel. 1988b. *The archaeology of the Israelite settlement.* Jerusalem: Israel Exploration Society.

Finkelstein, Israel. 1990. "The emergence of early Israel: Anthropology, environment and archaeology." *Journal of the American Oriental Society* 110: 677–86.

Firth, Raymond. 1930. "Report on research in Tikopia." *Oceania* 1, 1: 105–17.

Firth, Rosemary. 1943. *Housekeeping among Malay peasants.* Monographs on Social Anthropology, 7. London: London School of Economics and Political Science.

Fisher, William B. 1950. *The Middle East: A physical, social, and regional geography.* London: Methuen.

Flannery, Kent V. 1983. "Early pig domestication in the Fertile Crescent: A retrospective look." Pp. 163–88 in T. Cuyler Young, Jr., Philip E. L. Smith, and Peder Mortensen (eds.), *The hilly flanks: Essays on the prehistory of southwestern Asia.* Studies in Ancient Oriental Civilization, 36. Chicago: Oriental Institute of the University of Chicago.

Forlong, J. G. R. 1906. *Faiths of man: Cyclopedia of religions.* 3 vols. London: Bernard Quaritch.

Forsyth, T. D. 1875. *Report of a mission to Yarkand in 1873.* Calcutta: Foreign Department Press.

Fortes, M., and S. L. Fortes. 1936. "Food in the domestic economy of the Tallensi." *Africa* 9: 237–76.

Fosberry, M. 1868–69. "On some of the mountain tribes of the N.W. frontier of India." *Journal of the Ethnological Society of London* 1 (n.s.): 182–93.

Foster, B. O., Frank Gardner Moore, et al. (trans.). 1949–63. *Livy.* 14 vols. Loeb Classical Library. London: William Heinemann; Cambridge, Mass.: Harvard University Press.

Fox, Ernest F. 1943. *Travels in Afghanistan.* New York: Macmillan.

Frank, B. 1965. *Die Rolle des Hundes in afrikanischen Kulturen.* Studien zur Kulturkunde, 17. Wiesbaden.

Frankfort, Henri. 1961. *Ancient Egyptian religion: An interpretation.* New York: Harper and Row.

Frazer, James George. 1935. *The golden bough, a study in magic and religion.* Third edition. 12 vols. New York: Macmillan.

Frazer, James George. 1939. *The native races of Asia and Europe.* Anthologia Anthropologica. London: Percy Lund Humphries.

Frazer, James George (trans. and ed.). 1929. *Publii Ovidii nasonis fastorum libri sex: The Fasti of Ovid.* 5 vols. London: Macmillan.

Frazer, James George, et al. 1910–11. "Thesmophoria." Pp. 838–40 in Vol. 26 of *The Encyclopaedia Britannica.* Eleventh edition. 29 vols. New York: Encyclopaedia Britannica.

Freed, Stanley A., and Ruth S. Freed. 1981. "Sacred cows and water buffalo in India: The uses of ethnography." *Current Anthropology* 22: 483–502.

Freedman, David Noel (ed.). 1976. *Ancient synagogue excavations at Khirbet Shema^c, Upper Galilee, Israel, 1970–72.* Annual of the American Schools of Oriental Research, 42. Durham: Duke University Press.

Freeman, Michael. 1977. "Sung." Pp. 141–76 in K. C. Chang (ed.), *Food in Chinese culture: Anthropological and historical perspectives.* New Haven and London: Yale University Press.

Freitag, Sandria B. 1980. "Sacred symbol as mobilizing ideology: The North Indian search for a 'Hindu' community." *Comparative Studies in Society and History* 22: 597–625.

Frendo, Anthony J. 1992. "Five recent books on the emergence of ancient Israel: Review article." *Palestine Exploration Quarterly* 124: 143–47.

Friedländer, M. (trans.). 1956. *The Guide for the Perplexed by Moses Maimonides*. Second edition. London: Routledge and Kegan Paul.

Friedrich, Johannes. 1971. *Die Hethitischen Gesetze*. Documenta et Monumenta Orientis Antiqui, 7. Leiden: E. J. Brill.

Friters, Gerard M. 1949. *Outer Mongolia and its international position*. Baltimore: Johns Hopkins University Press.

Fritsch, G. 1868. *Drei Jahre in Süd-Afrika*. Breslau: Ferdinand Hirt.

Fritz, Volkmar. 1987. "Conquest or settlement: The Early Iron Age in Palestine." *Biblical Archaeologist* 50: 84–100.

Frobenius, Leo, and Ritter von Wilm (eds.). 1921–31. *Atlas Africanus*. 8 parts. Munich: C. H. Beck; Berlin and Leipzig: Walter de Gruyter.

Fryer, G. E. 1875. "On the Khyeng people of the Sandoway District, Arakan." *Journal of the Asiatic Society of Bengal* 44: 39–82.

Fryer, John. 1909–15. *A new account of East India and Persia*. Ed. W. Crooke. 3 vols. Hakluyt Society Works, series 2, nos. 19 (1909), 20 (1912), and 39 (1915). London: Hakluyt Society.

Frymer-Kensky, Tikva. 1987. "Utu." Pp. 162–63 in Vol. 15 of Mircea Eliade (ed.), *The encyclopedia of religion*. 16 vols. New York: Macmillan; London: Collier Macmillan.

Fuchs, Hanns. 1910. *Sagen, Mythen und Sitten der Masai*. Jena: Hermann Costenoble.

Fuchs, Stephen. 1950. *The children of Hari*. Vienna: Herold.

Fuchs, Stephen. 1960. *The Gond and Bhumia of eastern Mandla*. London: Asia Publishing House.

Fuhr, I. 1977. "Der Hund als Begleittier der Göttin Gula und anderer Heilgottheiten." Pp. 135–45 in B. Hrouda (ed.), *Isin—Išān Baḥrīyāt I*. Bayerische Akademie der Wissenschaften, Philosophisch-Historische Klasse, Abhandlungen, Neue Folge, 79. Munich: Bayerische Akademie der Wissenschaften.

Fürer-Haimendorf, Christoph von. 1943. *The aboriginal tribes of Hyderabad*. 2 vols. London: Macmillan.

Fürer-Haimendorf, Christoph von. 1946. "Agriculture and land tenure among the Apa Tanis." *Man in India* 26: 19–49.

Fürer-Haimendorf, Christoph von. 1963. "The social background of cattle-domestication in India." Pp. 144–55 in A. E. Mourant and F. E. Zeuner (eds.), *Man and cattle*. Royal Anthropological Institute, Occasional Papers, 18. London: Royal Anthropological Institute of Great Britain and Ireland.

Fürer-Haimendorf, Christoph von, and Elizabeth von Fürer-Haimendorf. 1948. *The Raj Gonds of Adilabad: A peasant culture of the Deccan*. Book 1, *Myth and ritual*. London: Macmillan.

Furon, Raymond. 1958. "The gentle little goat: Arch despoiler of the earth." *UNESCO Courier* (January): 30–32.

Gade, Daniel W. 1976. "Horsemeat as human food in France." *Ecology of Food and Nutrition* 5: 1–11.

Gaidoz, H. 1884. "À propos des chiens d'Épidaure." *Revue archéologique* (third series) 4: 217–22.

Gaillard, Claude. 1934. "Contribution à l'étude de la faune préhistorique de l'Égypte." *Archives du Muséum d'Histoire Naturelle de Lyon* 4: 1–126.

Galitzin, E. 1856. "Manners and customs of the Yacoutes." *Journal of the Ethnological Society of London* 4: 144–48.

Gamble, John. 1908–26. "Symbolism (Christian)." Pp. 134–38 in Vol. 12 of James Hastings (ed.), *Encyclopaedia of religion and ethics*. 13 vols. Edinburgh: T. and T. Clark.

Gamble, Sidney D. 1933. *How Chinese families live in Peiping.* New York and London: Funk and Wagnalls.

Gamble, Sidney D. 1954. *Ting Hsien, a North China regional community.* New York: Institute of Pacific Relations.

Gamkrelidze, Tomas V., and Vyachislav V. Ivanov. 1984. *Indo-European language and the Indo-Europeans.* (In Russian.) Tiblisi.

Gamkrelidze, Tomas V., and Vyachislav V. Ivanov. 1985a. "The ancient Near East and the Indo-European question: Temporal and territorial characteristics of Proto-Indo-European based on linguistic and historico-cultural data." *Journal of Indo-European Studies* 13: 3–48.

Gamkrelidze, Tomas V., and Vyachislav V. Ivanov. 1985b. "The migrations of tribes speaking Indo-European dialects from their historical habitations in Eurasia." *Journal of Indo-European Studies* 13: 49–91.

Gamst, Frederick C. 1969. *The Qemant: A pagan-Hebraic peasantry of Ethiopia.* New York: Holt, Rinehart and Winston.

Gandert, O.-F. 1975. "Beiträg zur Geschichte des Haushuhnes in der Hallstattzeit des nordwestalpinen Gebietes." Pp. 362–66 in A. T. Clason (ed.), *Archaeozoological studies*. Amsterdam and Oxford: North-Holland; New York: American Elsevier.

Gandhi, M. K. 1949. *Diet and diet reform.* Ahmedabad: Navajivan Publishing House.

Gandhi, M. K. 1950. *Hindu dharma.* Ahmedabad: Navajivan Publishing House.

Gandhi, M. K. 1954. *How to serve the cow.* Ahmedabad: Navajivan Publishing House.

Gangulee, Nagendranath. 1939. *Health and nutrition in India.* London: Faber and Faber.

Gardiner, Alan H. 1923. "The eloquent peasant." *Journal of Egyptian Archaeology* 9: 5–25.

Gardiner, Alan H. 1961. *Egypt of the pharaohs: An introduction.* Oxford: Clarendon.

Garrucci, Raffaele. 1872–81. *Storia della arte cristiana nei primo otto secoli della chiesa.* 6 vols. Prato: Gaetano Guasti.

Gaudefroy-Demombynes, Maurice. 1908–26. "Camel." Pp. 173–74 in Vol. 3 of James Hastings (ed.), *Encyclopaedia of religion and ethics*. 13 vols. Edinburgh: T. and T. Clark.

Geertz, Clifford. 1972. "Deep play: Notes on the Balinese cockfight." *Daedalus. Journal of the American Academy of Arts and Sciences* 101: 1–37.

Gejvall, Nils-Gustaf. 1969. *Lerna: A preclassical site in the Argolid.* Vol. 1, *The Fauna.* Princeton: American School of Classical Studies at Athens.

Geldner, K. 1908–26. "Aśvamedha." Pp. 160–61 in Vol. 2 of James Hastings (ed.), *Encyclopaedia of religion and ethics.* 13 vols. Edinburgh: T. and T. Clark.

Gelling, Peter, and Hilda Ellis Davidson. 1969. *The chariot of the sun and other rites and symbols of the northern Bronze Age.* New York and Washington, D.C.: Frederick A. Praeger.

Gening, V. F. 1979. "The cemetery at Sintashta and the early Indo-Iranian peoples." *Journal of Indo-European Studies* 7: 1–29.

Georgoudi, Stella. 1989. "Sanctified slaughter in modern Greece: The 'Kourbánia' of the saints." Pp. 183–203 and 259–68 in Marcel Detienne and Jean-Pierre Vernant (eds.), *The cuisine of sacrifice among the Greeks,* trans. Paula Wissing. Chicago and London: University of Chicago Press.

Gerard, Ralph W. 1952. *Food for life.* Chicago: University of Chicago Press.

Germani, Clara. 1985. "AID sparks a minor flap over a nearly extinct Indonesian pig." *Christian Science Monitor,* January 2, p. 5.

Ghirshman, R. 1977. *L'Iran et la migration des Indo-Aryens et des Iraniens.* Leiden: E. J. Brill.

Ghurye, G. S. 1979. *Vedic India.* Bombay: Popular Prakashan.

Gibson, H. E. 1935. "Animals in the writings of Shang." *China Journal* 23: 342–51.

Gimbutas, Marija. 1956. *Mesolithic, Neolithic and Copper Age cultures in Russia and the Baltic area.* Part 1 of *The prehistory of eastern Europe.* American School of Prehistoric Research, Bulletin 20. Cambridge, Mass.: Peabody Museum, Harvard University.

Gimbutas, Marija. 1958. *Ancient symbolism in Lithuanian folk art.* Memoirs of the American Folklore Society, 49. Philadelphia: American Folklore Society.

Gimbutas, Marija. 1961. "Notes on the chronology and expansion of the Pit-grave culture." Pp. 193–200 in J. Böhm and S. J. De Laet (eds.), *L'Europe à la fin de l'âge de la pierre.* Prague: Czechoslovak Academy of Sciences.

Gimbutas, Marija. 1970. "Proto-Indo-European culture: The Kurgan culture during the fifth, fourth, and third millennia B.C." Pp. 155–97 in George Cardona, Henry M. Hoenigswald, and Alfred Senn (eds.), *Indo-European and Indo-Europeans.* Papers presented at the Third Indo-European Conference at the University of Pennsylvania. Philadelphia: University of Pennsylvania Press.

Gimbutas, Marija. 1971. *The Slavs.* New York and Washington, D.C.: Praeger Publishers.

Gimbutas, Marija. 1977. "The first wave of Eurasian steppe pastoralists into Copper Age Europe." *Journal of Indo-European Studies* 5: 277–338.

Gimbutas, Marija. 1980. "The Kurgan wave #2 (c. 3400–3200 BC) into Europe and the following transformation of culture." *Journal of Indo-European Studies* 8: 273–315.

Gimbutas, Marija. 1982. *The goddesses and gods of old Europe: 6500–3500 B.C.* New and updated edition. Berkeley and Los Angeles: University of California Press.

Gimbutas, Marija. 1986. "Comments" [on David W. Anthony, "The Kurgan culture,

Indo-European origins, and the domestication of the horse: A reconsideration"].
Current Anthropology 27: 305–7.

Gimbutas, Marija. 1989. *The language of the goddess.* San Francisco: Harper and Row.

Ginzberg, Louis, et al. 1907. "Cock." Pp. 138–39 in Vol. 4 of Isidore Singer (ed.),
The Jewish encyclopedia. 12 vols. New York and London: Funk and Wagnalls.

Giraldus Cambrensis (Gerald of Wales). 1982. *The history and topography of Ireland.*
Trans. John J. O'Meara. Harmondsworth, Middlesex: Penguin.

Godbole, N. N. 1936. *Milk: The most perfect food.* Benares: Published by the author.

Goetze, Albrecht. 1962. "Critical reviews: Annelies Kammerhuber, *Hippologia Hethi-
tica.*" *Journal of Cuneiform Studies* 16: 30–35.

Goetze, Albrecht, and E. H. Sturtevant. 1938. *The Hittite ritual of Tunnawi.* American
Oriental Series, 14. New Haven: American Oriental Society.

Goldberg, Paul, and Ofer Bar-Yosef. 1982. "Environmental and archaeological evidence for climatic change in the southern Levant." Pp. 399–414 in John L. Bintliff
and Willem van Zeist (eds.), *Palaeoclimates, palaeoenvironments and human communities in the eastern Mediterranean region in later prehistory.* 2 parts. BAR International
Series, 133 (ii). Oxford: British Archaeological Reports.

Goldwasser, Orly. 1992. "On the date of Seth from Qubeibeh." *Israel Exploration
Journal* 42: 47–51.

Goldziher, I. 1901. "Islamisme et parsisme." *Revue de l'histoire des religions* 43: 1–29.

Golish, Vitold de. 1954. *Primitive India.* London: George G. Harrap.

Gonda, J. 1965. *Change and continuity in Indian religion.* The Hague, London, Paris:
Mouton.

Gonda, J. 1969a. *Aspects of early Viṣṇuism.* Second edition. Delhi, Patna, Benares:
Motilal Banarsidass.

Gonda, J. 1969b. *Eye and gaze in the Veda.* Verhandelingen der Koninklijke Neder-
landse Akademie van Wetenschappen, Afd. Letterkunde, n.s. 75, no. 1. Amsterdam and London: North-Holland.

Gonda, J. 1970. *Viṣṇuism and Śivaism: A comparison.* London: Athlone Press, University
of London.

Gonda, J. 1980. *Vedic ritual: The non-solemn rites.* Handbuch der Orientalistik, Abteilung 2, Band 4, Abschnitt 1. Leiden: E. J. Brill.

Gondal, Ram Pratap. 1948. "Changes in customs and practices among some lower
agricultural castes of the Kotah State." *Eastern Anthropologist* 1, 4 (June): 21–28.

Goodenough, Erwin Ramsdell. 1953–68. *Jewish symbols in the Greco-Roman period.*
13 vols. Bollingen Series, 37. New York: Pantheon Books.

Goody, Jack. 1971. *Technology, tradition, and the state in Africa.* London, Ibadan, Accra:
Oxford University Press.

Goody, Jack. 1982. *Cooking, cuisine, and class: A study in comparative sociology.* Cambridge: Cambridge University Press.

Gordon, Edmund I. 1959. *Sumerian proverbs: Glimpses of everyday life in ancient Mesopotamia.* With a chapter by Thorkild Jacobsen. Museum Monographs. Philadelphia:
University Museum, University of Pennsylvania.

Gottwald, Norman K. 1979. *The tribes of Yahweh.* Maryknoll, N.Y.: Orbis Books.

Gould, Sylvester E. 1945. *Trichinosis*. Springfield, Ill.: Charles C. Thomas.

Gould, Sylvester E. 1970a. "Clinical manifestations." Pp. 269–328 in Sylvester E. Gould (ed.), *Trichinosis in man and animals*. Springfield, Ill.: Charles C. Thomas.

Gould, Sylvester E. 1970b. "History." Pp. 3–18 in Sylvester E. Gould (ed.), *Trichinosis in man and animals*. Springfield, Ill.: Charles C. Thomas.

Gould-Martin, Katherine. 1978. "Hot cold clean poison and dirt: Chinese folk medical categories." *Social Science and Medicine* 12: 39–46.

Gourou, Pierre. 1936. *Les paysans du Delta Tonkinois. Étude de géographie humaine.* Publications de l'École française d'extrême-orient, 27. Paris: Éditions d'art et d'histoire.

Gourou, Pierre. 1945. *Land utilization in French Indochina.* Washington, D.C.: Institute of Pacific Relations.

Graham, W. A. 1924. *Siam.* 2 vols. London: Alexander Moring.

Grant, Michael. 1980. *The Etruscans.* New York: Charles Scribner's Sons.

Grattan, F. J. H. 1948. *An introduction to Samoan custom.* Apia, Western Samoa: Samoa Printing and Publishing.

Graves, Robert. 1927. *Lawrence and the Arabs.* London: Jonathan Cape.

Graves, Robert. 1957. "Mushrooms, food of the gods." *Atlantic Monthly* 200, 2 (August): 73–77.

Gray, John. 1957. *The legacy of Canaan: The Ras Shamra texts and their relevance to the Old Testament.* Leiden: E. J. Brill.

Gray, John Henry. 1878. *China: A history of the laws, manners, and customs of the people.* 2 vols. London: Macmillan.

Great Britain Admiralty. N.d. *A manual on the Turanians and pan-Turanianism.* London: H.M. Stationery Office.

Great Britain Admiralty, Naval Intelligence Division. 1944–45. *Jugoslavia.* 3 vols. Geographical Handbook Series. London: H.M. Stationery Office.

Great Britain Admiralty, Naval Intelligence Division. 1945. *Persia.* Geographical Handbook Series. London: H.M. Stationery Office.

Great Britain Colonial Office. 1953. *The improvement of cattle in British colonial territories in Africa.* Colonial Advisory Council of Agriculture, Animal Health, and Forestry, Pub. No. 3. London: H.M. Stationery Office.

Green, M. W. 1980. "Animal husbandry at Uruk in the Archaic period." *Journal of Near Eastern Studies* 39: 1–35.

Greenewalt, Crawford H., Jr. 1978. *Ritual dinners in Early Historic Sardis.* University of California Publications in Classical Studies, 17. Berkeley, Los Angeles, London: University of California Press.

Greenfield, Haskel J. 1984. "A model of changing animal exploitation strategies during the later prehistory of the Central Balkans." Pp. 45–56 in Caroline Grigson and Juliet Clutton-Brock (eds.), *Animals and archaeology.* Vol. 4, *Husbandry in Europe.* BAR International Series, 227. Oxford: British Archaeological Reports.

Greenfield, Haskel J. 1986. *The paleoeconomy of the central Balkans (Serbia): A Zooarchaeological perspective on the Late Neolithic and Bronze Age (ca. 4500–1000 B.C.).* 2 parts. BAR International Series, 304. Oxford: British Archaeological Reports.

Gregor, Walter. 1881. *Notes on the folk-lore of the north-east of Scotland.* London: Folk-Lore Society.

Griffis, William Elliott. 1882. *Corea: The hermit nation.* New York: Charles Scribner's Sons.

Griffith, Francis Llewellyn. 1910–11. "Hyksos." Pp. 175–76 in Vol. 14 of *The Encyclopaedia Britannica.* Eleventh edition. 29 vols. New York: Encyclopaedia Britannica.

Griffith, Ralph T. H. 1963. *The hymns of the Rgveda.* 2 vols. Chowkhamba Sanskrit Studies, 35. Benares: Chowkhamba Sanskrit Series Office.

Griffiths, J. Gwyn. 1960. *The conflict of Horus and Seth from Egyptian and classical sources.* Liverpool Monographs in Archaeology and Oriental Studies. Liverpool: Liverpool University Press.

Griffiths, J. Gwyn. 1970. *Plutarch's De Iside et Osiride.* Cardiff: University of Wales Press.

Griffiths, J. Gwyn. 1980. *The origins of Osiris and his cult.* Studies in the History of Religions, 40. Leiden: E. J. Brill.

Grigson, Caroline. 1982. "Porridge and pannage: Pig husbandry in Neolithic England." Pp. 297–314 in Martin Bell and Susan Limbrey (eds.), *Archaeological aspects of woodland ecology.* BAR International Series, 146. Oxford: British Archaeological Reports.

Grigson, Caroline. 1987. "Shiqmim: Pastoralism and other aspects of animal management in the Chalcolithic of the northern Negev." Pp. 219–33 in Thomas Evan Levy (ed.), *Shiqmim I: Studies concerning Chalcolithic societies in the northern Negev Desert, Israel (1982–1984).* 2 parts. BAR International Series, 356. Oxford: British Archaeological Reports.

Grigson, Caroline, John A. J. Gowlett, and Juris Zarins. 1989. "The camel in Arabia—A direct radiocarbon date, calibrated to about 7000 BC." *Journal of Archaeological Science* 16: 355–62.

Grist, D. H. 1936. *An outline of Malayan agriculture.* Malayan Planting Manual No. 2. Kuala Lumpur: Straits Settlements Department of Agriculture.

Grivetti, Louis Evan. 1980. "Dietary separation of meat and milk. A cultural-geographical inquiry." *Ecology of Food and Nutrition* 8: 203–17.

Groot, Gerard J. 1951. *The prehistory of Japan.* New York: Columbia University Press.

Groves, C. 1981. *Ancestors for the pigs: Taxonomy and phylogeny of the genus Sus.* Technical Bulletin, 3. Canberra: Department of Prehistory, Research School of Pacific Studies, Australian National University.

Gruner, O. Cameron. 1930. *A treatise on the Canon of Medicine of Avicenna.* London: Luzac.

Gryaznov, Mikhail P. 1969. *The ancient civilization of southern Siberia.* Trans. James Hogarth. New York: Cowles.

Gudger, E. W. 1926. "Fishing with the cormorant in China." *American Naturalist* 60: 5–41.

Gulliver, Pamela, and P. H. Gulliver. 1953. *The Central Nilo-Hamites.* Ethnographic Survey of Africa. East Central Africa, Part 7. London: International African Institute.

Gunn, Harold D. 1953. *Peoples of the plateau area of northern Nigeria.* Ethnographic Survey of Africa. Western Africa, Part 7. London: International African Institute.

Gunn, Harold D. 1956. *Pagan peoples of the central area of northern Nigeria.* Ethnographic Survey of Africa. Western Africa, Part 12. London: International African Institute.

Gurdon, P. R. T. 1904. "Notes on the Khasis, Syntengs, and allied tribes inhabiting the Khasi and Jaintia Hills District in Assam." *Journal of the Asiatic Society of Bengal* 73, Part 3, no. 4: 57–74.

Gurdon, P. R. T. 1907. *The Khasis.* London: David Nutt.

Gurdon, P. R. T. 1914. *The Khasis.* Second edition. London: Macmillan.

Gurney, Oliver R. 1940. "Hittite prayers of Mursili II." *Annals of Archaeology and Anthropology* 27: 3–163.

Gurney, Oliver R. 1977. *Some aspects of Hittite religion.* Oxford and London: Oxford University Press.

Gurney, Oliver R. 1990. *The Hittites.* London: Penguin.

Guthrie, W. K. C. 1962–81. *A history of Greek philosophy.* 6 vols. Cambridge: Cambridge University Press.

Gutmann, Bruno. 1926. *Das Recht der Dschagga.* Arbeiten zur Entwicklungspsychologie, 7. Munich: C. H. Beck.

Guys, M. Henri. 1863. *La Nation Druse.* Paris: Challamel Ainé.

Hahn, Eduard. 1896. *Die Haustiere und ihre Beziehungen zur Wirtschaft des Menschen.* Leipzig: Duncker und Humblot.

Hakker-Orion, Dalia. 1975. "Hunting and stock-breeding in Israel." Pp. 295–301 in A. T. Clason (ed.), *Archaeozoological studies.* Amsterdam and Oxford: North-Holland; New York: American Elsevier.

Hakker-Orion, Dalia. 1984. "The role of the camel in Israel's early history." Pp. 207–12 in Juliet Clutton-Brock and Caroline Grigson (eds.), *Animals and archaeology.* Vol. 3, *Early herders and their flocks.* BAR International Series, 202. Oxford: British Archaeological Reports.

Hall, Maurice C. 1938. "Studies on trichinosis. VI. Epidemiological aspects of trichinosis in the United States as indicated by an examination of 1,000 diaphragms for trichinae." *Public Health Reports* 53: 1086–1105.

Halpern, Joel Martin. 1958. *A Serbian village.* New York: Columbia University Press.

Hambly, Wilfrid D. 1934. *The Ovimbundu of Angola.* Field Museum of Natural History, Anthropological Series, 21, no. 2: 89–362. Chicago.

Hambly, Wilfrid D. 1935. *Culture areas of Nigeria.* Field Museum of Natural History, Anthropological Series, 21, no. 3: 365–502. Chicago.

Hambly, Wilfrid D. 1937. *Source book for African anthropology.* 2 vols. Field Museum of Natural History, Anthropological Series, 26. Chicago.

Hamilton, W. 1815. *The East India gazetteer.* London: John Murray.

Hamp, Eric P. 1987. "The pig in ancient northern Europe." Pp. 185–90 in Susan Nacev Skomal and Edgar G. Polomé (eds.), *Proto-Indo-European: The archaeology of a linguistic problem. Studies in honor of Marija Gimbutas.* Washington, D.C.: Institute for the Study of Man.

Hanauer, J. E. 1935. *Folk-lore of the holy land.* London: Sheldon.

Hanbury, R. D., P. B. Doby, H. O. Miller, and K. D. Murrell. 1986. "Trichinosis in a herd of swine: Cannibalism as a major mode of transmission." *Journal of the American Veterinary Medical Association* 188: 1155–59.

Handcock, Percy S. P. 1912. *Mesopotamian archaeology.* New York: G. P. Putnam's Sons.

Harcourt, R. A. 1974. "The dog in prehistoric and early historic Britain." *Journal of Archaeological Science* 1: 151–75.

Harlan, Lindsey. 1992. *Religion and Rajput women.* Berkeley, Los Angeles, Oxford: University of California Press.

Harle, James C. 1963. "Durgā, goddess of victory." *Artibus Asiae* 26: 237–46.

Harmer, Walter J. N.d. "Mother magic. An inquiry into the origin of domestic plants and animals." Unpublished manuscript.

Harmon, A. M. (trans.). 1960. *Lucian,* Vol. 2. London: William Heinemann; Cambridge, Mass.: Harvard University Press.

Harnack, Adolf, and Frederic C. Conybeare. 1910–11. "Manichaeism." Pp. 572–78 in Vol. 17 of *The Encyclopaedia Britannica.* Eleventh edition. 29 vols. New York: Encyclopaedia Britannica.

Harper, Edward B. 1959. "A Hindu village pantheon." *Southwestern Journal of Anthropology* 15: 227–34.

Harper, Edward B. 1964. "Ritual pollution as an integrator of caste and religion." Pp. 151–96 in Edward B. Harper (ed.), *Religion in South Asia.* Seattle: University of Washington Press.

Harrer, Heinrich. 1954. *Seven years in Tibet.* Trans. Richard Graves. New York: E. P. Dutton.

Harris, Marvin. 1966. "The cultural ecology of India's sacred cattle." *Current Anthropology* 7: 51–66.

Harris, Marvin. 1972. "The riddle of the pig." *Natural History* 81: 8, 32–38.

Harris, Marvin. 1973. "The riddle of the pig, II." *Natural History* 82: 2, 20–25.

Harris, Marvin. 1974. *Cows, pigs, wars, and witches.* New York: Random House.

Harris, Marvin. 1978. *Cannibals and kings.* New York: Vantage.

Harris, Marvin. 1985. *Good to eat: Riddles of food and culture.* New York: Simon and Schuster.

Harrison, Jane Ellen. 1955. *Prolegomena to the study of Greek religion.* New York: Meridian.

Harrisson, Tom. 1937. *Savage civilisation.* London: Victor Gollancz.

Hart, Donn Vorhis. 1954. "Barrio Caticugan: A Visayan Filipino community." Unpublished Ph.D. dissertation, Syracuse University.

Hart, Keith, and Louise Sperling. 1987. "Cattle as capital." *Ethnos* 52: 324–38.

Hartmann, R. 1883. *Abyssinien und die übrigen Gebiete der Ostküste Afrikas.* Leipzig: G. Freytag.

Hartog, François. 1989. "Self-cooking beef and the drinks of Ares." Pp. 170–82 and 256–59 in Marcel Detienne and Jean-Pierre Vernant (eds.), *The cuisine of sacrifice among the Greeks,* trans. Paula Wissing. Chicago and London: University of Chicago Press.

Hassan, Fekri A. 1984. "Toward a model of agricultural developments in Predynastic Egypt." Pp. 221–24 in Lech Krzyżaniak and Michal Kobusiewicz (eds.), *Origin and early development of food-producing cultures in north-eastern Africa*. Poznań: Polish Academy of Sciences, Poznań Branch; and Poznań Archaeological Museum.

Hassan, Fekri A. 1988. "The Predynastic of Egypt." *Journal of World Prehistory* 2: 135–85.

Hauck, H. M., S. Sudsaneh, and J. R. Hanks. 1958. *Food habits and nutrient intakes in a Siamese rice village*. Cornell Thailand Project, Interim Reports Series, 4. Data Paper, 29, Southeast Asia Program. Ithaca, N.Y.: Department of Far Eastern Studies, Cornell University.

Haug, Martin. 1978. *The Parsis: Essays on their sacred language, writings and religion*. Revised by K. W. West. New Delhi: Cosmo Publications.

Hauptmann, Gerhart Johann Robert. 1951. *The weavers. Hannele. The beaver coat*. Trans. H. Frenz and M. Waggoner. New York: Rinehart.

Hawass, Zahi, Fekri A. Hassan, and Achilles Gautier. 1988. "Chronology, sediments, and subsistence at Merimda Beni Salama." *Journal of Egyptian Archaeology* 74: 31–38.

Hawes, Charles H. 1903. *In the uttermost east*. London and New York: Harper and Brothers.

Hay, Stephen. 1969. "Between two worlds: Gandhi's first impressions of British culture." *Modern Asian Studies* 3: 305–19.

Hay, Stephen. 1970. "Jain influences on Gandhi's early thought." Pp. 29–38 in Sibnarayan Ray (ed.), *Gandhi, India and the world*. Philadelphia: Temple University Press.

Hayes, William C. 1965. *Most ancient Egypt*. Chicago and London: University of Chicago Press.

Hayes, William C. 1970. "Chronology. I. Egypt—to the end of the twentieth dynasty." Pp. 173–93 in I. E. S. Edwards, C. G. Gadd, and N. G. L. Hammond (eds.), *Prolegomena and prehistory*. Vol. 1, Part 1 of *The Cambridge ancient history*. Third edition. Cambridge: Cambridge University Press.

Haynes, Kingsley E., and Sherif M. El-Hakim. 1979. "Appropriate technology and public policy: The urban waste management system in Cairo." *Geographical Review* 69: 101–8.

Headland, Isaac Taylor. 1914. *Home life in China*. New York: Macmillan.

Hearne, Samuel. 1795. *A journey from Prince of Wales's Fort in Hudson's Bay to the northern ocean*. London: A. Strahan and T. Cadell.

Heber, A. Reeve, and Kathleen M. Heber. 1926. *In Himalayan Tibet*. Philadelphia: J. B. Lippincott.

Hecker, H. M. 1982. "A zooarchaeological inquiry into pork consumption in Egypt from prehistoric to New Kingdom times." *Journal of the American Research Center in Egypt* 19: 59–71.

Hehn, Victor. 1885. *The wanderings of plants and animals from their first home*. Ed. James Steven Stallybrass. London: Swan Sonnenschein.

Hellbom, Anna-Britta. 1963. "The creation egg." *Ethnos* 28: 63–105.

Hellwing, Salo (Shlomo). 1984. "Human exploitation of animal resources in the Early Iron Age strata at Tel Beer-sheba." Pp. 105–15 in Ze'ev Herzog, *Beer-sheba II: The Early Iron Age settlements*. Tel Aviv: Institute of Archaeology, Tel Aviv University.

Hellwing, Salo (Shlomo), and Yitzhak Adjeman. 1986. "Animal bones." Pp. 141–52 in Israel Finkelstein, *ʿIzbet Ṣarṭah: An Early Iron Age site near Rosh Haʿayin, Israel*. BAR International Series, 299. Oxford: British Archaeological Reports.

Hemmer, H. 1978. "Geographische Variation der Hirngrösse in *Sus scrofa* und *Sus verrucosus*—Kreis (Beitrag zur Problem der Schweindomestikation)." *Spixiana* 1: 309–20.

Henderson, Jeffrey (ed.). 1987. *Aristophanes Lysistrata*. Oxford and New York: Clarendon.

Henig, Martin. 1984. *Religion in Roman Britain*. London: B. T. Batsford.

Henninger, Joseph. 1948. "Le Sacrifice chez les Arabes." *Ethnos* 13: 1–16.

Henninger, Joseph. 1987a. "Sacrifice." Pp. 544–57 in Vol. 12 of Mircea Eliade (ed.), *The encyclopedia of religion*. 16 vols. New York: Macmillan; London: Collier Macmillan.

Henninger, Joseph. 1987b. "Scapegoat." Pp. 92–95 in Vol. 13 of Mircea Eliade (ed.), *The encyclopedia of religion*. 16 vols. New York: Macmillan; London: Collier Macmillan.

Herklots, Gerhard Andreas. 1921. *Islam in India*. London: Oxford University Press.

Hermanns, Matthias. 1949. *Die Nomaden von Tibet*. Vienna: Herold.

Hermanns, Matthias. 1954. *The Indo-Tibetans*. Bombay: K. L. Fernandes.

Herodotus. 1858. *The ancient history*. Trans. W. Beloe. New York: Derby and Jackson.

Herskovits, Melville J. 1926. "The cattle complex in East Africa." *American Anthropologist* 28: 230–72, 361–88, 494–528, 633–64.

Herskovits, Melville J. 1948. *Man and his works*. New York: Alfred A. Knopf.

Herskovits, Melville J. 1952. *Economic anthropology*. New York: Alfred A. Knopf.

Herzog, Edgar. 1967. *Psyche and death*. Trans. David Cox and Eugene Rolfe. New York: G. P. Putnam's Sons.

Herzog, Rolf. 1957. *Die Nubier*. Band 2, Völkerkundliche Forschungen, Sektion für Völkerkunde und Deutsche Volkskunde, Deutsche Akademie des Wissenschaften zu Berlin. Berlin: Akademie.

Hesse, Brian. 1986. "Animal use at Tel Miqne-Ekron in the Bronze Age and Iron Age." *Bulletin of the American Schools of Oriental Research* 264: 17–27.

Hesse, Brian. 1990. "Pig lovers and pig haters: Patterns of Palestinian pork production." *Journal of Ethnobiology* 10: 195–225.

Heydrich, M. 1931. "Koreanische Landwirtschaft: Beiträge zur Völkerkunde von Korea." *Abhandlungen und Berichte der Museen für Tierkunde und Völkerkunde zu Dresden* 19: 1–44.

Hickey, Gerald C. 1960. A study of a Vietnamese rural community—sociology. N.p. [Saigon?]. Viet-Nam Advisory Group, Michigan State University, mimeo.

Higham, C. F. W., A. Kijngam, and B. F. J. Manly. 1980. "An analysis of prehistoric canid remains from Thailand." *Journal of Archaeological Science* 7: 149–65.

Hiltebeitel, Alf. 1978a. "The Indus Valley 'Proto-Śiva', re-examined through reflections on the goddess, the buffalo, and the symbol of vāhanas." *Anthropos* 73: 767–97.

Hiltebeitel, Alf. 1978b. "The water buffalo, the sacrifice and the goddess." Pp. 44–46 in Franklin C. Southworth (ed.), *Symbols, subsistence and social structure: The ecology of man and animal in South Asia.* Philadelphia: South Asia Regional Studies, University of Pennsylvania.

Hilzheimer, Max. 1941. *Animal remains from Tell Asmar.* Oriental Institute of the University of Chicago, Studies in Ancient Oriental Civilization, 20. Chicago: University of Chicago Press.

Hinz, E. 1991. "Trichinellosis and trichinellosis control in Germany." *Southeast Asian Journal of Tropical Medicine and Public Health* 22 (Supplement): 329–33.

Hippocrates. 1959a. *Regimen.* Pp. 223–447 in Vol. 4 of *Hippocrates,* trans. W. H. S. Jones. Loeb Classical Library. London: William Heinemann; Cambridge, Mass.: Harvard University Press.

Hippocrates. 1959b. *The sacred disease.* Pp. 127–83 in Vol. 2 of *Hippocrates,* trans. W. H. S. Jones. Loeb Classical Library. London: William Heinemann; Cambridge, Mass.: Harvard University Press.

Hiralal, Rai Bahadur. 1925. "Some notes about marriage, food, drink, and occupations of castes affecting social status in the Central Provinces." *Man in India* 5: 56–68.

Hirsch, Emil G. 1907. "Fish and fishing." Pp. 403–4 in Vol. 5 of Isidore Singer (ed.), *The Jewish encyclopedia.* 12 vols. New York and London: Funk and Wagnalls.

Hivale, Shamrao. 1944. "The Laru Kaj." *Man in India* 24: 100–116.

Ho Ping-ti. 1975. *The cradle of the East: An inquiry into the indigenous origins of techniques and ideas of neolithic and early historic China, 5000–1000 B.C.* Chicago: University of Chicago Press.

Hodson, T. C. 1911. *The Naga tribes of Manipur.* London: Macmillan.

Hoffman, Michael A. 1974. "The social context of trash disposal in an Early Dynastic Egyptian town." *American Antiquity* 39: 35–50.

Hoffner, Harry A., Jr. 1967. "Reviews of books: *Die Kaškäer: Ein Beitrag zur Ethnographie des alten Kleinasien* . . . by Einar von Schuler." *Journal of the American Oriental Society* 87: 179–85.

Hoffner, Harry A., Jr. 1974. *Alimenta Hethaeorum: Food production in Hittite Asia Minor.* American Oriental Series, 55. New Haven: American Oriental Society.

Hoffpauir, Robert. 1977. "The Indian milk buffalo: A paradox of high performance and low reputation." *Asian Profile* 5: 111–34.

Hoffpauir, Robert. 1982. "The water buffalo: India's other bovine." *Anthropos* 77: 215–38.

Hollis, Alfred C. 1904. *The Masai: Their language and folklore.* Oxford: Clarendon.

Holmes, Maybel Marion. 1948. "A source book of Chinese food habits." Unpublished Ph.D. dissertation in home economics, Cornell University.

Homer. 1925. *The Iliad.* Trans. A. T. Murray. 2 vols. Loeb Classical Library. London: William Heinemann; New York: G. P. Putnam's Sons.

Homer. 1961. *The Odyssey.* Trans. Robert Fitzgerald. Garden City, N.Y.: Doubleday.

Hooton, Earnest A. 1925. *The ancient inhabitants of the Canary Islands*. Harvard African Studies, 7. Cambridge, Mass.: Harvard University Press.

Hopkins, David C. 1985. *The highlands of Canaan: Agricultural life in the Early Iron Age*. Social World of Biblical Antiquity Series, 3. Decatur, Ga.: Almond Press.

Hopkins, David C. 1987. "The subsistence struggles of early Israel." *Biblical Archaeologist* 50: 178–91.

Hopkins, Edward Washburn. 1894. "The dog in the *Rig-Veda*." *American Journal of Philology* 15: 154–63.

Hopkins, Edward Washburn. 1901. *India old and new*. New York: Charles Scribner's Sons; London: Edward Arnold.

Hopkins, Edward Washburn. 1969. *The great epic of India: Its character and origin*. Calcutta: Punthi Pustak.

Hopkins, Thomas J., and Alf Hiltebeitel. 1987. "Indus Valley religion." Pp. 215–23 in Vol. 7 of Mircea Eliade (ed.), *The encyclopedia of religion*. 16 vols. New York: Macmillan; London: Collier Macmillan.

Hornell, James. 1950. *Fishing in many waters*. Cambridge: Cambridge University Press.

Hornung, Erik. 1982. *Conceptions of god in ancient Egypt*. Trans. John Baines. Ithaca, N.Y.: Cornell University Press.

Horowitz, A. 1971. "Climatic and vegetational developments in northeastern Israel during Upper Pleistocene-Holocene times." *Pollen et spores* 13: 255–78.

Horwitz, Liora Kolska. 1987. "Animal offerings from two Middle Bronze Age tombs." *Israel Exploration Journal* 37: 251–55.

Horwitz, Liora Kolska. 1989. "Diachronic changes in rural husbandry practices in Bronze Age settlements from the Refaim Valley, Israel." *Palestine Exploration Quarterly* 121: 44–54.

Horwitz, Liora Kolska, and Eitan Tchernov. 1989. "Animal exploitation in the Early Bronze Age of the southern Levant: An overview." Pp. 279–96 in Part 2 of Pierre de Miroschedji (ed.), *L'Urbanisation de la Palestine à l'âge du Bronze ancien*. 2 parts. BAR International Series, 527. Oxford: British Archaeological Reports.

Hose, Charles, and William McDougall. 1912. *The pagan tribes of Borneo*. 2 vols. London: Macmillan.

Howey, M. Oldfield. 1923. *The horse in magic and myth*. London: W. Rider and Son.

Hrdlička, Aleš. 1912. *The natives of the Kharga Oasis, Egypt*. Smithsonian Miscellaneous Collections, 59, No. 1. Washington, D.C.: Smithsonian Institution Press.

Hrozný, Bedřich (Frédéric). 1922. *Code Hittite provenant de l'Asie Mineure, I*. Paris: Librairie orientaliste Paul Geuthner.

Hrozný, Bedřich (Frédéric). 1953. *The ancient history of western Asia, India and Crete*. Trans. Jindrich Prochazka. Prague: Artia.

Huffman, Ray. 1931. *Nuer customs and folk-lore*. London: Oxford University Press.

Hughes, J. Donald. 1975. *Ecology in ancient civilizations*. Albuquerque: University of New Mexico Press.

Hughes, Thomas Patrick. 1885. *A dictionary of Islam*. New York: Scribner, Welford.

Hulbert, Homer B. 1906. *The passing of Korea*. New York: Doubleday, Page.

Hull, Eleanor. 1928. *Folklore of the British Isles*. London: Methuen.

Humbert, André. 1980. *Le Monte dans les chaînes subbétiques centrales (Espagne du Sud)*. Publication 10. Paris: Département de géographie, Université de Paris–Sorbonne.

Hummel, Siegbert. 1955–58. "Der Hund in der religiösen Vorstellungswelt des Tibeters." *Paideuma* 6: 500–509.

Hummel, Siegbert. 1959–61. "Der Hund in der religiösen Vorstellungswelt des Tibeters. II." *Paideuma* 7: 352–61.

Huntingford, G. W. B. 1927. "Miscellaneous records relating to the Nandi and Kony tribes." *Journal of the Royal Anthropological Institute of Great Britain and Ireland* 57: 417–61.

Huntingford, G. W. B. 1953a. *The northern Nilo-Hamites*. Ethnographic Survey of Africa. East Central Africa, Part 6. London: International African Institute.

Huntingford, G. W. B. 1953b. *The southern Nilo-Hamites*. Ethnographic Survey of Africa. East Central Africa, Part 8. London: International African Institute.

Huntingford, G. W. B. 1955. *The Galla of Ethiopia; the kingdoms of Kafa and Janjero*. Ethnographic Survey of Africa. North-Eastern Africa, Part 2. London: International African Institute.

Hutchinson, R. H. Sneyd. 1906. *An account of the Chittagong Hill Tracts*. Calcutta: Bengal Secretariat Book Depot.

Hutson, James. 1921. *Chinese life in the Tibetan foothills*. Shanghai: Far Eastern Geographical Establishment.

Hutton, J. H. 1921. *The Angami Nagas*. London: Macmillan.

Hutton, J. H. 1963. *Caste in India*. Fourth edition. London: Oxford University Press.

Hutton, J. H. 1968. *The Sema Nagas*. Second edition. Bombay: Oxford University Press.

Hutton, J. H. 1969. *The Angami Nagas*. Second edition. Bombay: Oxford University Press.

Hyndman, David C. 1983–84. "Hunting and the classification of game animals among the Wopkaimin." *Oceania* 54: 289–309.

Hyvernat, Henry, and Emil G. Hirsch. 1907. "Forest." Pp. 433–34 in Vol. 5 of Isidore Singer (ed.), *The Jewish encyclopedia*. 12 vols. New York and London: Funk and Wagnalls.

Ibn el-Beïthar. 1877. *Traité des simples*, Vol. 1. Notices et Extraits des Manuscrits de la Bibliothèque Nationale et Autres Bibliothèques, 23, 1: 1–476.

Imperial Gazetteer of India. 1908. Provincial Series: Burma. 2 vols. Calcutta: Superintendent of Government Printing.

Imperial Gazetteer of India. 1909a. Provincial Series: Eastern Bengal and Assam. Calcutta: Superintendent of Government Printing.

Imperial Gazetteer of India. 1909b. Provincial Series: Kashmir and Jammu. Calcutta: Superintendent of Government Printing.

Inayatullah, Shaikh. 1942. *Geographical factors in Arabian life and history*. Lahore: Sh. Muhammad Ashraf.

Indian Notes and Queries. 1886. "Panjab—red food forbidden—Hindus." 4, 39 (December): 51.

Ingrams, Doreen. 1949. *A survey of social and economic conditions in the Aden Protectorate.* Asmara: British Administration.

Ingrams, W. H. 1936. *A report on the social, economic and political condition of the Hadhramaut.* Colonial Office Report, 123. London: H.M. Stationery Office.

Isaac, Erich. 1962. "On the domestication of cattle." *Science* 137, 3525 (July 20): 195–204.

Isaac, Erich. 1970. *Geography of domestication.* Englewood Cliffs, N.J.: Prentice-Hall.

Ivens, W. G. 1927. *Melanesians of the south-east Solomon Islands.* London: Kegan Paul, Trench, Trübner.

Izikowitz, Karl Gustav. 1951. *Lamet, hill peasants in French Indochina.* Etnologiska Studier, 17. Gothenburg, Sweden: Etnografiska Museet.

Jackson, A. V. Williams. 1928. *Zoroastrian studies.* Iranian Religion and Various Monographs. New York: Columbia University Press.

Jacobs, Joseph, and Solomon Schechter. 1907. "Eggs." P. 54 in Vol. 5 of Isidore Singer (ed.), *The Jewish encyclopedia.* 12 vols. New York and London: Funk and Wagnalls.

Jahn, Ulrich. 1884. *Die Deutschen Opfergebräuche bei Ackerbau und Viehzucht.* Breslau: Wilhelm Koebner.

Jaini, Padmanabh S. 1987. "Indian perspectives on the spirituality of animals." Pp. 169–78 in David J. Kalupahana and W. G. Weeraratne (eds.), *Buddhist philosophy and culture: Essays in honour of N. A. Jayawickrema.* Colombo: N. A. Jayawickrema Felicitation Volume Committee.

James, Andrew L. J. 1992. "The law and the chickens." *Christianity and Crisis* 52: 140–41.

Janssen, Jac J. 1975. *Commodity prices from the Ramessid Period.* Leiden: E. J. Brill.

Jastrow, Morris. 1898. *The religion of Babylonia and Assyria.* Boston: Ginn.

Jastrow, Morris. 1910–11. "Gula." P. 713 in Vol. 12 of *The Encyclopaedia Britannica.* Eleventh edition. 29 vols. New York: Encyclopaedia Britannica.

Jastrow, Morris. 1917. "Babylonian—Assyrian medicine." *Annals of Medical History* 1: 231–57.

Jayne, Walter Addison. 1962. *The healing gods of ancient civilizations.* New Hyde Park, N.Y.: University Books.

Jenkins, Frank. 1957. "The role of the dog in Romano-Gaulish religion." *Latomus* 16: 60–76.

Jenks, Albert Ernest. 1905. *The Bontoc Igorot.* Department of the Interior, Ethnological Survey Publications, 1. Manila: Bureau of Public Printing.

Jensen, P. 1886. "Das Wildschwein in den assyrisch-babylonischen Inschriften." *Zeitschrift für Assyriologie* 1: 306–12.

Jochelson, Waldemar. 1905–8. *The Koryak.* Memoirs, 10. New York: American Museum of Natural History.

Jochelson, Waldemar. 1906. "Kumiss festivals of the Yakut and the decoration of kumiss vessels." Pp. 257–71 in *Boas Anniversary Volume.* New York: G. E. Stechert.

Jochelson, Waldemar. 1926. *The Yukaghir and the Yukaghirized Tungus.* Memoirs, 13. New York: American Museum of Natural History.

Jochelson, Waldemar. 1928. *Peoples of Asiatic Russia*. New York: American Museum of Natural History.

Johnston, Harry Hamilton. 1895. *The river Congo*. London: Sampson Low, Marston.

Johnston, Harry Hamilton. 1910. *George Grenfell and the Congo*. 2 vols. London: D. Appleton.

Jolly, Julius (trans.). 1900. *The Institutes of Vishnu*. Vol. 7 of *The sacred books of the East*, ed. F. Max Müller. Oxford: Clarendon.

Jolly, Julius (trans.). 1908–26. "Food." Pp. 59–63 in Vol. 6 of James Hastings (ed.), *Encyclopaedia of religion and ethics*. 13 vols. Edinburgh: T. and T. Clark.

Jones, Rhys. 1978. "Why did the Tasmanians stop eating fish?" Pp. 11–47 in Richard A. Gould (ed.), *Explorations in ethnoarchaeology*. Albuquerque: University of New Mexico Press.

Joseph, Isya. 1919. *Devil worship: The sacred books and traditions of the Yezidis*. Boston: Richard G. Badger.

Joseph, Lawrence E. 1986. "Man and cormorant." *Audubon* 88, 2 (March): 38–41.

Josselyn, John. 1672. *New-England's realities discovered: In birds, beasts, fishes, serpents, and plants of that country*. London: G. Widdowes.

Julian. 1913. *Orations*. Vols. 1 and 2 of *The works of the Emperor Julian*, trans. William Cave Wright. Loeb Classical Library. London: William Heinemann; New York: Macmillan.

Junker, Wilhelm. 1891. *Travels in Africa during the years 1879–1883*. London: Chapman and Hall.

Junod, Henri A. 1913. *The life of a South African tribe*. 2 vols. Neuchâtel: Imprimerie Attinger Frères.

Justin. 1902. *History of the world*. Pp. 1–304 in *Justin, Cornelius Nepos, and Eutropius*, trans. John Selby Watson. London: George Bell and Sons.

Kaempfer, Engelbert. 1906. *The history of Japan*. 3 vols. Trans. J. G. Scheuchzer. Glasgow: James MacLehose and Sons.

Kaikini, V. M. 1951. "Vedic religion and Zoroastrianism." *Journal of the Anthropological Society of Bombay* 5, 2 (September): 37–50.

Kang, Shin T. 1972. *Sumerian economic texts from the Drehem archive*. Sumerian and Akkadian Cuneiform Texts in the Collection of the World Heritage Museum of the University of Illinois, 1. Urbana, Chicago, London: University of Illinois Press.

Kang, Shin T. 1973. *Sumerian economic texts from the Umma archive*. Sumerian and Akkadian Cuneiform Texts in the Collection of the World Heritage Museum of the University of Illinois, 2. Urbana, Chicago, London: University of Illinois Press.

Kang, Younghill. 1931. *The grass roof*. New York: Charles Scribner's Sons.

Karageorghis, Vassos. 1969. *Salamis: Recent discoveries in Cyprus*. New York, St. Louis, San Francisco: McGraw-Hill.

Karmarkar, A. P. 1944. "The fish in Indian folklore and the age of the Atharvaveda." *Annals of the Bhandarkar Oriental Research Institute* 24: 191–206.

Katsh, Abraham I. 1954. *Judaism in Islām. Biblical and Talmudic background of the Koran and its commentaries*. New York: New York University Press.

Kawaguchi, Ekai. 1909. *Three years in Tibet*. Madras: Theosophist Office.

Kay, S. 1834. *Travels and researches in Caffraria.* New York: B. Waugh and T. Mason.

Kees, Hermann. 1933. *Ägypten.* First section of *Kulturgeschichte des alten Orients* by A. Alt, A. Christensen, A. Götze, A. Grohmann, H. Kees, and B. Landsberger. Handbuch der Altertumswissenschaft, Abteilung 3, Teil 1, Band 3, Abschnitt 1. Munich: C. H. Beck.

Kees, Hermann. 1941. *Der Götterglaube im Alten Aegypten.* Mitteilungen der Vorderasiatisch-Aegyptischen Gesellschaft, Band 45. Leipzig: J. C. Hinrichs.

Kees, Hermann. 1961. *Ancient Egypt; a cultural topography.* Trans. Ian F. D. Morrow. London: Faber and Faber.

Keir, R. Malcolm. 1914. "Modern Korea." *Bulletin of the American Geographical Society* 46: 756–69, 817–30.

Keiser, Clarence Elwood. 1971. *Neo-Sumerian account texts from Drehem.* Babylonian Inscriptions in the Collection of James B. Nies, Yale University, 3. New Haven and London: Yale University Press.

Keith, Arthur Berriedale (trans.). 1914. *The Veda of the Black Yajus School entitled Taittiriya Sanhita.* 2 parts. Harvard Oriental Series, 18 and 19. Cambridge, Mass.: Harvard University Press.

Keller, C. 1901. *Madagascar, Mauritius, and other East-African islands.* London: Swan Sonnenschein.

Keller, Otto. 1963. *Die antike Tierwelt.* 2 vols. Hildesheim: Georg Olms.

Kemp, Barry J. 1987. "The Amarna workmen's village in retrospect." *Journal of Egyptian Archaeology* 73: 21–50.

Kemp, Barry J. 1989. *Ancient Egypt: Anatomy of a civilization.* London and New York: Routledge.

Kennedy, Raymond. 1953. *Field notes on Indonesia: South Celebes, 1949–50.* Ed. H. C. Conklin. New Haven: Human Relations Area Files.

Kerényi, C. 1959. *Asklepios: Archetypal image of the physician's existence.* Trans. Ralph Manheim. Bollingen Series 65, 3. New York: Pantheon Books.

Kern, H. 1918. *Verspreide Geschriften,* Vol. 8. The Hague: Martinus Nijhoff.

Khamboonruang, C. 1991. "The present status of trichinellosis in Thailand." *Southeast Asian Journal of Tropical Medicine and Public Health* 22 (Supplement): 312–15.

Khare, R. S. 1966. "A case of anomalous values in Indian civilization: Meat-eating among the Kanya-Kubja Brahmans of Katyayan gotra." *Journal of Asian Studies* 25: 229–40.

Khare, R. S. 1970. *The changing Brahmans: Associations and elites among the Kanya-Kubjas of North India.* Chicago and London: University of Chicago Press.

Khare, R. S. 1976. *Culture and reality: Essays on the Hindu system of managing foods.* Simla: Indian Institute of Advanced Study.

Khazanov, A. M. 1984. *Nomads and the outside world.* Trans. Julia Crookenden. Cambridge: Cambridge University Press.

Khin, U. 1948. *Fisheries in Burma.* Rangoon: Superintendent, Government Printing and Stationery.

Kidd, Samuel. 1831. *China.* London: Taylor and Walton.

Kilian, Lothar. 1983. *Zum Ursprung der Indogermanen.* Bonn: Habelt.

Kim, Charles W. 1983. "Epidemiology II: Geographic distribution and prevalence." Pp. 445–500 in William C. Campbell (ed.), *Trichinella and trichinosis.* New York and London: Plenum Press.

Kimble, George H. T. 1960. *Tropical Africa.* 2 vols. New York: Twentieth Century Fund.

Kingdon-Ward, F. 1949. *Burma's icy mountains.* London: Jonathan Cape.

Kinmond, William. 1957. *No dogs in China.* New York: Thomas Nelson and Sons.

Kinsley, David. 1986. *Hindu goddesses: Visions of the divine feminine in the Hindu religious tradition.* Berkeley, Los Angeles, London: University of California Press.

Kipling, John Lockwood. 1891. *Beast and man in India.* London and New York: Macmillan.

Kjaerholm, Lars. 1990. "Kula Teyvam worship in Tamilnadu: A link between past and present." Pp. 67–87 in Gabriella Eichinger Ferro-Luzzi (ed.), *Rites and beliefs in modern India.* New Delhi: Manohar.

Klein, Isaac. 1979. *A guide to Jewish religious practice.* Vol. 6 in the Moreshet Series, Studies in Jewish History, Literature, and Thought. New York: Jewish Theological Seminary of America.

Kler, Joseph. 1947. "The horse in the life of the Ordos Mongols." *Primitive Man* 20: 15–25.

Kohler, Kaufmann, and Solomon Schechter. 1907. "Dog." Pp. 630–32 in Vol. 4 of Isidore Singer (ed.), *The Jewish encyclopedia.* 12 vols. New York and London: Funk and Wagnalls.

Kolata, Gina Bari. 1974. "!Kung hunters-gatherers: Feminism, diet, and birth control." *Science* 185: 932–34.

Kolenda, Pauline Mahar. 1964. "Religious anxiety and Hindu fate." Pp. 71–81 in Edward B. Harper (ed.), *Religion in South Asia.* Seattle: University of Washington Press.

Koppers, Wilhelm. 1930. "Der Hund in der Mythologie der zirkumpazifischen Völker." *Wiener Beiträge zur Kulturgeschichte und Linguistik* 1: 359–99.

Koppers, Wilhelm. 1936. "Pferdeopfer und Pferdekult der Indogermanen." *Wiener Beiträge zur Kulturgeschichte und Linguistik* 4: 279–411.

Koppers, W., and L. Jungblut. 1942–45. "The water-buffalo and the zebu in Central India." *Anthropos* 37–40: 647–66.

Kozar, Zbigniew. 1962. "Incidence of *Trichinella spiralis* in the world and actual problems connected with trichinellosis." Pp. 15–67 in Zbigniew Kozar (ed.), *Trichinellosis.* Proceedings of the First International Conference on Trichinellosis. Warsaw: PWN—Polish Scientific Publishers.

Kozar, Zbigniew. 1970. "Trichinosis in Europe." Pp. 423–36 in Sylvester E. Gould (ed.), *Trichinosis in man and animals.* Springfield, Ill.: Charles C. Thomas.

Krader, Lawrence. 1955. "Ecology of Central Asian pastoralism." *Southwestern Journal of Anthropology* 11: 301–26.

Kramer, Samuel Noah. 1963. *The Sumerians: Their history, culture, and character.* Chicago: University of Chicago Press.

Kramer, Samuel Noah. 1981. *History begins at Sumer.* Third revised edition. Philadelphia: University of Pennsylvania Press.

Kretschmar, Freda. 1938. *Hundestammvater und Kerberos.* 2 vols. Stuttgart: Strecker und Schröder.

Kroeber, Alfred Louis. 1943. *People of the Philippines.* Second and revised edition. New York: American Museum of Natural History.

Kroll, Hubert. 1928. "Die Haustiere der Bantu." *Zeitschrift für Ethnologie* 60: 177–290.

Kümmel, Hans Martin. 1967. *Ersatzrituale für den hethitischen König.* Studien zu den Boğazköy-Texten, 3. Wiesbaden: Otto Harrassowitz.

Kunio, Yanagida. 1957. *Japanese manners and customs in the Meiji Era.* Trans. and adapted by Charles S. Terry. Tokyo: Obunsha.

Kurtz, Donna C., and John Boardman. 1971. *Greek burial customs.* Ithaca, N.Y.: Cornell University Press.

Laderman, Carol. 1983. *Wives and midwives: Childbirth and nutrition in rural Malaysia.* Berkeley, Los Angeles, London: University of California Press.

Laderman, Carol. 1984. "Food ideology and eating behavior: Contributions from Malay studies." *Social Science and Medicine* 19: 547–59.

Lagercrantz, Sture. 1950. *Contribution to the ethnography of Africa.* Studia Ethnographica Upsaliensia, 1. Lund, Sweden.

Lagercrantz, Sture. 1953. "Forbidden fish." *Orientalia Suecana* 2: 3–8.

Laing, Gordon J. 1963. *Survivals of Roman religion.* New York: Cooper Square Publishers.

Lal, Makkhan. 1984. *Settlement history and rise of civilization in the Ganga-Yamuna doab (from 1500 B.C. to 300 A.D.).* Delhi: B. R. Publishing Corporation.

Lambert, W. G. 1960. *Babylonian wisdom literature.* Oxford: Clarendon.

Lambert, W. G. 1967. "The Gula hymn of Bulluṭsa-rabi." *Orientalia* (Rome) (n.s.) 36: 105–32.

Landar, Herbert J. 1960. "The loss of Athapaskan words for fish in the Southwest." *International Journal of Linguistics* 26: 75–77.

Landon, Kenneth P. 1939. *Thailand in transition: A brief survey of cultural trends in the five years since the revolution of 1932.* Chicago: University of Chicago Press.

Lane, Edward William. 1908. *The manners and customs of the modern Egyptians.* London: J. M. Dent; New York: E. P. Dutton.

Langdon, Susan. 1989. "The return of the horse-leader." *American Journal of Archaeology* 93: 185–201.

Langkavel, B. 1881. "Das Hunde-Essen bei den verschiedenen Völkern." *Das Ausland* 54: 658–60.

Langkavel, B. 1888. "Pferde und Naturvölker." *Internationales Archiv für Ethnographie* 1: 49–60.

Langkavel, B. 1898. "Dogs and savages." Pp. 651–75 in the *Annual Report of the Smithsonian Institution for the Year Ending June 30, 1898.*

Lansdell, Henry. 1882. *Through Siberia.* Boston: Houghton, Mifflin.

Latham, James E. 1987. "Food." Pp. 387–93 in Vol. 5 of Mircea Eliade (ed.), *The encyclopedia of religion*. 16 vols. New York: Macmillan; London: Collier Macmillan.

Latourette, Kenneth Scott. 1964. *The Chinese, their history and culture*. Fourth edition. New York: Macmillan; London: Collier Macmillan.

Lattimore, Owen. 1929. *The desert road to Turkestan*. Boston: Little, Brown.

Lattimore, Owen. 1933. "The Gold tribe, 'Fishskin Tatars' of the lower Sungari." *Memoirs of the American Anthropological Association* 40: 1–77.

Lattimore, Owen. 1941. *Mongol journeys*. New York: Doubleday, Doran.

Lattimore, Owen. 1962. *Nomads and commissars: Mongolia revisited*. New York: Oxford University Press.

Laufer, Berthold. 1927. "Methods in the study of domestications." *Scientific Monthly* 25: 251–55.

Laufer, Berthold. 1931. "The domestication of the cormorant in China and Japan." *Field Museum of Natural History, Anthropological Series* 18: 201–63.

Lawrence, Walter R. 1895. *The Valley of Kashmir*. London: Henry Frowde.

Layard, Henry Austen. 1849. *Nineveh and its remains*. 2 vols. London: John Murray.

Leach, Edmund. 1964. "Anthropological aspects of language: Animal categories and verbal abuse." Pp. 23–63 in Eric H. Lenneberg (ed.), *New directions in the study of language*. Cambridge, Mass.: M.I.T. Press.

Leach, Maria. 1961. *God had a dog: Folklore of the dog*. New Brunswick: Rutgers University Press.

Leach, Maria (ed.). 1949–50. *Standard dictionary of folklore*. 2 vols. New York: Funk and Wagnalls.

League of Nations, Health Organization, Intergovernmental Conference of Far-Eastern Countries on Rural Hygiene. 1937. *Preparatory Papers: Report of French Indochina*. League of Nations Publications, Series 3: Health. Geneva: League of Nations.

LeBar, Frank M. (ed. and comp.). 1972–75. *Ethnic groups of insular Southeast Asia*. 2 vols. New Haven: Human Relations Area Files.

LeBar, Frank M., Gerald C. Hickey, and John K. Musgrave. 1964. *Ethnic groups of mainland Southeast Asia*. New Haven: Human Relations Area Files.

Lebkicher, Roy, George Rentz, and Max Steineke. 1952. *The Arabia of Ibn Saud*. New York: Russell F. Moore.

Lee, Richard B. 1968. "What hunters do for a living, or, how to make out on scarce resources." Pp. 30–48 in Richard B. Lee and Irven DeVore (eds.), *Man the hunter*. Chicago: Aldine.

Leitner, G. W. 1893. *Dardistan in 1866, 1886, and 1893*. Woking, England: Oriental University Institute.

Le May, Reginald. 1930. *Siamese tales old and new: The Four Riddles and other stories*. London: Noel Douglas.

Lemche, Niels Peter. 1985. *Early Israel: Anthropological and historical studies on the Israelite society before the monarchy*. Vetus Testamentum, Supplements, 37. Leiden: E. J. Brill.

Lemche, Niels Peter. 1988. *Ancient Israel: A new history of Israelite society.* Biblical Seminar, 5. Sheffield: JSOT Press.

Lemche, Niels Peter. 1991. *The Canaanites and their land: The tradition of the Canaanites.* Journal for the Study of the Old Testament, Supplemental Series, 110. Sheffield: JSOT Press.

Lepiksaar, Johannes. 1962. "Die vor- und frühgeschichtlichen Haustiere Süd-schwedens." *Zeitschrift für Tierzüchtung und Züchtungsbiologie* 77: 115–23.

Le Roux, Françoise, and Christian-J. Guyonvarc'h. 1987. "Epona." P. 135 in Vol. 5 of Mircea Eliade (ed.), *The encyclopedia of religion.* 16 vols. New York: Macmillan; London: Collier Macmillan.

Leroy, John D. 1978–79. "The ceremonial pig kill of the South Kewa." *Oceania* 49: 179–209.

Leshnik, Lawrence S. 1978. "The horse in India." Pp. 56–57 in Franklin C. Southworth (ed.), *Symbols, subsistence and social structure: The ecology of man and animal in South Asia.* Philadelphia: South Asia Regional Studies, University of Pennsylvania.

Lesko, Leonard H. 1987. "Seth." P. 178 in Vol. 13 of Mircea Eliade (ed.), *The encyclopedia of religion.* 16 vols. New York: Macmillan; London: Collier Macmillan.

Lessa, William A. 1975. *Drake's island of thieves: Ethnological sleuthing.* Honolulu: University Press of Hawaii.

Le Strange, Guy. 1905. *The lands of the Eastern Caliphate.* Cambridge: Cambridge University Press.

Leung, W. T. W., R. R. Butrum, and F. H. Chang. 1973. *Food composition table for use in East Asia,* Part 1. DHEW Publication No. (NIH) 73-465. Bethesda, Md.: U.S. Department of Health, Education and Welfare, and Food and Agriculture Organization of the United Nations.

Levchine, Alexis de. 1840. *Description des hordes et des steppes des Kirghiz-Kazaks ou Kirghiz-Kaissaks.* Trans. F. de Pigny. Paris: L'Imprimerie royale.

Levin, M. G., and L. P. Potapov (eds.). 1964. *The peoples of Siberia.* Chicago and London: University of Chicago Press.

Levine, Marsha A. 1990. "Dereivka and the problem of horse domestication." *Antiquity* 64: 727–40.

Levy, Thomas E. 1986. "The Chalcolithic Period: Archaeological sources for the history of Palestine." *Biblical Archaeologist* 49: 82–108.

Lévy-Bruhl, Lucien. 1923. *Primitive mentality.* New York: Macmillan.

Lewis, Albert Buell. 1932. *Ethnology of Melanesia.* Guide, Part 5. Chicago: Field Museum of Natural History.

Lewis, I. M. 1955. *Peoples of the horn of Africa.* Ethnographic Survey of Africa. North-Eastern Africa, Part 1. London: International African Institute.

Li Chi. 1957. *The beginnings of Chinese civilization.* Seattle: University of Washington Press.

Lilja, Saara. 1976. *Dogs in ancient Greek poetry.* Commentationes Humanarum Litterarum, 56. Helsinki: Societas Scientiarum Fennica.

Limet, Henri. 1987. "The cuisine of ancient Sumer." *Biblical Archaeologist* 50: 132–40, 144–47.

Lincoln, Bruce. 1979. "The hellhound." *Journal of Indo-European Studies* 7: 273–85.

Lincoln, Bruce. 1981. *Priests, warriors, and cattle.* Hermeneutics, Studies in the History of Religions, 10. Berkeley, Los Angeles, London: University of California Press.

Lindblom, Gerhard. 1920. *The Akamba in British East Africa.* Archives d'études orientales, 17. Uppsala: Appelbergs Boktryckeri Aktiebolag.

Lindeman, M. 1906. "Les Upotos." *Bulletin de la Société royale belge de géographie* 30: 16–32.

Ling, Stella, Janet King, and Virginia Leung. 1975. "Diet, growth, and cultural food habits in Chinese-American infants." *American Journal of Chinese Medicine* 3: 125–32.

Linton, Ralph. 1933. *The Tanala: A hill tribe of Madagascar.* Field Museum of Natural History, Anthropological Series, 22. Chicago: Field Museum.

Linton, Ralph. 1955. *The tree of culture.* New York: Alfred A. Knopf.

Liphschitz, Nili, and Yoav Waisel. 1986. "Palaeobotanical remains." Pp. 153–55 in Israel Finkelstein, *ʿIzbet Sarṭah: An Early Iron Age site near Rosh Haʿayin, Israel.* BAR International Series, 299. Oxford: British Archaeological Reports.

Liphschitz, Nili, Ram Gophna, and Simcha Lev-Yadun. 1989. "Man's impact on the vegetational landscape of Israel in the Early Bronze Age II–III." Pp. 263–68 in Pierre de Miroschedji (ed.), *L'Urbanisation de la Palestine à l'âge du Bronze ancien.* 2 parts. BAR International Series, 527. Oxford: British Archaeological Reports.

Little-known Asian animals with a promising economic future. 1983. Report of an Ad Hoc Panel of the Advisory Committee on Technology Innovation, Board on Science and Technology for International Development, Office of International Affairs, National Research Council. Washington, D.C.: National Academy Press.

Liu Chungshee Hsien. 1932. "The dog-ancestor story of the aboriginal tribes of southern China." *Journal of the Anthropological Institute of Great Britain and Ireland* 62: 361–68.

Liu Chungshee Hsien. 1941. "On the dog-ancestor myth in Asia." *Studia Serica* 1: 85–111.

Liu En-lan. 1937. "Pootu, a lost island." *Economic Geography* 13: 132–38.

Livingstone, A. 1988. "The Isin 'dog house' revisited." *Journal of Cuneiform Studies* 40: 54–60.

Lo, Kenneth H. C. 1971. *Peking cooking.* New York: Pantheon.

Lo, Kenneth H. C. 1979. *The encyclopedia of Chinese cooking.* New York: A and W Publishers.

Lockhart, W. S. A. (trans.). 1871. *Muraviev's journey to Khiva through the Turcoman country, 1819–20.* Trans. from the Russian by Philipp Strahl and from the German by W. S. A. Lockhart. Calcutta: Foreign Department Press.

Lodrick, Deryck O. 1981. *Sacred cows, sacred places: Origins and survivals of animal homes in India.* Berkeley and Los Angeles: University of California Press.

Lodrick, Deryck O. 1987. "Gopashtami and Govardhan Puja: Two Krishna festivals of India." *Journal of Cultural Geography* 7, 2 (Spring/Summer): 101–16.

Lodrick, Deryck O. 1991. "Cattle fairs and festivals in Rajasthan." Paper presented to the Second International Seminar on Rajasthan, Udaipur, December 17–23. 13 pp.

Lodrick, Deryck O. 1992. "Cattle rites and cattle festivals in northern India." *International Journal of Indian Studies* 2: 125–60.

Loeb, Edwin M. 1935. "Sumatra. Its history and people." *Wiener Beiträge zur Kulturgeschichte und Linguistik* 3: 1–303.

Loeb, Edwin M. 1962. *In feudal Africa*. International Journal of Linguistics, Vol. 28, No. 3, Part 2. Also Publications, Indiana University Research Center in Anthropology, Folklore, and Linguistics, 23. Bloomington: Research Center in Anthropology, Folklore, and Linguistics.

Long, Eleanor R. 1984. "How the dog got its days: A skeptical inquiry into traditional star and weather lore." *Western Folklore* 43: 256–64.

Lonsdale, Steven H. 1979. "Attitudes towards animals in ancient Greece." *Greece and Rome* 26: 146–59.

Lucian. 1913. *The Syrian Goddess*. Trans. H. A. Strong. London: Constable.

Lucian. 1959. *The Scythian or the consul*. Pp. 239–57 in Vol. 6 of *Lucian*, trans. K. Kilburn. Loeb Classical Library. London: William Heinemann; Cambridge, Mass.: Harvard University Press.

Lucian. 1961. *Dialogues of the dead*. Pp. 1–175 in Vol. 7 of *Lucian*, trans. M. D. Macleod. Loeb Classical Library. London: William Heinemann; Cambridge, Mass.: Harvard University Press.

Luomala, Katherine. 1960. "The native dog in the Polynesian system of values." Pp. 190–240 in Stanley Diamond (ed.), *Culture in history: Essays in honor of Paul Radin*. New York: Columbia University Press.

Lurker, Manfred. 1969. "Hund und Wolf in ihrer Beziehung zum Tode." *Antaios* 10: 199–216.

Lurker, Manfred. 1983. "Der Hund als Symboltier für den Übergang vom Diesseits in das Jenseits." *Zeitschrift für Religions- und Geistesgeschichte* 35: 132–44.

Lurker, Manfred. 1987. "Dogs." Pp. 395–97 in Vol. 4 of Mircea Eliade (ed.), *The encyclopedia of religion*. 16 vols. New York: Macmillan; London: Collier Macmillan.

Macalister, R. A. Stewart. 1912. *The excavation of Gezer 1902–1905 and 1907–1909*. 3 vols. London: John Murray.

Macalister, R. A. Stewart. 1965. *The Philistines: Their history and civilization*. Chicago: Argonaut.

McArdle, John. 1982. "Preliminary report on the Predynastic fauna of the Hierakonpolis project." Pp. 116–21 in Michael Allen Hoffman, *The Predynastic of Hierakonpolis—an interim report*. Egyptian Studies Association Publications, 1. Giza: Cairo University Herbarium; Macomb, Ill.: Department of Sociology and Anthropology, Western Illinois University.

McAuley, J. B., M. K. Michelson, and P. M. Schantz. 1991. "Trichinosis surveillance, United States, 1987–90." *MMWR CDC Surveillance Summaries* (Atlanta, Ga.) 40, 3 (December): 35–42.

McCall, Anthony Gilchrist. 1949. *Lushai chrysalis*. London: Luzac.

MacCana, Proinsias. 1987. "Celtic religion." Pp. 148–66 in Vol. 3 of Mircea Eliade (ed.), *The encyclopedia of religion*. 16 vols. New York: Macmillan; London: Collier Macmillan.

McCrindle, J. W. 1896. *The invasion of India by Alexander the Great*. Westminster: Archibald Constable.

MacCulloch, John Arnott. 1911. *The religion of the ancient Celts*. Edinburgh: T. and T. Clark.

MacCulloch, John Arnott. 1916–32. *The mythology of all races*. 13 vols. Boston: Marshall Jones.

McCulloch, Merran. 1951. *The southern Lunda and related peoples*. Ethnographic Survey of Africa. West Central Africa, Part 1. London: International African Institute.

MacDonald, David. 1929. *The land of the lama*. London: Seeley, Service.

MacDonald, Kevin C. 1992. "The domestic chicken (*Gallus gallus*) in sub-Saharan Africa: A background to its introduction and its osteological differentiation from indigenous fowls (Numidinae and *Francolinus* sp.)." *Journal of Archaeological Science* 19: 303–18.

Macdonell, Arthur A. 1897. *Vedic mythology*. Grundriss der Indo-Arischen Philologie und Altertumskunde. Band 3, Heft 1A. Strassburg: Karl J. Trübner.

Macdonell, Arthur Anthony, and Arthur Berriedale Keith. 1967. *Vedic index of names and subjects*. 2 vols. Indian Text Series. Reprint of 1912 edition. Delhi, Benares, and Patna: Motilal Banarsidass.

McGovern, William Montgomery. 1924. *To Lhasa in disguise: A secret expedition through mysterious Tibet*. New York and London: Century.

McKay, John W. 1973. "Further light on the horses and chariot of the Sun in the Jerusalem temple (2 Kings 23:11)." *Palestine Exploration Quarterly* 105: 167–69.

Macqueen, James G. 1975. *The Hittites and their contemporaries in Asia Minor*. Boulder, Colo.: Westview Press.

Macrobius. 1969. *Saturnalia*. Trans. Percival Vaughan Davies. New York and London: Columbia University Press.

Maguire, R. A. J. 1948. "Il-Torobo." *Tanganyika Notes and Records* 25: 1–27.

Mahmoud, Aly. 1984. "Arabs still cherish their camels." *Sacramento Bee* (California), June 17, p. F7.

Mainoldi, Carla. 1984. *L'Image du loup et du chien dans la Grèce ancienne*. Association des publications près les Universités de Strasbourg. Paris: Ophrys.

Majumdar, D. N. 1937. *A tribe in transition*. Calcutta: Longmans, Green.

Majumdar, Surendra Nath. 1924. "The Ao Nagas." *Man in India* 4: 41–82.

Malcolm, George A. 1951. *First Malayan republic: The story of the Philippines*. Boston: Christopher.

Malcolm, Sheila H. 1952. *Nutrition investigations in the New Hebrides*. South Pacific Commission, Technical Paper 23. Noumea, New Caledonia: South Pacific Commission.

Malinowski, Bronislaw. 1935. *Coral gardens and their magic*. 2 vols. New York: American Book.

Mallory, J. P. 1981. "The ritual treatment of the horse in Early Kurgan tradition." *Journal of Indo-European Studies* 9: 205–26.

Mallory, J. P. 1982. "Indo-European and Kurgan fauna I: Wild mammals." *Journal of Indo-European Studies* 10: 193–222.

Mallory, J. P. 1983. "Proto-Indo-European and Kurgan fauna II: Fish." *Journal of Indo-European Studies* 11: 263–79.

Mallory, J. P. 1989. *In search of the Indo-Europeans: Language, archaeology and myth.* London and New York: Thames and Hudson.

Mallowan, M. E. L. 1965. *Early Mesopotamia and Iran.* London: Thames and Hudson.

Malten, Ludolf. 1914. "Das Pferd im Totenglauben." *Jahrbuch des Kaiserlich Deutschen Archäologischen Instituts* 29: 179–256.

Malten, Ludolf. 1928. "Der Stier in Kult und mythischem Bild." *Jahrbuch des Deutschen Archäoligischen Instituts* 43: 90–139.

Malynicz, George L. 1970. "Pig keeping by the subsistence agriculturalist of the New Guinea Highlands." *Search* 1: 201–4.

Manwell, Clyde, and C. M. Ann Baker. 1983. "Origin of the dog: From wolf or wild *Canis familiaris?*" *Speculations in Science and Technology* 6: 213–24.

Manwell, Clyde, and C. M. Ann Baker. 1984. "Domestication of the dog: Hunter, food, bed-warmer, or emotional object?" *Zeitschrift für Tierzüchtung und Züchtungsbiologie* 101: 241–56.

Marcus, Amy Dockser. 1993. "Israeli, Russian Jews find themselves in a meaty debate. Ex-Soviets, unwilling to stop eating pork, are blamed for increasing social woes." *Wall Street Journal* (Western edition), April 19, pp. A1, 5.

Marinculic, A., D. Rapic, J. Brglez, N. Dzakula, and D. Stojiljkovic. 1991. "Epidemiological survey of trichinellosis in Yugoslavia." *Southeast Asian Journal of Tropical Medicine and Public Health* 22 (Supplement): 302–7.

Maringer, Johannes. 1981. "The horse in art and ideology of Indo-European peoples." *Journal of Indo-European Studies* 9: 177–204.

Marriott, McKim. 1968. "Caste ranking and food transactions: A matrix analysis." Pp. 131–71 in Milton Singer and Bernard S. Cohn (eds.), *Structure and change in Indian society.* Viking Fund Publications in Anthropology, 47. Chicago: Aldine.

Marsden, William. 1811. *The history of Sumatra.* Third edition. London: Longman, Hurst, Rees, Orme, and Brown.

Marshall, Harry Ignatius. 1922. *The Karen people of Burma: A study in anthropology and ethnology.* Ohio State University Bulletin, 26, No. 13. Columbus: Ohio State University Press.

Marshall, John. 1931. *Mohenjo-Daro and the Indus civilization.* 3 vols. London: Arthur Probsthain.

Marshall, William E. 1873. *A phrenologist amongst the Todas.* London: Longmans, Green.

Martial. 1919–20. *Epigrams.* 2 vols. Trans. Walter C. A. Ker. Loeb Classical Library. London: W. Heinemann; New York: G. P. Putnam's Sons.

Martial. 1926. *The Egyptians.* Trans. Henry H. Bohn. London: G. Bell.

Martin, Luther H. 1987. *Hellenistic religions: An introduction.* New York and Oxford: Oxford University Press.

Marty, Paul. 1930. "Les Nimadi, Maures sauvages et chasseurs." *Hespéris* 11: 119–24.

Marvin, Garry. 1984. "The cockfight in Andalusia, Spain: Images of the truly male." *Anthropological Quarterly* 57: 60–70.

Mason, F. 1868. "On dwellings, works of art, laws, and c. of the Karens." *Journal of the Asiatic Society of Bengal* 37: 125–69.

Mason, I. L. 1984a. "Camels." Pp. 106–15 in Ian L. Mason (ed.), *Evolution of domesticated animals*. London and New York: Longman.

Mason, I. L. 1984b. "Origins, evolution and distribution of domestic camels." Pp. 16–35 in W. Ross Cockrill (ed.), *The camelid: An all-purpose animal*. Proceedings of the Khartoum workshop on camels, December 1979. Uppsala: Scandinavian Institute of African Studies.

Maspero, G. 1901. *The dawn of civilization*. New York: D. Appleton.

Massé, Henri. 1938. *Croyances et coutumes persanes suivies de contes et chansons populaires*. Paris: Librairie Orientale et Américaine.

Masson, Olivier. 1950. "À propos d'un rituel hittite pour la lustration d'une armée." *Revue de l'histoire des religions* 137: 5–25.

Masson, V. M., and V. I. Sarianidi. 1972. *Central Asia: Turkmenia before the Achaemenids*. Trans. and ed. Ruth Tringham. New York and Washington, D.C.: Praeger Publishers.

Massy, A. 1890. "Quatorze mois chez les Thos et les Mans-tiens." *Bulletin de géographie historique et descriptive* 5: 332–84.

Masuoka, Jitsuichi. 1945. "Changing food habits of the Japanese in Hawaii." *American Sociological Review* 10: 759–65.

Mathews, L. 1980. "Hong Kong is talking about a dogmeat reversal." *San Francisco Examiner and Chronicle*. February 3, Sunday Punch Section, p. 1.

Mathur, K. S. 1964. *Caste and ritual in a Malwa village*. New York: Asia Publishing House.

Matthews, Washington. 1897. *Navajo legends*. Memoirs of the American Folk-Lore Society, 1897. Boston and New York: American Folk-Lore Society.

Matthews, Washington. 1898. "Ichthyophobia." *Journal of American Folk-Lore* 11: 105–112.

Matyushin, G. 1986. "The Mesolithic and Neolithic in the southern Urals and Central Asia." Pp. 133–50 in Marek Zvelebil (ed.), *Hunters in transition*. Cambridge: Cambridge University Press.

Maxwell, J. Preston. 1921. "Intestinal parasitism in south Fukien." *China Medical Journal* 35: 377–82.

Maxwell, W. E. 1881. "The folklore of the Malays." *Journal of the Straits Branch of the Royal Asiatic Society* 7: 11–29.

Mayer, Adrian C. 1960. *Caste and kinship in Central India*. Berkeley: University of California Press.

Maynard, Leonard A., and Swen Wen-yuh. 1956. "Nutrition." Pp. 400–436 in John Lossing Buck (ed.), *Land utilization in China*. Facsimile reprint of the 1937 edition published by the University of Nanking. New York: Council on Economic and Cultural Affairs.

Mayrhofer-Passler, E. 1953. "Haustieropfer bei den Indoiraniern und den anderen indogermanischen Völkern." *Archiv Orientální* 21: 182–205.

Mead, Margaret. 1930. *Social organization of Manua.* Bernice P. Bishop Museum, Bull. 76. Honolulu.

Meadow, Richard H. 1975. "Mammal remains from Hajji Firuz: A study in methodology." Pp. 265–83 in A. T. Clason (ed.), *Archaeozoological studies.* Amsterdam and Oxford: North-Holland; New York: American Elsevier.

Meadow, Richard H. 1983. "The vertebrate faunal remains from Hasanlu period X at Hajji Firuz." Pp. 369–422 in Mary M. Voigt, *Hajji Firuz Tepe, Iran: The Neolithic settlement.* Vol. 1 of Hasanlu Excavation Reports, ed. Robert H. Dyson, Jr. University Museum Monographs, 50. Philadelphia: University Museum, University of Pennsylvania.

Meadow, Richard H. 1984. "Animal domestication in the Middle East: A view from the eastern margin." Pp. 309–37 in Juliet Clutton-Brock and Caroline Grigson (eds.), *Animals and archaeology.* Vol. 3, *Early herders and their flocks.* BAR International Series, 202. Oxford: British Archaeological Reports.

Meadow, Richard H. 1985–88. "Faunal exploitation patterns in eastern Iran and Baluchistan: A review of recent investigations." Pp. 881–916 in Vol. 2 of Edenda Curaverunt, G. Gnoli, and L. Lanciotti (eds.), *Orientalia Josephi Tucci Memoriae Dicata.* 3 vols. Serie Orientale Roma, 56, 1–3. Rome: Istituto Italiano per il Medo ed Estremo Oriente.

Meadow, Richard H. 1991. "Faunal remains and urbanism at Harappa." Pp. 89–106 in Richard H. Meadow (ed.), *Harappa excavations 1986–1990: A multidisciplinary approach to third millennium urbanism.* Monographs in World Archaeology, 3. Madison, Wis.: Prehistory Press.

Meek, C. K. 1925. *The northern tribes of Nigeria.* 2 vols. London: Oxford University Press.

Meek, Theophile James. 1935. *Old Akkadian, Sumerian, and Cappadocian texts from Nuzi.* Vol. 3 of *Excavations at Nuzi.* Harvard Semitic Series, 10. Cambridge, Mass.: Harvard University Press; London: Oxford University Press.

Meggitt, M. J. 1965. "The association between Australian Aborigines and dingoes." Pp. 7–26 in Anthony Leeds and Andrew P. Vayda (eds.), *Man, culture, and animals.* Publication 78 of the American Association for the Advancement of Science. Washington, D.C.: AAAS.

Meier, Carl Alfred. 1967. *Ancient incubation and modern psychotherapy.* Trans. Monica Curtis. Evanston, Ill.: Northwestern University Press.

Meier, Carl Alfred. 1987. "Asklepios." Pp. 463–66 in Vol. 1 of Mircea Eliade (ed.), *The encyclopedia of religion.* 16 vols. New York: Macmillan; London: Collier Macmillan.

Meigs, Anna S. 1978. "A Papuan perspective on pollution." *Man* (n.s.) 13: 304–18.

Meissner, Bruno. 1924. *Babylonien und Assyrien.* 2 vols. Heidelberg: Carl Winters Universitätsbuchhandlung.

Mellaart, James. 1965. *Earliest civilizations of the Near East.* London: Thames and Hudson.

Menander. 1951. *The principal fragments*. Trans. F. G. Allinson. Loeb Classical Library. London: William Heinemann; Cambridge, Mass.: Harvard University Press.

Mendenhall, George E. 1962. "The Hebrew conquest of Palestine." *Biblical Archaeologist* 25: 66–87.

Mercer, S. A. B. 1908–26. "Water, water-gods (Egyptian)." Pp. 710–12 in Vol. 12 of James Hastings (ed.), *Encyclopaedia of religion and ethics*. 13 vols. Edinburgh: T. and T. Clark.

Merker, M. 1904. *Die Masai*. Berlin: Dietrich Reimer.

Merlin, R. H. A. 1971. *De canibus: Dog and hound in antiquity*. London: J. A. Allen.

Merriam, A. C. 1884. "Marvelous cures at Epidaurus." *American Antiquarian* 6: 300–307.

Merriam, A. C. 1885. "The dogs of Aesculapius." *American Antiquarian* 7: 285–89.

Mi Mi Khaing. 1946. *Burmese family*. Calcutta: Longmans, Green.

Middleton, John. 1953. *The Kikuyu and Kamba of Kenya*. Ethnographic Survey of Africa. East Central Africa, Part 5. London: International African Institute.

Mikesell, Marvin W. 1960. "Deforestation in northern Morocco." *Science* 132: 441–48.

Milgrom, Jacob. 1971–72. "Book of Leviticus." Cols. 138–47 in Vol. 11 of *Encyclopaedia Judaica*. 16 vols. Jerusalem: Keter Publishing House; New York: Macmillan.

Milisauskas, Sarunas. 1978. *European prehistory*. New York, San Francisco, London: Academic Press.

Miller, Robert L. 1990. "Hogs and hygiene." *Journal of Egyptian Archaeology* 76: 125–40.

Millet, Nicholas B., Gerald D. Hart, Theodore A. Reyman, Michael R. Zimmerman, and Peter K. Lewin. 1980. "ROM I: Mummification for the common people." Pp. 71–84 in Aidan and Eve Cockburn (eds.), *Mummies, disease, and ancient cultures*. Cambridge: Cambridge University Press.

Mills, J. P. 1926. *The Ao Nagas*. London: Macmillan.

Mills, J. P. 1937. *The Rengma Nagas*. London: Macmillan.

Milne, Mrs. Leslie. 1924. *The home of an Eastern clan: A study of the Palaungs of the Shan States*. Oxford: Clarendon.

Minns, Ellis H. 1913. *Scythians and Greeks*. Cambridge: Cambridge University Press.

Modi, Jivanji Jamshedji. 1911–34. *Anthropological papers*. 5 parts. Bombay: British India Press.

Modi, Jivanji Jamshedji. 1913–16. "The Pundits of Kashmir." *Journal of the Anthropological Society of Bombay* 10: 461–85.

Modi, Jivanji Jamshedji. 1926. "An American tribe and its buffalo and an Asiatic tribe and its fish." *Journal of the Anthropological Society of Bombay* 13: 432–37.

Modi, Jivanji Jamshedji. 1979. *The religious ceremonies and customs of the Parsees*. New York and London: Garland Publishing.

Moffatt, Michael. 1979. *An untouchable community in South India: Structure and consensus*. Princeton: Princeton University Press.

Monier-Williams, M. 1964. *Buddhism, in its connexion with Brahmanism and Hindu-*

ism and its contrast with Christianity. Chowkhamba Sanskrit Studies, 45. Benares: Chowkhamba Sanskrit Series Office.

Montelius, Oscar. 1888. *The civilisation of Sweden in heathen times.* Trans. from the second Swedish edition by F. H. Woods. London and New York: Macmillan.

Montesquieu, Charles de Secondat. 1977. *The spirit of laws.* Trans. David W. Carrithers. Berkeley: University of California Press.

Montet, Pierre. 1958. *Everyday life in Egypt in the days of Ramesses the Great.* London: Edward Arnold.

Moore, W. Robert. 1930. "Among the hill tribes of Sumatra." *National Geographic Magazine,* February, pp. 187–227.

Moreno, Manuel. 1992. "Pancāmirtam: God's washings as food." Pp. 147–78 in R. S. Khare (ed.), *The eternal food: Gastronomic ideas and experiences of Hindus and Buddhists.* Albany: State University of New York Press.

Mors, P. O. 1953. "Notes on hunting and fishing in Buhaya." *Anthropological Quarterly* 26: 89–93.

Moses, S. T. 1922–23. "Fish and religion in South India." *Quarterly Journal of the Mythic Society* 13: 549–54.

Mote, Frederick W. 1977. "Yüan and Ming." Pp. 193–257 in K. C. Chang (ed.), *Food in Chinese culture: Anthropological and historical perspectives.* New Haven and London: Yale University Press.

Motz, Lotte. 1982. "Freyja, Anat, Ishtar and Inanna: Some cross-cultural comparisons." *Mankind Quarterly* 33: 195–212.

Moyer, James C. 1983. "Hittite and Israelite cultic practices: A selected comparison." Pp. 19–38 in William W. Hallo, James C. Moyer, and Leo G. Perdue (eds.), *More essays on the comparative method. Scripture in context,* Vol. 2. Winona Lake, Ind.: Eisenbrauns.

Muffet, Thomas. 1655. *Health's improvement.* London.

Muhammad, G. 1905. "Festivals and folklore of Gilgit." *Memoirs of the Asiatic Society of Bengal* 1: 93–127.

Müller, Hanns-Hermann. 1984. "Zoological and historical interpretation of bones from food and sacrifices in early medieval times." Pp. 187–93 in Caroline Grigson and Juliet Clutton-Brock (eds.), *Animals and archaeology.* Vol. 4, *Husbandry in Europe.* BAR International Series, 227. Oxford: British Archaeological Reports.

Munro, R. H. 1977. "Comeback of the Chinese pet dog." *San Francisco Examiner and Chronicle,* April 10, Sunday Punch Section, p. 5.

Murdock, George Peter. 1958. *African cultural summaries.* Unpublished manuscript. New Haven: Human Relations Area Files.

Murdock, George Peter. 1959. *Africa: Its people and their culture history.* New York, Toronto, London: McGraw-Hill.

Murphey, Rhoads. 1951. "The decline of North Africa since the Roman occupation: Climatic or human?" *Annals of the Association of American Geographers* 41: 116–32.

Murphy, Edwin. 1990. *The antiquities of Egypt.* A translation with notes of Book 1 of *The library of history* of Diodorus Siculus. New Brunswick, N.J., and London: Transaction Publishers.

Murray, D. W. 1986. "On Keralan cattle: A response to Westen and Harris." *Current Anthropology* 27: 53.

Murray, G. W. 1935. *Sons of Ishmael: A study of the Egyptian Bedouin.* London: George Routledge and Sons.

Musil, Alois. 1928. *The manners and customs of the Rwala Bedouins.* Oriental Explorations and Studies, 6. New York: American Geographical Society.

Nachtigal, G. 1874. "Nachrichten von Dr. G. Nachtigal in Inner-Afrika. Die tributären Heidenländer Baghirmi's." *Petermanns Mitteilungen* 20: 323–31.

Nadel, Siegfried Ferdinand. 1947. *The Nuba.* London: Oxford University Press.

Nadel, Siegfried Ferdinand. 1951. *A black Byzantium.* London: Oxford University Press.

Naik, T. B. 1956. *The Bhils; a study.* Delhi: Bharatiya Adimjati Sevak Sangh.

Nalder, Leonard Fielding (ed.). 1937. *A tribal survey of Mongalla Province.* London: Oxford University Press.

Narasimhan, Chakravarthi V. 1965. *The Mahabharata.* New York and London: Columbia University Press.

Nath, Bhola. 1979. "Animal remains." Pp. 323–24 in Vol. 1 of F. Raymond Allchin and Dilip K. Chakrabarti (eds.), *A source-book of Indian archaeology.* New Delhi: Munshiram Manoharlal.

Nazli, B., and T. Inal. 1987. "Untersuchungen über das Vorkommen von *Trichinella spiralis* bei Haus- und Wildschweinen sowie aus diesen hergestellten Produkten in der Turkei." *Berliner und Münchener Tierärztliche Wochenschrift* 100: 187–90.

Neil, Robert Alexander (ed.). 1966. *The Knights of Aristophanes.* Hildesheim: Georg Olms.

Nelson, George S. 1970. "Trichinosis in Africa." Pp. 473–92 in Sylvester E. Gould (ed.), *Trichinosis in man and animals.* Springfield, Ill.: Charles C. Thomas.

Nemeroff, Carol, and Paul Rozin. 1989. "'You are what you eat': Applying the demand-free 'impressions' technique to an unacknowledged belief." *Ethos* 17: 50–69.

Nesbit, William M. 1966. *Sumerian records from Drehem.* Columbia University Oriental Studies, 8. New York: AMS Press.

Neumann, Erich. 1969. *The origins and history of consciousness.* Bollingen Series, 42. New York: Bollingen Foundation.

Neumann, J., and S. Parpola. 1987. "Climatic change and the eleventh–tenth-century eclipse of Assyria and Babylonia." *Journal of Near Eastern Studies* 46: 161–82.

Neusner, Jacob. 1973. *The idea of purity in ancient Judaism.* Leiden: E. J. Brill.

Newall, Venetia. 1971. *An egg at Easter.* London: Routledge and Kegan Paul.

Newall, Venetia. 1987. "Egg." Pp. 36–37 in Vol. 5 of Mircea Eliade (ed.), *The encyclopedia of religion.* 16 vols. New York: Macmillan; London: Collier Macmillan.

Newberry, P. E. 1928. "The pig and the cult-animal of Set." *Journal of Egyptian Archaeology* 14: 211–25.

Newcomb, Franc Johnson. 1940. *Navajo omens and taboos.* Santa Fe: Rydal.

Newman, L. F. 1946. "Some notes on foods and dietetics in the sixteenth and seventeenth centuries." *Journal of the Royal Anthropological Institute of Great Britain and Ireland* 76: 39–49.

Ní Chatháin, Próinséas. 1979–80. "Swineherds, seers, and druids." *Studia Celtica* 14/15: 200–211.

Ní Chatháin, Próinséas. 1991. "Traces of the cult of the horse in early Irish sources." *Journal of Indo-European Studies* 19: 123–31.

Niebuhr, Carsten. 1889. *Description of Arabia.* Trans. Major C. W. H. Sealy. Selections from the Records of the Bombay Government, 226, n.s. Bombay: Government Central Press.

Nietschmann, Bernard. 1973. *Between land and water.* New York and London: Seminar Press.

Nikhilananda, Swami (trans.). 1949–59. *The Upanishads.* 4 vols. New York: Harper.

Nilsson, Martin P. 1940. *Greek popular religion.* New York: Columbia University Press.

Nilsson, Martin P. 1949. *A history of Greek religion.* Second edition. Trans. F. J. Fielden. Oxford: Clarendon.

Nobis, G. 1974. "The origin, domestication and early history of domestic horses." *Veterinary Medical Review* 1974: 211–25.

Norbeck, Edward. 1954. *Takashima: A Japanese fishing community.* Salt Lake City: University of Utah Press.

Northampton, the Marquis of, W. Spiegelberg, and P. E. Newberry. 1908. *Report on some excavations in the Theban necropolis during the winter of 1898–9.* London: Archibald Constable.

Noth, Martin. 1960a. *Gesammelte Studien zum Alten Testament.* Munich: Chr. Kaiser.

Noth, Martin. 1960b. *The history of Israel.* Second edition. Trans. P. R. Ackroyd. New York and Evanston, Ill.: Harper and Row.

Noth, Martin. 1965. *Leviticus: A commentary.* Trans. J. E. Anderson. Old Testament Library. Philadelphia: Westminster.

Noth, Martin. 1966. *The Old Testament world.* Trans. Victor I. Gruhn. Philadelphia: Fortress.

Novak, David. 1976. *Law and theology in Judaism, second series.* New York: KTAV Publishing House.

Novak, David. 1987. "Kashrut." Pp. 270–73 in Vol. 8 of Mircea Eliade (ed.), *The encyclopedia of religion.* 16 vols. New York: Macmillan; London: Collier Macmillan.

Nweeya, Samuel K. 1910. *Persia the land of the Magi.* Philadelphia: John C. Winston.

O'Donovan, E. 1883. *The Merv Oasis: Travels and adventures east of the Caspian during the years 1879–80–81 including five months' residence among the Tekkés of Merv.* New York: G. P. Putnam's Sons.

O'Flaherty, Wendy Doniger. 1980. *Women, androgynes, and other mythical beasts.* Chicago and London: University of Chicago Press.

O'Flaherty, Wendy Doniger. 1981. *The Rig Veda: An anthology.* Harmondsworth, England: Penguin.

O'Flaherty, Wendy Doniger. 1987. "Horses." Pp. 463–68 in Vol. 6 of Mircea Eliade (ed.), *The encyclopedia of religion.* 16 vols. New York: Macmillan; London: Collier Macmillan.

Oiso, Toshio. 1976. "History of food and diet in Japan." *Progress in Food and Nutrition Science* 2: 35–48.

Ojoade, J. Olowo. 1990. "Nigerian cultural attitudes to the dog." Pp. 215–21 in Roy Willis (ed.), *Signifying animals: Human meaning in the natural world.* London, Boston, Sydney, Wellington: Unwin Hyman.

O'Laughlin, Bridget. 1974. "Mediation of contradiction: Why Mbum women do not eat chicken." Pp. 301–18 in Michelle Zimbalist Rosaldo and Louise Lamphere (eds.), *Women, culture and society.* Stanford: Stanford University Press.

Oldenberg, Hermann. 1988. *The religion of the Veda.* Trans. Shridhar B. Shrotri. Delhi: Motilal Banarsidass.

Oldenberg, Hermann, and F. Max Müller (trans.). 1892. *The Grihya-sūtras: Rules of Vedic domestic ceremonies,* Part 2. Vol. 30 of *The sacred books of the East,* ed. F. Max Müller. Oxford: Clarendon.

Olivieri, A. 1924. "Sacrifizio del gallo." *Rivista Indo-Greco-Italica di filologia-lingua-antichità* 8: 135–37.

Olmstead, A. T. 1968. *History of Assyria.* Chicago and London: University of Chicago Press.

Olsen, Stanley J. 1984. "The early domestication of the horse in North China." *Archaeology* 37: 62–63, 77.

Olufsen, O. 1911. *The emir of Bokhara and his country: Journeys and studies in Bokhara.* Copenhagen: Gyldendalske Boghandel Nordisk Forlag; London: William Heinemann.

Oppenheim, A. Leo. 1956. *The interpretation of dreams in the ancient Near East.* Transactions of the American Philosophical Society, 46, Part 3. Philadelphia: American Philosophical Society.

Orde Browne, G. St. J. 1925. *The vanishing tribes of Kenya.* London: Seeley, Service.

Ormeling, F. J. 1957. *The Timor problem.* Groningen and The Hague: J. B. Wolters and Martinus Nijhoff.

Orr, J. B., and J. L. Gilks. 1931. *The physique and health of two Africa tribes.* Medical Research Council (Great Britain). Special Report Series, 155. London: H.M. Stationery Office.

Osgood, Cornelius. 1951. *The Koreans and their culture.* New York: Ronald Press.

Otis, Laura P. 1984. "Factors influencing the willingness to taste unusual foods." *Psychological Reports* 54: 739–45.

Ouseley, William. 1819–23. *Travels in various countries of the East; more particularly Persia.* 2 vols. London: Rodwell and Martin.

Ovid. 1951. *Fasti.* Trans. James George Frazer. Loeb Classical Library. London: William Heinemann; Cambridge, Mass.: Harvard University Press.

Paine, Robert. 1957. *Coast Lapp society, I: A study of the neighbourhood in Ravsbotn Fjord.* Troms Museums Skrifter, 4. Troms, Norway.

Pallottino, Massimo. 1975. *The Etruscans.* Revised and enlarged. Trans. J. Cremona; ed. David Ridgway. London: Allen Lane.

Palmer, E. H. 1880. *The Qur'ān.* Vols. 6 and 9 of *The sacred books of the East,* ed. F. Max Müller. Oxford: Clarendon.

Palmieri, Richard Pietro. 1976. "Domestication and exploitation of livestock in the Nepal Himalaya and Tibet: An ecological, functional, and culture historical study of yak and yak hybrids in society, economy, and culture." Unpublished Ph.D. dissertation in geography, University of California, Davis.

Pandey, Lalta Prasad. 1971. *Sun-worship in ancient India.* Delhi, Patna, Benares: Motilal Banarsidass.

Panikkar, K. M. 1918. "Some aspects of Nāyar life." *Journal of the Royal Anthropological Institute of Great Britain and Ireland* 48: 254–93.

Parain, Charles. 1944. "The evolution of agricultural technique." Pp. 118–68 in Vol. 1 of John H. Clapham and Eileen Power (eds.), *The Cambridge economic history of Europe from the decline of the Roman Empire.* Cambridge: Cambridge University Press; New York: Macmillan.

Parel, Anthony. 1969. "The political symbolism of the cow in India." *Journal of Commonwealth Political Studies* 7: 179–203.

Parker, H. 1909. *Ancient Ceylon: An account of the aborigines and part of the early civilization.* London: Luzac.

Parker, Robert. 1983. *Miasma: Pollution and purification in early Greek religion.* Oxford: Clarendon.

Parkyns, Mansfield. 1868. *Life in Abyssinia.* London: John Murray.

Parpola, Asko, Seppe Koskenniemi, Simo Parpola, and Pentti Aalto. 1970. *Further progress in the Indus script decipherment.* Special Publications, 3. Copenhagen: Scandinavian Institute of Asian Studies.

Parry, N. E. 1932. *The Lakhers.* London: Macmillan.

Parry, O. H. 1895. *Six months in a Syrian monastery.* London: H. Cox.

Parsons, James J. 1962a. "The acorn-hog economy of the oak woodlands of southwestern Spain." *Geographical Review* 52: 211–35.

Parsons, James J. 1962b. *The green turtle and man.* Gainesville: University of Florida Press.

Paton, David. 1925. *Animals of ancient Egypt.* Princeton: Princeton: University Press.

Paton, Lewis Bayles. 1908–26a. "Ashtart (Ashtoreth), Astarte." Pp. 115–18 in Vol. 2 of James Hastings (ed.), *Encyclopaedia of religion and ethics.* 13 vols. Edinburgh: T. and T. Clark.

Paton, Lewis Bayles. 1908–26b. "Atargatis." Pp. 164–67 in Vol. 2 of James Hastings (ed.), *Encyclopaedia of religion and ethics.* 13 vols. Edinburgh: T. and T. Clark.

Paton, Lewis Bayles. 1908–26c. "Canaanites." Pp. 176–88 in Vol. 3 of James Hastings (ed.), *Encyclopaedia of religion and ethics.* 13 vols. Edinburgh: T. and T. Clark.

Paul, A. 1954. *A history of the Beja tribes of the Sudan.* London: Frank Cass.

Paul, Martha. 1981. *Wolf, Fuchs, und Hund bei den Germanen.* Wiener Arbeiten zur Germanischen Altertumskunde und Philologie, 13. Vienna: Karl M. Halosar.

Paulitschke, Philipp. 1893. *Ethnographie Nordost-Afrikas. Die Materielle Cultur der Danâkil, Galla und Somâl.* Berlin: Geographische Verlagshandlung Dietrich Reimer.

Paulus Aegineta. 1844–47. *The seven books of Paulus Aegineta.* 3 vols. Trans. F. Adams. London: Sydenham Society.

Pausanias. 1898. *Description of Greece.* 6 vols. Trans. J. G. Frazer. London: Macmillan.

Pawlowski, Zbigniew. 1983. "Clinical aspects in man." Pp. 367–401 in William C. Campbell (ed.), *Trichinella and trichinosis.* New York and London: Plenum.

Pearce, Nathaniel. 1831. *The life and adventures of Nathaniel Pearce.* 2 vols. Ed. J. J. Halls. London: Henry Colburn and Richard Bentley.

Pedley, John Griffiths. 1974. "Carians in Sardis." *Journal of Hellenic Studies* 94: 96–99.

Pelchat, Marcia Levin, and Paul Rozin. 1982. "The special role of nausea in the acquisition of food dislikes by humans." *Appetite: Journal for Intake Research* 3: 341–51.

Perlin, B. 1941. *Mongol'skaia Narodnaia Respublika.* Moskow: Politizdat.

Peschel, Oscar. 1906. *The races of man, and their geographical distribution.* New York: D. Appleton.

Peters, John Punnett. 1897–98. *Nippur, or explorations and adventures on the Euphrates.* 2 vols. New York: Knickerbocker.

Peters, John Punnett. 1913. "The cock." *Journal of the American Oriental Society* 33: 363–96.

Petrie, W. M. Flinders. 1892. *Medum.* London: D. Nutt.

Petrie, W. M. Flinders. 1908–26. "Egyptian religion." Pp. 236–50 in Vol. 5 of James Hastings (ed.), *Encyclopaedia of religion and ethics.* 13 vols. Edinburgh: T. and T. Clark.

Petrowitsch, M. 1878. "Die Volksmedicin bei den Serben." *Globus* 33: 348–51.

Philby, H. St. John B. 1928. *Arabia of the Wahhabis.* London: Constable.

Philby, H. St. John B. 1952. *Arabian highlands.* Ithaca, N.Y.: Cornell University Press.

Philip, J. A. 1966. *Pythagoras and early Pythagoreanism.* Phoenix, Journal of the Classical Association of Canada, Supplementary Vol. 7. Toronto: University of Toronto Press.

Phillips, E. D. 1965. *The royal hordes: Nomad peoples of the steppes.* London: Thames and Hudson.

Phillott, D. C. 1907. "Bibliomancy, divination, superstitions, amongst the Persians." *Journal and Proceedings of the Asiatic Society of Bengal* (n.s.) 2, 8: 339–42.

Philostratus. 1960. *The life of Apollonius of Tyana.* 2 vols. Trans. F. C. Conybeare. Loeb Classical Library. London: William Heinemann; Cambridge, Mass.: Harvard University Press.

Piggott, Stuart. 1983. *The earliest wheeled transport from the Atlantic to the Caspian Sea.* London: Thames and Hudson.

Plato. 1977. *Phaedo.* Pp. 193–403 in Vol. 1 of *Plato,* trans. Harold North Fowler. Loeb Classical Library. London: William Heinemann; Cambridge, Mass.: Harvard University Press.

Platt, Raye R., and Mohammed Bahy Hefny. 1958. *Egypt: A compendium.* New York: American Geographical Society.

Pliny. 1938–62. *Natural history.* 10 vols. Trans. H. Rackham et al. Loeb Classical Library. London: William Heinemann; Cambridge, Mass.: Harvard University Press.

Plutarch. 1871. *Symposiacs*. Pp. 197–460 in Vol. 3 of William W. Goodwin (ed.), *The writings of Plutarch*. Boston: Little, Brown.

Plutarch. 1936a. *Isis and Osiris*. Pp. 1–191 in Vol. 5 of *Plutarch's Moralia*, trans. Frank Cole Babbitt. Loeb Classical Library. London: William Heinemann; Cambridge, Mass.: Harvard University Press.

Plutarch. 1936b. *The Roman questions*. Pp. 1–171 in Vol. 4 of *Plutarch's Moralia*, trans. Frank Cole Babbitt. Loeb Classical Library. London: William Heinemann; Cambridge, Mass.: Harvard University Press.

Plutarch. 1955. *Pelopidas*. Pp. 339–434 in Vol. 5 of *Plutarch's Lives*, trans. Bernadotte Perrin. Loeb Classical Library. London: William Heinemann; Cambridge, Mass.: Harvard University Press.

Plutarch. 1956. *On superstition*. Pp. 451–95 in Vol. 2 of *Plutarch's Moralia*, trans. Frank Cole Babbitt. Loeb Classical Library. London: William Heinemann; Cambridge, Mass.: Harvard University Press.

Plutarch. 1957. *Whether land or sea animals are cleverer*. Pp. 309–479 in Vol. 12 of *Plutarch's Moralia*, trans. Harold Cherniss and William C. Helmbold. Loeb Classical Library. London: William Heinemann; Cambridge, Mass.: Harvard University Press.

Plutarch. 1959. *Romulus*. Pp. 87–187 in Vol. 1 of *Plutarch's Lives*, trans. Bernadotte Perrin. Loeb Classical Library. London: William Heinemann; Cambridge, Mass.: Harvard University Press.

Plutarch. 1971. *Life of Alexander*. Trans. K. J. Maidment. Auckland: Auckland University Press.

Polybius. 1922–27. *The histories*. 6 vols. Trans. W. R. Paton. Loeb Classical Library. London: William Heinemann; New York: G. P. Putnam's Sons.

Pool, Robert. 1987. "Hot and cold as an explanatory model: The example of Bharuch District in Gujarat, India." *Social Science and Medicine* 25: 389–99.

Pope, Marvin H. 1972. "A divine banquet at Ugarit." Pp. 170–203 in James M. Efird (ed.), *The use of the Old Testament in the New and other essays*. Studies in honor of William Franklin Stinespring. Durham, N.C.: Duke University Press.

Porphyry. 1965. *On abstinence from animal food*. Trans. Thomas Taylor. New York: Barnes and Noble.

Poultney, James Wilson. 1959. *The bronze tables of Iguvium*. Philological Monographs, 18. Baltimore: American Philological Association.

Powell, John B. 1945. *My twenty-five years in China*. New York: Macmillan.

Pozio, E., and G. La Rosa. 1991. "General introduction and epidemiology of trichinellosis." *Southeast Asian Journal of Tropical Medicine and Public Health* 22 (Supplement): 291–94.

Pozio, E., O. Cappelli, et al. 1988. "Third outbreak of trichinellosis caused by consumption of horse meat in Italy." *Annales de parasitologie humaine et comparée* 63: 48–53.

Pozio, E., G. La Rosa, K. D. Murell, and J. R. Lichtenfels. 1992. "Taxonomic revision of the genus *Trichinella*." *Journal of Parasitology* 78: 654–59.

Pozio, E., G. La Rosa, P. Rossi, and K. D. Murell. 1992. "Biological characterization of *Trichinella* isolates from various host species and geographic regions." *Journal of Parasitology* 78: 647–53.

Prakash, Om. 1961. *Food and drinks in ancient India*. Delhi: Munshi Ram Manohar Lal.

Préaux, Claire. 1939. *L'Économie royale des Lagides*. Brussels: Fondation égyptologique Reine Élisabeth.

Prejevalsky, N. 1876. *Mongolia, the Tangut country, and the solitudes of northern Tibet*. 2 vols. Trans. E. Delmar Morgan. London: Sampson Low, Marston, Searle, and Rivington.

Prins, A. H. J. 1952. *The coastal tribes of the north-eastern Bantu*. Ethnographic Survey of Africa. East Central Africa, Part 3. London: International African Institute.

Pritchard, James B. 1961. *The water system of Gibeon*. Museum Monographs. Philadelphia: University Museum, University of Pennsylvania.

Pritchard, William T. 1866. *Polynesian reminiscences*. London: Chapman and Hall.

Psarras, Con. 1983. "Ever since this protest, it's hard to find good horse meat in Utah." *Wall Street Journal* (Western edition), December 9, p. 25.

Pückler-Muskau, Herman Ludwig von. 1844. *Aus Mehemed Ali's Reich*. 3 vols. Stuttgart: Hallberger'sche Verlagshandlung.

Puhvel, Jaan. 1955. "Vedic *áśvamedha* and Gaulish *IIPOMIIDVOS*." *Language* 31: 353–54.

Puhvel, Jaan. 1970. "Aspects of equine functionality." Pp. 159–72 in Jaan Puhvel (ed.), *Myth and law among the Indo-Europeans*. Berkeley, Los Angeles, London: University of California Press.

Puhvel, Jaan. 1978. "Victimal hierarchies in Indo-European animal sacrifice." *American Journal of Philology* 99: 354–62.

Punekar, Vijaya B. 1959. *The Son Kolis of Bombay*. Bombay: Popular Book Depot.

Quin, P. J. 1959. *Foods and feeding habits of the Pedi*. Johannesburg: Witwatersrand University Press.

Radcliffe, William. 1921. *Fishing from the earliest times*. London: John Murray.

Rae, Edward. 1881. *The White Sea Peninsula: A journey in Russian Lapland and Karelia*. London: John Murray.

Raffles, Thomas Stamford. 1817. *The history of Java*. 2 vols. London: Black, Parbury, and Allen.

Raghavan, M. D. 1961. *The Karāva of Ceylon*. Colombo: K. V. G. deSilva and Sons.

Raikes, Robert L., and Robert H. Dyson, Jr. 1961. "The prehistoric climate of Baluchistan and the Indus Valley." *American Anthropologist* 63: 265–81.

Ramanujan, A. K. 1992. "Food for thought: Toward an anthology of Hindu food-images." Pp. 221–50 in R. S. Khare (ed.), *The eternal food: Gastronomic ideas and experiences of Hindus and Buddhists*. Albany: State University of New York Press.

Ramisz, A. 1985. "Current problems of epidemiology and epizootiology of trichinellosis." Pp. 190–200 in Charles W. Kim et al. (eds.), *Trichinellosis*. Proceedings of the Sixth International Conference on Trichinellosis, July 8–12, 1984. Albany: State University of New York Press.

Ramsay, H. 1890. *Western Tibet: A practical dictionary of the language and customs of the districts included in the Ladak wazarat*. Lahore: W. Ball, Government Printers.

Ramsay, W. M. 1890. *The historical geography of Asia Minor.* Royal Geographical Society, Supplementary Papers, 4. London: John Murray.

Ramsay, W. M. 1897. *Impressions of Turkey during twelve years' wanderings.* New York: G. P. Putnam's Sons; London: Hodder and Stoughton.

Randeria, Shalini. 1990. "Death and defilement: Divergent accounts of untouchability in Gujarat." Pp. 35–51 in Gabriella Eichinger Ferro-Luzzi (ed.), *Rites and beliefs in modern India.* New Delhi: Manohar.

Rao, V. V. 1974. "Bone remains from Bhokardan excavations." Pp. 225–33 in Shantaram Bhalchandra Deo (ed.), *Excavations at Bhokardan (Bhogavardhana), 1973.* Nagpur: Aurangabad.

Rappaport, Roy A. 1968. *Pigs for the ancestors: Ritual in the ecology of a New Guinea people.* New Haven: Yale University Press.

Raswan, Carl R. 1947. *Black tents of Arabia.* New York: Creative Age.

Ratzel, Friedrich. 1896–98. *The history of mankind.* 3 vols. London: Macmillan.

Raveret-Wattel, C. 1884. "Extraits des procès-verbaux des séances de la société. Séance générale du 13 Juin 1884." *Bulletin de la Société nationale d'acclimatation de France* 1 (fourth series): 599–607.

Raverty, H. G. 1859. "Notes on Káfiristán." *Journal of the Asiatic Society of Bengal* 28: 317–68.

Raverty, H. G. 1888. *Notes on Afghanistan and part of Baluchistan, geographical, ethnographical, and historical.* London: Eyre and Spottiswoode.

Read, R. N. Dick. 1962. "The Gidicho islanders of Ethiopia." *Geographical Magazine* 34: 507–23.

Reale Società geografica italiana, Rome. 1936. *L'Africa orientale.* Bologna: Zanichelli.

Recent archaeological discoveries in the People's Republic of China. 1984. Paris: United Nations Educational, Scientific and Cultural Organization; Tokyo: Centre for East Asian Cultural Studies.

Redding, Richard W. 1981. "The faunal remains." Pp. 233–61 in Henry T. Wright (ed.), *An early town on the Deh Luran Plain: Excavations at Tepe Farukhabad.* Memoirs of the Museum of Anthropology, 13. Ann Arbor: Museum of Anthropology, University of Michigan.

Redding, Richard W. 1984. "The faunal remains." Pp. 39–49 in Robert J. Wenke, *Archaeological investigations at El-Hobeh 1980: Preliminary report.* American Research Center in Egypt Reports, 9. Malibu: Undena.

Redding, Richard W. 1991. "The role of the pig in the subsistence system of ancient Egypt: A parable on the potential of faunal data." Pp. 20–30 in Pam J. Crabtree and Kathleen Ryan (eds.), *Animal use and culture change.* MASCA Research Papers in Science and Archaeology, Special Supplement to Vol. 8. Philadelphia: MASCA, The University Museum of Archaeology and Anthropology, University of Pennsylvania.

Reed, Charles A. 1965. "Imperial Sassanian hunting of pig and fallow-deer, and problems of survival of these animals today in Iran." *Postilla* 92 (November 5): 1–23.

Reed, Charles A., and Dexter Perkins, Jr. 1984. "Prehistoric domestication of animals in southwestern Asia." Pp. 3–23 in Günter Nobis (ed.), *Der Beginn der Haustierhaltung in der "Alten Welt."* Die Anfänge des Neolithikums vom Orient bis Nordeuropa, 9. Cologne and Vienna: Böhlau.

Reich, Eduard. 1935. *Die tchechoslowakische Landwirtschaft.* Berlin: Paul Parey.

Reichard, Gladys A. 1963. *Navajo religion; a study of symbolism.* Second edition. New York: Bollingen Foundation.

Reifenberg, Adolf. 1947. *The soils of Palestine.* Revised second edition, trans. C. L. Whittles. London: Thomas Murby.

Reifenberg, Adolf. 1955. *The struggle between the desert and the sown; rise and fall of agriculture in the Levant.* Jerusalem: Publishing Department, Jewish Agency.

Reinach, Salomon. 1884. "Les Chiens dans le culte d'Esculape et les *kelabim* des stèles peintes de Citium." *Revue archéologique* (third series) 4: 129–35.

Remig, J., and W. Froscher. 1987. "Akute Trichinose. Beobachtungen bei 193 Patienten einer Epidemie." *Deutsche Medizinische Wochenschrift* 112: 1855–59.

Renfrew, Colin. 1987. *Archaeology and language: The puzzle of Indo-European origins.* New York: Cambridge University Press.

Renner, H. D. 1944. *The origin of food habits.* London: Faber and Faber.

Report on the marketing of fish in India. 1946. Agricultural Marketing in India, Marketing Series, 52. Delhi: Manager of Publications.

Report on the marketing of fish in the Indian Union. 1951. Second edition. Agricultural Marketing in India, Marketing Series, 65. Delhi: Manager of Publications.

Rhys, John. 1972. *Celtic folklore, Welsh and Manx.* New York: B. Blom.

Riasanovsky, Valentin Aleksandrovich. 1937. *Fundamental principles of Mongolian law.* London: Kegan Paul, Trench, Trübner.

Richards, Audrey I. 1939. *Land, labour and diet in Northern Rhodesia.* London: International Institute of African Languages and Cultures.

Richards, C. J. 1945. *The Burman: An appreciation.* Burma Pamphlets, 7. Calcutta: Longmans, Green.

Ripinsky, Michael M. 1975. "The camel in ancient Arabia." *Antiquity* 49: 295–98.

Ripinsky, Michael M. 1985. "The camel in dynastic Egypt." *Journal of Egyptian Archaeology* 71: 134–41.

Risley, H. H. 1903. *India. Ethnographic appendices.* Census of India, 1901, Vol. 1. Calcutta: Superintendent of Government Printing.

Rissman, Paul. 1989. "The status of research on animal domestication in India and its cultural context." Pp. 15–24 in Pam J. Crabtree, Douglas Campana, and Kathleen Ryan (eds.), *Early animal domestication and its cultural context.* MASCA Research Papers in Science and Archaeology, Special Supplement to Vol. 6. Philadelphia: MASCA, The University Museum of Archaeology and Anthropology, University of Pennsylvania.

Ritson, Joseph. 1802. *An essay on abstinence from animal food as a moral duty.* London: Richard Phillips.

Ritter, Edith K. 1965. "Magical-expert (= *āšipu*), and physician (= *asû*). Notes on two complementary professions in Babylonian medicine." Pp. 299–321 in *Studies in honor of Benno Landsberger on his seventy-fifth birthday, April 21, 1965.* Oriental Institute, Assyriological Studies, 16. Chicago: University of Chicago Press.

Rivers, W. H. R. 1906. *The Todas.* London: Macmillan.

Rivers, W. H. R. 1914. *The history of Melanesian society,* Vol. 1. Cambridge: Cambridge University Press.

Robertson, G. S. 1896. *The Káfirs of the Hindu-Kush.* London: Lawrence and Bullen.

Robertson, Noel. 1982a. "Hittite ritual at Sardis." *Classical Antiquity* 1: 122–40.

Robertson, Noel. 1982b. "The ritual background of the dying god in Cyprus and Syro-Palestine." *Harvard Theological Review* 75: 313–59.

Robinson, A. E. 1936. "The camel in antiquity." *Sudan Notes and Records* 19: 47–70.

Robinson, J. A. 1935. *Notes on the nomad tribes of eastern Afghanistan.* New Delhi: Government of India Press.

Rockhill, William Woodville. 1900. *The journey of William of Rubruck to the eastern parts of the world, 1253–1255.* Hakluyt Society Works, second series, 4. London: Hakluyt Society.

Rockhill, William Woodville (trans.). 1884. *The life of the Buddha and the early history of his order.* Derived from Tibetan works in the Bkah-Hgyur and Bstan-Hgyur. London: Trübner.

Rola-Bustrillos, Nena. 1961. *Food management practices of homemakers in the rural areas.* Study Series, 12. Quezon City: Community Development Research Council, University of the Philippines.

Roscoe, John. 1915. *The northern Bantu.* Cambridge: Cambridge University Press.

Roscoe, John. 1923. *The Bakitara or Banyoro.* Cambridge: Cambridge University Press.

Rose, H. J. 1925. *Primitive culture in Greece.* London: Methuen.

Rose, H. J. (trans.). 1974. *The Roman Questions of Plutarch.* New York: Biblo and Tannen.

Rosenberg, Ellen M. 1973. "Ecological effects of sex-differential nutrition." Paper presented at the 72nd Annual Meeting of the American Anthropological Association, New Orleans, December 1, 29 pp.

Ross, Anne. 1967. *Pagan Celtic Britain. Studies in iconography and tradition.* London: Routledge and Kegan Paul; New York: Columbia University Press.

Rossier, E. 1984. "État actuel de la production et de la consommation de viande chevaline en France." Pp. 491–508 in Robert Jarrige and William Martin-Rosset (eds.), *Le Cheval: Reproduction, selection, alimentation, exploitation.* Paris: Institut national de la recherche agronomique.

Roth, Henry Ling. 1890. *The Aborigines of Tasmania.* London: Kegan Paul, Trench, Trübner.

Roth, Henry Ling. 1896. *The natives of Sarawak and British North Borneo.* 2 vols. London: Truslove and Hanson.

Routledge, W. Scoresby, and Katherine Routledge. 1910. *With a prehistoric people.* London: Edward Arnold.

Roux, Jean-Paul. 1959. "Le Chameau en Asie Centrale." *Central Asiatic Journal* 5: 35–76.

Rowley-Conwy, Peter. 1988. "The camel in the Nile Valley: New Radiocarbon Accelerator (AMS) dates from Qaṣr Ibrîm." *Journal of Egyptian Archaeology* 74: 245–48.

Rowton, M. B. 1967. "The woodlands of ancient western Asia." *Journal of Near Eastern Studies* 26: 261–77.

Roy, Sachin. 1960. *Aspects of Padam-Minyong culture.* Shillong: North-East Frontier Agency.

Roy, Sarat Chandra, and Ramesh Chandra Roy. 1937. *The Khāṛiās.* 2 vols. Rānchī, India: "Man in India" Office.

Rozin, Elisabeth. 1982. "The structure of cuisine." Pp. 189–203 in Lewis M. Barker (ed.), *The psychobiology of human food selection.* Westport, Conn.: AVI Publishing.

Rozin, Elisabeth. 1983. *Ethnic cuisine: The flavor principle cookbook.* Brattleboro, Vt.: Stephen Greene.

Rozin, Paul. 1988a. "Cultural approaches to human food preferences." Pp. 137–53 in John E. Morley, M. Barry Sterman, and John H. Walsh (eds.), *Nutritional modulation of neural function.* San Diego: Academic Press.

Rozin, Paul. 1988b. "Social learning about food by humans." Pp. 165–87 in Thomas R. Zentall and Bennett G. Galef, Jr. (eds.), *Social learning: Psychological and biological perspectives.* Hillsdale, N.J., Hove, and London: Lawrence Erlbaum Associates.

Rozin, Paul. 1990a. "Getting to like the burn of chili pepper: Biological, psychological, and cultural perspectives." Pp. 231–69 in Barry G. Green, J. Russell Mason, and Morley R. Kare (eds.), *Chemical senses.* Vol. 2, *Irritation.* New York and Basel: Marcel Dekker.

Rozin, Paul. 1990b. "Social and moral aspects of food and eating." Pp. 97–110 in Irvin Rock (ed.), *The legacy of Solomon Asch: Essays in cognition and social psychology.* Hillsdale, N.J., Hove, and London: Lawrence Erlbaum Associates.

Rozin, Paul, and April E. Fallon. 1987. "A perspective on disgust." *Psychological Review* 94: 23–41.

Rozin, Paul, and Carol Nemeroff. 1990. "The laws of sympathetic magic: A psychological analysis of similarity and contagion." Pp. 205–32 in James W. Stigler, Richard A. Shweder, and Gilbert Herdt (eds.), *Cultural psychology: Essays on comparative human development.* Cambridge: Cambridge University Press.

Rozin, Paul, and D. Schiller. 1980. "The nature and acquisition of a preference for chili pepper by humans." *Motivation and Emotion* 4: 77–101.

Rozin, Paul, and T. A. Vollmecke. 1986. "Food likes and dislikes." *Annual Review of Nutrition* 6: 433–56.

Rozin, Paul, Linda Millman, and Carol Nemeroff. 1986. "Operation of the laws of sympathetic magic in disgust and other domains." *Journal of Personality and Social Psychology* 50: 703–12.

Rubel, Paula G., and Abraham Rosman. 1978. *Your own pigs you may not eat: A comparative study of New Guinea societies.* Chicago: University of Chicago Press.

Ruel, Malcolm. 1990. "Non-sacrificial ritual killing." *Man* (n.s.) 25: 323–35.

Rushdy, Mahmud Effendi. 1911. "The treading of sown seed by swine." *Annales du Service des antiquités de l'Égypte* 11: 162–63.

Russell, Harris L. 1955. "Dog-slaying at the Argive sheep festival." *Classical Bulletin* 31: 61–62.

Russell, R. V. 1916. *The tribes and castes of the Central Provinces of India.* 4 vols. London: Macmillan.

Rutter, Owen. 1929. *The pagans of North Borneo.* London: Hutchinson.

Sachau, Eduard. 1883. *Reise in Syrien und Mesopotamien.* Leipzig: F. A. Brockhaus.

Sachau, Edward C. (trans.). 1971. *Alberuni's India.* Abridged edition, ed. Ainslee T. Embree. New York: W. W. Norton.

Saggs, H. W. F. 1962. *The greatness that was Babylon.* New York: Hawthorn.

Saggs, H. W. F. 1965. *Everyday life in Babylonia and Assyria.* New York: Dorset.

Saggs, H. W. F. 1984. *The might that was Assyria.* London: Sidgwick and Jackson.

Salonen, Armas. 1974. "Beiträge zur Geschichte des Schweines im Zweistromlande." *Studia Orientalia* (Helsinki) 43, 9: 3–11.

Salt, Henry. 1814. *A voyage to Abyssinia and travels into the interior of that country.* London: F. C. and J. Rivington.

Sangave, V. A. 1959. *Jaina community: A social survey.* Bombay: Popular Book Depot.

Sanjana, J. E. 1946. *Caste and outcaste.* Bombay: Thacker.

Sarna, Nahum M. 1987. "Biblical literature: Hebrew scriptures." Pp. 152–73 in Vol. 2 of Mircea Eliade (ed.), *The encyclopedia of religion.* 16 vols. New York: Macmillan; London: Collier Macmillan.

Sarytschew, Gawrila. 1806. *Account of a voyage of discovery to the north-east of Siberia, the frozen ocean, and the north-east sea,* Vol. 1. London: Richard Phillips.

Sathe, S. P. 1967. "Cow-slaughter: The legal aspect." Pp. 69–82 in A. B. Shah (ed.), *Cow-slaughter: Horns of a dilemma.* Bombay: Lalvani.

Sauer, Carl O. 1952. *Agricultural origins and dispersals.* New York: American Geographical Society.

Saunderson, H. S. 1894. "Notes on Corea and its people." *Journal of the Anthropological Institute of Great Britain and Ireland* 24: 299–316.

Sawitz, Willi. 1938. "The prevalence of trichinosis in the United States." *Public Health Reports* 53: 365–83.

Sayce, A. H. 1887. *Lectures on the origin and growth of religion as illustrated by the religion of the ancient Babylonians.* Hibbert Lectures, 1887. London: Williams and Norgate.

Sayce, A. H. 1902. *The religions of ancient Egypt and Babylonia.* Edinburgh: T. and T. Clark.

Sayce, A. H. 1908–26. "Bull (Semitic)." Pp. 887–89 in Vol. 2 of James Hastings (ed.), *Encyclopaedia of religion and ethics.* 13 vols. Edinburgh: T. and T. Clark.

Schafer, Edward H. 1950. "The camel in China down to the Mongol dynasty." *Sinologica* 2: 165–94.

Schafer, Edward H. 1977. "T'ang." Pp. 85–140 in K. C. Chang (ed.), *Food in Chinese culture: Anthropological and historical perspectives.* New Haven and London: Yale University Press.

Schäfer, Heinrich. 1917. *Nubische Texte im Dialekte der Kunûzi (Mundart von Abuhôr).* Abhandlungen der Königlich Preussischen Akademie der Wissenschaften, Phil.-

Hist. Klasse, Jahrgang 1917, No. 5. Berlin: Königlich Akademie der Wissenschaften.

Schapera, I. 1930. *The Khoisan peoples of South Africa*. London: Routledge and Kegan Paul.

Schapera, I. 1953. *The Tswana*. Ethnographic Survey of Africa. Southern Africa, Part 3. London: International African Institute.

Schapera, I., and A. J. H. Goodwin. 1950. "Work and wealth." Pp. 131–72 in I. Schapera (ed.), *The Bantu-speaking tribes of South Africa*. London: Routledge and Kegan Paul.

Schiffman, James R. 1985. "Korea is cleaning up its act to get ready for the '88 Olympics." *Wall Street Journal* (Western edition), November 14, pp. 1, 24.

Schilling, Robert. 1987. "Lupercalia." P. 53 in Vol. 9 of Mircea Eliade (ed.), *The encyclopedia of religion*. 16 vols. New York: Macmillan; London: Collier Macmillan.

Schlerath, Bernfried. 1954. "Der Hund bei den Indogermanen." *Paideuma* 6: 25–40.

Schneider, Harold K. 1957. "The subsistence role of cattle among the Pakot and in East Africa." *American Anthropologist* 59: 278–300.

Scholz, Herbert. 1937. *Der Hund in der griechisch-römischen Magie und Religion*. Berlin: Triltsch und Huther.

Schomberg, R. C. F. 1935. *Between the Oxus and the Indus*. London: Martin Hopkinson.

Schomberg, R. C. F. 1938. *Kafirs and glaciers: Travels in Chitral*. London: Martin Hopkinson.

Schrader, Otto. 1890. *Prehistoric antiquities of the Aryan peoples*. Trans. F. B. Jevons. London: Charles Griffin.

Schram, L. M. J. 1954. *The Monguors of the Kansu-Tibetan frontier: Their origin, history, and social organization*. Transactions of the American Philosophical Society, 44, Part 1. Philadelphia: American Philosophical Society.

Schwabe, Calvin W. 1978. *Cattle, priests and progress in medicine*. Minneapolis: University of Minnesota Press.

Schwabe, Calvin W. 1979. *Unmentionable cuisine*. Charlottesville: University Press of Virginia.

Schwabe, Calvin W. 1984a. "A unique surgical operation on the horns of African bulls in ancient and modern times." *Agricultural History* 58: 138–56.

Schwabe, Calvin W. 1984b. *Veterinary medicine and human health*. Third edition. Baltimore and London: Williams and Wilkins.

Schwabe, Calvin W. 1993, in press. "Animals in the ancient world." In Aubrey Manning and James Serpell (eds.), *Animals and society*. London and New York: Routledge.

Schweinfurth, Georg. 1873. *The heart of Africa*. 2 vols. London: Sampson Low.

Scott, James George. 1906. *Burma: A handbook of practical information*. London: Alexander Moring.

Scott, James George [Shway Yoe, pseud.]. 1910. *The Burman: His life and notions*. London: Macmillan.

Scott, James George, and J. P. Hardiman. 1900. *Gazetteer of Upper Burma and the Shan States*, Vol. 1, Part 1. Rangoon: Superintendent, Government Printing.

Scullard, H. H. 1967. *The Etruscan cities and Rome*. Ithaca, N.Y.: Cornell University Press.

Sebring, James M. 1987. "Bovidicy." *Journal of Anthropological Research* 43: 309–24.

Seeland, Nicolas. 1882. "Die Ghiliaken: Eine ethnographische Skizze." *Russische Revue* 21: 97–130, 222–54.

Seligman, Charles Gabriel. 1910. *The Melanesians of British New Guinea*. Cambridge: Cambridge University Press.

Seligman, Charles Gabriel, and Brenda Z. Seligman. 1918. "The Kababish, a Sudan Arab tribe." *Harvard African Studies* 2: 105–86.

Seligman, Charles Gabriel, and Brenda Z. Seligman. 1932. *Pagan tribes of the Nilotic Sudan*. London: George Routledge and Sons.

Selim, M. K., M. F. El-Sawy, A. A. Rashwan, and R. Barakat. 1981. "On the epidemiology of *Trichinella spiralis* in dogs and cats in Alexandria, Egypt." *Egyptian Journal of Veterinary Science* 18: 165–72.

Seth, S. K. 1978. "The desiccation of the Thar Desert and its environs during the protohistorical and historical periods." Pp. 279–305 in William C. Brice (ed.), *The environmental history of the Near and Middle East since the last Ice Age*. London, New York, and San Francisco: Academic Press.

Sextus Empiricus. 1933. *Outlines of Pyrrhonism*. Vol. 1 of *Sextus Empiricus*. Trans. R. G. Bury. Loeb Classical Library. London: William Heinemann; Cambridge, Mass.: Harvard University Press.

Shaffer, Aaron. 1974. "Enlilbani and the 'dog house' in Isin." *Journal of Cuneiform Studies* 26: 251–55.

Shaffer, Jim G. 1985–88. "One hump or two: The impact of the camel on Harappan society." Pp. 1315–28 in Vol. 3 of Edenda Curaverunt, G. Gnoli, and L. Lanciotti (eds.), *Orientalia Josephi Tucci Memoriae Dicata*. 3 vols. Serie Orientale Roma, 56, 1–3. Rome: Istituto Italiano per il Medo ed Estremo Oriente.

Shah, Haku. 1985. *Votive terracottas of Gujarat*. Ed. Carmen Kagal. New York: Maupin International.

Shakespear, J. 1912. *The Lushei Kuki clans*. London: Macmillan.

Shalash, M. R. 1984. "The production and utilization of camel meat." Pp. 231–47 in W. Ross Cockrill (ed.), *The camelid: An all-purpose animal*. Proceedings of the Khartoum workshop on camels, December 1979. Uppsala: Scandinavian Institute of African Studies.

Sharma, K. N. 1961. "Hindu sects and food patterns in North India." Pp. 45–58 in L. P. Vidyarthi (ed.), *Aspects of religion in Indian society*. Meerut: Kedar Nath, Ram Nath.

Sharma, R. R. P. 1961. *The Sherdukpens*. Shillong: Research Department, Adviser's Secretariat.

Sharma, R. S. 1974. "Iron and urbanization in the Ganga Basin." *Indian Historical Review* 1: 98–103.

Shaw, Ian. 1984. "Report on the 1983 excavations. The animal pens (Building 400)." Pp. 40–59 in Barry J. Kemp, *Amarna Reports I*. Occasional Publications, 1. London: Egypt Exploration Society.

Shaw, William. 1929. *Notes on the Thadou Kukis.* Calcutta: Asiatic Society of Bengal.

Sherring, C. A. 1906. *Western Tibet and the British borderland.* London: Edward Arnold.

Shinichirō, Takakura. 1960. *The Ainu of northern Japan.* Transactions of the American Philosophical Society, 50, Part 4. Trans. J. A. Harrison. Philadelphia: American Philosophical Society.

Shipley, A. E., Stanley A. Cook, and T. K. Cheyne. 1899–1903. "Swine." Cols. 4824–26 in Vol. 4 of T. K. Cheyne and J. Sutherland Black (eds.), *Encyclopaedia Biblica.* 4 vols. New York: Macmillan.

Shirokogoroff, S. M. 1924. *Social organization of the Mongols.* Extra Vol. 3. Shanghai: Royal Asiatic Society (North China Branch).

Shnirelman, Victor A. 1992. "The emergence of a food-producing economy in the steppe and forest-steppe zones of eastern Europe." *Journal of Indo-European Studies* 20: 123–43.

Shukla, Bramha Kumar. 1959. *The Daflas of the Subansiri region.* Shillong: North-East Frontier Agency.

Shulman, David. 1976. "The murderous bride: Tamil versions of the myth of Devī and the buffalo-demon." *History of Religions* 16: 120–46.

Sikes, Ernest Edward. 1910–11. "Hephaestus." Pp. 304–5 in Vol. 13 of *The Encyclopaedia Britannica.* Eleventh edition. 29 vols. New York: Encyclopaedia Britannica.

Silberman, Neil Asher. 1992. "Who were the Israelites?" *Archaeology* 45, 2 (March/April): 22–30.

Silbert, Albert. 1966. *Le Portugal Méditerranéen à la fin de l'ancien régime, XVIIIe-début du XIXe siècle.* 2 vols. Les hommes et la terre, 12. Paris: S.E.V.P.E.N.

Sillitoe, Paul. 1980–81. "Pigs in disputes." *Oceania* 51: 256–65.

Simmonds, P. L. 1885. *The animal food resources of different nations.* London: E. and F. N. Spon.

Simmons, James Stevens, et al. 1954. *The Near and Middle East.* Vol. 3 of *Global epidemiology: A geography of disease and sanitation.* Philadelphia: J. B. Lippincott.

Simon, Erika. 1983. *Festivals of Attica: An archaeological commentary.* Madison: University of Wisconsin Press.

Simoons, Frederick J. 1953. "Notes on the bush-pig (*Potamochoerus*)." *Uganda Journal* 17: 80–81.

Simoons, Frederick J. 1954. "The non-milking area of Africa." *Anthropos* 49: 58–66.

Simoons, Frederick J. 1958. "The use and rejection of hippopotamus flesh as food in Africa." *Tanganyika Notes and Records* 51: 195–97.

Simoons, Frederick J. 1960. *Northwest Ethiopia: Peoples and economy.* Madison: University of Wisconsin Press.

Simoons, Frederick J. 1970. "The traditional limits of milking and milk use in southern Asia." *Anthropos* 65: 547–93.

Simoons, Frederick J. 1973. "The sacred cow and the Constitution of India." *Ecology of Food and Nutrition* 2: 281–96.

Simoons, Frederick J. 1974a. "Fish as forbidden food: The case of India." *Ecology of Food and Nutrition* 3: 185–201.

Simoons, Frederick J. 1974b. "The purificatory role of the five products of the cow in Hinduism." *Ecology of Food and Nutrition* 3: 21–34.

Simoons, Frederick J. 1974c. "Rejection of fish as human food in Africa: A problem in history and ecology." *Ecology of Food and Nutrition* 3: 89–105.

Simoons, Frederick J. 1979. "Questions in the sacred-cow controversy." *Current Anthropology* 20: 467–76.

Simoons, Frederick J. 1981. "Dogs as human food in northwest Africa." *Appetite: Journal for Intake Research* 2: 253–66.

Simoons, Frederick J. 1991. *Food in China: A cultural and historical inquiry.* Boca Raton, Ann Arbor, Boston: CRC.

Simoons, Frederick J., and James A. Baldwin. 1982. "Breast-feeding of animals by women: Its socio-cultural context and geographic occurrence." *Anthropos* 77: 421–48.

Simoons, Frederick J., and Deryck O. Lodrick. 1981. "Background to understanding the cattle situation of India: The sacred cow concept in Hindu religion and folk culture." *Zeitschrift für Ethnologie* 106: 121–37.

Simoons, Frederick J., and Elizabeth S. Simoons. 1968. *A ceremonial ox of India: The mithan in nature, culture, and history.* Madison, Milwaukee, London: University of Wisconsin Press.

Simoons, Frederick J., Bärbel Schönfeld-Leber, and Helen L. Issel. 1979. "Cultural deterrents to use of fish as human food." *Oceanus* 22, 1 (Spring): 67–71.

Singh, L. Iboongohal. 1961. "The culture of Manipur." *Assam Quarterly* 1: 54–55.

Singh, Mohinder. 1947. *The depressed classes: Their economic and social condition.* Bombay: Hind Kitabs.

Sinor, Denis. 1981. "The Inner Asian warriors." *Journal of the American Oriental Society* 101: 133–44.

Skeat, Walter William, and Charles Otto Blagden. 1906. *Pagan races of the Malay Peninsula.* 2 vols. London: Macmillan.

Slater, Gilbert (ed.). 1918. *Some South Indian villages.* University of Madras, Economic Studies, 1. London: Oxford University Press.

Smith, Arthur H. 1894. *Chinese characteristics.* New York: Fleming H. Revell.

Smith, George. 1884. *Ancient history from the monuments. The history of Babylonia.* Ed. A. H. Sayce. London: Society for Promoting Christian Knowledge.

Smith, Sir William (ed.). 1893. *A dictionary of the Bible.* 3 vols. London: John Murray.

Smith, William Carlson. 1925. *The Ao Naga tribe of Assam.* London: Macmillan.

Smith, William Robertson. 1908. *The Old Testament in the Jewish church.* London: Adam and Charles Black.

Smith, William Robertson. 1914. *Lectures on the religion of the Semites.* New, revised edition. London: Adam and Charles Black.

Smyth, R. Brough. 1878. *The Aborigines of Victoria: With notes relating to the habits of the natives of other parts of Australia and Tasmania.* 2 vols. London: Trübner.

Sobania, Neal. 1988. "Fishermen herders: Subsistence, survival and cultural change in northern Kenya." *Journal of African History* 29: 41–56.

Sokolowski, Franciszek. 1962. *Lois sacrées des cités grecques*, Supplément. École française d'Athènes, Travaux et mémoires des anciens membres étrangers de l'École et de divers savants, 11. Paris: E. de Boccard.

Soler, Jean. 1979. "The dietary prohibitions of the Hebrews." *New York Review of Books* 26, 10 (June 14): 24–30. Trans. R. Forster from "Sémiotique de la nourriture dans la Bible," *Annales: Économies, sociétés, civilisations* 28 (1973): 943–55. Also published as "The semiotics of food in the Bible," pp. 126–38 in R. Forster and O. Ranum (eds.), *Food and drink in history*. Baltimore and London: Johns Hopkins University Press, 1979.

Sontheimer, Günther-Dietz. 1989. *Pastoral deities in western India*. New York and Oxford: Oxford University Press.

Sopher, David E. 1957. *Geography of Indian coasts*. Annual Summary Report, Office of Naval Research NR 388-041, Contract No. Nonr-2329(00), mimeo. Washington, D.C.

Sopher, David E. 1959. *Geography of Indian coasts*. Annual Summary Report, Office of Naval Research NR 388-041, Contract No. Nonr-2329(00), mimeo. Washington, D.C.

Sorokin, Pitirim A. 1942. *Man and society in calamity*. New York: E. P. Dutton.

Sowerby, Arthur de Carle. 1935. "The domestic animals of ancient China." *China Journal* 23: 233–43.

Speke, John Hanning. 1908. *Journey of the discovery of the source of the Nile*. London: J. M. Dent.

Spencer, Baldwin, and F. J. Gillen. 1904. *The northern tribes of central Australia*. London: Macmillan.

Spindler, Lloyd A. 1953. "Transmission of trichinae to swine through feces." *Journal of Parasitology* 39: 34.

Spiro, Melford E. 1949. "Ifalik: A South Sea culture." Unpublished manuscript submitted as a final report, Coordinated Investigation of Micronesian Anthropology. Washington, D.C.: Pacific Science Board, National Research Council.

Srinivas, M. N. 1955. "The social system of a Mysore village." Pp. 1–35 in McKim Marriott (ed.), *Village India*. American Anthropological Association Memoirs, 83. Menasha, Wis.: American Anthropological Association.

Srinivasan, Doris. 1975–76. "The so-called Proto-Śiva seal from Mohenjo-Daro: An iconological assessment." *Archives of Asian Art* 29: 47–58.

Srinivasan, Doris. 1984. "Unhinging Śiva from the Indus civilization." *Journal of the Royal Asiatic Society*, Part 1: 77–89.

Srivastava, L. R. N. 1962. *The Gallongs*. Shillong: Research Department, Adviser's Secretariat.

Stager, Lawrence E. 1985. "The archaeology of the family in ancient Israel." *Bulletin of the American Schools of Oriental Research* 260: 1–35.

Stager, Lawrence E. 1991. "Why were hundreds of dogs buried at Ashkelon?" *Biblical Archaeology Review* 17, 3 (May/June): 26–32, 38–42.

Stampfli, Hans R. 1983. "The fauna of Jarmo with notes on animal bones from Matarrah, the ʿAmuq, and Karim Shahir." Pp. 431–83 in Linda S. Braidwood, Robert J.

Braidwood, Bruce Howe, Charles A. Reed, and Patty Jo Watson (eds.), *Prehistoric archeology along the Zagros flanks*. Oriental Institute Publications, 105. Chicago: Oriental Institute of the University of Chicago.

Stanford University. 1956. *Taiwan (Formosa)*. Subcontractor's Monograph, HRAF-31, Stanford-5. New Haven: Human Relations Area Files.

Stannus, Hugh S. 1922. "The Wayao of Nyasaland." *Harvard African Studies* 3: 229–372.

Starkie, W. J. M. 1909. *The Acharnians of Aristophanes*. London: Macmillan.

Statius. 1961. *Silvae*. Pp. 1–337 in Vol. 1 of *Statius*, trans. J. H. Mozley. Loeb Classical Library. London: William Heinemann; Cambridge, Mass.: Harvard University Press.

Stayt, Hugh Arthur. 1931. *The Bavenda*. London: International Institute of African Language and Cultures.

Steedman, Andrew. 1835. *Wanderings and adventures in the interior of southern Africa*. 2 vols. London: Longman.

Steele, James H. 1970. "Epidemiology and control of trichinosis." Pp. 493–510 in Sylvester E. Gould (ed.), *Trichinosis in man and animals*. Springfield, Ill.: Charles C. Thomas.

Stefansson, Vilhjalmur. 1920. "Food tastes and food prejudices of men and dogs." *Scientific Monthly* 11: 540–43.

Stein, S. 1957. "The dietary laws in rabbinic and patristic literature." Pp. 141–54 in Kurt Aland and F. L. Cross (eds.), *Studia Patristica*, Vol. 2. Papers presented to the Second International Conference on Patristic Studies held at Christ Church, Oxford, 1955, Part 2. Berlin: Akademie.

Steinberg, David J., et al. 1959. *Cambodia: Its people, its society, its culture*. New Haven, Conn.: HRAF Press.

Steiner, Franz. 1956. *Taboo*. London: Cohen and West.

Stengel, Paul. 1880. "Die Pferdeopfer der Griechen." *Philologus* 39: 182–85.

Stevenson, H. N. C. 1954. "Status evaluation in the Hindu caste system." *Journal of the Royal Anthropological Institute of Great Britain and Ireland* 84: 46–65.

Stevenson, Margaret (Mrs. Sinclair Stevenson). 1920. *The rites of the twice-born*. London: Oxford University Press.

Stevenson, Margaret (Mrs. Sinclair Stevenson). 1930. *Without the pale*. London: Oxford University Press.

Stiebing, William H., Jr. 1989. *Out of the desert? Archaeology and the Exodus/conquest narratives*. Buffalo, N.Y.: Prometheus.

Stillman, Norman A. 1987. "Berber religion." Pp. 109–11 in Vol. 2 of Mircea Eliade (ed.), *The encyclopedia of religion*. 16 vols. New York: Macmillan; London: Collier Macmillan.

Stokes, Whitley. 1898. "The tragical death of Cúchulainn." Pp. 251–64 in Eleanor Hull (ed.), *The Cuchillin saga in Irish literature*. London: David Nutt.

Strabo. 1960–69. *Geography*. Trans. Horace Leonard Jones as *The Geography of Strabo*. 8 vols. Loeb Classical Library. London: W. Heinemann; Cambridge, Mass.: Harvard University Press.

Strathern, Andrew. 1971. "Pig complex and cattle complex: Some comparisons and counterpoints." *Mankind* 8: 126–38.

Stutley, Margaret. 1985. *Hinduism.* Wellingborough, Northamptonshire: Aquarian Press.

Stutley, Margaret, and James Stutley. 1977. *Harper's dictionary of Hinduism: Its mythology, folklore, philosophy, literature, and history.* New York, Hagerstown, San Francisco, and London: Harper and Row.

Suetonius. 1950–51. *The lives of the Caesars,* in Vols. 1 and 2 of *Suetonius.* Trans. J. C. Rolfe. Loeb Classical Library. London: William Heinemann; Cambridge, Mass.: Harvard University Press.

Sullivan, H. P. 1964. "A re-examination of the religion of the Indus civilization." *History of religions* 4: 115–25.

Sumner, William Graham. 1906. *Folkways.* Boston: Ginn.

Sundara Ram, L. L. 1927. *Cow-protection in India.* George Town, Madras: South Indian Humanitarian League.

Sverdrup, Harald Ulrich. 1938. *Hos Tundrafolket.* Oslo: Gyldendal Norsk Forlag. Trans. for the Human Relations Area Files.

Sykes, Ella C. 1910. *Persia and its people.* London: Methuen.

Sykes, Percy M. 1906. "The Parsis of Persia." *Journal of the Society of Arts* 54: 754–67.

Tacitus. 1889. *A treatise on the situation, manners, and inhabitants of Germany.* Pp. 286–342 in Vol. 2 of *The works of Tacitus.* 2 vols. The Oxford Translation. London: George Bell and Sons.

Talbot, William Henry. 1956. *Right food.* Tract No. 17. Third edition. Aliganj, Uttar Pradesh: World Jain Mission.

Tambiah, S. J. 1969. "Animals are good to think and good to prohibit." *Ethnology* 8: 423–59.

Tan, Swee Poh, and Erica F. Wheeler. 1983. "Concepts relating to health and food held by Chinese women in London." *Ecology of Food and Nutrition* 13: 37–49.

Taran, Mikhael. 1975. "Early records of the domestic fowl in ancient Judea." *Ibis* (London) 117: 109–10.

Taylor, F. H. N.d. *Save our soil.* [Jerusalem]: Soil Conservation Board, Government of Palestine.

Telegin, Dmitriy Yakolevich. 1986. *Dereivka: A settlement and cemetery of Copper Age horse keepers on the middle Dnieper.* Trans. V. K. Pyatkovskiy; ed. J. P. Mallory. BAR International Series, 287. Oxford: British Archaeological Reports.

Temple, O. 1922. *Notes on the tribes, provinces, emirates and states of the Northern Provinces of Nigeria.* Lagos: Church Missionary Society Bookshop.

Teston, Eugène, and Maurice Percheron. 1931. *L'Indochine moderne.* Paris: Librairie de France.

te Velde, H. 1977. *Seth, god of confusion.* Probleme der Ägyptologie, 6. Leiden: E. J. Brill.

Tew, Mary. 1950. *Peoples of the Lake Nyasa region.* Ethnographic Survey of Africa. East Central Africa, Part 1. London: International African Institute.

Thapar, Romila. 1961. *Aśoka and the decline of the Mauryas*. London: Oxford University Press.

Thaplyal, K. K. 1985. "Comments" (on Dilip K. Chakrabarti's "The issues of the Indian Iron Age"). Pp. 85–86 in S. B. Deo and K. Paddayya (eds.), *Recent advances in Indian archaeology*. Poona: Deccan College Post-Graduate and Research Institute.

Theal, G. M. 1910. *The yellow and dark-skinned people of Africa south of the Zambesi*. London: Swan Sonnenschein.

Thiel, E. 1958. *Die Mongolei*. Veröffentlichungen des Osteuropa-Institutes München, Band 13. Munich: Isar.

Thomas, Bertram. 1932. *Arabia Felix*. New York: Charles Scribner's Sons.

Thomas, N. W. 1908–26. "Animals." Pp. 483–535 in Vol. 1 of James Hastings (ed.), *Encyclopaedia of religion and ethics*. 13 vols. Edinburgh: T. and T. Clark.

Thomas, P. K. 1984. "The faunal background of the Chalcolithic culture of western India." Pp. 355–61 in Juliet Clutton-Brock and Caroline Grigson (eds.), *Animals and archaeology*. Vol. 3, *Early herders and their flocks*. BAR International Series, 202. Oxford: British Archaeological Reports.

Thomas, P. K. 1989. "Utilization of domestic animals in pre- and protohistoric India." Pp. 108–12 in Juliet Clutton-Brock (ed.), *The walking larder: Patterns of domestication, pastoralism, and predation*. London, Boston, Sydney, Wellington: Unwin Hyman.

Thompson, D'Arcy W. 1966. *A glossary of Greek birds*. Hildesheim: Georg Olms.

Thompson, Henry O. 1970. *Mekal: The god of Beth-shan*. Leiden: E. J. Brill.

Thompson, J. A. 1974. *Deuteronomy: An introduction and commentary*. London: Inter-Varsity Press.

Thompson, Laura. 1940. *Southern Lau, Fiji: An ethnography*. Bernice P. Bishop Museum, Bull. 162. Honolulu.

Thompson, R. Campbell. 1903–4. *The devils and evil spirits of Babylonia*. 2 vols. London: Luzac.

Thompson, R. Campbell. 1908. *Semitic magic: Its origins and development*. London: Luzac.

Thompson, Virginia. 1941. *Thailand: The new Siam*. New York: Macmillan.

Thompson, Virginia. 1943. *Post-mortem on Malaya*. New York: Macmillan.

Thomson, John Stuart. 1909. *The Chinese*. Indianapolis: Bobbs-Merrill.

Thomson, Joseph. 1885. *Through Masai land*. Boston: Houghton, Mifflin.

Thurston, Edgar. 1909. *Castes and tribes of southern India*. 7 vols. Madras: Government Press.

Thurston, Edgar. 1912. *Omens and superstitions of southern India*. New York: McBride, Nast.

Titcomb, M. 1969. *Dog and man in the ancient Pacific with special attention to Hawaii*. Bernice P. Bishop Museum, Special Publications, 59. Honolulu.

Tod, James. 1983. *Annals and antiquities of Rajasthan*. 2 vols. First Indian edition. New Delhi: Oriental Books Reprint Corporation.

Tooley, Angela M. J. 1988. "Coffin of a dog from Beni Hasan." *Journal of Egyptian Archaeology* 74: 207–11.

Torday, E., and T. A. Joyce. 1905. "Notes on the ethnography of the Ba-Mbala." *Journal of the Anthropological Institute of Great Britain and Ireland* 35: 398–426.

Torday, E., and T. A. Joyce. 1906. "Notes on the ethnography of the Ba-Yaka." *Journal of the Anthropological Institute of Great Britain and Ireland* 36: 39–58.

Towne, Charles Wayland, and Edward Norris Wentworth. 1950. *Pigs from cave to Corn Belt.* Norman: University of Oklahoma Press.

Townsend, Charles W. 1928. "Food prejudices." *Scientific Monthly* 27: 65–68.

Toynbee, J. M. C. 1973. *Animals in Roman life and art.* London: Thames and Hudson.

Trant, Hope. 1954. "Food taboos in East Africa." *Lancet* 267: 703–5.

Tregear, Edward. 1904. *The Maori race.* Wanganni, New Zealand: A. D. Willis.

Trimingham, J. Spencer. 1952. *Islam in Ethiopia.* London: Oxford University Press.

Tryjarski, Edward. 1979. "The dog in the Turkic area: An ethnolinguistic study." *Central Asiatic Journal* 23: 297–319.

Tsitsishvili, A. L. 1975. "Tierknochenreste aus Kurganbestattungen der mittleren Bronzezeit von Vardzia (Ostgeorgien)." Pp. 431–37 in A. T. Clason (ed.), *Archaeozoological studies.* Amsterdam and Oxford: North-Holland; New York: American Elsevier.

Tucci, G. 1956. *To Lhasa and beyond.* Trans. Mario Carelli. Rome: Istituto poligrafico dello Stato.

Tudor, D. 1969–76. *Corpus Monumentorum Religionis Equitum Danuvinorum (CMRED).* 2 vols. Études préliminaires aux religions orientales dans l'empire romain, 13. Leiden: E. J. Brill.

Turner, William Y. 1878. "The ethnology of the Motu." *Journal of the Anthropological Institute of Great Britain and Ireland* 7: 470–98.

Turville-Petre, Edward Oswald Gabriel. 1964. *Myth and religion of the north: The religion of ancient Scandinavia.* New York, Chicago, San Francisco: Holt, Rinehart and Winston.

Twitchell, K. S. 1953. *Saudi Arabia.* Princeton: Princeton University Press.

Ungnad, A. 1908. "Zum Genuss von Schweinefleisch im alten Babylonien." *Orientalistische Literatur-Zeitung* 11: 534–35.

University of California. 1956. *The economy of India.* 2 vols. Subcontractor's Monograph, HRAF-32, California–1. New Haven: Human Relations Area Files.

Ussishkin, David. 1978. *Excavations at Tel Lachish—1973–77. Preliminary Report.* Tel Aviv, 4, No. 1–2.

Vámbéry, Arminius. 1864. *Travels in Central Asia.* London: John Murray.

Van Buren, E. Douglas. 1939. *The fauna of ancient Mesopotamia as represented in art.* Analecta Orientalia, 18. Rome: Pontificum Institutum Biblicum.

Van Buren, E. Douglas. 1948. "Fish-offerings in ancient Mesopotamia." *Iraq* 10: 101–21.

Van Buskirk, J. D. 1923. "Some common Korean foods." *Transactions of the Korea Branch of the Royal Asiatic Society* 14: 1–8.

van der Toorn, K. 1985. *Sin and sanction in Israel and Mesopotamia: A comparative study.* Studia Semitica Neerlandica, 22. Assen/Maastricht: Van Gorcum.

Van Hoorn, G. 1953. "Kynika." Pp. 106–10 in Vol. 2 of George E. Mylonas and Doris

Raymond (eds.), *Studies presented to David Moore Robinson*. St. Louis: Washington University.

Vanoverbergh, Morice. 1936–38. "The Isneg life cycle." *Publications of the Catholic Anthropological Conference* 3, 2: 81–186; 3, 3: 187–280. Washington, D.C.: Catholic Anthropological Conference.

Van Seters, John. 1966. *The Hyksos: A new investigation*. New Haven and London: Yale University Press.

Van Zeist, Willem, and S. Bottema. 1982. "Vegetational history of the eastern Mediterranean and the Near East during the last 20,000 years." Pp. 277–321 in John L. Bintliff and Willem Van Zeist (eds.), *Palaeoclimates, palaeoenvironments and human communities in the eastern Mediterranean region in later prehistory*. 2 parts. BAR International Series, 133 (ii). Oxford: British Archaeological Reports.

Varro. 1912. *On farming*. Trans. L. Storr-Best. London: G. Bell and Sons.

Vayda, Andrew P. 1972. "Pigs." Pp. 905–8 in Vol. 3 of Peter Ryan (ed.), *Encyclopaedia of Papua and New Guinea*. Melbourne: Melbourne University Press.

Vayda, Andrew P. 1987. "Explaining what people eat: A review article." *Human Ecology* 15: 493–510.

Vayda, Andrew P., Anthony Leeds, and David B. Smith. 1961. "The place of pigs in Melanesian subsistence." Pp. 69–77 in V. E. Garfield (ed.), *Proceedings of the 1961 Annual Spring Meeting of the American Ethnological Society*. Seattle: University of Washington Press.

Vedder, H. 1928. "The Nama." Pp. 106–52 in *The native tribes of South West Africa*. Cape Town: Cape Times Limited.

Veith, Ilza. 1949. *Huang ti nei ching su wên: The Yellow Emperor's classic of internal medicine*. Baltimore: Williams and Wilkins.

Vermaseren, Maarten J. 1963. *Mithras, the secret god*. Trans. Therese and Vincent Megaw. New York: Barnes and Noble.

Vermaseren, Maarten J. 1977. *Cybele and Attis, the myth and the cult*. London: Thames and Hudson.

Vermeule, Cornelius. 1972. "Greek funerary animals, 450–300 B.C." *American Journal of Archaeology* 76: 49–59.

Vermeule, Emily. 1979. *Aspects of death in early Greek art and poetry*. Berkeley, Los Angeles, London: University of California Press.

Vernant, Jean-Pierre. 1989. "At man's table: Hesiod's foundation myth of sacrifice." Pp. 21–85 and 224–37 in Marcel Detienne and Jean-Pierre Vernant (eds.), *The cuisine of sacrifice among the Greeks*, trans. Paula Wissing. Chicago and London: University of Chicago Press.

Verrill, Alpheus H. 1946. *Strange customs, manners and beliefs*. Boston: L. C. Page.

Vickery, Kenton Frank. 1936. *Food in early Greece*. Illinois Studies in the Social Sciences, 20. Urbana: University of Illinois.

Virchow, Rudolph. N.d. *The life of the trichina*. Trans. Rufus King Browne. N.p.

Voigt, Mary M. 1983. *Hajji Firuz Tepe, Iran: The Neolithic settlement*. Vol. 1 of Hasanlu Excavation Reports, ed. Robert H. Dyson, Jr. University Museum Monographs 50. Philadelphia: University Museum, University of Pennsylvania.

Volkmar, Fritz. 1987. "Conquest or settlement? The Early Iron Age in Palestine." *Biblical Archaeologist* 50: 84–100.

von den Driesch, A., and J. Boessneck. 1985. *Die Tierknochenfunde aus der neolithischen Siedlung von Merimde-Benisalame am westlichen Nildelta.* Munich: Institut für Paläeoanatomie, Domestikationsforschung und Geschichte der Tiermedizin der Universität München und Deutsches Archäologisches Institut Abteilung Kairo.

von Grünau, Freiherr. 1899. "Bericht über meine Reise nach Siwah." *Zeitschrift der Gesellschaft für Erdkunde zu Berlin* 34: 271–80.

von Rohr Sauer, Alfred. 1968. "The cultic role of the pig in ancient times." Pp. 201–7 in Matthew Black and Georg Fohrer (eds.), *In memorium Paul Kahle.* Berlin: Töpelmann.

Vroklage, B. A. G. 1952. *Ethnographie der Belu in Zentral-Timor.* 3 vols. Leiden: E. J. Brill.

Waddell, L. Austine. 1899. *Among the Himalayas.* Westminster: Archibald Constable.

Waddell, L. Austine. 1939. *The Buddhism of Tibet or Lamaism.* Second edition. Cambridge: W. Heffer and Sons.

Wagner, Günter. 1949–56. *The Bantu of North Kavirondo.* 2 vols. London: Oxford University Press.

Waida, Manabu. 1987a. "Cocks." Pp. 551–52 in Vol. 3 of Mircea Eliade (ed.), *The encyclopedia of religion.* 16 vols. New York: Macmillan; London: Collier Macmillan.

Waida, Manabu. 1987b. "Pigs." Pp. 326–27 in Vol. 11 of Mircea Eliade (ed.), *The encyclopedia of religion.* 16 vols. New York: Macmillan; London: Collier Macmillan.

Walker, Benjamin. 1968. *The Hindu world.* 2 vols. New York: Frederick A. Praeger.

Walldén, Ruth. 1990. "Village-cult sites in South India in changing times." Pp. 89–93 in Gabriella Eichinger Ferro-Luzzi (ed.), *Rites and beliefs in modern India.* New Delhi: Manohar.

Walsh, Kathleen Dolan. 1989. "Cattle of the moon: Religion and ritual in the domestication and early history of *Bos primigenius* in the Mediterranean region." Unpublished Ph.D. dissertation in geography, University of California, Berkeley.

Wapnish, Paula. 1984. "The dromedary and Bactrian camel in Levantine historical settings: The evidence from Tell Jemmeh." Pp. 171–200 in Juliet Clutton-Brock and Caroline Grigson (eds.), *Animals and archaeology.* Vol. 3, *Early herders and their flocks.* BAR International Series, 202. Oxford: British Archaeological Reports.

Ward, William Hayes. 1910. *The seal cylinders of Western Asia.* Washington, D.C.: Carnegie Institution.

Warkworth, Lord (Percy, Henry A. G. P.). 1898. *Notes from a diary in Asiatic Turkey.* London: Edward Arnold.

Wasson, R. Gordon. 1982. "The last meal of the Buddha." *Journal of the American Oriental Society* 102: 591–603.

Wasson, Valentina Pavlovna, and R. Gordon Wasson. 1957. *Mushrooms, Russia, and history.* 2 vols. New York: Pantheon.

Watson, Virginia. 1965. "Agarabi female roles and family structure: A study in sociocultural change." Unpublished Ph.D. dissertation in anthropology, University of Chicago.

Watters, Thomas. 1904–5. *On Yuan Chwang's travels in India, 629–645 A.D.* 2 vols. Oriental Translation Fund, new series, 14. London: Royal Asiatic Society.

Webster, Hutton. 1942. *Taboo: A sociological study.* Stanford: Stanford University Press.

Weinfeld, Moshe, and Louis Isaac Rabinowitz. 1971–72. "Pentateuch." Cols. 231–64 in Vol. 13 of *Encyclopaedia Judaica.* 16 vols. Jerusalem: Keter Publishing House; New York: Macmillan.

Weinfeld, Moshe, et al. 1971–72. "Deuteronomy." Cols. 1573–83 in Vol. 5 of *Encyclopaedia Judaica.* 16 vols. Jerusalem: Keter Publishing House; New York: Macmillan.

Weiss, Barry. 1982. "The decline of Late Bronze Age civilization as a possible response to climatic change." *Climatic Change* 4: 173–98.

Weitz, Joseph. 1971–72. "Afforestation. Historical survey." Cols. 787–90 in Vol. 9 of *Encyclopaedia Judaica.* 16 vols. Jerusalem: Keter Publishing House; New York: Macmillan.

Welch, Holmes. 1967. *The practice of Chinese Buddhism, 1900–1950.* Harvard East Asian Series, 26. Cambridge, Mass.: Harvard University Press.

Wells, Ken. 1983. "Tongan chic in Utah is horsemeat luau and kava and rugby." *Wall Street Journal* (Western edition), May 13, pp. 1, 14.

Wenham, Gordon J. 1979. *The book of Leviticus.* New International Commentary on the Old Testament, 3. Grand Rapids, Mich.: William B. Eerdmans.

Wenke, Robert. 1985. "Excavations at Kom el-Hisn." *American Research Center in Egypt Newsletter* 129 (Spring): 1–11.

Wentzel, Volkmar. 1961. "Angola, unknown Africa." *National Geographic Magazine* 120: 346–83.

Werblowsky, R. J. Zwi, and Geoffrey Wigoder. 1966. *The encyclopedia of the Jewish religion.* New York, Chicago, San Francisco: Holt, Rinehart and Winston.

West, Barbara, and Ben-Xiong Zhou. 1988. "Did chickens go north? New evidence for domestication." *Journal of Archaeological Science* 15: 515–33.

West, Edward William. 1880–97. *Pahlavi texts.* Vols. 5, 18, 24, 37, and 47 of *The sacred books of the East,* ed. F. Max Müller. Oxford: Clarendon.

Westen, Drew. 1984. "Cultural materialism: Food for thought or bum steer?" *Current Anthropology* 25: 639–53.

Westermarck, Edward. 1924. *The origin and development of the moral ideas.* 2 vols. London: Macmillan.

Westermarck, Edward. 1926. *Ritual and belief in Morocco.* 2 vols. London: Macmillan.

Wheeler, Erica, and Swee Poh Tan. 1983. "From concept to practice: Food behaviour of Chinese immigrants in London." *Ecology of Food and Nutrition* 13: 51–57.

Wheeler, Mortimer. 1959. *Early India and Pakistan.* London: Thames and Hudson.

Wheeler, R. Richmond. 1928. *The modern Malay.* London: George Allen and Unwin.

Whitaker, Joseph I. S. 1921. *Motya: A Phoenician colony in Sicily.* London: G. Bell and Sons.

White, David Gordon. 1988–89. "Dogs die." *History of religions* 28: 283–303.

White, David Gordon. 1991. *Myths of the dog-man.* Chicago and London: University of Chicago Press.

White, David G. 1992. "You are what you eat: The anomalous status of dog-cookers in Hindu mythology." Pp. 53–93 in R. S. Khare (ed.), *The eternal food: Gastronomic ideas and experiences of Hindus and Buddhists*. Albany: State University of New York Press.

White, John. 1823. *History of a voyage to the China Sea*. Boston: Wells and Lilly.

Whitehead, Henry. 1916. *The village gods of South India*. London: Oxford University Press.

Wiedfeldt, O. 1914. "Wirtschaftliche, rechtliche und soziale Grundtatsachen und Grundformen der Atayalen auf Formosa." *Mitteilungen der Deutschen Gesellschaft für Natur- und Völkerkunde Ostasiens* 15, Part C: 7–55.

Wijesekera, N. D. 1965. *The people of Ceylon*. Second edition. Colombo: M. D. Gunasena.

Wilford, John Noble. 1993. "Old statuette traces horse to 2300 B.C." *New York Times*, January 3, 1, p. 10.

Wilkinson, J. Gardner. 1878. *The manners and customs of the ancient Egyptians*. 3 vols. London: John Murray.

Will, Ernest. 1985. "La Déesse au chien de Palmyre." *Syria: Revue d'art oriental et d'archéologie* 62: 50–55.

Williams. F. E. 1936. *Papuans of the Trans-Fly*. Oxford: Clarendon.

Williams-Hunt, P. D. R. 1952. *An introduction to the Malayan aborigines*. Kuala Lumpur: Government Press.

Wilson, Christine S. 1973. "Food taboos of childbirth: The Malay example." *Ecology of Food and Nutrition* 2: 267–74.

Wilson, Laurence L. 1947. *Apayao life and legends*. [Baguio, Philippines?]: publisher unknown.

Wilson, R. T. 1984. *The camel*. London and New York: Longman.

Winfield, Gerald Freeman. 1948. *China: The land and the people*. New York: Sloane.

Wirth, Albrecht. 1897. "The aborigines of Formosa and the Liu-Kiu islands." *American Anthropologist* 10: 357–70.

Wiser, Charlotte Viall. 1955. "The foods of a Hindu village of north India." *Annals of the Missouri Botanical Garden* 42: 303–412.

Wittwer, Sylvan, Yu Youtai, Sun Han, and Wang Lianzheng. 1987. *Feeding a billion: Frontiers of Chinese agriculture*. East Lansing: Michigan State University Press.

Wood, John G. 1870. *The uncivilized races, or natural history of man*, Vol. 1. Hartford, Conn.: American Publishing.

Wood, W. C. 1916. "The religion of Canaan from the earliest times to the Hebrew conquest." *Journal of Biblical Literature* 35: 1–133, 163–279.

Woodburn, James. 1968. "An introduction to Hadza ecology." Pp. 49–55 in Richard B. Lee and Irven DeVore (eds.), *Man the hunter*. Chicago: Aldine.

Woods, Barbara Allen. 1959. *The devil in dog form*. Folklore Studies, 11. Berkeley and Los Angeles: University of California Press.

Worthington, E. B. 1946. *Middle East science*. London: H.M. Stationery Office.

Worthington, S., and E. B. Worthington. 1933. *Inland waters of Africa*. London: Macmillan.

Wright, David P. 1987. *The disposal of impurity: Elimination rites in the Bible and in Hit-*

tite and Mesopotamian literature. Society of Biblical Literature, Dissertation Series, 101. Atlanta: Scholars Press.

Wright, G. Ernest. 1964. "Judean Lachish." Pp. 301–9 in Vol. 2 of Edward F. Campbell, Jr., and David Noel Freedman (eds.), *The Biblical Archaeologist reader.* 2 vols. Garden City, N.Y.: Doubleday.

Wyatt, Nicolas. 1989. "Aśvamedha and puruṣamedha in ancient India." *Religion* 19: 1–11.

Xenophon. 1914. *Cyropaedia.* 2 vols. Trans. Walter Miller. Loeb Classical Library. London: William Heinemann; New York: Macmillan.

Xenophon. 1958. *Anabasis.* Trans. W. H. D. Rouse as *The march up country.* Ann Arbor: University of Michigan Press.

Yakar, Jak. 1985. *The later prehistory of Anatolia: The Late Chalcolithic and Early Bronze Age.* 2 parts. BAR International Series, 268. Oxford: British Archaeological Reports.

Yamasaki, N. 1900. "Unsre geographischen Kenntnisse von der Insel Taiwan (Formosa)." *Petermanns Mitteilungen* 46: 221–34.

Yamashita, Jiro. 1970. "Trichinosis in Asia." Pp. 457–64 in Sylvester E. Gould (ed.), *Trichinosis in man and animals.* Springfield, Ill.: Charles C. Thomas.

Yang, Anand A. 1980. "Sacred symbol and sacred space in rural India: Community mobilization in the 'anti-cow killing' riot of 1893." *Comparative Studies in Society and History* 22: 576–96.

Yang, Martin C. 1945. *A Chinese village: Taitou, Shantung Province.* New York: Columbia University Press.

Yerkes, Royden Keith. 1952. *Sacrifice in Greek and Roman religions and early Judaism.* New York: Charles Scribner's Sons.

Yetts, W. Perceval. 1934. "The horse: A factor in early Chinese history." *Eurasia Septentrionalis Antiqua* 9: 231–55.

Young, Ernest. 1898. *The kingdom of the yellow robe.* Westminster: Archibald Constable.

Young, Oliver Gordon. 1961. *The hill tribes of northern Thailand.* Bangkok: Government of Thailand and the U.S. Operations Mission to Thailand.

Yü Ying-shih. 1977. "Han China." Pp. 55–83 in K. C. Chang (ed.), *Food in Chinese culture: Anthropological and historical perspectives.* New Haven and London: Yale University Press.

Zaganiaris, Nicolas J. 1975. "Sacrifices de chiens dans l'antiquité classique." *Platon* 27: 322–29.

Zaleskie, B. 1865. *La Vie des Steppes Kirghizes.* Paris: J.-B. Vasseur.

Zarins, Juris. 1978. "The domesticated equidae of third millennium B.C. Mesopotamia." *Journal of Cuneiform Studies* 30: 3–17.

Zarins, Juris. 1989. "Pastoralism in southwest Asia: The second millennium B.C." Pp. 127–55 in Juliet Clutton-Brock (ed.), *The walking larder: Patterns of domestication, pastoralism, and predation.* London, Boston, Sydney, Wellington: Unwin Hyman.

Zeder, M. A. 1984. "Meat distribution at the highland Iranian urban center of Tal-e Malyan." Pp. 279–307 in Juliet Clutton-Brock and Caroline Grigson (eds.), *Ani-*

mals and archaeology. Vol. 3, *Early herders and their flocks.* BAR International Series, 202. Oxford: British Archaeological Reports.

Zerfal, Adam. 1991. "Following the pottery trail—Israel enters Canaan." *Biblical Archaeology Review* 17, 5 (September/October): 28–47.

Zeuner, Frederick E. 1963. *A history of domesticated animals.* London: Hutchinson.

Zimmer, Heinrich. 1969. *Philosophies of India.* Ed. Joseph Campbell. Bollingen Series, 26. Princeton: Princeton University Press.

Zimmermann, Francis. 1987. *The jungle and the aroma of meats: An ecological theme in Hindu medicine.* Berkeley, Los Angeles, London: University of California Press.

Zimmermann, William J. 1970. "Trichinosis in the United States." Pp. 378–400 in Sylvester E. Gould (ed.), *Trichinosis in man and animals.* Springfield, Ill.: Charles C. Thomas.

Zohary, Michael. 1962. *Plant life of Palestine.* Chronica Botanica New Series of Plant Science Books, 33. New York: Ronald.

Zucker, Martin. 1972. "The sneaky pig and changing customs." *San Francisco Examiner and Chronicle,* Sunday Punch Section, May 21, p. 24.

INDEX

517

159, 164–166, 316, 383–384n. *See also* cock; divination, with chicken and eggs; eggs, embryonated; eggs, preserved; eggs, vegetarian

children: foods eaten by, and dietary discrimination against, 91, 160, 162, 209, 228, 231, 302, 303, 311, 316, 322–323, 341n, 384n, 430n

China: amount of animal foods consumed in traditional, 4, 5; animal fighting in, 120, 147; animal sacrifice and divination in, 58; bovines and beef in, 119, 122–124, 314; camel and camelflesh in, 194, 199, 395n; chicken and eggs in, 154, 166, 167, 316, 379n; cockfighting in, 377n; delicacies in, 84, 253, 426n; divination in, with chickens, 145; the dog and dog eating in, 202–203, 204, 208, 218, 220, 221, 240–241, 251; early exchanges of, with Vietnam, 56–57; fish and fishing in, 290, 291, 292, 425n, 426n, 429–430n; food prescribed and proscribed in, for pregnant and nursing women, 307, 316, 345n, 429n; foreigners' identification of the pig with the people of, 92, 319, 320; horse and horseflesh in, 176, 177, 388n, 389n; pigs and pork in, 46–48, 49, 56, 57, 79–80, 333n, 345n; symbolism of color red in, 379n; trichinosis in dogs of, 416n; vegetarians and vegetarianism in, 10, 292–295

Christ: Asclepius as a rival of, 380n; the cock as symbolic of resurrection of, 156; the dog, as seen by, 248; fish as symbolic of, 274; and the Islamic acceptance of camelflesh, 198; and New Testament references to pigs and pig keeping, 21; and the story of Peter and the cock, 380–381n; and the symbolism of eggs, 165

Christianity: attack of, on the cult of Asclepius, 380n; and the decline of horse eating in Europe, 187–88, 191, 193, 392n; and the fish and fish symbolism, 274–275; and the Levitican code, 32; and the pig and pork, 32, 33, 34, 40, 45, 54, 56, 59, 68, 78, 83, 342n; the pork-eating Moro group seen as converts to, 58; and the rejection of camelflesh, 198; and the rejection of dogflesh, 209, 211, 221, 231; and the role

and symbolism of the cock, 156, 380–381n; and the symbolism of fish, 419n; and the use and symbolism of eggs, 165, 315, 384n; vegetarianism among, 11; mentioned, 103. *See also* Catholicism, Roman

Christians, Chaldean: vegetarianism among, 11

Christians, Coptic (of Egypt): and pigs and pork eating, 33, 82, 340n; rejection of camelflesh by, 198

Christians, Ethiopian: and the pig and pork rejection, 41, 42, 343n; proper killing of animals required by, 302; rejection of camelflesh by, 198, 300; rejection of horsemeat by, 179

Christians, of India: common cattle and beef eating among, 113, 116; and fish and fish fishing, 287; pig keeping and pork eating among the St. Thomas, 54

Christians, of Nubia: pig keeping among, 41–42

clams, 254

Clason, A. T., 355n

Clavijo, Ruy Gonzalez de, 171

cleanness. *See* purity and pollution concerns

Clemens, 334

climate: adaptability of pig to, 72; as a factor in flesh use and avoidance, 40, 136–137

climatic change: deforestation as result of, and the decline of pig keeping in the Near East, 74–83, 359–360n; and Hebrew settlement in the hills of Canaan, 356–358n; and the rise of the sacred cow concept in India, 137, 138–140

Cline, Walter, 261

Clutton-Brock, Juliet, 355n

cock: in early Christianity, 380–381n; in Europe beyond Greece and Rome, 156; in the Greco-Roman world, 154–156, 157, 380n; among the Hebrews, 158, 381n; as herald of dawn, 145, 154, 156, 158, 160, 376n; in rainmaking in modern Palestine, 379n; sanctity of, in Southeast Asia, 145, 147, 376n; sanctity of, among Zoroastrians, 154. *See also* cockfighting; divination

cockfighting: in Africa, 160; in ancient Palestine, 157–158; Buddhist objections to, 145; in Christian Europe, 156; in the